EDITH KERMIT ROOSEVELT

Edith Kermit Roosevelt by Theobald Chartran,
1902

EDITH KERMIT ROOSEVELT

Portrait of a First Lady

SYLVIA JUKES MORRIS

COWARD, McCANN & GEOGHEGAN, INC.
NEW YORK

B
Roosevelt

Library of Congress Cataloging in Publication Data

Morris, Sylvia Jukes.
   Edith Kermit Roosevelt: portrait of a first
lady.

   Bibliography: p.
   Includes index.
   1.   Roosevelt, Edith Kermit Carow, 1861–1948.
2.   Roosevelt, Theodore, Pres. U.S., 1858–1919.
3.   Presidents—United States—Wives—Biography.
B757.3.R65M67   1980   973.91′1′0924 [B]   79-17851
ISBN 0-698-10994-5

Printed in the United States of America

To Edmund

Contents

A life of Aunt Edith should be written . . . she managed
TR very cleverly without his being conscious of it—no
slight achievement as anyone will concede.
                              —FRANKLIN DELANO ROOSEVELT

"Looking down from a second-floor side window
were Mr. Roosevelt's grandsons."
Lincoln's funeral procession, New York City, April 1865.

Introduction

On a sunny April afternoon in 1865, Abraham Lincoln's funeral procession moved slowly up Broadway. The President's body, having lain in state at City Hall, was on its way to the Hudson Ferry and a final tortuous journey to Springfield, Illinois.

Every building and column, as far as the eye could see, was draped with black muslin. Curtains were festooned with dark rosettes, flags drooped sadly at half mast, and even the street lamps were shrouded with black crepe hangings.

At the southwest corner of Union Square, the advance columns passed an immense property taking up the entire block from Fourteenth to Thirteenth Street. This was the four-story mansion of one of New York's richest men: investment counselor, real-estate agent, and plate-glass manufacturer Cornelius Van Schaak Roosevelt.[1]

Looking down from a second-floor side window onto the dense throng, massed fifteen feet deep along either curb, were Mr. Roosevelt's grandsons: Theodore, six and a half years old, and Elliott, five. With them was a fair, curly headed friend, Edith Kermit Carow, not yet four. In spite of the reassuring presence of her governess, Edith was frightened by the relentless blackness all around her, the sharp swords and bayonets glinting in the sun, the wailing

1

pipes, and never ending thud of drums. Presently, in the dusty distance, she saw a huge, dark shape approaching, preceded by a grotesque regiment of crippled soldiers—the Invalid Corps. As the catafalque drew near, little Edie began to cry. Irritated by her sniveling, the boys shunted her into a back room, and she saw no more of Lincoln's funeral.[2]

But, as Edith grew up in a neighboring town house, the fallen President became her hero. Time and again she walked across Union Square to gaze at Kirke Brown's statue of him. As her eyes traveled down from the troubled face, past the coat's stiff folds and the "smokestack" legs, they settled on the words at the base: "With malice toward none; with charity for all."[3]

Many years later, long after her marriage to the older of the two boys in the window, Edith told one of her sons that those "splendid words" of Abraham Lincoln had influenced her all her life.[4]

And it was a long life, spanning the best part of a century. Born in Lincoln's first term, Edith died while Truman was campaigning for his second. She lived through twenty-seven administrations of seventeen different Presidents, seven of whom she knew personally. Her own years as First Lady, from 1901 to 1909, coincided with America's rise to world power, under the exuberant guidance of her husband, Theodore, the best-loved President after Washington.

Today, in an age of declining expectations, nostalgia is growing for that peaceful, golden decade when the nation's prosperity seemed limitless, and when a large part of the globe joined in celebrating the Theodore Roosevelts and their six delightful children as the perfect American family. Never before or since have editors, cartoonists, and gossip columnists had such good copy from the White House. The young President and his attractive wife were high born and cultivated, yet they remained resolutely democratic. They were equally at ease entertaining Europe's imperial elite in the Executive Mansion (which Edith restored from top to bottom) and picnicking on the sandy shores of Sagamore Hill (where an observer "could not help remarking how pretty and young Mrs. R. looked in her bathing suit.")[5] The antics of the younger Roosevelts alone, from "Princess" Alice to the ingeniously mischievous Quentin, filled many miles of newspaper print.

If Theodore Roosevelt's place in history is well-documented and assured, that of Edith Kermit Roosevelt is not. She has thwarted several would-be biographers, for she was that strange anomaly, a public figure who remained private in the glare of the spotlights. While enjoying her husband's theatrical struttings on the world stage, she had no desire to "perform" herself, giving no speeches, granting no interviews, and permitting few photographs. Though offered large sums of money to write articles on any subject she chose, she steadfastly refused. When a servant showed her a yellow-press page full of pictures of herself and her family, she protested angrily. "One hates to feel that all one's life is public property."[6]

Privacy, indeed, was her passion. She would have nothing but contempt for the desire of some of her more recent successors to flaunt their weaknesses in confessional memoirs.

This distaste for self-revelation was lifelong, and it extended to her correspondence with her own friends and relatives. Time and again she exhorted them to destroy her letters, and took care that her diaries should remain concealed until long after her death. Fortunately thousands of those letters have survived, and diaries covering over forty years have recently come to light. At last it is possible to portray her in color and fine detail, and to award her the place she deserves in the gallery of presidential wives.

Although that place is high and prominent, Edith was by no means a political activist in the manner of her niece Eleanor Roosevelt. Her stature is rather that of the archetypal Victorian patrician lady, perfectly fulfilled as wife and mother, flawless in her interpretation of the role of First Lady, and "liberated" in the sense that she lived, with enthusiasm and contentment, exactly as she wanted.

Hers is first and foremost a love story, for from infancy to her death she adored one person "with all the passion of a girl."[7] Much as she cared for her children, shattered as she was by their later misfortunes and tragedies, her relationship with Theodore Roosevelt was her paramount obsession—even when he married another woman.

Despite this romantic preoccupation, Edith's life was full of drama in other respects—ranging from early impoverishment, family alcoholism and drug addiction, political assassination, attempted murder, suicide, and four major wars, through poignant and protracted old age. Consequently she experienced and understood more of the vicissitudes and mysteries of life than most women have, in her own time or ours.

In sexual mores, certainly, she was by no means repressed or naïve. The Washington of her early married life was known to be "one of the wickedest cities in the nation."[8] In New York, men of the highest social standing could be seen prowling the Waldorf-Astoria's "Peacock Alley" in search of prostitutes. During her White House years, *Town Topics,* the capital's notorious weekly scandal sheet, published stories of adultery, homosexuality, lesbianism, incest and sadism among the upper classes. Although Edith disapproved such flaunting of the moral code, her overall view of sex was earthy, and not without its humorous side. After reading Lewis Mumford's *Life of Melville* she said, "Alas, he suffers from the modern sex obsessions. Can't he stand silent on his peak in Darien and realize that what has swum into his ken was known by his ancestors, or he would not be here!"[9] Her own sensuality lasted until late in life. She once surprised a granddaughter by casually referring to "that wonderful silky private part of a woman."[10]

She was just forty years old when the assassination of William McKinley catapulted her husband into the position of Chief Executive. By then Edith had already spent twelve years in the public eye, yet she was an elusive personality to the press, to the general public, and, in many ways, to her friends. "I believe you could live in the same house with Edith for fifty years," said a classmate, "and never really know her."[11]

But when Edith entered the White House she visibly blossomed. Here, at last, her talents could be exercised to the full. The training had been long and sometimes arduous: seven years in Washington, where her husband was Civil Service Commissioner and, later, Assistant Secretary of the Navy, plus two years in New York.City as wife of the Police Commissioner. Added to these were the months of adulation that surrounded her and the hero of San Juan Hill, and two years in Albany as First Lady of New York State. Finally, there had been six months as consort of the Vice-President. Throughout, Edith supported her husband loyally and prudently. He, in turn, relied on her for behind-the-scenes counsel more than has been realized. "We all knew," their daughter once said, "that the person who had the long head in politics was Mother."[12] Roosevelt's valet remarked that she was a shrewder judge of people than Theodore, and the columnist Mark Sullivan wrote that she was, in the opinion of many, "greater

. among women than her husband among men."[13] The President himself confided that every time he had gone against his wife's advice he had paid for it. He also deferred to her in matters of literature. "She is not only cultured but scholarly," he said proudly.[14]

Hardly a day passed in her White House years without some brilliant social gathering. No other First Lady presided over as many official functions as Edith Roosevelt. She orchestrated every social event meticulously, from simple garden parties to elegant musicales, creating the maximum personal and intellectual harmony. Some evenings would be devoted to Washington's "inner set," some to the political establishment, and others to friends such as Henry Adams, Henry Cabot Lodge, John Hay, and John Burroughs. On the latter occasions, Edith's quiet wit sparkled, but seldom wounded.[15]

As First Lady, she was always simply gowned, and her dresses, at her own insistence, were completely American made. Princes, ambassadors, philosophers, and naturalists all admired her poise and graciousness. The Washington *Evening Star* described her social powers as "those of a real empress."[16] The President's closest aide concluded that in all her seven years in the White House she never made a mistake. "This will shine," he prophesied, "like a diamond tiara on her head someday."[17]

If Theodore Roosevelt's turbulent life can be described as cyclonic, his wife was the still center of the storm. Reserved to the point of aloofness, and given to the sternest self-discipline, Edith was a lifelong enigma even to members of her family. Yet no one denied her power and influence. She was "a sort of feminine luminiferous ether, pervading everything and everybody."[18]

Edith Kermit Carow, aged four.

Childhood
1861–1872

One

At that time we little thought that Col. Tyler's daughter would be the mother of a President's wife.

—William Lyman Gale.[1]

On Monday, June 6, 1859, two days before his marriage to Gertrude Tyler, thirty-three-year-old Charles Carow sailed into the harbor of Norwich, Connecticut, on a private launch. The June breeze ruffled his dark side whiskers and elegant mustache, and tossed the wavy hair on his high forehead. From where he stood he enjoyed a spectacular view of the town, sprawling over three hills at the confluence of three rivers. On either side, forested slopes rose steeply from the water's edge and tiers of houses nestled in groves of beech and maple.

Disembarking at the pier, Charles took a carriage and headed up Washington Street toward a clapboard mansion overlooking the Yantic River, in the most fashionable part of town. For a while he rumbled past bales and bollards and groups of longshoremen unloading freight. He felt at ease in nautical surroundings, since he was the son of one of the wealthiest shipping families in New York City. Charles had been born there on October 4, 1825, the seventh child of eight produced by Isaac Quentin Carow and Eliza

9

Mowatt. His French Huguenot ancestors, the Quereaus, had come to New York to escape the persecution of Protestants after the Revocation of the Edict of Nantes in 1685. On settling in America they had become Episcopalians, and most subsequent Quereaus were baptized, married and buried at Trinity Church, Wall Street. In 1797 Isaac had Anglicized the family name to Carow, "to the regret of his descendants."[2]

As a boy, Charles had lived on Cortlandt Street, only a gull's swoop away from the warehouse of his father and his uncle, Robert Kermit, on the northwestern corner of Maiden Lane and South Street. Their upper-floor offices overlooked the waterfront; the jib booms of Kermit & Carow clippers moored in the slips almost reached the windows.[3] In the storerooms below, Charles had watched the unloading of cargo from Liverpool and the West Indies: brass kettles, molasses, snuffer trays, cane sugar, ink powder, japanned bread baskets, rawhide whips, guns, saddles, thimbles, ivory combs, and violin strings.[4] At home in the evening he had played with exotic coins foreign passengers had used to pay their way across the Atlantic.[5]

Business prospered, and the Carows had moved uptown to fashionable St. Mark's Place, assembled an impressive library, and steadily ascended the social scale. As a Knickerbocker, Isaac qualified for membership in the exclusive St. Nicholas Society, founded to immortalize those of all nationalities who bore "the perils and struggles" of pre-Revolutionary days.[6] Charles shared a love of books with his father (his mother had died when he was twelve), but he did not have the family head for business. Nevertheless he had dutifully begun a commercial career, and was still learning his trade at the age of twenty-five, when Isaac Carow died.

Despite his good looks and wealth, Charles remained unmarried at thirty-two, when he met Gertrude Tyler of Connecticut, nine years his junior and recently returned from a finishing school in France. She was staying at the New York Hotel, a favorite stopping place for genteel New Englanders. Though not beautiful, Gertrude was cultured, poised and fashionably dressed, and these compensating virtues had attracted the mature Charles. One evening, as couples promenaded through the corridors of the hotel, he had steered Gertrude toward one of the long mirrors and told her to look at "the handsomest girl in the parade."[7]

After Gertrude returned to Norwich, Charles had corresponded with and from time to time called on her. During the last year their letters had begun to deal frankly, and sometimes testily, with touchy subjects. There had been the night, for instance, when he fell from his speeding carriage and broke both bones in one arm. Gertrude inferred, with apparent good reason, that her beau had been drinking, and suggested that he was more in need of a Doctor of Divinity than a Doctor of Medicine. Charles replied facetiously:

> MY SYMPATHIZING FRIEND
>   . . . Had I a "moral" fall, i.e. "been on a spree," there is a D.D. in Brooklyn who could have prescribed either soda water, wet cloths or "a hair of the dog" . . . no doubt he would also advise the "strait and *narrow way*," as you suggest . . . As it was a *physical* fall . . . I called on the M.D. instead of the D.D., also on whatever stray resolution of philosophy I could muster up.[8]

Eight months later, however, he was all sobriety in a letter to her father marked "Private."

> New York, 7th Mch 59
> MY DEAR SIR,
>   I have to ask of you the greatest favor that one man can ask of another.
>   I have won Gertrude's heart. Will you give me her hand.
>
> *Yours sincerely*
> CHARLES CAROW[9]

Daniel Tyler had no reason to refuse so terse yet graceful a request, and a June wedding was agreed upon. Charles had joyfully set about ordering a jeweled cross and chain for Gertrude ("I am told that in such cases the heavier the stones the more easily they are carried.") Not trusting Norwich florists, he also chose her bouquet in New York. "I hope you have not succumbed to the blues," he had written her in one of his last letters as a bachelor. "Keep as quiet as you can and don't get into any squabbles . . ."[10]

"I have won Gertrude's heart. Will you give me her hand."
Charles Carow and Gertrude Tyler at the time of their marriage.

Shortly after eight o'clock on Wednesday evening, June 8, 1859, Gertrude Elizabeth Tyler emerged from the family mansion on the arm of her father. She wore a simple-skirted heavy silk gown and point lace veil over her exquisitely coiffed dark hair. The face beneath the veil was extraordinarily pale, accentuating the darkness of her large eyes. Due to the softening effect of the lace, her long nose and too full mouth were less prominent than usual. Gertrude's graceful deportment bespoke an expensive education in the best schools of New York and Paris.[11]

Daniel Tyler IV helped his daughter into the waiting bridal carriage. He was a handsome silver-bearded man, who bore himself with the erect dignity of an artillery officer. Although he had graduated from West Point in 1819, and risen to the rank of Colonel in the regular army, he was now a man of many parts. He had traveled extensively in Europe (carrying with him letters of introduction from his cousin Aaron Burr to General Lafayette), translated French military books, and mastered the technology of English blast furnaces before returning to America and becoming a pioneer ironmaster in Pennsylvania and Alabama. Nothing delighted the Colonel more than resurrecting broken-down railroads, fixing up old ironworks, and restoring disused canals.[12]

This fascination with things industrial could be traced back to his colonial ancestor Job Tyler, who had emigrated to America in 1638 from Shropshire, England, birthplace of the Industrial Revolution. Daniel's more recent ancestors had been architects, gentleman farmers, and Harvard graduates. His mother, Sarah Edwards, had contributed a strain of New England Puritanism to the family, being a granddaughter of the great Protestant divine Jonathan Edwards.

Gertrude's mother, Emily Lee Tyler (now apprehensively awaiting her arrival in the church) was descended from Benjamin Lee, a Somerset-born naval commander and cousin to the William Pitts, Prime Ministers of England. Lee had settled in Massachusetts in 1784. The bride of Charles Carow therefore had many distinguished strains to contribute to the marriage, and to any future children of the union.

In a matter of minutes the carriage came to rest in front of Christ Episcopal Church, only a short distance along Washington Street. Whoever was responsible for the late hour of the wedding must have had a romantic turn of mind. The candlelit nave glowed with shimmering silks and satins; six women in the crowded congregation were wearing their own nuptial gowns. The Bishop of Connecticut, resplendent in ceremonial vestments, waited in the chancel. In front of him stood six groomsmen, and six bridesmaids in white silk with pink and blue shoulder-to-waist sashes. As Gertrude proceeded toward them, her pallor increased to the point where one of her cousins feared she would faint clean away.[13]

But the ceremony went smoothly. Afterward Mrs. Tyler (whose violet eyes showed the strain of sleepless weeks of preparation) hosted a 9 P.M. wedding reception in the Tyler mansion. She had had a last-minute crisis when a shipment of ices from New York City was spoiled with salt water by some carousing sailors. But the local confectioner had sent his young son with replacements just in time. Over forty years later the boy would still remember the Tyler-Carow wedding as a "very swell" affair. "The bride, although far from handsome, appeared highly educated, accomplished, and of noble traits."[14]

The reception ended at midnight, and Charles and Gertrude made their way back to the harbor, where the launch was waiting to transport them to New York.[15]

After this auspicious beginning, their marriage was soon struck by tragedy. Gertrude's first child, a boy born in Norwich on February 26, 1860, died at the age of six months. Less than a year later Gertrude returned to the Tyler home, and on August 6, 1861, produced her second child, a fair, blue-eyed daughter, Edith Kermit Carow.

Although the baby could not know it, as she lay in the comfortable security of her grandparents' house, the nation was already racked with civil war, and rapid changes were soon to affect the leisurely upper-class world into which she had been born. In March 1862 Daniel Tyler was appointed Brigadier General of the U.S. Volunteers, and ordered to join the Army of the Mississippi. In March 1864 Emily Lee Tyler died, and the Norwich home was broken up.[16] By then Gertrude and Charles had settled on Livingston Place, off East Fourteenth Street in New York, not very far from the Union Square mansion of Cornelius Van Schaak Roosevelt.

Two

Grave Alice, and laughing Allegra
And Edith with golden hair . . .

—Longfellow[1]

A thick veil descends on Carow family history after the closing of the Tyler home. Were it not for a few glimpses culled from Edith's association with the Roosevelts, and from the nostalgia of her old age, little could be told. She was to become an avid collector of information concerning her early ancestors, but throughout her life she compulsively destroyed data on her more immediate family, especially Charles Carow. "Mother . . . never told us stories about her childhood at all," complained her future stepdaughter.[2]

The reason why Edith did not reminisce was simple: the subject pained her. Despite her taciturnity, a few facts are certain. First, Charles was a failure in business; second, he was an alcoholic; third, he fell down the hold of one of his ships, hit his head, and was never quite stable afterward; fourth, Gertrude became increasingly hypochondriac; and, fifth, the family standard of living went into decline.[3]

At first, however, this decline was barely perceptible. During the war years, at least, life for the Carows went normally. On April 18, 1865, Gertrude's last child, Emily, was born and was placed, along

15

with her older sister, in the capable hands of an Irish nurse, Mary Ledwith. "Mame," as everyone called her, had emigrated in the 1840s in a sailing ship.[4] With her rosy cheeks and graying hair pulled back into a tight bun, she looked every inch an "amiable and solicitous tyrant."[5] Her fund of Gaelic sayings suited every occasion. "Better a finger off than aye wagging," she would caution the children in moments of indecision. If they were inclined to waste the food on their plates, she would recall the hard times in Ireland, when poor people needed "the ticket for soup and the letter for brandy."[6]

A week after the arrival of Emily, Edith went over to the Cornelius Van Schaak Roosevelt mansion to witness Lincoln's funeral procession. Since infancy she had been inseparable from the youngest Roosevelt grandchild, Corinne or "Conie." The two little girls were almost exactly of an age; as babies they had been wheeled side by side in Union Square.[7] Conie came often to visit Edith at Livingston Place; one day that summer she brought her brothers Theodore and Elliott as well. Their arrival caused some excitement.

"I was but four years old," Edith recalled, "when my mother came to the nursery to say that the Roosevelt children were coming to spend the day. I remember hiding my old and broken toys and my nurse explaining that the shabbiest of all might give the visitors the most pleasure."[8]

From the start Edith formed a special relationship with "Teedie," an asthmatic, shortsighted, and studious boy, three years her senior. She allowed him to play "house" with her, but five-and-a-half-year-old "Ellie" was excluded. Theodore soon came to depend on the friendship, and expressed disappointment at not seeing little "Edie" when he visited other homes.[9]

Mrs. Theodore Roosevelt, aware of the growing intimacy between Edie and her eldest son, invited the child to join him, Elliott and Corinne for kindergarten tuition in their brownstone at 28 East Twentieth Street. Gertrude, who was already feeling the effects of postwar inflation, happily agreed.

The head of the Roosevelt household, Theodore Senior, was the youngest son of Cornelius Van Schaak Roosevelt, who had made him a wedding present of the brownstone in 1854. At thirty-five he was a handsome, solid-looking man of enormous vitality, bent on increasing the Roosevelt fortune in plate glass and real estate, so that he could retire early and devote himself to his family and to philanthropy. "Mittie," as his wife Martha Bulloch Roosevelt was called, came from a plantation in Roswell, Georgia. She made no bones as to where her patriotic sympathies lay in the aftermath of the Civil War. Her fierce Southern loyalty was no doubt the reason why her husband had paid for a substitute soldier to fight for the Union in his place.[10]

Edith's first impression was of a magnificent-looking woman with jet-black hair and coral-tinged skin, just turned thirty. Fastidious to a degree, Mittie insisted that visitors leave their shoes in the hall of the Roosevelt brownstone, and provided a clean sheet for her doctor to sit on while he tended her. So elaborate was her toilette that she once missed a ball because she had taken so long to dress. Her eldest child, Anna, or "Bamie,"[11] never forgot one of her more elaborate outfits.

> She had on an enormous crinoline and a perfectly exquisite white muslin dress over a pink silk lining with all the little ruffles at the bottom edged with real lace, and the cloak . . . matched the dress, and the bonnet tied under her chin with great pink ribbons . . . and on the brim of the bonnet was a great big pink rose with perfectly realistic little green dragon flies. She also had a parasol with a real ivory handle and the lining of pink covered with muslin and trimmed with real lace . . .[12]

Mittie's unmarried sister, Anna Bulloch, lived at Twentieth Street, and in return for bed and board (she had lost most of her money during the war) taught the Roosevelt children in the second-floor nursery. Soft-voiced and violet-scented, "Aunt Annie" was to marry James K. Gracie in 1866, but she would continue as governess, supplementing her husband's income while he made his way in real estate. As a diehard Southerner, she had an inexhaustible fund of Br'er Rabbit stories, which she recited to the children in an animated drawl.[13] From these tales Edith graduated to the McGuffey Series of Readers, designed "to impart valuable information and to exert a decided and healthful moral influence" on young American minds. Teedie loved these books, too, and as President of the United States would often use pejoratives from McGuffey, such as "Meddlesome Matties," to describe his political opponents. The phrase "big stick" appears in Reader No. 3. McGuffey was the first of countless authors whom Theodore and Edith studied together. Notwithstanding her youth, she was sometimes seen, a little girl in a white dress, reading to Teedie on the steps of the Roosevelt brownstone.[14]

"She was sometimes seen . . . reading to Teedie on the steps."
The Roosevelt brownstone on East Twentieth Street, New York City.

Another series that absorbed them was "the very best magazine in the world," *Our Young Folks.* Such tales as "Pussy Willow," "Little Women," and "An Old Fashioned Girl" stressed the well-tried Victorian virtues of womanliness, manliness, good conduct, and decency upon their impressionable minds. Both Edith and Theodore kept bound volumes of this magazine all their lives.[15]

Edith's memories of her early learning experiences were not without the usual childhood distress. She once wrote of

> the schoolroom, the children around the table, and dear Mrs. Gracie training clumsy little fingers to write . . . I remember when in unison we recited Longfellow's *Children's Hour,* all eyes turned upon me, and all voices raised at the line "Edith with golden hair," until I was sunk in confusion and tears.[16]

Though naturally shy, Edith overcame her reticence to some extent as she grew older, but the desire for privacy and distaste for exhibitionism never left her. A picture taken in 1865 shows a composed, self-possessed little girl with eyes wise beyond her years, a strong nose and a firm mouth. There is, however, something vulnerable about her expression, and something apprehensive in the delicate circle formed by her thumb and forefinger. She looks like a child who already has some knowledge of the adult world. Her neatly matched headband and cummerbund and the well-starched ruff are clues to why she was known as "Spotless Edie."[17]

The air of remoteness about her was often mistaken for coldness or self-absorption. "When I was young," she later admitted to a son, "the other girls used to reproach me with 'indifference' and I fear you have inherited that trick of manner, which is all it is."[18] A shrewd friend observed that "she always seemed deeply detached from the external accidents of life. . . . her warmth and passion lay far beneath the surface. One felt in her a great strength of character and ineluctable willpower."[19]

A good part of every day at Twentieth Street was spent on physical exercise. Theodore Senior, a strong believer in cultivating the body as well as the mind, converted a back bedroom next to the nursery into an open-air twenty-by-twenty-five-foot piazza. Here in this "gymnasium" crippled Bamie (suffering from a congenital spinal defect, the result of Pott's disease), asthmatic Teedie, headachy Elliott, and Conie, also an asthmatic, strove to build up their strength and agility on parallel bars and ladders. Edith, whose own health was excellent, felt no need of such artificial exercise. In any case, she was never at ease in the gymnasium, and recalled her few attempts on the apparatus as being "painful and faltering." Her chief athletic feats were shinning down a wisteria vine which covered the piazza onto a pantry extension below, and climbing on top of a wardrobe to hide from the boys.[20]

The need for solitude was perhaps her most striking characteristic as a child, despite a capacity for close friendship. Once when she felt aggrieved she hid from her mother in an asparagus bed for hours, until Gertrude despaired that she had run away. Afterward Edith suffered great remorse for shattering an "already broken heart."[21]

That phrase is significant, for Gertrude Tyler Carow indeed had reasons to be unhappy. Her husband's drinking had increased in ratio to a disastrous drop in income from the Kermit & Carow shipping business.[22] Added to this, a ruinous rise in prices after the Civil War had forced the Carows to economize by moving in with Robert Kermit's widow, Aunt Ann Eliza. The old lady had a house which backed onto Cornelius Van Schaak Roosevelt's mansion on Union Square. Thus began a period of rootlessness which Edith was to remember all her life. From the time she was six, she said, her father never had a job or a home of his own, and was compelled to rely on the kindness of relatives to shelter his family. In winter this fell to the lot of Aunt Kermit; in summer to Grandfather Tyler, who kept a place near Red Bank, New Jersey. From both houses Charles made occasional forays in search of business.[23]

In 1867 events went from bad to worse. The year began inauspiciously. People crossing the East River on thin January ice had a close brush with death as it cracked into fragments. In April the government spent over $7 million buying Alaska from the Russians, with no apparent advantage to the economy. By December, while Dickens captivated the country reading from his own works, President Johnson was so unpopular as to face impeachment, and fifty thousand New Yorkers were out of work.

Edith, happily oblivious, retained her place in the Roosevelt inner circle. "Aunt Annie, Edith and Ellie send their love," wrote Theodore to his mother on April 28, 1868, as if his little chum were one of the family.[24] For the time being, at least, Gertrude and Charles were probably relieved to have it so. Their daughter was in good hands.

Aunt Annie, now Mrs. Gracie, expanded the girls' curriculum to include needlework. She held the classes at her furnished rooms on Fourth (now Park) Avenue. Edith became an accomplished needle-woman. She also enjoyed Aunt Annie's *al fresco* lunches of cold lamb and green pickles, which seemed to her the height of delightful dissipation in contrast to her regular nursery fare.[25]

Mittie, though increasingly impractical and fey, was another charming companion, reading to the children for hours on end, and telling them thrilling plantation stories of Negroes and hunting trips. Theodore Senior, busy as he was with his work for the Children's Aid Society, the State Aid Society, the Orthopedic Hospital, the Museum of Natural History, and the Museum of Art, took an active role in Edith's education. He produced plays for her to act in, devised topics for impromptu speeches, and organized nature trips along the Hudson and sailing jaunts on the Central Park swan boat. He was "the best man I ever knew," Theodore Junior would say long after meeting the greatest men of America and Europe.[26]

The Roosevelts were as generous with gifts as they were with their time. Fanny Smith (another of Teedie's little girl friends) recalled winning several valuable prizes for party games at Twentieth Street, including a black and gold enameled ring with a small diamond. Edith once received a tiny porcelain tea set, complete with ivory-handled knives and forks.[27] Mittie had deduced the girl's love of china from her habit of collecting broken shards.

Fanny Smith, writing her memoirs many years later, described the Roosevelts as "a family so rarely gifted that it seemed touched with the flame of 'divine fire.'"[28] Bamie, though less than four years older than Teedie, was counted as one of the "grown people."[29] She was dependable and organized, with an authoritative manner that few people questioned. As Mittie relinquished more and more household responsibility, Bamie energetically took it up. "She is a very good sister," declared Corinne, "and a splendid girl altogether although a little imperious every now and then."[30]

Plain and dark-skinned in an age when girls coveted fair complexions,[31] Bamie was further handicapped by a stooping gait due to her spinal disease. But what she lacked in beauty she made up in charm. She could seem "so absorbed in her companion of the moment as to make him feel of the utmost importance."[32] Riveted by her pale laughing eyes, swept along by the sweetness of her personality, and impressed by her competence, people forgot her physical defects.

Edith recalled being filled with "awe and admiration" at Bamie's skill in making her a doll's bonnet, and this awe carried over into adult life. Even in her sleep, Edith was all too aware of Bamie's powers of disapproval. "I had a dreadful dream last night," she once wrote, "in which you took me to a horse show and were very indignant because I removed my shoes and climbed the roof of a house. . . ."[33] There was awe, too, on Bamie's side. But it would be some years before Edith found this out.

Volatile, inquisitive, untidy Teedie was a trying brother for Bamie, but he was her favorite nevertheless. An all-consuming devotion to natural history, dissection, and taxidermy led him to make extraordinary demands on his family. "Bring home some mockingbird feathers," he commanded his mother when she was in the South, "and tell me how many curiosities and living things you have got for me."[34] And to his father: "You know what supple jacks are, do you not? Please get one for Ellie and two for me. Ask your friend to let you cut off the tiger cat's tail, and get some long moos and have it mated together . . ."[35]

Pets increasingly obsessed him, to the chagrin of his elders. A live mouse once leaped out of a Dutch cheese passed to Theodore Senior at table. The Roosevelt's cook was horrified to discover a dead one, destined for Teedie's scientific purposes, stored in the icebox. On a streetcar one day, a friend of Mittie's was struck dumb when Teedie politely tipped his hat and several frogs landed at her feet.

Ellie also balked at some of his brother's pastimes. At the family summer home he drew a line between their two beds, beyond which Teedie's snakes ventured at their peril. As he grew older he became disinclined to share a room with him because of the stench of entrails and arsenic.

Elliott's gentle good looks and generous nature made him the darling of the nursery, and the apple of Aunt Annie's eye. Since he craved love, and was very demonstrative in return, women especially indulged him. To Fanny Smith he was "quite irresistible."[36] Socially and athletically Ellie was much more mature than his brother; intellectually and morally he was much weaker. As he approached puberty he began to suffer debilitating nervous attacks, brought on, it appears, by feelings of inferiority and self-doubt. Eventually, these bouts prevented him from leading a normal school life.

The mutual attraction of Corinne and Edith was, for the most part, one of opposites. While the former was vital, fanciful and gregarious, the latter was moody, serious, and solitary. They shared a love of poetry, and boundless admiration for Teedie. Outside the family, Edith was the person Corinne cared for most.

In the spring of 1869, Ulysses S. Grant was inaugurated President of the United States. America, her civil strife behind her, prospered again. In the West, the construction of the massive Union Pacific and Central Pacific Railroads neared completion. In the East, Frederick Law Olmsted put the final touches to his $15-million landscaping of Central Park. Now, on sunny afternoons, open-top victorias driven by liveried coachmen and drawn by ornately bridled bobtailed chestnuts and strawberry roans could be seen circling the carriage-ways. Inside them splendidly attired matrons nodded at passing gentlemen riders, while younger ladies of leisure twirled their parasols in the Mall.

But the Roosevelt family was looking beyond its immediate horizons for amusement. All winter they had studied travel books and pored over maps in preparation for a year-long tour of Europe. By the time sailing day arrived on May 12, the children were resigned to this dread excursion, with the exception of ten-and-a-half-year-old Teedie. He hated to leave his live "buggie" creatures and his stuffed dead ones. Even more, he hated to leave Edith Carow, and cried profusely on the way to the docks. "It was verry *[sic]* hard parting from our friend," he wrote in his diary.[37]

Arriving at Liverpool on May 21, the Roosevelts spent ten days with relatives of Mittie before going on to Scotland. On the train from Glasgow to York Teedie said again how very sad he had been "to part with Edith, and cousins Jimmie and Emlen." Edith was proud to know that "I came first."[38]

Six months and nine countries later Teedie jubilantly calculated: "We have been half the time we are to stay abroad! hip! hurrah!" Travel did not improve his health. In Paris on November 15 he was so sick that he left the hotel only for a Russian bath and then came back and "wrote a letter to Eideth *[sic]*." She was never far from his thoughts. On November 22 he recorded a poignantly misspelled diary entry: "In the evening mamma showed me the portrait of Eidieth Carow and her face stired up in me homesickness and longings for the past which will come again never, alack never."[39] He

"Her face stired up in me homesickness
and longings for the past . . ."
Theodore Roosevelt, aged ten,
and Edith Carow, aged seven.

told Edith she was his "most faithful correspondent," and two of her
childhood letters to him have miraculously survived.[40] They are
written on minute hand-lined notepaper embossed with red initials.
The first appears to have been written in the fall of 1869.

DEAR TEEDIE
    The little picture in your last letter pleased me very
much you are the first one to whom I have written with
this pen it is a dear little gold one a present for having
some teeth drawn and filled. The filling was more
painful than the drawing because laughing gas was
given when the teeth were drawn. When I took the gas I

thought I was in the green house and I felt no pain at all. I send you a sensitive leaf if you hold it in your hand it will curl all up. I shall send Conie another we are just leaving the country

goodbye yours
EDITH[41]

In her other letter written from Red Bank she told him a funny story about little Emily, and, remembering his passion for animals, announced: "We have got a pig that has been all around the world in one of Papas ships he is as fat as he can be . . ."[42]

At Christmas she must have written again, and Teedie, who was by then in Sorrento, replied early in the New Year.

MY DEAR EIDIE,

We came from Naples today. I have recieved your interesting letter and reply to it on paper recieved on Christmas. Yesterday we made the ascent of Mt. Vesuvius. It was snow covered which heightened our enjoyment. We went first in caraiges for a long while. We then got out and mounted ponies. We mounted now pretty steadily. At first we walked but after a while Papa, Ellie and I galloped ahead with two guides and one strange gentleman. These guides were the only ones mounted. We galloped along until we came to a gulley coated with ice on which the horses walked with 2 legs on one side and 2 legs on the other side. We got to a house where we dismounted to wait for the others and as Conie came up she gave me a great big snowball on the side. I would have thrown another at her but we had to mount and Ellie and I galloped ahead till we came to the place where we got off our horses. I made a snowball and as Conie came up hit her. We then began the ascent of snow covered Mt. Vesuvius. I went first with one guide with a strap in which I put my hands. One place where the side was steeper than any alp I have been on the guide and I fell We recovered ourselves right away. Our Alpine stocks went down farther and our guide had to go down to get them. I got up to near the top we went inside of a wall where the snow ceased and it was quite warm. We then went on untill we came to a small hole through which we saw a red flame inside the mountain. I put my alpine stock in and it caught fire right away. The smoke nearly suffacated us. We then went on and saw a larger hole through which I could fall if I liked. We put some pebbles down and they came up with pretty good force. We here sat down to lunch. We ate some of the eggs boiled in Vesuvius sand. Ellie and I played with some soildiers and then we began the decent. This was on the opposite side of the mountain. I was the last, then Mama with Papa on one and a guide on the other side of her and then the rest. We went down the side in loose dirt in which I sunk up to my knees. The decent was verry steep. Mama was so exausted she could hardly walk. When we got to the bottom we mounted our horses and went along a miserable road. There were places where the men who were on foot could hardly walk so it was verry hard for the horses. We then drove to the hotel. But now goodby

Evere your loving friend,

T. Roosevelt[43]

While Teedie went on to Rome and Florence, Edith began to feel lonely. She was glad not to be spending the winter in the city, she told Conie, "for I shall miss you much and if I stay here I can play with a beautiful sled that Uncle Guss gave me . . ."[44]

With the Roosevelts away the nursery classes had been abandoned, and there was some talk of sending Edith to school. But her enrollment was postponed, purportedly because "Mammma thinks my eyes are not very strong." In a complaint common to bookish children, Edith added: "She and Mame whenever they see a book in my hands give me no peace till I lay it down."[45]

Every week, however, she attended classes at Mr. Dodsworth's famous school for dancing and deportment, at the corner of Twenty-sixth Street and Fifth Avenue. The strict old dancing master and his wife taught succeeding generations of New Yorkers not only how to waltz and polka on the wide slippery floor, but also how to conduct themselves in society. A later pupil remembered them both vividly.

*   *   *

Mr. Dodsworth was the impersonation of elegance and etiquette, coupled with a stinging sarcasm and discipline. We left our coats and little fur-lined shoes in the room downstairs. We then shook hands and curtsied to Mrs. Dodsworth, whose hair had the stiffest ondulé, whose voice had the most liquid modulation, and whose person was sheathed in a dress covered with spangles or embroidered with pearls, or poured into a creation of cloth of gold. She sat at a painted Louis XV desk with a register to mark our attendance which she did with a fine pen and holding her little finger slightly extended while she wrote. Mr. and Mrs. Dodsworth were the visible expression of all that it meant to be a lady and a gentleman in those days.[46]

When the Roosevelts returned in the spring of 1870, they joined Edith at the dancing school, and quickly became the nucleus of an exclusive group. Fanny Smith was a member. "There was no fear of being a wallflower because we had . . . special badges and pledged either definitely or otherwise only to dance with one another."[47]

Years later, an outsider reminded Edith that "for every dance there was a scramble on the part of four Roosevelts, 'Teddy,' Elliott, Alfred and Emlen to secure you for a partner." Apparently Theodore usually triumphed, because Edith saved the dance programs "on which his name was written oftener than any other boy's."[48]

Three

If you would be happy and enjoy life at any time, you must fulfill honestly and faithfully the duties of the hour; for from the time we can distinguish good from evil, every hour has its duties and responsibilities.

—General Daniel Tyler to Edith Carow[1]

Very little remains, in a physical sense, of the New York City of Edith's childhood. But it lives on vividly in the prose of Edith Wharton, her distant cousin and contemporary, who saw it as "a cramped horizontal gridiron of a town without towers, porticoes, fountains or perspectives," cursed with a "universal chocolate-covered coating of the most hideous stone ever quarried."[2]

What brownstones lacked in exterior grace they compensated for in interior luxury. Large marble fireplaces, heavy damask draperies, tall ormolu mirrors, and ornate glass chandeliers overwhelmed the narrow rooms. English porcelain, leatherbound books, and ivory fans crammed shelves and display cabinets. As possessions outstripped space, Astors, Goelets, and Roosevelts poured their surplus wealth into real estate, and built mansions in vacant lots uptown. Until the early 1870s Manhattan's fashionable citizens had clustered below Fiftieth Street in such exclusive neighborhoods as Union Square,

"A cramped horizontal gridiron of a town . . ."
The New York City of Edith's childhood.

Gramercy Park, and Madison Square. As these areas became crowded, and as commerce moved in, society migrated to grander homes farther north.

The first to break with brownstone tradition was not one of the old Knickerbocker "nobs," but one of the nouveau-riche "swells," department-store prince Alexander T. Stewart. This sandy-haired Scot, whose fortune was second in size only to that of the Vanderbilts, had the audacity to build a $1.5-million palazzo, at Fifth Avenue and Thirty-fourth Street, right opposite the solid town house of society leader Mrs. William B. Astor.[3] Stewart stuffed his mansion with over a thousand of the finest canvases, statues, and art objects ever assembled by one collector. But sheer wealth did not admit a man automatically to the higher echelons—at least not yet—and the Astors elected not to call on the harsh-voiced haberdasher.

Gradually, over the next two decades, old established Oelrichs and Stevenses and newly arrived Fricks and Carnegies began to settle side by side in Fifth Avenue mansions which edged out the scattered shanties that had long bordered Central Park. Wealth, not breeding, now determined where people might live. The Roosevelts were able to follow the prosperous migration north; but other well-bred Knickerbockers who, like the Carows, had fallen on hard times were forced to choose less exalted neighborhoods.

In 1870 New York's population, having almost tripled in thirty years, approached a million. Yet expansion was still entirely lateral. Skyscrapers did not exist, and Trinity Church spire remained the only vertical thrust of any stature. Large tracts along Fifth Avenue and Broadway consisted of empty lots, while Madison Avenue ended abruptly at Forty-second Street. Harlem was a small country town, and the riverside between West Seventieth and West 110th Streets was nothing more than a village.

Carriages, stagecoaches and four railroads running at street level created tremendous noise and smoke in midtown. Ill-paved roads littered with horse manure, and slimy gutters scavenged by pigs were breeding grounds for malaria and typhoid. Barefoot street urchins huddled in doorways and over gratings for warmth. Sanitation hardly existed in rat-ridden tenements; an average of seventy-eight people shared each slum privy. When cholera struck, as it frequently did, medical help was scarce. The infant-mortality rate was thirty percent, and life expectancy averaged only forty years.

Crime "was never so bold, so frequent, and so safe" according to the diarist George Templeton Strong. "We breathe an atmosphere of highway robbery, burglary and murder. Few criminals are caught and fewer punished . . . We must soon fall back on the law of self-preservation."[4]

About two miles south of the Carow house was Five Points, the most notorious district in New York. Radiating from City Hall Place (euphemistically known to locals as Paradise Square) were pungent alleyways crammed with cheap taverns, gambling dens and brothels. Even the slum-hardened Charles Dickens was appalled by the extreme poverty and vice and "bloated faces" of neighborhood alcoholics. "All that is loathsome and decayed is here," he wrote in his *American Notes*.[5]

Although the rich suffered no such indignities, some of them endured lives of real vacuity. Weak-chinned opportunists vied for the favors of homely heiresses, spoiled matrons spent fortunes on the latest Paris fads, and clad their flunkeys in opulent livery; decadent industrialists plied their yachts of ill repute along the Eastern seaboard.[6]

In this diverse social climate, precariously poised between the opulence of Fifth Avenue and the squalor of downtown, Edith Kermit Carow grew up.

On July 17, 1871, as deprived Irish immigrants rioted in New York City, Edith heard that Cornelius Van Schaak Roosevelt had died. The dust had hardly settled on his grave when plans were announced to tear down his splendid mansion, with its tesselated marble floors and silver doorknobs, and replace it with a sewing-machine warehouse.[7] With commerce moving into Union Square it was clearly time for the Carows and Aunt Kermit to relocate as far uptown as they could afford.

That August, while Charles hunted for a house, Gertrude, Edith, Emily, Mame, and Lily the cat set off for a vacation in Pennsylvania. Since it had been decided that Edith would go to school in the fall, this was to be her last spell of childish freedom.

Two days after her tenth birthday the party arrived in Renovo, on the west branch of the Susquehanna. "We can see three large mountains," she wrote her father from the hotel, "and a beautiful river like a silver thread so shallow that this morning I saw a horse and wagon drive across it."[8] Charles Carow replied with long and charming letters addressed to "My Dolly." Anxious to hear as much from her as possible, he sought to reassure her: "No matter about the spelling when you write to me. Say what you want to say and don't lose time thinking about the words . . . just write whatever comes in your head." He encouraged her burgeoning interest in plants with snippets of horticultural news: "Isabel brought or sent a slip of myrtle for you and I have planted it. I think that it is the same plant that you know under the name of vinca, except that the leaf is not edged with white." He urged her to read his long letters without assistance, as she had "no fried sums or stewed geography dishes to cook."[9]

During the following two weeks the children took buggy rides, climbed hills, picnicked in the woods, fished in the streams, played croquet, and acted in tableaus of Red Riding Hood and Tom Thumb. Edith, already showing promise as a horsewoman, practiced riding. "I have got Spency the pony to face up and down the walks and go slow when I turn him round."[10]

Meanwhile Gertrude, who at thirty-five found few joys left in life, complained in a shaky hand of a lack of husbandly letters, of too much dust, of unrelenting headaches and chronic back pain. When news finally came that Charles had let the Fourteenth Street house, she querulously hoped he would be able "to find one to replace that will please."[11] By the same mail Edith, with all the optimism and enthusiasm of youth, wrote her dear Papa: "Won't it be fun packing up to move."[12]

That fall the Carows and Aunt Kermit settled down in a town house at 200 West Forty-fourth Street. It was now time for Edith to begin the formal stage of her education. She accordingly enrolled at Miss Comstock's School, an exclusive private establishment occupying two brownstones at 32 and 34 West Fortieth Street. It had been recommended by Fanny Smith's father; Fanny was to be a student there, too.

Wearing her new uniform of red-piped plaid dress and flat-heeled boots, her fair hair braided, Edith arrived for her first day's schooling.[13] She was welcomed by a black doorman, and shown into a parlor. Except for its painted floor and chairs, it did not look in the least like a classroom. There was a central table, large enough to accommodate ten or twelve pupils, a bureau with little mats and cologne bottles, a mantelpiece adorned with photographs and ornaments, a corner table with books, and a basket of fruit. Boarders, who slept in rooms opening to left and right, had arranged the parlor "in this pretty manner."[14]

Miss Louise Comstock, the headmistress, had "flashing dark eyes and clear-cut features." She held a "terrifying charm for the more impressionable of her pupils."[15] But as they got to know her high ideals in matters of conduct, morality, and learning, they learned to respect and even love her. "The foundation of her life," recalled one student, "was built upon religion, and all her teachings were along inspirational lines."[16]

Edith, influenced by Miss Comstock, grew up to be deeply religious and conscientious, with a highly developed moral sense weaker mortals often found disconcerting. The assistant teachers also left their stamp. Miss Ward, a strict disciplinarian, taught her self-control; Miss Watson encouraged her love of literature, and gave her high grades for essays and neatness; Mrs. Luddington, a specialist in English history, knew everything worth knowing about the Wars of the Roses, and stimulated the girl's curiosity in other people and places. Edith had a better appreciation of the general than the particular, and though she learned "dozens of things," the "'names of battles dates of kings' my mind let slip with marked success."[17]

Then there was Miss Winters, who conducted a select Latin class of only three pupils: Edith, Fanny, and a "high-minded" girl named Alice Post. While Fanny and Alice found the *Aeneid* "a treat," Edith lacked enthusiasm, and even resisted her Virgil-loving father's attempts to give her supplementary lessons. She also had "no success" with German, but persevered with French, the main language of the Comstock classroom, and became quite fluent, peppering her conversation and letters with Gallic phrases. Even so, at the end of her life she still lamented being "so very stupid about languages."[18]

The only sciences Edith studied were zoology, botany, and physiology, which consisted of learning the names of the parts of the body in Latin. Higher mathematics were not, to her relief, included in the Comstock curriculum. One of "the advantages of being a girl," she always avowed, was not having to take geometry.[19]

Miss Comstock's schedule of required textbooks was formidable. A partial list featured Oswald's *Etymology*, Colburn's *Mental Arithmetic*, Cooley's *Natural Philosophy*, Harkness's *Latin Grammar*, Caesar, *Principia Latina, Comédies et Proverbes, Fables de La Fontaine, Malheurs de Sophie*, Dickens's *Child's History of England*, the Bible, *Tales of the Saxons, Birds and Flowers*, and the *Letters of Chatham*.[20]

Edith's best subject was English literature. When Gertrude, who was perennially worried about the children's financial future, tried "to make believe that I had an accomplishment, [she] hit upon what she called 'Belles Lettres.'"[21] If the worst came to the worst, Gertrude fantasized, Edith could perhaps support the family by writing.

Her taste for Shakespeare, stimulated by Taine's *Abridged History of English Literature*, turned into a lifelong passion. "Shakespeare says everything for me always." *As You Like It* was her favorite comedy, and she believed that if by some misfortune the play were lost, she would be able to "write it out." Of the tragedies, she preferred *Macbeth,* and, to her mind, *Romeo and Juliet* was "the most beautiful love story ever written."[22] A copy of Shakespeare accompanied her on most journeys, and she was once seen sitting on a stack of trunks reading *King John* aloud.

Edith's love of literature so interfered with other studies that she made a rule for herself not to read poetry or novels during the school week, because "one gets too absorbed."[23]

As for music, Comstock's offered a much more extensive education than the usual patriotic and religious fare served up at American public schools of the period. Edith regularly went to symphony concerts at Steinway Hall, and choral performances at the Academy of Music, both on Fourteenth Street. She played no musical instrument herself, and had a rather ordinary singing voice, but she developed a deep reverence for the classical masters, and appreciated such shocking modernists as Liszt and Wagner long before they were fashionable. The violinist Heifetz, while still a mere "gangling shock-haired boy of 18," left her "absolutely dazed with emotion."[24]

One of Edith's classmates was the granddaughter of P. T. Barnum, and when the old showman brought his circus to the Hippodrome she became the most sought-after girl in school. Other popular pastimes, as Edith and Fanny approached adolescence, were going to Shakespeare matinees at the new Edwin Booth Theater, promenading on Fifth Avenue, and taking the trolley to Astor Place to ogle the dashing Seventh Regiment at drill.

> Sometimes [wrote Fanny] Edith and I would spend the afternoon together in the dim dusty precincts of the Society Library on University Place. There we would find the books not always accessible at home. Rhoda Broughton's *Red as A Rose is She* and *Goodbye Sweetheart* would have been considered dangerous fare by my father and mother but in the remote security of the Society Library I was able utterly to lose myself in their deliriously romantic pages. Whether Edith also indulged in forbidden fruit I don't remember but I know that usually her taste in reading was for the best.[25]

Such excursions, of course, were the exception rather than the rule. Month after month, year after year, the strict regimen of school dominated Edith's activities, even down to the basic skill of handwriting. Miss Ellis, Comstock's specialist in the art, taught the girls a style invented and vigorously promoted by Platt Rogers Spencer, which became the standard script of three generations of Americans. Using both old-fashioned quills and the new metallic pens, Edith practiced the chief Spencerian characteristics: round, flowing curves, combining legibility with grace. As she mastered the form she gave it her own individual stamp. Experts may divine imagination and quick thinking in the racy angularity of her pen strokes. Often she writes at such speed that letters and words merge; *t* crosses fly way above their stems; dots are scattered far from the parent *i;* periods have an impatient resemblance to dashes. Unmistakably, her style says, "I, too, am somebody."[26]

Edith and Emily Carow in early adolescence.

Youth
1872–1886

Four

I have a feeling for Edith which I have for no one else, a tender kind of feeling. . . . Every time I see her I notice what a clever girl she is.

—Corinne Roosevelt[1]

On October 16, 1872, the Roosevelt children said goodbye to Edith and sailed for "another terrible trip" abroad.[2] Theodore Senior had accepted the post of American Commissioner to the Vienna Exposition of 1873, and proposed to spend the intervening winter in Egypt and the Levant.

Soon letters began to arrive at 200 West Forty-fourth Street, bearing exotic postmarks, and relating adventures in the mummy pits of Edfoo, atop the Great Pyramid of Cheops, and around the Temple of Karnak. Theodore also sent lists of specimens he had bagged for the new "Roosevelt Museum of Natural History" which he had established on the third floor at Twentieth Street, such as ibis, cranes, storks, and pelicans. While he was having a thoroughly good time, Corinne was nostalgic for home.

"My own darling Edie," she wrote from Thebes on February 1, "don't you remember what fun we used to have out in the country, and don't you remember the day we got Pony Grant up in the

Chauncey's summer house and couldn't get him down again, and how we were always losing Teedie's india rubber shoes?"[3]

The Roosevelts arrived in Constantinople on April 6, 1873. The next day Teedie, who had suffered only three attacks of asthma and one of cholera morbus in the previous six months, wrote Edith:

> I think I have enjoyed myself more this winter than I ever did before. Much to add to my enjoyment Father gave me a gun at Christmas, which rendered me happy and the rest of the family miserable.
>
> I killed several hundred birds with it, and then went and lost it! I think I enjoyed the time in Egypt most, and after that I had the most fun while camping out in Syria . . . we were on horseback for several hours of each day, and as I like riding ever so much, and as the Syrian horses are very good, we had a splendid time. While riding I bothered the family somewhat by carrying the gun over my shoulder, and on the journey to the Jordan, when I was on the most spirited horse I ever rode, I bothered the horse too, as was evidenced by his running away several times when the gun struck him too hard. Our tent life had a good many adventures in it. Once it rained very hard and the rain went into our open trunks. Another time our tents were almost blown away in a rough wind, and once I hunted a couple of jackals for two or three miles as fast as the horse would go. Yours truly,
>
> T. ROOSEVELT, JR.[4]

Significantly, this letter to Edith deals exclusively with his own manly attributes of courage and daring, while others written to relatives at the same time lyrically describe ruins, and make childish jokes about native nudity and Mittie's indigestion.

In the spring of 1873 the Roosevelts split up. While Theodore Senior took up his position in Vienna, Bamie accompanied her mother to Carlsbad to take the waters, and the three younger children traveled to Dresden to spend the summer studying with a German family. There Theodore mastered the heroic *Nibelungenlied*, excelled at boxing and wrestling, and plagued his hosts with smelly experiments on mice and hedgehogs. In spite of this, his German tutor, Fräulein Anna Minkwitz, perceived that he was an extraordinarily gifted boy. When Mittie came to collect the children, and asked Anna, "I wonder what is going to become of my Teddy?" the young woman replied, "You need not be anxious about him. He will surely be one day a great professor, or, who knows, he may become even President of the United States."[5]

The Roosevelts' boat docked in New York on November 5, 1873, and Theodore Senior took his family directly to their new townhouse at 6 West Fifty-seventh Street. He had returned from Europe ahead of them to supervise its construction. Edith Carow paid her first visit shortly afterward, and found an infinitely grander house than the Twentieth Street brownstone, with ornate wood paneling, richly carved furniture, and luxurious Persian rugs. The rooms shimmered with glass and crystal, and gleamed with polished brass and silver.

Against this sumptuous background Edith and Theodore renewed acquaintance. She found him more mature in every way. The puny "pig-chested" boy of thirteen months before had been transformed into a tall, serious, bespectacled youth.[6] His personality, too, had changed. He had developed a sense of chivalry, and become something of a prude, contemptuous of boys who swore and told risqué jokes. Juvenile traits of willfulness and self-importance remained. As his cousin Maud Elliott noted, Theodore was still sure that "he could do things better than anyone else."[7]

A few weeks later Edith saw him again at Bamie's New York debut.[8] She was the youngest of four hundred guests, and the brilliance of the gathering merely served to emphasize what she already sensed: that a wide gulf now existed between her twelve-year-old self and this newly accomplished naturalist, linguist and pugilist. Theodore's travels and strange experiences set him apart from his peers, and from her. He had already begun intensive private tuition in preparation for Harvard, and several years must pass before they would recapture the closeness they had known as children. As if to underline her immaturity, she found herself being bundled off to bed with Corinne when the German dances began at 2:30 A.M.

Coincidentally or not, Edith's friendship with Corinne now took on a new dimension. In Dresden Corinne had belonged to a literary club, which she sought to imitate in New York City. Accordingly she appointed herself its president and invited Edith to be secretary. Another close friend, Fanny Smith, and nine other girls made up the membership. They met once a week, fortified themselves with doughnuts and lemonade, and read aloud their own poems, stories, and essays. The club was called P.O.R.E., an abbreviation first interpreted as "Paradise of Ravenous Eaters." But as the members grew older (their association appears to have lasted about three years) they settled on the more prosaic name "Party of Renowned Eligibles."

After each meeting Edith copied the literary offerings into notebooks, which soon ran to several volumes. On a typical Saturday the program included an essay entitled "A Continental Tour," a romance called "The Modern Sleeping Beauty," and Edith's poem "The Four-Leaved Clover." This last was full of Keatsian compound adjectives, and described a little girl "hammock-swung" with her mother in "a cool vine-draped corner." The mother muses on her daughter's childish ways, which are "not unlike the ways of men." The penultimate verse reads:

> *Is it not so? Some valued prize we seek,*
> *Feel fortune-favored when we it do find*
> *And yet but vanished have a few short days*
> *When we move on, and leave our prize behind.*[9]

Some of Edith's P.O.R.E. stories were typically adolescent, with heroines in pale wraps and feathered slippers finding true love in the final paragraph. But her poetry, which Fanny Smith remembered as being the most finished of the group, was more complex, and dealt with adult themes of loss, despair, regret, resignation and renewal. In one verse, sadness is dispelled by the arrival of a man to whom the heroine can minister; in another, joy at the arrival of a new baby quickly moves to

> *Soon those helpless tiny fingers*
> *By life's thorns will wounded be*
> *Holding close the cruel roses*
> *Plucked from life's deceptive tree.*[10]

"Doughnuts and lemonade . . . stories and essays."
P.O.R.E. members. From left: Edith, Fanny,
Corinne, Grace Potter, unidentified.

Grasp the roses nevertheless, and embrace life "in every flying moment," was the poet's sage advice.

As Edith entered her teens, the United States slid into another depression, which was to last for six years. This renewed economic crisis seems to have further affected Charles Carow's health. A letter from Gertrude to Edith, who was accompanying her father on a recuperative trip to New Jersey, reads enigmatically: "I hope your father has recovered from his fatigue he is not strong and must be careful." More revealing is a series of rough drawings and captions scribbled on the same notepaper by Edith. They suggest that all was not well in the parental relationship. One shows a cadaverous figure in a doorway, with Cupid hovering behind panes of glass. Below is written: "Poverty coming in at the door and love flying out at the window." Another sketch is of a lady reaching to tweak a jester's cap. The caption beneath reads: "When lovely woman stoops to folly." A third has someone blowing on a wick, and the inscription: "Out, out, brief candle."[11]

The next three summers of Edith's young life were divided between the beaches of Monmouth County, New Jersey, and Tranquillity, the Roosevelt seaside place at Oyster Bay, Long Island. There were "not many country seats," she disappointedly observed, on the shores of New Jersey. Most settlements consisted of fishermen's and farm hands' shacks, and the cottages of laborers from inland tomato canneries. In between rose such semifashionable resorts as Long Branch, Oceanic and Sea Bright, patronized mainly by wealthy German Jews.[12] Oyster Bay, in contrast, was almost exclusively WASP, with immaculate white mansions and yachts.

The chief attraction of New Jersey, for Edith, was General Tyler's house, Barbary Brae, on the banks of the Shrewsbury River near Red Bank. Here the old General raised Alderney cows, grew pears, plums, and asparagus, and served delicious suppers of soft-shelled crabs and freshly caught trout. Wisteria and honeysuckle clambered over the large piazza. Maples, elms and willows shaded the spacious gardens, and one large oak sheltered "a little summer house . . . reached by winding stairs." The gardens were a riot of color: gold and purple pansies, red sweet william, brown imperials, Persian lilacs, snow berries, and clumps of white sweet-scented lily of the valley. Marble statues entitled *Cross Husband* and *Good Natured Wife* stood on either side of the white gravel walks edged with moss and clove pinks.[13]

Edith spent long warm days gratifying her nature-loving eye and ear. The sight of fishnets strung out on sable sands, purple beach plums dangling from dark twigs, and speckles of bright marsh flowers bordering the blue inland lagoons, the scent of ripening fruit, the tang of pine on the salty air, the sounds of mewing gulls, and the pounding surf rushing toward the strand stirred her well-tuned senses.

She loved to swim, and to watch the antics of adult bathers. It was *de riguer* in those days for gentlemen in loosely buttoned flannel trouser suits and ladies in skirted jackets, pantaloons, wide-brimmed hats and rubbers to run briskly up and down before entering the water. Police officers patrolled the sands to discourage scandalous flashes of calf.[14]

When her parents took an afternoon drive, and more energetic friends headed for the tennis courts or bowling alleys, Edith went for long country rambles, picking armsful of "goldenrods and the vivid scarlet cardinal and white marsh flowers," which she afterward arranged in an "immense blue pitcher in the dining room."[15] Her knowledge of wildflowers was so developed in the fields of New Jersey that as an adult she would be able to identify the most obscure North American varieties.

Sometimes she climbed up Rumson Neck, a hilly spit of land separating the Shrewsbury and Navesink Rivers. From here she could peer between elegant homes, pavilions, and gingerbread hotels and see the holly forests of Sandy Hook. On a clear day the whole glittering spread of New York Bay, teeming with sailboats and pleasure steamers, spread out before her.

Teedie came to Sea Bright in the last week of July, 1874. But judging from his personal "Notes on Natural History," he had more eyes for local wildlife than for Edith Carow. The little booklet is full of observations of meadowlarks, bitterns, yellowthroats, and, "most conspicuous," the fish hawk, which whistled and boomed as it plunged down on its prey.[16]

Edith was nevertheless invited to visit Oyster Bay in turn. Traveling there, as she soon found out, was a long and complicated business. But as summer followed summer and invitation followed invitation, she learned to treat it as a pleasant ritual, full of anticipatory excitement. She would either take a boat from Port

Washington to New York or make the journey in four separate stages: by coach to Oceanic, train to Jersey City, carriage to Hoboken, and powerful sidewheel ferry across the Hudson River to West Twenty-third Street. In New York she hired a hansom which whisked her to the East Thirty-fourth Street pier, where she took another ferry across to Long Island City, starting point for the train to Syosset. Relaxing in the parlor car, she would select thirst-quenching peaches or pears from straw baskets lined with leaves, and watch the shabby outskirts of the city give way to farmland streaming past the window. The last six miles of her journey, from Syosset to Oyster Bay, were usually made in her host's buggy.

"The children were left pretty much to their own devices."
Tranquillity, Oyster Bay. Mr. and Mrs. Roosevelt on porch;
Corinne and Edith (foreground) on lawn.

A place less tranquil than Tranquillity when full of Roosevelts, their numerous cousins and guests, would be hard to imagine. But the two-storied white clapboard building was stately enough, with its four classical columns fronting on a wide verandah overlooking the bay. The children were left pretty much to their own devices, except for one or two activities which Theodore Senior liked to organize. After church on Sundays he had the children read their own synopses of the sermon. He also encouraged them to perform amateur theatricals, coaching them in acting and advising on costumes and makeup. Fanny Smith, who regarded her annual visit to Oyster Bay as "a week in Paradise," was so improved by Roosevelt cosmetics that Elliott invited her one night to "a sinister-looking structure on a rise of land behind the house" for a cozy assignation.[17]

On riding trips through the thick forests and leafy lanes of the promontory known as Cove Neck, the Roosevelts and their guests recited the poems of Shakespeare, Shelley, Browning, Swinburne, and Tennyson, and discussed their favorites in front of a camp fire. At picnics on the buttercup-covered Yellow Banks facing Oyster Bay they presented critical essays on such weighty topics as Plutarch's *Lives*, William Wordsworth's sonnets, and Washington Irving's folklore.[18] At night they often sailed out of Cold Spring Harbor for cruises on the Sound.

Edith was also taken for many daylight excursions across the bay by Teedie, "who loved to row in the hottest sun, over the roughest water, in the smallest boat." But she was by no means his only choice of companion. He liked to ride with Fanny Smith, picnic with the "very nice" Annie Murray, and enjoy an occasional "lovely long row" in the moonlight with Nellie Smith. Nevertheless it was the name Edith that he painted on the stern of his rowboat, and it was she whom he asked to work a flag "for your namesake."[19]

In October 1875 Teedie turned seventeen. He was now a wiry five feet eight inches tall, and weighed about 124 pounds. He admitted to being timid by nature, but toughened himself with hard and often dangerous physical feats. He studied systematically for long hours, and had already achieved a sophistication of mind far beyond his years. Edith Carow was attracted by this aspect of his character more than any other. Girls in general found him clumsily appealing when he condescendingly patted them with his riding crop, or dropped sandwiches into the charlotte russe. Boys, on the other hand, disliked his moral rejection of "certain usually condoned activities."[24] Yet few

"It was the name Edith he painted on the stern of his rowboat."
Elliott, Theodore, Corinne and Edith c. 1876.

could deny Teedie's "unquenchable gaiety," which pervaded any room he entered. Fanny dreaded being put next to him at formal gatherings, "lest I become so convulsed with laughter at his whispered sallies as to disgrace myself." [20]

A curious ambivalence toward Edith is discernible in Corinne's diaries and letters during 1876.

> I have a feeling for Edith which I have for no one else [she wrote], a tender kind of feeling. I am always careful of her and then I know quite well that I love her much more than she does me in fact. I often feel that she prefers Grace [Potter] to me. . . . Every time I see her I notice what a clever girl she is, she reads more and writes better than any girl I know.

Then, in a letter dated June 10, she calls Edith "my evil dearest." This love-hate theme continues in a note for Edith's fifteenth birthday, on August 6:

> . . . The chrysalsis is already cracked only three years more before it will be entirely opened. Why child, your hair will soon be turning gray. . . . I send you fifteen "I love you's" and twice that amount of "I hate you's" to counteract each other.

After this there is an embarrassed conclusion: "The only person to whom I try to be faithful is my dear Edith, and she thinks my letters stupid! This last thought overpowers me . . ."

Corinne was even ambivalent about Edith's looks. She "is tall and fair, with lovely complexion and goldeny hair," she wrote in her diary on October 6. "Otherwise she is not really pretty though at times she looks perfectly lovely." Three weeks later, Edith is "certainly a very pretty girl." [21]

Corinne's feelings were a portent for the future. Her Southern warmth and Edith's New England coolness had become more pronounced at the onset of adolescence. Corinne was intimidated by Edith's seriousness and self-discipline, and jealous of her literary prowess. Edith, for her part, envied Corinne's spontaneity and social ease. There was also a growing rivalry for Teedie's affection, complicated by Corinne's desire to have Edith exclusively for herself. It was a situation never to be entirely resolved, even by the death of the object of their devotion.

Five

'Tis one of Providence's wise dispensations
That each day bringing joy and pain anew
Shall drop a curtain twixt the last day's ruins
Where lie our old pains and old pleasures too.

　　　　　　　　　　　　　　　—Edith Kermit Carow[1]

Dressed in a festive white piqué dress and blue sash, Edith attended Corinne's fifteenth birthday party at Tranquillity on September 27, 1876. The occasion was not entirely happy, since on the same day Teedie left for Cambridge, Massachusetts, to begin four years of study at Harvard.[2] If he felt as much of an ache as Edith did at their parting, he recovered his humor soon enough, as a letter to Mittie shows:

> When I arrived here on Wednesday night I found a fire burning in the grate, and the room looking just as cosy and comfortable as it could look. The table is almost *too* handsome, and I do not know whether to admire most the curtains, the paper or the carpet. What would I have done without Bamie . . .
>
> I do not begin work until Monday, when I shall start

51

with seven or eight hours a day. I rise at 7:15, attend
prayers at 7:45 and at 8 take breakfast at commons,
where the food is very fair. We have lunch at half past
twelve, and dinner at half past five.

Please to send on in the valise, as soon as possible,
with the paper and ink stand, my skates.

Clearly he intended to play as well as study. His next few letters
home made no mention of Edith. The person he missed most,
apparently, was Theodore Senior, whom he considered his "best and
most intimate friend."[3] To please him, Teedie vowed that while in
college he would drink very little and smoke not at all, a policy he
continued for the rest of his life.

When Corinne arrived home in New York from Oyster Bay on
October 31, she found Fanny Smith and Edith waiting for her at 6
West Fifty-seventh Street. Fanny was not quite comfortable in
Edith's society. "Edith Carow," she confessed many years later,
"caused me to suffer acute pangs of jealousy, because of her intimacy,
long antedating mine, with Corinne Roosevelt."[4]

The three friends sauntered down to the National Academy of
Design, on the northwest corner of Fourth Avenue and Twenty-third
Street, where they spent the morning looking at paintings by modern
American artists. Edith enjoyed art, and seldom missed an important
exhibition.

That night she held her annual "unhallowed" Halloween party in
the Carows' kitchen. "We pulled molasses candy," Fanny remembered, "ducked for apples, or shivering, sought our fate in the mirror
of a darkened room. I think it was in that kitchen that young
Theodore Roosevelt [once] drank thirteen cups of tea in rapid
succession, and where Fred Osborn, younger brother of Henry
Fairfield Osborn ate 30 cookies in some competition, without fatal
results." Afterward Gertrude Carow played the piano, muttering
under her breath, "Callow goslings," as her daughters and their
friends practiced the dance steps so painstakingly learned at
Dodsworth's.[5]

Teedie's exuberant presence was missed at the celebration of 1876,
and though he made a brief appearance in New York at Thanksgiving, it was not until December that Edith saw much of him.

At the first party of the Christmas season he danced a flamboyant german with her. Edith "looked as pretty as a picture," Teedie told Elliott afterward, "and was very sweet." Next Aunt Anna Gracie entertained a crowd of young people at her new house on East Thirty-fourth Street. The supper was lavish: tongue, chicken salad, stewed oysters, ice cream and cakes, and a punch bowl of lemonade. Guests were allowed to go upstairs late in the evening for what Aunt Annie fondly imagined to be a look at her prize painting, *The Ancient Mariner*. "Tedie took Edith, Archie Murray took Conie," Mrs. Gracie innocently noted, "until nearly everybody went up and down in couples—made it very sociable." At one point in the evening Conie and her partner went into the morning room, which was "dimly and suggestively lit" by a low gaslight and glowing fire, "for the express purpose of interrupting Thee and Edith, who had gone in there for a cosy chat." Teedie seems to have enjoyed the "chat" exceedingly, for early the following morning he was on hand to thank his aunt for "the success of the season."[6]

Back in Cambridge in early January 1877, Teedie wrote home to boast that classmates who visited him in New York thought Annie Murray and Edith Carow "the prettiest girls they had met" there. Soon, however, Cambridge social life caught him up afresh. "Some of the girls are very sweet and bright, and a few are very pretty," he wrote Bamie. "'Still oh Anneth I remain Faithful to Thee!' (the proper name in the above beautiful rhapsody is a compound of Annie and Edith)." Two weeks later he told Corinne of a sleighing party for "forty girls and fellows and two matrons in one huge sleigh" dragged through the Boston suburbs by eight horses. "One of the girls," he continued, "looked quite like Edith—only not nearly as pretty as her Ladyship: who when she dresses well and do'n't frizzle her hair is a very pretty girl."[7]

Edith, meanwhile, aware of her shaky standing in the affections of the gregarious freshman, read an unconsciously revealing poem to the P.O.R.E., entitled "My Dream Castles."

> *I have many noble castles*
> *In the air*
> *Buttress, battlements and turrets*
> *Showing fair*

Clear defined each age-dark story
'Gainst a rosy sunset glory
*   Pure and rare.*

To my castles none may enter
*   But the few*
Holding to my inmost feelings
*   Love's own clue*
They may wander there at will
Ever welcome finding still,
*   Warm and true.*

Only one, one tiny room
*   Locked they find,*
One thin curtain that they ne'er
*   Gaze behind.*
There my lost ambitions sleep,
To their tear-wept slumber deep
*   Long consigned.*

This my lonely sanctum is;
*   There I go*
When my heart all worn by grief
*   Sinketh low*
Where my baseless hopes do lie
There to find my peace, go I,
*   Sad and slow.*

But my fairy castles still
*   Bravely stand*
'Neath the summer skies sweet
*   Fancy land*
Silken pennants flutt'ring gay
From their towers and wanton play,
*   Zephyr fanned.*[8]

The sentiments expressed in this poem bear an extraordinary
resemblance to those of Edith's distant relative Edith Wharton, in

one of her earliest stories, "The Fullness of Life," published in 1893—sixteen years after Edith's verses were written:

> I have sometimes thought that a woman's nature is like a great house full of rooms: there is the hall, through which everyone passes in going in and out; the drawing room where one receives formal visits; the sitting room, where the members of the family come and go as they list; but beyond that, far beyond, are other rooms, the handles of whose doors are never turned; no one knows the way to them, no one knows whither they lead; and in the innermost room, the holy of holies, the soul sits alone and waits for a footstep that never comes.[9]

Teedie spent Easter with friends in Massachusetts. But he missed his family, and shortly afterward invited them to visit him in Cambridge. "We would have jolly fun," he promised, so "be sure and come, and *make* Maud [Elliott] and Edith come." Edith needed no persuasion, and late on Thursday, May 24, she arrived in Boston with Theodore Senior, Bamie, Corinne, Elliott and Maud. Next day they drove over to Harvard.

The Yard had fewer buildings then than now. Its lawns, protected only by low granite posts and shaded by stately elms and pine trees, made a quiet refuge from the clatter of horsecars on the surrounding cobblestone streets. Teedie lived in a second-floor bedroom and study at 16 Winthrop Street, only two blocks from Harvard Square. Here Edith met two of her host's friends, Johnny Lamson and Harry Jackson. The long weekend began with "a lovely long drive" through Cambridge in two carriages, and included an evening at the theater, a formal luncheon in Johnny's rooms, meetings with other classmates, and a quiet Sunday, during which Edith and Theodore had plenty of time to talk as they used to do as children. "The last three days have been great fun," Teedie wrote after his guests left. The visit was still on his mind three weeks later when he wrote Corinne: "I do'n't think I ever saw Edith looking prettier; everyone, and especially Harry Chapin and Minot Weld admired her little Ladyship intensely, and she behaved as sweetly as she looked." He would

like to have them all come again next year, he added, and ended with:
"Best love to Maud, and when you write to Edith tell her I enjoyed
her visit *very* much indeed." [10]

Edith was prompt in sending Theodore a note which nicely
combined formality and affection.

> My dear Theodore,
>
> I feel like writing immediately now that I am back in
> New York, to thank you for the pleasant time I had in
> Boston, for indeed I enjoyed to the utmost every minuite
> *[sic]* of my stay.
>
> May I ask you to say to all your friends that I
> appreciate Harvard freshmen as much as Mr. Jackson
> does New York girls, and tell Mr. Lampson *[sic]*
> especially that I shall long remember that pleasant
> lunch in his rooms.
>
> So with a clear recollection of what were to me at
> least, three perfectly happy days,
>
> Believe me,
Most sincerely yours,
Edith K. Carow
>
> New York, May 29
> 200 West 44
> P.S. Mamma having consented to my keeping a
> *conditional* promise, may I trouble you to send me the
> exact shade of your sofa? [11]

There is no mention of Edith in Teedie's diary for the summer of
1877, even though he spent several days with Corinne and Elliott at
Oceanic, New Jersey, rowing, driving and, as usual, having "great
fun."

Edith returned to Oyster Bay with Corinne in mid-August, and
during the following two weeks enjoyed picnic teas on Cooper's Bluff
and more "lovely moonlight rows," unaware that her next visit to
Tranquillity would be in greatly changed circumstances for the
Roosevelts. [12]

During the summer, Theodore Senior had "strained himself in
some way," and shortly after developed what appeared to be

peritonitis. Teedie came down from Harvard on December 21 and was shocked by his forty-six-year-old father's changed appearance. By Christmas Day, however, the patient seemed "brighter," and on the twenty-eighth Teedie felt sufficiently easy about him to escort Edith to Aunt Anna Gracie's for cream taffy.[13]

New Year's Day saw the customary round of calls by the rich and fashionable upon one another. Those receiving left their drapes partly drawn, so that passersby would be attracted by their brightly lit drawing rooms. Teedie, energetic as ever, visited about twenty friends, and particularly enjoyed calling on "singularly sweet" Annie Murray, "pure religious" Fanny Smith, and Edith Carow, who "makes up my trio of *freundinnen.*"[14]

Theodore Senior, who was, unknown to his family, suffering from inoperable bowel cancer, lingered on for another six weeks, his torment relieved only by merciful doses of ether and chloroform. "I have sat with him some seven hours," Corinne wrote Edith in the last days. "He slept most of it, but at times was in fearful agony. Oh Edith, it is the most frightful thing to see the person you love best in the world in terrible pain, and not be able to do a thing to alleviate it."[15] Finally, at 11 P.M. on February 11, Theodore Senior died. The "dearest of his children" was too late to see him alive.[16]

Throughout the spring and summer of 1878 Teedie lamented the death of his father. "Sometimes when I fully realize my loss I feel as if I should go wild," he confided to his diary. "He was everything to me. . . . I have lost the only human being to whom I told *everything*. . . . I had been so accustomed to go to him for advice that I hardly know how to decide for myself . . ." By July he felt more self-reliant: "It seems to me that I have aged very much since that bitter day." He was at home at Oyster Bay now, "deep mahogany from the waist up," gradually forgetting his grief in a frenzy of riding, swimming and rowing.[17]

Theodore, as he now preferred to be called, remembered Edith's seventeenth birthday on August 6, and sent her a bonbonnière. Corinne sent greetings, and remarked on how old they were getting:

> One short year more and the brook will be past [*sic*]
> . . . Dear little girl, whom I have known in truth, ever
> since you were a little bit of a girl, I hope that the next

> 17 years of your life will be as peaceful and sheltered (I
> know they have not been untroubled) as those past. I
> often think of your future and wonder what it will be,
> and whether we will always be so placed as to see much
> of each other. But the future is very secretive of what it
> will bring forth . . ."[18]

If Edith felt herself singled out as a special object of Theodore's
affection during her summer visit to Oyster Bay, it was not without
cause. He seemed to want her with him in most of his activities
during the first few days. On August 19 he took her sailing, on the
twentieth rowing, and on the twenty-first drove her to Cold Spring,
where they picked water lilies together. Next day, after tea, they went
up to the summerhouse.[19]

Here, apparently, for some unforeseen, inexplicable reason, their
growing tenderness exploded into hostility—or at the very least a
violent disagreement. History is silent as to the nature of this lover's
quarrel. Theodore, years afterward, would admit only to "a break" in
their "very intimate relations." At this time, he added, "we both of us
had . . . tempers that were far from being of the best." His own rage,
or frustration, after the summerhouse episode can be read between
the lines of his diary, which significantly omits all reference to Edith
in the weeks that followed. On August 22 he speaks of riding his
horse "so long and hard" that he feared the animal was injured. On
the twenty-fourth he shoots a dog to death for bothering him. On the
twenty-sixth he takes a cruise in the Sound, firing his gun at
everything that bobbed up in the water, "from bottles or buoys to
sharks and porpoises."[20]

One theory to do with the quarrel is that Theodore asked Edith to
marry him, and was refused. Edith herself recalled in later life that he
proposed to her more than once in 1877 and 1878. Her cousin, Edna
Tyler, qualified this claim, saying that the proposals were "common
knowledge in the family," but added that Grandfather Daniel Tyler
forbade any engagement, partly because Edith was too young, and
partly because the Roosevelts had "a history of scrofula." (No such
history has ever been uncovered.) Years later Corinne said that on
the contrary Theodore Senior had discouraged the match at a family
conference shortly before his death. The reason given was that he
disapproved of Charles Carow's drinking habits. Edith never ex-

plained the estrangement herself, except to say vaguely that Theodore had "not been nice."[21]

The break clearly upset him, and he sublimated his disappointment in hard work and abnormal physical activity. Edith appears to have successfully concealed her feelings, for after her departure from Oyster Bay on August 30 Corinne wrote: "We all miss you so much, but still I think I would go through the pain of another goodbye for another such a pleasant two weeks." The driver of Edith's coach "had entirely succumbed" to her charms, Corinne went on. "I always said you were a beguiling young person."[22]

Theodore's schedule, as he began his junior year in September 1878, was a heavy one. His curriculum of nine subjects involved twenty hours of lectures, recitations and laboratory work each week, but by studying two hours daily before breakfast and five or six after, he had most afternoons and evenings free.[23] As a result, his letters and diary for this period are full of references to his social life. He had been elected to several clubs, including the prestigious Porcellian, was attending partridge suppers, and playing whist and billiards. His female acquaintances multiplied, and new names appeared, including that, on October 18, of a Miss Alice Hathaway Lee, the cousin and neighbor of his friends Dick and Rose Saltonstall. She lived in a "homelike" Victorian mansion on Chestnut Hill, Brookline, a six-mile buggy ride from Harvard Square. After his first weekend walking, dancing, and gathering chestnuts with the fair seventeen-year-old Alice (she was just eight days older than Edith), he declared her "a very sweet, pretty girl"—as he did Edith and countless other females he favored.

From Theodore's twentieth birthday on, Alice figures more and more frequently in his diary. But it seems he had not dismissed Edith entirely from his mind. Having accepted an invitation to spend Thanksgiving with the Saltonstalls, he asked Corinne to remember him to Annie and Fanny, and give his love to Edith "if she's in a good humor; otherwise my respectful regards. If she seems *particularly* good-tempered, tell her that I hope that when I see her at Christmas it will not be on what you might call one of her off days."[24]

He spent the long weekend playing tennis and strolling with Rose Saltonstall and Alice Lee. "I have gotten very well acquainted with both of them," he wrote. "Rose is a very good pleasant girl, and as for pretty Alice Lee, I think her one of the sweetest most ladylike girls I have ever met." At this point two pages have been torn out of his diary. It may be that he wrote more specifically of his feelings for Alice on those missing pages, since he later admitted making a vow that same weekend to woo and marry her.[25]

Anxious, for the time being at least, to conceal his emotions, Theodore kept up an appearance of impartiality in his outward relationship with Rose and Alice, going so far as to give expensive gifts to Rose when he gave none to Alice, and to flirt with others in her presence. If Edith Carow had any inkling of Theodore's growing obsession, she tried not to show it. On April 3, 1879, she met him at Aunt Annie's, and seemed to him "just the same sweet little flirt as ever." Later that month, when Edith won a prize in the *World* literary competition, Theodore asked Bamie to "congratulate her for me." His letter was written from Chestnut Hill.[26]

In May 1879 Theodore invited Corinne, Bamie, Elliott, Aunt Annie and his mother to spend a few days in Cambridge to meet some of the belles of Boston. "They are a very sweet set of girls; and I really now know them better than I do most of my former New York friends—Rose and Alice in fact I know better than I do any New York girls . . ."[27] Being excluded from the party, after she had shone as the star of the previous one, and having her intimacy with Theodore so publicly usurped was deeply wounding to Edith.

Some time during the early summer of 1879, Theodore proposed marriage to Alice Lee. Nobody, least of all Edith Carow, knew about this; the secret came out only years later. At any rate Alice refused, or postponed her answer, perhaps because she was unsure of her feelings for the eccentric undergraduate who came to tea reeking of arsenic.

It was a season of loss and disruption for Edith. On June 30, 1879, seventy-five-year-old Aunt Kermit died in Oceanic. The brother who had shared her home for so many years was her sole heir, and he kindly passed on the old lady's writing desk to Edith. Shortly afterward the Carows moved yet again, to an imposing town house at 114 East Thirty-sixth Street.

As usual, Edith found solace in reading. Among the books she listed that summer were Swinburne's *Life of Blake*, Gilmore's *Life of Coleridge*, Brown's *Life of Southey*, Henry James's *Watch and Ward*,

Thackeray's *Pendennis,* and second readings of Dickens's *Great Expectations* and *Tale of Two Cities.* On August 6 she received a copy of *Lucille,* a long poem by Owen Meredith, inscribed "To Edith K. Carow on her eighteenth birthday, from her sincere friend Theodore Roosevelt."[28]

Theodore spent the early summer months at Oyster Bay, and then set out for a hunting trip in Maine. On the way he called at Chestnut Hill and found Alice "so bewitchingly pretty" that he was sorely tempted to cancel his vacation plans. When he returned to Brookline "tough as a pine knot" in September, he felt he had come home.[29] Absence, it appears, had warmed Miss Lee's cooling heart.

With a lighter schedule in his senior year, Theodore threw himself into extra-curricular activities. He took on the roles of President of the A.D.Q., Vice-President of the Natural History Society, President of the O.K., Secretary of the Pudding, Editor of the *Advocate,* and Librarian of the Porcellian.[30]

Determined to have a final fling, he bought a dogcart in which to make his social calls, and fitted himself out with an elegant wardrobe. He saw Alice Lee often, and later confessed that he had been unable to sleep—on some nights had not even gone to bed—fearful that her final answer to his proposal, when it came, would be no.[31]

In New York, briefly on November 16, he had a delightful visit with Edith, now graduated from Miss Comstock's. Literature must have formed a large part of her conversation, for afterward he declared her "the most cultivated, best-read girl I know."[32]

It would appear from Theodore's behavior at this period that he had not entirely made up his mind as to what he wanted in a woman. Nineteen months before, he had pondered in his diary: "I so wonder who my wife will be! 'A rare and radiant maiden,' I hope; one who will be as sweet, pure and innocent as she is wise."[33] Now he seemed bemused, oscillating restlessly between Alice and Edith. The former was certainly "radiant" and "innocent," but she was not "wise"; the latter was merely attractive, but capable of stimulating him intellectually to a degree far beyond the reach of her rival.

Later that month, for example, Lees and Roosevelts exchanged visits, and Theodore spent five days over Thanksgiving at Chestnut Hill. Then, on Christmas Eve, he called on Edith Carow, singling her out from among ten other "very pretty girls."[34] On the twenty-sixth, the two old friends also had lunch together. That same evening,

Alice, her sister Rosy, and Dick and Rose Saltonstall arrived in New York to spend a week at Fifty-seventh Street. The days passed pleasantly, with drives in Central and Jerome Parks, and evenings of formal dinners and parties. At some point during the seven days, it is safe to assume, Edith Kermit Carow first laid eyes on Alice Hathaway Lee.

She saw a tall, athletic person with a graceful carriage, wavy corn-colored hair, pale gray eyes, a slight mouth, and a retroussé nose. Though less boisterous than Theodore, Miss Lee was by nature gay and quick-witted, and the pair complemented each other perfectly. Alice, in turn, saw a mature girl somewhat shorter and less expensively dressed than herself. Edith's figure was unathletic and curvaceous, her personality private and austere. The two young women, in both looks and temperament, were natural rivals.

When Alice returned to Chestnut Hill her mind was made up. Whatever doubts she had about her ardent suitor (always irresistible on his home ground) were dispelled by the warmth of her reception in the Roosevelt home. On Sunday, January 25, 1880, the day before the Harvard semiannual examinations, she agreed to marry him. Theodore was ecstatic. "The aim of my whole life shall be to make her happy," he wrote in his diary, "and oh, how I shall cherish my sweet queen!"[35]

The following weekend Theodore went to New York to buy a ring, and tell his family of his engagement. Everyone was "delighted and too sweet for anything" at the news, he wrote, "though very much surprised." Though the betrothal was not to be formally announced until February 16, Theodore told Edith Carow before anyone else outside the family.[36]

The effect of this stunning revelation upon Edith can be imagined. For sixteen years she had lived in the closest intimacy, both physical and emotional, with Theodore. She had shared his education, his home life, his vacations, his dreams and desires. In 1878, indeed, she had herself been on the point of betrothal to him. Try as she might to conceal her disappointment and desolation, her shock, to perceptive observers, was so great that Roosevelt family members recalled it vividly half a century later.[37] True to her lifelong practice of suppressing any intimation of her romantic feelings, she neither said nor wrote a word in reaction to Theodore's letter—at least none that has survived.

"A tall, athletic person . . . gay and quick-witted."
Alice Hathaway Lee.

Her reading list that February included a book called *Splendid Misery.*[38]

In June Theodore graduated Phi Beta Kappa, twenty-first in a class of 177. Most of July and early August he spent with Alice at Oyster Bay or Chestnut Hill or Bar Harbor, Maine, before going west with Elliott for a hunting trip. This strangely timed excursion had a purpose. A Cambridge doctor told Theodore that he had a weak heart, and that if he wished to live a normal span he must forgo strenuous activity and take up an undemanding profession. Theodore preferred to die rather than live like an invalid, and set out to prove the physician wrong. Out West he began a death-defying regimen "to build me up."[39]

On Wednesday, October 13, 1880, Edith Carow gave a dinner party for Theodore Roosevelt. If there was any tension he seemed unaware of it. Two days later Fanny Smith wrote in her diary: "He is as funny and delicious as ever and wild with happiness and excitement. I went with him to see the wedding presents he is going to give Alice. I hope she is very fond of him."[40]

Edith arrived in Boston on Monday night, October 25, two days before the wedding. She checked into the Brunswick Hotel, sharing a suite with Grace Potter and Fanny on the upper floor, while the Roosevelts and the Gracies shared two parlors below. Theodore took a bachelor room elsewhere in the hotel. "The next day people called and we explored the city at intervals," Fanny remembered. "Most of the party dined together at a big table, and in the evening the ushers came—we had great fun." Theodore himself was in "wild spirits," and "indulged in one of his favorite pastimes," tipping back Fanny's chair so far that she was in terror of disgracing herself with a back somersault.[41]

The following morning, Theodore's twenty-second birthday, Edith and Fanny drove to the Unitarian Church in Brookline together. The day was sunny and so warm that the male guests left off their topcoats. "It was the dearest little wedding," Fanny wrote. "Alice looked perfectly lovely and Theodore *so* happy and responded in the most determined Theodorelike tones."[42] At the reception afterward Edith Kermit Carow defiantly "danced the soles off her shoes."

Six

She knew that someday, somehow, she would marry Theodore Roosevelt.

—Nancy Roosevelt Jackson[1]

After an overnight stay in Springfield, Massachusetts, Theodore and Alice spent their first two weeks of married life at Tranquillity, where they slipped into the easy domesticity of well-matched temperaments. On returning to West Fifty-seventh Street for the winter, Theodore resumed his studies (begun earlier in the fall) at Columbia Law School, and Alice settled into the routine of a lady of leisure. She enrolled in Drina Potter's Tennis School, and began to hold Tuesday afternoon tea parties in her own parlor, quite separate from Mittie's.

Fanny Smith spoke for many in the Roosevelt circle when she said that Theodore's wife was "lovable in every way."[2] Only one of their intimates appeared to disagree, and of her coolness Alice was only too aware. Why, she asked Corinne, when everybody else was so cordial, could she not seem to get anywhere with Edith Carow?[3] The two women nevertheless found themselves often in each other's company. In December, for example, they accompanied Corinne on an excursion to Morristown, New Jersey, "the Southern Newport."

Walking together through its snowy streets, Edith and Alice admired the Italianate villas and made polite but distant conversation.[4] All through the season, in New York City, they shopped at the same stores, dined at the same tables, attended the same theaters, and danced at the same balls.

As Knickerbockers, the Carows and the Roosevelts were naturally expected to socialize on a grand scale, along with the more acceptable members of New York's growing population of new rich, such as the Vanderbilts. Since the 1860s, when a portly Georgian named Ward McAllister settled in Manhattan, society had had an arbiter "to band together the respectable element of the city."[5] The bushy-browed McAllister was well versed in the etiquette and cuisine of the grand palaces of Europe, and he introduced these attributes of Continental life to American society at a series of cotillion dinners held in Delmonico's restaurant at Fifth Avenue and Fourteenth Street. Here he fed people on his favorite dishes: terrapin, Newport turkey raised on grasshoppers, nesselrode, "king of the ices," and urged connoisseurs to sip, not gulp, their wine. He also organized his famous series of Patriarchs' Balls, glittering events subscribed to by twenty-five of New York's leading families, such as the Astors, the Schermerhorns, the Livingstons, the Van Rensselaers, and the Rutherfurds. The patriarch of each family was entitled to bring five men and four women to each event; an additional fifty distinguished visitors to the city were also allowed to attend, making a total of three hundred.

At various Patriarchs' Balls during the season of 1880–81, Mr. and Mrs. Theodore Roosevelt attracted "much attention," he with his "superb waltzes," and she with her graceful, blond beauty.[6] Edith, who deliberately avoided the social spotlight, was occasionally among the onlookers. But more often than not she forsook the balls for a quiet evening at home reading Addison, Jane Austen and Browning.

One of the big events of the season was Corinne Roosevelt's debut on December 8, 1880. Her oldest friend was among the five hundred people who braved cold winds and freezing temperatures to make their way to Fifty-seventh Street. Corinne, wearing a muslin-and-Valenciennes dress with a corsage of daisies, received her guests in the heavily paneled dining room. Beside her stood Mittie, plumper now but elegant as ever, and Alice, exquisite in her wedding gown, white flowers nestling in her fair hair.[7]

Soon the house was absolutely jammed. Aunt Anna Gracie, who despite an attack of what "appeared to be cholera" considered the party too important to miss, found the crowd so oppressive she had to retire upstairs. Bamie, heedless of the cries of a group of rheumatic Frenchmen, threw open the windows to let in air. Theodore graciously did his duty handing out cigars to all and sundry. The only family member missing was Elliott, who had gone to India to hunt.[8]

At eleven o'clock the Lauder Quintet, stationed behind a decorative Christmas screen, began to play softly rhythmic music. Edith went to the main-floor parlor to exercise the skills she had acquired at Dodsworth's. About midnight her partner escorted her to the morning room for a champagne supper catered by Pinard.

The name of the young man has not survived, but it is supremely irrelevant. If Edith dwelt on her own romantic prospects, as she passed from room to room, she must have found them wanting. The time for her own debut had come and gone. Charles Carow's fortune continued to erode, and his health continued to decline. There seemed little hope now of taking her rightful place in society; her best chance of marital happiness had already slipped away. She was in her twentieth year, and there was no suitor she cared for in comparison to the one she had lost. Since Theodore had gone out of her life, indeed, she had earned the reputation of having "an utter lack of susceptibility."[9] By Victorian standards, she was irrevocably headed for spinsterhood—unless, of course, she gave up all notions of a romantic alliance and married for money.

About this time, according to family tradition, Edith briefly contemplated the latter option in order to replenish the Carow coffers. But she did not find it in her character to do so. The truth of the matter was that in her heart of hearts she had no doubt that "someday, somehow, she would marry Theodore Roosevelt."[10]

Corinne's introduction to society, delayed by the death of Theodore Senior, was a mere formality, since she had already, in the summer of 1880, met her future husband.

Douglas Robinson, a huge, plain Scot, was heir to a real-estate fortune. Though gruff and irascible in manner, he had a tender heart, and loved the ultrafeminine Corinne with a consuming passion. Unfortunately the feeling was not reciprocated, and she cried and agonized secretly for months before agreeing to an engagement. "I hope all will be right," Mittie wrote her sister, with some insincerity, for it was she who had encouraged the match, apparently for economic reasons.[10] Edith, acknowledging Corinne's announcement in mid-February 1881, wrote with a note of diffidence: "I know I shall like Mr. Robinson (if he will let me) . . . and I rejoice with you in your happiness my own dear little girl."[12]

But Corinne could not rejoice. Warm and emotional as she was, and ready to laugh or cry with anyone as the mood demanded, she was, unlike her friend, sadly destined to live and die without experiencing romantic love.[13]

If the past year had been the most wretched of Edith's life, it had been the happiest of Theodore's. At times he could not believe his good fortune in winning "the fairest and purest and sweetest of women." Yet at other times there were signs of restlessness. A surfeit of domestic life as the solitary male head of a household of four females showed itself when letters from Elliott arrived describing glorious hunting successes in India. As Mittie read them aloud, he would pace up and down "like a caged Lynx." If Alice protested he would stop and smother her with kisses, reassuring her that it was just a momentary longing for the wilderness and a gun.[14]

But there were other yearnings too. He was, after all, only twenty-two years old. He missed the all-male bonhomie of the Harvard campus; the hardy tramps in Maine; the flirtatious teasing of Fanny Smith or Annie Murray, not to mention the deep intellectual exchanges he had known with Edith Carow. His legal studies did not satisfy a growing longing for action and commitment, and he began to cast about for other outlets. One day he climbed the steps of Morton Hall, the headquarters of the Twenty-first Assembly District, or "Silk Stocking District," Republican Club, and became a member. In these bare, smoky rooms he found his milieu. From now on, with brief interruptions, politics would be his life.

If Alice had difficulty making common ground with Edith, Theodore felt no such strain. No sooner had Alice left for a spring visit to her parents in Chestnut Hill than he "took Edith to drive." Their destination was probably his favorite Riverside Park, where they could watch sailboats bobbing on the blue-green waters of the Hudson River under the sunset-pink sky. Squeezed side by side in the dogcart seat, they talked almost as they used to so many years ago. Edith missed that lost intimacy more than she cared to admit. No one in her small circle was Theodore's intellectual equal. None so understood or appreciated her, and none made her laugh as he did. He was, indeed, inimitiable and irreplaceable. In six weeks' time he would leave for a four-month trip to Europe, on a belated honeymoon, and the prospect of this long absence must have filled her with dread.

While Theodore was mountain climbing in Switzerland in July, President James A. Garfield was shot at a Washington railroad station by an enraged spoilsman. This "meant work in the future for all men who wish their country well," Theodore recorded in his diary. Consciously or not, he was preparing himself for just such labor. While in Europe he continued to write his first book, *The Naval War of 1812*, and as soon as he returned to New York in early October he resumed work at the law school. Then, on October 28, 1881, the day after his twenty-third birthday, he was nominated Republican candidate for the New York State Assembly in the Twenty-first District. The time had come, party stalwarts felt, for someone young, wellborn, and scrupulously honest to counter the burgeoning power of city Democrats. On November 8 he was elected. "Don't think I am going to go into politics after this year," he told a friend, "for I am not."[15]

A month after Theodore's election, Edith gave a large party at 114 East Thirty-sixth Street to celebrate. Mittie, Alice Lee, Corinne and Douglas were there, and Theodore, resplendent in a brightly colored satin waistcoat, led the cotillion in his eccentric bouncing style. Yet the gathering had sad overtones, for in three weeks he and his wife would move to Albany for the opening of the 1882 Legislature, and they would stay away for the rest of the winter. There was even talk of their buying an upcountry farm in the summer. "I do dread parting with Teddie, and Alice," Mittie wrote Elliott. "Alice has endeared herself to me and she is so companionable and always ready to do what I ask her and I do love her, and I think she loves me."[16]

On April 29, 1882, Edith was one of eight bridesmaids who stood beneath a bower of palms and smilax in the Fifth Avenue Presbyterian Church at the wedding of Corinne Roosevelt to Douglas

Robinson. After the ceremony she felt bereft, and wrote Corinne: "I kept realizing that you were leaving your old life behind, and if we live to be ninety years old we can never be two girls together again."[17]

Now that Corinne too was going to live out of town much of the year (Douglas had a large house in Orange, New Jersey), Edith came more and more to depend on her own family for social life. At the end of August 1882 she went to Canada and stayed with Grandfather Tyler at St. Hilaire Mountain, a resort about thirty miles from Montreal. The General had grown inordinately fond of her, if not of seventeen-year-old Emily, and had especially requested her presence. A friend of the family remembered: "He wrote me of her talents, of her writings and of how he loved her, evidently doating on the dear child and drawing from her so much pleasure." Although Edith did not know it, it was to be their last vacation together. After their return the old soldier, now eighty-three, collapsed in his rooms at the Fifth Avenue Hotel. On November 30, 1882, surrounded by children and grandchildren, he died. His body was taken south to Anniston, Alabama, over the rail tracks he had built, in a special train. No fewer than two thousand mourners visited the cemetery where he was buried on December 5.[18]

Shortly before his passing he had written his granddaughter: "Old age, my dear Edith, as I know by experience, requires much patience and consideration on the part of those who administer to its wants, and who are sometimes sorely tried by its caprices. The only recompense that remains is conscious discharge of duty, to be repaid, perhaps, in kind, in due time, when our old age overtakes us."[19] Edith kept this letter, and took its contents to heart.

General Tyler willed five parts of his $193,000 fortune to his children, but Gertrude's share of $47,000 had to remain invested, with the interest of approximately $5,000 a year paid semiannually "during the entire period of her natural life." On her death, the interest was to continue to be paid in equal parts to Edith and Emily. Evidently the old man did not trust Gertrude and her improvident husband to manage the income sensibly, for his other daughter, Mary, received her full share outright, as did his three sons.[20]

Theodore Roosevelt, meanwhile, after a spectacularly successful debut in the New York State Assembly, had been reelected to a second one-year term. Alice had been bored by Albany provincial life, and all thought of an upstate farm had consequently been abandoned. Instead they purchased a Manhattan brownstone at 55 West Forty-fifth Street. Since Alice had not yet had the responsibility of running a household, Aunt Annie helpfully drew up a list of duties for her two maids.

The days at Forty-fifth Street were blissful and hospitable. Theodore came down from Albany as often as possible, and invited friends to dine, play cards, and spend the night. "I can imagine nothing more happy in life than an evening spent in my cosy little sitting room, before a bright fire of soft coal, my books all around me, and playing backgammon with my own dainty mistress," he recorded in his diary.[21]

The 1882–83 social season got under way in December with subscription and regimental balls, plays, concerts, operas, private musicales, theatrical entertainments, and elaborate dinner parties. Lily Langtry made her first American appearance at Wallack's Theater; Adelina Patti performed in *Lucia di Lammermoor* at the Academy of Music (a favorite haunt of Edith's); Nilsson and Albani gave recitals. Not to be outdone, Aunt Annie Gracie advertised an "Amateur Dramatic" in her home. Edith, Theodore and Alice Lee dutifully attended.[22]

Perhaps Aunt Annie sensed Edith's loneliness, for as the winter progressed she seemed to see more of her than usual. They went together to art exhibitions, concerts, Bible readings, and birthday parties. Then, on March 13, 1883, came an ominous entry in the old lady's diary: "Edith's father ill she cannot lunch here."

Years of business worries and alcohol abuse had taken their toll of Charles Carow. Now, after collapsing at the age of fifty-eight, he was too weak to respond to treatment, and lay dying at home. The doctor came and went, leaving the three anxious women with little hope and many memories of their troubled life together. Edith was inclined to remember only the good times. From early childhood her father's love of books and nature had stimulated her own. He had coached her in Latin and in horseback riding, and encouraged an interest in the world beyond her own immediate horizons, to compensate for the narrow outlook of her introspective mother. He had indulged her fondness for fantasy, propping her on his knee as a child and spinning yarn after yarn for her; later, as she approached adolescence, he had taken her to theater after theater. (All her life she would cherish the program of every play she had seen with him.) In more recent years they had reaffirmed their essential closeness as they sat in the window at East Thirty-sixth Street, listening to the whippoorwill that paid them evening visits.[23]

Finally, on March 17, 1883, after seven days of struggling for breath, Charles Carow died. The official causes of his death were pericarditis (inflammation of the heart muscle and membranes), pneumonia (inflammation of the lungs), and asthenia (general debility and weakness)—all diseases endemic to the habitual drinker. The *Times* obituary column next day carried a brief announcement, with the cold request "Please omit flowers."[24]

The funeral took place at St. Mark's-in-the-Bowery on Tuesday, March 20. Corinne, who was eight months pregnant, did not attend, nor did Theodore, up in Albany, but Alice Lee Roosevelt and Aunt Annie Gracie joined the family at the simple service. No record appears to exist of Gertrude's feelings at the time. In correspondence later, she hardly ever mentioned her husband. Edith also was reticent on the subject of Charles Carow, but thirty-five years after his death, when she acquired a new mount, she called it Oriole, "after a favorite horse of my father's." Seeking in her old age to sum up his character, she could only say that he had been "an angel."[25]

Charles was buried during Holy Week. Not far west of his gravesite the windows of the stores along Ladies' Mile were bright with spring fashions. Edith, clad in deepest mourning, had a special reason to view the displays wistfully, for her father's death had occurred, ironically, only days before what would have been the most brilliant social event of her life so far. She had been chosen to dance the Star Quadrille at Alva Vanderbilt's Easter Monday "Ball of the Century," and now was forced to decline.

And so on March 27, the day after the ball, Edith had to content herself with reading newspaper articles that likened the quarter-million-dollar extravaganza to the pagan festivities of Cleopatra and Alexander the Great. All the most brilliant luminaries of society had attended, wearing fancy dress of unprecedented lavishness. Ward McAllister came as the Count de la Mole, in purple velvet and scarlet silk; Mrs. Chauncey Depew as Ondine, in sea-green satin with clusters of water lilies; Richard Morris Hunt, architect of the

Vanderbilt mansion, as the fourteenth-century Florentine Cimabue, in white cloth of gold, capuchin hood, and pointed shoes; Mrs. Cornelius Vanderbilt "as the Electric Light, in white satin trimmed with diamonds, and a magnificent diamond head-dress." Younger women, many of them Edith's close friends, went dressed as princesses, peacocks, peasants, and hornets. Few missed Edith in the Star Quadrille; one commentator, indeed, thought the replacement dancer in rose-colored silk was her.[26]

The spring of 1883 was an eventful one for the Roosevelts. In April Corinne's first child, Theodore Douglas, was born. In May, Alice Lee conceived after two and a half years of marriage, and in June Elliott became unofficially engaged to twenty-one-year-old Anna Rebecca Hall.

The beautiful, socially gifted but shallow Miss Hall lived at Tivoli, on the banks of the Hudson River, some twenty miles north of the Hyde Park home of the Roosevelts' baby cousin Franklin Delano Roosevelt. The family approved the match, and hoped rootless, hard-drinking "Nell" would now "settle down with a definite purpose in life."[27]

On December 1, 1883, Edith went to the wedding. "You know a chap loves to be ruled over by a lovely woman," the young husband had once written. The bride was certainly lovely, but whether she would be able to rule him remained to be seen. Anna was lazy, and incapable of creating the disciplined domestic framework Elliott needed. On the contrary, she looked to him to provide the excitement she craved, and hoped he had not formed an ideal of her "that I shall shatter hereafter."[28]

In the meantime, the prospect of fatherhood was affecting Theodore's health. He began to suffer severe attacks of asthma and cholera morbus, as he had done in the past when change was imminent. His characteristic remedy was to go west and hunt buffalo. Before leaving for Dakota in early September, he bought ninety-five acres of land on Cove Neck at Oyster Bay, to add to an original sixty secured in the winter of 1880. He subsequently resold twenty-eight of these to Bamie, and thirty-two to Aunt Annie.[29]

By early 1884 the stables and lodge on his remaining ninety-five-acre property were complete, and Theodore and Alice began to study

plans for a hilltop residence, which they intended to build immediately. For the time being they let their West Forty-fifth Street house
to the Elliott Roosevelts, and returned to Fifty-seventh Street, so that
Alice would have companionship in the last weeks of her pregnancy.
If Theodore noticed a puffy look around her eyes, or heard her
complain of badly swollen ankles, he did not allow it to worry him.
Mittie, however, had commented some time before on how "very
large" Alice was.[30]

Theodore went up to Albany as usual on Monday, February 11,
and the following day his wife went into labor. The Assemblyman
knew nothing of it until he received a telegram on Wednesday
morning, announcing the birth of a daughter. A few hours later a
violently contrasting cable summoned him home.

Fog in the Hudson Valley delayed his train, and it was almost
midnight before he groped his way through dimly gaslit streets to the
Roosevelt mansion. Here he received the news that not only was
Alice dying of Bright's disease, but also his mother was mortally
stricken with typhoid.

At three o'clock in the morning on February 14, 1884, Mittie died
surrounded by her children. She was only forty-nine years old, and
her velvet-black hair had not a single strand of gray.[31] Theodore, his
heart breaking, climbed back to the third floor to resume his vigil at
Alice's bedside. She was barely conscious, and made no gesture of
recognition. At two o'clock that afternoon, Alice Hathaway Lee
Roosevelt died.

Edith joined a packed congregation at the Fifth Avenue Presbyterian Church for a double funeral service. The atmosphere was
charged with emotion as the clergyman spoke in a choking voice of
Theodore's terrible double tragedy. He prayed that the young man
be given strength "to address himself afresh" to the duties God had
ordained for him.[32]

The interments, in neighboring graves at Greenwood cemetery,
Brooklyn, took place in the presence of the immediate family and a
few close friends. All were "utterly demoralized," one witness
remarked, "and Theodore is in a dazed, stunned state. He does not
know what he does or says."[33]

Bewildered and utterly unable to comprehend his loss, Theodore
wrote in his diary on February 16: "We spent three years of
happiness greater and more unalloyed than I have ever known fall to

the lot of others. For joy or for sorrow my life has now been lived out."

But life inevitably went on. Baby Alice Lee's baptism took place on Sunday the seventeenth, and two days later Theodore returned to Albany. His despair was all-consuming, but he would not speak of it, to his family now, or ever.[34]

Seven

The keenness of joy and the bitterness of sorrow are now behind me.

—Theodore Roosevelt[1]

A week after the funeral 6 West Fifty-seventh Street was sold, and its contents were divided among the surviving family.[2] In late May, Bamie, now surrogate mother to Baby Lee, moved into a townhouse at 422 Madison Avenue. From now on Theodore would make this his New York *pied à terre*. In return he offered Bamie the use of Leeholm, his still-unfinished house at Oyster Bay, even then rising huge and grim on its muddy hilltop. Doubtless he and his sister and his daughter would spend many summers there, and many winters together in town; but Bamie from the start insisted that they finance their respective households separately and independently. This, she said, would make for "a much easier relationship to break" than if they pooled their resources.[3] Perhaps she sensed that Theodore, for all his protestations of remaining faithful to the memory of Alice Lee, would not be long a widower.

As things turned out, she saw very little of her brother during the rest of 1884. In June Theodore went to Chicago to serve as delegate-at-large at the Republican National Convention. There he cemented an alliance with a fellow Reform Republican, Henry Cabot Lodge of

Massachusetts. Ten years his senior, Lodge was to become the most important political influence in his life. Together they supported a decent, dull reformer, George F. Edmunds of Vermont, for the Presidency, rather than the incumbent Chief Executive, Chester A. Arthur, or party favorite James G. Blaine, "the Continential Liar from the State of Maine." Despite their efforts, the nomination went to Blaine, but he was fated to lose the race against Grover Cleveland in November, thus bringing to an end twenty-four years of Republican rule.

Too sick at heart to seek reelection to the State Assembly in the fall, Theodore continued west to Dakota. In September 1883, during his buffalo hunt, he had made a substantial investment in the local open-range cattle industry, purchasing four hundred head of cattle and hiring two leathery local cowboys, William Merrifield and Sylvane Ferris, to take care of them at the Maltese Cross Ranch. Now he impulsively decided to establish a second ranch, called Elkhorn, in the Bad Lands of the Little Missouri north of Medora. He announced that he would import William Sewall and Wilmot Dow, his old Maine hunting guides, as managers of a new thousand-head herd. For the foreseeable future he would make ranching his "regular business."[4] With yet another stock purchase, made against the advice of his financial counselor, his investment would total $85,000, over half of his entire inheritance.[5]

In spite of this enormous stake in the West, Theodore's thoughts frequently turned east. He began to collect antelope heads for his "famous hall at Leeholm," and urged Bamie to stir up the builders every now and then.[6]

Thirteen hours a day in the saddle, week after week, month after month, toughened Theodore, while the austere Dakota landscape soothed his spirit. Yet according to Bill Sewall he was "very melancholy at times," and protested that his life had no meaning. Sewall disagreed with him. "You have your child to live for," he said. "Her aunt can take care of her a good deal better than I can," Theodore replied.[7] Merrifield (also recently widowed) tried to console him, but he would not be persuaded. "Don't talk to me about time will make a difference—time can never change me in that respect."[8]

Edith Carow's activities in the summer and early fall of 1884 are more scantily documented than any other period of her adult life. It was as though without Theodore she did not exist. The only mention of her in Mrs. Gracie's diary occurs on November 20: "Miss Edith Carow and Mr. Stratton to dine at 7 o'clock." Who Mr. Stratton was, and how often she saw him, remains a mystery. There is no correspondence between Edith and Theodore, for the very good reason that he did not wish to see her, much less hear from her. During brief trips to New York, he had told his sisters not to invite Edith home when he was staying with them. Evidently he was afraid of resurrecting old, uncontrollable emotions—Theodore subscribed to the sentimental Victorian belief that second marriages were wrong, in that they were a betrayal of the spirit of the departed.

Literature afforded some distraction. During the winter of 1884–85 he wrote a 95,000-word book called *Hunting Trips of a Ranchman*. The work exhausted him and accentuated his already haggard frailty. A St. Paul reporter who met him in April 1885 on one of his periodic trips between New York and Dakota described him as "a boyish-looking young fellow with a slight lisp, a short red mustache, and eyeglasses . . . the typical New York dude."[9] But the pallid reediness of early manhood proved short-lived. In the next nine weeks he put on an incredible thirty pounds in weight, and became bronzed and sturdy. When he passed through St. Paul again on June 22 there was "very little of the whilom dude in his rough and easy costume," and his slow, upper-class drawl had entirely disappeared.[10]

In that same month Edith went to stay at Aunt Annie's new Oyster Bay residence, Gracewood. A short walk through the woods brought her to Leeholm, where Bamie was preparing for a five-week visit from Theodore. Now, for the first time, she saw looming through the trees a three-storied gabled structure sitting solid and squat on the brow of a wheat field. Along its south and west sides ran a broad verandah, which provided the only shade on the bare, exposed hilltop. To the north and west the grass sloped down to blue expanses of shining sea water; in the distance she could see the shores of Connecticut.

Wandering through the house's twenty-two rooms (eight of them with fireplaces, and dumbwaiters to lift logs from the cellar), Edith could not but wonder what on earth a cowboy widower with only one child could want with so much space.

Theodore arrived ten days later, but Edith was by then discreetly removed to Corinne's seventy-two-acre estate in Orange, New Jersey. Innumerable visitors flocked to Oyster Bay that summer, but she was not among them. Personally, she had no particular reason to avoid Theodore, except the knowledge that he would find her presence disturbing. He was, she knew, sensitive about their aborted juvenile romance, and idealistic about the dead Alice Lee. Time would tell if this artificial separation was doomed to become permanent; in the meantime she had her own immediate future to consider.

It had been decided by Gertrude, Emily and herself that the sharply reduced Carow fortune necessitated their living abroad, in some such cheap yet fashionable country as Italy. First, however, they would treat themselves to a prolonged vacation in England and Europe, sailing in the spring of 1886.

Politics brought Theodore back from the Bad Lands in mid-September 1885, to campaign on behalf of the New York State Republican gubernatorial candidate. Edith stayed away from Bamie's house, as usual, on days when he was there. For nineteen months now they had successfully avoided each other. But sometime early that fall, either by chance or design, they met.

The encounter took place as Edith was leaving Bamie's parlor and descending the stairs. Perhaps the conversation of the two women had been so absorbing that her departure was delayed—or maybe Theodore returned earlier than planned. Whatever the case, the two bumped into each other in the hallway.[11]

Edith had seen little, if anything, of Theodore since Alice's funeral, and remembered him as he was then, thin, pale and distraught. Now his physique was range-hardened, his face nut-brown and leathery. Sorrow had made him more of a man, and less of a boy, yet beneath a subdued personality she sensed the old, exuberant "Teedie."

When former intimates meet unexpectedly after a long parting, the shock of encounter sets off an explosion of conflicting emotions and disparate memories. Edith and Theodore had known each other for twenty-one years; what passed through their minds at that poignant moment can only be imagined. There were so many old things to remember, so many new things to adjust to. Together they had been nursery companions, riding, rowing and dancing partners, celebrants at weddings and mourners at funerals. Once as close as brother and sister, they were now as estranged as thwarted lovers. Yet, as the first awkward words of greeting passed between them, long-suppressed feelings surfaced. It was clear to both that these fleeting moments in the hallway had irrevocably changed their lives.[12]

Soon afterward Theodore began to call on Edith again in her East
Thirty-sixth Street parlor. At first their meetings were private—even
secret—and then, as the social season progressed, they met in public,
as old friends might. Theodore even put off returning to his ranch for
the winter.

"At first their meetings were private."
Edith's parlor at 114 East 36th Street.

Once he had recovered from the shock of their resumed relationship, he found that Edith had blossomed physically and was
temperamentally more equable than the angular, moody teenage girl

of the seventies. She was composed and self-assured and, behind the steely control, more tolerant, sympathetic, and wise. This last attribute, however, was not new; her friends liked to say that Edie had been "born mature."[13]

Fanny Smith (now married to Will Dana and just recovering from a miscarriage) saw Edith and Theodore together many times that winter, but had not the slightest inkling of a romantic attachment.[14] Nor did Bamie and Corinne suspect the growing intimacy, and were not surprised when Theodore invited Edith to the Meadowbrook Hunt Ball. It was to be held on Saturday, October 26 (the eve of his twenty-seventh birthday) in his Oyster Bay house, newly named Sagamore Hill.[15]

The hunt itself took place earlier that same day. Theodore led the chase for at least a third of the first ten miles of the run. About half way, his big horse fell, and rolled on top of him, breaking his left arm. Managing somehow to remount, he finished the course, taking some twenty more fences with the broken arm hanging limply at his side.

That night, irrepressible as ever, he attended the ball at Sagamore Hill. Arm in a sling, his scratched face plastered, he twirled Edith about the floor with cheerful abandon. "I am always willing to pay the piper when I have had a good dance," he told Henry Cabot Lodge, "and every now and then I like to drink the wine of life with brandy in it."[16]

On November 17, 1885, little more than three weeks after the ball, Theodore (his arm still in a sling) proposed marriage to Edith. Her answer, predictably, was yes. The betrothal was secretly solemnized with a ring, a watch, and a pearl necklace.[17] For the time being they would tell absolutely no one, not even their closest kin. Theodore had been a widower for less than two years, and did not wish to remarry with unseemly speed. There was also the question of where they would live. Edith, a cultivated Easterner, could hardly be expected to settle in the wild West, while he, having invested so heavily in his ranches, could not afford a winter town house as well as Sagamore Hill. Besides this he had to consider with the utmost delicacy what to do about Bamie and Baby Lee, whose lives had become deeply intertwined. Gertrude and Emily also had to be considered, since they were counting on Edith to help them set up a home abroad. All in all, the situation was fraught with difficulties. Only time could resolve them.

The couple decided, therefore, that Edith should go to Europe as

"She was self-assured and wise."
Edith about the time of her engagement.

planned. In a year or so, when Theodore had a clearer idea of whether he was to be a cowboy, a politician, or a writer, they would announce their engagement, fix a wedding date, and decide where and how to live.

As 1886 began, Theodore resumed regular diary entries of his social life for the first time since the death of Alice Lee. He and Edith attended operas, plays, private theatricals and dinner parties. On February 14, the second anniversary of his wife's death, he drew a heart, pierced by an arrow. Yet morbid thoughts were quickly dispelled, for by early March day after day is marked simply with the letter "E."

With marriage on the horizon, however distant, the purely social life of a man-about-town soon lost its charm for Theodore. Consequently, when Houghton Mifflin asked him to write a life of Thomas Hart Benton, he leaped at the opportunity for useful and absorbing work. Throughout February he had been a hive of industry, and gathered material for the book in such quantities that he was soon ready to head west to his ranch and begin writing. Edith was not due to sail for Europe until late April, but he had been too long absent from his Dakota managers, and decided to quit New York more than seven weeks before her.

Their last days together were difficult ones. Soon five thousand miles of land and ocean would lie between them, and as the time approached the futility of separation became harder to bear. Yet both were captives of the hidebound forces of Victorian propriety and convention, and when March 15 came they dutifully said goodbye.

At the Elkhorn Theodore occupied himself with rounding up cattle, presiding over the Stockmen's Association, planning a hunting expedition to the Idaho Rockies, and writing *Benton*. In New York, meanwhile, Edith busily prepared for her move to Europe. Apparently there was some doubt as to the permanence of their emigration. "The Carows have sold their house and are going abroad on the 24th of April, probably for 18 months," Corinne wrote on March 29. "I trust not for more. It makes me quite blue . . ."[18] How and in what circumstances Edith would eventually return, Corinne of course did not know, while Theodore, who did, feigned ignorance. "What day does Edith go abroad and for how long does she intend staying?" he slyly wrote Corinne on April 12. "Could you not send her when she goes some flowers from me? I suppose fruit would be more useful, but I think flowers 'more tenderer' as Mr. Weller would say."[19]

Edith sent long and frequent letters to Theodore, numbering every one to make sure he read them in the correct sequence. Only one complete letter of this series has survived. Apparently Edith, when burning her intimate correspondence in old age, could not bring herself to destroy this one, so full of tenderness and youthful ardor.

London
Tuesday, June 8 [1886]

DEAREST,

I felt so reproached when your letter of the 24th told me you had only heard from me once, that I immediately answer it, though I wrote only Saturday.

Indeed you have no excuse for being a sensitive plant, since if you have sent me 17 letters this is my 14th . . .

I meant to explain about the Arabian Nights last week. Almost the first thing I remember is being told about Sinbad the Sailor when I was a tiny girl and used to climb up on my father's knee every evening and beg him to "spin me a yarn." Children are such queer little people and all their imaginings are so matter of fact, drawn from their own experience which necessarily is very limited, and from whatever they hear or read which impresses them very deeply. Put the Arabian Nights in the hands of most children and it opens a new world to them, full of glowing Eastern light and colour. If this were only done there would possibly be fewer commonplace grown-up people,—certainly the bane of society; indeed, my dearest Mr. T.R. I think imagination is one of the greatest blessings of life and while one can lose oneself in a book one can never be thoroughly unhappy. I don't for a moment defend the morale of the Arabian Nights. Indeed I rarely open them now, and most of the heroes and heroines never seemed more than glittering phantoms hung with gold and jewels; but it is the whole atmosphere of the book which is so fascinating and somehow Kubla Khan and Aldrich's little lyric

"When the sultan goes Ispahan," give me the same feeling. I have always had a passion for fairy tales, and it is the same feeling which makes me linger over Boucher's or Watteau's pictures, while Emily tries to drag me away and says they are neither life nor nature. I know it all quite well, but they are Arcadia, Utopia, Fancy Land, and take me out of myself more than pictures with real soul, which after once seeing one can never forget.

I cannot explain very coherently on paper but some very hot day, I will pull my tattered old copy of the *Arabian Nights* from the bottom of the box where it now reposes and show you what I mean.

I have never read "Sordello," so can't be teased about it, but I daresay if Jerrold had read it over often enough he would have gotten something out of it. That is the trouble with Browning; he takes such a lot of digging. One might as well learn a language.

Please tell me if you keep up your Spanish, or if all those somnolent hours of study were profitless . . .

London is perfectly lovely now, everything is so bright and gay. Last night we heard your cousin Mr. Scovell, poor Marcia Roosevelt's husband, sing in *Carmen*. He is middle aged, ugly and uninteresting with not enough voice to redeem his bad acting. His one idea of making love is to seize the prima donna's arm and shake her, violently. I am so glad it is not your way. It is such fun driving in the park and seeing all the people. You may not believe it, but I never used to think much about my looks if I knew my dress was all right; now I do care about being pretty for you, and every girl I see I think "I wonder if I am as pretty as she is," or "At any rate I am not quite as ugly as that girl." Mame told me today I had never taken any care of my complexion, but she hoped I would now, but when I asked why, she could give no satisfactory reason. You should have seen her walking down Baker Street holding an umbrella over my head. She is always so pleased when she brings me a letter from you, and after considerately giving me plenty of time to read it, she comes back to ask if you are quite well.

The Doctor has advised Mamma not to go to any baths,—which is an immense relief to Emily and myself as we hated the idea of Karlsbad,—but to travel slowly and enjoy herself, so I have not an idea where we shall go after we leave London. When you tell me when to expect you we will decide when we will return to England. You know I love you very much and would do anything in the world to please you. I wish I could be sure my letters sound as much like myself as yours do like you; or that they are what you like. You know all about me darling. I never could have loved anyone else. I love you with all the passion of a girl who has never loved before, and please be patient with me when I cannot put my heart on paper.

Mamma says I must tell you that I am very practical and know a great deal about money. Please send me your photo in hunting costume. Not that there is any danger of my forgetting you but I want to show it to Emily.

I am more glad than I can say that you have been enjoying the western life and do hope the cattle will turn out well, but be good and patient and do not worry too much; please take your hunting trip for I am quite sure it will pay for itself.

You must take me out west, or I shall repent all my life not having seen the place my dearest is so fond of. I am quite sure I should be comfortable. Could I have afternoon tea without asking Mr. and Mrs. Seawell [sic] and Mr. and Mrs. Dow and all the little Seawells and Dows to join?

I have got the most entrancing hat, all tipped down over my nose and tipped up over one ear, with pale pinky-lilac flowers drooping around. It is almost too pretty to wear since you are not here to see it.

Of course you absurd Mr. T.R. I do not wish you to write often if you do it as a duty, but if you do it for pleasure (as I write you) then we both enjoy your letters.

"Please send me your photo in hunting costume."
Theodore Roosevelt in buckskins, 1885.

I wish I could see *Benton*. When do you suppose it will be published?

I perfectly love your description of the life out west for I almost feel as if I could see you and know just what you are doing, and I do not think you sentimental in the least to love nature; please love me too and believe I think of you all the time and want so much to see you.

Mamma and Emily ask me to send you their love, and you know you have all of your

EDITH

P.S. Do you think I wish you to hire Windsor or Buckingham for a honeymoon that you say that you can't give me such a one as you would wish?[20]

Throughout the early summer Theodore openly showed pictures of Edith to his ranching friends, but kept up the pretense with his family that he had lost the "restless caged-wolf feeling" of yore, and was entirely happy as a cowboy. Then suddenly, on July 5, 1886, his letters began to strike a different tone, as if preparing his sisters for what was to come. "It will fairly break my heart to have to give up this life," he wrote Corinne. "However if I continued to make long stays here I should very soon get to practically give up the East entirely."[21]

A reason other than his impending marriage for this change of heart can be found in one sentence of a July 4 speech that he made in Dickinson, Dakota:

> If you fail to work in public life as well as in private for honesty, and uprightness, and virtue, if you condone vice because the vicious man is smart, or if you in any way cast your weight into the scales in favor of evil, you are just so far corrupting and making less valuable the birthright of your children.

After the oration, Roosevelt told a reporter "that he believed he could do better work in a public or political way than in any other." The reporter replied, "Then you will become President of the United States." Theodore expressed no surprise, and gave the impression of having arrived at precisely the same conclusion.[22]

Three days later he left for New York, looking "bright, eager, impulsive and positive," according to a newsman who met him en route. He spent a month in the East completing *Benton*, looking into the possibility of a post as President of the New York City Board of Health, and still concealing the fact of his engagement.

From Europe Edith's letters continued to arrive. She was clearly reveling in the myriad stimulations of the Old World. "If I were only sure you had never been to Prague I would tell you all about the cathedral with its crumbling little chapel inlaid with mosaics and the bronze candelabra from Jerusalem, and the fountain cast by Peter Vischer, and the narrow little streets of the Josephstadt . . ." But again her thoughts returned to him in lovingly protective tones: "Please try not to break your other arm until I can take care of you." [23]

By August 7 Theodore was back out West, again lauding the cowboy existence. ". . . I am greatly attached to the Ranch and the life out here, and am really fond of the men. It is in many ways ideal; we are so very rarely able to, actually and in real life, dwell in our ideal 'hero land.' The loneliness and freedom, and the half-adventurous nature of existence out here, appeals to me very powerfully." [24] But when he returned from the Idaho Rockies on September 18, a serious problem confronted him. The price of cattle in the overstocked Bad Lands had fallen so disastrously that Sewall and Dow, seeing no future there, had decided to return to Maine. To make matters more distressing, he discovered that in his absence the following item of gossip had been published in the social columns of *The New York Times:*

> The engagement was announced during the week of ex-Assemblyman Theodore Roosevelt and Miss Carow of New York. Miss Carow has long been an intimate friend of Mr. Roosevelt's sisters. Mr. Roosevelt is a widower, his first wife, formerly Miss Gray *[sic]*, of Boston, having died some three *[sic]* years ago.

Then, a week later, a retraction, probably inserted by Bamie or Corinne:

> The announcement of the engagement of Mr. Theodore Roosevelt, made last week, and which came from a supposedly authoritative source, proves to have

been erroneous. Nothing is more common in society than to hear positive assertions constantly made regarding the engagement of persons who have been at all in each other's company, and no practice is more reprehensible.[25]

Annoyed and shamefaced, Theodore now had the unenviable task of explaining his deception to his elder sister.

Elkhorn Ranch,
Medora, Dakota Sept. 20, 1886.

DARLING BAMIE,

On returning from the mountains I was savagely irritated by seeing in the papers the statement that I was engaged to Edith Carow; from what source it could have originated I cannot possibly conceive.

But the statement itself is true. I am engaged to Edith, and before Christmas I shall cross the ocean to marry her. You are the first person to whom I have breathed one word on the subject; I am absolutely sure that I have never betrayed myself in any way, unless some servant has seen the address on the letters I wrote. When it finally became absolutely impossible to keep it longer from them, Edith told her mother and sister, but under such conditions (especially as they are abroad) that I can scarcely believe either of them told anyone else. When I was back in July I would have told you, but at that time I was uncertain whether it would not be a year before we were married, for reasons which I will give you in full when we meet. On returning to Medora I received letters giving definite shape to my plans; I did not write you at once, because a letter is such a miserably poor substitute for talking face to face; and I should not write you now, had it not been for this report; for I will see you before you have time to answer me.

I utterly disbelieve in and disapprove of second marriages; I have always considered that they argued weakness in a man's character. You could not reproach me one half as bitterly for my inconstancy and unfaithfulness, as I reproach myself. Were I sure there were a heaven my one prayer would be I might never go there, lest I should meet those I loved on earth who are dead. No matter what your judgment about myself I shall most assuredly enter no plea against it. But I do very earnestly ask you not to visit my sins upon' poor little Edith. It is certainly not her fault; the entire blame rests on my shoulders. Eight years ago she and I had very intimate relations; one day there came a break, for we both of us had, and I suppose have, tempers that were far from being of the best. To no soul now living have either of us ever since spoken a word of this.

As regards yourself, my dearest sister, I can only say you will be giving me the greatest happiness in your power if you will continue to pass your summers with me. We ourselves will have to live in the country almost the entire year; I thoroughly understand the change I will have to make in my life. As I have already told you, if you wish to you shall keep Baby Lee, I of course paying the expense.

I will write to Elliott and Anna, Corinne and Douglass, and Aunt Annie and Uncle Jimmie. No other person is to be told a word about it.

I will explain everything in full when I see you. *Forever your loving brother,*

THEODORE ROOSEVELT

As I do not care to see Rosy Lee I shall return about Oct. 6, '86.[26]

This extraordinary letter, with its intimations of guilt, embarrassment, cowardice, and lack of parental interest, has been suppressed for almost a century. In fairness one must admit that Theodore was under considerable stress when he wrote it. His ranches were failing, his sisters (who had promptly issued a denial of his engagement) bewildered and annoyed at discovering the clandestine nature of his relationship with Edith. He continued to be tortured by remorse over Alice Lee. Friends in Dakota heard him pacing his room for hours bemoaning his lack of "constancy." He even courted death by offering to raise a company of horse-riflemen to quell a Mexican border dispute.[27] Worst of all, perhaps, was his attempt to appease Bamie by offering her Baby Lee, as if the child were a consolation prize for his having deceived her.

In late September, Theodore shut up the Elkhorn Ranch, consolidated his herds under Merrifield and Ferris, and headed east, arriving in New York in early October. He found Bamie in a new house at 689 Madison Avenue, bravely determined to make the best of a painful situation. She was "too lovely about it for anything," and even agreed to accompany him to London, where the wedding ceremony was to be held. As for Corinne, she found the whole situation "all terribly incomprehensible." The prospect of sharing her beloved brother with her oldest friend, whom both she and Bamie suspected would be a possessive wife, was not pleasing. But Theodore, having fully explained himself to them, at least to his own satisfaction, now seemed "thoroughly happy in his engagement."[28]

In mid-October, Theodore accepted a surprise nomination by the State Republican Party to run in a three-way race for Mayor of New York City. He doubted that he could win, but as a pragmatist he wanted to keep in good standing with the Republican kingmakers, lest he should want to resume his political career sometime in the future. In any case he ran an excellent campaign against the Democrat Abram S. Hewitt, and the labor leader Henry George—perhaps the best mayoralty race the city has ever seen—with lofty issues addressed in a clean fight. Bamie kept her future sister-in-law informed of the candidate's progress, writing with enthusiasm on October 23:

> MY DEAREST EDITH
>
> You will be astonished at another letter so soon, but though of course Theodore writes you of everything, still you will wish to hear what I try to write; of the wonderful enthusiasm he certainly inspires; never mind what the results . . . it is astounding the hold he has on the public . . . Douglas has been as always a trump having organized "the Roosevelt Campaign Club of Businessmen" which brings in many active workers. Theodore breakfasts and sleeps at home where he is comfortable . . . by half after nine he is in the Head Quarters at the Fifth Avenue never leaving except for

lunch and dinner . . . even then he can but spare a short time; he is very bright and well considering the terrific strain which of course will be worse constantly until the second [of November] is past. It is such happiness to see him at his very best once more; ever since he has been out of politics in any active form; it has been a real heart sorrow to me, for while he always made more of his life than any other man I knew, still with his strong nature it was a permanent source of poignant regret that even at this early age he should lose these years without the possibility of doing his best and most telling work; in that there should be the least chance that he might find his hold over the public gone when he once more came before them and this is the first time since [Assembly] days that he has enough work to keep him exerting all his powers. Theodore is the only person who had the power except Father who possessed it in a different way; of making me almost worship him and now it is such a desperate feeling to realize that in all this excitement I cannot help him in the least except that he knows how interested I am. I would never say or write this except to you, but, it is very restful to feel how you care for him and how happy he is in his devotion to you . . . I go back again tomorrow [to Sagamore Hill] to remain over the Hunt Ball. I wish you were to be there this year also as you were last . . . I send you the pieces from this mornings Times they are samples of what happens daily of course of the favorable side, those most against him can find nothing but his youth, supposed wealth, and being born a gentleman to say as detrimental. . . .[29]

As expected, Theodore did not win the mayoralty, running a poor third to Hewitt. On the night of November 5 he and Bamie sat up late writing preliminary notes of his engagement to close friends. The official announcement would not be released until November 8, well after their departure. To Mrs. Henry Cabot Lodge Bamie wrote:

Theodore is radiantly happy and we sail on Saturday for England. . . . Theodore has against my will insisted on my keeping Baby, in fact for the present at least we will go on just as we are. . . . Edith we have known intimately always. She is very bright and attractive and I believe absolutely devoted to Theodore so I think their future looks most promising. . . .[30]

When Cousin James West Roosevelt heard the news he wrote Theodore in pleased surprise:

. . . Now that you are to marry a girl who has been one of my best friends, a girl whose main characteristic is truth, I am very much delighted. . . .

I know that you will be happy, and your happiness is much to me. I know that you will be a better man because you will have a fuller life. You are marrying a woman who can enter into your plans and who can appreciate your aims. . . . You are marrying one also who will love you—that is best of all.[31]

And so, on November 6, Theodore and Bamie sailed on the S.S. *Etruria* for England.

Edith and Kermit, 1890.

Marriage and Motherhood 1886–1901

Eight

I would I could adopt your will,
See with your eyes, and set my heart
Beating by yours, and drink my fill
At your soul's springs—your part my part
In life for good and ill.

—Robert Browning[1]

Waiting in London for Theodore's arrival, Edith had ample time to ponder the nature and character of the man she was about to marry. During their eight months' separation she had taken comfort in the knowledge that women, on the whole, interested him little, and that he preferred male conversation and masculine pastimes.

Yet Theodore was not as unsusceptible as she imagined. That very summer, while visiting out West, he had been greatly impressed by Mrs. Martha Selmes, the wife of a fellow rancher. "She is I think very handsome," he wrote Bamie. "She is very well-read, has a delicious sense of humor and is extremely fond of poetry—including my new favorite Browning, as well as my old one Swinburne." In another letter he had rhapsodized: "As you know, I am no judge of looks but I think her really handsome."[2] (Sooner or later, Edith learned about the striking rancher's wife, and conceived a jealousy of her so ill-disguised that people hesitated to mention Mrs. Selmes in her presence.)

Theodore's views on male and female roles in society changed little over the years. He contended that the best policy for a man was to marry at the earliest opportunity; and that the greatest vocation for a woman was to be a good wife and mother. To him the family was more important than the state, domestic life infinitely superior to any other "makeshift and starveling substitute." Celibacy, therefore, should be heavily taxed. Simultaneously, he acknowledged the rights of women to education and self-fulfillment, and the opportunity to work and excel in their own careers. (In college he had written a thesis on "The Practicability of Giving Women Equal Rights," and had even suggested that a wife be allowed to keep her maiden name.)[3] When the time came he would support woman suffrage—even though Edith was lukewarm about it, and Bamie felt it merely compounded the "stupid" vote.

Since boyhood, Theodore had disliked risqué jokes and sexual innuendo. He also deplored the double standard of morality that most men applied to sexual conduct. If chastity was desirable for spinsters, it was equally so for bachelors. Women should not tolerate infidelity, and rapists—far and away the worst criminals in society—should be punished like murderers.

Edith herself shared most of Theodore's views on life and society, and had others, equally strong, of her own, which she would in time impress upon him. In her hands he would become more disciplined, more prudent, and more wary of his political and personal rivals. Could Edith Carow have been aware of the caliber and vast ambition of the man who would shortly become her husband, and the high destiny they faced together?

Theodore's boat docked in Liverpool in the early afternoon of November 13. He took the first train to London, where Edith awaited him in Buckland's Hotel on Brook Street, in the fashionable heart of Mayfair. His own suite was reserved at Brown's Hotel on Dover Street, a short walk away and convenient for both of them as a refuge from the over-attentive Mrs. Carow and Emily.[4]

Brown's was a discreetly luxurious setting for their reunion, with its heavy lace curtains, plush drapes, and dim, cozy alcoves. But stiff horsehair seats protected by antimacassars discouraged too much lingering. In any case, Edith preferred the privacy of Theodore's suite, where they could huddle over the fire and express all the intimacies they had been unable to say in letters. So reclusive were they in those first days that they annoyed the American Ambassador by neglecting to tell him of their presence in the capital. Theodore was, after all, a well-known political and literary figure who was expected to do a certain amount of socializing.

Their solitude, as it happened, was short-lived. Soon Bamie arrived from visiting Bulloch relatives in Liverpool, and then came Cecil Spring-Rice, a British diplomat whom Theodore had met during the crossing and persuaded to act as best man. Edith, who was not inclined to easy familiarity, took an immediate liking to "Springy," as his friends called him. He was just a few months younger than Theodore. After graduating from Eton and Balliol College, Oxford, Spring-Rice had joined the Foreign Office, and was appointed Private Secretary to the Earl of Granville. Next he became assistant to the Earl of Roseberry. His recent visit to the New World had stimulated a lively interest in the United States, and now, after meeting the "amusing" Theodore Roosevelt, he was determined to secure an appointment there.[5]

In appearance, Spring-Rice was typical of his class and breeding. He had a long face, broad forehead, aquiline nose, and pale smoothed-down hair. The almond-shaped eyes, framed by unruly brows, were frank and warm, and Edith recognized in him the combined qualities of an aesthete and a gentleman. He, in turn, found her "charming."

Under Springy's influence, Theodore became a social lion during the two weeks before his wedding. He was put down for the Atheneum, the St. James, and other "swell" clubs. He dined daily with eminent statesmen, including Joseph Chamberlain, the progressive Liberal thinker. He rode to hounds, and turned down numerous invitations to shoot for lack of time. Edith, meanwhile, was busy with wedding preparations, and saw very little of Theodore during the daytime. "You have no idea how sweet Edith is about many different things," Theodore wrote Corinne almost querulously. "I do'n't think even I had known how wonderfully *good* and unselfish she was; she is naturally reserved and finds it especially hard to express her feelings on paper."[6]

An archetypal London pea-soup fog settled down on Thursday,

"The combined qualities of an aesthete and a gentleman."
Cecil Spring-Rice.

December 2, the day of Edith and Theodore's marriage. Bamie had
to be led by link bearers to Buckland's Hotel, where she helped Edith
arrange her Valenciennes-lace gown and orange-blossom veil. At the
same time, Cecil Spring-Rice put on a frock coat and went to Brown's
to collect Theodore. Oblivious to the thick mist, and the necessity of
making an early start for St. George's, Hanover Square, the two men
were soon "intensely occupied in a discussion over the population of
an island in the South Pacific." Their debate continued on the way to
the church, until Springy stopped the cab, darted into a haber-
dasher's shop, and returned with a pair of orange gloves for the

groom.[7] Edith's reaction as she walked up the nave and saw Theodore's orange fists, luminescent even through the haze, may well be imagined.

The ceremony, conducted by Charles E. Camidge, Canon of York, was private and brief. In the registry afterward with Spring-Rice and Emily as witnesses, the new Mr. and Mrs. Theodore Roosevelt signed the church register. Edith described her previous self as a twenty-five-year-old spinster with no profession; Theodore called himself a widower of twenty-eight and gave his profession as ranchman. He could not have known just how short-lived the latter designation would be.[8]

Meanwhile, back in North Dakota, Theodore's cattlemen were boggling over a highly imaginative announcement of the marriage in the *Badlands Cowboy:*

> While Mr. Theo. Roosevelt has gone to England to get him a wife, it is an American lady whom he is to marry. His prospective bride is just nineteen years old and is the youngest daughter of Governor Carroll of Maryland, a family famous for its wealth and blue blood. Her sister recently married an English nobleman. It is there that Miss Carroll is staying. The young lady is a grandchild of the late Royal Phelps and entered New York society about five years ago. Mr. Roosevelt is about thirty years old and has been a widower for two years. He is very wealthy.[9]

Immediately after the wedding breakfast Edith and Theodore left for Dover. From here Theodore wrote Bamie: "We are having the most absolutely ideal time imaginable." They went on to Paris, Lyons and Marseilles, and by December 13 had reached the balmy Mediterranean town of Hyères, in Provence. Both Edith and Theodore loved the stately palms, the red and white rose hedges, the olive orchards and orange groves, and the quaint Provençal language and costumes. "It is delightful to idle one's days here with a clear conscience," Theodore wrote Bamie, "for the time is all our own this winter and is to be spent for nothing else. We walk and drive over the hills and along the seashore, and have a lovely suite of rooms from which we can look over the bay." One window faced west across

steep pine-clad hills. Through it, in the evening, they would watch
daylight fade, and recite in unison, "The dying sunset kindled
through the cleft . . ."[10]

Taking a private carriage, they left Hyères and drove along the
French and Italian Rivieras to the "beautiful bay of Spezia." Cozily
ensconsed in the Grand Hotel, they ate chicken, peas, omelet and
partridge, and drank beer and Chianti before their own crackling
wood fire.[11] At about this time Edith conceived her first child.

Their idyllic honeymoon was interrupted in the new year of 1887,
when they joined Mrs. Carow and Emily in Florence. At the same
time Theodore began to receive reports of catastrophic blizzards in
Dakota. Preliminary estimates indicated that his loss of livestock
would be so severe that he must "think very seriously of closing
Sagamore Hill and going to the ranch for a year or two."[12]

Depressed and worried about money, he worked hard at six
chapter-length articles on hunting and ranching for the *Century
Magazine* (later published in book form as *Ranch Life and the Hunting
Trail)*, and tried to think of ways to economize. Should he sell his
hunter, or cut the gardening staff, or "see if it pays to get my own hay
and fodder?"[13] But living a circumscribed life was not Theodore's
style, and his thrifty intentions were short-lived. Soon he was
purchasing an elaborately carved Florentine sideboard, dining table,
and chairs for Sagamore Hill, asking his brother-in-law's advice on
where to buy fine English shoes, and engaging a suite of rooms in
Rome, while the Carows had to be content with scantier quarters four
flights up.

The winter days passed quickly. He finished his articles, "read
them aloud to Edith," and was grateful for her "most valuable"
literary advice and corrections. Try as they might to enjoy the rest of
their stay abroad, domestic problems continued to plague them. Even
larger than finance loomed the question of Baby Lee's custody.
Bamie, unmarried, and facing a lonely middle age, obviously (despite
her protest to Nannie Cabot Lodge) longed to raise the child as her
own. Theodore would have happily accepted this arrangement, but
his new wife objected the moment he broached the subject. "I hardly
know what to say about Baby Lee," he wrote Bamie in great
embarrassment. "Edith feels more strongly about her than I could
have imagined possible. However, we can decide it all when we
meet."[14]

Eager as he was to postpone a decision, Edith had made up *her* mind. The very idea of Theodore visiting Madison Avenue in order to see his own daughter was repellent to her; she would not hear of it.

On January 16, the Roosevelts and the Carows reached Naples. Next day they all drove to Pompeii, where Theodore had' been seventeen years before. He remembered little of it, however, and this second visit therefore had "the charm of almost absolute novelty." Besides he had the added pleasure of being here with Edith, who liked to sightsee as he did—without a Baedeker. In Sorrento a few days later, they slipped away from the Carows to see a tarantella, and took a flying trip to Capri in a chartered sailing boat. "I had no idea that it was in me to enjoy the *dolce far niente* even as long as I have. Luckily, Edith would hate an extended stay in Europe as much as I would," he wrote Corinne on January 22. But there were unmistakable signs of restlessness. He took vigorous daily walks up and down the surrounding hills, as well as more leisurely strolls with Edith, and wrote of the hazards of "sedentary seclusion" and "daily overeating."[15]

Back in Rome on February 5, Edith bid a sad farewell to her mother and sister, who still had no settled home in mind. The parting was particularly hard for Gertrude, since Edith was by far the more affectionate and competent of her two daughters. Life without such a companion held few charms for Mrs. Carow—not to mention the less patient and sympathetic Emily, to whom Gertrude's increasing hypochondria was becoming a sore trial. Edith could not fail to realize what a lucky escape she had had in marrying Theodore. The alternative—ceaseless wandering as one of an impecunious expatriate trio—seemed worse than death.

In Venice, Edith and Theodore, alone again for the first time in five weeks, resumed their honeymoon. Celebrating in longed-for solitude, they rented huge, splendid, but chilly rooms looking across the water to San Giorgio Maggiore. They spent days admiring the "florid barbarism" of Venetian architecture, indulged in languorous gondola rides along the winding canals, and, at night, drank in the beauty of the moonlit piazzas. A snow storm, which made the city infinitely more strange and romantic than before, came as a fitting climax to their stay.[16]

Edith was awed by the lofty grandeur of Milan Cathedral, but

Theodore, who was beginning to show signs of homesickness, longed for his "beloved woods and mountains and great lonely plains."[17] To all intents and purposes the trip was over. His recently published *Benton* had just come in the mail, and although it was "rough" in places, he was sufficiently encouraged to want to tackle some more ambitious historical work.

In Paris, in mid-February, they visited an old friend, Augustus Jay, the Second Secretary at the American Embassy, and dined with the esoteric Boston Buddhist William Sturgis Bigelow. Reaching London in the last week of the month, Theodore sent subtle news to Corinne: "Edith has been feeling the reverse of brightly for some little time."[18]

Her indisposition did not prevent them from being once again taken up by London society. They had lunch with the revered historian George Otto Trevelyan, were escorted to the House of Commons by a Member of Parliament, and accepted an invitation from the Honorable William North for a three-day stay at Wroxton Abbey, on the Warwickshire-Oxfordshire border. "I wanted Edith to see a really first-class English country house," Theodore explained to Lodge, "but isn't it funny to think of a rabid American like myself having every courtesy extended him by Lord North? Edith, thank Heaven, feels as I do, and is even more intensely anti-anglomaniac; and I rather think our utter indifference, and our standing sharply on our dignity, have been among the main causes that have procured us so hospitable a reception."

After the visit to Wroxton Abbey Theodore had had enough of Europe. "I shall be glad to get home," he confessed to Bamie. "I am an American through to the backbone."[19]

There remained only a meeting with Robert Browning. The poet was then almost seventy-five years old, and much lionized by London society. Since their teenage years Edith and Theodore had loved his work, and knew much of it by heart. Theodore was particularly fond of quoting "Love Among the Ruins," written after Browning's elopement to Italy with Elizabeth Barret:

> *When I do come, she will speak out, she will stand,*
> *Either hand*
> *On my shoulder, give her eyes the first embrace*
> *Of my face,*

> *Ere we rush, ere we extinguish sight and speech*
> *Each on each.*

Seeing and hearing Browning was a romantic climax to a new, ecstatic experience, which Edith ever after looked back upon as the most idyllic period in her life. Fourteen years later she would write to her husband: "I love you all the time in my thoughts and think of our honeymoon days, and remember them all one by one, and hour by hour . . ."[20]

Nine

I think I become more bound up in Edie and the children every day.

—Theodore Roosevelt[1]

On Sunday, March 27, 1887, Edith and Theodore disembarked in New York, and drove straight to Bamie's house at 689 Madison Avenue, their temporary home until May. Three-year-old Alice, wearing her best dress and sash, greeted them with a bunch of pink roses. While Edith settled in and became acquainted with her stepdaughter, Theodore entertained two friends from Washington who had come north to welcome them back. One was none other than Cecil Spring-Rice, newly appointed to the staff of the British Legation. In return for the Englishman's hospitality in London, Theodore introduced him to New York society, and put him up at the Century Club, which Spring-Rice considered to be "a glorified Savile."[2]

The other visitor was rather more formidable than the gentle Springy, and Edith was apprehensive about meeting him. He was the distinguished Boston Congressman Henry Cabot Lodge, Theodore's colleague at the 1884 Republican Convention and now fast becoming his closest friend. Edith's first impression was of a tall, slight, energetic person, with a closely clipped beard and a tightly controlled demeanor. Lodge had an intimidating habit of dropping his mouth at the corners and screwing up his hazel eyes, as if in disapproval of everyone and everything. When he spoke, his Boston Brahmin voice rasped like the tearing of bed linen. But behind this chilly façade lay warm inner spaces to which only intimates were admitted. Edith was relieved to gain access, not merely by virtue of her marriage to Theodore, but because she and Lodge shared a love of belles lettres. Cabot soon came to have "a great deal of confidence" in Edith's critical taste and judgment. "He is one of the few men I know who is as well-read as she is in English literature," Theodore told Bamie, "and she delights to talk with him."[3]

Edith, for her part, had leisure to ponder many curious parallels between the lives of Cabot and Theodore. Both had been delicate children who built their bodies by strenuous exercise. Both had attended Harvard, and married beautiful Bostonians shortly after graduating (a parallel Edith did not care to dwell on). Both had broadened their minds with extensive European travel, and had written books and studied law before embarking on their careers in politics. Lodge had a fuller classical education than Theodore, was a wittier conversationalist, and more polished orator. But, on the whole, Theodore considered their minds well matched "personally, politically and in every other way." Lodge, in return, thought Roosevelt "one of the most lovable as well as one of the cleverest and most daring men" he had ever met, and "the best friend I have in the world." Edith approved of their closeness, to the extent of saying, in a moment of feminine morbidity, that if Theodore died, Lodge was the one person she would care to see.[4]

Sagamore Hill, which had been closed all winter, remained so until late spring. On April 4, leaving Baby Lee once more with Bamie, Edith took Theodore to Philadelphia to meet some of her Tyler relatives. After a day or two he went on alone to North Dakota to assess the impact of the recent blizzards on his stock. It was even worse than he had anticipated. "I am bluer than indigo about the cattle," he wrote Bamie. "I wish I was sure I would lose no more than half the money ($80,000) I invested out here. I am planning how to get out of it." He became more depressed as the days went by. "For the first time I have been utterly unable to enjoy a visit to my ranch," he told Lodge. "I shall be glad to get home."[5]

Both Edith and Theodore were back at Madison Avenue in early

"Bamie, unmarried . . . longed to raise the child as her own."
Anna Roosevelt and Alice Roosevelt.

May, preparing for their move to Sagamore Hill. To soften the blow
of parting from Baby Lee, Bamie spontaneously left 689 before they
did, and went South for a vacation. Theodore and Edith were left
alone with their child for the first time. Awkwardly, no doubt, they

learned to sit on the floor with her, peopling her block houses with "visionary beings whose careers were varied and picturesque to a degree."[6]

Alice was permitted only two weeks with her new "Mother" (Edith insisted on this appellation) before being packed off to Chestnut Hill to stay with her grandparents. The Roosevelts had a serene Victorian confidence in the adjustability of infants. It was decided that Alice would spend three weeks of every spring and fall in Boston from now on. The doting Lees spoiled the child, but Edith was grateful for their "loyalty" in that they never tried to alienate Alice from her.[7]

The new Mrs. Roosevelt was now free to establish herself in the home she would occupy for the rest of her life. Try as she might on first moving in, she could not escape painful associations. Sagamore Hill had been built for one woman and ruled by another. Its twenty-two rooms reflected the maternal hopes of the dead Alice Lee, and its furniture the taste of the departed Bamie. Fortunately she was able to put her own stamp on the house at once, installing old Kermit and Carow pieces as well as some new ones bought in Italy.

For the first week she and Theodore worked "like a couple of dusty, not to say grimy, beavers," placing furniture, hanging up game heads, and arranging hundreds of books.[8] Edith resigned herself to the heavily masculine décor of Sagamore Hill, with the exception of one first-floor room which she appropriated as her own personal parlor. It faced south onto the front piazza and lawns, and west toward the blue waters of the bay. She furnished it simply with pale floral button-back sofas and two armchairs, two side chairs, delicate side tables and lamps, and the small writing desk inherited from Aunt Kermit. This was to be her refuge from the cares of running a large household, a quiet space where she could read and write and find relief from her sometimes over-boisterous husband.

Theodore, in turn, established himself across the paneled hall in the library, full of southern sunshine during the day and cozily crackling with wood fires at night. There was a massive desk here where he could work, under the benign oil-painted gaze of his father.

Farther down the hall past the stairs was a small dining room, which they filled to bursting with a heavy oak Florentine suite. An interconnecting pantry opened out into the kitchen, whose size bespoke the importance of food in Theodore's life. For their bedroom, they selected a rather drafty second-floor room facing north and east.

"This was to be her refuge."
Edith's parlor at Sagamore Hill.

The rest of the floor was given over to spare bedrooms (shrouded, for the time being, in white dust covers). Above were the maids' rooms, trunk and linen closets, and Theodore's private sanctum, the "gun room," facing west over the tops of trees. Here, among his burgeoning collection of weapons and Western memorabilia, he soon began to write his fourth book, a biography of Gouverneur Morris. With no prospect of government appointment under the present Democratic Administration, and with sharply decreased expectations as a rancher, the career of literary gentleman was the only one left to him.

That first summer of their marriage established a pattern of work and recreation that changed little over the years. Edith spent her mornings organizing the household, sewing and answering letters, while Theodore went to his study to write. In the afternoon they walked in the woods, swam, rode or boated through the "marshy lagoons and curious winding channels." As Theodore pulled on the oars, Edith would read aloud from Browning, Thackeray, Matthew Arnold, and other of their favorite authors. Occasionally, on calm Sundays, they would row clear across Oyster Bay to Christ Episcopal Church in the village.[9]

One of the first people to interrupt their solitary idyll was Cecil Spring-Rice, who arrived in early June and stayed for a week. Edith by now felt entirely at ease with his unceremonious manner and self-deprecating wit. His untidy appearance, indifference to food, and casual disregard of his health brought out her motherly instincts, and during his visit she adopted him as one of the family. He had a delightful facility for composing witty rhymes and sketching carica-tures, as well as an inexhaustible fund of ghost stories, with which he would amuse his hosts on chilly evenings around the fire. He also had the habit, disconcerting to Theodore, of reading Dante and Homer in the original Italian and Greek. But he was no match for the Roosevelts on horseback. After a shaky canter on Caution, the polo pony, he acknowledged his limitations: "I never met a pony that had such a thorough command over its rider."[10]

Bamie, despite Theodore's standing invitation to regard Sagamore Hill as her summer home, came to stay only twice in 1887. On the second occasion she brought with her a lanky, well-born and adoring young Scotsman, Robert Hector Munro Ferguson, better known as "Fergie" or "Bob." She had met him in London the previous winter. At eighteen, he was fourteen years her junior. Her attitude toward him was half maternal and half romantic: she fretted over his weak lungs, and simultaneously enjoyed his attentions as she introduced him to New York society. Like Cecil Spring-Rice and Henry Cabot Lodge, Fergie was to become a staple member of the Sagamore Hill circle.

Edith was almost eight months pregnant on August 6, 1887, when she celebrated her twenty-sixth birthday. Plans had been made to accommodate her mother and sister, who were due to arrive in time for the confinement. But at the last minute the hypochondriacal Gertrude telegraphed to say she was ill and could not sail. Edith was not too upset. "I do not think she feels her absence," Theodore wrote

Bamie. "She has never reposed any trust in her sickness and trouble."

Like most pregnant women, Edith nevertheless instinctively wanted a close female companion in the house. Bamie, back in New York, was now the obvious choice; yet Edith preferred to rely on her old nurse. Her motive in bypassing Bamie was clear. Having only just taken the place in Theodore's and Alice's life formerly occupied by her sister-in-law, she wanted to keep her at arm's length for a while. It was left to an embarrassed Theodore to explain: "Mame is devoted; you know how much she is to Edith; I do not think there is need of anyone else." [11]

In early September, Theodore sent his *Gouverneur Morris* to the publisher. Now, with nothing to do but contemplate the impending birth of his second child, and remember the tragedy attending the birth of his first, Theodore suffered the worst attack of asthma he had had in a long time. Fortunately, Baby Lee provided some distraction. She watched him shave, supervised his tennis, and demanded his company on long walks. Edith went with them occasionally, but she was heavy and sickly now. Although her confinement was not due until the second half of the month, Theodore was not too surprised when at nine o'clock on the evening of September 12 she suddenly went into labor. The nurse who was to help with delivery and stay on for postnatal care had not yet arrived, but fortunately Cousin West Roosevelt, who was a doctor, lived nearby and was quickly summoned. In a final rush, at 2:15 A.M., Edith gave birth to an eight-and-a-half-pound son, Theodore Junior. "She was extremely plucky all through," Theodore Senior told Bamie. "Aunt Annie spent the night here and took charge of Baby . . . I am very glad our house has an heir at last!" [12]

The birth caused great rejoicing throughout the Roosevelt clan, which had been plagued by a "sending of girls" in recent years. One uncle "drove about with the dashboard of his wagon decked with goldenrod, and an orange ribbon in his whip, and sent the baby a gold piece because a Dutch boy had come." [13]

Meanwhile Edith submitted meekly to the customary Victorian practice of being wrapped from bosom to hips in tough muslin bandages a yard wide, and pinned fast in front and down both sides. Thus mummified, she remained in bed for two weeks before being helped up, unwrapped, and allowed to lie on the sofa in corsets. She suffered acutely from postnatal depression. "I used to cry by the hour," she remembered afterward, "and yet . . . I am not a tearful person, nor was I really ill." Even when Theodore escorted her on a recuperative drive, she wept and begged him to take her home.[14]

Alice drew her little rocking chair up to the new baby's crib, and after close scrutiny declared him to be "a howling polly parrot." She soon became devoted to him, and continued to watch him closely, "especially when he 'eats Mamma.'" She said she did not want to go to Chestnut Hill for her fall visit unless she could take little Ted with her.

Bamie was finally invited to come and see the baby on October 1. Two days before, Theodore dashed off an abrupt note: "Edie is still pretty weak, and the small boy has colic, but I guess it will be all right. I probably hunt Saturday so I may not be able to meet you myself. Yours ever, Thee. P.S. Edie wants a pair of nursing corsets."[15]

The winter of 1887–88 was the mildest in seventeen years until a freakish blizzard in mid-March paralyzed New York City for two days. Edith and Theodore had moved into town in January, and, with Bamie away, were comfortably settled at 689 when the storm struck. Theodore found the waist-high snow drifts and hurricane-force winds "great fun" at first, but with Edith absorbed in the two children, and himself housebound, he soon began to feel the lack of a serious occupation. "I should like to write some book that would really take rank as in the very first class," he wrote a former Assembly colleague.[16] The wish was father to the action, and by the end of March he was well into research for what developed into his magnum opus, *The Winning of the West,* a four-volume history of America's expansion from the time of Daniel Boone through the American Revolution.

In April the Roosevelts moved back to Oyster Bay, and in mid-May Alice left for her spring stay at Chestnut Hill, accompanied by Mame. Ted, now in short clothes, took great delight in playing with two dogs and a litter of newly born kittens, freeing Edith at last for time alone with Theodore. They would occasionally drive together in the high phaeton to see Elliott and Anna Roosevelt, now living in Hempstead. On the way back they would dawdle awhile on the plains of Syosset to admire great beds of violets and clumps of flowering dogwood in full bloom. Edith cherished these moments alone with Theodore, which unhappily became rarer as spring gave way to summer. Her preference for solitude, and his for company, called for adjustments that had to be made in this early stage of their married life. To Edith, Sagamore Hill was a refuge from the turbulent world, where she could raise her children, be a companion to her husband, and immerse herself in books. Theodore, on the other hand, relished people, politics, stimulating talk and strenuous games. Theirs was a clash of interests and personalities which called for loving compromise—on Edith's side rather more than Theodore's. "One should not live to oneself," she conceded years later to a son. "It was a temptation to me, only Father would not allow it. Since I have grown older and realized that it is a great opportunity when one has a house that one can make pleasant for younger—and also older—people to come to, I have done better."[17] To please her husband she reluctantly took up tennis (a game at which her predecessor had excelled), and tried to be tolerant of his growing addiction to polo, which slowed his writing to two pages a day. But Theodore also made some concessions, as he admitted to Ted at the time of the latter's engagement. "Greatly tho I loved Mother, I was at times thoughtless and selfish, and if Mother had been a mere unhealthy Patient Griselda I might have grown set in selfish and inconsiderate ways. Mother . . . when necessary, pointed out where I was thoughtless, instead of submitting to it. Had she not done this, it would in the end have made her life very much harder, and mine very much less happy."[18]

That this conflict of opposing wills had not been resolved by midsummer 1888 is confirmed by a disapproving letter from Corinne to Bamie, written during a visit to Oyster Bay.

> Teddy of course, must work in the mornings and Edith takes very little interest in outdoor sports. She has been simply too sweet for anything to us, and I cannot admire her too much for her tender consideration of Alice and her delightfully managed and beautiful home, but it certainly is a great pity that she has allowed herself to become indifferent to all people; it cannot help resulting in a depressing effect on everybody.[19]

Edith's reluctance to entertain notwithstanding, there was a steady stream of visitors to Sagamore Hill that year. Cousin Nellie Tyler came and lounged luxuriously on the piazza sofa. She was followed by Cabot Lodge, and then by Gertrude and Emily Carow. Alice liked these new relatives from the start, and commandeered Emily to escort her to Gracewood, where Aunt Annie Gracie was giving lessons to a second generation of Roosevelts.

Few people shared the little girl's fondness for Emily Carow. At twenty-three she was an unflattering caricature of her sister: her figure was reedier, her nose more sharp, her mouth thinner and wider. She was a confirmed pessimist, and this aspect of her personality was not improved by her years of wandering through southern Europe in the company of her gloomy mother. Nieces and nephews were quite fond of Aunt Emily when they were small, but in later years her increasing crabby strictness led them to dub her "the Mediterranean Menace."[20]

Fast becoming a nuisance of another kind was Elliott Roosevelt. His constitutional weakness for drink, aggravated by peer pressure in the racy Long Island circles in which he and his society-loving wife moved, had turned him into an alcoholic. There had been one or two embarrassing incidents that summer, which caused Theodore to ponder "if it would do any good to talk to him seriously about his imprudence!" He concluded not, but wished that Elliott would "come to me for a while; but I guess Oyster Bay would prove insufferably dull."[21]

The first week of July was socially hectic, at least as far as Edith was concerned. She had to endure a garden party, a yacht race, and a polo game before leaving with Theodore for a short vacation with friends in Geneseo, Livingston County, New York. Their host was William Austin Wadsworth, a country squire and expert hunter, who lived at Homestead, a Colonial mansion full of heirlooms in the midst of a vast estate. There was a fine stable of horses, some of whom were frisky enough to show Edith her husband's cowboy ability to avoid being thrown. One horse bucked so violently that Theodore "sat on its ears" and had to use his legs "as a throat latch" before scrambling back into the saddle. Everybody, Edith included, howled with laughter.[22]

Perhaps because he sensed that his reclusive wife was at last beginning to relax in the society of his friends, Theodore hugely enjoyed himself. "He sleeps till ten o'clock," Edith wrote Lodge fondly, "writes two lines a day and is fatter than ever." About this time she discovered that she was once again pregnant. Announcing the fact to Bamie, Theodore said that Alice's "wish for 'another brother or sister' will, I rather regret to say, probably be gratified about the end of next January."[23]

On July 29, Edith went to watch Oyster Bay play Meadowbrook at polo. The game was exciting and without mishap until the final moments, when Theodore rushed after Elliott at terrific speed as he took the ball downfield. There was a thump of horseflesh as brother tried to ride brother out. Suddenly—no one saw how—Theodore was thrown, and knocked unconscious. For several minutes, Corinne wrote, "he neither moved nor stirred, and seemed like a dead man." After getting up, he staggered about, "rambling in his head," for a couple of hours, and was not fully himself for several days. Edith, outwardly imperturbable, "behaved with great presence of mind at the time," but just over a week later, two days after her twenty-seventh birthday, she had a miscarriage.[24]

"You may perhaps be relieved that your house will not be used for confinement purposes this winter," Corinne shrewishly wrote her sister. (Dr. West Roosevelt had insisted Edith avoid the isolation of Long Island in winter for the birth.) "The whole thing has been most mysterious, and neither Anna nor I think there would have been any mishap, had not the tendency to it been acquiesced in by all parties." Then, fearing she might have gone too far, Corinne added: "However there may have been some complication about which we know nothing."[25]

Edith stayed in bed for twelve days after losing her baby, during which time Theodore continued to play polo. On August 21, the day after she came downstairs, he started off for a hunting trip in the Rockies, leaving the Carows in charge.

He stayed West all through September, returning to Oyster Bay on October 5. Two days later he left home again to campaign for the Republican presidential candidate, Benjamin Harrison, in Minnesota and Michigan. This time Edith went with him. "At last she will see the wonderful Mrs. Selmes," Theodore informed Bamie.[26] The tour was "immense fun" for them both. Edith had ventured from her domestic shell once more, and seemed to find the world agreeable.

Throughout the early part of 1889 Theodore struggled to finish the first volume of *The Winning of the West*, but the life of a writer was too sedentary for so active a man. He longed above all to enter the political arena, and to be in Washington in some official position of responsibility, like Henry Cabot Lodge and Cecil Spring-Rice. In May his wish was fulfilled, for, on the urging of various powerful friends, and as a reward for his campaigning, President Harrison appointed him to the post of Civil Service Commissioner at a salary of $3,500 a year. When he assumed office on May 13, Edith was once again pregnant.

Ten

The American woman of the nineteenth century was much better company than the American man.

—Henry Adams[1]

Since the long hot months of summer were approaching, Edith elected to postpone her move to Washington until the end of 1889, after the birth of her child. In the meantime, Theodore, who disliked hotels, and wanted to economize, would use Lodge's house on Connecticut Avenue as his *pied à terre*.

The post of Civil Service Commissioner, though not politically desirable, had its challenges, and Theodore threw himself into work with his customary zeal. In the first few weeks he investigated examination fraud in the New York Custom House, rooted out corruption in Midwestern post offices, and enforced the law "without fear or favor."[2] The position was not as ineffectual as he had suspected, but he was not entirely reconciled to a bureaucratic career. In mid-June, when Volume I of *The Winning of the West* was published to favorable reviews and sales, he veered again toward the independent life of a writer. "Literature must be my mistress perforce," he wrote the historian Francis Parkman, to whom he had dedicated his book.[3]

Theodore went north very little that summer, spending most of his weekends in Washington. When he did appear at Sagamore Hill, however, he devoted all his time to Edith and the children. Polo was temporarily abandoned, but not without qualms. "I am rapidly sinking into a fat and lazy middle age," he complained, though he was not yet thirty-one. When he left for his annual trip to the Rockies on August 7 he felt "acute physical terror" at the thought of climbing the first mountain.[4]

Edith fell into a deep depression immediately after Theodore left. It seemed to her that whenever she was pregnant her husband absented himself for long periods, leaving her with the responsibility for managing his children, his household, his farm, and his finances. This year her loneliness was compounded by the fact that he no longer lived at home anyway. On August 15 she wrote him a letter full of love and anguish:

> . . . Do be very careful. I try not to worry about you, but it is hard, and though of course you have been away so much I am accustomed to not seeing you in the house, still it has been a hopeless kind of summer to look back on, and all I can think of are the times you have been here; our lovely rows, and that long drive . . .
>
> Even though you felt blue on arriving at Medora, I know you will soon be well and enjoying yourself. As for the money you lost there we are far better off without it than we should be without what it bought for you—your health and books.
>
> This evening there was a beautiful autumn sunset. I sat a long time on the fence of Smith's field watching it and wishing for you. I am trying to make Alice more of a companion. I am afraid I do not do rightly in not adapting myself more to her . . .
>
> I wish I were gayer for the children's sake. Alice needs someone to laugh and romp with her instead of a sober and staid person like me.
>
> My darling you are all the world to me. I am not myself when you are away. Do not forget me or love me less.
>
> EDITH

She wrote again on August 31, even more despairingly: "It is four weeks tomorrow evening since you left, so more than half the weary time has gone . . . I miss you every minute, awake or asleep, and long for you beyond all expression. After this we will be together if all goes well. I am looking forward so much to the time when the baby comes and you are with me."[5]

Theodore replied cheerfully. He was, as she predicted, enjoying himself ("I never was in more superb health and condition"), although he was at pains to emphasize the unpleasant aspects of life in the wild.

> The last week I went off with pack ponies . . . made a great bag, of two moose, a mountain bison, two bear and a cougar. One of the bears charged me in the most determined way. At the end of the trip the hunter got very drunk on my whiskey, which he succeeded in ferreting out, and we had very nearly a stand-up fight; and I came in alone, with my pack pony after two or three days travel.
>
> . . . I thus got my game much earlier than I expected; my proposed expedition with the wolf hounds has fallen through . . . and I cannot say I am sorry, *for I am dreadfully homesick without my darling*, and now I hope to be home even before the 20th . . .

In guilty acknowledgment of the reproof implicit in her own letter, he made a compensatory promise: "Next year there will be [no pregnancy] and you must come to the Yellowstone with me; then I can start you home, and take a little hunt after you have gone, and so not be away from you so long."[6]

Theodore was back in Washington on October 10 when a telegram arrived from Sagamore Hill. Edith had given birth, prematurely, to a boy. Arriving in Long Island City too late for the last train to Oyster Bay, the anxious father chartered a special locomotive, reaching home about four o'clock in the morning. Bamie (who, having been trained to keep her distance, now apparently rated as an acceptable guest) was there already, and stayed on for a few days to send off birth announcements. "Edith can't say enough of what a comfort you were to her," Theodore wrote later. "Again and again she says, 'Oh that *dear* Bysie.'"[7]

"Baby bruvver Kermit miaows," Ted observed at the christening of the fair-haired squalling newcomer in Edith's parlor on Sunday, November 3, 1889. "Man in Nana's clothes," he went on loudly, staring at the priest's voluminous surplice.[8] He was quickly shuttled across the hall to the library, and out of earshot.

In late December, Edith left her children with Bamie and joined Theodore in Washington to set up house. He had rented a small establishment at 1820 Jefferson Place, N.W. In contrast to Sagamore Hill the house was laughably tiny: a dressing room would have to do double duty as a guest room if ever people came to stay. With so little space to fill, and several pieces of her old furniture from East Thirty-sixth Street available for distribution through the rooms, Edith soon had everything "homelike and comfortable."[9]

With the house arranged, and the children not due until after Christmas, Edith had time to explore Washington. She discovered that the capital was in effect two very different places: the elegant city of L'Enfant, whose diagonal tree-shaded avenues intersected streets to form circles and squares graced with bronze and marble statues, and the shabbier city of vacant lots, slum tenements and Negro shanties which lay behind and in between the five-story mansions of the wealthy.

With a population of only 200,000, Washington gave an impression of spaciousness and leisure. Edith, who had always disliked the dirt and bustle of New York City, appreciated the quiet cleanliness of Washington's streets. She gazed with interest at the horse-drawn machines whose rotating spirals of twigs swept debris to the roadside to be gathered up and carted away. With streetcars humming along on smooth rails, noise was minimal, and the peaceful thoroughfares were disturbed only by the occasional clatter of a hansom or the rumble of a "herdic." The latter was a glassed-in omnibus which she could hail at will. She entered at the back, dropped a nickel into a slot at the front and then settled into a cushioned seat in the olive-green compartment, keeping an eye out for drops of oil from the swinging paraffin lamps.

Center Market, where she soon became a regular customer, was a venue for all kinds of people. Upper-class matrons, with basket-carrying servants in tow, selected terrapins for soup, eggs for soufflés, chickens for aspic, and fruit for sherbet. Side by side with them shopped hoteliers, boarding-house keepers, private chefs, and black housewives.

Elsewhere she noticed that classes and races separated sharply. None of the city's sixty thousand blacks, no matter how high their rank, profession, or political standing, fraternized socially with whites. And few of Washington's transitory residents, including Cabinet officers, Senators, and soldiers, were invited to the homes of socially established Washingtonians like the Leiters, the McLeans, the John Hays, and Henry Adams.

Culturally, Washington was still a backwater, compared to European capitals. The National Theater, and a few vaudeville and burlesque houses, provided little in the way of good drama. Musical offerings were confined to Sousa's Marine Band, scattered German lieder groups, and Negro church choirs. "Washingtonians," said one social observer, "care less about symphonies than about tea."[10]

No national art gallery yet existed, but Edith was pleased to discover that the Smithsonian Institution was assembling a nucleus of paintings. She spent many hours at the Institution, and would return there many times with her children during the seventeen years she was to live in Washington.

Another establishment that lured her was Fischer's, an antique store that equaled the best in Europe, full of furniture, silver, etchings, autograph letters, and rare books. Edith loved to burrow or, as she phrased it, "snoop" in stores of this kind. She had an infallible nose for a bargain, and spent many happy hours combing through Fischer's ever-changing stock, looking for treasures to install in her new house.

Washington's social season began officially with the White House New Year's Day Reception on January 1, 1890. At about 10:30 A.M., Edith and Theodore set off to pay their respects to Benjamin Harrison. Rain drizzled down as they drove past long lines of common citizens in Pennsylvania Avenue waiting to shake the Chief Executive's hand. Snatches of martial music wafted out on the cold air as the Roosevelts' carriage drew up at the North Portico of No. 1600. The door opened to admit them to the crowded vestibule, bright with gaslight, and decorated with tropical plants. A servant took Edith's wrap, and she was rather shocked to see it rolled up tightly and stuffed into a ticketed pigeonhole. Space, clearly, was at a premium in the first house of the nation. Edith and Theodore joined the press of dignitaries crowding the Main Corridor en route to the President's parlors.

At eleven o'clock, "Hail to the Chief" signaled that Harrison and his party were descending to the Blue Room to begin three hours of ritual handshaking. First to be received were his Cabinet officers and scores of brilliantly uniformed and bemedaled diplomats. Next came Supreme Court Justices, and Congressmen led by Theodore's especial friend, the enormously tall and triple-chinned Speaker, Thomas B. Reed. Gold-draped Army and Navy officers followed, and finally, at about noon, members of the departmental branch of the Government, including the Civil Service Commissioners and their wives. The Roosevelts had difficulty reaching the Blue Room because Theodore's friends, whose numbers seemed to be legion, kept coming up to pump his hand.[11]

The music became appropriately solemn as Edith and Theodore entered the elliptical Blue Room. Thirteen years had passed since Edith first entered the White House as a teenage sightseer, but this parlor, she noticed, had changed hardly at all. There were the same blue cut-velvet circular sofa in the center, the same rococo chairs against the walls, and the same large mirror and pier table. Shaded chandeliers and sidelights brought out the blueness of the décor. Massed in the three tall windows were palms, rubber trees, red poinsettia, pink azaleas and ferns, almost blocking out the view of President's Park and the Potomac River.

The President seemed pleased to see Theodore and his colleagues. "Nobody got a heartier reception than the three Commissioners," wrote the Washington *Post* reporter, "Mr. Roosevelt being very demonstrative in his protestations of good wishes to the President for the coming year." But Edith knew that privately Theodore thought Benjamin Harrison lacked backbone, and that the Senators had "flannel legs."[12]

Standing before the President with a less jaundiced eye, she saw a short, stout, square-faced man with a full sandy beard. His blue eyes were genial, but behind them she sensed an immense reserve that matched her own. It was something of a disappointment not to meet

the First Lady, who was in mourning for a relative. Carolina Lavinia
Scott Harrison was considered the best housekeeper the White House
had so far seen, and Edith knew of her plans to enlarge the Mansion,
preserve its historic furniture, and establish a presidential china
collection. As the wife of a lowly government appointee, she herself
could hardly have foreseen that she would one day execute and
improve on the plans that "Carrie" Harrison did not live to
complete.

Brilliant social occasions followed fast on one another for Edith and
Theodore that first January in Washington: White House receptions
for the Diplomatic Corps, officers of the Army and Navy, and
Supreme Court Justices; balls, theater parties, and champagne
suppers. It was a revelation to Theodore to see how his "pretty" wife
blossomed in this sophisticated environment. "I have not seen Edith
since her marriage enjoy going out as much as she has enjoyed the
dinners here," he wrote Bamie.[13]

The month was climaxed by a banquet for twenty-eight at the
Vice-President's mansion on Rhode Island Avenue. Levi P. Morton
had the grandest house in town. It was once owned by Alexander
Graham Bell, and had been extravagantly remodeled with a white
and gold entrance hall, a magnificent carved staircase, and a grand
salon hung with pale blue damask and gilt French mirrors. James
McMillan, one of the Republican Party's most powerful Senators,
escorted Edith in to dine at an "extremely handsome" table. The
conversation sparkled, and she relished the sensation of rubbing her
mind against first-class intellects. Though Theodore might have to
work with and for ordinary people, "for pleasure and instruction"
both he and she preferred to relax in an environment such as this.[14]

The Roosevelts' own entertaining was on a necessarily smaller
scale, and consisted mostly of tea parties and Sunday-evening
suppers where "the food was of the plainest and the company of the
best." At these gatherings—usually for no more than eight—
Theodore held everyone enthralled with tales of cowboy fights,
grizzly bear hunts, and other adventures in the Bad Lands. "There
was a vital radiance about the man," wrote Margaret Chanler, his
frequent guest, "a glowing unfeigned cordiality towards those he
liked that was irresistible." As for the hostess, she was "more difficult
of access," and praise "could not reach or define her. Just as the

camera is focussed she steps aside to avoid the click of the shutter." To this astute observer, Edith seemed "deeply detached from the external accidents of life . . . her family was the all-important continuum."[15]

Important as her husband and children were to Edith, she nevertheless enjoyed the society of an imposing roster of people during her first season in Washington. Most eminent among them was Henry Brooks Adams, the short, crusty historian and philosopher. Adams liked well-bred women, and found the new young Commissioner's wife especially "sympathetic."[16]

Since the death of his own wife from a dose of chloride in December 1885, the fifty-two-year-old Adams had lived a semi-reclusive life on Lafayette Square. His elegant town house, designed

"A stable companion to statesmen."
Henry Brooks Adams, drawn by J. B. Potter.

in the New England Romanesque style by Henry Hope Richardson, complemented that of his friend and neighbor John Hay, who had employed the same architect. As a descendant of two Presidents Adams was fascinated by politics and power. But no President had ever seen fit to call on his prodigious talents, and he himself had never sought elective office. "He wanted it handed to him on a silver plate," said Oliver Wendell Holmes. Adams felt a failure because, in consequence, he had little direct influence on government. He consoled himself by saying that "as far as he had a function in life, it was as a stable companion to statesmen, whether they liked it or not." [17]

His house, full of rare books, Japanese art, Chinese bronzes, English watercolors, Italian drawings and Mexican marble, was a unique aesthetic experience for Edith. Intellectually, too, it was a challenge. She would find sitting in the low-slung "nursery altitude" maroon leather chairs such luminaries as the great sculptor Augustus St. Gaudens, the artist John La Farge, the poet and biographer John Hay, and the geologist Clarence King. [18]

Edith knew that Henry Adams had accepted her as one of his inner circle (recognized as the most exclusive in Washington) when after nine months' acquaintance he sent her a gift copy of the first volume of his *History of the United States from 1801–1871*. This work was printed mainly for friends, and to receive one was a sign of high favor. [19]

"Only women are worth cultivating," Adams once wrote his good friend Henry James. The historian was amused to note how effectively Mrs. Roosevelt, in her quiet way, controlled Theodore. "He stands in such abject terror of Edith . . . What is man that he should have tusks and grin!" [20]

Anna Cabot Lodge, known to her friends as "Nannie," was perhaps the most admired woman in Adams's circle. Her beauty was striking: she had dark violet eyes, set in a pale chiseled, patrician face. Her looks were enhanced by the unusual elegance of her gowns, made from the finest materials, and by the velvet or pearl band which she always wore high at the neck. Adams considered her one of "the chief dispensers of sunshine" in the capital. "Where Mrs. Lodge summoned," he wrote years later, "one followed with gratitude." Spring-Rice (another member of the Adams circle) adored Nannie, as did Winthrop Chanler: "She is as sympathetic, as witty, as understanding, companionable, lovable, as no other woman . . . I have never known her equal and would do violence to any catiff hound who does not agree with me."[21]

Women also fell under her spell. "She was the most charming woman I have ever known," said Margaret Chanler, "an exquisite presence in the workaday world. She had great wit; it was the only weapon she ever used in self-defence, and Cabot was a little afraid of its winged shafts."[22]

Edith became close friends with Nannie, and also with Elizabeth Cameron, who was if anything even more exquisite. At thirty-two, Mrs. Cameron was almost a quarter-century younger than her husband, the senior Senator from Pennsylvania. Petite, vital and Titian-haired, she was considered to be the most beautiful woman in Washington, as well as a brilliant talker and a gracious hostess at her mansion on the east side of Lafayette Square. Adams was deeply, secretly, in love with her, admiring her to the point of idolatry.

At the end of the season Edith "lapsed into a quiet vegetative life" through summer, most of which she and the children spent at Sagamore Hill.[23] Theodore remained in the capital, desperately trying to finish a history of New York City in between bouts of work at the Civil Service Commission. He had not forgotten his promise to take Edith to Yellowstone, and came home at the end of August to escort her West.

At 4:30 A.M. on September 2, 1890, they arrived in Medora, their first stopping place en route. Theodore wanted to show Edith his Elkhorn Ranch before proceeding. With him he had also brought Bamie, Corinne, Douglas Robinson, Bob Ferguson, and Henry Cabot Lodge's sixteen-year-old son "Bay." Rain fell in torrents as the party left the train, and Edith's skirt was caked with "glutinous slime" by the time she reached the depot. Here they were met by Sylvane Ferris and Bill Merrifield, who took them to Joe Ferris's store across the street. Edith at last had the opportunity to scrutinize Theodore's closest Western friends. Sylvane was a sunburned, broad-browed man with clear blue eyes and a red neckerchief. His brother Joe was short and stocky, with a drooping mustache and a gaze that Edith felt she could trust. She could not say the same for Merrifield. Despite Theodore's protestations that Bill was basically all right, Edith believed that he was "on the make," an opinion shared by the citizens of Medora, who also found him "big-headed."[24]

Leaning against the store counter, as Mrs. Joe Ferris cooked breakfast, was another cowboy, straight out of a Remington painting. Lanky and wild-looking, he spat with unerring aim, and carried a brace of pistols with the air of one who knew how to use them. This was the famous local sheriff, Hell-Roarin' Bill Jones, "a thoroughly good citizen when sober," Theodore said, "but . . . a little wild when drunk."[25]

At dawn, in the damp and misty air, the men mounted horses, and Edith, Bamie and Corinne climbed into an unsprung wagon to begin the thirty-three-mile journey north to Elkhorn. Edith's first impression of the Bad Lands under the gray morning light was that it was the most desolate, depressing countryside she had ever seen. Ugly bare hills, split by shadowy canyons and sodden clay valleys, rose on every side. There was no road whatsoever; twenty-three times that morning they had to cross and recross the winding Little Missouri River. Its banks were so steep that they needed to hurtle down one side at breakneck speed in order to have enough impetus to splash through the water and up the other side.[26]

The river widened as they neared the ranch, and the landscape changed dramatically. Sandstone buttes streaked with scoria thrust tall and taller and glowed red in the climbing sun; grasses waved on the plateaus; cottonwoods shimmered along the bottoms. The air cleared, and Edith, her mood improved, began to feel invigorated. Finally, at noon, they reached the last ford, and she glimpsed the Elkhorn compound, nestling under a clump of trees across the river.

The two-storied slope-roofed ranch house was little more than a cabin built out of great logs caulked with oakum. It measured sixty feet long and thirty feet wide. There were eight rooms with fireplaces, and a porch facing the Little Missouri, where Theodore as a widower had spent many hours reading in a rocking chair. Guns, antlers and bear rugs formed the chief décor. The master bedroom, complete with rubber bathtub and books, awaited Edith's occupancy for the first and only time.

Mrs. Merrifield, "a most refined little woman from Ottawa," entertained the visitors with a copious lunch. Afterward Theodore gave them a tour of his property. They climbed a butte, picked their way gingerly through fields infested with rattlesnakes, and crept up on a prairie-dog town. But as soon as they drew close the fat little rodents sunbathing beside their holes dived out of sight.

"The master bedroom awaited Edith's occupancy
for the first and only time."
The Elkhorn Ranch

Edith, despite her genteel upbringing, had a lusty taste for life in the rough, and thoroughly enjoyed her stay at the ranch. Riding a brisk little horse called Wire Fence, she laughed at Corinne trying to "wrastle" a calf, watched punchers lasso heifers for branding, tracked deer through the cottonwoods, ate a cowboy's lunch of beef, potatoes, hominy biscuits and stewed apricots served from a roundup wagon on the plains, and galloped home in the glowing evening light across grassy meadows. Like Theodore before her, she came to love the strange, wild scenery of the Bad Lands, the remoteness and freedom of life on the range. She felt healthy and alarmingly sturdy (her weight had increased to 131 pounds, six more than usual), and was sorry when it was time to leave.[27]

From Medora, on September 9, the group continued west by train to Livingston to begin their expedition through Yellowstone Park. Theodore's guide provided a string of horses, which Bamie suspected (and Edith soon found out) had never been ridden sidesaddle before. Her first mount, indeed, bucked so frighteningly that the boy who replaced her on it fainted from the exertion of trying to stay on.

The first night out was icy cold, and after a perfunctory splash in a brook the campers snuggled under blankets and tried to keep warm. Theodore, ever the practical joker, crept over to Corinne's tent, pretended to be a bear, and scared her half to death. Next morning everyone ate a hearty breakfast of ham, tomatoes, "greasy cakes" and coffee, followed, after a few hours on the trail, by a lunch of bread and cheese. This daily diet, unaccountably furnished by a fiery-tempered Chinese cook, was monotonous, but nobody dared to complain.

On the second day they followed Gardiner River to a series of terraces formed by sulphurous and alkali pools, which reminded Edith of highly colored coral beds. On the third, they climbed up Golden Gate Canyon, and on the plateau beyond discovered boiling pools, extinct craters, and strangely tinted formations. The weather—cloud-free days and crisp starry nights—was perfect, and the flora and fauna astonishingly varied. Edith identified gentians, hare bells, lupins, goldenrods and asters, while Theodore pointed out black bears, elk, peregrine falcons, golden eagles, Canada geese, bitterns, chickadees, water ousel, sun birds, grass finches, and yellow-crowned warblers.

One night, 7,500 feet up among the pine trees, the men made fires of tree trunks and the women added layers of extra clothing—thick under-flannels, woolen petticoats, Shetland jackets, wrappers, shawls, and fur cloaks. Even then Edith needed six blankets before going to sleep. By morning, the camp's pail of water had frozen solid, and she felt so numb it was painful to dress.

Pressing on toward Gibbon Falls, they passed mud cauldrons the consistency of thick paint, and after a long agonizing ride descended through tortuous ravines to Fountain Geyser. As the cook prepared ham and potatoes for dinner that night, he complained in lugubrious Oriental tones of being "heap sore."[28] The following morning the geyser erupted in a roaring tunnel of steam for an entire hour before subsiding to its former placid green mirrorlike surface.

The campers rested at Yellowstone Lake, where Edith marveled at the prismatic color changes of reflected rose and amethyst peaks. From here she followed Theodore along a peninsula of eagle-nesting rocks to see the miraculous view from Inspiration Point. To their right brilliant canyon formations stretched away to Yellowstone Falls, and to their left lay a deep gorge of rocks and pines, with the river running like a green thread through it.

On the return journey Edith's horse reared suddenly at the sound of blasting, and threw her to the ground. She escaped with a bruised leg and a few abrasions, but was so shaken she could not climb the ten-thousand-foot Mount Washburn, as she had hoped.

Afterward Theodore wrote Mrs. Carow:

> I have rarely seen Edith enjoy anything more than she did the six days at my ranch, and the trip through Yellowstone Park; and she looks just as well and young and pretty and happy as she did four years ago when I married her—indeed I sometimes almost think she looks if possible even sweeter and prettier, and she is as healthy as possible, and so young looking and slender to be the mother of those two sturdy little scamps Ted and Kermit.[29]

Eleven

I live in constant dread of some scandal of his attaching itself to Theodore.

—Edith Kermit Roosevelt[1]

The Roosevelts celebrated Christmas 1890 at Jefferson Place. Notwithstanding their modest income, they spent lavishly on gifts for the children. Alice at six and Ted at three were of an age to appreciate such generosity. Even little fourteen-month-old Kermit, wrote Theodore, "really liked his stocking and toys, though in abject terror of the menagerie of squeaking woolly animals which covered his table. Soon after seven Alice and Ted fairly galloped into our room to look for their stockings . . . Such nice stockings, with such an entrancing way of revealing in their bulging outlines the promise of what was inside . . . " After breakfast the family moved into the library where the larger presents were laid out: trains, Noah's Ark complete with animals, Buffalo Bill, Indians, soldiers, horses and dolls. "I suppose Alice and Ted came as near to realizing the feelings of those who enter Paradise as they ever will on this earth," their father concluded.[2]

It was a particularly joyful Christmas for Edith, for she found herself again pregnant. Motherhood agreed with her, to the bewilderment of some of her fashionable friends. She seemed "disgustingly pleased," a disapproving Elizabeth Cameron wrote Henry Adams in Samoa. "When I think of their very moderate income, and the recklessness with which she brings children into the world without the means either to educate them or provide for them I am quite worked up . . . she will have a round dozen I am sure . . . It is a shame."[3]

Fortunately fatherhood also agreed with Theodore. He believed that the upper classes should produce very large families, in order to compensate for the fecundity of the lower. Himself a boy at heart, he loved to read adventure stories to the children, and recite his favorite nursery song, handed down by his Dutch ancestors:

> *Trippel, trippel toontjes,*
> *Kippen in de boontjes,*
> *Koetjes in de klaver,*
> *Paardjes in de haver,*
> *Eendjes in de water plas,*
> *'K wow dat kindje grooter was.*[4]

Every evening, before the boys went to bed, he played bear to their baby raccoon or badger, exciting and terrifying them at the same time. Edith, meanwhile, concentrated on the more advanced taste of their sister, reading her *Grimm's Fairy Tales* and stories from *The Arabian Nights*, just as Charles Carow had done to his daughter a quarter of a century before. Alice was also required to take Bible lessons, and to pray for "my mother who is in heaven." This led to some understandable confusion about Edith's own identity. "Alice was much surprised to learn that I was not Papa's sister," she wrote in her "Baby's Journal." Compounding the confusion was Theodore's refusal to mention the dead parent at all. Alice's annual visits to her Lee grandparents, and the occasional appearance of Grandmother Carow added to the puzzle. Only "Auntie Bye" (Bamie) ever talked to the child about Alice Lee, saying how pretty and warm a person she had been, and how much they had all loved her.

Edith's personal view was more caustic. If Alice had lived, she contended, she would have bored Theodore to death.

Early in 1890 Elliott Roosevelt's drinking began to threaten the good name of the Roosevelts. Bamie and Corinne, though sympathetic, dreaded having him to dinner, while Theodore saw as little of

"He loved the fast Long Island hunting set."
Elliott Roosevelt in his mid-thirties.

him as possible. There was no hope that Elliott's society-loving wife
would ever act as a stabilizing influence. Her "utterly frivolous life,"
Theodore said, had "eaten into her character like an acid."[5] In his
opinion, Elliott should take a drastic cure under the supervision of an
authoritative doctor. "Half measures," he wrote Bamie, "simply put
off the day, make the case more hopeless, and render the chance of a
public scandal greater."[6]

Deaf to this advice, Elliott had decided simply to lease his town
and country houses, forsake the fleshpots of New York and the fast

Long Island hunting set, and take his family to Europe. But by the fall of 1890 it was clear that the sojourn abroad was a disaster. Anna, burdened with two children, was unable to control her husband's drinking and extravagance. Moving from country to country and spa to spa cost them $1,500 a month; spread over a year, this rate of spending would exceed Elliott's investment income.

Then, shortly before Christmas, Anna had written to say that she was pregnant again, and afraid of her husband's drunken rages. She begged Bamie to cross the Atlantic and keep her company.

"Elliott seems to be quite out of his head," Elizabeth Cameron wrote Adams early in 1891, "so Bamie sails next week to take care of her [Anna] before returning to do as much for Mrs. Theodore." Bamie left at the beginning of February. "Edith and I . . . wish we could be with you," Theodore wrote insincerely, "for we know what a terrible trial you have to go through."[7] But Bamie, as usual, was perfectly capable of looking after herself, not to mention Elliott and Anna. Things began to happen as soon as she met up with them in Vienna. She had "a thorough consultation" with a local specialist about her brother, then escorted Elliott to a sanitarium in Graz for treatment. Not trusting him out of her sight, she persuaded the authorities to give her a room there "although it was against the rules."[8] By April Elliott appeared sufficiently improved to remove to Paris, where the party rented a house in Neuilly. A noted doctor was engaged to take care of Anna, and on June 2, 1891, a boy, Hall, was safely born.

Meanwhile, in New York, fresh problems were developing for Elliott. One of his former maidservants, Katy Mann, announced that he was the father of her recently born baby, and began legal action to obtain financial aid. The figure she had in mind was enormous by nineteenth-century standards: ten thousand dollars. Theodore and Edith were disinclined to believe the woman's claim until a professional investigator, suspecting mere blackmail, went to see the baby. "He came back," Theodore reported to Bamie, "convinced from the likeness that Katy Mann's story was true. It is his business to be an expert in likenesses."[9]

The news could not be kept from Elliott, who had begun to drink heavily again after the birth of his legitimate child. He became so violent and suicidal that Bamie had no choice but to follow Theodore's advice to leave him in an asylum outside Paris for six months, and return to America with Anna and the children.[10] She arrived in early August, in good time, as Mrs. Cameron had predicted, for Edith's own confinement.

Edith had been at Sagamore Hill since late spring, while Theodore remained at Jefferson Place in Washington, keeping "bachelor's hall" with Cecil Spring-Rice. The Englishman found him a compatible, if eccentric, companion. "I have experienced a variety of curious habits of Teddy's . . . One is to walk up and down (with creaky boots) when he is thinking . . . another is to eat chicken like a wild animal. Otherwise I don't see anything in the way of his being perfect to live with; and he is one of the people who are absolutely dependable and sure."[11]

As the time for the birth of Edith's baby drew near, Spring-Rice joined Theodore at Sagamore Hill. He found Gertrude and Emily Carow in residence, and was far from impressed with the latter. "Miss Carow is really one of the most dismal people I ever met," he told Elizabeth Cameron, "for she talks obsessionally about her romantic conquests in Rome. I don't think I ever met such a bore."[12]

On August 13 Edith's contractions became severe, and West Roosevelt was summoned. She had a long and difficult labor, and he stood at the foot of the bed reminding her that she was "not responsible for an orphan asylum—only for one little baby."[13] She finally gave birth to a sturdy girl, Ethel. The baby reminded Theodore so much of his stocky Dutch ancestors that he called her "Elephant Johnny."

He left for a six-week hunting trip in September, and was back before the Carows sailed for Europe at the end of October. They had been at Sagamore Hill for nearly five months, and Edith for one was not sorry to see them go. She promised that when her investments improved she would cross the Atlantic and taste their hospitality. "I shall certainly pay you a visit," she wrote sweetly, "of a week or so."[14]

When Edith returned to Washington that winter, it was to a larger, more comfortable, but luckily no more expensive house at Jefferson Place and Nineteenth Street. The extra space was essential, not only because of the new baby, but because the other children were growing fast now. Alice was tall and pretty, with golden hair, a straight little nose, and white, even teeth. Because the wealthy Lees paid for her clothes, Edith could be extravagant on her behalf. "I got Alice a beautiful dress at Stern's," she wrote Emily, "dark large plaid with navy blue velour . . . Forty-two dollars, and her coat rough blue cloth lined throughout with plaid silk will be $45. Mrs. Lee wishes it, and I am glad as Alice is a child who needs good clothes, and would look quite as forlorn as Eleanor in makeshifts."[15]

This was an invidious comparison, as far as Alice was concerned, for, as Edith herself said, Elliott's daughter was "plain" and "her mouth and teeth seemed to have no future." Eleanor was eight months Alice's junior, but already stood taller and more gawky. Edith conceded in an afterthought that "the ugly duckling may turn out to be a swan." For some reason—probably Elliott's erratic behavior—Edith did not want the cousins to see much of each other.[16]

As for Ted, he was, in his father's fond opinion,

> the most loving, warm-hearted gallant little fellow who ever breathed . . . I often show him and Alice books; the great, illustrated Milton, the *Nibelungenlied,* or hunting books; and Ted knows any amount of poetry from Scott to Longfellow. I tell them how I hunted the game whose heads are on the wall; or of Washington crossing the Delaware, or of Lincoln or Farragut. We have most entrancing plays in the old barn, and climbing trees in the orchard, and go to Cooper's Bluff; Ted usually having to come back part of the way piggy-back. He wears big spectacles, which only make him look more like a Brownie than ever; and delights in carrying a tin sword, at present, even in his romps. It is an aweinspiring sight to see him, when Alice has made a nice nest in a corn-stack, take a reckless header in after her, with sword and spectacles, showing a fine disregard both of her life and his own.[17]

If Ted was a fireball of mental and physical energy, Kermit was the opposite. He was slight and ethereal in appearance, with hair the color and texture of spun gold. Introspective by nature, he preferred his own or his mother's company to anyone else's. While the others played noisy games, he liked to sit in the window and gaze at the moon. Though less active than his brother, Kermit was so limber that he could use his toes to scratch his nose, and frame his face by putting the soles of his feet on his cheeks.[18]

Ethel, who looked angelic with her plump, fair-skinned features, small eyes and button nose, was actually a "jolly, naughty, whacky baby." She liked to play with people rather than toys; a favorite occupation was to have her mother lie flat on the nursery floor while she pulled out her hairpins. Strong and vigorous, Elephant Johnny performed every action with a jump, so that Edith could barely control her. Whatever displeased her she dropped on the floor, and she would grapple fiercely with Mame or her mother in order to have her own way. There were times when Edith feared that, given the strength, "she would kill us both."[19]

With two homes to run, twice-yearly migrations to and from Washington to finance, and four children to feed and clothe, the Roosevelts found that their family budget, always precariously balanced, was by now seriously strained. When Theodore accepted the Civil Service post he had been forced to curtail his literary output, with the result that his income dropped by nearly $1,000 to $7,500 a year. Washington's cost of living was proportionately higher in the late nineteenth century than the late twentieth. A moderate-sized house rented at $2,500 a year; fuel cost $300; milk $420; and the children's doctors' bills amounted to $556 in 1891 alone. Edith found it increasingly difficult to make ends meet. In one desperate month she managed to reduce her butcher's bill from $165 to $110, and the grocer's from $95 to $75, but several other "dreadful" bills remained unpaid. "The repairs of the carriages . . . hangs over me like a nightmare." Their deficit one year was $1,155.79. "How many bills do you think you can pay?" she asked Theodore. "I enclose the Harvard Club bill . . . Are your dues ten or twenty dollars? Could you resign?"[20]

She had a better business sense and more patience for detail than her hasty, profligate husband, and gradually took over all the family finances. She kept meticulous accounts of expenditures, paid out on the first of the month promptly, though it made her "quite limp," and meted out a daily allowance to Theodore. A friend who met the latter in a bookstore watched as he fumbled in his pocket for cash to make a purchase. Finding only twenty-five cents, Theodore laughed:

"Every morning Edie puts twenty dollars in my pocket, and to save my life I never can tell her afterward what I did with it!"[21]

In April 1892 there was a break in the clouds. John Carow, an uncle who had died childless in Liverpool, England, left Edith and Emily approximately $35,000 each. But Edith, whose business instinct told her to discount great expectations until they materialized in cash, received the news cautiously. "I try not to think too much about it for it may all come to nothing." Gertrude Carow was more optimistic: "I am so very thankful that Emily and you have inherited so handsomely . . . God has surely been good to me in my old age."[22] Because John Carow owned property in both England and America, settlement of his estate was delayed, and the two nieces did not receive their inheritance—$1,200 each annually—for almost two years. Emily, who already had visions of a childless death herself, willed her share to Ted, with the proviso that he take care of Gertrude should his grandmother survive her. Edith, in turn, found John Carow's investments so "wonderfully good" that she put her previously inherited Elevated-Railroad stock into an education fund for the boys.[23]

Although on paper the Roosevelts' financial prospects seemed to be brightening, 1893 was a panic year for the country as a whole. The U.S. Treasury's gold reserve, depleted by excessive imports, fell to less than $1 billion. Between May and July alone three hundred banks failed, prices and wages dropped, markets for goods vanished overnight, unemployment and strikes multiplied. There were bread lines in major cities. Theodore became morbid about his investments, hinting that he might have to give up Sagamore Hill, or alternatively close his Washington house, send the family to Oyster Bay, and rent a simple room for himself in the capital. Edith was strongly against the latter option. She saw little enough of Theodore as it was in summer: to be separated in winter as well was unthinkable. Unappealing as the prospect of renting out Sagamore Hill was, she preferred "that dire resort."[24]

To make matters worse, Theodore's accountants miscalculated his 1893 income and expenditures, and he found himself nearly $2,500 short in December. "Theodore feels the poorhouse is impending," Edith wrote Bamie, but she knew no more than he what to do. Privately, she was glad that her own affairs (and those of her Carow relatives) were handled by the reliable firm of Cruikshank and Sons, even though Mr. Cruikshank grumbled that Gertrude, who had converted to Catholicism, gave too much money "to that damned Pope."[25]

A year of even greater austerity was called for. "If we again run behind," said Theodore, "I see nothing to do save leave Sagamore." In early 1894 he made a last-ditch effort to retrench, and sold a field behind the Sagamore Hill barn to James A. Roosevelt. He also discussed economizing on cultivation of the farm. Edith was embarrassed and skeptical. "I fear no particular result can come of it," she confided to Bamie, "but my way of managing has been an evident failure. I shall be only too glad to try his."[26] As if in penance, she began to make her own tooth powder from ground-up cuttlefish bones, dragon's blood, burnt alum, arris root, and aromatic ingredients.[27]

In March the first payment from John Carow's estate arrived, and made a welcome dent in their indebtedness. But the country's financial situation did not improve. Mills and mines closed down by the hundreds, and paper money was so scarce that Edith had to pay the servants in gold. "I am more thankful than I can say that Theodore is not in business," she wrote Gertrude. "I believe that he would go mad with anxiety."[28]

As it was, Theodore was extremely depressed about his future. He felt that his career had been a useful and honorable one for a man with extensive private means, but not for a man without. The children would have reason to reproach him, he said, for not having chosen a money-making profession. Mrs. Carow fondly hoped he might improve matters by running for Congress. Edith concurred, but feared "that is a dream never to be realized."[29]

The Roosevelts' financial problems through 1891, 1892, and 1893 were compounded by worries about Elliott's continuing alcoholic and moral decline. After Bamie and Anna returned to the United States in August 1891 they had joined Theodore in a petition to have Elliott declared legally insane, and his fortune of some $175,000 placed in trust for his family. The news had made front-page headlines in all major newspapers, but Theodore, to whom the welfare of Anna and her children was paramount, insisted that "the only thing to do is go resolutely forward."[30]

Elliott, incarcerated in Château Suresnes, his asylum outside Paris, had replied with a formal denial of insanity, published in both the

European and the American editions of the New York *Herald*. During the months that followed, he also wrote his brother many "terribly harrowing" letters, which Theodore, bewildered, described as "so sane, yet so absolutely lacking in moral sense."[31]

In December 1891 a commission was appointed to pass judgment on the case. Theodore decided this was a propitious moment to cross the Atlantic, explain the situation to Elliott, and persuade him to sign away his property voluntarily. On the ninth day of the new year he set sail, and Edith and Bamie waited anxiously for news from Paris. Word came within the month that Elliott, "utterly broken, submissive and repentant," had agreed to deed two thirds of his property to Anna, take a further cure in the United States and live apart from his wife and children until he had proved his worthiness of them.[32]

In February Elliott returned to America and submitted to "Dr. Keely's Bi-Chloride of Gold Cure" in Dwight, Illinois, for five weeks. Corinne and Aunt Annie thought Theodore unduly harsh in insisting on Elliott's long probation and separation from his wife. Theodore was adamant. If Elliott reneged on the agreement, Anna could and would "get a divorce."[33]

No sooner had Elliott completed his "cure" than he begged to be readmitted to the family hearth. But Anna stood firm, and insisted on at least one year's proof of sobriety. Douglas Robinson came to his aid and offered him a managerial post at the Robinson family holdings near Abingdon, Virginia, and Elliott gratefully accepted.

Throughout the summer of 1892 he kept informing his mother-in-law of his successful battle against alcohol. "Neither from heat or fatigue, thirst or weakness, from despondency, discouragement, hopelessness or any other cause have I experienced the slightest inclination to drink."[34]

In November, Anna, now twenty-nine, moved into a new town house on East Sixty-first Street in New York City, and began to reconstruct her life, perhaps in anticipation of her husband's eventual return. But during the same month she contracted diphtheria, and on December 7, after a brief struggle, died. She had refused to see Elliott during her illness, but he came north for the funeral. Anna was buried, as stylishly as she had lived, in an elegant pink silk wrapper fringed with white lace at the throat and wrists. Elliott seemed to be devastated, but by Christmas he was showing alarming signs of his former conviviality. His behavior at the house of Anna's sister earned Edith's stern disapproval. ". . . Though his wife was but a fortnight in her grave," she reported to Emily, "he was as gay as a butterfly and singing all the comic songs." Theodore was so "worn" by all this that his wife forced him to see more people. "When he dines out and *must* exert himself he forgets . . ."[35]

Elliott returned to Virginia, and in February rumors of fresh dissipation reached the Roosevelts. "Elliott has been giving the Abingdon people a taste of his mettle," Theodore told Bamie. "Recently, while sitting 'reading' stark naked, he upset a lamp and burnt himself badly." The Commissioner was asked to go south to "influence" his brother, but he declined. "I explained to them it was absolutely useless."[36]

Two more deaths in 1893 succeeded in further upsetting Elliott's delicate equilibrium. First in late May came that of his son Ellie, followed two weeks later by that of his aunt and long-time defender, Mrs. Gracie. "Poor Elliott is wandering about New York Heaven knows where," Edith told Emily soon afterward. "He rarely spends a night at his rooms and drinks a great deal . . . it wears on Theodore dreadfully and if he gets thinking of it he cannot sleep."[37]

Elliott now abandoned his position in West Virginia for good, and moved into an apartment on West 102nd Street, New York, with a Mrs. Evans. Under such circumstances it was unthinkable that he see any more of his children, who were now living with Anna's mother. Edith suggested that nine-year-old Eleanor be sent away to a good boarding school, otherwise "I do not feel she has much chance poor little soul."[38] The result was that Eleanor was sent in due course to Bamie's old school, Allenwood, in Wimbledon, England. Edith's advice proved to be perspicacious: under the tutelage of Allenwood's famous headmistrees, Mademoiselle Souvestre, the "ugly duckling" developed, if not into a swan, at least into a young woman capable of captivating a future President of the United States.

In late July 1894 Elliott was thrown out of his carriage and seriously hurt. "Much as I miss Mrs. Gracie," Edith wrote her mother, "I feel she was taken from evil to come. Elliott has sunk to the lowest depths. Consorts with the vilest woman, and Theodore, Bamie and Douglas receive horrid anonymous letters about his life. I live in constant dread of some scandal of his attaching itself to Theodore." The latter's comment was, "Poor fellow; if only he could have died instead of Anna."[39]

A little over two weeks later, on Tuesday, August 14, Elliott had an attack of delirium tremens and went berserk. He tried to jump from his apartment window, ran violently up and downstairs, stumbled, stiffened into a convulsive attack, and died. "He looked like our old Elliott," Corinne wrote Bamie, who was in London. "The terrible bloated swelled look was gone, and the sweet expression round the forehead made me weep bitter tears. . . . Theodore was more overcome than I have ever seen him—cried like a child for a long time." [40]

Theodore gave Bamie a graphic account of his brother's last hours and rites:

> . . . He would have been in a straight jacket had he lived forty-eight hours longer. It was his fall, aggravated by frightful drinking, that was the immediate cause; he had been drinking whole bottles of anisette and green mint, besides whole bottles of raw brandy and of champagne, sometimes half a dozen a morning. But when dead the poor fellow looked very peaceful, and so like his old, generous, gallant self of fifteen years ago. The horror, and the terrible mixture of sadness and grotesque, grim evil continued to the very end; and the dreadful flashes of his old sweetness, which made it even more hopeless. I suppose he has *[sic]* been doomed from the beginning; the absolute contradiction of all his actions, and of all his moral even more than his mental qualities, is utterly impossible to explain. For the last few days he had dumbly felt the awful night closing on him; he would not let us come to his house, nor part with the woman, nor cease drinking for a moment, but he wandered ceaselessly everywhere, never still, and he wrote again and again to us all, sending me two telegrams and three notes. He was like some stricken, hunted creature; and indeed he was hunted by the most terrible demons that ever entered into man's body and soul.
>
> His house was so neat and well-kept, with his bible and religious books, and Anna's pictures everywhere, even in the room of himself and his mistress. Poor woman, she had taken the utmost care of him, and was broken down at his death. Her relations with him had

been just as strange as everything else. Very foolishly, it had been arranged that he should be taken to be buried beside Anna, but I promptly vetoed this hideous plan . . . and he was buried in Greenwood beside those who are associated with only his sweet innocent youth, when no more loyal, generous, brave, disinterested fellow lived.

All his old friends came to the funeral; the church was filled. It was very, very sad; and behind it followed the usual touch of the grotesque and terrible, for in one of the four carriages that followed to the grave, went the woman, Mrs. Evans, and two of her and his friends, the host and hostess of the Woodbine Inn. They behaved perfectly well, and their grief seemed entirely sincere. . . .

Katy Mann came in to Douglas' office with the child which she swears was his; I have no idea whether it was or not; she was a bad woman, but her story *may* have been partly true. But we cannot know. Well, it is over now; it is fortunate it is over; and we need only think of his bright youth . . . Poor Anna, and poor Elliott![41]

Edith's grief over Elliott's death was largely on behalf of Corinne, who had struggled harder than anyone else to rescue the tortured man. "I have been thinking of you and longing to be with you," she wrote after the funeral. "These last years of sorrow and shame seem blotted out and I can only remember what happened long ago, how Elliott would take us sailing and how everyone loved and admired him . . . But each year he lived would have done its part toward killing that very memory. Thank God that blow fell while you can still mourn, and while little Eleanor can have loving and tender last words from her father to treasure."[42]

Twelve

Better get the moon, Father.

—Kermit Roosevelt[1]

The peace and security of Edith's household, disturbed by the turmoil of her brother-in-law's last two years, was also disturbed by a change of administration in Washington. In November 1892, Benjamin Harrison lost the election to his Democratic predecessor, Grover Cleveland. There followed six months of uncertainty while Theodore waited for the new President to establish himself. Then, in late April, the Civil Service Commissioner handed in his resignation. Cleveland declined it, asking him to stay on for at least one or two years more. Theodore was delighted, since Henry Cabot Lodge had just been elected Senator from Massachusetts. Edith too was pleased, and told Emily she would hate to give up "this pleasant life."[2]

She was now an established member of the Henry Adams circle, enjoying the great man's affection and esteem, as well as that of his scintillating friends. Of these, the sculptor Augustus St. Gaudens radiated an especial glow in the spring of 1893, for he had been appointed sculptor-in-chief at the Chicago World's Fair. On his account alone, Edith and Theodore would have been happy to go to the exhibition, which celebrated the four hundredth anniversary of

Columbus's discovery of America. The additional appointment of Bamie Roosevelt as a Lady Manager of the event made an extended visit all the more desirable.

They joined Bamie in Chicago on May 11, for an eleven-day stay, and were just as astonished as twenty-four million other visitors that year at the wonders their countrymen had wrought. Six hundred acres of sandy, swampy wasteland of the Windy City had been transformed into landscaped islands with dazzling vistas of Greek- and Renaissance-style buildings, all apparently solid. They were actually moulded from "staff," a plaster-like substance that could be carved into the most delicate classical motifs. Illuminated by searchlights at night, the façades shone like white marble, while occasional bursts of fireworks bathed them in myriad colors. Edith, floating past them for hours in a hired gondola, listening to the strains of open-air orchestras, felt herself "in fairyland."[3] She lamented that the palaces were not permanent. There was also a wealth of statuary. Theodore, ever the archpatriot, admired those of Presidents of the United States, while Edith, whose artistic horizons were wider, preferred St. Gaudens's figures of Columbus in the Grand Basin, and Diana atop the Hall of Agriculture.

Returning to the Fair by day, she endlessly explored Plaisance Mile, with its exotic Javanese Quarter, Egyptian Street, Turkish Music Hall, Japanese Temple, and Eskimo Village, where she picked up "a cunning doll for Kermit dressed in white fur."[4]

The summer of 1893 ensued, its lazy calm broken by Theodore's occasional, but always turbulent, appearances at Oyster Bay. He was still feeling pessimistic about his future, and feared that "only a very mild and moderate success" was in store for him.[5] Edith, accustomed to these attacks of self-doubt, realized they came, more often than not, when work was slack; if Theodore was not occupied every waking moment, he felt as guilty as a wanton shirker.

She found that the best way to dispel his gloom was to involve him with the children. This was not difficult to do, since they were becoming increasingly entertaining. Tomboy Alice continually pestered Edith for trousers and short hair like her brothers, and from time to time announced (in polite company) her intention of giving birth to a monkey. Ted was a hyperactive quicksilver as he darted about plunging his tin sword into imaginary enemies, and riding so recklessly on fat Pony Grant that Edith half jokingly doubted he would live to adulthood. Kermit, willful and quietly mischievous, could barely be restrained from eating the Fourth of July firecrackers, which he fancied were some delicacies. His favorite "toy" was a "dushtpan" with which he helped the maids keep the house tidy. Little Ethel was preoccupied with all kinds of pets, particularly rodents. "Come out of your ness, cunning guinea piggies," she would cajole. At night when Edith tucked her in, like as not there would be

"Her oldest and rather worst child."
Edith's snapshot of Theodore playing ball at Sagamore Hill.

one or two malodorous hamsters already huddled under the blankets. Theodore got such boyish delight out of playing with his "bunnies" that Edith began to refer to him as her "oldest and rather worst child."[6]

Nevertheless she was desolate, as usual, when he left for his annual hunting trip on September 1. "I had a dreadful dream last night," she wrote him two weeks later, "where I loved you so much and you turned from me."[7]

She was now about two months pregnant with her fourth child.

Bamie did not appear much at Sagamore Hill that year. First there had been the Fair; then she had to nurse her beloved Bob Ferguson through scarlet fever; then in November she sailed for England to act as hostess to her distant cousin James Roosevelt Roosevelt, First Secretary of the American Embassy in London.[8] "Rosy" had been recently widowed, and left to raise a boy of fourteen and a girl of twelve. Bamie's charitable gesture would keep her abroad uninterruptedly for the next nine months, win her a presentation at Queen Victoria's Court, and change her life in a way she could hardly have anticipated.

Although Edith's pregnancy was noticeable as the 1894 season began, she continued with her Washington social life right into the spring, dining out three or four times a week with Theodore, and entertaining at Jefferson Place most other nights. During their few evenings alone together she sewed or read while he made "ineffective bolts" at his next volume of *The Winning of the West*.

On Thursday, February 1, the Roosevelts dined for the first time at the White House. Ironically, they had never been invited there by the Republican Harrisons (Theodore had been too much a thorn in the side of that Administration), yet the Democratic Clevelands deemed them worthy company for Justices of the Supreme Court and members of the House and Senate judiciary committees. At seven-fifteen the President greeted Edith and Theodore in the East Room, against a background of potted foliage illuminated by red, white and blue lights. At his side stood the tall and darkly beautiful Frances Folsom Cleveland, twenty-seven years his junior. She was wearing a striking gown of black velvet, with a red satin underskirt and white lace bodice. Since marrying her in 1886, Grover Cleveland had grown more tolerant of social life. As a bachelor President he had openly disliked the formal French meals served at the White House, preferring to slip out to a saloon for large quantities of pickled herrings, pork chops, and lumps of Swiss cheese. Thus fortified, he would return to his desk to continue work till midnight. Bull-necked, immensely fat (three hundred pounds), and impatient of small talk, he had only gradually become tolerant of his wife's brilliant entertaining.

Shortly after seven-thirty Theodore took Mrs. Cleveland's arm and escorted her into the State Dining Room. Richard Watson Gilder, the poet, biographer and editor of *Century Magazine*, followed with Edith. When she took her place at his right she found that her other neighbor was none other than the President.

All around her she was conscious of a warm red glow. Oval plaques of scarlet tulips stretched the whole length of the table, red tapers burned in the candelabra, and the mantelpieces were a mass of crimson flowers. Yet as much as she and Theodore appreciated the honor being paid them, they were not dazzled by the Clevelands' hospitality. "As the only Republican present, we felt rather out of it and had to be most guarded in our conversation." Summing up the evening, Edith wrote: "I have been to more cheerful feasts but also more gloomy ones."[9]

Most of the Roosevelts' acquaintances at this time stood high in the political or literary world. But on occasion they attended purely social dinners with Washington's wealthiest families, such as the millionaire Levi Leiters, who lived in a marble mansion on Dupont Circle, and were famous for their hundred-dollar terrapins. Mrs. Leiter, six feet tall with a classic head and large bejeweled bosom, delighted in sculptures, objets d'art, fine silver and handsome urns. But her most beautiful possessions were her three young daughters, one of whom, Mary, was admired by Cecil Spring-Rice. Unfortunately for Springy, Mrs. Leiter's sights aimed higher than lowly diplomats, and Mary was soon engaged to a more brilliant Englishman, the egotistical Lord Curzon, future Viceroy of India.

On the whole the Roosevelts preferred simpler meals with intellectually compatible friends. Among these were the Winthrop Chanlers, a wealthy, sophisticated couple who had spent years living abroad. Margaret, a niece of Julia Ward Howe and a devout Roman Catholic, had been raised in Italy. "Winty," now in his early thirties, was a fun-loving, adventurous spirit who looked and acted like a nine-teenth-century Sir Walter Raleigh. Theodore detected faunlike qualities in him, and could not bear to think of him suffering the misfortunes of common humanity.

Washington's spring was later than usual that year, and on the crisp last day of March, Edith, Theodore, Ted, Alice and a few friends went for a long scramble up Rock Creek. The park was as wild in parts as the Far West. Edith walked briskly for a woman in the ninth month of pregnancy, checking the dogwoods, laurels and azaleas for signs of bloom. Theodore thought she had never looked better, in contrast to Fanny Dana, who "had many wrinkles and looked many years older." Edith herself was calmly confident about her looks: "I suppose as long as I keep my colour I am all right, and with plenty of sleep and exercise I hope to do that for some years yet," she wrote Gertrude. "Theodore would be really distressed if I got old and haggard."[10]

On April 9, 1894, ten days after the walk in Rock Creek Park, Edith gave birth to her fourth child and third son.

> She suffered less than ever before [Theodore reported to Bamie in London], and is now *so* happy; and so darling and good, in bed with the wee blanketed bundle . . . it was over so quickly that Mame, who was upstairs, did not hear anything. When at one, I went up to tell her, Ted waked up and overheard and went wild with delight, promptly rushing in to tell Sister.[11] Then they sat up in Mame's bed chattering like parakeets, and hugging two large darkey rag dollies which they always take to bed. They were overjoyed, and Edie was so well, that I finally let them put on their wrappers and slippers and tiptoe down to see Edie and the baby. They were as cunning about him as possible, and were far too excited to do much sleeping for the remainder of the night.[12]

Every morning during Edith's recovery, Theodore and the children picked pink roses from a bush which grew outside the morning-room balcony, and presented them to her at breakfast. Theodore loved the newcomer "more than he ever had so small a baby." [13] Ted made a gift of his own silver cup, and Ethel begged to be allowed to hold "the long-clothes boy." Kermit eyed the latest addition to the family with suspicion, and said he cared more for his "dushtpan." Later, however, he succumbed to the infant's undisputed charm "because he had such berry tiny feet!" [14]

The baby was baptized on Sunday, June 10, at 5 P.M. in Edith's parlor at Sagamore Hill. He smiled angelically as the priest named him Archibald Bulloch, in honor of Mittie Roosevelt's great-grandfather, a former President of Revolutionary Georgia.

There was the usual steady stream of visitors to Sagamore that summer, including Grandma Lee, who spoiled Alice with many expensive gifts (it was nothing for her to present the girl with a pony, and then a cart to go with it). Henry Adams came to stay, accompanied by Cecil Spring-Rice. More sophisticated houses beckoned Springy, but for the most part he preferred the one on the hill "swarming with bunnies."

Swarming it certainly was in 1894. Every child in the family could entertain a cousin his or her own age from the Yellowbanks home of Emlen and Christine Roosevelt, or from Waldeck, home of James West and Laura Roosevelt. Alice paired off with Emlen's daughter Christine, Ted with his son George, and Kermit with his son John. Ethel was friendly with West's daughter Lorraine, and Archie would in time become inseparable from her brother Nicholas. Besides these there were Elliott's and Corinne's children, who often stayed at Gracewood, making sixteen cousins in all.

Theodore, stocky and muscular in a one-piece bathing suit buttoned down the front, enjoyed teaching his sons, daughters, cousins, nephews and nieces to swim. His dubious tuition consisted of forcing each child to jump cold turkey off the dock into the ocean. Alice cried copiously, and Eleanor quaked with fright, but nobody drowned. Edith usually joined them, decorously dressed in heavy skirt and ankle-length pantalets.

When it came to land activities, Theodore was equally inflexible. "Under or over but never around" was his philosophy, as he led a long file of relatives through woods, over haystacks, and headlong down Cooper's Bluff to the beach, just as he had as a boy. Edith evaded these excursions. She preferred to sit reading in a cool balloon-sleeved white muslin dress, or to sew under her wisteria arbor overlooking the Sound. Or she would put on a shady sailor hat and stroll down to Yellowbanks for a chat with Theodore's aunt Mrs. James A. Roosevelt.

"Aunt Lizzie" was a wealthy Philadelphia Quaker who claimed to be descended from the Plantagenets. Though aging and dropsical, she retained her queenly bearing as she held court from a horsehair sofa on the porch. Cookies and lemonade stood at her elbow for anyone who happened to stop by. When the heat became too much for her, she would be ferried out to the bay to catch the ocean breezes as she lay on the deck of her steam launch. Edith was "very fond" of the old lady, admired her well-stocked mind and command of languages, and in time came to look on her as her best friend.[15]

Refreshed by these excursions, Edith was again able to face the hurly-burly of life with five young children. Kermit was particularly trying at the moment. He had developed water on the knee, and had one leg encased in irons. But this did not stop him from scrapping with bossy Ethel, and when she bit him he stood on his head and gave her a mighty thump with his brace.

Constitutionally unable to join in rough-and-tumbles as Theodore did, Edith was content to serve her children in less strenuous ways. She understood all their dreams and expectations, and indulged their mischief to such a point that one son remarked, "When Mother was a little girl, she must have been a boy!"[16] Her knowledge of plants, animals, history and poetry was so extensive that the children wondered where she learned it all. "From that military gentleman, General Information," she would tease.[17]

That August of 1894 New York City reformers approached Theodore and asked him to be their candidate for mayor in the fall elections. He was inclined to accept the offer, but before doing so discussed the matter with Edith. She made no secret of her preference for staying in Washington: besides, she said, they could not afford to entrust their future to a fickle electorate. Theodore, therefore, declined to run, and left for the West in early September, cruelly depressed. Only when Bamie arrived on a short visit from England on September 12 did Edith learn from her just how badly Theodore had wanted the mayoralty. Full of remorse, she told her sister-in-law that she felt "terribly" at having failed Theodore. Then in a rush of bitterness and guilt:

> He never should have married me and then would have been free to make his own course . . . I never realized for a minute how he felt over this, or that the mayoralty stood for so much to him; and I did not know it either just in what way the nomination was offered; in fact I do not know now for I did not like to ask too much.
>
> I am too thankful that he is away now for I am utterly unnerved and a prey to the deepest despair . . . if I knew what I do now I should have thrown all my influence in the scale with Corinne's and helped instead of hindering him.
>
> You say that I dislike to give my opinion. This is a lesson that will last my life, never to give it for it is utterly worthless when given,—worse than that in this case for it has helped to spoil some years of a life which I would have given my own for. I shall be myself again by Saturday when the darling gets back.[18]

Theodore, with three weeks out West to mull over the choice he had made, concluded that it had been a mistake. "The prize was very great; the expense would have been trivial and the chances of success were good," he wrote Bamie. "But it is hard to decide when one has the interests of a wife and children to consider first." To Lodge he was more candid:

> . . . The last four weeks, ever since I decided not to run, have been pretty bitter ones for me; I would literally have given my right arm to make the race, win or lose. It was the one golden chance, which never returns; and I had no illusions about ever having another opportunity; I knew it meant the definite abandonment of any hope of going on in the work and life for which I care more than any other. You may guess that these weeks have not been particularly pleasant ones; but outside of my immediate family no one but you

knows this. At the time, with Edith feeling as intensely as she did, I did not see how I could well go in; though I have grown to feel more and more that in this instance I should have gone counter to her wishes and made the race anyhow. It is not necessary to say to you that the fault was mine, not Edith's; I should have realized that she could not see the matter as it really was, or realize my feelings. But it is one of the matters just as well dropped . . .

My civil service work here, now, seems to me a little like starting to go through Harvard again after graduating."[19]

For the first time in almost eight years of marriage, Edith's relationship with Theodore was in crisis. Bamie came to the rescue. Seeing how the incident had strained her sister-in-law's nerves, she whisked her and the children off for a vacation. Nothing cured Edith's ills better than long country walks, and after two weeks of trekking across Vermont's broad meadows she was ready to face Theodore again. Thanks to their mutual love and understanding, the crisis passes.

William L. Strong, who duly won the mayoral race on the reform ticket, offered Theodore the position of Commissioner of Street Cleaning. After careful consideration (which Edith described as "three days suspended like Mahomet's coffin between heaven and earth") Theodore refused, saying that the work was "out of my line." However, he hinted to a friend of Mayor Strong that he would not mind being New York City's Police Commissioner, a role he could "afford to be identified with."[20] Beside, his usefulness at the Civil Service Commission was coming to an end. The service was double the size that it had been when he took office, and the law better enforced. He felt it was time to move on.

In the meantime, Edith was confined to the house with two ailing children, and one, Baby Archie, who after eight months on the breast was now being weaned. Kermit, "a cranky little mortal," was still in irons, and Alice, whose ankles were weak (the tendons in her heels were too short and turned her feet on one side) also needed braces.

The doctor's treatment consisted of strapping her leg to an instrument and turning a key which gradually forced the heel and foot into the proper position painlessly. Edith had to continue stretching and massaging Alice's leg at home—with such success that the child was eventually able to walk normally.

What with mounting doctor's bills, physical strain and chronic "neuralgia"—migraine headaches which increasingly plagued Edith—she was soon exhausted, and in January 1895 spent two weeks with Corinne in Orange. Theodore hoped the rest would do her good. He was worried about her because "she will *not* take care of herself, do what I can."[21]

Edith returned to Washington at the end of the month feeling "a little stronger," and resumed her active social life. Several times that season she and Theodore dined with Rudyard Kipling and his "quite impossible" American wife, Caroline.[22] The Englishman, not yet thirty, was already world-famous as the author of *Barrack-Room Ballads,* and an unmistakable genius. He was a compulsive talker, even more so than Theodore, who consequently thought him "rather underbred," and crossed swords with him when he criticized America. Edith, however, detected an intrinsic good nature in Kipling's creased, shortsighted eyes and "common little monkey face."[23] Thanks to her diplomatic mediation, he and her husband soon grew to respect each other.

In early spring, Edith succumbed to the bicycling craze then sweeping the nation. She found the lessons difficult—"the wheel wobbles in every direction as if it were alive"—and to straighten her at shaky moments the instructor pulled at a handled belt strapped round her waist.[24] But before she could master the art, Theodore was at last offered the job of New York City Police Commissioner at a salary of six thousand a year.

He officially resigned from the Civl Service Commission on April 25. For Edith, winding up six years of life in Washington, where she had been so happy, might have been a painful business, but she scarcely had time to brood, since the move had to be made in a matter of days. Also a marriage, a sickness, and a death conspired to distract her. On April 22, Mary Leiter married Lord Curzon in a shower of fashionable confetti. About the same time, the Roosevelts visited Tilden Selmes, who was dying of liver cancer in a Baltimore hospital. The beautiful Mrs. Selmes was so heartbroken that she was unable to face her long-time admirer and his wife. Then, on Sunday, April 27, a cable arrived from Turin, announcing the death, at the age of fifty-nine, of Gertrude Tyler Carow. Lacking further information, Edith could only assume that her mother had died of a combination of long-familiar ailments—rheumatism, neuralgia, grippe and gout, complicated by a medical addiction to morphine.[25]

Shocked as she was at Gertrude's sudden passing, her sorrow was not profound, as it had been for Charles Carow. A steady stream of whining, neurotic letters over the years had hardened her heart to maternal comparisons between her own happy marriage and the loneliness of the two expatriate women. "Always you are in my thoughts and heart," Gertrude had written, "and sometimes when I am suffering and Emily does not see then I cry like a spoiled baby for you . . . life would be nothing without you and the darlings to think about also Theodore . . ."[26] There was no news yet of Emily's future plans, but Edith assumed that her sister would come straight to America after the burial.

On May 2, the Roosevelts had a farewell lunch in Washington with Henry Adams. By the middle of the month they were comfortably settled at 689 Madison Avenue in New York City. Soon Edith was "rapidly recovering her tone," and Theodore was finding his new job "absorbingly interesting."[27]

Thirteen

His wife and children gave him a kind of spiritual bath that sent him back to the city refreshed and ready for what might come.
—Hermann Hagedorn[1]

Edith saw very little of her husband in his first few months as Police Commissioner. Although he moved out to Sagamore Hill with her for the summer, he left home at seven-thirty every morning, cycling to the Oyster Bay Station, and often as not staying in town overnight, working up to forty hours at a stretch in a "perfect whirl" of activity.[2] But Edith was not entirely alone with the children, since Emily Carow arrived at the beginning of June for a six-month stay. Both sisters would remain in deep mourning for their mother well into the winter.

Theodore was only one of four New York City Police Commissioners, but his prompt election as President of the Police Board put him in a position of some power and much publicity. Reporters flocked around him from the moment of his daily arrival at the white marble Police Headquarters on Mulberry Street. They would sit in his office as he tore through his morning paperwork and castigated corrupt policemen, then accompany him to the Old Vienna Bakery, and watch him gobble his lunches of bread and milk or squab chicken and *café au lait*.[3] In the afternoon, they covered his performance in the judge's box at police trials. After dark they would follow him on all-night patrols looking for shirking officers.

At thirty-seven years of age Theodore Roosevelt appeared to one reporter to be a man of "unusual physical strength" and "unlimited vitality." He was no longer dapper as in his Assembly days; his sandy hair was too close-cut to be stylish, his neck too thick and his face too florid for him to qualify as a handsome man. He had a habit of squinting and polishing his spectacles furiously as though the very act would give him clearer vision. His wide grin revealed fine, strong teeth, but there was, for some, a touch of mockery in the smile, and he seemed to strain for a cordiality he did not quite feel.[4]

If he appeared tense at times it was not without good reason. As the most actively reform-minded of the four commissioners, he had taken it upon himself to enforce the most unpopular law in the New York statute book, the Sunday Closing Act. This long-abused measure banned all sales of alcoholic beverages on the Lord's Day. Theodore thought the Act was ridiculous himself, but so much bribery and political corruption arose out of willful infractions that he felt compelled to enforce it to the letter.

As a result he antagonized powerful members of the State Legislature, both Democratic and Republican, Tammany Hall, the "yellow" press, and, most of all, hundreds of thousands of thirsty New Yorkers, who saw no good reason to forgo their traditional pails of cool beer on their one day off.

The furor against him mounted as the summer wore on, and Theodore began to talk of giving up his controversial post. He felt he should abandon all future hope of a career in politics, and retire to Sagamore Hill to become a "literary hermit."[5] But those who knew him best saw only ambition in his restlessness, and unfulfilled talent in his indecision. They sensed that no task yet undertaken by Theodore Roosevelt had stretched him to the full. Bob Ferguson, who accompanied him on a raid of New York's worst red-light districts one night, was confirmed in his view that what Theodore really needed was "a great and glorious war" to "give effective outlet to his more natural and active inclinations."[6] Roosevelt himself increasingly extolled the tenets of the Monroe Doctrine, and talked of the desirability of America taking Canada from the British, and driving the Spaniards out of Cuba.

"He seemed to strain for a cordiality he did not quite feel."
Theodore Roosevelt, aged thirty-seven.

On July 3, 1895, to Edith's great surprise, a cablegram came announcing Bamie's engagement to Lieutenant William Sheffield Cowles. Her fiancé was a naval attaché to the United States Embassy in London, whom she had met shortly after arriving there in December 1893. At that time she had asked Edith if she had known Will in Washington. "Lieutenant Cowles flourished here for several years," Edith replied. "I used to see him occasionally, but never thought much of him one way or the other. I believe he is divorced from his wife . . ."[7] Lieutenant Cowles was indeed divorced as far as Washington law was concerned, but the much stricter laws of New York State defined him as still technically married, which meant that if he set up house with Bamie in Manhattan she might be threatened with property confiscation, and he with prosecution for bigamy. Theodore consulted with New York lawyers on their behalf, and came up with two unappealing alternatives. Will could either get relief by "returning to his domicile and suing his wife for adultery" or, when the couple eventually came back to America, they could relocate in a more tolerant state, such as California.[8] Fortunately, it turned out that Will had an ancestral home in Farmington, Connecticut, and the laws of that state would recognize his remarriage.

The world at large might be surprised at the sudden engagement of the crippled forty-year-old spinster, but the Roosevelts, knowing her charm and social powers, could understand how she had captivated the forty-nine-year-old officer. Though Will was not the brightest or the wittiest man who moved in Bamie's orbit, Edith remembered him as kind and dependable and solidly distinguished-looking, with his walrus mustache and gold epaulettes. If Bamie was not deeply in love, she was at least very affectionate, and called him her "dear old bear."

Henry Cabot Lodge, who encountered Bamie in Paris that fall as she was buying her trousseau, approved of Will as a "Republican and a jingo," but affected to disapprove of him as her husband. "Why on earth should you get married?" he teased. "You have Theodore and myself."[9] Rosy Roosevelt, too, was full of chagrin at losing his housekeeper, nanny and diplomatic hostess, and he left London in a huff while the wedding preparations were under way.[10]

Unable to cross the Atlantic for the ceremony, Edith and Theodore sent a five-hundred-dollar check, which, combined with another from the Robinsons, purchased Bamie's wedding collaret and five-star "tiara." Corinne and Douglas represented the immediate family at the marriage service in St. Andrew's Church, Westminster, on November 25, 1895. Bob Ferguson and his brother Ronald acted as ushers. "Will simply adores her and cannot take his eyes off her," Corinne told Edith later. She went on to describe Bamie's progress up the aisle on Rosy Roosevelt's arm, looking "a little twitchy" in her simple white dress and veil under the glittering tiara. Will also appeared frightened to death throughout the ceremony, and incapable of harming a fly, which did not deter Corinne from solemnly exhorting him to "be tender" with her sister, at the packed reception afterward.[11]

To keep Bamie and Will occupied during their honeymoon in France, Corinne dumped her children on them, while she toured the Loire châteaus. Not until the couple returned to London to settle in a house on fashionable West Eaton Place did they gain some measure of privacy.[12]

It soon became apparent that no matter how harmless and accommodating Will and Bamie had been as single people, as a couple they were more assertive. Theodore and Edith were informed that since Will's appointment would keep them in England for at least another eighteen months, 689 Madison Avenue would henceforth be rented rather than be made freely available to members of the family. Edith was no doubt upset at the prospect of losing the town house she had grown accustomed to have the run of for the last nine years. After discussing the matter with her husband, she offered to pay $1,800 (or $450 per month, January through April) and promised Bamie meekly to "see to all cleaning and take the best care of your things, though I am not as good a housekeeper as you are . . ."[13]

Although Theodore, in his first six months as police commissioner, managed to diminish crime, enforce the Sunday Closing Act, and improve working conditions for the force, it was not without great cost to his own well-being. By the end of October he had run himself to a virtual standstill, and was so overwrought and edgy that one friend suspected he was on the verge of a nervous breakdown. On top of all "the grinding labor and the worry," there now came demands for him to speak two or three times a night for Republican candidates in the state and municipal elections. Being a good party man with latent political ambitions, he could not refuse. Edith, concerned about his health, began to insist on going into town with him when work was going to keep him away overnight.[14]

Edith's period of mourning for Gertrude Carow was almost over when she moved back to 689 in January 1896. She was never quite reconciled to the loss of her stimulating social life in Washington, but she could at least take advantage of New York's cultural riches. She splurged on a fashionable black silk evening dress at Altman's, and began to go out again. In a packed Metropolitan Opera House she heard Melba and de Reszke in *Faust,* and went to the latest exhibitions of contemporary art. There were dinners with architect Grant La Farge and her very good friend Mary Cadwalader Jones, an aunt of Edith Wharton and an intimate of Henry James.

As for the children, they also benefited from the sophisticated facilities of New York City. They were instructed by the best tutors, and treated by the best doctors. Alice and Ted began to take dancing lessons with Mr. Dodsworth, and Edith, who chaperoned them, no doubt felt a pang or two of nostalgia for the days when she and Theodore had learned to waltz and polka under this same stern gaze. But after hours and hours of watching Alice (now so developed that she had to wear a corset) and Ted making painfully slow progress, she felt "like an animal in a cage."[15]

Despite Theodore's professional worries and her own financial ones ("It seems to cost so much to merely exist in New York," she complained to Bamie), Edith, at thirty-four, was yearly more happy in her marriage. The children, too, luxuriated in a domestic atmosphere of love and security. When James West Roosevelt died in April, after long suffering from weak lungs, alcoholism, and morphine dependency, Kermit remarked sadly, "Oh, Mother, I wish we had the water of life to give to our friends."[16]

By the summer of 1896 Theodore's difficult relations with his colleagues at Police Headquarters had flared into open wrangling. It was plain he could achieve nothing more there, and he began to dream instead of a government post under William McKinley, the Republican party's new and promising candidate for the Presidency. His first move was to invite two old mutual friends of himself and the nominee to Sagamore Hill at the beginning of August. He and Edith had known Mr. and Mrs. Bellamy Storer since early Washington days, and Theodore now asked them to recommend him to McKinley as the potential Assistant Secretary of the Navy. The Storers agreed to do what they could.

With the election still three months off and the campaign not due to open officially until September, Theodore could expect no immediate change for the better in his career. He found solace from his struggles at Mulberry Street in the innocent entertainment afforded by his family. "Their gay doings, their odd sayings," a friend remembered, "cleansed him of the smoke and grime of the battle . . . His wife and children gave him a kind of spiritual bath that sent him back to the city refreshed and ready for what might come." [17]

"I wish you could see [the boys'] costumes," he wrote Bamie, "especially Kermit's; he wears the blue overalls, which are perhaps the finest triumph of Edith's genius, and which are precisely like those of our hired man, with a cap like that of a second-rate French cook, a pair of shabby tennis shoes, and as his hands are poisoned [from ivy], a pair of exceedingly dirty kid gloves. When, in this costume, turning somersaults on the manure heap, he is indeed a joy forever." [18]

Alice, now almost thirteen, was a "great romping girl," who could ride Pony Grant bareback, both astride and sideways. Pretty and very intelligent, she nevertheless preferred smart town life to the rustic simple existence at Sagamore Hill.

Ethel, who increasingly resembled Auntie Bye, had grown very plump, with legs as sturdy as bedposts. A plain yoked frock, with no discernible waist, was the only becoming style for her. When riding an old polo pony called Diamond, she liked to wear bloomers which did double duty as a place to store vast quantities of apples.

Archie, whose big eyes and mass of yellow hair reminded Edith of the Christ-child in a Murillo painting, was, in her opinion, "quite the prettiest of the family." He said little, but was active and full of mischief. Theodore, whom the boy adored, said he had "lots of character, all of it bad." [19]

The first of the children to receive public education was nine-year-old Ted, who was enrolled by his parents in Cove Neck School for the fall term of 1896. Here, in a white clapboard building, sat the children of gardeners and coachmen from nearby estates, far outnumbering those of landowners and professional men. Ted was "very happy studying with little Gallaghers and Brenners," Edith wrote Cecil Spring-Rice, "and will rather miss it when we go to town and he falls under the sway of Alice's governess."[20]

In November William McKinley defeated Democrat William Jennings Bryan by a half a million votes, the biggest majority ever recorded against a presidential candidate.

The Storers now redoubled their efforts to have McKinley nominate Theodore as Assistant Secretary of the Navy, but as the winter days shortened, no encouraging word came from the President-elect's home in Canton, Ohio. McKinley, it was rumored, feared that Theodore's bellicosity might affect America's delicate relations with Spain over Cuba. However, McKinley did not give a flat no to the appointment.

This continuing ambiguity had the customary unsettling effect on Theodore. During one December weekend, Edith reported to Corinne, he "played bear so hard with the children that he brought on a violent attack of asthma; then a dead bough fell on his arm when he was chopping and made a big bruise; then he bumped his head so hard against the mantlepiece in putting a log on the fire that he cut his forehead; next he tumbled while skiing and strained his finger and last of all his shoulder was very stiff from carrying the skiis . . ."[21]

The proponent of the Strenuous Life left for New York on Monday morning "in a dilapidated condition," but returned undaunted on Christmas Eve for more fun. That afternoon he went down to Cove School, and urged the children to stand up for their rights, be kind to animals, and do "something worth while when they grew up"—a speech he was to make there, with minor variations, for the rest of his life. Then, after listening to the pupils' songs and recitations, he presented them gifts of their own choosing—skates, sleds, railway trains, dolls—bought by Edith at Bloomingdale's, where she could "get the best value for money."[22]

After the presentations, the family had a six-o'clock dinner, then drove in a sleigh to Christ Church for carols. When they reached home, they found Bob Ferguson waiting for them, and, after some reviving tea, milk punch, toast and jam the adults filled the stockings.

It was bitterly cold when the children awoke them next morning at six o'clock, clamoring for gifts. Everyone huddled around a bright fire in Edith's bedroom. "I muffled Archie in my blue shawl," she told Bamie, "Bob with a sofa blanket decently but scantily draping his legs was most picturesque and Theodore in his old brocade wrapper which only flourishes on such occasions was not far behind him. After breakfast we had the big presents in the gun room, where the climate was like nothing but the North Pole. After lunch we succeeded in getting warm by playing 'pillow-dex'—very idiotic but very funny." [23]

In Henry Adams's opinion, the coming of the new Republican Administration ended the dullest quarter century in American history, but the change was at great cost to his own social life. Not only did he lose John Hay, whom McKinley appointed Ambassador to the Court of St. James's, but the beautiful Elizabeth Cameron closed her house on Lafayette Square, and also left for Europe. With Cecil Spring-Rice now serving in Germany, only the Lodges remained of the old Adams circle, and even they were more and more taken up by politics, now that the G.O.P. was back in power.

Adams was therefore pleased to hear, in early April 1897, that his "sympathetic" friend Edith Kermit Roosevelt would soon return to town. After tireless lobbying on Theodore's behalf by the Storers, John Hay, Henry Cabot Lodge, Speaker Tom Reed and Judge William Howard Taft, Theodore had been finally appointed Assistant Secretary of the Navy under Secretary John Davis Long.

It was with little regret that Theodore quit his post as Police Commissioner, although he confessed to having enjoyed his effective work at grass-roots level. The move to Washington would bring him prestige, glamor, and national prominence. Whether it would add to his reputation as a political reformer remained to be seen. Somehow he felt that the large social problems of the day could be solved only by "working right in the mire." [24]

Fourteen

I would have turned from my wife's deathbed to have answered that call.

—Theodore Roosevelt[1]

"I feel you will not pleased to hear that you may expect a niece or nephew in the first week of December," Edith wrote Emily on May 10, 1897. "I know you thought the stork had paid enough visits here . . ."[2]

Pregnancy caused a postponement of Edith's move to Washington with Theodore when he took up his position as Assistant Secretary of the Navy. Once again the hospitable Lodges accommodated him. A few days before Theodore's arrival Cabot received a letter from their mutual friend William Sturgis Bigelow. "I have an almost superstitious feeling about [Theodore]," he wrote, "that he has a great deal depending on him ten or twenty years hence. There is nobody else just like him above the horizon."[3]

Certainly there was no one like him above Secretary John D. Long's horizon. Theodore was careful at first to conceal his enormous ambitions. The white-haired valetudinarian was pleased to have an enthusiastic, hard-working assistant on whom he could rely when he felt like stepping out to see a doctor, or a podiatrist, or a masseur.

What he did not foresee was that the New Yorker, once he had his arm on the rudder of the Navy Department, would, before too many months had passed, be commander of the whole ship.

One of the first to benefit from Theodore's influence was Will Cowles, who reported to America for sea duty just as his brother-in-law arrived in Washington. He had been given the command of an antiquated gunboat, but Theodore had him transferred 'to an auxilliary cruiser, the *Topeka*, where he would be of much more direct use in the event of war.

Bamie did not immediately return to the United States with her husband, but stayed behind to close up their London house. Neither Theodore nor Edith could meet her when her ship docked on May 1, 1897. However, he and Cabot Lodge were already laying plans to persuade the social doyenne of Eaton Place (Bamie's house had been described by the London *Times* as "the pleasantest" transatlantic rendezvous in town[4]) to spend the winter in Washington.

Among the Fourth of July guests at Sagamore Hill that year was fifteen-year-old Franklin Delano Roosevelt, Theodore's fifth cousin and a student at Groton. He was an attractive extrovert with a handsome, if willowy, build. Contemporary members of the family considered him to be something of a "featherduster," lacking the rugged, sporty qualities they admired.[5] Edith could hardly have guessed, as she entertained this remote cousin, how closely his career would follow Theodore's, nor that some thirty-five years hence she would be mistaken for his mother and, more improbably, his wife.

She went to the capital for ten days in early August to organize the furnishings of their newly rented house at 1810 N Street, opposite the British Embassy. Fortunately for Edith, who was now six months pregnant, the weather was unusually cool, and she grappled energetically with pieces of "mesozoic or horsehair furniture" that had belonged to her own and Theodore's grandparents. When she returned to Sagamore Hill Theodore stayed on, "having immense fun running the Navy."[6] Secretary Long had gone on vacation.

In 1897 the United States fleet was in relatively poor standing, compared to the British, Russian, and Japanese navies. Theodore immediately set out to increase the number of American battleships to eight, and to acquire more cruisers and torpedo boats. To galvanize his superiors, he wrote a pamphlet listing the hawkish opinions of former Chief Executives on the Navy. He discussed these with President McKinley at dinner, and on afternoon drives, and promised him that the Department would be "in the best possible shape" if war with Spain should come.[7]

Theodore's belligerent talk was not so outrageous, nor so individual, as it may appear. Imperialist ambitions had surfaced in Harrison's Administration, when the Hawaiian Islands first became available for annexation; and the Navy began to seek bases in the Caribbean. Then, in 1895, had come news of colonial disturbances in Cuba, where native insurgents were trying to throw off Spanish rule. That struggle was now, after two and a half years, fiercer than ever; Spanish atrocities in reprisal were being shrilly publicized in the American "yellow" press of Joseph Pulitzer and William Randolph Hearst, and there was serious talk of the United States going in to liberate the island. This pleased Theodore Roosevelt, who felt that war with Spain "would result at once in getting us a proper Navy and a good system of coast defence." He told the President that he would go to war himself in order to liberate Cuba. McKinley, smiling, asked what Mrs. Roosevelt would think of such an action. Theodore replied that both she and Henry Cabot Lodge would regret it, but it was the one situation where he "would consult neither." The President laughed and said he would guarantee Theodore the opportunity he sought, "if war by any chance arose."[8]

In late October Edith and the children joined Theodore in Washington in time for his thirty-ninth birthday. The following morning Kermit and Archie were enrolled at the local public school, and Edith settled happily back into the familiar surroundings of her favorite city.

On November 9, 1897, the Roosevelts' fifth child, a boy, was born unexpectedly. "Edith is doing well," Theodore wrote Bamie. "By the aid of my bicycle I just got the Doctor and Nurse in time. We are very glad and much relieved." Within two hours of his son's birth he had entered him for Groton. The baby was baptized Quentin, in honor of Edith's grandfather, Isaac Quentin Carow. Cabot Lodge attended the christening, to Theodore's amusement, "with gloomy reluctance." It was "against his principles to sanction anything so antimalthusian as a sixth child."[9]

By Christmas Edith was already "beginning to look and feel herself," her husband reported. "When she is well she will enjoy

"Edith settled happily back
into the familiar surroundings of her favorite city."
Washington, D.C., in the 1890s.

Washington more than ever . . ." But Edith was not as well as at first
appeared. On Twelfth Night she was stricken with "grippe," only
thirty-six hours before Theodore was due to leave for an important
series of social and business engagements in New York. For two days
she was sicker than he had ever seen her (he suspected that she might
have typhoid fever), and although he desperately wanted to keep his
appointments, he decided he had better not go. He called in a trained

nurse, and shipped the younger children to friends. Alice, who was in "the habit of running the streets uncontrolled with every boy in town," remained at home, as did Ted.[10] The boy was an additional source of worry to his father, for he suffered acutely from nervous headaches, and none of five separate doctors could diagnose the cause.

Edith developed acute "neuralgia" pains on January 17, followed on the twentieth by fever and "sciatica" so intense she could not sleep. "It is of course a plain case of exhaustion," wrote the sympathetic Elizabeth Cameron to Henry Adams.[11]

Actually, Edith's malaise was much more serious. There was no improvement during the next four weeks, and her fever never fell below 101 degrees. It became necessary to send Alice away from home to stay with Bamie in New York. Ted remained too ill to move.

About February 22, 1898, Edith noticed an ominous swelling in her abdomen near the pelvis. Theodore, "extremely anxious," sent for the great Sir William Osler of Johns Hopkins University. The small, lithe, dark-eyed Celt, who was a world expert in abdominal tumors, said that Edith was "critically ill" with an abscess in the psoas muscle, and recommended an immediate operation. But Theodore, feebly relying on "a lot of perfectly incompetent doctors, taxidermists and veterinarians, good sportsmen and excellent athletes" (to quote Winthrop Chanler), decided to wait and see if surgery could be avoided. "Such cattle for doctors I have never known," Elizabeth Cameron exclaimed in disgust. Edith's fever continued to rage. Finally, on March 5, Theodore called in a gynecologist, who confirmed Osler's diagnosis, and operated the following day.[12]

"Everything went well," Theodore told Bamie, "but of course it was a severe operation, and her convalescence may be a matter of months. She is now well over the effects of the ether and the shock, but of course exceedingly weak. She behaved heroically; quiet and even laughing, while I held her hand until the ghastly preparations had been made."[13]

Edith was still feverish afterward, and slept little while the open wound drained. Weeks passed. At times Theodore could not tell whether his wife would live or die. But slowly, "very slowly," he wrote Brooks Adams on March 21, "she is crawling back to life."[14]

The same could mercifully be said of Ted, whose strange nervous prostration was at last on the mend. As soon as the boy could travel, his father sent him to join Alice in New York, where he received remedial treatment from Dr. Alexander Lambert. The unexpected diagnosis was that Theodore had long been driving him too hard, both physically and mentally. Theodore, chastened, promised never again to press Ted, who had "bidden fair to be all the things I would like to have been and wasn't." Luckily for the other children, Edith observed later, he was too busy in the years that followed to exert the same pressures on them that he had on Ted.[15]

Alice stayed away happily all spring. At first she resented living under the kind but firm hand of "Auntie Bye," and having to submit to a regimen of lectures and concerts, as befitted a young lady of fourteen. She had complained to her stepmother that it was "worse than boarding school," whereupon Edith replied that that was why she had been sent there.[16] Alice now found that she enjoyed the intellectual stimulation furnished by Bamie's friends, and announced that she had no desire to return to Washington.

Concurrent with Edith's and Ted's private crises were public ones of equal seriousness to Theodore. On February 15, 1898, The U.S.S. *Maine,* which was paying a "courtesy visit" to Cuba, blew up in Havana Harbor, killing 264 Americans. Congress, the press, and young jingoistic Republicans such as Theodore and Lodge suspected the Spaniards of mining the ship, and redoubled their clamor for war. Theodore went further: he wrote William Astor Chanler, Winty's brother, urging him to raise a regiment for Cuban service, and to take him along as Lieutenant Colonel. "I shall chafe my heart out if I am kept here instead of being at the front," he wrote on March 15, as Edith lay at death's door.[17]

But President McKinley would not declare war, pending an investigation of the *Maine* disaster. As Assistant Secretary, Theodore managed to see an advance copy of the court of inquiry's report within the next week; it stated that the explosion had been caused by an "external device," and this in his mind was conclusive grounds for war.

On March 27, the day before the report was made public, with Edith still weak and "terribly wasted," Theodore wrote his eldest son: "Today I took a hard walk with Doctor Wood and we both discussed how we could get into the army that would go to Cuba."[18] Leonard Wood was a new close friend, the President's personal physician, and a career soldier who had distinguished himself against Geronimo during the Apache uprising.

By April 4, with the younger children back in the house, Edith felt at last so much better that she was able to come downstairs and summon a carriage for a drive in the warm spring air. On impulse she directed it to the Metropolitan Club, hoping to surprise Theodore, who lunched there every day. Outside the club entrance she recognized the sandy hair and rolling walk of Leonard Wood, and asked him to go in and tell Theodore that a lady wanted to speak to him. The Assistant Secretary emerged unsuspecting, and when he saw his wife came running toward her. "I wish," Edith told Ted, "you could have seen his face of surprise and delight."[19]

On April 11 McKinley sent the inevitable war message to Congress, and twelve days later he was authorized to raise three volunteer cavalry regiments to swell the regular army. That same day the Secretary of War offered Roosevelt the command of one of the regiments, but he did not consider himself fully qualified, and agreed instead to serve as Lieutenant Colonel, under Colonel Leonard Wood.

All of Theodore's intimates—Lodge, Chanler, Bigelow, Hay, Adams, and Douglas Robinson—were against his decision to enlist. "I really think he is going mad," wrote Winty. "The President has asked him twice as a personal favor to stay in the Navy Department, but Theodore is wild to fight and hack and hew. It is really sad. Of course, this ends his political career for good. Even Cabot says this."[20]

Other friends wondered how he could desert his wife and children at a such time. But Theodore chillingly replied that, thanks to investments and insurance, they were not dependent on him for their support, and his death "would not very materially affect their income." He also told Dr. Lambert that his decision, while agonizing, was inevitable. Having publicly advocated war with Spain for at least a year, he now felt compelled to practice what he had preached, otherwise his political future would have been compromised.[21] Years later he admitted to another friend:

> When the chance came for me to go to Cuba with the Rough Riders Mrs. Roosevelt was very ill and so was

Teddy. It was a question if either would ultimately get well. You know what my wife and children mean to me; and yet I made up my mind that I would not allow even a death to stand in my way; that it was my one chance to do something for my country and for my family and my one chance to cut my little notch on the stick that stands as a measuring-rod in every family. I know now that I would have turned from my wife's deathbed to have answered that call.[22]

Bracing herself against the storm of criticism, Edith, still frail, loyally supported her husband's decision. "I can never say what a help and comfort Edith has been to me," her husband wrote gratefully.[23]

And so, on May 6, 1898, Theodore Roosevelt resigned as Assistant Secretary of the Navy and prepared to join his regiment at training camp in San Antonio, Texas. In spite of her fears for his safety, and dread of the domestic responsibilities about to fall entirely on her shoulders, Edith tried to make Theodore's last two weeks in Washington pleasurable. They dined with friends, went out driving through the countryside, and spent as much time as possible with "the cunning children." On May 12, summoning all her considerable reserve of spiritual strength, Edith hid her feelings of desolation as the Lieutenant Colonel packed his Brooks Brothers blue Cravenette cavalry uniform and twelve spare pairs of steel-rimmed spectacles. Kermit proudly reported his departure that evening to Aunt Emily. "Father went to war last Thursday. I sted up untill he left which was at 10 . . ."[24]

Fifteen

Come back safe darling 'pigeon' and we shall be happy, but it is quite right you should be where you are.
— Edith Kermit Roosevelt[1]

Theodore's eight-hundred-strong regiment, the First U.S. Volunteer Cavalry (soon to be known as Roosevelt's Rough Riders) was made up of Western cowboys and stockmen, Southern farmers, Indian braves, Mexican Americans, Ivy Leaguers, and Eastern socialites, including young Bob Ferguson. At the end of May, Theodore cabled Edith to say that their training was complete. Men and horses were being packed into railroad cars and moved to Tampa, Florida, where they would board transport ships to Cuba.

> When Ted heard of your telegram [Edith wrote], and was shown Tampa on the map, he said 'I suppose Father will get the war wind full in his face.' He says he should think every boy should want to go to war and wished you could have taken him just to clean your guns for of course he would not expect a shot at the enemy! He subsequently remarked he was sure he would get angry in a battle and ping away at the foe as fast as he

> could cram in cartridges. . . . Ted hopes there will be
> one battle so that you can be in it, but come out safe.
> Not every boy has a father who has seen a battle he
> says."[2]

She went on to give Theodore other comforting details of domestic
life, yet try as she might to sound lighthearted, her loneliness çame
through. "Always I have the longing and missing in my heart, but I
shall not write about it for it makes me cry."[3]

Since Theodore would be in Tampa for a few days prior to
embarkation, Edith set out to join him there on June 1. Her train
journey south was through desolate country: "All white sand and low
palmetto bushes, and tall melancholy pines draped with gray
moss. . . . and occasionally a little cluster of shanties with pickanin-
nies sleeping at the door while their mammies hoed corn in the little
fields adjoining."[4]

She did not look for Theodore at the Tampa railroad station the
next evening, knowing he would not be released from camp in time to
meet her there. They had fixed their rendezvous under the rotunda of
the Tampa Bay Hotel, where he had reserved "a comfortable room
with a bathroom."[5]

The hot little town was crowded with sailors from warships
anchored in the bay as well as some thirty thousand soldiers. It was
with some difficulty that Edith's cab made its way through the sandy
streets to the bizarre Moorish-style hotel. This luxurious folly, with
its silver minarets and domes, operated during the winter as a resort
for the rich, and was usually closed in summer. Now, however, it had
been taken over by the Army as its headquarters for the Cuban
invasion.

Edith followed her porter up the hotel steps onto a street-wide
porch teaming with uniformed officers and white-trousered newsmen.
Some guests were Civil War veterans, rocking impatiently in the
shade, waiting for their last chance in battle; others were pink-faced
youths fresh from West Point. There were monocled attachés from
Germany and Russia, military observers from Britain, France, and
Japan, some harrassed Washington bureaucrats, and not a few good-
looking women in suspiciously bright clothes.

Lieutenant Colonel Roosevelt was waiting for her in the lobby,
looking "thin but rugged and well." He had exciting news: Colonel

"They had fixed their rendezvous under the rotunda."
The Tampa Bay Hotel, summer 1898.

Wood had given him permission to be with Edith overnight for the duration of her stay—although he would have to return to camp at 4 A.M. for reveille. "We were both very hungry for our supper," Edith wrote the children next day, "and glad to get at bed at once."[6]

Next day Colonel Wood and Theodore came to lunch with her, and afterward took her to see their camp, ten miles away on a sandy plain ringed by palmettos and pine. Khaki-shirted Rough Riders were moving like ants in and out of white tents erected neatly in long "streets." Edith greatly enjoyed meeting the officers in her capacity as visiting Colonel's lady. She watched the cavalry at drill, saw the horses being led to water, and was introduced to two regimental mascots, a little dog named Cuba and a temperamental mountain lion cub. (Later these were joined by a bald eagle named Teddy.)

She returned to camp on June 6 to watch the entire cavalry complement at mass drill. Members of the press corps were present, including the famous Richard Harding Davis of the *Herald,* and several representatives of foreign governments. Edith soon struck up an acquaintance with a dapper young British military observer, Captain Arthur Lee, whom Davis had already introduced to her husband. ("Good heavens, don't you know Theodore Roosevelt? You must meet him this very minute. He is the biggest thing here and the most typical American living."[7] Lee had immediately fallen under Roosevelt's spell. In his memoirs, written forty years later after a lifetime of friendship with Theodore and Edith, he said that the Rough Rider was "the most alive, the most compelling, the most entertaining human being with whom I had ever come in contact."[8]

The stately maneuvers of long lines of cavalry that day formed a fitting climax to Edith's stay. The following morning, after a second wrenching farewell, she left for New York.

Later in the day, Wood, Theodore and the Rough Riders boarded the S.S. *Yucatan,* one of thirty-two crowded transports bobbing on a fetid canal off Port Tampa. Here, due to a naval scare, they were to remain for the next eight days, in semitropical heat with the threat of dysentery hanging over them. For six of these days, Theodore did not even leave his cabin, because the decks were too crowded. The name "Rough Riders" was now a misnomer, in that there was no room on the transport for any but a few officers' horses, and several of those soon died of the heat.

Winthrop Chanler saw Theodore on a short spell of shore leave, "sitting at table in a little Hotel at the pier unable to get anything he wanted, in the uniform of a Lieut. Col., dry and hungry . . . gnashing his teeth at the whole disgraceful performance of embarkation." In spite of Theodore's quitting his job at the Navy Department where "he might have been running the best part of the show," Chanler felt, correctly as it turned out, that "his political future has been benefitted rather than hurt."[9]

Finally, on June 14, to the sound of bands playing "The Star Spangled Banner" and "The Girl I Left Behind Me," the transport fleet moved out of Tampa Bay, and steamed south "through a sapphire sea, wind-rippled under an almost cloudless sky."[10] At Key

West a convoy of twelve naval vessels joined them, making a total of some seventeen thousand officers and men, and they proceeded to Cuba.

Back at Oyster Bay, Edith had taken to looking anxiously out of the window for the mailman cycling up the hill with letters from Theodore. She realized that there would be a hiatus now until the first dispatch bags came from Cuba about June 25. Meanwhile, she could only search the newspaper columns for mention of his name. Thanks to Theodore's gift for publicity, these were plentiful, enabling her to piece together his movements.

On June 22 he disembarked at Daiquirí, near Santiago, with a large invasion force. The port had no usable pier, and several soldiers were drowned in the heavy surf. One cargo boat overturned, losing a quantity of blankets and cartridge belts. Some of the horses, pushed out of the transport to swim for land, headed out to sea instead. Fortunately, a bugler on shore had the presence of mind to blow a battle call, whereupon the horses wheeled about and swam toward him.

The Rough Riders set up their dog tents that night on the borders of the Daiquirí River, surrounded by soaring mountains, palm trees, mangroves and bamboo thickets. It was decided that they would begin to march on Santiago next day. Supplies for the march were critically inadequate, but Brigadier General Shafter, the invasion commander, was in such haste to attack the enemy before tropical diseases weakened his force (summer was the height of the yellow-fever season) that no delay could be tolerated.

So on June 24, the Rough Riders set off along the coast to Siboney, moving at a killing pace in tremendous heat. They had only the wool uniforms they wore when they landed, and heavy packs of unnourishing food, mainly fat bacon, hardtack, and coffee. Of quinine, the most essential drug against fever, they had none; for the next two weeks they would have to fan away ubiquitous mosquitoes and drink water from contaminated streams.

They made Siboney that night, and next morning pushed on north into the interior mountains. The high grasses teemed with rabbit-sized land crabs, tarantulas, lizards and snakes, and the heat was so insufferable that they soon began to jettison tents, coats and blankets.

Wood and a small advance guard led the way along the hill trail toward Las Guásimas, while a regiment of regular soldiers took a parallel road below. The Volunteers were talking and laughing loudly as they approached the junction of the two trails, when suddenly Spaniards, invisible in the densest part of the jungle, opened fire upon them with deadly smokeless Mausers. The newspaper reports made this sound embarrassingly like an ambush, but Theodore, in one of his first Cuban letters to Edith, was at pains to give a different impression.

> Yesterday we struck the Spaniards and had a brisk fight for two and a half hours before we drove them out of their position. We lost a dozen men killed or mortally wounded, and sixty severely or slightly wounded. . . . One man was killed as he stood beside a tree with me. Another bullet went through a tree behind which I stood, and filled my eyes with bark. The last charge I led on the left using a rifle I took from a wounded man; and I kept three of the empty cartridges we got from a dead Spaniard . . . for the children. Every man behaved well; there was no flinching. The fire was very hot at one or two points where the men around me went down like ninepins . . .[11]

Edith's overwhelming relief that Theodore had been spared in battle so far was tempered by alarm at his insalubrious living conditions, which he proceeded to enumerate in graphic detail.

> I have been sleeping on the ground in the mackintosh, and so drenched with sweat that I haven't been dry a minute day or night. . . . My bag has never turned up, like most of our baggage . . . I have nothing with me, no soap, toothbrush, razor, brandy, medicine chest, socks or underclothes . . .
>
> For four days I never took off my clothes . . . and we had no chance to boil the water we drank . . . The morning after the fight we buried our dead in a great big trench, reading the solemn burial services over them, and all the regiment joining in singing "Rock of Ages." The vultures were wheeling overhead by hundreds.

> They plucked out the eyes and tore the faces and the
> wounds of the dead Spaniards before we got to them,
> and even one of our own men who lay in the open. The
> wounded lay in the path, a ghastly group; but there were
> no supplies for them . . . The woods are full of land
> crabs . . . when things grew quiet they slowly gathered
> in gruesome rings around the fallen.[12]

Theodore went on to other paragraphs, which Edith chose not to
include when she sent copies of his letters to Corinne. They were no
doubt intimate and tender, for in her first reply on June 27 she wrote:
"Last night I slept better because I held your dear letters to my heart
instead of just having them under my pillow. I felt I was touching
you when I pressed against me what your hand had touched."[13]

On June 30 the Rough Riders were ordered to bivouac in the
jungle near the San Juan range of hills, in preparation for a major
battle the following day. Shafter's plan was to charge the two major
entrenchments still separating him from Santiago. Due to sickness in
the command, Leonard Wood had just been promoted to Brigadier
General, and Theodore replaced him as Colonel and commanding
officer of the first Volunteers. That evening the two leaders stood for
a while on the brow of El Pozo staring at the distant silhouette of San
Juan. They were an oddly matched pair. Observers noticed a distinct
contrast in their personalities and methods. Roosevelt was of the
"Biff-bang-do-it-right-now-can-not-put-it-off-another-minute"   sort,
said Sergeant Dave Hughes of the Rough Riders. He was a daring
extrovert, full of energy and ambition, while Wood was more cool and
cautious. The latter had long been aware that sooner or later he
would be "kicked upstairs to make room for Roosevelt."[14]

Yet, decisive and courageous as Theodore appeared to his men, he
admitted afterward that that night he did not dare think of Edith or
his children, lest it "unman" him.[15]

On the morning of July 1, 1898, as he made his final preparations
for the decisive fight of the war, Edith lay on a chaise longue on the
west porch of Sagamore Hill. Kermit was curled up beside her;
Archie sat on her legs, and Alice, who had a pronounced interest in

the material things of life, was asking why their income had been reduced during her father's absence. Comforting though it was to have the children near, Edith could not prevent her heart from thumping with alarming force and irregularity (it had suffered an "enlargement" after Theodore's departure, and would not be normal again until his return).[16]

At 1 P.M. she and the children went in to lunch. Simultaneously, fifteen hundred miles away to the south, Theodore, who had just received permission to storm the Spanish entrenchments, jumped onto his pony Little Texas and, with a wave of his hat and blue bandana, led the Rough Riders in a grand charge up Kettle Hill, the first of the San Juan Heights. The hail of fire coming down the hill was so withering that he had to abandon the horse halfway, and continue on foot. Miraculously no Mausers struck him, and before cresting the top he killed a fleeing Spaniard with his revolver. With a rush the surviving Rough Riders came up and joined him. Now, as thickets of Spanish bullets pranged against the iron sugar-boiling kettle which gave the hill its name, they covered the advance of Regulars up San Juan Hill proper, to their left. But Theodore was not content with this backup activity for long, and soon was leading another charge in support of the general thrust toward Santiago.

The battle raged most of the afternoon. Shrapnel screamed all around; stinging particles of sand whirled in the air; cannonballs plowed up the ground. Of 490 Rough Riders, eighty-six were killed or wounded, the heat prostrated forty, and six were reported missing. But the worst that happened to Theodore was that his elbow was scraped by a bullet. The day ended in victory. For the new Colonel, it had been "aside from Edith, *the* time of my life."[17] A letter from Bob Ferguson, which she received a few days later, confirmed it:

> DEAR MRS. THEODORE
>   . . . No hunting trip so far has ever equalled it in Theodore's eyes . . . when I caught up with him . . . he had just "doubled up a Spanish officer like a Jackrabbit" . . . and all the way down to the next line of entrenchments he encouraged us to "look at these damned Spanish dead!" . . . I really believe firmly now they can't kill him . . . Some of the men insist on his

taking some shelter sometimes, and he is becoming more amenable to discipline.[18]

This last remark at least was music to Edith's ears. Young Ted, who still wanted to act as his father's batman in Cuba, eagerly followed stories of the Santiago campaign in each day's newspapers. When he heard that a piece of shell had ripped his father's shoe heel on San Juan Heights, he issued instructions to "save the boot." Archie, too, followed the news in his fashion. On hearing that the Spanish commander, General José Torral, had agreed to a cease-fire, he promptly told the coachman to go and pick up his father at the station.[19]

In mid-July, Edith's eye alighted on a letter to the editor of the New York *Sun* from three Democrats recommending that the people of New York State nominate Theodore Roosevelt for Governor. She cut it out and sent it to him as a portent of things to come.

With no further battles to dread, Edith could relax somewhat, although the threat of a fatal fever epidemic grew worse every day the army remained in Cuba. But her emotional state was still precarious when, ironically, death struck closer to home. On Friday, July 15, Uncle James A. Roosevelt died in a commuter train. Edith, who had been fond of the old man, did not dare allow herself to weep, for, she confessed to Theodore, "if I once break down all the longing for you and the terrible suspense and loneliness comes over me in a wave that I am helpless against." It was at such moments that she marveled at the endurance of women in the Civil War, "who lived through four years of this."[20]

By July 19, thousands of Spanish bodies rotting in the Cuban heat had spread fever and dysentery through the American regiments. "The mismanagement had been something beyond belief, and the suffering of the troops great in consequence," Theodore wrote Douglas Robinson. "We have no adequate transportation or hospital facilities nor a proper supply of food . . . the few delicacies—if beans and tomatoes can be called such—which they have I had to purchase myself . . . Of the six hundred with whom I landed, less than three hundred are left; the others are dead or in the hospital . . ." The beans, he neglected to add, he had carried eight miles on his own back up a deep mud mountain path.[21]

Theodore worked tirelessly to make his men as comfortable and healthy as possible until they could be shipped out of Cuba. "This fellow worked for his troopers like a cider press," wrote Stephen Crane, correspondent for Pulitzer's *World*. "He tried to feed them. He helped build latrines. He cursed the quartermasters and the— 'dogs'—on the transports to get quinine and grub for them. Let him be a politician if he likes. He was a gentleman down there."[22]

If Theodore Roosevelt was instrumental in some measure in getting the army into Cuba, he now had to exert pressure to have it moved out. A letter he wrote to General Shafter sharply criticizing the War Department's management of troops and supplies was leaked to the press, and caused a national outcry. (This was the most likely reason why Theodore was not later awarded the Medal of Honor, for which he was recommended by his brigade, division, and corps commanders. Edith later wrote that it was "one of the bitter disappointments" of his life.[23])

Coincidental or not to the letter, the army was promptly ordered to sail for Montauk, Long Island.

On Monday, August 15, Edith received a confidential telephone message to come to Montauk. Despite a strict order of quarantine which had been placed over Camp Wickoff, the Rough Rider's billet for the next few weeks, her husband had made special arrangements to see her. She needed no further bidding, but after a five-hour rail journey she was met with the unwelcome news that yellow fever had broken out, making the quarantine even stricter. But having come so far, she was not to be stopped by this. "I carry a picture in my heart always," wrote the *Evening Sun* correspondent Jacob Riis, "of Mrs. Roosevelt hooded and cloaked against a threatening storm on the board seat of an army wagon bound for the Montauk hills, to receive her lover-husband back from the war."[24]

Edith found a young officer who was willing to smuggle Theodore out of the camp for a clandestine reunion. Their meeting was necessarily brief. Afterward all she would say was that Theodore looked well, "but very thin."[25]

That night she stayed in a Red Cross hut. The following day she moved to an unappealing room in a house on a nearby bluff surrounded by wastes of sand and bay bushes. Somehow she managed to inveigle herself into the camp by volunteering as an assistant in the hospital. For the next four days she worked as never before in her life, tending the sick and wounded. For lack of cots, several hundred men were forced to sleep on blankets on the hard wooden floor. There was a shortage of nourishing food. Theodore was told by one freckled nurse that "these sick boys need egg nogs, and we haven't supplies for making them!" He said nothing, but later that day men came up the hill carrying great baskets of eggs, cans of milk, sacks of sugar, a case of brandy and whiskey and a case of champagne addressed to "The Red-Haired Nurse, Diet Tent, Detention Hospital, Montauk."[26]

The beverage was dispensed "with Colonel Roosevelt's compliments," and made the men feel they were back in God's Country. Years later one of the recipients said that "Mr. Roosevelt won many friends and votes that night."[27]

On Saturday, August 20, Theodore was at last free to leave Camp Wickoff temporarily, and return home with his wife for four days' leave. Crowds at Oyster Bay were so enthusiastic that they had to fight their way to a tasseled surrey waiting at the station. As they drove home past their own bank, Edith noticed a display of candles reading "OUR TEDDY."[28]

If the couple expected peace at Sagamore Hill, they were quickly disappointed. Newsmen, politicians, relatives, and neighbors disturbed their once-tranquil hilltop with persistent questions about Theodore's gubernatorial plans. Edith, coming up from a swim one day, was shocked to find "camera fiends" sitting on the fence taking snapshots. "It is something horrid," she told her sister, "but will not last long."[29]

Reporters also pestered the children. One asked Archie, "Where is the Colonel?" "I don't know where the Colonel is," replied the boy, "but Father is taking a bath."[30]

The New York newspapers were lavish in their praise of the hero of San Juan Hill, and almost unanimous in suggesting that he accept the Republican nomination for Governor. Even Senator Thomas Collier Platt, party boss and Theodore's avowed enemy since Police Commissioner days, reluctantly sent a delegate to sound him out. But

Theodore was noncommital. Since his disappointing loss of the mayoralty in 1886, and the crisis over his wanting to run again in 1894, he had been cautious of reentering the political arena. Beside, he had been offered large sums of money by *Scribner's* and other magazines to write his reminiscences of the Cuban campaign—so much, indeed, that Edith said she would be relieved "in a way" if he were not nominated.[31]

Nevertheless Theodore cabled Grant La Farge and Henry Cabot Lodge and asked them to come to Oyster Bay to discuss his prospects. Grant advised him to take the nomination, if offered, because he was destined for "big things." Lodge was still mulling over the pros and cons when Theodore, hearing of renewed sickness at Camp Wickoff, cut short his leave and returned to Montauk.

The children were naturally dying to see the camp and meet the Rough Riders their father talked so much about. So two weeks later, on a perfect September day, Edith took the four eldest on a twenty-four-hour visit with their father. By then quarantine was less strict, and they could move in and out of the camp as they pleased. Alice basked in the admiring glances of the young army officers when she lunched at their mess. That night Ted and Kermit slept in their father's tent, one occupying his cot and the other his air mattress, while the Colonel tried to get a few winks on the hard board table.[32]

Before leaving Montauk Edith paid a last visit to the camp. In her honor, the men raised a new gold-fringed silk flag in place of their old battle-faded and bullet-rent colors.[33]

On September 13, 1898, a month after arriving at Long Island, the Rough Riders were mustered out. Before leaving they presented Theodore with a reproduction of Frederic Remington's bronze *Bronco Buster*. As the men filed by to shake their Colonel's hand in a last farewell, many of them were crying. Theodore's own eyes glistened with tears, and the bronze would remain one of his most prized possessions through life.

The day after he arrived back at Sagamore Hill, he met with Senator Platt at the Fifth Avenue Hotel to discuss his prospects as a gubernatorial candidate. The talk was "entirely satisfactory," Theodore wrote Lodge afterward. "Apparently, I am going to be nominated."[34]

Sixteen

We like being Governor very much thank you.
—Edith Kermit Roosevelt[1]

Edith's private hope that Theodore would now settle down to a quiet literary life was quickly dispelled when, on Monday, October 3, 1898, a committee arrived at Sagamore Hill bringing the official notification of his nomination for Governor. As Theodore stood on the west piazza making his acceptance speech, Edith leaned against the balustrade, smiling, eyes cast down. Only the tightly clasped hands revealed a certain apprehension at being thrust so suddenly into prominence. After the ceremony, she served lunch to thirty people, a gesture which marked the beginning of her own public career.[2]

Simultaneously, the financial clouds which had been hanging over the Roosevelts throughout their twelve years of marriage began to lift. Theodore set to work on a series of high-paying articles on his war experiences, eventually to be published in book form as *The Rough Riders;* the Red Cross reimbursed him the seven hundred dollars he had spent on regimental supplies in Cuba; and Edith rid herself of the lease on the no-longer-needed Washington house for the same price she had paid for it. If Theodore was now elected Governor at a

salary of ten thousand dollars a year, with a house maintained at
state expense included, Edith's account book would at last swing
dramatically into the black.

Strictly speaking, Theodore might well have been ineligible for the
position of Chief Executive of New York State. The law required that
any candidate be a resident of the state for five years preceding his
nomination. But early in March 1898, while Assistant Secretary of
the Navy, Theodore had signed an affidavit declaring Washington his
official residence, in order to avoid paying taxes in New York City.
Fortunately, Elihu Root, a highly respected party member, and wily
legal advocate, spoke up for Theodore at the State Convention. Root
cited an earlier affidavit saying that Roosevelt was a resident of
Oyster Bay. To the relief of the Republican organization this
argument went unchallenged, and Theodore was nominated without
further ado.

On October 5, Edith arrived at a flag-draped Carnegie Hall to
hear her husband launch the gubernatorial campaign. Seven thousand people packed the auditorium to overflowing. They clapped
wildly as Theodore came onto the platform with twelve Rough
Riders, and responded approvingly to his speech about America's
growing role in world affairs—a theme more suited to a national than
a state campaign. "I was glad I had gone," said Edith, who as a rule
preferred to avoid such gatherings. "There was so much enthusiasm
that I had no opportunity of feeling nervous as I usually do when I
hear Theodore."[3]

Rough Riders were again in evidence on October 15, when
Theodore began a train tour of the state. Their flamboyant appeal to
the voters was not lost on his campaign managers. Every stop was
heralded by a bugler sounding a cavalry charge, and spontaneous
oratory was provided by Sergeant Buck Taylor: "Vote for my
Colonel! And he will lead you, as he led us, like sheep to the
slaughter!" The candidate was convinced that such gaffes gained
rather than lost him support.[4]

Theodore campaigned with all his formidable vigor, making 102
speeches in one week alone, most of them in the open air, in grimy
industrial towns. Edith fretted about her husband's exposure to
possible violence. Since Chicago's Haymarket Riot in 1886 a growing
anarchist movement had identified with labor in the United States,
and the threat of assassination was real for an upper-class Re-

publican hero figure like Theodore Roosevelt. At least in Cuba there had been a known enemy. But now, as the New York *Sun* sympathetically remarked, Mrs. Roosevelt "no sooner felt she saw him by Scylla than Charybdis loomed up."[5]

To distract her mind during the anxious weeks before the election, Edith helped Amy Cheney, daughter of the editor of the Oyster Bay *Pilot,* whom Theodore had hired as his temporary secretary. The two women, sometimes assisted by Alice, worked in the third-floor schoolroom. At first Edith found the work fatiguing, but she persevered, and soon took charge. "Miss Cheney is a good stenographer," she told Emily, "but neither she nor Alice are capable of more than the mechanical part."[6] In effect she became her husband's surrogate, sorting and dictating answers to huge quantities of mail.

Under Edith's management, Amy recalled, the atmosphere of Sagamore Hill was "one of order and harmony except when . . . Teddy got too careless with his pet snakes or toads."[7]

Although Bamie was passionately interested in politics, she took no part in the campaign. Crippled and increasingly arthritic, she had amazed both family and friends by falling pregnant at the age of forty-three. Now in her ninth month, she was unable to see her brother on the stump, and regretted that she could not entertain his Republican cronies at policy-making breakfasts at 689. She looked uncomfortably large, and felt understandably nervous at her approaching confinement. "If things should not go rightly," she cautioned Will, "let Edith and Corinne help you . . . they care more for me than any others do and they are the best women I know."[8]

Fortunately, her fears were unfounded. On October 18, Edith received a telegraph urging her to come to town at once, since Mrs. Cowles was in labor. But by the time she arrived her sister-in-law had, with the aid of instruments, given birth to a healthy ten-and-a-half-pound boy. He was named William Sheffield, and, in Edith's opinion, looked "absurdly like his father." Bamie herself was "wonderfully well," so, after three days, Edith returned to Sagamore Hill and resumed her clerical duties.[9]

John Pierpont Morgan, one of the richest men in America, had a reputation for never backing a loser. His last-minute contribution of ten thousand dollars to the Roosevelt campaign set Wall Street's seal of approval upon "the boy candidate," and on November 8 Theodore

Roosevelt defeated the Democratic contender, Augustus Van Wyck, by 17,786 votes. Edith received a jubilant telegram from Joe Murray, Theodore's earliest political mentor: "YOUR HUSBAND WON THE NOMINATION AT SAN JUAN HILL HIS PERSONALITY WON THE ELECTION."

"I have played it in bull luck this summer," Theodore wrote Cecil Spring-Rice. "I know perfectly well that the luck will not continue, and it is not necessary that it should."[10]

In early December, Edith went upstate to look over the Executive Mansion, which was to be her winter home for the next two years at least. Emerging from the station, she felt that Albany, with its domes and spires and rows of elegant town houses, pleasingly resembled a small English cathedral town. Yet it held a painful association for her. She knew that the Tub apartment house, on her left as she drove up State Street toward the Capitol, was where Theodore as a young Assemblyman had roomed with Alice Lee, and that many of his old associates in the Legislature would inevitably be comparing the second Mrs. Roosevelt with memories of her "very charming" predecessor.[11] Edith could only put the past aside, and turn her gaze to the future as the carriage swung south along the top of the hill into Eagle Street. Just ahead, in spacious grounds overlooking the Hudson Valley—and, to her alarm, some insalubrious slums— towered the Governor's residence.

It was a massive three-story structure, profuse with a forty-year accumulation of architectural gingerbread in the form of turrets, cupolas, balconies and porches. Edith had heard from some people that it was the handsomest building in town. Others had told her it was a dreary pile of masonry, full of stuffy rooms. Her own first impression was reassuring: the house was solid and comfortable, with space to spare for all six "bunnies," their pets, and any number of overnight guests.

Mrs. Black, the outgoing Governor's wife, met Edith at the door, and hospitably escorted her on a tour of the house. The first pleasant feature to catch Edith's eye was a huge hall fireplace glowing with logs. She knew Albany to be one of the coldest towns in the country, and was relieved to hear that the furnaces below the carriage house (stoked by three men around the clock, and consuming 350 tons of coal a year) were paid for by the state.

Off the entrance passage to the right was a reception room and

"The house was solid . . . with space to spare for all six 'bunnies.'"
The Executive Mansion, Albany.

music room, and to the left an office. Next to this was a spacious dining room, with seating for thirty-two people. This opened onto a delightful conservatory with views to the south. At the north end of the house was a large drawing room added in the 1880s, with a splendid wood floor for dancing. Nine bedrooms led off from the second-story hall, and a similar number fanned out on the third floor. The kitchen was in the basement. With an annual appropriation of three thousand dollars for repairs and renovation, Edith looked forward to making some improvements, but on her own and Theodore's account she feared that "the entertaining will be expensive."[12]

On their way north after Christmas, the Roosevelts stopped off in New York City to see the Cowleses. Henry Adams later relayed

Bamie's "humorous picture of the military Teddy's march to Albany, tumbling in on her, all the children and nurses dropping with grippe and Edie sweetly drawling that she had forgotten to order cabs, while Teddy had appointed a meeting of politicians and patriots for every hour of the day in her drawing room."[13]

By the time they reached Albany on Friday, December 30, ·Edith, too, was ailing with influenza. During dinner with Governor and Mrs. Black she found the glare of electric light and the effort of keeping up a conversation unbearable, and retired early. The Blacks had already packed their belongings, and they moved out that same evening. The following day, Saturday, Theodore took the Oath of Office privately in the Secretary of State's room. Since January 1 fell on a Sunday, there would be no public ceremony until Monday, giving the family time to settle into their new home.

One of the first to welcome the Roosevelts to Albany was Fanny Smith Dana, now widowed and remarried to James Russell Parsons and living in the capital. Fanny had recently become an author of some note, having published a best-selling book on wildflowers.

She found her old friend pacing up and down the Executive Mansion as though "laboring under the excitement of a new and great experience." Edith was also, no doubt, feverish, but that night she managed to accompany Theodore to a quiet ball in the State Armory. On Sunday morning she attended a service in the Victorian Gothic All Saints' Cathedral, but felt so weak when she arrived home that the doctor ordered her to bed along with the rest of the sick household. Only Theodore was able to accept an invitation to dine at the Parsons'. Garrulous as ever, he stayed so late talking of his future plans that the servants unwittingly locked him out of the Executive Mansion. Not wanting to disturb his ailing family, the new Governor broke a window and climbed through.[14]

Icy cold gripped Albany on Inauguration Day. At breakfast time the temperature was six degrees below zero, and crisp snow half a foot deep enshrouded the city. It was packed so glacier-hard that sleighs climbing the steep hill to the Capitol were in danger, should the horses lose their footing, of hurtling down again. When the Governor's military escort arrived to take him to the swearing-in ceremony, their bugles froze, leaving only drum taps to sound on the still, thin air. But the Inaugural Parade, the most brilliant seen in the State Capitol since the Civil War, warmed the crowd, and their cheers in the snappy temperature made up for the paucity of music.[15]

Edith felt sufficiently well to take her place near the dais in the Assembly Chamber, which was lavishly decorated in a blaze of red, white, blue and gold. Alice, looking very grown-up in pink silk and sable furs, sat next to her. Together they watched Theodore enter to be sworn in as thirty-sixth governor of New York State. He blew a kiss to Ted in the gallery, touching off a storm of applause.[16]

In reply to ex-Governor Black's welcoming address, Theodore made a typically Rooseveltian speech, appealing for practical morality and manly virtue in government. The sentence, "It is absolutely impossible for a Republic long to endure if it becomes either corrupt or cowardly" had the ring of his earlier speeches made as a State Assemblyman eighteen years before. "It was a most solemn and impressive ceremony," Edith wrote Emily later. "I could not look at Theodore or even listen closely or I should have broken down."[17]

Back in the Executive Mansion at two-thirty she braced herself to receive between five and six thousand people waiting in line. She wore, as planned, her white watered-silk dress, with its high chiffon waist. Diamond buttons sparkled on the collar; in one hand she held a bouquet of green and brown orchids, and in the other a bunch of white hyacinths and lilies of the valley. It was clear to the crowds and the newspapermen that this smiling but reserved woman was determined to break with the tiring and, to her, overfamiliar practice of shaking hands with the multitude.[18]

Theodore, dignified in a long frock coat and under-the-collar tie, had no such scruples. He grinned unfailingly as he kept up an average of five words to each handshaker. A double line of soldiers encouraged the guests to move briskly. At the end of two hours, Edith's first major public ordeal was over. Afterward she served tea in the drawing room to a select group of friends and politicians, noting acerbically that while Bamie and Corinne looked well dressed in white and lilac, "Laura and Leila and the other cousins were rather shabby."[19]

Across the room, her husband, as usual in moments of triumph, was forecasting his own political demise. With the Governorship, he told Fanny Parsons, he had "shot his last bolt." He would be humbly satisfied thereafter if he could leave his children "a legacy of work well done."[20]

Edith, still sick, spent most of her first week at Albany in bed. She passed the time writing letters, crocheting, reading Henry Cabot Lodge's recently published *Story of the Revolution,* and browsing through fashions of the 1850s in old *Harper's* magazines. With Alice and Ethel now in the capable hands of an English governess, Quentin and Archie under the stern supervision of Mame, and Ted and Kermit enrolled in the Albany Military Academy, she was freer of everyday responsibilities than at any time since the birth of her first child. As soon as she recovered, therefore, she set about the task of brightening up the neglected mansion, which, Theodore complained, reminded him of a Chicago hotel.[21]

First she replaced some of its "unspeakable" old paintings with more contemporary works by her favorite artists, including La Farge, Bonsel, and Seton Thomas. Rummaging around in numerous nooks and crannies, she found a "really pretty" marble bust, some ornaments for the drawing-room clock, and plenty of good extra furniture, which she distributed throughout the cavernous house. Matching tables and chairs which had strayed from one another over the years were effectively reunited. Later she turned a cloakroom into a bedroom, made space for a schoolroom downstairs, and converted a billiard room on the third floor into a gymnasium for Theodore and the children. "I get a great deal of amusement out of this house," she wrote Emily happily.[22]

When her sister heard of all the creative activity she offered to come over from Italy and "help." But Edith, suspecting that Emily might be hoping for a permanent place in the bosom of the newly prosperous family, declined with surprising harshness. "I certainly do not want you to come home," she wrote, "as you do not care for America and Americans and with the new responsibilities of this position on my hands I have to be selfish to attend to everything properly."[23]

It had taken many years to rid herself of guilt about her spinster sister. But if fate had led them along different paths, that was Emily's misfortune. Adding insult to injury, Edith condescendingly promised to send over some old gowns at the end of the season, because "in such a small place as this I feel I should not appear in exactly the same garments two years in succession."[24]

After such discouraging signals from her nearest relative, Emily seems to have decided to make a permanent home in Italy. She rented a small villa on a hill overlooking the Mediterranean near Genoa, and seriously considered proposals from at least two doubtful suitors. But Edith, realizing that Emily was not in love, advised caution. While happy married life was "far better in every way for a woman than independence," she wrote, an unsuitable match could be "hell on earth." Single life, on the other hand, might "never be worse than lonely."[25]

During his first session as Governor, Theodore was in frequent conflict with the New York State Republican machine, led by Senator Thomas Collier Platt. Roosevelt won many of these encounters with the wily, arthritic boss, but good-humoredly accepted defeat when politics made it inevitable. One important success for Theodore was the appointment of his own nominee to administer the Erie Canal, which had hitherto been a corrupt source of political patronage. He also strong-armed the Legislature into passing a bill that ended the tax-free advantage of corporations enjoying state franchises. Platt angrily warned that this could result in a loss of campaign contributions, should Theodore decide to run for a second term. The Governor paid no heed to this thinly veiled threat.

Administrative work consumed long hours and left Theodore little time for relaxation. Until Edith had the Executive Mansion gymnasium ready, his only exercise came from walking along Eagle Street to the Capitol, and running up the 117 marble steps to his second-floor office. He was delighted when workers installed a horizontal bar and a punching bag, and soon was in such trim that he invited Mike Donovan, Director of the New York Athletic Club, to spar with him.[26]

Although Albany's social life did not compare in sophistication to that of Washington, Edith enjoyed the little Hudson town in many different ways, throwing herself into various activities with the energy of a teenager. She joined the Friday Morning Club, an organization of intellectual young women who amused themselves by reading prepared papers on topical subjects. As winter eased its icy grip on the countryside she went on long botanical rambles with Fanny Parsons, and helped her collect rare specimens. Edith had a quick eye for unusual plants, but having collected one, she moved on rapidly to the next. Fanny, who liked to linger, had difficulty in keeping pace with her restless step.[27]

At official functions Edith danced many "giddy" cotillions with

Theodore's aides, and afterward would tuck the favors she received under the boys' pillows. When small-town culture palled, she would board a train for Washington to spend a few days with the Lodges, or go to New York City for a revitalizing round of opera and theater. That season she saw Henry Irving and Ellen Terry in Shakespeare, and a new production of *Cyrano de Bergerac*. The latter, she casually assured Emily, "lost greatly in translation."[28]

When the Governor had an appointment in New York with Senator Platt, he and Edith stayed at 689 Madison Avenue. After Bamie moved to Washington later that year to be near Will at the Navy Department, they stayed with Corinne at 422. Here, while Edith had breakfast in her room, Theodore would join his sister and a dozen or so friends downstairs, talking and eating prodigiously, and consuming cup after cup of heavily sweetened coffee. "I'm not hungry," he used to say, "but thank God I'm greedy." Then, with an expression of mock guilt on his face, he would point to the ceiling and say, "I feel Edie's stern disapproval trickling down from the third floor."[29]

It was no secret that Theodore adored his wife and coveted her favor. She, in turn, loved him as intensely as always. But her perceptive niece, "Corinney" Robinson, noticed signs of great possessiveness. "She . . . seemed to me, as a child, to dominate him by withholding the outward and visible signs [of affection]." The girl also found her aunt remote, and "as calm and imperturbable as a Buddha." The timbre of Edith's voice was high and incisive, well modulated with cultivated English tones, and her words could be lightly sarcastic. "You do not like books the way our children do," she would say, smiling, "but I hear, my dear, you like to dance." Such a remark gave little Corinney the instant feeling that she "belonged to a class of morons who were uselessly frivolous."[30]

Bamie's son, Sheffield, was also "rather terrified" of his Aunt Edith. "She was a brilliant and erudite woman, but I mistrusted what she would say of us the minute she left the room." Even adults were in awe of her. "The only person I ever knew Auntie Bye to be a little afraid of was Aunt Edith," said another relative. Both Bamie and Corinne "were watching their Ps and Qs a little bit when they were with her." Once Edith decided she disliked a person it was impossible to win back her good graces. "Mother never took any prisoners," one of her children observed.[31]

These, however, were the subjective views of family intimates. To friends such as Fanny Parsons, Edith in her Albany years was "especially pretty" and "greatly admired." To Elizabeth Cameron she appeared "absurdly young-looking" in spite of her "necessary queenliness." The devoted Springy, languishing in Persia, followed her progress with fascination. "I wish I could see you at an official reception," he wrote. "Perhaps I may live to kiss your hand at the White House." [32]

Entertainments in the Albany mansion ran smoothly under the management of Theodore's aide Colonel Treadwell. He took care of the food, seating arrangements, and music, while Edith supervised the flowers. She liked to choose striking combinations of spring hyacinths, tulips and daffodils, and summer carnations, roses and maidenhair, all grown in the greenhouses on the grounds.

Sometimes the children were allowed to sit at the top of the stairs to watch the guests and listen to the musical ensemble. But they were not always satisfied with such docile amusement. During one function they climbed down from their bedrooms into the gardens, and were caught snowballing in their pajamas. On another occasion they planted a billiard ball in a bowl of luscious-looking plums on the dining table, causing one absent-minded guest to nearly crack his teeth. One warm spring night, as Edith entertained a fashionable crowd in the executive drawing room, she was appalled to smell a powerful zoological odor wafting up from downstairs. Investigation disclosed that it represented the accumulated winter droppings of several dozen pet rabbits, hamsters, and guinea pigs, which the children housed in the cellar.

The guinea pigs were named after real people, without regard to sex. There were, for example, the clerics Bishop Doane and Father O'Grady, and the military men Admiral Dewey and Fighting Bob Evans. One day Archie burst in on his parents and their guests shouting excitedly, "Father, Father, Bishop Doane has had twins!" [33]

A gift from Theodore's West Virginia Republican supporters of a small bear to Alice increased the animal population downstairs. It was named Jonathan Edwards, after Edith's ancestor, since, according to Theodore, it showed "a distinctly Calvinistic turn of mind." [34]

Gifford Pinchot, Chief Forester of the United States, once arrived for an overnight stay to find the Executive Mansion "under ferocious attack from a band of invisible Indians, and the Governor of the Empire State was helping a houseful of children to escape by lowering them out of a second-story window on a rope." After the children had been "saved," the athletic Pinchot proved his own worth by knocking Roosevelt "off his very solid pins" in a boxing match. Only then did the two men get down to a scheduled discussion of forestry.[35]

Given her natural reserve, Edith was surprisingly tolerant of her children's more embarrassing pranks. When Kermit set up a row of clay devils beside him in her church pew, and pulled out a baby tooth during the sermon, holding the gory specimen up for all to see, she feigned absorption in prayer.[36]

All the children enjoyed life in Albany, with the exception of fifteen-year-old Alice, who grew prettier and more flirtatious daily, and found the stolid old Dutch capital unexciting. "She cares neither for athletics nor good works," her stepmother wrote, "the two resources of youth in this town!"[37] There had been talk of sending Alice to Miss Spence's School in New York City, but she rebelled against any form of regimentation, and threatened to do something "disgraceful" until her parents abandoned the idea. When she decided against being confirmed, Theodore and Edith, who believed that their children should be encouraged to think for themselves, did not insist.

Alice longed to be grown up, and liked nothing more than to wear a bridesmaid's dress, which made her look eighteen. Edith, sensing that her stepdaughter would blossom brilliantly in a state debut, hoped that Theodore would be elected for a second term in 1900, so that Alice could be "brought out" with appropriate pomp and circumstance in the Executive Mansion.[38]

After a long and harshly cold winter, ice gorges began to lumber downriver, and spring at last arrived. The legislative session ended on April 28, and Theodore joined his wife and four older children for a celebratory picnic in the Hudson countryside. Wearing a sports skirt and blouse, Edith tramped through the pine woods delighting in the first trailing arbutus, delicate-flowered hepaticus and clusters of rare sweet-scented white violets. At lunch time she built a fire, roasted jacketed potatoes, and then rested under a tree before heading home hot, sunburned, and dusty. This was the kind of excursion she loved, and it left her feeling in avowedly better health than she had ever been in her life.[39]

School ended for Ted and Kermit on June 9, and the next day

"All the children enjoyed life in Albany,
with the exception . . . of Alice."
From left, Ted (seated), Ethel, Alice, Quentin, Kermit, Archie.

Edith moved her household to Oyster Bay. Later in the month Theodore traveled to Las Vegas, New Mexico, for the first Rough Riders' reunion. People greeted him with the noisy enthusiasm usually afforded presidential candidates. "My reception caused some talk," he confided to Henry Cabot Lodge, "so I thought it better to come out in an interview that of course I was for President McKinley's renomination."[40]

The "talk" then changed to his prospects of the vice-presidential spot on a McKinley-Roosevelt ticket. Theodore had no objection to this at first, but Edith was decidedly against it. She liked her roomy Albany mansion, and the handsome allowance that went with it, not to mention Theodore's salary of ten thousand dollars. As Vice-President he would earn two thousand less, and would not even be provided with a house. To Edith, enjoying her new-found prosperity and security, such a sacrifice was best not contemplated. In any case, the prospect was highly unlikely, since Vice-President Garret A. Hobart would most probably run again.

While Theodore was out West, Sagamore Hill began to fill up with summer guests. Among them was Arthur Lee, the young English Army Captain Edith had met in Florida. After the war he had fallen in love with Ruth Moore, the pretty eldest daughter of a founder of the Chase Manhattan Bank. He was reluctant to return home until he had won her. Edith found Lee an agreeable substitute for Spring-Rice: refined in manner, sensitive to women, knowledgeable about art, and well versed in literature and politics.

In Theodore's absence she entertained rather more grandly than had been her usual practice. She hired a launch to transport her guests to a clambake in Huntington Harbor, and invited them to dine at the swell Seawanhaka Yacht Club in Oyster Bay, which Alice had already given the seal of her sophisticated approval.

Theodore arrived home in time for the July Fourth celebrations. He made a speech in the village, and in the evening neighborhood children came to Sagamore Hill for a pyrotechnical display. The *pièce de résistance* was an enormous firework likeness of the Governor himself, and its ignition was accompanied by a regal salute of twenty-one bombs.[41]

With a few spare weeks on his hands, Theodore decided he would now write a life of Oliver Cromwell.[42]

Becoming less and less reclusive as her enjoyment of the position of First Lady of the State grew, Edith went with Theodore on September 28 to greet Admiral Dewey, the returning hero of the battle of Manila, on his triumphant arrival in New York Harbor. She was welcomed aboard the S.S. *Olympia* by the "small active nervous" admiral, who after lunch proudly pointed out shell holes in his sister ship *Indiana*.[43]

One of the unexpected advantages of Theodore's new job was that Edith was able to be with him on many public occasions, with the result that they saw more of each other now than they had since the early days of their marriage. She accompanied him on visits to county fairs, showing the enthusiasm of a seasoned campaigner, sat in his box at concerts, stood at his side at numberless receptions, and entertained a variety of official and foreign guests, including the Governor-General of Canada, Lord Minto, and a rude young English war correspondent named Winston Churchill.[44] Theodore's growing appreciation of Edith as a political ally and helpmeet was apparent in a letter he wrote Arthur Lee that fall, congratulating him on his engagement to Ruth:

> There is nothing in the world—no possible success, military or political which is worth weighing in the balance for one moment against the happiness that comes to those fortunate enough to make a real love-match—a match in which lover and sweetheart will never be lost in husband or wife. I know what I am writing about, for I am just as much devoted to Mrs. Roosevelt now as ever I was—

Here Edith came in and interrupted the eulogy.[45]

Although Theodore seldom remembered his wife's birthday ("He did not know me at that time," Edith wryly explained), he always acknowledged their wedding anniversary on December 2, and was determined to do so lavishly in the year 1899. She was unusually hard to please when it came to gifts. It was her contention that if people took the trouble to know her and her tastes they would not go wrong. If they failed, she felt misjudged, and could make her displeasure felt

"It is the only photograph of Edith that I have ever cared for."
The "goddess" picture, 1900.

merely by the way she eyed the present. From the family and close friends she prized small, old, exotic things, such as decorative moccasins, a tiny gold Aztec frog, an antique pewter sardine server. For official gifts she understandably preferred things "of perishable nature," like a crate of juicy pears, a box of wild rice, or a sack of Indian corn. Theodore was consequently a little apprehensive as he gave his wife an expensive blue-faced watch in celebration of their thirteenth anniversary. But he need not have worried. Never, he told Lodge, who helped him choose it, had Edith liked a present so much.[46]

Her approval of the gift reflected a general feeling of personal warmth and well-being at this time. Both home life and public career were entirely satisfying, and for once she had money to spare. (Theodore was able to save all his salary as Governor, because of the high fees he now commanded for his articles and books). Yet a little nostalgia crept into one of Edith's letters to Cecil Spring-Rice. "I cannot describe the feeling," she wrote, "with which I look back to those years in Washington when we were all young." It was flattering at thirty-eight to be so often complimented on her youthful appearance, but "it is one thing to look young,—and quite another to be young."[47]

On December 17, Edith went to New York City to meet her sister, who had at last been invited to spend some time in Albany. Bob Ferguson also joined the Roosevelts for Christmas in the Executive Mansion, which followed well-established rituals. Emily, in spite of the apparent failure of her most recent romance, was in good spirits, and chatted happily with Edith as they all sat round the yule-log fire. Bob, on the other hand, brooded on Britain's prospects in the Boer War, while Theodore speculated about his political future. What he would most like, as he wrote Springy, was the Governorship of the Philippines. Alice hoped for that, too. She dreamed of living in Manila "among the palm trees in a 'palace' surrounded by young officers in white uniforms." But privately Theodore confided to Henry Cabot Lodge an even greater dream of his own. Vice-President Hobart had just died: this meant that if President McKinley were in turn to die "tomorrow" he, Theodore Roosevelt, might be "seriously *considered* as his successor."[48]

His immediate prospects, however, were rather less grand. Pressure was mounting for him to take Hobart's place on the Republican ticket next year. Edith was still against this, and Lodge, though he had no doubt that Theodore would one day be President of the United States, was reluctant "to urge him to follow a course in the slightest degree against his judgment." As for the Governor himself, he had no firm idea on the matter, beyond musing that the Vice-Presidency might be a good steppingstone to the Presidency in 1904. But he knew that American political life was like "a kaleidescope" and was capable of throwing up many new and talented men between now and then.[49]

The year 1900, Edith's second in Albany, began with a customary formality, the New Year's Day reception. Senator Platt, by staying away, showed his disapproval of Theodore's forthcoming legislative plans to regulate large corporations and make statements of their earnings available to the public. To the conservative leader, Roosevelt's intentions were alarmingly socialistic. It was therefore desirable, in Platt's opinion, that the Governor be nominated this coming

June for the politically powerless position of Vice-President.

But he did not take into account the influence of Roosevelt's strong-willed wife, working, as always, behind the scenes. Before January was out Theodore began to express reservations, mainly financial ones. "Even to live simply as Vice-President," he explained to Lodge, "would be a serious strain upon me, and would cause me, and especially would cause Edith, continual anxiety about money." To forestall a movement on his behalf, Theodore went on, he intended to declare publicly that he would be a candidate in the fall only for another term as Governor. McKinley would have to look elsewhere for a running mate. "Edith bids me to say," he concluded, "that she hopes you will forgive her!"[50]

Confident that the matter of the Vice-Presidency was settled, Edith left with Emily on March 7 for a visit to Cuba, now under United States protection. She wanted to see for herself, she joked, just how formidable a hill San Juan really was.

As her ship steamed into Havana Harbor on March 10, Edith thrilled with patriotic pride at the sight of Old Glory streaming above Morro Castle. The Governor-General of Cuba, who was none other than Leonard Wood, waited at the gangplank for their disembarkation, and took them to his official palace. For the next two weeks Edith and Emily luxuriated in southern sunshine, and enjoyed their V.I.P. status as General Wood's guests. Courteous guides ferried them all over the island, which, although scarred by war, was still the most beautiful in the Caribbean. This was Edith's first experience of the tropics, and she became instantly addicted to the sight of palm and orange groves, banana and breadfruit trees, waving fields of sugarcane, "the bright flowers, the blue and pink houses . . . the brown skinned people with soft dark eyes, and the women draped with mantillas."[51]

As for Theodore's renowned incline, it was neither as impressive nor as steep as she had been led to expect. "It looks so quiet now," she wrote Ethel, "and in the trenches our soldiers have made nice little gardens of lettuce and radishes."[52]

Edith returned to Albany rested and refreshed after almost a month away. Travel obviously agreed with her. She looked, said her doting husband, "just like a girl."[53]

The Republican National Convention was only six weeks off when Edith and Theodore arrived in Washington on May 8, 1900, for a four-day visit. L'Enfant's white city was at its loveliest, with dogwood blooming in the squares, but tension over Theodore's prospects of becoming his party's vice-presidential nominee hung in the air. His name was on everybody's lips, much to Edith's distress. Theodore still hoped for a further term as Governor, and tried to ascertain if Washington's "inner circle" was as anxious to have him on the ticket as state party members seemed to be.

The Roosevelts met the Lodges, the Hays, and the Roots, and dined with President McKinley himself. "I felt rather puffed up at the White House," Edith wrote Fanny Parsons, "when I realized how very much younger Theodore and I were than any of the other prominent people." [54]

In spite of her reluctance to have Theodore's name on the Republican ticket, Edith had already reserved a box for herself at the Convention hall in Philadelphia. "As I have never attended a National Convention," she told Judge Alton B. Parker, a dinner guest back in Albany, "I am expecting to have a good time."

"Oh!" replied Parker, "you will have the most wonderful time of your life . . . Just a bit late, you will see your handsome husband come in and bedlam will at once break loose, and he will receive such a demonstration of applause from the thousands of delegates and guests as no one else will receive. And being a devoted wife, you will be very proud and happy . . . You will see your husband unanimously nominated for the office of Vice-President of the United States, and—"

"You disagreeable thing," Edith interrupted, "I don't want to see him nominated for the Vice-Presidency!"

Her anxiety was so apparent that the judge afterward regretted his prophetic remarks. "In common with the men in Albany at that time, I held her in high regard." [55]

Edith and Theodore arrived in Philadelphia on June 16, 1900, and checked into the Hotel Walton. From the outset they were pestered by Western delegates who roamed the corridors playing fifes and drums and chanting, "We Want Teddy! We Want Teddy!" The bedlam continued for most of the next week. Edith could only beg Theodore to say nothing that would damage his chances of remaining Governor. She helped him and some friends draft a statement designed to forestall a Roosevelt stampede. The essence of it was that he could best serve the party and the public by remaining Governor of New York State.[56]

On Thursday, June 21, the climactic day of the Convention, Edith took her seat in the gallery box, looking pale in a black hat, a black skirt and a pink silk shirtwaist. Reporters scrutinized her intently. "She is not according to artistic standards a beautiful woman," wrote the *World* correspondent, "but she would be at any time an interesting one."[57]

Just as Judge Parker had predicted, Theodore entered the hall "a bit late," and strode to his place with the New York delegates below her, wearing a broad-brimmed hat craftily reminiscent of Cuba. His appearance brought loud and prolonged applause—much to the annoyance of Party Chairman Marcus Alonzo Hanna. "Don't you realize," he chastized Roosevelt supporters, "that there's only one life between this madman and the White House?"[58]

More thunderous shouts and clapping greeted Theodore as, jaw set firmly, he mounted the platform to make a speech seconding McKinley's renomination. Catching a glimpse of Edith in the gallery, he waved reassuringly at her. "As he did so," reported the New York *Tribune*, "the sun broke through an opening in the roof and its rays played for a moment like an aureole about his head. He actually flushed, but for a moment only, and then he faced the shouting throng once more. For the first time, practically, the real hero of the convention stood in full view of the admiring thousands."[59]

Theodore's nomination as Vice-Presdient was now inevitable. As a loyal Republican, he could not possibly resist it. "Roosevelt might as well stand under Niagara Falls and try to spit water back," said Platt. When McKinley told Hanna that he had no objection to Theodore as his running mate, the Chairman retorted: "Your duty to the country is to *live* four years from next March."[60]

As the band struck up Theodore's theme tune "There'll Be a Hot Time in the Old Town Tonight," he glanced up again at Edith. "With just a little gasp of regret," noted one reporter, "Mrs. Roosevelt's face broke into smiles, as she, once for all, accepted the situation with a grace worthy of a true patriot."[61]

Seventeen

I ought to find out why those men are going up the trail.
—Edith Kermit Roosevelt[1]

Everybody was talking about "the fabulous Roosevelts" when they arrived in Washington two days before the Inauguration. The capital, after a winter lean in White House functions, was starved for glamor and excitement, and looked to the handsome vice-presidential family to provide it.[2]

The last six months had been exceptionally busy ones for Edith. While Theodore campaigned for the continued occupation of the Philippines and against the policy of free silver, she pasted up his news clippings, sorted his mail, prepared Ted for Groton, and deposited the boy there at the end of October. On November 6, President McKinley and "gallopin'" Teddy defeated the Democratic ticket of William Jennings Bryan and Adlai E. Stevenson by 849,000 votes. The strain of Theodore's absence in the campaign, and the prospect of having him "in such a useless and empty position" as Vice-President, caused Edith to lose weight to the point where her neck bones showed. Theodore, however, preferred her thin and told Emily she looked "prettier than ever."[3]

As 1900 came to an end Edith received for the last time in Albany, and, feeling "rather blue," moved out of the Executive Mansion "where we have been so happy."[4] As the twentieth century began, she nursed Ted through asthma and bronchitis, took Quentin to New York for the removal of his adenoids, skated with Alice, coasted with Archie, planted hyacinths with Ethel, and read *Rob Roy* and *The Legend of Montrose* to Kermit. Conscious of her growing historical importance as the wife of a public figure, she began to keep a daily diary, a practice she would continue almost without interruption until the last years of her life.

In February, Theodore left for a seven-week hunting trip in the Rockies. Besides writing to him almost daily, she attended the village sewing guild, took German lessons, heard Melba at the Met, negotiated the rental of the Storers' house in the capital for three thousand dollars a year, and engaged a private railroad car to take the family to Washington for the Inaugural ceremonies.

The Douglas Robinsons, Uncle James Gracie, Bob Ferguson, Theodore's Albany secretary William Loeb, and his colored valet Pinckney all traveled south with the Roosevelts on March 2. Edith had arranged for a lunch of cold meat, baked potatoes, fruit, milk and coffee to be served en route, and asked the railroad company to send her the bill. This practice of always paying personal expenses, even when on public business, was one day to earn Theodore Roosevelt the accolade of being "the only President who ever *insisted* on paying a doctor's bill."[5]

Edith planned to spend just two full days in Washington before returning to Oyster Bay for the spring and summer. So she stayed at Bamie's newly rented Victorian row house at 1733 N Street, near Connecticut Avenue.

On Monday, March 4, Inauguration Day, Edith came downstairs to the parlor and found workmen erecting a gigantic floor-to-ceiling floral tribute to Theodore from an anonymous donor. The lavishness of this three-thousand-dollar arrangement shocked Edith's Puritan scruples, and its size left scant room for the Roosevelts, Lodges, Hays and Roots when they assembled for a champagne breakfast. At ten-thirty a military guard formed in the narrow street outside to escort the Vice-President-elect to the Capitol. The others prepared to follow in barouches half an hour later. Quentin stated flatly that he did not intend to go and "hear Father pray at the Senate."[6] Mindful of her son's further threat to talk throughout the ceremony if forced to go, Edith sensibly left him with Pinckney.

Rain was falling as her closed carriage drew up at the Senate

Chamber. When she entered the gallery to take her seat for the swearing-in, Washington's newspapermen obviously did not recognize her, or mistook somebody else in the party for Mrs. Roosevelt. One reporter noted that she was wearing a dark tight-fitting suit and velvet toque, while another described her dress as light tan trimmed with blue velvet and brown fur, and worn with a chiffon hat. Throughout her official life Edith was to frustrate the press in its efforts to capture her elusive looks and personality. Ted, who had been instructed to bring his smartest clothes from Groton, wore odd trousers, vest and jacket—the three best pieces from three different suits. Ethel's and Kermit's clothing was scarcely visible under a profusion of McKinley-Roosevelt campaign buttons, flags, and other assorted emblems.

Edith felt proud as Theodore, looking tanned and "so young and handsome" in his well-fitting frock coat and red carnation buttonhole, entered the Chamber. Quiet and very dignified, he took the oath in an uncharacteristically low but distinct voice. His more familiar high staccato tones were heard in the rousing imperialistic speech which followed. "A great work lies ready to the hand of this generation," he prophesied. "As we do well or ill, so shall mankind in the future be raised or cast down." [7]

When she emerged into the still-falling rain, Edith found that she was under the protection now of a special policeman. He summoned a cab to take her to the White House for lunch. President McKinley, standing portly and jovial beside his invalid wife's chair, greeted her warmly. Brilliant diamonds sparkled in Ida McKinley's wispy hair, but her eyes were dull with sedation. During the lunch she sat as usual directly to the right of the President, so that he could act quickly to cover her face with a napkin, should she be struck by an epileptic convulsion.

Quentin, who had been brought on by Pinckney, was in no better mood. Asked by Mrs. Root if he knew what his father now was, he replied, "Just Father." [12] Ted, in contrast, enjoyed himself hugely. He downed two glasses of champagne, thinking it was fizzy water, with no apparent ill effects, "which speaks volumes," said Edith, "either for Ted's head or the President's champagne." [8]

After lunch, Edith took the children to Thompson's Drug Store at the corner of Fifteenth Street and Pennsylvania Avenue. Here, for two hundred dollars, she had rented a room three flights up to watch the Inaugural Parade. The rain had stopped, but there was still no sun when the presidential carriage hove into view. Theodore followed in another coach, and Edith could barely restrain the younger children from falling out of the window in their excitement. The ambitious Alice, however, who looked on President and Mrs. McKinley as "usurping cuckoos,"[9] was more thoughtful. As she compared McKinley's embonpoint and pallid complexion with her father's bronzed flesh and taut figure, she could not help wondering if the President could survive a second term.

That night, dressed in a white, silver and chenille-embroidered dress and train, and carrying a large bunch of violets, Edith took her seat in the presidential box in the gallery of the Pension Office Building for the Inaugural Ball. Below, in the vast hall, electric lights shimmered on the pale yellow draperies as a thousand dancers circled the great central mound of ferns and pink flowers. Mrs. McKinley, in a stunning gown of pearl-embroidered satin, was too frail to dance. Alice, who yearned to join the whirling throng, and resented having to wear a childish white point-d'esprit dress, perched unselfconsciously on the arm of the First Lady's chair. After an hour or so, the presidential party retired for supper and early bed. Edith was not sorry, for she had reserved a car on the ten-o'clock train for New York next morning. Theodore would stay behind to preside over the Senate until the session ended in four days' time. Then, his vice-presidential duties over until the fall, he would join the family at Oyster Bay. "I really enjoyed the trip," Edith told her sister. She had been full of forebodings, but now "felt happy that all had gone so well . . ."[10]

By April she found Theodore already restless and complaining that the Vice-Presidency "ought to be abolished." At least he could divert himself with letters describing the civilian escapades of his regiment. Some Rough Riders were always in need of money for dubious purposes, which they did not hesitate to "borrow." Others had homicidal problems. "Dear Colonel," one reported, "I write you because I am in trouble. I have shot a lady in the eye. But Colonel I did not mean to shoot that lady. It was all an accident, *for I was shooting at my wife.*" Such letters led Edith to feel, from time to time, that she and Theodore were "the parents of a thousand very large and very bad children."[11]

In May, Fanny and Jim Parsons visited Oyster Bay for a weekend. Fanny remembered that Sagamore Hill "was at its loveliest, with the orchard bursting into bloom and the woods speckled with the spreading wraith-like branches of the flowering dogwood." Theodore was his usual vital and stimulating self, but Fanny discerned a change in him. "The spur of combat was absent. It was another atmosphere."[12] Edith, on the other hand, seemed happy and carefree. For the first time in six years, she was enjoying an uninterrupted idyll with her husband.

Later in the month, the Roosevelts went to the opening of the Pan-American Exposition in Buffalo. Here Edith particularly admired the St. Gaudens statue of Sherman, and Cecilia Beaux' beautiful brushwork in a picture of the Gilder children.[13] Theodore, meanwhile, powwowed with Indians, and Alice "rolled around on the backs of camels," and watched the hoochee-koochee, a dance which soon caught on in fashionable circles.

On the way home they stopped for a few days with the Wadsworths in Geneseo. Luxuriating in her temporary freedom from domestic responsibilities, Edith roamed through woods studded with wild phlox and late ferns. When it rained, she buried herself happily in books.

That summer Edith acquired a brown mare, which she named Yagenka, after the heroine of a romance by Sienkiewicz. Wearing a blue cloth riding habit and a black fedora, or a straw hat and veil, she rode out with Theodore in good weather or bad, her preferred speed being "a good smart gallop." Since she did not hunt to hounds, Edith could not be called a first-rate horsewoman; but she had responsive hands, and controlled her mount expertly.[14]

It was not, as it happened, a summer without trials. Archie caught chicken pox, Quentin somehow managed to lodge a mothball up his nose, and Edith had a bout with poison ivy. Things grew more serious in August, when Alice, who had been visiting friends, came home with an abscess in her jaw and loose front teeth. She thought it was the result of being kicked at a dance. Edith rushed her to Roosevelt Hospital in New York. Doctors there wanted to remove the teeth, but Edith "insisted on saving them."[15] She did not want her daughter to make her début with dentures. Next, Theodore came back from hunting in Colorado, suffering from bronchitis, and

"She rode out with Theodore . . .
her preferred speed being 'a good smart gallop.'"
Edith on Yagenka.

Quentin followed Alice into the hospital with an infected ear. It was a trying time for Edith, and when everyone had recovered. she treated herself to a below-the-knee Louis XV–style black taffeta coat with lace at the collar and cuffs.

At the end of August Theodore left on a speaking tour, while Edith took the children to the Adirondack Mountains, where she had rented a four-room cottage facing the Tahawus Club for a two-week vacation. The weather was rainy and cool; for the first day or two Edith wrote letters, Archie chatted to no one in particular, and the others curled up with books in front of the open fire.

On September 7 Edith and Ethel set out for a friend's lakeside camp, where Theodore, returning from his trip, had promised to meet them for lunch. But at the Lower Works, a horse-watering place en route, Edith found a telephone message waiting for her. It was from Theodore, telling her that he would not be able to keep their rendezvous. President McKinley had been shot.

A crazed Pole had approached the President at the Pan-American Exposition in Buffalo, carrying a gun concealed beneath a hand-kerchief. McKinley was not dead, but the wound was serious, and Theodore had been summoned to his bedside.

Edith was appalled and bewildered. "The President is not a man to inspire personal hatred . . . it must be an anarchist."[16] Shaken, she continued on to the camp, through country "as wild as if the Indians still lived there."[17]

Next morning, Sunday, Theodore telegraphed to say McKinley was so much better that he now felt free to begin his interrupted vacation. Three suspenseful days later, he arrived at Tahawus. On Thursday, September 12, the Vice-President joined Edith, Ethel, Miss Young, and three friendly youths on an excursion to Camp Colden, five or six miles away. In spite of rain, the tramp through rough woodland was stimulating, and they all had a good appetite for supper. They ate in front of a blazing fire, then stretched out to sleep on balsam-bough cots in log huts nearby.

After breakfast the following morning the men went on to climb the 5,344-foot Mount Marcy, while Edith and the others started back to the club. On the way they met two guides coming toward them. The men hurried past, saying only that they had a message for "one of the Marcy party."[18] Edith was on the point of calling after them, but the men were already moving out of earshot.

Back at Tahawus, she learned that President McKinley had suffered a relapse. Theodore arrived at about six that evening, damp, bedraggled, and hungry. He sent at once to the Lower Works for the latest news from Buffalo. After dinner there was still no word from below. At nine the Vice-President went to bed, saying to Edith, "I'm not going unless I'm really needed. I have been there once and that shows how I feel. But I will not go to stand beside those people who are suffering and anxious."[19]

While Edith and Theodore slept, Corinne Roosevelt Robinson's house in Orange, New Jersey, was besieged by reporters wanting to

"At Tahawus she learned that President McKinley had suffered a relapse."
McNaughton's Cottage on Mt. Marcy.

know where her brother could be found. Exhausted from answering their questions, Corinne withdrew to her writing room and tried to relax by looking through a box of old letters Edith had written years before. She picked one out at random. It was dated Washington, 1877, and read:

DEAREST CORINNE:

Today for the first time I went to the White House. Oh, how much I wished for you. It seemed so wonderful to me to be in the old mansion which had been the home of President Lincoln, and which is so connected with all our country's history. It gave me a feeling of awe and excitement. I wish you could have been here to share the

feeling with me, for I don't suppose it is likely that we
shall ever be in the White House together, and it would
have been so interesting to have exchanged our memories of things that had happened in that wonderful old
house. But how unlikely it is that you or I shall ever
come in contact with anything connected with the White
House. . . .[20]

Shortly before midnight, Edith and Theodore were awakened by
loud knocking. Fresh dispatches brought the news that President
McKinley's condition was critical. Theodore left immediately on a
buckboard. Relays of fresh horses had been arranged at intervals
along the dark, precipitous mountain road to North Creek, thirty-five
miles away. There a special train was waiting to speed him to
Buffalo.

After breakfast, Edith bundled the children into a carryall cart and
followed the same bumpy route that Theodore had traveled a few
hours earlier. The vacation was over anyway, and not a moment too
soon: Archie was feeling wretched with tonsilitis, and Quentin had
earache again. They clamored for their mother's attention while she
tried to unravel her tangled thoughts. As the cart pulled in at the
Lower Works, she was handed a message: "PRESIDENT MCKINLEY
DIED AT 2:15 THIS MORNING. THEODORE ROOSEVELT."[21]

That was all. The formal signature spoke volumes. At forty-two,
Theodore Roosevelt had become the twenty-sixth President of the
United States, the youngest man ever to hold that office. At forty,
Edith Kermit Roosevelt was now the First Lady of the land.

An overwhelming feeling of tiredness and apprehension swept over
Edith as she transferred her young charges to a train at North Creek
for the second leg of their long journey home. Fears for Theodore's
safety, anxiety about the children, and regrets for the lack of privacy
which would now be their lot were uppermost in her mind.

At 6 P.M. the train pulled in at Saratoga Springs. A reporter
brought Edith the news that Theodore had taken the Oath of Office
that afternoon in the Wilcox house in Buffalo in the presence of the
majority of the McKinley Cabinet.

But even at this most dramatic moment of her life, Edith was
confronted with the mundane responsibilities of a wife and mother.

At Albany she shunted her party on board the Hudson River night boat to Manhattan. It did not arrive at Canal Street until early Sunday morning. By then they had been traveling nonstop for twenty-four hours. Bone-weary as she was, Edith could not go on to Oyster Bay immediately, since she had to search out an aurist for her youngest son. "Small pebble came out of Quentin's ear," she noted afterward, in amused relief.[22]

It was lunchtime before she at last reached Sagamore Hill and sought out the solacing company of Aunt Lizzie. As Edith unburdened herself of the conflicting emotions of hopes fulfilled and fears for the future, she knew she could count on the old widow's sympathy and understanding.

Friends reacted promptly. "Just suppose Theodore had refused the Vice-Presidency," Winty Chanler speculated, "and some stuffed dummy had taken the place. We have a lot to be thankful for." Theodore, said Spring-Rice, "will make things hum." And from Chestnut Hill came a poignant letter from Grandmother Lee, whose own daughter, had fate not so cruelly intervened, would now perhaps be First Lady. "Theodore can't want to be congratulated under such sad circumstances, and yet I feel so thankful that he is to fill the high position to which he has been so suddenly called, and for you too dear Edith, to do the honors of the White House is so exactly what you are fitted for . . ."[23]

Edith Kermit Roosevelt in 1901.

First Lady
1901–1909

Eighteen

Being the centre of things is very interesting, yet the same proportions remain.

—Edith Kermit Roosevelt[1]

Men doffed their hats, and women bowed as the Jersey City trainmaster escorted the thickly veiled First Lady to the 10:32 express waiting to transport her to Washington for President McKinley's funeral. While the actions of the people made Edith doubly aware of her august position, the name of the private car, Oceanic, stirred childhood memories. What strange fate had brought little Edie Carow from the sandy shores of Oceanic, New Jersey, to the like-named Pullman bearing her to the White House?

That Monday afternoon, September 16, 1901, was cloudy and dull as Edith's train pulled into Sixth Street Station. Crowds waiting for the evening special from Buffalo bringing McKinley's body and Theodore to the capital confronted her as she stepped out onto the platform. The press was quick to note that she had "made her hurried trip unaccompanied by a maid," and lauded this as an example of "her simple habits and democratic tastes."[2] Will Cowles had a carriage waiting at the baggage entrance, and whisked Edith away to 1733 N Street. This modest home was to be in effect "the

Little White House" until Mrs. McKinley had recovered sufficiently to move out of the Executive Mansion.

By the time Edith had settled into a room on the second floor, Theodore arrived, "looking very grave and older," having escorted the dead President to 1600 Pennsylvania Avenue. However, he was "not at all nervous" at the prospect of what lay ahead, for he knew that the whole country was behind him. Edith had no doubt that he could handle the responsibility, but did wonder how he would cope with "this life of confinement," as she put it.[3]

A dreary rain was falling next morning when Edith and Theodore started for the White House at nine. Assembling with other funeral guests in the Red Parlor, Edith noticed a familiar rotund figure, and impulsively went up to him. "Oh, Mr. Cleveland, my husband is so young!" "Don't worry," said the former President, "he is all right." Nothing, she remembered later, could have given "as much support and satisfaction" as that simple remark.[4]

Riding with Will, who had been pressed into service as Naval Aide, Theodore and Edith followed McKinley's hearse to the Capitol in a carriage drawn by four splendid black horses. Its side windows were open, so that the crowd had a fine view of the new President, who had recovered his good spirits overnight, and was animatedly talking. As they rode along Pennsylvania Avenue, Edith heard running through the crowd, like a series of firecrackers, the exclamation "There's Roosevelt! There's Roosevelt! There's Roosevelt!"[5] But nearer to the Capitol, a profound silence settled over the people. Suddenly, as the hearse turned the corner to ascend Capitol Hill, a frightful wail disturbed the calm, startling Edith and everybody else. The weird cry came from a bent old black woman, waving her arms and grieving in soulful Southern tones. As the Presidential carriage mounted the incline, her voice was drowned by the band of the guard of honor striking up "Nearer My God to Thee." The first words of this hymn had been McKinley's last.

Edith and Theodore alighted, and began to follow the coffin up the steps to the Rotunda. The crowd, thinking they would now be allowed access to the corpse, broke through the police lines and swept like a tidal wave across the square. Alarmed officers began wielding batons, but to no avail. Women screamed as they fell and were trampled underfoot. Not until artillerymen posted on the steps aimed their carbines and yelled, "Get back!" was order restored.

Safely inside, but still trembling, Edith found the brief obsequies "impressive," but the whole experience was "one of the saddest" in her life.[6]

Mrs. McKinley, grief-stricken, declined to see anyone after the ceremonies. "Really all her life is gone poor lady," Edith noted.[7] Later she wrote the widow a letter of sympathy, and sent flowers, but knew that nothing could assuage her predecessor's desolation.

After dinner that evening Theodore left for McKinley's home town of Canton, Ohio, where the President was to be buried. Edith, meanwhile, prepared to return to Oyster Bay to organize the family move to Washington. She also needed a chance to reflect on the violent change in her life. "I suppose in a short time I shall adjust myself to this," she wrote Emily from the train next day, "but the horror of it hangs over me, and I am never without fear for Theodore. The secret service men follow him everywhere. I try and comfort myself with the line of the old hymn, *Brought safely by His hand thus far, why should we now give place to fear?*" With this thought she brightened. After all, "the life will be far easier than that of the Vice-President's wife. For one thing, I shall not have to count the pennies; for another I shall have no calls to make . . ."[8] On the contrary, society must henceforth come to her, and she and Theodore would be able to choose whom to receive, and whom not.

Back at Sagamore Hill for her last precious week of private life, Edith had much to do and more to ponder. The sight of dolls lined up on the nursery bed wearing black armbands ("For President McKinley," Quentin explained) made her aware of the supreme importance of preserving her children's innocence in the face of a curious and all-encroaching world. She dreaded exposure to public scrutiny, and the praise and censure of the press, but knew it was inevitable, so she must handle it as best she could. Already pressures were beginning to build up. "You can't think how much anxiety pervades the country about the children's education," she complained to Theodore. "I receive letters from schools and tutors every day."[9]

Theodore moved into the Executive Mansion (which he would soon officially dub the White House) on September 23, and dined there quietly that night with the Cowleses and the Robinsons. Edith,

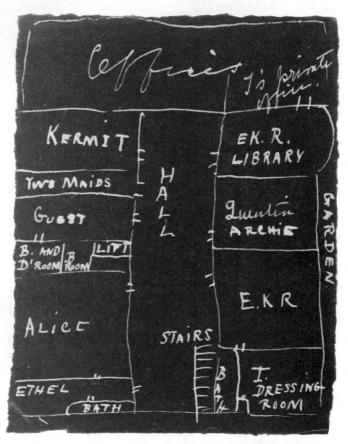

"Edie says it's like living over the store."
Edith's sketch plan of the White House,
showing offices adjacent to living quarters.

Ethel, Kermit, the cook and two maids arrived two days later. As a
teenager, Edith had been in awe of the splendid halls that Lincoln
once roamed, but now she found them disappointingly gloomy, with
their heavy gilt, plush Victorian furniture, and age-darkened frescoed
ceilings. What was more, the second-floor living quarters were
impossibly cramped for such a large family as hers. "Edie says it's
like living over the store," Theodore told a friend.[10]

Except for a small private dining room, the main floor of the
Mansion was devoted to public rooms. Straight away, however,
Edith elected to use the Red Parlor to receive personal acquain-

tances. She could not even call the second floor entirely her own, since the space over the East Room was given over to executive offices. Only a glass screen separated these from the family quarters. The latter consisted of a huge drafty hall, five bedrooms, two ancient bathrooms, a guest room, a maid's room, and an oval library.[11] Clearly, this accommodation was inadequate for a family of eight, and something drastic would have to be done if they were to live in any degree of comfort for the next three and a half years. Should Theodore win election in his own right in 1904, and then again in 1908, this could be their home for *eleven* and a half years.

In the meantime, Edith allocated the large southwest bedroom, with its private dressing room and bath, to herself and Theodore. From here they could enjoy pleasant views of the gardens, the Washington Monument, the Tidal Basin, and, in the distance, the silvery Potomac River. Alice was given the room opposite, facing the Hay and Adams mansions across Lafayette Square. Ethel took the room next door on the northwest corner, from where she could see her father's old Navy office. Kermit shared the room overlooking St. John's Episcopal Church with Ted, who was conveniently away at Groton most of the time. Mischievous Archie and Quentin were put between the library and their parents' bedroom, where Edith could keep an eye on them day and night. The maids, Rose and Mary, had to share a small room next to Kermit's, while Annie and Anna would have to make do with a basement room near the kitchen—or go to the attic, where Edith despairingly ordered "some pen-like bed chambers built."[12] Mame, whom she suspected of having "vague desires of a government place," was a source of "endless bother." The crusty nurse could hardly be expected to share a room with the fast-growing boys, and there was simply no other place for her. Fortunately for Edith, Mame's health prevented her coming to Washington right away. Plagued by what seemed to be a stone, the old woman was recuperating at Sagamore Hill, and would later go to relatives in New York while her employer decided what to do with her.[13]

Edith's first symbolic gesture in the White House was to throw open the windows to let in sunlight and fresh air and dissipate the dark, musty atmosphere. Next she rearranged furniture, filled bookshelves with favorite tomes, and ordered fresh flowers from the Executive greenhouses.

After three or four days the household was "partly settled," and Edith collapsed into "a heavy sleep of exhaustion" for forty-eight hours. "To me the shadow still hangs over the White House," she wrote Emily as she began to recover, "and I am in constant fear about Theodore . . . He is well, but I find I have to consider him at every turn to make all go smoothly."[14]

A token of the First Lady's determination to remain a part of the President's life was her appropriation of the upstairs oval library as her personal sitting room. A door connected this room to Theodore's office, making it possible for him to consult with her between appointments, and for her to tap lightly if he stayed up too late working.

The children soon made themselves at home in Washington. They raced new bicycles around the White House grounds, found the high-ceilinged halls ideal for stilt-walking, and roller-skated in the cavernous basement. These pleasures were curtailed when school began in October. Edith arranged for Kermit and Archie to go to local public schools, and enrolled Ethel as a boarder from Mondays to Fridays at the Cathedral School on Woodley Street in the Cleveland Park section of the city. Alice successfully evaded the same fate by staying with Bamie at Farmington. She seemed to resent the fuss made by her peers as they dwelt on the privileges attending a President's daughter, and determinedly remained away until the end of the month, by which time she was reconciled to exploring the advantages of the White House for herself.

Edith gradually established a routine which would change little over the next few years. She had breakfast with her husband and the children at eight-fifteen, after which she and Theodore walked in the garden. At nine o'clock she dealt with her voluminous mail, read and clipped the newspapers, made a list of visitors she wished to see, and consulted with the steward, the chef and the maids about the day's activities and menus. (She had decided to break with tradition and abolish the office of Housekeeper, preferring to supervise things herself.) Between eleven and twelve every Tuesday she entertained the wives of the Cabinet officers in her sunny sitting room. Enthroned in a heavy armchair, and flanked on either side by her guests, formally arranged on two long sofas, she conducted a genteel discussion of topics of the day. On other weekdays at this time, she had French conversation lessons, or went for a drive in her carriage, occasionally stopping off at stores and antique shops. At one-thirty Theodore invariably brought several people to lunch. Afterward Edith received callers, and at about four o'clock went riding in Rock Creek Park or the Virginia countryside with her husband. Theodore's horse was a huge jumper named Bleistein, shipped to him by the Wadsworths. Edith accompanied him on Yagenka, looking "so young," said Theodore, that people mistook her for his daughter.[15]

Before dinner the First Lady spent half an hour to an hour reading and talking in her room with the children. Often as not the President, who could never resist a boy's story, would also appear. "He always

"Before dinner the First Lady spent half an hour . . . with the children."
Edith, Archie and Quentin.

came in and kissed her hand," a maid's daughter recalled, "and then had a rough-and-tumble play on the floor with the children . . . When the allotted time was up Mrs. Roosevelt would say, 'Theodore, it is time to dress for dinner.'" Instantly, "like well-disciplined soldiers," the scrappers rose from the carpet and trooped to their quarters.[16]

One of the most successful innovations Edith made in the first weeks in the White House was to appoint Isabelle Hagner, a plumply handsome young woman, as her Social Secretary at a salary of fourteen hundred dollars a year. The First Lady needed help with correspondence, and preparing schedules of whom to receive. "Washington is always filled with strangers," Edith observed, as she sifted and scrutinized the endless applications for admittance to the Mansion. No one with the shadow of a scandalous reputation would be admitted, if she could help it. Even the President's sisters were required to make appointments. "Belle" was exactly suited to help handle such matters. The job called for discernment, a knowledge of society (she came from an old District family), and the utmost tact. These qualities she had in abundance. She was also resourceful and companionable, and fitted into the Roosevelt ménage perfectly. In time she became Edith's "snooping" accomplice in incognito forays to antique shops, and a popular friend of the children. Her sense of the ridiculous was perhaps her most endearing trait. At one White House gathering, the statuesque secretary was dancing with a dwarf-sized diplomat, when they tripped and fell. The little official disappeared beneath his partner's red velvet train, and when he wriggled out he was grinning from ear to ear. Most women would have been embarrassed, but Belle was even more amused than he.[17]

"Theodore is very well and of course bears all this responsibility with the utmost ease," Edith told Fanny Parsons. He was, indeed, more than equal to the task, resisting friends' overtures for official posts, making judicious appointments strictly on merit, and clearing his desk routinely by the end of each day. "Edith is too sweet and pretty and dignified and wise as mistress of the White House; and is very happy with it," Theodore wrote in his turn. "She is forty," he told John Hay, "and I do not think I deceive myself when I say that she neither looks nor acts nor feels as if she was [yet] thirty."[18] There was no doubt that the new President and his wife were thoroughly qualified for and ideally suited to their position. They were, after all, the first aristocrats to preside over the Executive Mansion since the John Quincy Adamses, and even *Town Topics*, which was notoriously quicker to blame than to praise, observed that Edith was "a lady who does not have to depend on dressmakers or books of etiquette to make her presentable, and one to whom the duties of her high position . . . come rather as a right than a revelation." [19]

The presidential salary of fifty thousand a year, and generous appropriations for upkeep, fuel, lighting and stationery, meant that Edith at last could entertain in a style for which she had a taste, but had not hitherto been able to afford. For the moment, however, while Washington was still in mourning for McKinley, the most she could do was hold afternoon teas graced by lace doilies, colored ribbons, matching flowerpieces and elaborate confections. But soon there would be garden parties with uniformed bands, and huge marquees packed with refreshments; and, most expensive of all, several sumptuous State banquets every season lavish with orchids and champagne.

John Hay's attitude to Theodore Roosevelt was that of "a benevolent and amused uncle." To his neighbor Henry Adams he wrote: "Teddy said the other day, 'I am not going to be a slave of the tradition that forbids Presidents from seeing their friends. I am going to dine with you and Henry Adams and Cabot whenever I like. But' (here the shadow of the crown sobered him a little) 'of course I must preserve the prerogative of the initiative.'" [20]

Crown or no crown, Theodore certainly used the initiative in a startling way when, on October 16, he invited Booker T. Washington, the Negro head of Tuskegee Institute, to dine at the White House. No black had ever done so before, and when Washington's name appeared on the list of the day's callers there was an uproar, particularly among Southern whites. The President, they raged, was fomenting dangerous ideas of racial and social equality. In defense, Theodore said he had had no intention other than that "of showing some little respect to a man whom I cordially esteem as a good citizen and good American." Actually, Roosevelt's intention in inviting Washington had been to discuss hard political business. "We talked at considerable length," the black man wrote afterward, adding that he felt that Roosevelt "wanted to help not only the Negro, but the whole South."[21] In doing this the President needed to recruit Washington's help in finding suitable Southerners for federal posts, and forming the Republican Party's Southern election strategy. Amid all the hysteria that followed, "Mr. Dooley," the satirist Finley Peter Dunne, was a voice for sanity. "From all I can larn, he hung his hat on th' rack and used proper discrimination between th' knife an' th' fork, an ast f'r nawthin' that had to be sent out f'r." An inventory of the spoons, remarked the columnist, showed that Washington "had used gintlemanly resthraint." The furor eventually died down, but no other black dined at the White House during Theodore Roosevelt's tenure.[22]

"Simplicity Marks the White House Thanksgiving," headlined the New York *Journal* on November 28, 1901. "There were no formal functions, but everybody had a good time, plenty of turkey and trimmings . . . and a social gathering in the Red Parlor."

The Douglas Robinsons and the Lodges joined the Roosevelts for the traditional dinner, and Corinne wrote a friend that she had "never seen Theodore more darling and gay and natural." Edith was "looking very attractive in her pure white gown, the children playing about and an atmosphere of home and hospitality permeating everything." Bamie, who had visited Edith shortly before, found her sister-in-law "so calm and with time for everything—her great sunny room and she sitting quietly embroidering make a tranquil-feeling spot in life."[23]

Christmas was more festive. Edith and Theodore went to a Christmas Eve party at the Cowleses', hung stockings on the White House library mantel, and entertained twenty-six to dinner on Christmas night, followed by dancing in the East Room. Next day, Edith took the children for a three-day cruise down the Potomac on the Presidential yacht *Dolphin.* In later years she fondly recalled such excursions "where we used to go ashore and have the most wonderful oyster roasts."[24] After three months as First Lady, Edith Kermit Roosevelt was clearly in full command of her official duties, at peace with herself, and, above all, having fun.

After this quiet season, 1902 began with an eleven-o'clock fanfare of trumpets heralding the New Year's Day reception. It was the signal for Edith, wearing a white corded-silk gown and carrying a bouquet of orchids and lilies of the valley, to descend the White House staircase on the President's arm. Behind her, to the sound of martial music played by the red-uniformed Marine Band (concealed in a bank of thick holly), followed members of the Cabinet, their black suits contrasting somberly with the profusion of red and green tropical plants in every niche, and the brilliant glow of Roman torches. Edith and Theodore led the procession to the Blue Room. Here they began to receive according to strict laws of protocol. First came a coruscating parade of foreign ambassadors: the German representative resplendent in white-plumed hat, blue cape and scarlet coat ablaze with gold and jeweled decorations; the Russian in blue and gold effulgent with medals; and the Chinese legation in sumptuous Oriental silks and satins. Next came the robed Supreme Court Justices, followed by Senators, Congressmen, Army and Navy officers and hundreds of other dignitaries. Finally there were some five thousand ordinary citizens, trooping through reverently to shake hands with their new Chief Executive. As she had in Albany, Edith sweetly discouraged contact by holding her bouquet with both hands and simply smiling and bowing. At 1:30 P.M. Theodore told her she had done her part. He, however, would continue so as not to "disappoint the people who had stood so long in the cold."[25]

The following night, Edith was hostess at her first Cabinet Dinner. Fifty people assembled in the East Room, which was decorated with poinsettia blooms from the White House conservatory. Then Theodore and Edith—dressed in a pale-blue "picture" gown—led their guests through all the public rooms to the State Dining Room at the west end of the house. Here an enormous hour-glass-shaped table, decorated with a blazing mass of pink begonias edged with maidenhair fern, was illuminated by gilded candelabra. Conversation across such an elaborate arrangement was difficult; the President, sitting opposite his wife, complained that he could not see her for foliage. But the atmosphere was warm and friendly, and Edith had every reason to congratulate herself for carrying the evening off so smoothly.

Alice's début took place the very next night. Most young women of her age (she would be eighteen in six weeks' time) might have relished the experience of coming out in the White House. No President's daughter, indeed, had ever made her début here; the event was regarded as the most important ball at 1600 Pennsylvania

Avenue since the days of Dolley Madison. Alice, however, was not easy to please. For one thing, the young lady did not like the East Room's bourgeois décor of circular padded seats, endless strands of smilax, and potted palms. She also found the waxed linen crash tacked across the floor for the five hundred dancers "humiliating." The serving of punch, instead of the champagne customary at the parties of her sophisticated New York friends, was another "horrid blow." Even worse was the lack of a cotillion with its ever changing partners and the chance to receive expensive "favors"—gold watches, pearl necklaces, jeweled evening bags, and silver cigarette cases. Her cost-conscious stepmother forbade such extravagance. Alice was prepared to finance the champagne and the favors out of her own independent income (a quarterly stipend of $500 from the Lees), but Edith insisted that the party was her parents' responsibility and she must have what they could afford.[26]

The reception began in the Blue Room at 10 P.M. Alice, looking exquisite in white chiffon appliquéd with white rosebuds, her light-brown hair arranged in a fashionable pompadour, greeted the guests with Edith at her side. All of New York and Washington society seemed to be there. Among those filing by were the fabulous Leiter girls; the daughters of the British Ambassador, Sir Julian Pauncefote; Alice's handsome cousin Franklin Delano Roosevelt; her wealthy boy friends Ogden Reid, Payne Whitney and Robert Goelet; and Countess Marguerite Cassini, the Russian ambassador's pretty daughter, who would become Alice's close friend and, later on, her romantic rival.

If the debutante herself was less than buoyant, no one noticed. There were more than enough millionaires to keep her amused, and she whirled happily in their arms to the strains of the "Hop Long Sing" two-step, Sousa's "Bride Elect" polka, and a recently composed tune called the "Sagamore Hill" waltz. "Alice had the time of her life," wrote her Aunt Corinne, "men seven deep around her all the time, Edith a gracious hostess, Theodore perfect . . . such go to it all. We did not leave until two o'clock and I think everyone had a good time. The beautiful conservatories were perfect for sentiment and it was so pretty to see the girls' gay dresses and many a uniform and college athlete hidden among the plants."[27]

Not everyone was as enamored of White House functions as Corinne. Melancholic Henry Adams was among the disapprovers. A week after Alice's dance he dined with Edith and Theodore at the Executive Mansion (having not been there since 1878, when the Hayeses were his hosts). He described his visit of January 12, 1902, to his dear friend Elizabeth Cameron:

> . . . That the house is to me ghastly with blood and dreary associations way back to my great-grandmother a hundred years ago, seems no particular reason why it should always depress me, or why it should seem to entomb a little family party of very old friends, in the private dining-room, and upstairs afterwards to smoke in the cheery octagon; but it did. We were only eight, Cabot and Nanny Lodge and a Mrs. Selmes[28] of Minnesota, whom I must have known in the Hayes epoch, and who came on me like a ghost. We waited twenty minutes in the hideous red drawing-room before Theodore and Edith came down; and we went in to dinner immediately with as much chaff and informality as though Theodore were still a Civil Service Commissioner. We chattered round talk; Cabot was bright; Hay was just a little older and a thought more formal than once we were; Edith was very bright and gay; but as usual Theodore absorbed the conversation, and if he tried me ten years ago, he crushes me now. To say that I enjoyed it would be, to you, a gratuitous piece of deceit. The dinner was indifferent, very badly served, and, for some reason, nothing to drink but a glass of sherry and some appollinaris. Theodore's talk was not exactly forced or unnatural, but had less of his old freshness and quite as much of his old dogmatism. . . . He lectures me in history as though he were a high-school pedagogue. Of course I fall back instantly on my favorite protective pose of ignorance, which aggravates his assertions, and so we steadily drift apart.[29]

Although Edith could not cure Henry Adams's habitual gloom, she could at least do something about the "hideous red drawing-room," not to mention the rest of the neglected mansion. But that would have to wait until the end of her first social season.

Theodore Roosevelt's early months in the Presidency were stimulating to the political observer and the ordinary citizen alike. Winds of change were in the air, and even though Roosevelt had promised to continue McKinley's policies, he was doing so in his own cyclonic fashion. It was clear from the outset that the new President's Administration would be innovative, and the country welcomed this. Politically a liberal-conservative, Roosevelt was open to fresh ideas from all manner of people—scientists, business and labor leaders, reformers, cowboys, farmers, suffragettes—and while respecting the past, he looked resolutely to the future.

In his first message to Congress on December 3, 1901 (at twenty thousand words the longest ever written), he made it clear that he did not accept the nineteenth-century status quo. It was time for industry, which had grown beyond all imagining since the Civil War, to be regulated, and its vast wealth shared more equitably. This curbing of rampant free enterprise would not be easy. Immigrants pouring in from south and east Europe kept wages low and slowed union attempts to organize. At the same time, small businessmen were being squeezed by mergers and by giant corporate trusts. Roosevelt, a Hamiltonian in philosophy, believed it was the federal government's responsibility to break up such groups to ensure the small businessman "a square deal," and to see that the public in general was protected from the unfair pricing of monopolies. Such companies as U.S. Steel, which combined the assets of magnates like Henry Frick and Andrew Carnegie; Standard Oil, controlled by John D. Rockefeller; and J. P. Morgan's New England Steamship Lines all eventually came under scrutiny.

If Roosevelt's storm appeared to gather force slowly on the issue of trust-busting, it was because he wanted to be fair to big business. This apparent ambiguity prompted Mr. Dooley to satirize the President's thoughts: "Th' trusts . . . are heejous monsthers . . . On wan hand I wud stamp thim undher fut; on th' other hand not so fast." [30]

One of the few people with whom Edith kept up a regular correspondence outside the family during these years was Cecil Spring-Rice, now reluctantly serving as British Commissioner in Cairo. Theodore modestly invited Springy to come and "see for yourself how I manage things," [31] and Edith repeated the invitation in a revealing letter written on January 27, 1902.

>MY DEAR MR. SPRING-RICE:
>   It was good to hear from you and it will be even better to see you. Last night the Lodges and Mr. Adams and Austin Wadsworth and his wife were here and we talked of you and of the empty place which you have left. I count on long misty moonlight evenings on the White House porch, Theodore in his rocking chair, you and Cabot settling world affairs over your cigars, while Mrs. Lodge and I meekly listen as becomes our sex and position. Being the centre of things is very interesting, yet the same proportions remain. When I read "The World is too much with us" or "Oh for a closer walk with God" they mean just what they did, so I don't believe I have been forced into the "first lady of the land" model of my predecessors. You would have understood this in the old days, so I hope you do now.
>   I want you to see the children. Alice is exceedingly pretty, and has a remarkably steady head though in some ways very child like. Ted is a good boy and stands well at school. Kermit is odd and independent as always, and Ethel is just a handful. She is a replica of Mrs. Cowles. Archie we call "the beautiful idiot" and Quentin is the cleverest of the six.
>   I am sending you a Scribner with an essay on Washington which I like exceedingly . . .
>   Goodbye
>   E.K.R. [32]

· Fanny and Jim Parsons came to occupy the solitary guest room at the end of January. The dark draperies and heavy old furniture made Fanny feel lonely until Theodore, "laughing and welcoming," came and filled the somber chamber with his warm presence. Edith, wrote Fanny, appeared "serene . . . Her marriage—a singularly happy one through the long years—was perhaps never more perfect than at that time." At meals, Fanny observed, everyone stood until the President sat, and he was always served first. "It's hard to remember *not* to be a gentleman," Fanny heard him mutter. The conversation at lunch, with William Howard Taft just returned from the Philippines, and Secretary of War Elihu Root exercising his caustic wit in the face of Theodore's exuberance, was scintillating. Coming after a morning of hearing the President dictating a multitude of letters at high speed and on different subjects, it furnished Fanny with memories for life.[33]

Edith's extreme happiness changed to great distress in mid-February when news came that Ted had been stricken with pneumonia at Groton. She went to him at once, and nursed him through a thirty-six-hour crisis during which he lay close to death. By February 22, Ted was sufficiently recovered to return with his mother to Washington and convalesce. But Edith herself had little time to rest, for two days later Prince Heinrich, brother of the German Kaiser, arrived on a state visit. Ostensibly he had come to America for the launching of the Emperor's racing schooner, built in a New Jersey shipyard. But his more important mission was to establish friendlier relations with the new Administration.[34]

"Edith fortunately does not care a rap about meeting Prince Henry or any other imperial or non-imperial potentate in the wide world," Theodore wrote. "Doubtless Edith has her faults," he added mischievously, "but she is wholly free from any exaggerated reverence for adventitious rank and pomp." His wife nevertheless liked the bearded prince in the dark blue gold-trimmed admiral's uniform, and Alice, too, found him "unaffected and agreeable."[35] Prince Heinrich, for his part, welcomed this American visit and the fuss made of him. It was a refreshing change from his usual function—acting as his brother's envoy at European funerals.

The State dinner held in the East Room on February 24 was a stag affair. Edith saw, however, that the crescent-shaped table looked its best, decorated with roses and primroses, and illuminated by thousands of elecric lights in the nautical shapes of anchors and ropes. "An amusing incident," reported *Town Topics,* "was the serving of beer in steins at the dinner table—a bad breach of etiquette according to German forms." The steins were rented from a local restaurant, and as the Prince emptied his he almost choked in surprise. Printed on the bottom he read: "Stolen from Gersternberg's."[36]

Edith traveled to Shooter's Island off Jersey City next day to see Alice launch the Kaiser's boat. The sky was overcast, but this did not detract from the success of the occasion. "In the name of His Majesty, the German Emperor, I christen this yacht *Meteor*," said the poised girl in a firm voice, as she swung the silver-encased champagne bottle against the hull, splattering her blue velvet gown in the process. Then, with a silver hatchet, she severed the last rope, and the craft slipped into the water. Prince Heinrich kissed her hand and proposed in a strong German accent, "Three hearty cheers for Miss Roosevelt."[37] At the lunch which followed on the Prince's own steamer, *Hohenzollern,* Edith, lulled by the music of the excellent German band, looked on as His Royal Highness presented Alice with a diamond bracelet from the Kaiser. This prompted the press to speculate on whether Wilhelm II was encouraging his brother to ask for the hand of the blue-eyed daughter of the President of the United States.

Whatever the case, she was known from now on as "Princess Alice," and seemed to be a natural choice to go as her father's representative to the upcoming Coronation of Edward VII. But this was not to be. Only the offspring of an officially recognized sovereign could be seated in Westminster Abbey; so Alice was consoled with a trip to Cuba instead.

Almost every First Lady since Martha Washington had held a weekly reception of some kind at the White House. Edith's gathering took the form of a musicale, usually held on a Tuesday or Friday evening during the season. "Mrs. Roosevelt and I had quite a discussion," the profoundly unmusical Theodore told a reporter, "as to what form of entertainment would be fitting in the President's house, and she finally concluded that this was it."[38]

The musicales continued into April. Every evening began with dinner at eight o'clock for a select group of twenty or so in the State Dining Room. At ten o'clock Edith went to the Green Room to welcome the several hundred guests invited for the performance. The audience was seated on gilt chairs arranged in the East Room. Theodore came in at the last moment, and took a seat in the front row, where he could greet the artists as they entered by the north door, and thank them after each performance. His idea of a suitable reward, after a mellifluous violin recital, was to present an autographed copy of *The Rough Riders*.[39] Edith sat near the south door to receive latecomers.

After the concert, guests were served ices and punch, while Edith and Theodore circulated among them. At eleven-thirty the First Lady returned to the Green Room to bid everybody good night. "She has a fashion of seeming to have been looking and longing for just the particular one who is greeting her," wrote a newsman, "and her gentle hand-pressure, a thing apart from the cold, flabby society 'shake,' sends you on your way rejoicing."[40]

Edith's early programs were simple, consisting mostly of songs and other light chamber music. Then, on April 3, the world-renowned flamboyantly hirsute pianist Ignace Jan Paderewski came to play. He dined with the Roosevelts before giving his recital to a worshipful audience. The artist Cecelia Beaux recalled the evening in painterly detail, in a letter written next day:

> The yellow head of the Lion shone gloriously against the satin of the Blue Room . . . He and Madame were standing alone, as were all the other couples, whispering . . . It is a thrilling moment when the Sovereigns come in, and we all rise, if we have been seated, an act which would turn the head of any ordinary civilian. They went the rounds, and made each of us happy. The President is too delicious when he drops his great square head on one side, with an air of exchanging a confidence with the Country's guest . . . The East Room was crowded . . . I sat with the St. Gaudenses, the Proctors, and Mrs. West Roosevelt. . . . The President was near with Mrs. Lodge. Paderewski outdid himself, though he was a little cold at first. By the time he got to the ["Military"] Polonaise . . . I think it may have been better than hearing Chopin himself.[41]

On another evening the austere but spectacularly handsome Ferrucio Busoni performed, and later came a promising young Spanish cellist named Pablo Casals. He played a Boccherini sonata and Saint-Saëns's undulating "Le Cygne." Sixty years would pass before Casals returned to the White House to perform for the John Fitzgerald Kennedys.

Edith's other musicales were even more ambitious. She brought in the Vienna Male Voice Choir from Europe, and on another occasion the entire Philadelphia Orchestra. No other White House hostess, remarked Countess Marguerite Cassini in 1956, "surpassed the good taste" of Edith Kermit Roosevelt at her musical evenings. Many leading society women sought to emulate her, and paid high fees to lure such luminaries as Nellie Melba, Ernestine Schumann-Heink, Jan Kubelik, and Josef Hofmann to their homes.[42]

In the spring of 1902 Cecilia Beaux, who had come to Washington to paint an unofficial portrait of the First Lady, found herself charged with a double assignment. "It was to have been of Mrs. Roosevelt only," the artist remembered, "but her daughter Ethel consented to literally 'jump in,' greatly enlivening, I hope, her mother's hours of attention to posing." The painting was done in the Red Parlor (by then also being used for family breakfasts), with Edith and Ethel seated on a broad upholstered bench. The rosy walls of the room infiltrated the picture, suffusing it with a warm glow. The President occasionally looked in on the sittings to cast a benign eye over the canvas, and the children interrupted constantly, competing for attention. Edith was "entirely unruffled" by the din they made reciting Scott's poems in unison, and even contributed to the noise herself as she prompted the stumblers in any of the parts and verses. When the portrait was finished Theodore did not like it, but St. Gaudens declared it "a masterpiece."[43]

That same spring a rumor circulated in Washington that the First Lady was expecting a child. Most people dismissed the story as idle gossip, but a joyful letter of April 24 to Emily Carow confirms that Edith was indeed pregnant. "I have the most enormous appetite at present, though I loathe anything sweet, can't touch wine and care but little for tea and coffee! Meat seems to appeal to me!" However, on Friday, May 9, there is a cryptic entry in her diary: "Was taken sick in night." She remained in her bedroom for the next twelve days, attended by a nurse, and the happy exclamation marks faded from her letters.

The welcome arrival of Cecil Spring-Rice at the end of a busy season, and his prolonged occupation of the only guest room, confirmed Edith's opinion that the White House in its present form was inadequate for both private and public purposes. No matter how she organized and shuffled the family around, there never seemed to be enough upstairs space, while downstairs, at large state gatherings, people were so crammed into the main hallway that they barely had room to remove their wraps.

Fortunately the present First Lady was not alone in her desire to expand and renovate the Executive Mansion. Presidents Benjamin Harrison, Grover Cleveland, and William McKinley had all submitted plans of varying grandiosity, but Congress had been unwilling to vote the huge sums necessary, and doubted the wisdom of tampering with James Hoban's hallowed design. Now the Roosevelts, taking advantage of the obvious needs of their large family, and a growing movement to beautify the city of Washington as a whole, presented new plans to Congress.

Unlike their predecessors, Theodore and Edith were anxious to return the White House to its eighteenth-century purity. Any restoration must be in such style as George Washington might have approved: any expansion must be along the lines already conceived by Thomas Jefferson. The prestigious architectural firm of McKim, Mead and White was requested to prepare plans with these considerations in mind.

Congress, impressed by the beauty and practicality of the blueprints, voted an appropriation of over half a million dollars. Of this sum, $65,916 was to be spent "at the President's discretion" on building a new West Wing of executive offices, connected to the house by Jefferson's original colonnade, which was now swallowed up by greenhouses. This would free the vast space above the East Room for Edith to create two suites, each consisting of two guest rooms with adjoining baths. The remaining $475,445 was to go toward reconstruction and visual improvements. Chief among these was the removal of the west stairway, to increase the size of the State Dining Room. The east stairway, which used to lead to the second-floor offices, could now be exclusively devoted to private use. Other changes called for the stripping of architectural excrescences which had been accumulating since Zachary Taylor's tenure, and the removal of Chester Arthur's giant Tiffany screen, situated between the vestibule and the main corridor. The rest of the money would be spent on new and reupholstered furniture, high-quality cabinetwork, lighting fixtures, heating systems, and modernized plumbing.

Outside, too, major changes were planned. The inappropriate

greenhouse built in 1857 would be dismantled, and the gardens re-landscaped, with a new porte cochere on the East Wing and elegant cast-iron gates.

All of this construction work meant that the Roosevelts would have to move out of the White House for about six months. "One thing I want definitely understood," Theodore wrote McKim in May, ". . . and that is the question of expedition. Without fail we must have . . . the office building and all of the present living apartments finished completely by October 1st."[44] This was no hardship to Edith, who was looking forward to a long, relaxing spell at Oyster Bay. Since the chief architect, Charles Follen McKim, was based in New York, she could meet and correspond with him regularly during the summer to discuss the progress of the renovation. Accordingly, on June 9, she sailed down the Potomac on the Presidential yacht *Dolphin*, accompanied by her four youngest children. Theodore, meanwhile, would move into temporary quarters on Jackson Place. When the hottest weather began he would follow the family to the cool shores of Long Island.

Sagamore Hill was besieged by reporters that summer, the first of Theodore's presidency, and they wrote such colorful accounts of his activities that he was moved to protest to the editor of the *Sun*. ". . . I am living here with my wife and children just exactly as you are at your home. . . ."[45] The stories, however, continued of the President of the United States camping out on remote islands protected only by a bodyguard of three small boys; of toiling in the fields with his groundsmen, drinking out of the same bucket, and insisting he be paid at scale for the day's work; of chopping down trees by way of relaxation; and of risking life and limb on dangerous cross-country gallops.

In between all this physical activity, Theodore conducted affairs of state as usual. Senators Lodge and Hanna came to talk about the trusts; Chief Forester Gifford Pinchot discussed land reclamation and conservation; Governor Odell reported on the state of New York State. As well as receiving unprecedented numbers of officials, Edith entertained the usual quota of family and friends, including Fergie, Theresa Richardson, and Dr. Lambert. Only one guest was not welcome. She refused point blank to meet the touring Russian Grand Duke Boris, whose reputation as a womanizer had preceded him

across America. The First Lady absented herself before he arrived at
Sagamore Hill, leaving Theodore to give the truthful explanation that
she was out to lunch. His Royal Highness was free to make what he
wished of it.

On September 3, as Edith was planning to sail across the Sound to
meet Theodore on his way back from a New England speaking tour,
she received a message. The President had been involved in a serious
accident. A trolley had collided with his carriage in Pittsfield,
Massachusetts, throwing him out and killing his favorite Secret
Service man, William Craig. Edith hurried to Bridgeport and found
Theodore with only a bruised cheek and a scraped leg. He had had a
lucky escape, but his injuries turned out to be not as superficial as at
first appeared.

Monday afternoon, September 15, the Roosevelts played host at an
extraordinary garden party for their Nassau County neighbors.
Invitations went out via the local press and pulpits, and thousands
responded, pouring into Oyster Bay by train and carriage. Awareness
that President McKinley had been assassinated at just such a public
gathering led to unusual security arrangements. Sixty New York City
policemen, and several hundred private citizens, sworn in as depu-
ties, stopped everybody some distance from the flag-bedecked house,
insisting they leave their umbrellas, parasols, cameras, and
lunchboxes on the lawns. A double line of Secret Service men,
stationed immediately in front of the President, kept a close look out
for anyone with hands suspiciously concealed. Among the most
vigilant guards was Edith. Although she looked cool and calm in a
creamy embroidered voile dress and a sun hat, her eyes were
watchful and rarely strayed far from Theodore.

"Dee-lighted! Bless my soul, it's Jake!" the President exclaimed as,
for three hours, he pulled his guests by at a rate of sixty a minute,
propelling them inexorably in the direction of raspberry shrub and
ginger snaps being served on the other side of the porch. Three
thousand crystal punch cups engraved "Theodore Roosevelt, 1902"
were dispensed as souvenirs that afternoon, and demand greatly
exceeded the supply. Clearly, the campaign of 1904 had already
begun.[46]

Nineteen

If Roosevelt had never done anything else, the metamorphosis of the White House from a gilded barn to a comfortable residence . . . would entitle him to his country's gratitude.
—Ellen Maury Slayden[1]

Howls of protest from preservationists greeted the Roosevelts' plans to renovate the presidential mansion in 1902. It was, said a sympathetic observer, "as though every battered bracket and what-not had been the cherished possession of Martha Washington and must be kept forever sacred."[2] The truth was, of course, that although the father of the nation had selected the site and approved the design of the White House, he and his wife had never lived there. John Adams had been the earliest occupant, and the only surviving heirloom from his tenure was Gilbert Stuart's portrait of Washington. Everything else, except the outer walls, had been destroyed when the British set fire to the "palace" in 1814. Afterward the White House had been tastefully reconstructed by its original architect, James Hoban, in the classical style and reopened by President Monroe. But subsequent occupants had seen fit to impose their own accretions of early-, middle- and late-Victorian bric-a-brac. In the process they gradually replaced most of the American Federal and French

Empire–style refurnishings. President Chester A. Arthur alone had shipped twenty-four wagonloads out of the mansion in 1882, before calling in Louis Tiffany, the leading Art Nouveau craftsman of his day, to redecorate.

As a result, about all that the Roosevelts inherited from the Monroe period was a suite of Bellangé gilt furniture, a large surtout table, a few marble mantels and busts, several gilded bronze clocks, and a trunkful of silver. These delicate items were hardly noticeable in the congested half-house, half-office building of 1902.

Even the preservationists could not deny the needs of the First Family for more space. As the nation had expanded, so had presidential responsibilities, bringing increased numbers of politicians, office-seekers, employees, and guests to the White House. This phenomenal growth had succeeded in diminishing both living and working quarters, and led every Chief Executive since Tyler to clamor for enlargement, or for separation of the executive offices from the mansion. Only the Roosevelts had the determination, in spite of criticism, to forge ahead with the long-overdue changes. Now, as a reward for their perseverance, they could look forward to living in a White House restored to its classical simplicity, yet streamlined to handle the increased pace of twentieth-century living.

Charles McKim soon found out during his meetings and correspondence with Edith that summer that the new First Lady was determined to play a major role in the transformation process.

Sagamore Hill
August 21, 1902

DEAR MR. McKIM:

This is about pictures. The President and I have consulted, and we hope it is possible for you to put all the ladies of the White House, including myself, in the downstairs corridor that the dressing rooms open on; also the busts. It could then be called the picture gallery, and you know a name goes a long way. I am afraid the Presidents will still have to hang in the red and green rooms, and I suppose Washington and Mrs. Washington and Lincoln must remain as before, in the East Room. I do not remember whether you intended to have them paneled in the wall. I do not think you said so to me, but sometimes being paneled in lends a certain importance to a portrait.

I wish you would write me what you think about all this. Will you have someone come on Thursday next with samples of wallpaper for the upstairs rooms; and I also hope you are attending to the designs of the bedroom furniture. If Davenport does the papering, I might tell him at the same time what I think is necessary in the bed-rooms, unless you have already done so, and he is preparing designs for me.

I hear from Washington that the house is going on apace.

Sincerely yours
EDITH KERMIT ROOSEVELT[3]

When the architect submitted an unsuitable design, she did not hesitate to reject it in imperious tones. "I do not like my writing desk at all," she wrote in response to one blueprint, "I think it ought to be made to match the furniture which is rosewood, carved with big birds, I should say about fifty years old. Perhaps it would be a good thing to have a photograph taken of the bed. In any case I think the drawing of the writing table is ugly and inconvenient."[4]

Before deciding on the shade of silk hangings and covering for the Blue Room, she consulted Theodore and Alice as to their preference, and then demanded full design details from McKim. "I would like to know exactly how you propose it should look completed." Twenty-four hours, in her opinion, was enough time for him to comply with this request. "I shall be in New York on the *Sylph* at East 23rd St. tomorrow, Friday, evening, and if you prefer seeing me to writing these explanations, I shall be glad to have you dine with me at half past seven."[5]

Understandably, in view of Edith's intense interest in every last detail of the renovation, McKim preferred to have her stay away from the White House, at least until major construction work was finished. She undertook not to move her family back until November, but the appearance of an abscess on Theodore's injured leg made her hurry to join him in Washington on September 24.

"Even the President's sisters were required to make appointments."
Edith at her White House desk.

She found him laid up in their temporary quarters at 22 Jackson
Place, having had to abandon a planned Western trip. The leg had
been operated on in Indianapolis the previous day, and highly secret
medical reports had revealed that two ounces of "pure serum" had
collected around the bone.[6] Four days of enforced rest gave him no
relief, and as a last resort the doctor decided to operate again. Using
only cocaine as a sedative, the surgeon "made a gash nearly two
inches long and scraped his shin bone," Edith reported to Kermit
(who had just started at Groton), "and as soon as it was over he was
lifted back into his wheeled chair and came into the sitting room
where is he now reading."[7]

Theodore never quite got over the effect of his accident. "The shock," he confessed years later, "permanently damaged the bone." Whenever he was tired, or received an unexpected jar, the leg ached, although he was careful to conceal his discomfort in public.[8]

The renovation of the White House was proceeding ahead of schedule, and so, on October 1, Edith paid her first visit to the new mansion. In spite of the clangorous presence of workmen, thick layers of plaster dust, and a strong smell of paint in the main-floor rooms, she found the house "wonderfully improved" in its harmonious new color scheme of white and buff, reminiscent of Federal days. Mounting to the upper-floor hall, she was inspired by the sight of fresh green-burlap-covered walls with rods "at the proper height"— an ideal gallery to hang her own collection of small pictures. For the west wall, given new importance by the removal of the ugly stairway beneath it, she had a bold plan. One of the valuable items "lost" to the White House was a lusty oil by George Watts entitled *Love and Life*, which her prudish predecessors had banished to the Corcoran Gallery. Edith resolved to retrieve the painting and hang it on this very wall, "where it can't shock the multitude." She intended to set up her own writing desk, duly redesigned by McKim, directly opposite, making the whole gallery in effect her private office. Thus established at the heart of the family living quarters, Edith would be in stately command of all activities affecting the private and public affairs of the house.[9]

Despite the huge decorating appropriation Congress had placed in the President's hands, Edith exercised thrift in spending it just as assiduously as she did her own money. Some hardly worn hangings which were no longer suitable for the main floor were used to reupholster upstairs furniture, and several perfectly good carpets were relaid in the family quarters. One room was scarcely touched at all—the "cheery octagon" or library, which Adams had so liked. Edith consented, for the time being, only to its being rewired and repainted. Where it was necessary to spend money, however, she did not hesitate to do so lavishly. The new bedrooms over the East Room were sumptuously refurnished, as was the President's study next to the library.[10] Theodore was treated to fresh maple floors, and plain buckram wall covering, which set off the variegated bindings of his favorite books. Over his marble mantle Edith affixed a historical inscription: "THIS ROOM WAS FIRST USED FOR MEETINGS OF THE

CABINET DURING THE ADMINISTRATION OF PRESIDENT JOHNSON.
IT CONTINUED TO BE SO USED UNTIL THE YEAR MCMII. HERE THE
TREATY OF PEACE WITH SPAIN WAS SIGNED."

The President's desk was made from oak timbers of the British ship
Resolute, which had been found abandoned in the Arctic Circle by a
U.S. whaler in 1855. Purchased and refitted by Congress, the ship
had been sent to Queen Victoria "as a token of goodwill and
friendship." When it was eventually broken up, the Queen ordered
that a desk be made from its hulk, and sent to President Hayes in
1880 "as a memorial of the courtesy and loving kindness which
dictated the offer of the gift of the President."[11]

Edith was particularly pleased with the success of her plans for the
master bedroom. It made a sunny refuge, with its southward-facing
windows, pink-and-green-garlanded curtains, and matching sofa.
Theodore, too, approved the room, because Edith had installed some
furniture that had been used by the Lincolns. He said he liked to
imagine the Emancipator shambling about the mansion, his face
deeply furrowed and racked in thought.[12]

By mid-October the Executive Office Wing west of the restored
colonnade was ready—the first presidential working quarters to be
separate from the White House since fire destroyed those built by
Jefferson.[13] It was a graceful one-story structure, low and unobtru-
sive, yet with ample space for the President and his thirty-eight
assistants and members of the press.

Theodore, now able to hobble on crutches, immediately moved in.
Crossing the reception hall, he entered his own suite, dominated by a
large square fifteen-by-fifteen-foot office. The room was simply
decorated with olive burlap walls and matching curtains. There was
a fireplace opposite the big mahogany desk, and over the mantel
hung an oil portrait of Lincoln. Bookshelves, a divan, several
comfortable chairs, and an Art Nouveau lamp completed the official
décor. Theodore's personal touch was already evident in a globe of
the world, a photo of a bear, and a framed autographed copy of
"Opportunity," a sonnet by the late Senator Ingall:

> *Master of human destinies am I.*
> *Fame, love, and fortune on my footsteps wait;*
> *Cities and fields I walk; I penetrate*
> *Deserts and seas remote, and passing by*

Hovel, the mart, and palace, soon or late
I knock unbidden once at every gate!
If sleeping wake—if feasting, rise before
I turn away. It is the hour of fate,
And they who follow me reach every state
Mortals desire, and conquer every foe
Save death; but those who doubt or hesitate,
Condemned to failure, penury, and woe,
Seek me in vain, and uselessly implore,
I answer not, and I return no more.[14]

Edith's own personal touch was a large bunch of purple flowering heliotrope, a traditional symbol of a happy marriage.

"High windows faced south onto a tennis court."
The new Executive Office wing and grounds
during the Roosevelt Administration.

Sliding doors opened eastward into the Cabinet Room, whose nine deep leather armchairs sported silver name-plates, giving a pleasing (if illusory) sense of permanence to their occupants. High windows faced south onto a tennis court, which Edith, who was concerned about her husband's weight, had ordered constructed. Here, in time, a "Tennis Cabinet" would form, consisting of such accomplished players as the United States Forester Gifford Pinchot, Secretary of the Interior James R. Garfield, and Assistant Secretary of State Robert Bacon, as well as some of the fitter members of the Diplomatic Corps.[15]

A vivid picture of Roosevelt at work in the Executive Office Wing has survived in the writings of William Bayard Hale, a *New York Times* reporter, who spent many hours watching the phenomenal routine of the nation's twenty-sixth President.

> Here, in the Cabinet Room, those who call to see the President are usually received by him, from 10 A.M. to 1:30 P.M. Between ten and twelve Senators and Representatives have the entrée without the need of an appointment. Others must make an appointment with Secretary Loeb. Sometimes a score of people will be in the Cabinet Room at one time, and the President goes from one to another, making the circle of the room half a dozen times in a morning, always speaking with great animation, gesturing freely, and in fact talking "with his whole being, mouth, eyes, forehead, cheeks and neck all taking their mobile parts." He stands for the most part as rigid as a soldier on parade, chin in, chest out, the line from the back of the head falling straight as a plumb line to the heels . . . When the President sits, it may be on the divan or on the Cabinet table, he is very much at his ease, and half the time one foot is curled up under him. Curiously whenever he tucks one foot under him his visitor is very likely to do the same thing.
>
> A hundred times a day the President will laugh, and, when he laughs he does it with the same energy with which he talks. It is usually a roar of laughter, and it comes nearly every five minutes. His face grows red with merriment, his eyes nearly close, his utterance becomes

choked and sputtery and falsetto, and sometimes he doubles up with paroxysm. You don't smile with Mr. Roosevelt; you shout with laughter with him, and then you shout again while he tries to cork up more laugh and sputters: "Come, gentlemen, let us be serious . . ."[16]

Though always first to deny that he was a man of genius, except perhaps as a leader, Theodore Roosevelt nevertheless had an abnormal capacity to comprehend and absorb the most intractable problems and data. In a manner reminiscent of Napoleon Bonaparte, he wore out his secretaries and stenographers with endless hours of dictation. Every subject, ranging from the habits of the water ousel to the political future of Manchuria, interested him. He would finish dictating a thirty-thousand-word critique of a recently published book, and call immediately for another "shorthand man" to handle a government matter, while the first staggered into the General Office in a state of exhaustion. William Loeb, who had been the only stenographer Theodore could depend on to stay after office hours in Albany, furnished the same service as Private Secretary in the White House. "He is always on the spot," said the President, "and that means everything to me."[17]

No news item or article, no matter how unfavorable to him or his Administration, was kept from Theodore Roosevelt. A staff member would read between three hundred and five hundred newspapers each day, and mark for the President's attention anything which reflected the opinions or mood of the country. Edith liked to sift through these selections as well as read three or four newspapers of her own choosing, and then call Theodore's attention to "any item which she thought he should know about."[18]

In spite of the splendor of her new surroundings, and the importance of her administrative duties, Edith privately continued to find her identity in motherhood. "I have been busy in my trunks today," she wrote Emily after returning to Oyster Bay to collect the children the following Sunday. "The baby trunk made me rather sad . . . I shall keep the little things another year in the hope of using them."

His wife's longing for a sixth child (or seventh, counting Alice) was not shared by Theodore. Even after the birth of Archie he had said that his particular branch of the Roosevelt family tree was quite prolific enough. Nor did the White House doctor, Admiral Preston Rixey, find the First Lady's desire to become pregnant at forty-one "reasonable."[19] But Edith remained quietly optimistic.

The Roosevelts made their formal move into the new White House on November 5, 1902. The Main Floor reception rooms were still far from finished, and there was still so much dust about that Edith's personal maid protested every time she was asked to lay out a fresh tea gown. The continued presence of workmen, however, did not deter Theodore from entertaining. To one of his first lunches came Helen Nicolay, Secretary of the Washington Literary Club, who described the gathering in a letter indicating that Edith's redecoration, at least of the Red Room, was not to everyone's taste.

> The whole lower floor of the White House is in a mess, undergoing alterations that will improve it immensely. There was a strong smell of turpentine everywhere, and we were relieved of our wraps while standing in the great vestibule, on one foot, so to speak, clutching our skirts to keep them out of the carpenters' dust on the floor. Then we were ushered into the Red Parlor, whose walls have been covered with deep red velvet, with results rather startling. At least to my mind, they combine the fascinations of a pall and a sleeping car. The room is at present furnished with a misfit collection of leather chairs and lounges. The real furniture is being made to order we are told. It also is to be covered with leather, because the room is to be used for smoking on occasion, and the furniture must not be of a material to hold the smoke. Fancy—with those walls!
>
> In a few minutes Mr. Von Briesen was ushered in. Then Mrs. Roosevelt appeared, dressed in white wool. She has a wonderfully pleasant voice and a sweet face . . . When a little after two o'clock the door opened and the President came in—teeth and all—no time was lost in making for the dining room. He took out Mrs. Hay, the rest of us followed in a group. Mrs. Roosevelt stopped a moment at the door of the state dining room to point out some change, and the President, having

seated his lady, came bouncing back, like a rubber ball, to see why we did not come on. The poor man was frankly hungry, having been on his feet since 9:20 A.M. seeing people, deciding questions all in a minute, and emphatically leading the strenuous life. He said he felt as though he had been galloping. He talked most entertainingly throughout the meal, and managed besides to dispose of a goodly amount of food. You will laugh when I give you the menu—*bouillon,* salt fish, chicken with rice, rolls, and baked beans. Of beans and the salt fish the President had a second helping. For dessert there was Bavarian cream, served with preserves and cakes. There was one kind of wine, which most of the party declined, and tea, poured by Mrs. Roosevelt, who made it for all the rest just as her husband liked his "and no questions asked." Cigars were passed after the meal and lighted by the two lawyers. Mr. Roosevelt did not smoke.

The china was miscellaneous: nice enough but not extraordinary. I only remember some pretty Haviland, and that the bread and butter plates were in the form of flags of the different nations. The President had the Star Spangled Banner, the rest of us got what was left. The German [von Briesen] drew the tricolour; I the Union Jack. The waiters were two spry slim coloured youths, not in livery, and they were kept rather busy. My impression is that they were always moving toward the President.

If my life depended on it I could not tell you about the centerpiece. There must have been one; but the truth is that Mr. Roosevelt was so rattlingly lively, yet so earnest and dignified, his wife so kind and unaffected, and the whole meal so informal in character, that what was on the table dwindled to minor importance. Theodore, Jr. appeared after we were all seated, shook hands all around, took part in the talk with the aplomb of young America, and excused himself before dessert to go riding with his small sister—having meanwhile extracted from his mother permission to use her horse.

It was just a nice lively United States family entertaining with heartiness and pot-luck chance visitors of the hour. The only visible difference was that the President was served first, then Mrs. Roosevelt, and after them the guests. Oh, yes. Another detail not customary. U.S. was embroidered on plate doilies. The President and Mrs. Roosevelt sat opposite each other at the sides, not the ends, of the oval table.

The talk ranged over many subjects—importunate Senators; Colonel Hay's Bavarian ancestors; the Negro problem; the impossibility of [Roosevelt's] doing more than establish certain fixed principles in his own mind and live up to them regardless, and his feeling of the deep obligation he was under, as President, to do this; anecdotes of pet riding horses and a humorous account of a portrait recently painted of him, which was, he said, the only portrait of himself he had ever liked. He liked it because it did not resemble him in the least, but looked as he would like to look. It was a picture he wished to leave to his grandchildren, if he ever had any.

In spite of his almost incessant talk, I was impressed with the care he took—the care of a generous, thoughtful host—to bring up topics that would interest and draw out the best from each one of his guests in turn. Von Briesen had worked with him in civic matters in New York, and his praise caused the German to turn shy and rosy as a girl.

References to books and authors showed much reading the President managed to do, while the rapidity with which his mind worked kept us all on the jump. He seemed to follow the usual processes of reasoning, but to do so at twice or thrice the usual rate of speed, with the result of apparently leaping from conclusion to conclusion, while the rest of us hurried breathlessly after him . . .

But the impression above all others is of a man *living* with every fibre of his being, ardently as well as arduously, and having the best time of anybody who ever inhabited the White House.[20]

The State Dining Room, where this luncheon took place, was (aside from the East Room) the most dramatically changed of all the Mansion's public chambers. By the removal of the west staircase which had been adjacent, the seating capacity was increased from sixty to 107. Its oak-paneled walls were embellished with Corinthian pilasters and hung with two seventeenth-century Flemish tapestries. An Indian carpet of solid green covered the floor, and the windows were draped with emerald velvet, in contrast to the elaborate stucco ceiling and silver chandelier. The furniture consisted of lustrous mahogany tables, Regency–style consoles supported by eagles, and high-backed Queen Anne chairs. A large stone chimneypiece was installed in the center of the west wall. It was decorated with two carved lion heads—much to the irritation of Theodore, who would later change them for the American buffalo.[21] McKim was also unable to stop him from ornamenting the carved cornice with stuffed moose and deer heads.

Henry Adams found the room "charming" but was amused at the unintentional irony of its size. "Theodore innocently delights in its space which dwarfs him. Mrs. Roosevelt, who has in her mild way, rolled Bammy [*sic*] quite out of the house, and very properly . . . accepts the state-rooms with even more pleasure than Theodore does, and looks less lost in them, although she too needs a crown."[22]

Now that the State Dining Room could seat over a hundred people, Edith found that she had an embarrassing insufficiency of matching china. She had inherited what remained of large sets of French porcelains purchased by Mary Lincoln, Lucy Hayes, and Caroline Harrison, and parts of smaller sets bought by Frances Cleveland and Ida McKinley. None, however, had enough pieces to serve more than eighty guests at a time. Edith therefore ordered a complete set of 1,320 pieces of creamy white English Wedgwood—(enough for 120 place settings) decorated with a two-inch-wide Colonial motif, incorporating the Great Seal of the United States, and enameled in traditional red, brown and yellow.[23]

When first laid out on the great tables, the Roosevelt china was handsomely complemented by existing pearl-handled, gold-bladed knives, cut glass engraved with the United States coat of arms, and a thirteen foot gilded bronze surtout de table centerpiece. Edith now undertook a project first conceived, but never realized, by Mrs.

Harrison. She not only collected together the known sets of presidential china, but began to search for the rarer pieces which previous administrations had scattered. Her efforts were amazingly successful. By 1904 she would have recovered enough historic White House china to merit its display. With the help of Abby Gunn Baker, a Washington journalist, she arranged a selection of the best pieces in specially made cabinets installed in the Ground Floor Corridor. Before she left the White House the exhibit featured relics of almost all twenty-five previous Administrations.[24]

Determined that future Presidents and their wives should not be as cavalier with White House heirlooms as her predecessors, Edith had a complete inventory made of all china, glass, and furniture in her care. Thereafter it was the rule not to dispose of objects of historic value at any President's whim.

Two of Edith Kermit Roosevelt's claims to enduring recognition remain that she established the White House China Collection and created the gallery of portraits of First Ladies, emphasizing the role that she and other presidential wives have played in the nation's history.

Henry Adams was cautiously pleased with the rest of the restored mansion. "It is now quite a gentleman's place," he told Elizabeth Cameron, "mostly done in white." He felt, however, that the parts done in red and green were "less successful." Even so, few could deny that the Red Room, when finally completed, was a vasty improved parlor. Gone were the Romanesque Revival motifs and mahogany mantle of Chester Arthur's time. In their place were classical patterns, and a small, more refined Italian marble fireplace removed from the State Dining Room. Red Venetian silk velvet covered the walls, and red damask upholstery the furniture. In place of the portraits of Presidents' wives, which Edith had removed to her downstairs gallery of First Ladies, she hung three or four of the finest presidential portraits available. Supreme over the fireplace was the great Stuart study of Washington, which she considered the most valuable possession of the White House.[25]

Another mantlepiece, also taken from the State Dining Room, was placed in the Green Room, where its proportions showed to better advantage. This elegant parlor, with its cool-looking Genoese velvet walls, developed a silvery sheen at certain times of day, when the light from outside streamed horizontally through the windows.

McKim had removed most traces of nineteenth-century décor, returning the room to its original pure lines, and illuminating nine further presidential portraits with a magnificent crystal chandelier.

Before the renovation, the Blue Room had had baby-blue hangings, outdated ornaments, and furniture more suitable for a lady's boudoir than the chief reception room in the nation. Now the walls were covered with steel-blue corded silk edged with yellow Grecian embroidery, and the windows draped with matching fabric. The new furniture was in French Empire style, upholstered in blue and gold. A door was cut in the east wall to match one cut earlier on the west side to facilitate the passing of guests through to the Green and Red Rooms and from there to the East Room and the State Dining Room respectively.

The most dramatically transformed chamber of all, as far as the visiting public was concerned, was the huge East Room. Stripped of its grimy frescoed ceiling, dark wallpaper and faded carpets, it now seemed full of radiant space, as opposed to Victorian gloom. McKim installed ornamental stucco, enameled panels, low-relief sculpture by the Piccirilli brothers, and polished oak floors, achieving a grand but spare simplicity.

Three electric chandeliers, each hung with 3,500 pieces of crystal, and four bronze Roman standards substituted for the bulbous lighting installed by President Grant. In place of dusty padded sofas and heavy curtains, McKim had ordered carved, gilded banquettes covered with silk velour, and warm yellow damask draperies. Marble-topped consoles and enormous mirrors gave the room a brightness appropriate to the many festivities the Roosevelts intended to hold there.

Edith allowed the children to make a garden beneath the East Room windows, so that when spring came guests could look out onto colorful pansies and geraniums.[26]

One intentional side effect of McKim's redesign was a streamlining in the flow of large numbers of visitors. Ordinary White House guests no longer crowded the hallway struggling to remove and check their outer garments, as Edith herself had done on New Year's Day 1890. Instead they alighted from carriages at a newly built porte cochere opposite the Treasury Building, and proceeded to cloakrooms in the resurrected East Terrace.[27] Here, to right and left of the entrance, were rows of umbrella stands and 2,500 boxes to store wraps.

Eminent guests shed their cloaks in separate dressing rooms

"Stripped of its grimy frescoed ceiling . . .
it now seemed full of radiant space."
The East Room before and after the restoration of 1902.

located under the East Room, and were received in an ellipse beneath and echoing that of the Blue Room, which was called the Diplomatic Ante-Room. McKim had created both of these extra spaces by dropping a boiler, and its attendant pipes and ducts, into trenches below the basement floor.

From the East Wing and the Ground Floor Corridor (now comfortably furnished with sofas and decorated with potted plants) visitors reached a fifteen-foot-wide staircase leading to the Main Floor reception rooms. Overnight guests could ascend from the basement to the upper floors by a splendid new elevator, made of oak roof trusses from the Old South Church in Boston. The interior was mirrored and embellished with a carved frieze and a rolling grille of brass poles.[28] This novel conveyance provided endless amusement to the children, who somehow found a way to arrest its progress between floors by pushing exterior buttons, to the irritation and bewilderment of adult passengers.

"The White House, first a work of art, then by changes an architectural aberration, is now by restoration a charming and refined mansion," was the verdict of the Secretary of the American Institute of Architects. Edith's opinion was more prosaic, but no less heartfelt. "It is a great pleasure to have guests now that I can make them comfortable," she wrote Aunt Lizzie. "Every day I am more thankful to Mr. McKim for all the changes that he made." Theodore's view was that the presidential home had been transformed "from a shabby likeness to the ground floor of the Astor House into a simple and dignified dwelling for the head of a great republic." Addressing future generations, he emphasized the importance of preserving "a perpetual eye of guardianship" over the Executive Mansion "to see it is kept unchanged and unmarred from this time on."[29]

Mr. Dooley fervently agreed. In his opinion, Roosevelt had changed things too much already.

> Up to his time th' White House was a place where any gintleman cud live but wudden't if there was a hotel handy. But it wasn't good enough for this jood. He changed it around . . . to suit th' ideas iv archytecture in New York. He put th' coal cellar on th' roof, th' kitchen

in th' treasury departmint an' arranged it so that guests enthered through th' laundhry an' proceeded up through th' ash chute to a pint where they was picked up by an autymatic disthributor and disthributed—th' leg in the East Room, th' arms in the West Room, an' so on . . . In this palace he lives like a king, an' onaisy lies th' head that wears a crown.

. . . All this takes money, Hinnissy, an' where does it come fr'm? Out iv my pocket an' ye'er's, me boy. It's you an' me that's payin' f'r this here oryental splindhor.[30]

Twenty

She was the perfection of "invisible government."
—Owen Wister[1]

In spite of the political difficulties of his first fifteen months in office, Theodore Roosevelt thoroughly enjoyed guiding the "great machinery" of government. He felt confident in his position, and secure in the knowledge that his wife was more than equal to her duties as First Lady. "I do not think my eyes are blinded by affection," he wrote Maria Storer on December 8, 1902, "when I say that she has combined to a degree I have never seen in any other woman the power of being the best of wives and mothers, the wisest manager of the household, and at the same time the ideal great lady and mistress of the White House."[2]

Ten days later the Roosevelts hosted their first annual Cabinet dinner,[3] signaling the approach of the first social season in the renovated Mansion. Its official arrival was marked by the flinging open of wrought-iron gates at the foot of the White House's new east stairway on January 1, 1903. Edith and Theodore descended to the traditional blare of trumpets to begin their New Year's reception. One by one the time-honored sequence of entertainments followed: the Diplomatic Reception on January 8, the Diplomatic Corps

Dinner on January 15, the Judicial Reception on January 22, the Supreme Court Dinner on January 29, the Congressional Reception on February 5, and the Army and Navy Reception on February 12— interspersed with nightly balls, musicales, theater parties and suppers.

With the opening of the season, the remodeled Mansion was exposed to curious and critical eyes eager to see what changes Edith had created. Important guests arriving for the Diplomatic Reception on January 8 passed through the new south entrance and were surprised to see busts and portraits of First Ladies in "a warm and spacious corridor" where previously there had been nothing but boilers and pipes. A few people grumbled that it was a "desecration" to exhibit such hallowed relics in "the cellar," but the general reaction to the new First Ladies' Gallery was favorable. "It seems to me it has rescued those admirable females from oblivion," wrote Ellen Maurey Slayden, wife of a Senator from Texas. "The light is good, there is plenty of room and anyone who wants to gaze at Mrs. Van Buren's bobbing curls or Mrs. Hayes's blue velvet dress 'all buttoned down before' can do it at leisure without incommoding other people."[4]

Dominating the gallery was a magnificent new canvas of Mrs. Roosevelt by Théobald Chartran, presented as a gift from the French people. The mistress of the White House was portrayed seated on a white bench in the garden, against a background of the classic columns of the South Portico. She was wearing a white chiffon ruffled dress, a black coat and a black Gainsborough hat. Her right hand held a pair of white gloves, and her left lightly clasped a fine ebony parasol. The pose characteristically combined informality with regality and the calm that was always Edith's most noted attribute.

While the two thousand guests were assembling in the East Room (which struck some as "white and bare"[5]) the Roosevelts entertained a select few to dinner. Among those invited were the Owen Wisters, who arrived late, embarrassed, and panting. But Edith quickly put them at their ease, so much so that Wister remembered every detail of the evening that followed, and wrote an evocative account of it:

> Mrs. Roosevelt was gracious and consoling; she had not known of our arrival or they would not have sat down. Various shiftings of places were caused by our coming, but the company was not large. It was all easy

and informal and gay, as Roosevelt most liked to have it. . . . This particular dinner . . . was my first meal there since the whole place had been done over beneath the guiding taste of Mrs. Roosevelt. He [TR] knew how a room ought to look, but less minutely how to make it look so . . .

Inkpots, waste baskets, frosted glass doors, clicking typewriters, the whole back-stairs of office running, removed from the front stairs where it had been suffered to encroach, and put decently out of sight. Very handsome admirable dining room, new furnished; simple, dignified new wainscoting of natural wood; and round about, the solemn heads of moose and elk. All the rest of the house in keeping; a sense of quiet throughout, instead of the ugly sights and sounds of business rattling away just outside the bedroom doors. No display, everything simple—but dignified—as the President's house ought to be.

As to the food itself, there was never a piling on of courses, it was always good—and simple, with sherry and white wine . . .

. . . he allowed us but a short time for our cigars . . . the procession was formed and we marched down to the blue room . . . The President and Mrs. Roosevelt stood side by side at the head of the room, roped off from us guests. I do not see how the natural welcome of a hostess and the dignity of a great position could be more perfectly blended and expressed. She also looked very well; not tired, which seemed wonderful, considering the exactions that she had to meet every day. . . . Next [to] the President stood a Secret Service man, a truly ambrosial creature with shining hair, a yellow mustache, a man's fine figure, and an eye that must certainly have turned the heads of many distracted females. The President told me that he was a mountaineer from West Virginia. Cabot Lodge said while I was looking at him and commenting on his impressive appearance: "Yes; and it's not pleasant to reflect that as he stands there, his hand is on his revolver from start to finish."

And so for two hours the American people with each

name announced passed in at the door to the President's left, and across the space roped off, and out at the door to the right . . .

One of the people addressed Mr. Roosevelt as well as her husband, saying: "Good evening, Mrs. President."

. . . After the great crowd was gone, about eleven, certain invited guests went up to the hall above, and then sat at little tables and were refreshed with much needed bouillon; and champagne, and ice cream.[6] My wife and I came wandering along the hall, and were hailed by Cabot Lodge and Mrs. Rhinelander Jones, and Dooley . . . They called us to come and sit at their table, which we were glad enough to do. It was not long before we saw the President approaching, stopping at each table to see that his guests were comfortable; and so he gradually made his way to us. He checked our rising with a quick gesture, as he often did, and then placing his hand on Dooley's shoulder, he addressed us in a strong Irish accent:

"'I haven't time f'r to tell ye th' wurruk Tiddy did in ar-rmin' and equippin' himself, how he fed himself, how he steadied himself in battles an' encouraged himself with a few well-chosen wurruds whin' th' sky was darkest. Ye'll have to take a squint into th' book ye'ersilf to l'arn thim things.'

"'I won't do it,' said Mr. Hennessy. 'I think Tiddy Rosenfelt is all r-right an' if he wants to blow his hor-rn lave him do it.'

"'Thrue f'r ye," said Mr. Dooley . . . "But if I was him I'd call th' book 'Alone in Cubia.'"

His recitation was longer than I have quoted; and all the time that he was delivering it with the most vigorous gusto and a countenance beaming with mirth and appreciation, his hand lay on the shoulder of the man who had written it. . . . It was one of Dooley's most brilliant satires, written when the story of the Rough Riders had been published after the Spanish War, and while he was Governor of New York. It was an example of the President's astonishing power to retain what he read. . . .

"By George, that was bully!" said the President to Dunne. "I did enjoy that!" And he laughed with the rest of us.

Dunne, purple-faced during the recitation, managed to recover his composure and have the last word.

"Do you know, Mr. Roosevelt," he said solemnly, "the appearance of your cabinet is a great disappointment to me. *I don't believe one of them has ever killed a man.*"[7]

Because the White House kitchens were unable to handle the huge numbers of guests at state banquets, Edith relied on the services of Washington's leading caterer, Rauscher. While each menu was being prepared she would arrange the seating with her majordomo, and send the list to the President for his approval. Usually he accepted her plans without question, only checking to ensure there would be no bores in his immediate vicinity. No matter how politically desirable a dinner guest might be, Theodore could not tolerate bad talkers or, worse still, bad listeners.

The dinner menu Edith served the Diplomatic Corps on January 15, 1903, survives as an example of one of her more elaborate banquets. The selection of dishes was deliberately international, and was printed in a curious mixture of French and English.

Cape Cod Oysters on Ice Plates
Croutes Panachées

———

Potage Consommé Printanier aux
Quenelles de Volaille

———

Stuffed Olives   Curled Celery
Salted Almonds

———

Tartalettes à la Moelle

———

Mousse of Lobster à la Richelieu,
Sauce Corail

———

Poulards Braisé Montesquieu

Aloyan of Beef à la Diplomate
Timbales Chartreuse   Potatoes Palestine

— Sorbet —
Granité au Champagne

English Pheasant Roasted
Salade of Season

Paté de Foie Gras en Bellevue

Cheese   Pull Bread

— Glâcé —
Fantasie

Petits Fours Glacé   Cerises Fondantas
Marrons Glacé

Peppermints   Bonbons Fourrés

— café —[8]

Sherry, Sauternes, Bordeaux Rouge, Ruinart, Appolinaris and liqueurs accompanied the banquet. The Marine Band, stationed in the North Vestibule, played a program of music which was as international as the food, including Brahms's Hungarian Dances, some American marches, and a grand fantasia from Verdi's *Il Trovatore*. Not surprisingly the dinner took much longer than the customary one and a half hours. Afterward ladies returned to the East Room, while the gentlemen took coffee and cigars in the Private Dining Room.[9]

Rauscher's fee for banquets such as this was $7.50 a plate, rising to ten dollars a plate if wines were included. The President paid the entire amount out of his own pocket. Theodore also insisted on ordering champagne and cigars, saying he wanted "only the best served at the White House." As a result he spent more than any previous Chief Executive on entertaining, but he did so cheerfully, explaining that he had "a horror of trying to save any money out of his pay."[10]

When Theodore and Edith dined privately their tastes were simple, but even then Theodore could not resist turning every meal into a social event. The First Lady would order a light lunch for two, and then "the President would come in with three or four people, and there was no time to add to the menu." Guests therefore left hungry. Ike Hoover, the White House usher, overheard one mutter to another, after an inadequate serving of liver and bacon, "Let's go to the hotel and get something to eat."[11]

Edith was unable to attend her last musicale of the season before Lent. During the preparatory dinner she felt faint, and had to retire upstairs. For the next two days she was confined to her bed. *Town Topics* was quick to notice "Mrs. Roosevelt's abrupt disappearance from society," and reminded its readers of a similar withdrawal the previous spring. No doubt the culprit was again "the stork."[12]

Once more the magazine was right, and once more the stork proved an elusive bird. "I am now feeling quite myself," Edith sadly wrote Emily on March 22, ". . . the Doctor says that he likes me to ride unless I should get into that condition again, when I must stop at once and be very careful." But she still did not give up hope of having another child. "My two spring experiences have made me cautious about having clothes made up," she wrote in another letter, adding that if she did manage to conceive again, "I would not come downstairs to any function so as to give myself every chance . . ."[13]

Meanwhile Theodore, though working exceptionally hard, managed to find time to have two portraits painted. One was by Chartran, the other by John Singer Sargent. He disliked the Chartran, because it reminded the family of "a mewing cat," and made veiled threats to have it destroyed before he left the White House. The Sargent, on the other hand, pleased him. Even before it was finished the President wrote that it was "going to be great . . . He is painting it on the landing of the big stairs . . . because he said the light was best there." The portrait, showing Roosevelt pausing in mid-descent, with his hand on the bannister knob, soon went on display at Fischer's. Henry Adams described it to Elizabeth Cameron with his usual perspicacity and spleen. "The portrait is good Sargent and not very bad Roosevelt. It is not Theodore, but a young intellectual idealist with a taste for athletics, which I take to be Theodore's idea of himself. It is for once less brutal than its subject, and will only murder everything in the White House. Of course we all approve it." [14]

The First Family broke up temporarily at the approach of spring. Alice made a goodwill visit to Puerto Rico; Theodore left for a two-month cross-country tour; Edith took her three youngest children on a cruise in the naval yacht *Mayflower*. With Ted and Kermit away at school, the White House was silent for the first time in months. Then, on Easter Monday, April 13, it resounded again with happy shrieks. Thousands of young Washingtonians arrived carrying baskets of hard boiled eggs, which they proceeded to roll down the gently sloping lawns. Edith did not approve of this old custom. "It seems such needless destruction of the lovely grass." Almost worse was the game called "picking eggs," when pairs of children tapped their respective eggs together to see whose cracked first. The huge number of broken eggs gave off a combined odor that could be smelled three squares away,[15] and Edith was relieved when the contest came to a conclusion.

Nine-year-old Archie missed the fun, having been stricken by both measles and whooping cough. He was also depressed about the death of "Jack Dog," a favorite black-and-tan fox terrier. Edith had Jack buried in a glass-topped coffin and promised reinterment in the "Faithful Friends" pet cemetery at Sagamore Hill later. But Archie was inconsolable. To cheer him up, Quentin enlisted the aid of a footman in coaxing Algonquin, Archie's calico pony, into the White House elevator. The 350-pound animal was understandably nervous at first, but soon became interested in his own reflection in the elevator mirror, enabling the footman to press the second-floor button. The sight of Algonquin trotting into Archie's bedroom did wonders for the invalid, who immediately began to mend. In no time at all he was up and dressed in his riding costume of Rough Rider hat, blue knickerbockers, and yellow leggings, and galloping around the White House grounds again.

The Roosevelt children and their ever-growing menagerie of eccentric pets came as a godsend to the Washington press, who had

"The sight of Algonquin trotting in . . . did wonders for the invalid."
Quentin Roosevelt mounted, with White House policeman.

been starved of humorous copy since the days of Abraham Lincoln. In addition to Algonquin there was Tom Quartz, "the cunningest kitten," who once seized Speaker Joe Cannon by the ankle half way down the grand staircase; there was Kermit's kangaroo rat, who had to be fed lumps of sugar at the breakfast table; there were Eli the blue macaw and Loretta the parrot, who periodically filled the Executive Mansion corridors with their cackling; and there was Emily Spinach, the emerald green snake (named after the unfortunate Miss Carow) whom Alice took to fashionable parties in her purse. "A nervous person had no business around the White House in those days," remembered Ike Hoover. "He was sure to be a wreck in a very short time."[16]

Edith would have been the first to agree. No sooner had she waxed, polished and finished the new East Room's handsome parquet floor than the staff found it crisscrossed with spiral-rutted lines. "We thought it would make a fine roller-skating ring," the young culprits explained, "and we found it dandy."[17]

"Not one of my children ever wants to be told or directed about anything whatever!" Edith admitted to Ethel's piano teacher. It was no use appealing to Theodore, who had been known to slip into the nursery before a Diplomatic Reception for a romp with "two small persons in pink tommies," emerging with his dress shirt so "mussed" that it had to be changed. "He thinks children should be given entire freedom for their own inclinations," the First Lady complained.[18]

On May 3, Edith dined at Henry Adams's house with a group of friends, to say goodbye to the historian, who was about to sail for Europe. Adams was in a feisty frame of mind, and harped on his favorite theme—the superiority of the American female to her male counterpart. "The American man is a failure!" he ranted. "Has not my sister here more sense than my brother Brooks? . . . Wouldn't we all elect Mrs. Lodge Senator against Cabot? Would the President have a ghost of a chance if Mrs. Roosevelt ran against him?" Someone remarked that these women were not average, and Adams replied that neither were the men. Edith, who was always stimulated by such conversation, enjoyed herself hugely. "Everyone was as pleasant as possible," she wrote her husband afterward, carefully neglecting to tell him exactly what Adams had said.[19]

Theodore returned from his transcontinental tour on June 5, 1903. Edith heaved a deep sigh of relief when she saw his carriage drive up to the White House portico. Although she believed that the West was "the one place in his domains" where he could "escape the ubiquitous reporter," she felt drained by her two anxious months of worrying about his safety.[20] The children could hardly contain themselves for excitement, and waited with bated breath to see what gifts he had brought. The favorite was a badger named Josiah, who waddled about "like a little bear submitting with perfect equanimity to being picked up." Archie was pleased to discover that "he bites legs sometimes but he never bites faces."[21]

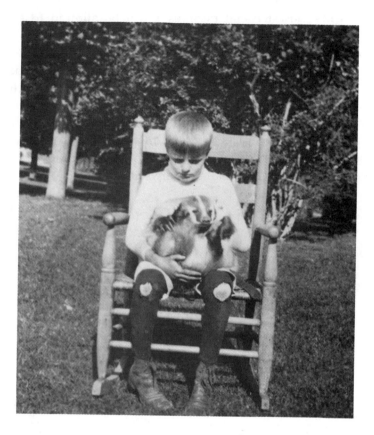

"He bites legs sometimes but he never bites faces."
Archibald Roosevelt with Josiah the badger.

The President looked bronzed and healthy and rested. He had managed to squeeze into his itinerary two field trips to Yosemite and Yellowstone with the naturalists John Muir and John Burroughs. (The latter was of the opinion that "the most interesting thing in that wonderful land was, of course, the President himself.") Inspired by the splendors he had seen in the parks, Theodore was determined to put Yosemite under national control. "I want to go just as far in preserving the forests and preserving the game and wild creatures as I can lead the public sentiment."[22]

Despite his excitement at being home, Theodore did not fail to notice that Edith had put on one of her dresses he most admired, and that she had lost a flattering amount of weight. "It is not good taste to speak about one's wife," he confided to Lodge next day, "but in writing to my closest friend perhaps I can be allowed to say that though Edith looked frail she looked so pretty that upon my word she seemed to me just as attractive as seventeen years ago when I crossed to England to meet her." A few days later he was still rhapsodizing to Taft. "I take the keenest pride in seeing Mrs. Roosevelt at the head of the White House—a gentlewoman, who gives to all the official life . . . an air of gracious and dignified simplicity, and who with it all is the ideal of a good American wife and mother who takes care of her six children in the most devoted manner . . . Mrs. Roosevelt comes a good deal nearer my ideal than I do myself."[23]

Twenty-One

*At the Roosevelts' there was a great bubble and hum in the air,
with Mrs. Roosevelt, loveliest and wisest of hostesses, keeping
table talk off the rocks.*

—Julia Foraker[1]

"We have had a lovely summer—as lovely a summer as we have
ever passed," Theodore told Corinne just before returning to
Washington on September 28. "Alice," he added disapprovingly,
"has been at home very little—spending most of her time in Newport
and elsewhere, associating with the Four Hundred—individuals with
whom the other members of the family have exceedingly few
affiliations."[2]

Life was a giddy whirl for the beautiful nineteen-year-old "Princess
Alice." As the President's daughter she was naturally the belle of
American society, and frantically pursued by the press. Her position,
though one of privilege, carried no responsibilities, and as an
unabashed hedonist she made the most of it. Newsworthy escapades
made better copy than praiseworthy duties, such as laying foundation
stones and attending demure tea parties. Headline after headline

"A young wild animal . . . put into good clothes."
Alice Roosevelt, aged eighteen.

recorded her comings and goings. Alice had taken a submarine plunge to the bottom of the ocean; she had been seen dancing at midnight on the Vanderbilts' roof; she had raced a Panhard, unchaperoned, from Newport to Boston at the reckless speed of twenty-five miles an hour; she had placed bets at a racetrack, engaged in poker games, and even smoked cigarettes in public. She was, said Ruth Lee, "like a young wild animal that had been put into good clothes." Arthur Lee was less critical. He liked Alice's "golden sense of humour," and said that there was "enough of her father in her" to captivate his affections.[3]

Certainly, given the opportunity, Alice could comport herself flawlessly. She was quite capable in Edith's absence of standing in "with a brilliant manner and a friendly conception of her duty to her father's guests . . . very competent, thoughtful, picturesque, with an inexhaustible stock of pleasant surprises."[4]

Alice liked the role of official hostess, and shone on the rare occasions the President called upon her to play it. Usually, however, he kept his eldest child at a distance. Perhaps her presence was a painful reminder of his intense feeling for the first Alice Lee; perhaps her pranks were a desperate cry for his attention. Whatever the case, Edith went out of her way to compensate the girl for lack of paternal warmth. Theodore's flesh, in her opinion, was her own flesh. But no amount of stepmotherly affection ever quite made up for Alice's deprivation. The hurt went deep, concealed behind a gaily defiant façade.

"Father doesn't care for me," Alice wrote in her diary, "that is to say one eighth as much as he does for the other children. It is perfectly true that he doesn't, and, Lord, why *should* he. We are not in the least congenial, and if I don't care overmuch for him and don't take an interest in the things he likes, why *should* he pay any attention to me or the things that I live for, except to look on them with disapproval."[5]

From time to time Theodore tried to enforce discipline upon her. He vainly berated her for her lack of family feeling, forbade her to smoke under his roof, and attempted to separate her from the flighty Marguerite Cassini, whom he considered a bad influence. Governing the United States was one thing; controlling Alice was another, he said despairingly.[6]

His daughter's *cris de coeur* grew ever louder and brasher. She took to enlivening dull parties by firing off dynamite caps and flaunting her bilious-looking snake. She also made a habit of emerging from her room at midday, to emphasize how late she had been out the night before. "Sister continues to lead the life of social excitement, which is I think all right for a girl to lead for a year or two, but which upon my word I do not regard as healthy from the standpoint of permanence," Theodore wrote Ted. "I wish she had some pronounced serious taste. Perhaps," the President added, without much conviction, "she will develop one later."[7]

That fall Alice did develop a serious taste, for the short, muscular, balding, well-bred new Congressman from Ohio, Nicholas Longworth. At thirty-four, "Nick" was fifteen years older than Alice, and a man of the world for whom a dazzling career in politics was forecast. No doubt much of his appeal for her lay in his resemblance to her father; but his urbane conversation and polished manner made him attractive to many other young women. Men were drawn to him as well. He had a reputation as a gourmet and an oenophile (his family were noted Cincinnati viniculturalists) and always entertained lavishly. Besides, he was so musically gifted that even the supremely unmusical Theodore Roosevelt acknowledged him to be "much the best violinist who ever left Harvard."[8]

Despite Alice's obvious political and sexual appeal, not to mention her ill-concealed love for him, Nick was more taken with the dark Russian charms of Marguerite Cassini at first. He wooed the latter extravagantly, with large quantities of long-stemmed roses, and repeatedly asked if she would care to live "in a little red brick house in Cincinnati." (By this he meant Rookwood, his palatial family home.) Marguerite would laughingly reply that she preferred "a little white *isba* on the steppes of Russia." Nick's ardent purposefulness was too much for the flirtatious countess, and when Alice asked point-blank if Nick had proposed, Marguerite said that she had turned him down. "He is the second person [Charles de Chambrun was the first] that I vowed to have and that she has reft [?] from me. So I suppose there will be a third," Alice wrote in her diary. "I don't think he should have been as nice to me as he has been . . . oh why am I such a desperate pill." From then on the relationship between the girls was noticeably cooler.[9]

Acknowledging defeat, Nick now began to turn his attention to Alice.

The season of 1904 heralded a presidential election year, and White House entertainments were on a markedly splendid scale. Unprecedented numbers of richly dressed millionaires and famous artists and writers appeared at the various functions, and people began to talk about the regal style the Roosevelts had brought to the Presidency. Henry Adams, recently returned from Europe, was invited to the Diplomatic Reception on January 17, and was astonished by the monarchical trappings and imperial manners everywhere in evidence. Small Oriental ministers in peacock-embroidered kimonos jostled against the epaulettes of European and South American dignitaries, and the jewel-encrusted bosoms of American society ladies, for an hour and a half before being rewarded by Theodore's handshake and Edith's smile. After a further hour of "rattling with the court," Adams obeyed Belle Hagner's summons to join a procession of privileged guests and march upstairs for supper.

"I was a good deal bewildered by this style of royalty," the historian wrote Elizabeth Cameron, "but I was completely staggered by what followed." Acting for all the world like an absolute monarch, Theodore overwhelmed his guests with a "torrent of oratory" on every political issue ranging from the Boer War to the Panama Canal. To Adams's philosophic mind, the President's obsessive use of the personal pronoun was "mere cerebral excitement," but the frenzied tone of his monologues disturbed him nevertheless. "The town is hot and smoking with tales of the Imperial Court," Adams reported, "and our quiet simple little Edie of ten years ago has flowered into the chief object of attack." [10]

If Edith had any inkling of this criticism, she paid no attention. The White House might have become a "court," but her private life went on much as before, and she kept up with her old friends.

On January 20 a letter arrived from Cecil Spring-Rice (who was now First Secretary at the British Embassy in St. Petersburg) announcing his engagement to Florence Lascelles, daughter of the British Ambassador to Berlin. The cautious Springy was almost forty-five, and had known his fianceé for eight years. He therefore felt there was a "certain amount of safeness" in the match, and hoped Edith would approve. "I am rather accustomed mentally to ask about a contemplated action, 'What would T.R. think of it?' and of a contemplated *person* 'What would E.R. think of it?' The answer in this case was satisfactory. I am quite sure you would like her if you knew her."[11]

The news of Spring-Rice's subsequent marriage in June to the inconspicuous-looking Florence (who at an Embassy reception for impoverished gentlewomen was once mistaken for one of the guests) came as a surprise to Washingtonians. They knew that in the past he had preferred pretty, well-dressed women such as Elizabeth Cameron and Mary Leiter. But Florence apparently had compensating virtues. She was practical and musical, and liked "exactly the same things" as her husband. After three weeks of honeymoon Spring-Rice admitted that he was "quite ashamed of being so happy."[12]

On February 1, 1904, Elihu Root resigned his post as Secretary of War and returned to private life. The President was quick to say how much he would miss this disinterested adviser, even though Root had fought him on every policy with which he disagreed.

Root's replacement was William Howard Taft, a genial Ohioan with walrus mustache and ample girth (he weighed over three hundred pounds). He was conventional, sluggish, and lacking in dynamism—"a fat mush," said Adams.[13] Taft had a brilliant legal mind, but, as Edith shrewdly pointed out, was too much of a yes-man to be able to give such bold, impartial advice as Root.

The First Lady looked for fearlessness and candor in the men surrounding her husband, but seldom found it. The President was such an intimidating personality, with strong opinions, forcefully expressed, that subordinates who dared to dispute his judgment were few. Theodore's tendency to like everyone who agreed with him compounded the problem. All the more fortunate, said one correspondent, that he should be blessed with a wife with "infinitely superior insight" into character than he, who could save him "many a slip."[14] Her misgivings about Taft were, as it turned out, entirely justified.

Theodore had further reason to lament Root's departure on February 8, 1904, when the Japanese attacked Port Arthur in Manchuria, to protest Russia's failure to maintain an "Open Door" trade policy in that country. America was weary of Russian intransigence, and, like Japan, would prefer to see Manchuria given over to the Chinese. But for the time being Theodore was too preoccupied with domestic concerns to involve himself actively in Asian affairs. A strike was threatened in the Government Printing Office, extensive fraud had been uncovered in the Post Office, and the rich were threatening to support Mark Hanna as Republican national candidate. Worst of all, the Rooseveltian style of living had come under attack. "Fads, Frauds and Follies Cripple Nation's Finances," ran a headline in the Brooklyn *Eagle*. The new presidential stables, the three yachts, the grand banquets, and even the White House tennis court were all targets. Theodore felt compelled to defend his integrity by writing to Lawrence Fraser Abbot, president of the *Outlook*, in the hope that he would "make public what the real facts are."[15]

The request for new stables, he explained, had not come from him but from the Superintendant of Public Buildings, who felt the old ones stood on unhealthy ground and made the horses sick. As for traveling by yacht, it was obviously a more efficient way than moving the presidential entourage by land, and the expense involved was "too trivial to be considered." White House entertaining, he insisted, cost the taxpayer nothing, since "I pay the butcher, the baker, and the grocer at Washington just as I do at Oyster Bay." The tennis court, he conceded, had cost the nation something—four hundred dollars—but its upkeep was less expensive than the greenhouses it replaced.[16]

If Theodore was damned for spending too much, Edith was damned for spending too little. "The wife of the President, it is said, dresses on three hundred dollars a year," sneered Mrs. Stuyvesant Fish, a leader of the Four Hundred, "and she looks it."[17] This slight, coming as it did from a woman famous for vulgar display, struck the First Lady as a compliment to her thrift, and she pasted it in her scrapbook.

Few presidential wives could have been as frugally elegant as Edith Kermit Roosevelt. "I have had my last year's black velvet hat done over with black roses very prettily," she told Emily in 1904. Mrs. Roosevelt was not, as one columnist wrote, "a woman who centers her attention on clothes. Her gowns last sometimes three seasons, with the sleeves altered now and then to bring them up to date." Nevertheless she managed to maintain what Owen Wister called an "exquisite and very personal simplicity of dress . . . attained as all art is attained by gift united to cunning thought."[18]

This, combined with her still-youthful good looks, attracted compliments even from her husband's archrival, Senator Hanna.

Once at a White House ball a pretty Parisian-gowned girl, angling for compliments, asked the Senator who was the best-dressed woman in the room. Hanna jerked his head in Edith's direction. The girl said she saw nothing remarkable about Mrs. Roosevelt's black dress; it was simply a nice frock. "That's all a lady has to have, sis," said the Senator.[19]

His respect for Edith went far beyond her personal appearance. He once happened upon a small boy who stood in Dupont Circle talking to Quentin and the First Lady in a victoria. As the carriage drove away, Hanna's cane poked the boy in the spine: "You! You ought to take your hat off when any woman speaks to you. When Mrs. Roosevelt speaks to you, keep it off a week!"[20]

The "restless agitation" and "chronic excitement" which Theodore Roosevelt brought to the White House may have made Henry Adams feel tired, but the country at large marveled at their President's energy and zeal.[21] The same degree of force he applied to governing he applied to all his activities. Exercise was done strenuously or not at all; magazine articles were not so much read as demolished, every page torn off after reading and thrown on the floor; hands were not shaken but pulverized, and even the most unimportant callers were greeted like long-lost brothers.

But as the 1904 election approached, there was a marked change in Roosevelt's demeanor and conversation. Adams was among the first to note it at a White House dinner on March 9. "Theodore has stopped talking Cowboy and San Juan," he told Elizabeth Cameron. "Every idea now centres on the election, and he talks about that with all the fluency and *naïveté* of a schoolboy. That he is still a bore as big as a buffalo I do not deny, but at least he is a different sort."[22]

Aware of his insecure status as an accidental President, Theodore was anxious to reassure the American voter that he was a solid, judicious executive, worthy of a full term in his own right. His pace became less febrile, his cordiality more discriminating, and his method of procedure better organized. Administrative problems were no longer given equal weight, and he delegated increasing amounts of responsibility. Always a consummate politician, he now began to look statesmanlike. As a member of the Cabinet grudgingly put it, "He has settled down to his job and is moving as steadily and as safely as an old horse in the plowing."[23]

Edith and Theodore took special pleasure in Washington's blossoming locust trees and honeysuckle vines that spring, knowing that if the electorate voted "with its back to the future" in November they would not be there to see them the following year. "I do not think that any two people ever got more enjoyment out of the White House than Mother and I," the President wrote Ted. "We love the House itself without and within, for its associations, for its stateliness and its simplicity. We love the garden. And we like Washington. We almost always take our breakfast on the south portico now, Mother looking very pretty and dainty in her summer dresses . . ."[24]

According to Taft, Theodore Roosevelt loved the South Portico as he did no other part of the White House. He made his "most brilliant sallies of wit" on that spot, and "when the world seemed to be all awry" it was there that he and Edith sat, "and his tempestuous nature would receive just that influence that made him one of the greatest figures the country has ever seen."[25]

The Roosevelts were sitting on the Portico after lunch on June 23, 1904, when Secretary Loeb brought the news that Theodore and Charles Warren Fairbanks had been nominated Republican candidates for President and Vice-President at the Chicago Convention. The news was not surprising to Theodore, given the fact that his only serious challenger, Senator Hanna, had died earlier that year. His opponent would be Alton B. Parker, a conservative Gold Democrat and anti-imperialist. Edith remembered Parker as the New York State judge who had so accurately forecast Theodore's nomination as Vice-President in 1900. Knowing Parker to be a colorless personality, she saw no threat in his candidacy.

Edith went to Oyster Bay next day. Theodore remained behind; he would spend much of that summer in Washington, pondering his prospects in the fall election. "If defeated," he wrote Bamie, "I shall feel disappointed, yet I shall also feel that I have had far more happiness and success than fall to any but a very few men; and this aside from the infinitely more important fact that I have had the happiest home life of any man whom I have ever known."[26]

"The nearer the election comes the more anxious and uneasy I get," Edith wrote Emily in early October. But her fears were unfounded. Parker's campaign collapsed like a pricked balloon. A Democratic attempt to smear Roosevelt, for receiving seventy-two percent of his more than two million dollars in contributions from Wall Street, failed to sway the voters. Nevertheless, in the final week before balloting, Edith became so restless with suspense that she lost five pounds in weight.[27]

On polling day itself Theodore returned to Washington after voting in Oyster Bay. Edith stood at the White House door and watched him climbing the steps toward her. "It makes no difference how it goes," he said. "I have had a vision on the train, and it was of you and the children. Nothing matters as long as we are well and content with each other."[28]

Inside the house, he found Archie covered with campaign buttons, running excitedly back and forth to the telegraph office in the Executive Wing with the early returns. Buffalo and Rochester showed large gains for the Republican ticket, followed by Chicago, Connecticut, New York and Massachusetts with evidence of an enormous drift to the GOP.

Edith had invited members of the Cabinet, their wives, and a few close friends to stop by afterward for "a little feast which can be turned into a festival of rejoicing or into a wake as circumstances warrant."[29] But by seven-thirty, when Mrs. Cortelyou, wife of the Chairman of the Republican National Committee, joined the Roosevelts and the Cowleses for dinner, Theodore's election was almost assured. The President beamed with pride and happiness as Archie continued to shower him with telegram after telegram confirming his overwhelming victory and showing the largest popular and electoral majorities ever given a presidential candidate.

Later that evening Theodore Roosevelt made what some considered to be the worst political mistake of his career. In the exuberance of victory he announced, "On the fourth of March next I shall have served three and a half years, and this three and a half years constitutes my first term. The wise custom which limits the President to two terms regards the substance and not the form. Under no circumstances will I be a candidate for or accept another nomination."[30]

Edith, standing nearby as he made this rash proclamation, was seen to flinch. She later told Owen Wister that had she known what Theodore was going to say she would have done all in her power to prevent it. The reason was not her own ambition to remain in the White House, but the knowledge of the severe handicap any

President places on himself with Congress and the people in announcing his intention not to seek reelection at the outset of his term. But the damage was done, and she was helpless to undo it.[31]

As for Theodore, he continued to rejoice in his good fortune. Americans had given him a term in his own right. It was the most triumphant day he ever had, or could have, he told Kermit. But, he went on in sonorous tones (Alice called this one of his "posterity letters"), "it was a great comfort to feel, all during the last days when affairs looked doubtful, that no matter how things came out the really important thing was the lovely life I have with Mother and with you children and that compared to this home life everything else was of very small importance from the standpoint of happiness."[32]

Twenty-Two

These are stirring times to live in, and sometimes I feel like a child before Christmas and can hardly wait for it to happen.
—Edith Kermit Roosevelt[1]

The March sky threatened rain as coachman Charlie Lee, "proud as a peacock" in his blue livery, drove a four-horse landau up to the White House. Promptly at ten o'clock the President-elect emerged and climbed into the carriage for the ride to the Capitol. He was wearing the customary frock coat and top hat, and a ring from John Hay which contained strands of Lincoln's hair. The Secretary of State had wanted his friend to wear it because he was "one of the men who most thoroughly understand and appreciate Lincoln."[2]

Theodore's military escort included forty Rough Riders (barely sober after a week of carousing) and a group of Civil War veterans who, according to Edith, were a trifle "shaky on their poor old pins."[3]

The First Lady, wearing a dark-blue cloth coat and matching skirt, left for the inauguration an hour later, riding with Alice and Ted. In the next carriage came Mame, looking not a day over sixty though she was nearer eighty, in charge of Ethel, Kermit, Archie and Quentin. They were followed by house guests Corinne and Douglas Robinson, and Christine and Emlen Roosevelt. Then came Bamie with the newly-engaged cousins Franklin and Eleanor Roosevelt, and the Cabinet ladies brought up the rear.

The sun broke through as Theodore stepped out onto the platform for the swearing-in ceremony, and a cool breeze ruffled the fine white hair of Chief Justice Fuller as he administered the Oath of Office. Below the East Portico of the Capitol stood army and navy cadets, and beyond them thousands of ordinary citizens straining to hear the Inaugural speech. In a distinct voice, muffled by high winds, the President spoke of the need for America to avoid complacency and vainglorious pride, and to recognize that with great wealth went responsibility toward the less fortunate.

A severe headache sent Edith hurrying back to the White House for a dose of phenacetin and a brief rest before joining nearly two hundred guests for a buffet lunch. "There was an unusual amount of individuality in the Inaugural parade that followed," she told her sister. "Seth Bulloch [Sheriff of Deadwood, South Dakota] was there with a band of cowboys, and a lot of Harvard men in college gowns and caps, black with red facing. As they passed our box they gave the Harvard cheer, and two nice old gentlemen came down from the stand into the street to join with them."[4]

Theodore beamed with pride as group after group passed the reviewing stand on Pennsylvania Avenue. Detachments of Puerto Rican and Filipino troops ("rejoicing in their shackles," remarked the President) marched by.[5] Roosevelt's face lit up at the sight of a posse of Bad Lands ranchers, and a tribe of Indians riding green-, blue-, red- and yellow-painted horses and armed with spears and tomahawks. He was having the time of his life jigging to the rhythm of the bands, and laughing uproariously as a Rough Rider lassoed an unsuspecting bystander and hauled him into the street.

On and on came the parade. Alice, in a white cashmere outfit, struggled to keep her wheel-sized ostrich-plumed hat in place, while the other children had a glorious time mingling with the crowds and snapping photographs with their box Brownies.[6]

At six o'clock Edith and Theodore returned to the White House for an informal reception of the Rough Riders, and then they served dinner at seven-thirty to sixteen close family and friends. But the day was still far from over. Following the custom begun by President Madison, the Roosevelts were to attend the Inaugural Ball at the Pension Office Building on Fourth Street. Arriving there, they found between six and seven thousand people assembled to greet them. The vast hall was decorated to resemble a Venetian garden, with forty-foot-high palms, eagles on tall standards, and blue draperies festooned with American Beauty roses. In the middle of the floor a square was roped off, around which Edith and Theodore and Vice-President and Mrs. Fairbanks solemnly processed before going to a to a box in the gallery to watch the dancing.

Edith, in the tradition of Martha Washington, wore a gown that was completely American made. The fabric, a robin's egg blue silk brocade with raised gold pattern of ostrich feathers and medallions, had been woven in Paterson, New Jersey. To prevent its being reproduced, the design was afterward destroyed. The square-necked, short-sleeved gown was tailored in New York, and featured a bodice insertion of rose-point lace, a family heirloom over two hundred years old.[7] It had a dropped waistline, a heavily pleated skirt, and a three-yard train. With the dress Edith wore a rose diamond necklace and a blue aigrette in her hair.

From time to time throughout the evening Edith and Theodore moved to the edge of the gallery to receive the applause of the dancers. The First Lady soon learned not to press against the railings, which had recently been painted and had added a bronze imprint to her gold-encrusted skirts.[8] The evening ended with a light supper for the Cabinet and the Inaugural Committee, after which Edith and Theodore and their house guests went back to the Executive Mansion for a "back hair" talk.

Just as they were all going to bed, Theodore remembered a round bottle of old cherry liquer that someone had sent him, and insisted on opening it for a nightcap. The party reassembled in Edith's bedroom in various stages of undress, and drank the President's health from huge tumblers. They talked of old times and childhood days, laughing "immoderately" and feeling "so gay, so full of life and fun" that they "could hardly bear to say 'goodnight.'"[9]

The Inauguration was but a brief interlude in a year of high drama for the Roosevelts. Since January, when Port Arthur had surrendered to the Japanese, Edith herself had become secretly enmeshed in a long series of diplomatic maneuvers.

The British Ambassador, Sir Mortimer Durand, and President Roosevelt did not see eye to eye. Durand was a respected diplomat of the old school: courteous, deferential, circumspect and slow. Theodore, who liked to deal frankly and directly with foreign envoys, found it impossible to communicate with him. So did Edith, who also found Lady Durand uncongenial. "One cannot talk of anything important," she complained to Arthur Lee, "because Sir Mortimer freezes up and puts on his official manner at once—and one cannot talk of anything amusing because they do not see the point and merely appear bewildered."[10] The Roosevelts made no bones about the fact that they would infinitely prefer Cecil Spring-Rice in the post. Springy was articulate and knowledgeable and shared the President's views on changing international dynamics in the twentieth-century world. The British Foreign Office appreciated this, and knew that Spring-Rice had the ear of the American Chief Executive. But Her Majesty's Government deemed it inappropriate that a diligent senior officer like Sir Mortimer should be replaced by a junior, especially one who had once served under him.

The fall of Port Arthur, however, made the lack of communication between Roosevelt and Durand critical. It was essential for the Foreign Office to have an immediate exchange of views with the American President on the developing imbalance of world power. As luck would have it, Spring-Rice was in London on leave at the time, and in late January 1905 he was ordered to proceed to Washington for secret talks with Roosevelt.

Springy slipped into the capital, ostensibly on a private visit, and stayed with Henry Adams. No one was fooled by this decoy. Diplomats and press rumbled that he was there to act as mediator between President and Ambassador, and to enlighten both men as to the true situation in Asia.

On Sunday January 29, the visitor dined alone with Edith and Theodore. "His tales of Russia were such as to make one feel that rebellion against such a government is a holy war," Edith wrote Emily later. "Cold shivers ran down my back as they did when I was small and read tales of the Indian wars and massacres."[11]

Spring-Rice had long contended that it was Russia's ambition "to occupy the whole of Asia." Japan's determination to thwart that desire, climaxed by the capture of Port Arthur, hurt the pride of the Russian people, and they took to the streets in nonviolent protest. Springy gave the Roosevelts a first-hand account of how the Russian government handled the demonstrations. Strikers marching in front of the Winter Palace were bombarded with rifle fire. Students parading red flags were ridden down by mounted police, "swords cutting and slashing." Jews merely going about their daily business had also been subjected to cruel persecution.[12]

Theodore was convinced by Springy's stories and views that no country could long prosper in the face of such "crushing despotism." The more Spring-Rice talked, the more necessary it seemed to maintain contact with him after he returned to Russia. Spring-Rice, for his part, wanted to see Theodore Roosevelt "play an even bigger part on an even bigger stage" than he had already.[13] They therefore devised a clandestine method of communication, bypassing the State Department and the British Embassy. In future, Springy would address all strategic letters to the First Lady, a willing party in the conspiracy.

In his first letter, postmarked St. Petersburg, March 13, 1905, Spring-Rice confessed that as a mere official he felt uneasy writing to a "sovereign." He added that he heartily prayed "for the time when you descend from the throne." There followed a long explanation of the current political situation in Russia.

> It cannot be said that the cause of reform, advocated by about one million out of a people of 140 millions, has much chance of success. But what is certain is that the whole fabric of society is falling, and that disorders are increasing and that the only hope of the Government now lies in allying itself with the ignorant masses against the thinking element—which is not an element which can organize or act. The only people who are capable of action are the bombists, and the future lies with them.

And then, in an ominous paragraph:

> The Government for centuries has lived by the poverty and ignorance of the masses; and the country and especially the educated people will have to pay for it. In the meanwhile the Emperor lives quietly, a prisoner like the Sultan at Yildiz, in his palace garden; and plays with his baby and will hear nothing but baby

> talk. If you come with disagreeable truths, he listens and
> says nothing. His ideas, if he has any, are to maintain
> the autocracy undiminished and to continue the war
> until he has gained "the mastery of the Pacific." Doesn't
> the expression sound odd? Where is America? Has she
> no interest in the Pacific? Or is she to confine her
> interests to Russia's care? It is really stupendous.[14]

Spring-Rice's rhetoric was duly transmitted to the President by the
First Lady, and did not fall on deaf ears. In preparation for the
growing Russo–Japanese threat, Theodore's main objective now
became "to keep America in trim, so that fighting her shall be too
expensive and dangerous a task to likely be undertaken by anybody."[15]

The clandestine correspondence continued throughout the year.
"How I pester you with politics!" Springy wrote Edith. "But you are
quite a politician now aren't you, and so I treat you."[16]

Socially as well as politically the 1905 season was especially
interesting for Edith. A brilliant roster of artists and writers regularly
lunched at the White House. On January 12, for example, her guest
list included America's most eminent historian, its finest stained-
glass artist, most brilliant sculptor, and greatest novelist—Henry
Adams, John La Farge, Augustus St. Gaudens, and Henry James.

As always when surrounded with minds of high quality, Theodore
was at his loquacious best—or worst, in Adams's opinion. La Farge
and St. Gaudens were somewhat ill at ease in the resultant avalanche
of oratory, although the latter gave an impression of fascinated
absorption in what the President was saying. La Farge explained
afterward to Lodge that the sculptor's intense stare was deceptive: he
was merely "studying and measuring the proportions of the speaker's
face—'His nose is three quarters of an inch—his forehead so much
and so forth.'"[17]

Adams deflated Theodore from time to time with prickly sallies,
while James, who was revisiting his native land after a long sojourn
abroad, ponderously searched for the precise word to express his own
matchless thought. The novelist's slowness of speech, however, belied
the rapidity and accuracy with which he had already summed
Theodore up. Roosevelt was "a really extraordinary creature for

native intensity, voracity, and *bonhomie,*" playing his role "with the best will in the world." James granted Theodore's "amusing likeability," but was critical of his attempt "to make a 'court.'"[18]

Edith described the lunch as "the pleasantest thing I've done this year," and declared Henry James "one of the most charming and delightful people whom I have ever met." In concurring, Theodore did an about-face: he had previously dismissed the expatriate writer (whose subtle complexities of prose eluded him) as "the little emasculated mass of inanity."[19]

James returned to the White House that night for the Diplomatic Reception, and at dinner afterward was seated to the right of the lady on the President's right. From his closer vantage point he "got a rich impression" of Theodore Roosevelt, "and of his being verily, a wonderful little machine." With the perspicacity of genius, he added: "—destined to be overstrained perhaps, but not as yet, truly, betraying the least creak. It functions astonishingly, and is quite exciting to see. But it's really like something behind a great plate-glass window on Broadway."[20]

Edith was so enchanted with the author that she invited him to join her on a spring cruise to Mount Vernon. She never forgot him, and once when she saw a rotund woodchuck sitting on a fence, "eyeing the world with mingled dignity and disgust," she said it looked exactly like the Master.[21]

Another talented visitor to the White House that winter was John La Farge's architect son Grant, who came to discuss plans for enlarging Sagamore Hill. Edith and Theodore wanted to add a large drawing room to the north end of the hall, to facilitate the entertaining of ever growing numbers of guests. La Farge stunned Edith with the news that the room, as planned, would cost sixteen thousand dollars, almost exactly as much as the entire house had cost in 1884. This sum was, she thought, "far more than we can possibly afford," but Theodore was determined to go ahead, and signed a contract for the work to begin in March and be completed by mid-June.[22]

Meanwhile there was a family wedding to attend. At three-thirty on March 17, St. Patrick's Day, Edith and Theodore arrived at a pair of adjoining private houses on East Seventy-sixth Street in New York City for the marriage of their niece Eleanor to Cousin Franklin. The

President was to give the bride away, in his dead brother's stead. Since Eleanor also had no mother, Edith had offered to send out the invitations and hold the ceremony in the White House, "to do for you as we should for Alice."[23] But Eleanor had declined, preferring to marry in rather less grand surroundings.

The "ugly duckling" had indeed grown, if not into a swan, at least into a tall, almost regal young woman, with a mind of her own. Eleanor's years as "the most important person" in Mademoiselle Souvestre's finishing school had provided stability as well as intellectual and social polish. The headmistress, a woman of great charm and intelligence, had cared for Eleanor deeply, and been appreciative of her remarkable qualities. As a result she returned to America more poised and confident, capable of encouraging her "featherduster" fiancé to become a man worthy of succeeding her beloved Uncle Ted. She identified with the President's bold activism, and wanted one day to emulate it. "I could not, at any age," she later said, "be content to take my place in a corner by the fireside and simply look on."[24]

At the conclusion of the service, Theodore, wearing a shamrock buttonhole, kissed the bride and said to the groom, "Well, Franklin, there's nothing like keeping the name in the family." With that he headed for the dining room. All the guests followed, hanging on the President's every word, and leaving the newlyweds standing alone. Theodore Roosevelt, as Alice remarked, wanted to be "the bride at every wedding and the corpse at every funeral."[25]

Among the 340 wedding presents the couple had received was a small watercolor of children wading, framed by Fischer. The picture had originally been a gift to the President from a Dutch genre painter named Blommer, but it had not pleased the First Lady. "It is really good of its kind," she told Emily drily, "but a kind which I don't happen to care for."[26]

An April cruise on the *Sylph* through the St. John's River wilderness in Florida prompted Edith to look for a primitive country retreat near Washington. Accordingly in early May she went to investigate a small timbered shack in the foothills of the Blue Ridge Mountains in Albemarle County, Virginia. The shack belonged to Will Wilmer, an old Carow family friend, and stood on his five-hundred acre estate, Plain Dealing Farm. To reach it, she had to walk about a mile, across a stream of clear water, through a meadow speckled with violets and mountain pinks, and into a pine forest. Then the trees gave way so suddenly to the cabin that she found herself right at its front door. She saw at once it was just what she wanted. The cabin certainly was primitive. It consisted simply of one room downstairs and two upstairs, with rough plank walls and a dilapidated roof. That was all. Will had said she could have it for $195, with five acres of surrounding land.

The more Edith considered her find, the more excited she became. Washington was only about 125 miles away, and the nearest railroad station a mere fourteen, along a red dirt road. There was rural mail delivery—all she had to do was "put out a box"—and a store a brief horseback ride away, where she could buy supplies of pork, potted ham, codfish, crackers and ginger snaps, as well as axle grease and cartridges. Whenever possible, of course, the family would subsist on wild game—quail, partridges and deer, which "the braves" would hunt and "the squaws" would cook.[27]

She began to list a few items of furniture and equipment she would need—plank tables, benches, straight-back rockers, a dish cupboard, a meat block, a bread box, an earthenware water-jug, a swinging crane and andirons.

Edith named the cabin "Pine Knot" and went home to tell Theodore about it.

She returned on Thursday, June 8, to prepare the hut for his first visit, taking the minimum amount of kitchen pots and pans, and the maximum number of gray blankets, for the weather was crisp.

The President arrived late next day, and after dinner at Plain Dealing went over to Pine Knot, looking forward to a weekend alone with his wife. "It is really a perfectly delightful little place," he wrote Kermit later.

> Mother is a great deal more pleased with it than any child with any toy I ever saw, and is too cunning and pretty and busy for anything. . . . In the morning I fried bacon and eggs, while Mother boiled the kettle for tea and laid the table. Breakfast was most successful, and then Mother washed the dishes and did most of the work, while I did odd jobs like emptying the slops etc. Then we walked about the place . . . admired the pine trees and the oak trees and then Mother lay in the

"Mother is . . . more pleased with it than any child with any toy."
Pine Knot, Albemarle County, Virginia.

hammock while I cut away some trees to give us a better view from the piazza . . . It was lovely to sit there in the rocking chairs and hear all the birds by daytime and at night the whippoorwills and owls and little forest folk . . . there was no one around the house to bother us at all. As we found that cleaning dishes took up an awful time we only took two meals a day . . . On Saturday evening I fried two chickens for dinner, while mother boiled the tea and we had cherries and wild strawberries, as well as biscuits and corn-bread. To my pleasure Mother greatly enjoyed the fried chicken, and admitted that what you children had said of the way I fried

> chicken was all true. In the evening we sat out a long
> time on the piazza, and then read indoors and went to
> bed. Sunday morning we did not get up until nine. Then
> I fried Mother some beefsteak and some eggs in two
> frying pans, and she liked them both very much. We
> went to church . . . dined soon after two at "Plain
> Dealing," and then were driven over to the station . . .[28]

By late Sunday afternoon Edith noticed that the lines had
smoothed out of Theodore's face, and the ruddy color reappeared in
his cheeks.

Time and again, winter and summer, they returned to the little
cabin for what Edith called "rest and repairs." Sagamore Hill no
longer offered refuge: when Theodore went there, reporters, politicians and favor-seekers followed in such numbers that he was kept as
busy as he was in the White House. Pine Knot became the only place
near at hand where he and Edith could escape the pressures and the
limelight of their position. Here, as out West in his youth, Theodore
could slake his perpetual thirst for nature.

On rare occasions soul mates were invited to join him. One of these
was the great naturalist John Burroughs, who the President ingeniously suggested might "help him name his birds."[29] (Actually
Theodore knew them all already, and had a boyish desire to show off
his ornithological expertise.) After leaving the train and driving some
ten miles past fields of corn and rye, they left the wagon and walked
the rest of the way to Pine Knot. The spring migration was under
way, and the warm air was loud with birdsong. Burroughs took off
his overcoat, and the President insited on carrying it. They identified
several warblers en route, among them the blackpoll, the black-
throated blue, and Wilson's black cap. "He knew them in the trees
overhead as quickly as I did," Burroughs said afterward.

It was late afternoon when they reached the cabin. But Theodore
was eager for another walk, so they set off across fields and marshes
and through the woods at his usual breakneck speed. "Mrs.
Roosevelt took him to task," Burroughs remembered, "when she saw
the heated condition in which we returned." Shamefaced, the
President agreed "that was no way to go after birds."

That night when Burroughs went to bed he found a nest of flying

"When Burroughs went to bed he found a nest of flying squirrels."
John Burroughs, author and naturalist.

squirrels in his room. He took them down because they disturbed him, but Edith and Theodore put the nest up in their room, and tucked the two squirrels back in it.[30]

In the three days that followed, Theodore and Burroughs searched at a more leisurely pace, and were able to spot over seventy-five species of birds. The President identified all of them but two, which

Burroughs, to his chagrin, could not recognize, either. The naturalist was also amazed at his host's botanical knowledge. "Roosevelt seemed to know the flowers as well as he did the birds."

The time spent in the cabin was almost as diverting as that spent outdoors.

> One evening as we sat in the lamplight, he reading Lord Cromer on Egypt and I a book on the man-eating lions of Tsavo, and Mrs. Roosevelt sitting near with her needlework, suddenly Roosevelt's hand came down on the table with such a bang that it made us both jump, and Mrs. Roosevelt exclaimed in a slightly nettled tone, "Why, my dear, what *is* the matter?"
>
> He had killed a mosquito with a blow that would almost have demolished an African lion.

As they sat there in that isolated hut, Burroughs began to think of "how risky it was for the President of the United States to be so unprotected—without a guard of any kind," and raised the subject of possible assassination with Theodore.

"Oh," he answered, slapping his hand on his hip pocket, "I go armed, and they would have to be mighty quick to get the drop on me."[31]

Shortly after that Burroughs went outside to stretch his legs and listen to the night sounds in the woods. He took a turn round the cabin, and almost immediately heard what he assumed was an animal lumbering off through the trees. He thought at first it might be a dog, but Edith enlightened him privately. The question of security at Pine Knot, which he had himself raised, had long ago occurred to her. There had been nights when she had lain awake in "terror-stricken panic." The children had sensed her fears; even little Archie put a gun beside his bed, "just in case." So she had quietly arranged for two Secret Service men to come every night at nine, stand on guard till morning, and hide in a nearby farmhouse during the day. She did not let the President know of their presence "because it would irritate him."[32]

Returning to Sagamore Hill on June 26, 1905, Edith found that the new North Room had opened up the house in a most unexpected way. Fully forty feet long and thirty feet wide, it was nothing less than a wooden baronial hall with a high, angled-arched ceiling, Ionic columns, and a dramatically sunken floor reached by a short stairway. A huge windowed alcove, recessed in the west wall, gave extra breadth as well as light. Opposite was a large fireplace with a

"It opened up the house in a most unexpected way."
The North Room, Sagamore Hill.

mantlepiece of Philippine camagon wood, surmounted by panels embossed with the initials "TR" and "EKR." Centered between the two north windows was a laurel wreath encircling an American eagle carved by Gutzon Borglum.

Within a short time of Theodore's arrival a few days later, two buffalo heads were placed on the east wall, and two elk heads opposite, with his Rough Rider hat and sword hanging from their antlers. Regimental colors added a further touch of military display. Two prized sculptures, both gifts of his personal staff, commemorated his Cuban colonelcy and Governorship of New York State—Frederic Remington's bronze *Bronco Buster,* and St. Gaudens's *Puritan.*

Whatever Edith might have thought about some of her husband's additions, she and he were united in their decision to grace the north room with a "really first-class piece of American art"—Marcius Simons's large oil landscape *Where Light and Shadow Meet.* In time it would be joined by two other Symbolist works by the same artist, *Porcelain Towers,* and (Theodore's favorite) *The Seats of the Mighty.*[33]

The President admitted to La Farge that he liked the room better than any in the White House, "which, as you know, is my standard of splendor!"[34]

News of John Hay's death at his home in New Hampshire on July 1, 1905, cast a chill on the Roosevelts' summer. The Secretary of State had been seriously ill with angina pectoris and a prostate condition, which a protracted visit to Europe had failed to cure or alleviate. Edith, who had last seen him in Washington eleven days before, "never for a moment realized he was fatally ill."[35]

Theodore was genuinely sorry to lose such a close friend and adviser. "John Hay's house was the only house in Washington where I continually stopped," he told Lyman Abbot. "Every Sunday on the way back from church I would stop and have an hour's talk with Hay. We would go over foreign affairs and public business generally, and then I would usually get him to talk to me about Lincoln—for as you know, Lincoln has always meant more to me than any other of our public men, even Washington."[36]

The President considerably modified his warm words about Hay after the publication of the Secretary's letters, many of which were satirical of him. Incensed, Roosevelt wrote a long "posterity letter" to Lodge, granting that Hay was a delightfully epigrammatic conversationalist, and one of the best correspondents of his time. But he had not been a good administrator, and therefore not a good Secretary of State. "He had a very ease-loving nature and a moral timidity which made him shrink from all that was rough in life . . .

He was at his best at a dinner table or in a drawing-room." What was more, he went on, Hay never "initiated a policy or was of real assistance in carrying through a policy." Roosevelt did allow, however, that the Secretary "sometimes phrased what I desired said in a way that was of real service."[37]

Elihu Root replaced Hay in the Cabinet at a critical moment in world history. The issue of the Russo–Japanese War—sovereignty of Manchuria, in particular the Kwantung Peninsula and Port Arthur—was still not resolved. Theodore had been "growing nearly mad" for months trying to persuade the two sides to settle their differences at the conference table.[38] Finally he succeeded in being accepted as a mediator, and on July 2 it was announced that Japan's Minister of Foreign Affairs, Baron Komura, and her minister to the United States, Baron Takahira, would meet with Russia's President of the Council of Ministers, Sergius Witte, and Ambassador von Rosen, on the U.S. naval yacht *Mayflower* in Oyster Bay, preparatory to conferring at Portsmouth, New Hampshire. The date of the meeting was set for August 5, leaving the State Department only thirty-four days of frantic preparations.

Meanwhile the summer air at Sagamore Hill was thick with rumors of romance. Just before leaving on an official tour of the Far East, Alice had shown unmistakable signs of lovesickness. It had been announced that Representative Nick Longworth would join her party at San Francisco as a member of the House Foreign Affairs Committee. "ALICE IN WONDERLAND," trumpeted the newspaper headlines. "How First Maiden of Land Will Travel in Orient . . . Representative Longworth to Go Along—Tropical Romance Anticipated."[39] Alice had promptly taken to her bed with indigestion, toothache, and eczema, and lost five pounds in weight.

En route across the Pacific she succeeded in capturing not only Nick's attention but also that of the world press, by jumping fully clad into the ship's swimming pool. By the time the party reached Japan interested observers on board saw that "there was something more than mere friendship" between the President's daughter and the Congressman. They spent much time together during the next ten days, lunching with the Emperor and sauntering through the Imperial Gardens. "The charming scenery of Japan is conducive to love-making," Representative Grosvenor told a reporter afterward, "and I guess none of it was wasted."[40]

As head of the delegation, Secretary Taft felt some avuncular responsibility. "I think I ought to know if you are engaged to Nick," he repeatedly asked. To which Alice invariably replied, "More or less, Mr. Secretary, more or less."[41]

Edith seldom had the opportunity to see her children together these days, but had every reason to be proud of them. Ted had left Groton a year early, in order to study under a tutor for entry into Harvard that fall. Kermit, almost sixteen, was of all the brood "the most devoted" to his mother. He was still a solitary, independent character. "Very few outsiders care for him," said Edith, "but if they like him at all they like him very much." Horseback riding and shooting interested him very little, but he loved cycling, collecting autographs and rare books, and accumulating strange objects ranging from fragments of quartz to broken strawberry boxes.[42] He had a better-developed and finer literary taste than the others, and had recently introduced his parents to the work of the young Maine poet Edwin Arlington Robinson. The President liked Robinson's book of dramatic lyrics entitled *Children of the Night* so much that he wrote a review for the *Outlook*. He also gave the poet an easy $2,000-a-year post in the New York Treasury, so that he could pursue his literary work free of financial worry. Robinson, a descendant of the Colonial writer Anne Bradstreet, justified the Roosevelts' faith in him, and went on to win three Pulitzer prizes.

Ethel, at fourteen, was a conscientious student, a fine horsewoman and an efficient child-minder who helped her younger brothers with arithmetic and Latin. She could be relied on to manage the house and the servants and supervise the gardening in her parents' absence. Ethel was also public-spirited, teaching a Sunday-school class of black boys at St. Mary's Chapel in Washington.

"Archie is a little trump, so loving and polite and honorable," Theodore (for whom the pugnacious boy was always on his best behavior) wrote Aunt Emily.[43] At eleven, the third son was not scholastically bright, but had "sobriety of character." He was devoted to animals, and to sailing, and at this stage in his young life craved a naval career.

Quentin was a handful, who "may cause more trouble both to others and to himself [than Archie]," his father warned.[44]

Saturday, August 5, was a perfect summer day as Edith and the children set off for Cooper's Bluff with books, needlework and cards. A servant followed, carrying a large picnic basket, for the family intended to spend the afternoon watching the arrival and departure of the Japanese and Russian peace emissaries in the bay. Anchored directly offshore were the *Mayflower* and the *Dolphin*, and just outside the entrance to the Sound lay the convoy ship *Galveston*. Between these vessels bobbed flotillas of small craft, multinational flags unfurled.

Shortly before 12:30 P.M. a twenty-one-gun salute boomed the approach of the presidential launch, and hearty cheers echoed across the water as Theodore, in frock coat and top hat, climbed the gangway of the *Mayflower* to prepare for his ministerial guests. At 12:35 P.M. Edith saw the cruiser *Tacoma*, flying the Japanese sun flag, drop anchor about a mile away, and transfer its bevy of diplomats to a launch. Half an hour later the *Chattanooga* discharged the Russian envoys. They crossed the bay flying the Russian white, red and blue colors, to the sound of a nineteen-gun ambassadorial salute.

While Edith sat high on the bluff, gazing down at the microscopic figures on the deck of the *Mayflower*, she knew that her husband faced the most delicate diplomatic maneuver of his career. She could almost hear his fluent but ungrammatical French as he introduced the bearlike Russians to their pint-sized adversaries. She knew exactly what would happen next. Theodore would take Witte and Komura by the arm and steer them toward the dining saloon, talking all the while, so that neither minister was aware of who crossed the threshold ahead of the other. Awaiting them was a buffet lunch, but no sit-down tables, to circumvent the awkward question of who merited the place of honor at the President's right. After lunch Theodore would propose a toast, and Edith well knew the words he had rehearsed in advance. "I drink to the welfare and prosperity of the sovereigns and peoples of the two great nations whose representatives have met one another on this ship. It is my most earnest hope and prayer . . . that a just and lasting peace may speedily be concluded among them."[45]

It was after three o'clock when Edith saw the President disembark from the *Mayflower*. Gathering the children, she made her way back to Sagamore Hill to join him.

Next day Edith Kermit Roosevelt turned forty-four. The best birthday present she could have was the unanimous praise of Theodore as mediator in the morning newspapers. "One is so frequently disappointed by one's heroes," a Russian diplomat had told a *Sun* reporter. "But your President is so real and vital and full of magnetism." An enthusiastic letter from Spring-Rice soon arrived, telling Edith that Premier Rouvier of France had cited her husband as "the greatest moral influence of the age." [46]

After four weeks of wrangling at Portsmouth, the Russians and the Japanese finally announced a peace settlement at midday on August 29, 1905. Theodore was in the library answering correspondence as the Associated Press bulletin was relayed to him by telephone. "This is splendid! This is magnificent!" he said. His face broke into smiles as he rushed from the room to find Edith. When he returned he was still beaming. It was a good thing for both parties, he said to Secretary Loeb, and, thumping his chest, "a mighty good thing for *me* too!" [47]

Details of the agreement came after lunch. The sovereignty of Manchuria was to be restored to China. Japan was ceded the major influence in Korea, the lease of Port Arthur, and half the island of Saghalien. In return she relinquished her claim to war indemnity from Russia, as Theodore had advised.

Congratulations poured in to Sagamore Hill from Tsar Nicholas, Kaiser Wilhelm, King Edward VII and the Mikado, not to mention the Archbishop of Canterbury and the head of the Salvation Army. The world's press had nothing but superlatives for Theodore Roosevelt's accomplishment. "A master of diplomacy such as does not otherwise exist," wrote a Berlin correspondent. "He held the mandate of the civilized world and he made his task epochal." [48]

America and her President had come of age.

Twenty-Three

*As a team they produced a judgment that was not infallible, of
course, but dangerously near it, humanly and politically.*
> —Frederick M. Davenport[1]

All Washington turned out to welcome the President and First
Lady when they returned to the capital on September 30, 1905. The
worshipful clamor of the crowd on Pennsylvania Avenue that fall day
indicated that Theodore Roosevelt was the best-loved President since
George Washington. Blessed with superhuman vitality and drive, he
was revered by his countrymen and foreigners alike. Even Southern
Democrats had forgiven him for entertaining Booker T. Washington
in the White House.

The new devotion of the South became apparent on October 18,
when the President began a speaking tour of Virginia, Georgia,
Alabama, Florida, Arkansas and Louisiana. Edith went with him as
far as Atlanta and "enjoyed the trip immensely since Theodore was
received everywhere with the greatest enthusiasm."[2]

At Charlotte, North Carolina, she herself was honored with an
extraordinary gesture of hospitality when the widow of Stonewall

Jackson boarded the train and invited her across the street to meet some friends. There, strolling about under the trees in the dusk, stood all the ladies and young girls of Charlotte, anxious to shake hands with her. They escorted her to Mrs. Jackson's parlor for a few minutes of polite Southern conversation. It was as simple and natural as possible, Edith told Kermit, "like a page from an old tale."[3]

On the morning of October 20 the Roosevelts reached Roswell, a village just north of Atlanta in the foothills of the Southern Appalachians. Here, on the banks of the Chattahoochee River, Theodore's mother, Mittie Bulloch, was raised and married. Roswell could have changed little, Edith thought, since those days, except that it was now inhabited almost exclusively by widows. They lived in frame houses built by Theodore's grandfather, supporting their families by working in cotton factories nearby. Bulloch Hall, one of Georgia's few antebellum mansions to have survived Sherman's devastating march, sat on a hill in a cedar grove against a beautiful backdrop of mountains. It was a Greek Revival mansion with marbled blue and gray Doric columns, green shutters and brown and gold trim.

Theodore's mother had told him so much about the place that he felt as if he knew every nook and cranny, and as if it were haunted by the ghosts of all who had lived there. The house was in such good repair that Edith felt a lingering regret that it was no longer owned by a Roosevelt. It made her sad to see the violet bed and the old well that Mittie had talked so much about; to be introduced to the family nurse, Mam Grace, and to Daddy William, an old Negro who had been a slave in Theodore's grandfather's time. "I can't say how much went through my mind," Edith wrote Aunt Lizzie later. "I felt fairly choked, and longed to shut myself up quite alone in one of the rooms and think. The people were more than kind but I resented their very existence in the house."[4]

Moving on to Atlanta, Edith received about a hundred ladies in the Governor's Mansion, and then returned to Washington, leaving Theodore to go on to Florida. "She was the feature of the occasion everywhere, and it was great fun having her along," Theodore told Ethel. "I felt very melancholy when she went away."[5]

Alice arrived home from her four-month Pacific tour on October 27, 1905, (her father's forty-seventh birthday) looking "very thin and worn."[6] She had lost twenty pounds in weight, and appeared nervous, overwrought and ill, but Edith thought it better not to comment on the fact.[7] Something was troubling her stepdaughter that she was not yet prepared to discuss.

The truth was that Nick had at last asked Alice to marry him, and she felt shy about telling the family. It took the girl four weeks to summon up enough courage. Finally one night she followed Edith into the bathroom, and told her the news "while she was brushing her teeth, so that she should have a moment to think before she said anything." Meanwhile, Nick was in Theodore's study, asking for Alice's hand in marriage "with great formality."[8]

If Alice's fears were of possible parental disapproval, they turned out to be groundless. Both her father and stepmother were "well satisfied" with the match. The fifteen-year age difference was outweighed, in Edith's view, by Nick's cleverness, his serious interest in his political career and his "comfortable income according to our not over-ambitious ideas." The union looked even better as the weeks went by. "Alice is really in love," Edith told Aunt Lizzie, "and it is delightful to see how softened she is." But, "I still tremble when I think of her face to face with the practical details of life."[9]

Mrs. Longworth, who had fondly hoped that her bachelor son would never marry, lunched at the White House on December 13. Next day the engagement was officially announced, and the wedding date set for February 17, 1906, creating an anticipatory air of excitement throughout the world.

Edith became exhausted by a "perfect whirl" of dinner engagements in the months preceding the ceremony. There were seven hundred invitations to send out, for, as *Town Topics* remarked, everyone who had ever given "Princess Alice" a cup of tea expected to be asked. There were also over two hundred thank-you notes to write for the gifts which poured in from nations anxious to flatter the peacemaker of Portsmouth. There was a Gobelin tapestry from the President of France, a length of gold cloth embroidered with white chrysanthemums from the Emperor of Japan, and a string of fabulous pearls valued at $25,000 from the Cuban people. There was also a cornucopia of other presents, ranging from a bronze head of Victory by Augustus St. Gaudens to a hogshead of popcorn. Alice, gleefully totting up the combined monetary value, refused nothing, no matter how trivial or vulgar. A White House aide remarked that she would accept anything but a red-hot stove, "and will take that if it does not take too long to cool." She was not entirely mercenary, however. One of her favorite gifts was a string of amber beads Kermit had bought at Fischer's for fifty dollars; she wore it "all the time."[10]

Saturday, February 17, was a bright mild day, and the White House staff was busy early preparing for the most splendid function ever held in the historic house. Edith, bracing herself for the ordeal to begin at noon, spent the first couple of hours at an upstairs window, knitting and talking to Grandma Lee. Grandpa Lee was out walking with Douglas Robinson. Theodore, making the most of spare moments as usual, was in his office firing off letters on fraud in municipal elections and the wisdom of scheduling jujitsu as a form of exercise at the Naval Academy.

Shortly before twelve Edith entered the East Room on Ted's arm, and found the huge chamber full to bursting with friends, government officials, and diplomats. All eyes were on her as she walked up an aisle formed by ropes of white ribbon toward her front-row seat on the left. She wore a brown brocade of Japanese design—an unfortunate choice, in that it accentuated her tired pallor. After five successive seasons of increasingly brilliant entertaining at the pinnacle of American society—not to mention her large family responsibility—the First Lady was beginning to feel and show the strain. As Theodore said, "Edith is all right as far as her tether goes, but her tether is not a long one."[11]

An improvised altar placed over an Oriental rug stood on a platform erected in front of the east window. On either side were two large Satsuma vases filled with Easter lilies, in simple contrast to the banks of azaleas, American Beauty roses, and white rhododendrons elsewhere in the room. As the corridor clock chimed the hour of noon, and the Marine band struck up the march from *Tannhäuser*, Alice appeared on her father's arm.

Appropriately she wore a princess-style gown of white satin. The yoke and short sleeves were trimmed with the same lace that her own mother and grandmother had worn on their wedding days. A circlet of orange blossom anchored a voluminous veil to her soft pompadour. Round her neck was a diamond necklace from Nick, and she carried a bouquet of white orchids. No bridesmaids attended her. Alice wanted no competition—not that she would have had any. The President's daughter, declared *The New York Times*, "looked as pretty as she ever did in her life." [12]

Bishop Henry Yates Satterlee began to recite the service in a voice which reminded one guest of an auctioneer's. At one point the bride "turned her head almost wistfully" toward her stepmother. The President, who wore no buttonhole, seemed subdued. When the moment came for him to give her away, his voice, in contrast to the bishop's, was scarcely audible.

As soon as the ceremony ended Alice crossed to her stepmother, arms outstretched. Edith rose in some surprise. Placing both hands on the First Lady's shoulders, Alice affectionately kissed her. Then, holding her at arms' length, she spoke a few words and kissed her again. [13]

This display of spontaneous warmth was charged with emotion for both women. For nineteen years Edith had nurtured the girl as though she were her own, feeling all along that anyone who was part of Theodore was inevitably part of herself. Now, at the high point of Alice's life, here was proof, if such was needed, that the care was appreciated and the affection returned. Almost seventy years later Alice would admit that while she loved her father she was "never particularly close to him." On the other hand, "I enjoyed my stepmother." [14]

Nick, who looked so happy that a *Times* reporter compared him to "one broad beam of sunshine," also embraced his mother-in-law, while Cousin Franklin made himself useful arranging Alice's long silver brocade court train for the photographers. [15] Theodore joined the bride and groom for a stiffly formal group portrait, and then they adjourned to the State Dining Room for the wedding reception.

Among the throng waiting in line to congratulate them was Nellie Grant Sartoris, daughter of the great general, herself a White House bride thirty-two years before. Alice greeted her with due formality, but nobody received preferential treatment after the first champagne cork popped. Servants, aides, newsmen, and distinguished guests alike had democratic carte-blanche to help themselves to pâté, salad, claret, punch, strawberries and petit fours. "If the Secretary of State ranked the chambermaid no one worried about it this day," noted Ike Hoover, the White House usher. There was no stinting in the flow of food and wine. Even Hoover, who was inclined to think the Roosevelt fare inadequate, conceded: "It can be truthfully said that

"The President's daughter
'looked as pretty as she ever did in her life.' "
Mr. and Mrs. Nicholas Longworth with the President, 1906.

this was once, and only once, in this house when everybody was amply supplied with all the inner man might desire."[16]

As the afternoon wore on, close friends and family gathered in the private dining room adjoining to see the bride cut the cake. With the help of a military aide's saber, the slices fell away "like snow under a hot sun." By the time Alice went upstairs to change, Edith was "dropping with fatigue." Her stepdaughter knew "what a relief it was to her to have the wedding over at last and me off."[17]

The children showered their departing sister with rice, and when that grain gave out, Archie switched to black beans. Alice and Nick made a devious escape to thwart reporters, and spent the night at a secret hideaway just outside Washington. From here they went on to Cuba for a two-week honeymoon. Then, in June, they sailed for an extended tour of Europe, where they dined with King Edward, the Kaiser, and the President of France. "It was all very pleasant," said Alice nostalgically, "but there was no feeling of another world and time as there had been in the Orient."[18]

One possible reason why Theodore had looked so grim at Alice's wedding was the news that his eldest son and namesake was not doing well scholastically at Harvard. "A record of Cs and an occasional D does not allow much margin for accidents," he acidly informed Ted. Then, on February 23, news came that the young man's marks had deteriorated to the point where he had actually been put on probation. Theodore told his son to give up athletics and social life instantly, and "to peg away as hard as you know how." Edith minded her son's lapse very much, "coming when Father has so much to worry and bother him."[19]

Added to this domestic worry was the gradual realization that she was not the only one to feel the cumulative exhaustion of high office. Theodore, as he approached forty-eight, was beginning to display signs of premature age. Although he had "hardly a grey hair in his head, and hardly a wrinkle in his face," his weight was approaching two hundred pounds, and he complained of a stiffness in some of his movements. His frantic exercise regime, far from helping him, was a positive hindrance, since he sustained so many injuries from it. Parrying at single sticks with Leonard Wood resulted in swollen wrists and knuckles, Japanese wrestling aggravated his rheumatism, and a recent boxing blow, received while sparring with Edith's cousin

Dan Tyler Moore, had ruptured an artery in his left eye and blinded him—a closely guarded White House secret.[20] On top of all this was the fact that he had been suffering from arteriosclerosis for about eight years. Now, for the first time in his presidency he determined to have a long summer vacation. "Too violent exercise does not rest a man when he has had an exhausting mental career," Theodore concluded.[21]

Edith went to Groton in mid-March 1906 for Kermit's Confirmation, and though she was gone only four days, Theodore kept her informed of family activities. One of the few surviving letters from him to his wife shows the close and natural simplicity of their relationship.

> DARLING,
> Did you send me the little volume of Birrell's essays? I enjoyed them hugely.
> I am very much better; as comfortable as possible. It's a shame that you should have such weather; all the trees are now coated with ice; but I hope that the heavy rain which is falling will take it off. Ethel and Quentin, very cunning, have just gone off in the brougham to their respective schools. The two little boys were absorbed last evening with the "Legend of Montrose;" and I was nearly as much interested as they were, and *very* grateful that you were reading such an interesting book to them. Tonight the ferrets came, for the rats, and Archie anticipates an hour or two of delirious rapture.
> Yesterday I had to work after six; then I took half an hour's walk in the rain. . . .
> Give my dearest love to blessed Kermit, and tell [him] I think of him all the day. . . .
> YOUR OWN LOVER[22]

On May 9 the English novelist H. G. Wells, who was working on a series of articles about America for the London *Tribune*, lunched at the White House. Theodore admired his guest's imaginative gift (the greatest since Dickens, in the opinion of some critics) but was less sanguine about his extreme socialistic philosophy. The author, on the other hand, felt skeptical of Roosevelt's seemingly naïve optimism, yet was impressed by his love of country and his outstanding intellect. The President said that if America must eventually lose "the impetus of her ascent" to greatness, as other nations had done, he nevertheless chose to live as if this would not happen. After a postprandial stroll the two men parted beneath the colonnade. Roosevelt's last words (a reference to the writer's *Time Machine)* were: "Suppose, after all, that should prove to be right, and it all ends in your butterflies and morlocks. *That doesn't matter now.* The effort's real. It's worth going on with. It's worth it. It's worth it—even so. . . ."

Wells went away feeling that the President of the United States was symbolic "of the creative will in man." The passing years did not change his high opinion of Theodore Roosevelt. He was, Wells wrote later, "the most vigorous brain in a conspicuously responsible position in all the world in 1906."[23]

In spite of his election-night statement that he would not run for a third term, Theodore was far from being a lame-duck President. That year he succeeded in putting through a great deal of controversial legislation. On March 18, the Senate passed the Hepburn Act, regulating railroad rates so that they did not favor large corporations. June saw the passage of the Pure Food Bill, as well as an act permitting government inspection of meat-packing houses. Roosevelt accomplished the latter by threatening to publish even more grisly details of dirt, disease, and fraudulent ingredients than had already appeared in a report of presidential inspectors and in Upton Sinclair's sensational novel *The Jungle.*

Meanwhile, Theodore's most ambitious undertaking, the construction of the Panama Canal, was moving ahead. A waterway linking the Atlantic and Pacific oceans had been talked about for four hundred years, and attempted twice already, first by an American company in Nicaragua and more recently by a French one in Colombia. Both projects had been thwarted by rocketing costs, tropical rains and mud, and a cripplingly high death rate from tropical diseases.[24] The first of these handicaps posed no problem to the prosperous United States; the second could be overcome by modern engineering, and the third by enlightened sanitary and pest-control methods. So, on June 28, 1902, Congress had authorized the President to purchase the French-held concession for $40 million, with the proviso that the Colombian government would grant the United States a lease on a ten-mile wide Canal Zone across the Isthmus of Panama for $10 million, plus an annual rental of $250,000. The Colombians, reluctant to sacrifice sovereignty, and greedy for a percentage of the price paid the French, had rejected the offer. There seemed no way out of this impasse until November 4, 1903, when a revolutionary junta seceded from Colombia and proclaimed the new Republic of Panama. At Theodore's urging the United States promptly recognized the new republic—too promptly, in international opinion—and within two weeks Secretary Hay had concluded a treaty with the *insurrectos*.

And so work on the isthmian canal had resumed under a new commission, which shipped in large numbers of Jamaicans used to heavy manual labor in a tropical climate. A brilliant American medic, Major William Crawford Gorgas, worked tirelessly to overcome the malaria and yellow-fever problem by eliminating the mosquito-breeding puddles. His success was phenomenal: not a single death occurred among twelve thousand whites in one three-month period. Hopes ran high that the canal—a triumph for American engineering and medicine in general, and for Theodore Roosevelt in particular—would be open for shipping in August 1914, and fully complete six years after that.

In the fall of 1906 Theodore announced he would go to Panama to see the work on the canal in progress. This would make him the first American President to travel abroad while in office.

At 4 P.M. on Thursday, November 8, Edith and Theodore boarded the *Mayflower*, sailed down the Potomac River to Chesapeake Bay and transferred to the S.S. *Louisiana* off Piney Point. The 16,000-ton battleship had been refitted for their comfort in the Brooklyn Navy Yard.[25] The Captain's and the Admiral's quarters in the after part of the gun deck were now combined into a suite consisting of a bedroom, a modern bathroom, a dressing room and two dining rooms, one with seating for thirty, another one for private use.

The *Louisiana* took the Windward Passage route to Panama, sailing between the bold mountains of Cuba and Haiti, past the east end of Jamaica and through the Caribbean to Colón. All six days at sea were calm and sunny. Wearing cool linen dresses, Edith spent her time reading Sabatier, "walking up and down the deck, or sitting at the stern and watching the two great cruisers which are Theodore's convoy, and feeling very magnificent." She thought of the old buccaneers and sea dogs who had pirated these waters since Columbus and Balboa, and "pored over the maps of the canal, until I literally dream of it at night."[26]

Theodore felt "a little bored," as he always did at sea. For a while he occupied himself reading Milton, Tacitus and a German novel, but soon the urge to govern and reform came over him, and he fired off a letter to Secretary of the Navy Bonaparte, criticizing the size of the ship's guns, and its coal delivery arrangements.

The *Louisiana* dropped anchor at Colón at 3 P.M. on Wednesday, November 14. That evening President and Mrs. Amador, Chairman of the Canal Commission Theodore P. Shonts, the Chief Engineer, John F. Stevens, Dr. Gorgas, James Bucklin Bishop, Secretary of the Commission, and Frederick Palmer, the official presidential news correspondent, went on board to greet the visitors. The Roosevelts slept overnight on the ship, but rose early next morning to take a rail trip southwestward across the Isthmus from Colón to Panama. Suitably garbed in white duck suits and broad-brimmed hats, Edith and Theodore climbed on the waiting car, and rolled off through groves of plantains and bananas, steaming jungles and swampland. Rain began to fall in torrents, until the rails beneath them sank in slime, and the odor of mildew pervaded the air. Edith wondered how the laborers could possibly work in such seas of mud for eight months of every year. At stopping stations along the way, "little groups of chocolate drops," as she called them, sang patriotic songs and waved the American flag. The sight of them made Edith ponder the ironies of imperialism. "There was an indescribable mixture of pathos and humor in these poor little scraps of humanity, born of Jamaican negroes mostly, singing 'Land where my fathers died, Land of the pilgrims' pride.'" Nevertheless she was pleased to note that at every settlement the canal company had erected two-storied gray and white buildings with double piazzas and mosquito netting for white married and single laborers, and separate quarters with bathrooms "for the better class." Negro huts stood on less salubrious ground, with a raised platform in the yard to keep the chickens from drowning in floods.[27]

The Roosevelts eschewed a restaurant lunch, preferring to eat instead at the employees' canteen in La Boca, so that Theodore could

"The rails beneath them sank in slime
and the odor of mildew pervaded the air."
Edith and Theodore in Panama, November 1906.

get first hand knowledge of the food. They smilingly refused a
"Panama cocktail"—a mixture of quinine and brandy—and took
their own three-grain quinine pill instead. Then they helped themselves to vermicelli soup, native beef, mashed potatoes, peas, beets,
chili con carne, plum pudding, ice cream, tea and coffee. Theodore
gave the meal qualified praise. It was "as good as one can get for fifty
cents in the ordinary American hotel." Afterward he made a surprise
inspection of the kitchen, firing off questions at the rate of thirty a
minute for a solid half hour. He listened attentively to complaints
from black and white alike about too much overtime, too little pay,

and the low quality of yams. Nothing escaped him; nothing was too insignificant. He seemed, said a reporter, "to understand everything."[28]

The Roosevelts spent the night at the Hotel Tivoli, which was still under construction but had one hastily completed wing to accommodate the presidential party. Next day brought the Zone its worst storm in ten years—over four and a half inches of rain. But they carried on as planned with their visit to the Culebra Cut. A ninety-five-ton steam shovel was working to scoop mud and rock and gravel from the mountainside onto trains, which in turn dumped the waste in the jungle and at dam sites. Theodore naturally could not resist climbing into the driving seat of the monster shovel, and having his picture taken by the press.

On their last day in the Zone the Roosevelts visited the site where the Chagres River would be converted into the twenty-three-mile Gatún Dam. After two days of rain, the hilly route, which lay through tropical forest, was magical with exotic orchids, brilliant-plumed birds, colorful butterflies, lizards and snakes. "All my old enthusiasm for natural history seemed to revive," Theodore told Kermit, "and I would have given a good deal to have stayed and tried to collect specimens." It occurred to him that in a few years ships would be passing a hundred feet above where the railroad now ran.[29]

The euphoria common to all travelers who venture into insalubrious climes and then head safely home permeated the entire battleship as it drew near U.S. waters. One night the sailors built an improvised stage on the quarterdeck to entertain their illustrious passengers. The performance began with an overture by the ship's orchestra, and was followed by a minstrel show, a clog dance, a cakewalk, and (in a sly homage to the new Mrs. Longworth) a solo rendition of "Alice, Where Art Thou?" The show ended with three boxing bouts, which the President enjoyed more than anything.[30]

Some ten weeks later, the First Lady was finishing lunch in the company of the Mexican Ambassador and Secretary Root when her husband entered and said, "Edie, I want you to come into the next room. There is somebody there to see you." Mystified, she did as he asked, and found an officer and "three huge jackies" from the *Louisiana* waiting for her. They were holding a large silver Tiffany loving cup. Shyly, they explained that all sailors were superstitious of having women aboard, believing that they brought bad luck. But the voyage with Mrs. Roosevelt had been so safe and fine that the enlisted men wished to give her the cup as a memento of it. "She was so overcome," Belle Hagner recalled, "that her serenity almost deserted her."[31]

Twenty-Four

I have had the happiest home life of any man I have ever known.
—Theodore Roosevelt[1]

Edith's twentieth wedding anniversary on December 2, 1906, came and went with no special celebration at the White House. The Washington *Post,* however, did not allow the day to pass without editorial comment. "No couple better fitted to maintain and improve social traditions ever occupied the Executive Mansion," wrote the columnist, and urged citizens to raise their hats to "all that is best and wholesome in American family life."

If that included nine-year-old Quentin Roosevelt, his teacher at the Force School, Miss Virginia Arnold, could hardly agree. The boy, in a word, was a terror, so much so that she was obliged to write a letter of complaint to the President. His reply came promptly on White House stationery:

> DEAR MISS ARNOLD:
>   I thank you for your note about Quentin. Don't you think it would be well to subject him to stricter

discipline? . . . Mrs. Roosevelt and I have no scruples whatever against corporal punishment. . . . I do not think I ought to be called in merely for such offences as dancing when coming into the classroom, for singing higher than the other boys, or for failure to work as he should at his examples, or for drawing pictures instead of doing his sums. . . . If you find him defying your authority or committing any serious misdeeds let me know and I will whip him. . . .[2]

Edith thought that her "fine little bad boy" was the cleverest but most difficult to handle of all her children. He was strong-willed and independent-minded, with a degree of physical fearlessness that frightened her. No nook or cranny of the White House was sacred to him. Quentin climbed on the roof, crawled between the rafters, and squeezed into the eaves of the attic, penetrating places previously inhabited only by rats. He liked to scale the great magnolia tree beneath his mother's window, and thread "streams of official red tape to its topmost boughs." He was on terms of "affable familiarity" with Secret Service men, aides, servants and policemen, although his practical jokes often strained relations. Once he hid on top of the North Portico, and rolled a gigantic snowball onto the head of the officer on duty below. His father, who was just then emerging to greet an important visitor, was furious, not so much at the undignified spectacle of the law spraddled on the ground, but because the incident made him laugh so much.[3]

"Quentin is a roly-poly, happy-go-lucky personage," Theodore wrote Nannie Lodge, "the brightest of any of the children, but with a strong tendency to pass a very happy life in doing absolutely nothing except swim or loaf about with other little boys."[4]

These friends, known around town as "The White House Gang," included Charley Taft, the sturdy son of the Secretary of War; pale-browed Bromley Seeley, freckly Dick Chew, wiry Edward Stead, tiny Walker White and Earle Looker, the future chronicler of their exploits.

The gang's crimes were legion, and their punishments swift. When they fired spitballs at the portrait of Andrew Jackson (three on his forehead "like an Arabian dancer," Quentin said, two on his ear lobes, one on the end of his nose and a "gob over each of the buttons on his coat") the President banished the gang from the White House for a week. When they bounced sunbeams from mirrors onto the windows of the State-War-Navy Building, a uniformed figure appeared on the roof with flags and duly semaphored the following: "Y-O-U U-N-D-E-R T-R-E-E-S [pause] . . . A-T-T-A-C-K O-N T-H-I-S B-U-I-L-D-I-N-G M-U-S-T I-M-M-E-D-I-A-T-E-L-Y C-E-A-S-E H-A-L-T S-T-O-P [pause] C-L-E-R-K-S C-A-N-N-O-T W-O-R-K [pause] G-O-V-E-R-N-M-E-N-T B-U-S-I-N-E-S-S I-N-T-E-R-R-U-P-T-E-D [pause] R-E-P-O-R-T T-O M-E W-I-T-H-O-U-T D-E-L-A-Y F-O-R Y-O-U K-N-O-W W-H-A-T [pause] T-H-E-O-D-O-R-E R-O-O-S-E-V-E-L-T."[5]

Presidential dignity notwithstanding, Theodore could barely resist joining in some of their pranks himself. One day the boys were traveling in the back of a streetcar, and noticed the President following behind in his carriage. They began to make the worst faces they knew how at him. He responded immediately and in kind, producing "terrifying and extraordinary grimaces, which were witnessed with the utmost amazement by passengers on the car."[6]

The White House nursery, sandwiched between the library and Edith's bedroom, was the scene of much devilment. It was scantily furnished, so that spare beds could be easily installed to accommodate Quentin's overnight guests. During one pajama party the boys were in the middle of a pillow fight when they heard footsteps coming along the hall. Instantly, they turned off the light. The door opened, and a shadowy figure, partly obscured by a screen and chair, stepped inside. Without warning, each member of the gang let fly a pillow and felled the unidentified person with a crash. "The restored light disclosed TR in full evening dress," Bromley Seeley recalled, "half on the chair and half on the floor, submerged under pillows and nearly covered by the capsized screen. In the brief abashed silence his characteristic (and much caricatured) grin relieved our doubts, and his laughter as he regained his feet and replaced the screen was joined by our own . . . when he left he was enshrined more securely than ever in the hearts of six small boys."[7]

Edith was also a victim of gang antics. When she was entertaining an Italian diplomat and an army officer in the upstairs hall, Quentin and his friends, including Earle Looker, climbed to the skylight above in order to spy on them.

> The Italian's monocle convulsed us. Our own monocles—crystals from old watches—were promptly

brought into service . . . Quentin—softly at first—began to talk what he fondly imagined to be Italian. The syllables were too contagious for us to remain silent, and soon we were all gibbering away, louder and louder.

"Quentin!" Mrs. Roosevelt called, and four small boys, each with a glittering monocle in his eye . . . stared down from the edge of the skylight. The Italian opened his eyes in astonishment, and dropped his eyeglass into his tea![8]

In spite of necessary reproofs from time to time, Looker had the distinct impression that Edith "considered it a misfortune to be a First Lady, and, therefore, not able to romp with us through rooms and halls of the White House." He felt her "quick understanding of when it was wise to interfere with Gang plans—and when to look the other way . . . Her judgment in these matters was keen, because she was alive to the hourly changes of pitch of childhood spirit."[9]

The children were sensitive to the tenderness in the President's voice whenever he spoke his wife's name, and they grew to love "the gracious lady" with undiminished affection. "She was benign, affable, motherly, and, above all, interested in us all," Earle Looker remembered. What was more, she "knew more about the mind of a child . . . than any teacher of child psychology."[10]

This did not mean that Edith turned a blind eye to all of Quentin's peccadillos, and would ask Theodore to discipline him from time to time. But she always retired from the room "much agitated when the final catastrophe became imminent."[11]

Quentin was more like his father than her other sons, even Ted. He had the same spontaneous enthusiasms, was quick to anger and equally quick to forgive. He was frank, impetuous, aggressive, imaginative (he once compared his sunburned legs to a Turner sunset) and had the same explosive way of speaking. "His tow head was always mussed," according to Looker, "his tie coming untied . . . his stockings refusing to stay up. His head seemed too large for his body. He was as irrepressible mentally as he was physically, and, either way, there was no holding him down or back."[12]

He nearly always had the last and most pertinent word. When his father told him that he could not walk across the flower beds on stilts, because the gardener objected, he said contemptuously, "I don't see what good it does for you to be President. You can't do anything here." Once when he was starting out for school and his mother said, "It is not necessary to say that I hope you will be a good boy," he replied, "No, that would be a bromide."[13]

Quentin was more than a match for inquisitive reporters. Asked for some personal details about the President, he said, "I see him sometimes, but I know nothing of his family life."[14]

Theodore and Edith were often astonished at his enterprise and his ability to strike up democratic friendships. Rather than ask his parents to buy a beehive, he acquired his own with the aid of "a mongrel-looking small boy" whose father kept a fruit stand. When Mr. Schmid, the owner of a Washington pet shop, needed a pig, Quentin "called on an elderly darkey" in the country, bought one from him for one dollar, carried it under his arm to town on the cars, and sold it to Schmid for $1.25. "I don't know how I can keep him in order," said Edith in despair. "He is forever doing things and knows every mucker in town."[15]

He was certainly no respecter of dignified persons, nor, for that matter, the orderly conduct of government. During a meeting in the Executive Office between the President and the Attorney General, Quentin roller-skated in and deposited a large king snake, along with two smaller ones, in his father's lap. The President suggested that he go into the next room and wait his turn with four Congressmen. Quentin obediently rumbled off, "with the assurance that he would there find kindred spirits. They at first thought the snakes were wooden ones," Theodore told Archie later, "and there was some perceptible recoil when they realized they were alive. Then the king snake went up Quentin's sleeve—he was three or four feet long—and we hesitated to drag him back because his scales rendered that difficult. The last I saw of Quentin, one Congressman was gingerly helping him off with his jacket so as to let the snake crawl out of the upper end of the sleeve."[16]

On December 10, 1906, Theodore Roosevelt became the first American to win a Nobel Prize—for his efforts in bringing about the Russo-Japanese peace accord. After discussing with Edith what he should do with the $40,000 prize, he cabled the Norwegian Minister of Foreign Affairs that the most fitting way to use the money would be to establish a permanent Industrial Peace Committee to strive for more equitable relations between workers and management. Privately he explained to Kermit that he could not in good conscience accept financial reward merely for doing his job. "Altogether Mother and I felt that there was no alternative and that I would have to apply the money to some public purpose. But I hated to have to come to the decision," he said wistfully, "because I very much wisht [sic] for the extra money to leave to all you children."[17]

The radical tone of the President's message to Congress at the end of 1906, declaring that all big business was engaged in interstate commerce and should therefore be under Federal control, made Wall Street tremble. Rumors of a drop in the stock market proliferated. In the spring of 1907, waves of selling shook world exchanges. Businesses failed across the country, prices fell, and unemployment rose sharply. To stave off panic, Roosevelt softened his verbal attacks on corporations, while allowing Federal investigations into improper business practices to continue. But it was an exhausting time, and the strain on Theodore began to show.

"The general impression of this town is that we all feel tired," Henry Adams wrote on March 26, 1907. "Three or four persons close to the President have assured me that, for the first time, even he complains of fatigue and shows it. . . . The President is trying to find out what effect a dose of hard times and unemployed labor will have on the Republican vote. For the first time he is transparently hesitating."[18] Two days later, Theodore took to his bed with toothache.

Edith now had three patients to nurse, for Ted had boils, and Archie was still recuperating from a near-fatal attack of diphtheria. For the next seven months the economic situation was to continue uncertain. A government probe of the Union Pacific Railroad, and a fine of $29 million assessed against the Standard Oil Company further staggered the business establishment. In June, the American Steel Company failed, the credit became tight in spite of a Treasury surplus. Finally, in mid-October, speculators attempting to corner the copper market with funds drawn from unstable trust companies as well as from the sound Knickerbocker Trust Company of New York caused a national panic. Desperate depositors waited on line all night to withdraw their money from banks, until the Knickerbocker collapsed completely and the Trust Company of America threatened to do the same.

The market stabilized on October 23, when J. P. Morgan deposited large sums of private money in the latter. Next day the U.S. Treasury followed suit, with $25 million in government funds. Morgan rallied other businessmen to do likewise, and the panic was checked.

Late one unbearably hot night in the early summer of 1907 the President of the United States "sat solemnly in scanty attire" with his daughter Ethel on the piazza of Sagamore Hill. They were alone in the big house, except for Quentin, who was asleep upstairs. Edith had sailed up the Sound with Archie in the *Sylph* to pick up the two eldest boys.

Bright moonlight streamed across the piazza, and "as always happened on moonlight nights," the male servants began to sing somewhere on the property. Theodore identified the voices of his two black housemen and two white stablemen, harmonizing with the duet of his black coachman and groom. Both father and daughter listened enchanted until the music died away.[19]

Ethel, now sixteen, had begun to lead "just about such a life as Edith herself led at her age," Theodore wrote Henry Cabot Lodge.[20] She was always going away to parties in town, riding on country estates at weekends, and inviting her special friends home. All the children, for that matter, were growing up with alarming speed. Ted, now in his second year at Harvard, was about to leave on an extended trip to Minnesota. Seventeen-year-old Kermit was also going west to camp with the Thirteenth Cavalry, and to hunt prairie chickens and deer. In the fall, Archie would be off to Groton, like his brothers before him. Then there would be only Quentin left.

For the time being, however, Archie was still a boy who loved to sail his little dory in the bay, with his inseparable seagoing companion, Skip, the mongrel. All the family loved the animal except Edith. He was "a cunning little fellow and friendly, of course," she concluded. "In fact he's friendly with everyone. Personally I never cared for a cur; but then it is a mere matter of taste."[21] She, too, anticipated the boy's departure for Groton with dread. The accidental death of Skip, just two days before Archie left, evoked a surge of maternal protectiveness. Her son, she knew, had plenty of character, but he was frail and prone to fierce headaches, and intensive study did not agree with him. "I think the petition in the Litany, 'Strengthen those who stand, comfort the weak-hearted, raise up

"All the children were growing up with alarming speed."
The Roosevelt family in 1907.

those who fall, and finally beat down Satan under our feet' is especially for boys going out into the big world," she wrote Emily. "I have added it to my prayers and hope you will do so too." [22]

The household moved back to Washington on September 25, 1907. Four days later, Theodore left for a three-week speaking tour of the

West and the South—taking time out for a bear hunt in the
Louisiana canebrakes. The First Lady embarked on a heavy schedule
of entertaining and theater-going, but as always her heart was with
her husband, and she scanned each day's mail eagerly for letters. The
President had to be careful what he wrote her, since curious postal
employees had been known to open his personal mail and packages.[23]
Edith herself was so jealous of their privacy that she had extracted a
promise from him to destroy all her letters on receipt. Even so
Theodore could not resist a certain tenderness whenever he addressed his wife:

> Tenesas Bayou
> Thurs. Oct. 10, 1907 P.M.
>
> DARLING EDIE,
>
> All your dear, dear letters have come; I love them so;
> and after reading them again and again I can hardly
> make up my mind to tear them up. What a time you and
> Ethel did have with Fidelity in the mudhole! It was
> more exciting than any adventure *I* have had. Tell Ethel
> I loved her letter; I can't answer it now because I must
> write Kermit and Archie, and letter writing in camp is
> difficult, for there are no conveniences, and we are in the
> saddle literally from sunrise to sunset. Tell her I entirely
> agree with her criticism of Chesterton. . . . I am very
> homesick for you; whenever I wake up at night, or stay
> still waiting to hear the hounds in the day I find myself
> counting the days before I get back—a little less than
> thirteen now, my darling sweetheart.
>
> But I really think the outing has been very good for
> me. This camp is comfortable; I have no hard exercise;
> but I ride slowly, from 6–12 hours a day thru these
> magnificent woods, with frequent long halts; and I am
> getting in first class condition. There are no bear here. I
> have seen one deer, running like a race horse thru the
> cane; and by a lucky, and difficult shot I killed it—
> delighting the dear doctor John McIlhenny, and win-
> ning undeserved praise from all the party. The first four
> days were as hot as Hades, with continual rain; but the
> last two days have been cool, clear, a delight in every

way. All the party are as nice as possible. We are now
going to move round to camp elsewhere, to try to find
bear; I have not much hope of success; but the trip is all
right anyhow.

YOUR OWN LOVER[24]

Commenting to Aunt Lizzie on Theodore's success with the deer,
Edith said, "He never admits that he makes a good shot except by
luck!" As for his fitness, "he certainly must be if he admits it, for he
usually tells me that he is an old and broken man."[25]

Four days after returning to Washington, Theodore celebrated his
forty-ninth birthday. As an experiment, Edith gave him an ultra-
modern wallet, which held both bills and visiting cards. But he could
not conceal his disappointment. "He was dear about it," she told
Kermit, "but it is a kind they did not have when he was a boy . . . so
I think he is a little shy of it." She made amends five weeks later on
their twenty-first wedding anniversary, by presenting to him a
beautiful edition of Isaak Walton's *The Compleat Angler,* of which he
heartily approved. In the evening they went to see Winchell Smith's
play *Brewster's Millions,* "which was so funny that it even amused
Father all through, though I had meant to send him home," Edith
told Kermit.[26]

The President's Annual Message to Congress at the end of 1907
was so insistent on ever-progressive reforms that the legislative body
chose largely to ignore them. Incensed, Theodore sent up a second
Message early in the New Year, which not only reiterated his
previous proposals, but contained his most aggressive attack yet upon
big business.

He urged a new employers' liability act, and a comprehensive act
to compensate government employees injured on the job. (The
President particularly had in mind Panama Canal workers, some of
whose injuries he had seen during his visit to the Isthmus.) He also
called for increased government control of railroads and industrial
corporations, as well as for Federal control of securities issues.

Theodore's chief advisers were all against these radical proposals,
"Councils of war never fight," he complained. But Edith was solidly
behind him. "Mother really likes the message," the President wrote
Kermit, "and I am sure it is on the right track."[27]

Only his first two requests were granted by the Sixtieth Congress; the others would come later, in the Taft and Wilson administrations. In political ideas and ideals Theodore Roosevelt was way ahead of his contemporaries, and so, it appears, was his wife.

"I feel that Mrs. Roosevelt has given poise to the White House," Theodore told an aide, in an attempt to explain why his wife was, in his opinion, an incomparable First Lady. What was more, she, not he, was largely responsible for his reputation as a patron of the arts. "It is my wife who often reminds me of some new struggling author, and suggests that he be invited to visit us . . . I often get the credit of doing things to which she is entitled." He claimed that she was better educated, better read, and a better critic than he, "and I know she scorns secretly my general knowledge of literature."[28]

Be that as it may, there was no doubt that he was a little intimidated by Edith, and that she took advantage of this sometimes to remind him that, despite his worldwide reputation as a superman, he was but human after all.

One evening early in 1908 she watched with amusement while Theodore lost track of a dinner guest's story and tried to redeem his lack of concentration by asking a lot of questions. Edith had been suffering from neuralgia, and felt "very woe begone," but this, as he ruefully told Archie afterward, "seemed to be the turning point in her evening, and she brightened up and got over her headache, every now and then making a sudden little assault upon me, just as I have seen a bird ruffle up its little feathers and give a sudden peck; then she would feel heart-smitten lest she had been too severe, and pet me to make up."[29]

Twenty-Five

Gentle to the last, I thought, and wondered when the White House would again have such a mistress.

—Archibald W. Butt[1]

As her last year as First Lady began in March 1908, Edith sat for a pastel sketch by the Hungarian painter Philip Alexius Laszlo de Lombos. A noble portrait of the President by the same artist showing him with cloak and riding crop had just been finished, and both Edith and Theodore liked it "better than any other."[2] Theodore was equally "delighted" with Laszlo's drawing of Edith's head, which was eventually to hang in her sitting room at Sagamore Hill.

Theodore Roosevelt now began to make plans for the transition from public to private life which he would face in twelve months' time. Instinct told him that it would be wise to leave, not only Washington, but the country itself for a while, to allow his hoped-for Republican successor to establish himself. He did not want to be "an old cannon loose on the deck in the storm."[3]

Accordingly, he wrote to the great African big-game hunter Frederick Courtenay Selous, asking for advice on the feasibility of mounting a major zoological specimen-collecting expedition through Kenya and Uganda. His chief backers would be the Smithsonian Institution and the American Museum of Natural History, and he intended to take Kermit along. Selous was encouraging, and arrangements for the trip took shape. Theodore estimated he would be in the wilderness at least six months, and Edith prophesied that she would be "a little bit of thread" by the time he returned. But this would be "a cheap price to pay for any journey which can interest him after the life he has led for eight years."[4]

Theodore now began to talk "continually" of the safari, at the same time trying to convince Edith of how much he disliked the idea of going. She was not fooled, but accepted that given his still-youthful restlessness "there would be endless complications if he tried to stay at Sagamore."[5]

Besides, Scribners was willing to pay handsomely for articles written during the expedition, and expanding these into a book would mercifully occupy Theodore at least through the summer following his return.[6] Once it was settled that a doctor, Major Mearns of the United States Medical Corps, would accompany her husband, she felt easier about tropical health hazards. She was also relieved that the antelope heads and skins would go to the Institution, and not end up on her own walls.

The question of who would follow him as President had occupied Theodore ever since the fateful day he announced he would not seek reelection. Several possible candidates had emerged. Perhaps the most suitable heir to Roosevelt's political and economic policies was Charles Evans Hughes, Governor of New York State. But he was too proud and independent a spirit to accept automatic nomination by the incumbent as kingmaker. Elihu Root was the most gifted intellect in the Republican Party, but his business interests and conservative outlook ill became the progressive times. In the end Theodore's personal liking for William Howard Taft tipped the scales in his favor, and he announced that the Secretary of War would be his choice for a successor. Taft would have preferred a seat on the Supreme Court, and his mother forecast that "the malice of politics" would make her genial son miserable. But the Secretary's wife was ambitious to be First Lady, so he reluctantly agreed to run.

Thus on June 19, 1908, at the Chicago Convention, Taft received the Republican nomination; but not until after a forty-nine-minute demonstration in favor of a third term for Roosevelt.

With Theodore increasingly busy battling Congress and the trusts, organizing a nationwide conference on conservation, and equipping himself for his safari, Edith welcomed the arrival at the White House of a new walking and riding companion. He was Archibald Willingham Butt, a portly red-haired Southerner with a clipped mustache, the successor to Charlie McCauley as White House military aide.

"Archie," as he was known to friends, came from distinguished Georgian and Massachusetts Colonial stock, and was endowed with a combination of traits guaranteed to endear him to Edith. He was courteous without being pompous, chivalrous without being familiar, moral but not prudish, capable of intimacy without being indiscreet, and of literary talk without being pedantic.

Unmarried at forty-two, he was three years Edith's junior, and his years of closeness to a widowed mother made him an ideal companion and confidant to the First Lady. In the ten months that remained of her White House tenure, Butt was to become an admirer of Edith Roosevelt, seeing himself "in the role of knight for a mistress so gentle, so sweet, and so altogether lovely." [7]

Butt was a born reporter, and practiced his natural gift in a series of diary-letters to his mother and sister-in-law, describing in almost daily detail the personalities and events of life in the inner circle of the Executive Mansion. He took up his duties on Friday, May 8, while Edith and Theodore were at Pine Knot with John Burroughs. His first luncheon at the White House was on Wednesday, May 13, in company with President Hadley of Yale, the Cowleses and the Lodges. A Rhine-wine cup was served with the meal, and the President remarked it always amused him to serve alcohol to big temperance leaders when they came to dine. They usually drank it, and afterward at their conferences "calmed their conscience by protesting against the bibulous habits at the capital." [8]

Since there had been many recent assaults on unescorted ladies in and around Washington, the President ordered Captain Butt to accompany Edith whenever she went out alone. This, the stout aide soon discovered, involved a lot of exercise: Edith thought nothing of

"He saw himself in the role of knight."
Captain Archibald Willingham Butt.

striding out for miles at a time, stopping only for iced tea or lemonade when the weather was hot. Archie wrote admiringly that she was "a pretty good walker, and knew all the out-of-way paths.[9] They talked of many subjects on these long rambles, including the art of "snooping," or tracking down antique bargains in junk shops. Edith told Butt one day, with what he would always remember as "that inimitable little laugh of hers":

> Snoopers are born not made. Now Ethel thinks she is a snooper, but she really isn't, and does not know the first principle of snooping. No amount of training would make the President a snooper. He would possibly pass over the most charming articles of china or bronze and end by buying a brass bedstead. Alice is better, but of all my children Kermit is the ideal . . . He has the nose of a perfectly bred snooper.[10]

As she warmed to the sympathetic Southerner, the First Lady became uncharacteristically frank, going so far as to discuss details of personal finances with him. She confessed that she and Theodore "had not saved any of the President's pay; that it had all gone in the effort to keep up the White House as they thought it should be kept up."[11]

On September 13, 1908, Ted celebrated his twenty-first birthday. He had recently graduated from Harvard, and in spite of his rather wayward career there, he had now developed signs of an unswerving ambition to make a lot of money in business fast, and then go into politics. As a result he had turned down the opportunity to go to Africa with his father and Kermit, preferring instead to take a millhand's job in a Connecticut carpet factory, and work his way up from the bottom. Theodore, while applauding his independence, was reassured to note that he had not lost his Rooseveltian love of books. "Ted . . . quite spontaneously reads Virgil and Horace for his own amusement before going to bed."[12]

Kermit, too, loved the classics, and planned to include Homer in Greek among the books he would take on safari. But first he intended to enter Harvard, and stay there six months before taking a year off for the expedition (which had doubled in length as Theodore's plans grew more elaborate). "I am confident you will do well at college and avoid some of the mistakes Ted made," his mother wrote after he left for Cambridge in September. "But after all they were but follies and he has told me since how glad he is that he never did anything shameful. You are too much your father's son to find any attraction in immoral impurity. Refinement as well as principle will keep you from that temptation." Fate was to clothe these remarks with tragic irony in later years.

Archie, she went on, seemed to be "safe" at Groton, but Quentin she was "sometimes anxious about." In a last-ditch effort to wean her youngest child, now almost eleven, from the Washington "muckers," Edith enrolled him as a boarder at the Episcopal High School, a sixty-year-old establishment near Alexandria, Virginia. He had long wanted to go, unlike her "other little birds," who had all been reluctant to leave the nest.[13]

"It's awfully nice," Quentin wrote his mother on his second day. "Up here the boys have fags or squids . . . I am g.g. whites squid. It isnt bad all I have to do is call him at quarter past seven and carry water for him." But twenty-four hours later he felt miserable. "The cat [i.e., himself] is sad. His joy has had a reaction. Yesterday he had a terrible attack of homesickness . . . My nick name is 'rooster.' Last night all we new kids were taken into the gynmasium and run [hazed]. I had to stand on a gym horse and speak on prohibition then four of us had to sing ('I never smoke I never chew that nasty dirty weed') to the tune of *Auld Lang Syne*."[14]

Edith drove over to fix Quentin's room on September 26, and found him "very brave and manly." On the twenty-eighth he was sent home ill, and he stayed there until October 2. He did not tell his parents the reason for his nausea, but confessed to Archie he had been "hazed a good deal," had his bed dumped and turned over on him, and was made to smoke a cigarette morning and evening, "getting deathly sick each time." He was also forced to box a boy twice his weight. "I might have made a good show if I hadn't been sick," he concluded.[15]

At the end of October, the headmaster, suspecting that Quentin was congenitally unsuited to boarding-school life, suggested that he become a day boy for a while. Edith was more than glad "to have him where I can tuck him into bed and we can have breakfast and dinner together." After Christmas he became a boarder again, but was never entirely happy in the role.[16]

Traveling back from the Episcopal High School one day, as Edith frequently did that fall, she saw a small house on fire, and stopped her carriage to console the owner, a black laundress. The thunderstruck woman described her afterward as "the beautifullest lady I ever did see, in the finest cloe's I ever see and the biggest pocketbook I ever see . . . she give me twenty dollars right on de spot and a sweet face to it . . . when she rolls on past, I drap on my marrow bones and pray so loud de Lawd couldn't he'p hearing me praise Gawd from whom all blessin's flows."[17]

Few people realized the extent of Edith Roosevelt's charity. Donations of money and supplies were made quietly, spontaneously, and often anonymously. Jacob Riis was "more than once the almoner" for her in dispensing money to the poor during a hard winter in New York. But she always insisted that he find out "the exact facts" of each case, so that the help could be applied wisely. "Carrying" people when they should "learn to walk" was not her philosophy.[18]

The needy, both near and far, benefited from her largesse. Baskets of food, fuel and clothing were dispatched to impoverished Washingtonians; a Michigan woman threatened with eviction was sent a small sum of money, and her husband was helped to find a job; a one-hundred-dollar bill was sent to a sick family in a church she once attended; ten-dollar bills to clergymen and various charities were mailed regularly, as a matter of course. On one typical day the First Lady sent ten dollars to the Washington Hospital for Foundlings, to the Hope and Health Mission, to the Children's Hospital, and to the Washington Home for Incurables. Her favorite way of giving alms, according to Belle Hagner, was to have doctors hand out cash to charity patients as they were discharged from hospital free wards.[19]

Friends in trouble could also depend on a discreet check from Edith; large donations often went to Rough Riders who had fallen on hard times. "Compassion filled her heart," commented one aide. Another said that no one's presence was more "felt," however subtly, by Americans. "The world at large admired and respected her—but to those of us who knew her well, she was an Angel."[20]

By the fall of 1908, Theodore's plans for his postpresidential safari were nearly complete. He would sail from New York in late March 1909, and it was decided that Edith would meet up with him in Egypt in mid-March 1910. There was no question of their returning immediately to the United States; the crowned heads of Europe were already showering invitations upon them to stay in their palaces and receive the plaudits of their peoples. One night at dinner Theodore wondered aloud as to what a former President should wear at ceremonial functions in foreign courts. He strongly objected to the diplomatic garb of knee breeches and black stockings, and asked Captain Butt if the military dress uniform of a Colonel of Cavalry would be an appropriate substitute. The aide (who liked gaudy uniforms, and had himself portrayed in one) said that it would. The uniform under consideration—the most ostentatious in the Army— was embellished with yellow plumes and gold lace. Theodore said that he would wear it with patent-leather boots, confirming Edith's oft-stated opinion that all Georgians were "peacocks." She interrupted the discussion quickly and firmly. "Theodore . . . if you insist upon doing this I will have a *vivandière's* costume made and follow you throughout Europe."

The President took her teasing good-naturedly, and said nothing more about military finery that evening. Edith told Butt afterward that her husband's weak spot was not liking the family to laugh at him. "I will not have him wear a uniform in Europe," she went on, "for they would ridicule him in this country." She told the captain to postpone ordering any such outfit, and in the end had her way: Theodore agreed to wear an ordinary frock coat.[21]

The subject of the African expedition was a constant one during the last months of Roosevelt's administration. One day the President received a call from the head of the Associated Press, who wanted to have a representative accompany him to Africa. Theodore refused, but the man persisted, saying that the "yellow" newspapers would almost certainly send their reporters, and that the Associated Press could not afford to be scooped "if anything should happen."

"What do you mean by anything happening?" asked the President.

"Well," came the reply, "I don't like to anticipate evil, but should a lion really do his duty as a lion . . ."

Theodore recounted this story with glee over dinner. His guests laughed, but Edith did not. It seemed to Archie Butt that she turned "a trifle paler."[22]

Many friends voiced their concern about Theodore venturing into tropical jungle, but he would say, "It does not do to try to live too long . . . I am ready to rest my career here, or . . . after I have had a little fling in Africa." Edith could only console herself with reflecting that as President of the United States he was daily "a target for every crank who comes to these shores." [23] In Africa, at least, he would be free of that threat. He assured her that he would keep away from unhealthy and dangerous regions. "But," she wrote Cecil Spring-Rice (who was just appointed to a post in Sweden), "I might as well try to control a hunter with a gossamer bridle as to bind him with promises." [24] This did not reassure the nervous Springy, who began to bombard Edith with literature on the medical dangers of life in the tropics. Theodore, amused, tried to put him at ease.

> Oh! you beloved Mrs. Gummidge! If you feel as melancholy over my trip in Africa as you do over the future of the race generally, at least you must not share the feeling too fully with Mrs. Roosevelt. I laughed until I almost cried over your sending her the pamphlet upon the "sleeping sickness," and explaining in your letter that it was perfectly possible that I would not die of that, because (in the event of my not previously being eaten by a lion or crocodile, or killed by an infuriated elephant or buffalo) malarial fever or a tribe of enraged savages might take me off before the sleeping sickness got at me! I am bound to say, however, that the letter gave Mrs. Roosevelt a keen though melancholy enjoyment, and she will now have the feeling that she is justified in a Roman matron-like attitude of heroically bidding me to go to my death when I sail on a well-equipped steamer for an entirely comfortable and mild little hunting trip.
>
> Seriously, both of us were really touched and pleased with your letters and with your thought of me. I feel excessively melancholy at being separated for so long from Mrs. Roosevelt, and I shall be so homesick, especially when, as I suppose will be the case, I have a slight attack of fever or something of the kind, that I shall not know quite what to do with myself. But I am convinced that it is the wise thing for me to go, and also I freely admit that I am looking forward to the trip! I should like to have stayed on in the Presidency, and I make no pretense that I am glad to be relieved of my official duties. The only reason I did not stay on was

> because I felt that I ought not to, and I am exceedingly
> glad that I am to have the interest of this African trip
> before me . . .[25]

On November 3, 1908, the Republican ticket of William Howard
Taft and James S. Sherman won a great victory in the presidential
elections. Theodore was "simply radiant" over the party's triumph,
and saw the result as an endorsement of his own policies. "We have
them beaten to a frazzle," he said over and over again.[26]

Mrs. Taft lost no time in making her plans as the next First Lady
known. On November 30, Edith learned that she intended to
dispense with the Executive Mansion's frock-coated ushers and
replace them with liveried servants. "Oh it will hurt them so," Edith
exclaimed to Archie Butt, her voice breaking. For a moment she
could not speak. "Don't think me foolish," she continued, "but if you
knew how those men had served us and how kind and thoughtful
they have been in times of illness and trouble, you would understand
me now."

Seeing how strongly she felt about the ushers, Butt arranged that
the ones she cared for most would be kept on as head men in charge
of the footmen; the others were "promoted" to the Executive Office
staff.[27] But Mrs. Taft would replace the police guards at the main
entrance with black footmen.

The Roosevelts' last Christmas in the White House was celebrated
in the company of over fifty relatives and friends. The table was
decorated with ferns and red leaves, and Archie Butt was intrigued
by a new novelty beside each plate: "tissue paper packages which
popped when opened, and everyone wore some sort of paper
headgear, from fool's cap to crown." The turkey was supplied by
Horace Vose, the Rhode Island "Turkey King" who had been
shipping birds to the Executive Mansion since President Grant's
days.[28] Plum puddings followed, "ablaze with burning brandy," and
the meal ended with miniature ices of Santa Claus holding a
Christmas tree and a lighted taper. Afterward Edith took the women
and children to the crypt, where she had dressed a tree with gifts—
toys for the children, and books for the adults.

Three days later Edith and Theodore introduced their second
daughter to Washington society with a celebration more elaborate,
but inevitably less memorable than that attending Alice's debut.

Ethel was still only seventeen, and was quiet and retiring in contrast to the flamboyant "Princess" of 1902. But her parents wanted her to have the same privilege of coming out in the White House that her half-sister had had. Four hundred and forty guests attended, and the problem of feeding them all was solved by seating them at tables in the basement, leaving the first-floor salons free for promenading and dancing.

Ethel received in the Blue Room, wearing white satin studded with crystals, and Edith stood at her side in dark-blue brocade, which matched the surrounding décor.

Although the First Lady incurred the President's displeasure by forbidding him to partake of midnight supper (late snacks gave him twinges of gout), she made up for it at another ball for Ethel ten days later by allowing him to partner her in his typically energetic hops around the floor. "She looked so pretty and shy," he said, "and evidently had much the same feeling that she would have had if we had been secretly engaged and she was afraid that such a public attention might compromise her!"[29]

The season of 1909 was as splendid and eventful as its seven predecessors, but a certain elegiac tone crept in to all the proceedings. The brief golden age of the White House was coming to an end. The President-elect was jolly and popular, his wife graceful and cultivated, and their children seemed pleasant enough; but as a First Family the Tafts somehow lacked the magic—and the fun—of the Roosevelts. Already, cartoonists and columnists were lamenting the prospect of four uninspiring years, and the White House staff looked glum as they began the long process of sorting and packing the Roosevelt's belongings.

Edith and Theodore began to think of suitable mementos for their friends and aides. She was inclined to plan her gift-giving carefully, but he showed early signs of rashness—wanting to give all of his presidential relics away. One night he stayed up late after his wife had gone to bed, and started systematically to strip his study for the benefit of souvenir-hunting guests. Ethel warned her mother of what was going on, but Edith only laughed. She deliberately stayed awake in order to see him "tiptoeing about, knowing that he had been doing something naughty."[30]

In spite of her careful inventory of White House possessions, and her disinclination to profit by her tenure as First Lady, there were two items that Edith could not bring herself to leave behind. The first was a pair of Sèvres figures, given to her by the Rochambeau Commission in 1902 and used at state banquets. Mrs. Taft thought them to be the most beautiful objects in the Mansion, and would be disappointed to find them gone; but Edith considered the figures to be a personal gift, and said she had "the documents to prove it."[31] She therefore felt she could keep them with a clear conscience.

The other item presented more of a problem, in that it was definitely part of the Mansion's furniture. It was a small antique mahogany sofa which she had bought in 1901 for forty dollars to lend tone to the Red Room. After the restoration of 1902 she had transferred it to the Upper Hall, and had grown unaccountably fond of it. Unknown to Edith, the President wrote to Speaker of the House Joe Cannon, asking for her "to be permitted to take it and to replace it with a new sofa." As soon as she found out she tried to have the letter withdrawn, saying the matter was "too trivial" for official correspondence. But subsequently a newspaper article appeared, implying that the First Lady wanted to remove furniture from the White House without paying for it. Edith considered the release of the contents of Theodore's letter to be a malicious act on the part of the Speaker or his secretary, and exploded in front of Archie Butt. "Before I leave Washington I am going to tell Speaker Cannon what I think of his action, how little and petty I think it to be. It is the first time since I have been in the White House that I have been dragged into publicity of this kind." As for the "wretched little sofa," she said she no longer wanted it, "now that all the associations with it are of a most disagreeable character." This was the only occasion on which the aide saw "anything akin to anger" in Edith Roosevelt.[32]

Not for almost two years would her disappointment be assuaged, by the kindly intervention of her husband's successor.

THE WHITE HOUSE
Washington, D.C.
Dec. 31st 1910.

My Dear Mrs. Roosevelt:

It came to me sometime ago upon authority I could not doubt that when you left the White House there was a mahogany settee which you had purchased for the

White House about which clustered many pleasant associations, and that you attempted through Col. Bromwell, to secure this settee for your use at Oyster Bay, purposing to replace it in the White House by another just like it. Through what I may call the density of Col. Bromwell, and the assumption of authority to speak by Mr. Cannon your purpose was defeated. The custom is well established by which Cabinet officers leaving office take away their cabinet chairs, replacing them with new ones equally serviceable. Why the real head of the White House, the wife of the President, should be denied the same privilege, and especially in respect to a chair or settee that she herself bought for the White House and which has not therefore acquired value by long years of use in the White House I can not see. Neither the Army engineer in charge of the Public grounds, nor the Speaker of the House has anything to say about it.

I have ventured to substitute for the settee which you bought for the Government and put in the White House and which was out of repair, a new settee just like it and this new piece of furniture is now in the place of the old one and available for use of future presidential families without any additional expense to the Government.

Meantime I have taken the liberty of sending to you by express at Oyster Bay, the old settee which has become mine to bestow by exchange, and I hope you will accept it as a New Year's token of my earnest wish that the coming year may be full of happiness for you and yours. I hope the settee will bring back to you the pleasantest hours at the White House . . .

Believe me *sincerely yours*

WM. H. TAFT[33]

The final two weeks before Taft's Inauguration were among the busiest of Edith's life. While Theodore worked from dawn to midnight completing the business of his administration, she had Archie Butt smash all cracked or chipped presidential china (instead of selling it or giving it away, a practice she thought "cheapened the

White House."). She also had him burn the unpopular Chartran portrait of Theodore, because it showed him "in a coy attitude with his head on one side, looking sentimentally out from the canvas." She rounded up forlorn acquaintances they had not yet entertained in the Executive Mansion, and, by way of a swan song, gave the last of her many musicales. The audience was exclusively female and united by strong ties of friendship. A string quartet played appropriately somber pieces, and the throbbing violins and cello caused a "general breakdown." Many women were still weeping as they said goodbye to the First Lady; Belle Hagner stood at a window and cried "as if her heart would break." But Edith's extraordinary public poise— Butt thought it her greatest characteristic—as usual did not desert her. She seemed "apparently as unmoved as if she were an iceberg." In her room afterward, however, she had "one good wholesome weep," and then emerged "smiling through her tears." [34]

On Sunday, February 21, Edith came home from church "to find the terrible news of Stewart Robinson's death." Corinne's youngest son, only twenty-one-years old, had just fallen from the window of his Hampden Hall room at Harvard, and been killed. Like the drunken showoff Dolohov in Tolstoy's *War and Peace,* he had lost his balance, and toppled to the ground. Since he was the most lighthearted, fun-loving and endearing of all her children, Corinne was utterly devastated. [35]

Edith and Theodore had no time to absorb this frightful shock; they had to leave at once for Hampton Roads to meet "the Great White Fleet," due to return from its round-the-world cruise the following day. Edith looked "bowed with sorrow" when she left the White House, but as she boarded the *Mayflower* at five o'clock "she assumed the role of First Lady and carried off the duties with great composure and dignity."

Early next morning, she and Theodore stood on deck just inside the Virginia Capes, with two thousand small craft bobbing all around them. Presently Edith caught her first glimpse of the pale ships looming majestically through curtains of rain and sea haze. "That is the answer to my critics," Theodore shouted triumphantly. "I could not ask a finer concluding scene to my administrations." [36]

Precisely at eleven o'clock, as scheduled, the *Connecticut* came abreast of the *Mayflower,* followed at regular intervals by the other cruisers. The combined bedlam of sea whistles and twenty-one-gun salutes was deafening. The President lifted his hat, and cheers rang out from sixteen decks, as the *Mayflower* steered between the double line of cruisers to take its place at the head and to receive the admiral and other officers.

Because of their sudden state of mourning for their nephew, Edith and Theodore could not stay for the celebratory dinner that evening. As darkness fell, their yacht steered out of the Roads and sailed slowly back up the Potomac.

The following day Edith left to be with the Robinsons, and to attend Stewart's funeral on the twenty-fourth. Her two eldest sons met her train in New York. "I can't stop thinking of it all," she wrote Kermit later. "Auntie Corinne is my life long friend and her grief is mine. My heart swelled with pride when you and Ted were beside me as we walked down the station. It was the one bright spot in the dreadful day. I love and trust you both and if I can see Archie and Quentin follow in your steps I can sing my *'nunc dimittis'* and say 'of those Thou hast given me I have not lost one.'"[37]

By February 28, 1909, the White House was at last stripped of all the Roosevelts' personal belongings. Edith had worked herself "almost to death" to make sure that every surface and each piece of linen was immaculately clean.

The last two days passed rapidly. On Monday, March 1, Theodore held a luncheon for thirty-one male guests. They included the "Tennis Cabinet," old hunting companions, such as Bill Sewall, various friends and acquaintances who had helped him in difficult times, and one or two "who have been arrested . . . for holding up trains and killing desperadoes."[38]

After the waffles and syrup had been served, Theodore rose to speak, and soon "there was not a dry eye" at the table. Sinewy Seth Bullock, Sheriff of Deadwood, was supposed to make a speech in reply. But he was so overcome with emotion that he merely choked, and, leaning forward, plucked wordlessly at the flower centerpiece. Crouched beneath the foliage was a magnificent bronze cougar by Proctor, a gift from those present.

Edith joined Theodore that afternoon for tea at the Townsends.' When she returned to the White House to change for dinner with the Bacons, she found a package on her bureau from a group of the society women she had so frequently entertained over the years. It was a single-strand necklace of solitaires inlaid in platinum. Edith had never owned such precious jewels, and was completely overcome. Ethel, too, began to cry, and the President, "when he tried to cheer them broke down himself." [39]

It was snowing on the evening of March 3 as Edith and Theodore came down to their last dinner in the White House. Fires burned brightly in every room, warming the chill of imminent departure. Ten guests were awaiting them: President-elect and Mrs. Taft, Bamie and Will Cowles, Nick and Alice Longworth, Elihu and Mrs. Root, Archie Butt and Mabel Boardman, a close friend of the Tafts. The sadness of the occasion sat heavily on everyone. Root looked glum and tearful; even Alice (who did not trust Taft to carry on Roosevelt's policies) was not her usual ebullient self; she realized what a gap her father's departure from Washington would make in her own life.

Edith, though she professed not to be tired, was unusually pale in her black silk and lace gown, contrasting starkly with Mrs. Taft's white satin and filmy tulle. No mention was made of the coming transfer of housekeeping power, and not a single domestic detail was discussed. Theodore managed to keep the conversation buoyant. "He puts most of the macaronis about the clubs to shame in the matter of sheer social chat," noted Captain Butt. [40]

Mr. and Mrs. Taft had been invited to spend the night, and after dinner, when all the guests except Captain Butt had gone, Edith rose and announced that she was retiring. Taking Mrs. Taft's hand, she "expressed the earnest hope that her first night in the White House would be one of sweet sleep."

"Thoughtful and gentle to the last," mused Archie Butt, and wondered "when the White House would again have such a mistress." Tomorrow his orders were to accompany Mrs. Taft to the Capitol, and from then his allegiance must be to the new President. When he said goodbye to Edith in the hallway, he felt he had "closed the book" on her, "for tomorrow she will only wear a mask to conceal the real heart pain." [41]

Henry Adams, despite his pose of cynical disapproval of "the friend with tusks and eyeglasses," had for many months been dreading the departure of the Roosevelts from the Washington scene.

"Whatever charges his enemies made against him, they never included dullness," he once wrote of Theodore. In January 1909 he had told a friend, "My last vision of fun and gaiety will vanish when my Theodore goes . . . Never can we replace him." In the end he could not bring himself to cross Lafayette Square to say goodbye, and explained why in a poignant letter to Edith:

> MY DEAR MRS. ROOSEVELT:
>
> Of all earthly trials, farewells are the worst. At the end of life they become intolerable. Is it not enough that I should have to look out of my window every moment, and that, whenever my eye falls on the White House the thought that you are not there should depress me, without having also to assume an air of cheerfulness and go to bid you goodbye as though we both like it?
>
> I have bid goodbye to my friends until I am quite broken up by it, and cannot go through the form any more. Washington is a city of tragedy. No other place ever has, or ever can approach it. Only in this last year I have lost nearly all of the persons and houses on whom I have been dependent; and nothing takes their place. . . .
>
> You are still a mere child and have lots to care for and to do, but I am a remnant,—Andrew Jackson and I,—in a sort of Niagara whirlpool, wobbling round and round, while my friends float gently down the river to the sea.
>
> I send you this wail only to explain why I failed to see you off. The least decorative object that I know is my own figure at a ceremony. The least cheerful animal on earth is myself at a farewell. The woodchuck is best in his hole, and at least spares you his shadow. . . .
>
> *Ever yrs*
>
> HENRY ADAMS[42]

Theodore's reluctance to quit the Executive Mansion was well known. "I have had a great run for my money," he wrote Kermit, "and I should have liked to stay in as President if I had felt it was right for me to do so; but there are many compensations about going, and Mother and I are in the curious and very pleasant position of having enjoyed the White House more than any other President and his wife whom I recall, and yet being entirely willing to leave it, and looking forward to a life of interest and happiness . . ."[43]

Edith, who preferred to keep her deepest emotions private, would admit only to feeling "a little sad" at the thought of relinquishing "the lovely White House." But she would not allow her thoughts to dwell on it; "rather on Sagamore in the spring."[44]

Rain and snow had been pouring down for several days before the Inauguration of William Howard Taft, and by Thursday morning, March 4, Washington looked sodden and battered. Along the whole length of Pennsylvania Avenue "crude and unsightly" scaffoldings awaited the expected crowds; early arrivals froze in the coldest temperatures the capital had experienced since the blizzard of 1899. Flags and bunting snapped angrily in a tearing east wind, and the overcast skies made a grim backdrop to the garlanded white columns in front of the Treasury Building.

Roosevelt and Taft left for the ceremony in a heavy snowstorm. Because of the weather, it was decided that the Oath of Office would be administered in the Senate, rather than on the Capitol steps. Edith watched them go, and then drove with Bamie, Belle, and Quentin to lunch with Alice. Ethel had already gone north to prepare Sagamore Hill; Kermit was in New York, and Ted at work. "That cheerful small pagan" Quentin was feeling rather less buoyant than usual today: he confessed to "a little hole in the stomach" at the thought of leaving the White House. Nevertheless, he was determined to watch the Inaugural Parade from the President's box with Charley Taft. He would be the only Roosevelt "anywhere in evidence" after the swearing-in, since he had to finish his term at school in Virginia.[45]

A first hand, characteristically unpunctuated account of the Senate ceremony was relayed to Edith later by Bamie, as it was told her by Senator Newlands:

> He said Theodore sat absolutely motionless except during the Inaugural address he moved his head as though in approbation the moment the address was over before any one could realize what was occurring he went up the steps to the Speakers desk and then bade Mr. Taft an affectionate farewell turned went down the steps instantly out of the small door then suddenly the people

> realized he had gone and the whole place clapped and
> applauded and Mr. Newlands said that scarcely a dry
> eye could have been seen . . . he said the terrible feeling
> that it was over and he was gone was horrible you felt as
> though there were a wave of feeling all about you. . . .[46]

Clutching a jar of terrapin Belle had brought for Theodore to eat in the train, Edith went directly from Alice's to the railroad station. Theodore joined her early in the presidential waiting room. He had not been asked to escort the new President back to the White House; Mrs. Taft had created a precedent by doing so herself.

Edith and Theodore walked through two deep lines of well-wishers, many of them crying. As the train pulled out they stood together on its rear platform. "Goodbye! Good luck!" Theodore shouted as he waved his hat. Edith, her mask in place, smiled.

Edith Kermit Roosevelt by Philip de Laszlo, 1908.

Mistress of
Sagamore Hill
1909–1919

Twenty-Six

I want him to be the simplest American alive, . . . and . . . he wants to be also . . . but the trouble is he has really forgotten how to be.

—Edith Kermit Roosevelt[1]

Early in the morning of March 23, 1909, Edith waved goodbye to Theodore and Kermit from the Sagamore Hill piazza as they left to board the S.S. *Hamburg* on the first leg of their year-long expedition. She disliked protracted farewells, and had no desire to fight her way through well-wishing dockside crowds. In any case she had done all she could for Theodore, packing nine spare pairs of spectacles, ample supplies of medicine, and a jungle-proof pigskin-bound "library" comprising thirty-seven literary classics. The selection of titles reflected her own taste as well as his, with volumes of Spenser's *Faerie Queene*, Bacon's *Essays*, and Crothers's *Gentle Reader* interspersed with the *Nibelungenlied, Huckleberry Finn, Rob Roy* and Bret Harte's *Luck of Roaring Camp*.

Kermit, looking back at his mother as the carriage rolled away, thought she looked perfectly calm and self-possessed. But nevertheless he had the feeling that "her heart was almost broken."[2]

Edith spent the rest of the day walking in the woods, talking to her

347

remaining children, and trying to imagine what Theodore was doing. By eight that evening she was emotionally exhausted, and crawled into bed. "It was a dreadful day," she recalled. "I have never known but one like it; that day when Archie's fate was in doubt [from diphtheria] and we did not know if he would live or not."[3]

Theodore, meanwhile, was already at sea and fighting off boredom, as well as people who wanted to introduce themselves to a former President. After three days he was "desperately homesick for Edith," while Kermit lay on a sofa reading Homer and strumming his mandolin.[4]

In Theodore's last week at Sagamore Hill, between fifteen and twenty thousand farewell letters had poured in. Edith had no hope of answering them all. Even so, she made a valiant attempt to be at her desk immediately after breakfast each day, answering the more personal letters, and attending to "each little bill as it comes in."

No matter how prepared she had thought she was for the transition from public to private life, the violent suddenness of it took her by surprise. Barely three weeks before, she had been at the center of national affairs, surrounded by aides, secretaries, fashionable women and powerful men; her days had been full of business, order and dispatch. Her six children had been constantly in and out of the house, and her husband working only a few doors away. Now she found herself once again simply "the mistress of Sagamore Hill," on a chilly, isolated promontory with only a handful of servants and one grown-up daughter who was much out of the house. Fortunately Quentin and Archie would soon be coming home for the Easter vacation.

"If it were not for the children," she admitted, "I would not have the nervous strength to live through these endless months of separation from Father. When I am alone and let myself think I am done for, for self control is a moral muscle which exercise strengthens."[5]

And so she continued to plow through her mail every morning. In the afternoons she discussed estate matters with the gardener, planted spring bulbs, rode her new horse Nicolette, went to the local sewing guild, and read aloud with Ethel. Her letters to Kermit are replete with details of neighbors, the weather, plants, animals, house-decorating plans"chronicles of small beer" which she told her son to tear up. "I can write posterity letters," she went on with a touch of querulousness, "not as well perhaps as Father and Senator Lodge, still I too can write them, and the question is would you care as much to read them . . ."

Within two weeks of Theodore's departure, her weight had climbed from its customary 125 pounds to 140 pounds.[6]

And so the time passed.

One of the last things Theodore had done before sailing was to make a plea to Archie Butt (who had come north to see him off) to go and visit Mrs. Roosevelt. The White House aide was not able to do so until mid-June, when he passed through Oyster Bay on his way to the Taft summer residence in Beverly, Massachusetts. As he drove up the hill he saw Edith walking across the lawn in a pale blue dress and a large white hat. She looked well, he thought, "and her interest in everything was just as keen and kindly." They discussed the accuracy of newspaper reports of the safari—ten lions killed already and twenty animals shipped. Edith told Kermit that the captain "asked a thousand questions" about him and his father, "and talked and talked and talked for he said there was no one to whom he could speak freely." Butt gave her all the latest news from Washington. Apparently, when President Taft received politicians and delegations he constantly asked his aide what TR would do or say in similar situations. As for Mrs. Taft, a recent stroke had rendered her a virtual invalid. She was having to have special therapy, and lived in constant fear of further paralysis. How few happy First Ladies there had been, remarked Edith; only herself, Mrs. Cleveland, and perhaps Mrs. Grant as far as she could recall. "I doubt if even I was entirely happy," she added, "for there was always that anxiety about the President . . . I never realized what a strain I was under continuously until it was over."[7]

After lunch Butt took his leave of her and motored back to New York, taking Ethel, who would be spending the night in town. Edith remained behind in the silent house, brooding about Mrs. Taft. "I hate to think of people being in sorrow where we were so happy," she wrote to Kermit that night.[8]

Eleven days after Butt's visit, Edith sailed with Ethel, Archie and Quentin on the S.S. *Crete* for Europe. She had ten thousand dollars in her pocketbook and intended to spend the next five months on "an endless sightseeing tour," educating the children.[9] It had been twenty-three years since she last crossed the Atlantic before marrying Theodore. Now she was following him with plans for a second honeymoon.

Emily was at Genoa to meet her relatives on the morning of July 12, and by late afternoon they were all squeezed into her tiny rented Villa Magna Quies—House of Great Quiet—outside Porto Maurizio. The villa was set in the Ligurian hills looking out over olive groves, vineyards and the Mediterranean Sea. A Secret Service man immediately took up station outside the front gate; even here, it seems, the safety of a former First Lady was not guaranteed. The children acquired bicycles, and began daily lessons in French, Italian and Latin at the Franciscan monastery on a nearby mountain. Quentin, dressed in Italian style breeches was soon so much at home with the tonsored holy fathers that he let them cut his hair.

Relieved of domestic responsibility, Edith settled into a tranquil routine. She took walks in the orchards, preferring those behind the house in order to escape the notice of the Secret Service men. Sometimes she strolled along a donkey trail to an earthquake-ruined town across the mountains. She rowed in a green boat looking for opal-colored jellyfish with deep-purple edges, and took daily swims in the azure sea. The pebbly beach caused her much discomfort at first, and an "admiring crowd of at least six people" would collect to watch her coming ashore on hands and knees. So she bought a pair of bathing shoes to regain her dignity.[10]

At the end of July, Edith said goodbye to Ethel and Archie, who had been invited to join the American ambassador to Italy, Lloyd Griscom, and his wife, on a tour of Provence. She and Quentin would meet them later in Lyons. It was a relief to have more space to herself in the villa. "I felt a vivid sympathy for families who live in close quarters that I have never known," she wrote Theodore. She set down her pen as a cool breeze blew through the window, and looked out on "the wide blue Mediterranean set in a frame of pine trees."[11]

Accompanied by a Swiss maid, who acted as courier, Edith and Quentin reached Avignon on Thursday, August 5. Next day they explored the Palais des Papes, saw a play at the amphitheater in Orange, and went on to Lyons. At forty-eight, this was her first experience of independent foreign travel, and she discovered that she had a taste for it. "I begin to feel a little more confident in my powers of looking out for myself," she told Aunt Lizzie.[12]

By August 11, the reunited family was in an apartment in the Avenue Gabriel in Paris, lunching with the Jusserlands and Dr. Sturgis Bigelow, dining with Henry Adams, and beginning an intensive program of visits to museums, palaces, and cathedrals.

On September 11, Archie and Quentin, who had to return to school, sailed home with an adult escort. Edith and Ethel left Paris soon afterward to visit Switzerland, Milan, Verona, Venice, Padua and Turin, before returning to Porto Maurizio on October 8 in time to witness Emily's formal signing of the title deeds to Villa Magna Quies. To Edith's private relief, this committed her sister to spending the rest of her life in Italy.

Later in the month Edith made a trip south to Florence, Siena and Rome. In the Holy City in the early hours of November 6, she was awakened with a "terrible rumor about Theodore." Unconfirmed reports said that he had been killed in Africa. At five that afternoon a cable arrived from Nairobi to say the news was unfounded. But the shock "took something out of me which can't come back until I see him," she confided to Cecil Spring-Rice.[13]

Edith and Ethel sailed from Sorrento to New York on November 12. On that same day Theodore sat writing to his wife in his camp on the N'zoi River, near Mount Elgon in British East Africa. His letter was so full of tenderness and yearning for her that it, along with her own youthful love letter to him from London in 1886, would remain too precious to destroy.

> Oh, sweetest of all sweet girls, last night I dreamed that I was with you, and that our separation was but a dream; and when I waked up it was almost too hard to bear. Well, one must pay for everything; you have made the real happiness of my life; and so it is natural and right that I should constantly [be] more and more lonely without you. The other day here I sat down under a tree and found my clothes covered with "pitch-forks"; and laughed so as I thought of the Sweet Cicily at home. Do you remember *all* about the Sweet Cicily, you darling? Do you remember when you were such a pretty engaged girl, and said to your lover "no Theodore, that I cannot

allow"? Darling, I love you so. In a very little over four months I shall see you, now. When you get this three fourths of the time will have gone. How very happy we have been for these twenty-three years! Five days hence, on the 17th, is the anniversary of our engagement. . . .

We are now camped on one of the streams that make up the headwaters of the Nile; a rapid, muddy river, with hippos and crocodiles in it. The banks are fringed with strange trees; and the country is covered with grass so high as to make it well nigh hopeless to look for lions. But we have killed many antelopes of kinds new to us; their names would mean nothing to you—bohor, sing sing, oribi, lelwel, kob. This seems to be a healthy country for men; but half of our horses have died, and we may have to go into the railroad on foot.

I have no idea how my articles in Scribners have done, or whether they have been failures; at any rate I hope you have liked them. I have worked faithfully at them; and it has been a very real resource to have them to do. Of course I never in the world would have taken this as a mere pleasure trip. Kermit solemnly reads over the articles, with a strong proprietary feeling. He and I are really attached to our personal attendants—poor funny grasshopper-like black people!

Kiss Ethel and the two little boys for me—they really are hardly "little boys" any longer. Give my dearest love to Aunt Lizzie; and Laura, and Christine and Emlen.

YOUR OWN LOVER [14]

"The country is crazy-mad about Father," Edith wrote Kermit on her return. "The poor President must have a horrid time. The newspapermen in New York who dine together every Saturday have formed a 'Back from Elba' club and formally drink the toast at each meeting." [15]

Taft had been in office only nine months, but already his refusal to acknowledge the progressive Republican movement had created alarming dissent within his own party. While the insurgent wing wanted Roosevelt to take up their neglected cause of reform, the conservative wing was urging him to stay away from America for at least another year, until after the congressional elections in the fall of 1910. "Why not for life?" inquired Henry Adams, reassuming his pose as malicious elder statesman.[16]

"In the abstract they are right," Theodore wrote Bamie, "but in the concrete I have'n't the slightest intention of allowing myself, and poor Edie, to be kept longer away from our home and children."[17] In mid-December he and Kermit left British East Africa for less hospitable regions of Uganda, "the land of sleeping sickness and the fever tick." When they emerged at Khartoum in the Sudan three months later, they had collected a total of thirteen thousand specimens and three thousand skins, listed 296 categories of species, and taken numberless photographs.

On March 14, 1910, they were waiting on the dusty local railroad platform as Edith and Ethel drew into the station. To his wife's great relief, Theodore was not only "in splendid condition," but he had "lost that look of worry and care" that had been almost habitual during the White House years.[18] Kermit was sturdier. Evidently, his daring encounters with lions and rhinos had transformed the last remnants of spindly youth into hardy manhood.

The British Sirdar, Sir Reginald Wingate, had sent his aide-de-camp to receive the Roosevelts, and had put his palm-fringed white Khartoum palace at their disposal. From these luxurious quarters (where the great General Gordon had died defending the city against Mahdi dervishes in 1885), Edith made sightseeing trips into the inhospitable desert. She visited the battlefield of Omdurman, site of history's last great cavalry charge in 1898, watched native dancers, saw a splendid parade of Sudanese troops, and visited the exclusive Egyptian and Sudanese Officers' Club.

On March 17, Theodore, Edith, Kermit and Ethel left Khartoum on the evening northbound train. They were enthralled by mirages in the darkening sands moving past their carriage window. Next day at Wadi Halfa they boarded the steamer *Ibis* for the rest of the journey along the White Nile to Cairo. They stopped at Abu Simbel to see the temples of Rameses II, and at Luxor to see the great Roman ruins of Karnak by moonlight—"a glimpse of the ineffable, of the unutterable," as Theodore had described them as a boy. On March 30, the Roosevelts sailed on the "dirty and uncomfortable" *Prinz Heinrich* for Naples.[19]

Here Theodore received another reminder that he was still

"She took sightseeing trips into the inhospitable desert."
Edith in Egypt, March 1910.

considered a world leader despite his status as a private American
tourist. Arriving late one night at a performance of the opera *Andrea
Chenier,* he was greeted by a ten-minute ovation, while the singers
stood helplessly silent. In the intermission a stream of people came
up to introduce themselves to him. The experience, he reflected, was
reminiscent of his presidential tours in the United States—"the same
courtesies and kindnesses, and the same wearing fatigue and hurry." [20]

Emily joined them on April 3 in Rome, where Theodore was
plunged into yet another controversy. He had wanted to meet the

Pope, and the American Ambassador had requested an audience, but there were unacceptable strings attached. Merry del Val, the Vatican Secretary of State, said that a meeting could take place only on condition that the former President did not also meet with a certain group of American Methodist evangelists in Rome. Apparently, one of the latter, Ezra Tipple, had recently denounced the Holy Father as "the whore of Babylon." Theodore made a public announcement that the Pope could choose his own visitors, but he, as a free American, reserved the right to see whom *he* pleased. He then added fuel to the flames by seeing neither.[21]

Relations with the Italian monarchs were considerably smoother. The Roosevelts had a "very pleasant" dinner at the palace, discussing the early history of the House of Savoy with the King, and the poetry of the Balkan Slavs with his Montenegrin Queen.

After leaving Rome on April 6, Edith and Theodore began to retrace their honeymoon trip along the Italian Riviera—in reverse—by taking the train to Spezia, and driving a three-horse carriage to Rapallo. The first day, a lovely one of "sun and shadow," was spent crossing the mountains to Sestri Levante, where they stayed at an old hotel and lay in bed listening to the waves lapping against the walls beneath their balcony.[22] But even here their privacy was invaded. Municipal officials paid a call, followed by a band which discordantly serenaded them. By the next day, as they drove on to Chiavari, people were already lining the route ahead of them, and so the second honeymoon came to an abrupt end.

Emily, Ethel and Kermit, who had been in Pisa, rejoined them at Genoa, and all traveled on to Porto Maurizio together. Here the children stayed with their aunt, in Villa Magna Quies, while their parents went to a larger house on the same hillside, owned by Emily's good friend Madame Rappis. On Sunday, April 10, Theodore was made a citizen of the little town, and a road was named after him. As it turned out, this was his last day of relative tranquillity. The next morning Gifford Pinchot, of all people, arrived at Porto Maurizio, and Theodore was instantly plunged into a seething cauldron of American political intrigue. As the result of a rancorous dispute with President Taft's Secretary of the Interior, Richard Ballinger, Pinchot had been forced to resign as Chief Forester of the United States. But he had grievances other than the compromising of conservation policies, and he spent the entire day closeted with his former chief airing them. "One of the best and most satisfactory talks with T.R. I ever had," the former Cabinet member recorded in his diary. But the subject matter of the lengthy discussion was never revealed. It is enough to say that the same day Theodore wrote Lodge: "I very earnestly hope that Taft will retrieve himself yet, and if, from whatever causes, the present condition of the party is hopeless, I most emphatically desire that I shall not be put in the position of having to run for the Presidency, staggering under a load which I cannot carry, and which has been put on my shoulders through no fault of my own."[23]

As early as January, Edith had written Kermit: "The Ballinger-Pinchot investigation has begun and I don't feel at all happy over it, for it puts the President in such a difficult position. I do feel so sorry for him. His very good qualities are disadvantages. If he would have 'roared' at them a bit, things might never have come to this pass." Now she wrote Corinne: "I hate the political outlook more and more."[24]

Theodore decided that the changing political situation in America must in no way interfere with his tour of Europe. Accordingly he and Kermit left Porto Maurizio on April 13 for quick visits to Vienna and Budapest. Edith and Ethel went to Paris ahead of them, to stay with Robert Bacon, Theodore's old college friend and last Secretary of State. Taft had appointed Bacon ambassador in place of Henry White, enraging Roosevelt, who thought White was the best man in the entire diplomatic corps. He had no personal objection to Bacon, but the firing of White, coupled with the removal of Pinchot, seemed like a double repudiation of his own former policies.

During her ten days in the French capital Edith shopped at Worth's, heard *Manon* and *Samson et Dalila* at the Opera, saw *Oedipus Roi* at the Théâtre Français, met the great sculptor Rodin in his own house, and dined at the Élysée Palace, where she was seated between President Armand Fallières and former President Émile-François Lubet. On April 23 she heard her husband make a favorably received speech, "Citizenship in a Republic," at the Sorbonne. From now on Edith and Theodore were increasingly treated like royalty by royalty. In Brussels they dined with the King and Queen at Laeken Palace, and next day they had lunch in The Hague with Queen Wilhemina. The last was the only ruler that they disliked; she struck them as exceedingly unattractive, conceited, commonplace, and, in Edith's word, "stupid."[25] Wilhemina bullied her fat, dull husband, snapping at him ferociously in their presence.

Diplomats throughout Europe and Scandinavia were amazed at the enormous popular demonstrations for the Roosevelts, and at their being asked to stay in the royal palaces, "something hitherto unheard of in the case of any but actual sovereigns."[26]

On Thursday, May 5, Theodore battled a sore throat and bronchitis as he made his delayed Nobel Prize speech at the university in Christiania (Oslo). In it he called for a limitation of naval armaments, and for the formation of a "League of Peace," anticipating Woodrow Wilson's League of Nations by ten years. Two days later the Roosevelts moved on to Stockholm. Since the King of Sweden was away, they stayed with the Crown Prince and Princess. It was "no use trying to talk of books with these or any other of the royalties, excepting the Italians and the Queen of Belgium," Theodore remarked disapprovingly. On the whole, however, he liked and respected most of the monarchs he met, finding them, "serious people, with charming manners . . . anxious to justify their own positions by the way they did their duty . . . each sovereign was obviously conscious that he was looking a possible republic in the face, which was naturally an incentive to good conduct."[27]

While they were in Sweden, news came of the death of England's King Edward VII. Out of consideration for his nephew, Kaiser Wilhelm, the Roosevelts stayed with their own ambassador when they arrived in Berlin early on May 10. But they lunched that day with His Imperial Majesty at Sans Souci Palace in Potsdam. Edith sat next to him, and he asked her if she liked paintings. She said yes with such enthusiasm that the Kaiser immediately took her off to show her the palace treasures. Theodore looked after them helplessly, and was not able to conceal his jealousy when they returned. He was beginning to feel that if he met just one more monarch "I should bite him."[28]

Later on during their stay Theodore became the only private citizen ever to be allowed to review the German troops at their Kaiser's side. Photographs were taken of the five-hour maneuvers, including a set of pictures mounted between glass, so that both sides could be put on display at Sagamore Hill.[29]

President Taft asked Theodore to act as his Special Ambassador at King Edward's funeral. Consequently, when the Roosevelts arrived

in London on May 16, they took up official residence with the
American Ambassador, Whitelaw Reid, at Dorchester House. Alice
arrived the same afternoon, already well equipped with mourning
clothes, since Grandfather Lee had died two months before.[30] Spring-
Rice was also in the metropolis. Edith spent a pleasant morning with
him visiting Eton College, and an afternoon at the National Gallery.

At the funeral service on May 20 in St. George's Chapel, Windsor,
Edith sat with Ambassador Reid in the choir. Notwithstanding the
magnificent service, all eyes were on Theodore. "With Roosevelt and
the Kaiser at King Edward's funeral," Archie Butt remarked, "it will
be a wonder if the poor corpse gets a passing thought."[31] President
Taft, also, was astonished at the attention lavished on his predecessor:

> I don't suppose there was ever such a reception as
> that being given Theodore in Europe now. It does not
> surprise me that rulers, potentates, and public men
> should pay him this honor, but what does surprise me is
> that small villages which one would hardly think had
> ever heard of the United States should seem to know all
> about the man. The receptions which are accorded him
> in small obscure towns and hamlets are most significant.
> It illustrates how his personality has swept over the
> world, for after all no great event transpired during
> either of his administrations, and no startling legislation
> was enacted into law. It is the force of his personality
> that has passed beyond his own country and the capitals
> of the world and seeped into the small crevices of the
> universe.[32]

On May 25 Edith had an audience with Queen Mother Alexandra
and her sister the Dowager Empress of Russia. Both women were
remarkably friendly toward the former First Lady, and at the end of
the visit asked if they might kiss her. "Being half of New England
blood, and not of an expansive temperament," Theodore amusedly
wrote later, she "endured rather than enjoyed the ceremony."[33]

The grieving Queen Mother saw Theodore separately, and almost
hysterically bemoaned the fact that she now had to leave Buckingham Palace for Marlborough House, having so reluctantly done

the reverse when her husband became king. Then, abruptly changing the subject to that of Edward's corpse, she said, "You see he was so wonderfully preserved. It must have been the oxygen they gave him before he died."[34]

Next morning the Roosevelts left for Cambridge, where Theodore was to address the College Union and receive an honorary degree. The undergraduates responded to the latter enthusiastically by lowering a Teddy bear from the ceiling. From here Edith, Alice and Theodore went to the Arthur Lees' beautiful old country home, Chequers, in Buckinghamshire, for the weekend. An unusually brilliant roster of guests had been marshaled by their hosts, including Cecil Spring-Rice; Lord Roberts, winner of the Victoria Cross in the Indian Mutiny and Commander of the British forces in the Boer War; Frederick S. Oliver, biographer of Alexander Hamilton; Alfred Lyttelton, a nephew of Gladstone and a Conservative Party Colonial Secretary; and Lord Arthur James Balfour, the cerebral and aristocratic former Conservative Prime Minister.

Theodore and the last took to each other almost at once during dinner the first night. Behind Balfour's mantle of "cool ruthlessness" was a mind of eclectic versatility, which Theodore opened up by saying that he himself "never demanded of knowledge anything except that it should be valueless." Balfour immediately became communicative and intimate.

To Edith's delight both men were soon at their dazzling best, rubbing their diamond-sharp intellects one against the other in an "almost ceaseless play of coruscating talk." Arthur Lee saw that on Balfour's part, at least, it was "a case of love at first sight." Lord Roberts seemed a little overpowered by his dinner companions. But Theodore, who found the author of *Forty-one Years in India* "gentle, moderate and considerate," treated him "with a deference and almost boyish hero-worship" which greatly touched Roberts's heart.

Lord Kitchener, conqueror of the Sudan, joined the house party for lunch on Saturday, May 28, and Edith took an instant dislike to his overbearing manner. Theodore, too, found him "exceedingly bumptious, and everlastingly posing as a strong man." Kitchener attacked Roosevelt in a loud voice on the subject of the Panama Canal, insisting against all protests that *he* would have built it at sea level. Theodore diplomatically put an end to the discussion by saying that he would sooner trust the engineer George Goethals's opinion on the

Isthmus, which Kitchener had never seen, just as he would trust the Englishman's on matters relating to the Sudan.[35]

Spring-Rice was impressed with the stature of his old friend among such giants. "Roosevelt has turned us all topside down," he wrote a few days later; "he has enjoyed himself hugely and I must say, by the side of our statesmen, looks a little bit taller, bigger and stronger."[36]

Edith and Theodore returned to London on Monday, May 29. On the thirtieth the former President was summoned to the American Embassy to consult with Elihu Root, who brought messages from the White House. Root spent an hour defending President Taft's conservative policies, and urged Roosevelt to stay out of politics for at least sixty days after his return to America.

Nine days after the talk with Root, Theodore wrote to President Taft. "I am of course much concerned about some of the things I see and am told; but what I have felt it best to do is say absolutely nothing . . ."[37]

Edith spent her final day in London revisiting the Wallace Gallery and saying goodbye to the Reids, while Theodore went to the New Forest in Hampshire to take an ornithological walk with the British Foreign Secretary, Sir Edward Grey. His companion was an expert bird watcher, and the two men spent all day listening to and identifying songs. That night they stayed at an inn on the edge of the woods. Theodore enjoyed his twenty-four hours with the high-minded knight more than any others he had spent in Europe. Only Leonard Wood, he said, had so impressed him after so brief an acquaintance. Grey, in turn, saw enough of Theodore Roosevelt "to know that to be with him was to be stimulated in the best sense of the word for the work of life."[38]

Edith, Alice, Ethel and Kermit joined Theodore next day at Southampton. At midday they boarded the *Kaiserin Auguste Victoria*, and began their eight-day voyage to America, which Theodore had not seen for fourteen months.

Twenty-Seven

He sat down at the President's desk and said how natural it seemed to be there.
                —Archibald W. Butt quoting Irwin H. Hoover[1]

An unprecedented welcome awaited the Roosevelts when their boat sailed into New York Harbor on Saturday, June 18, 1910. The bay was filled with yachts and skiffs of citizens anxious to toot their whistles at the first sight of "Teddy," as well as a flotilla of destroyers and one big battleship. Early-morning rain had cleared by 6:30 A.M., when a launch carrying the reception committee circled the steamer as it lay off quarantine. In the small boat were Secretary of the Navy George von L. Meyer, Secretary of Agriculture James Wilson, Senator Henry Cabot Lodge, Congressman Nick Longworth, and Captain Archie Butt, representing the White House. The crew of S.S. *Kaiserin Auguste Victoria* let down a ladder and the men climbed up.

Theodore was in his sitting room, and Butt handed him a welcoming letter from the President. When Edith joined them the aide gave her one from Mrs. Taft:

361

My dear Mrs. Roosevelt:

I write to extend to you and President Roosevelt and your family a hearty welcome. I congratulate you that your husband and Kermit have returned to you safe and sound. Mr. Taft has invited you and President Roosevelt to visit us at the White House soon after your return. I earnestly second that invitation. I am sorry that I shall be at Beverly after June 22nd where I go to recuperate after the season. If you find it impossible to come to Washington now, Mr. Taft and I would be delighted to have you and Mr. Roosevelt visit us in the White House next December after Congress meets.

With best wishes

Yours sincerely
Helen H. Taft[2]

The extraordinary use of the terms "President Roosevelt" and "Mr. Taft" by the First Lady echoed the attitude of her husband, who had confessed in the early days of his term to looking over his shoulder for Roosevelt whenever he was addressed by his official title. Edith declined her invitation, as did Theodore, explaining that they did not think it appropriate for a former President to to go Washington except when Congress was in recess. The Tafts felt rebuffed by this shallow excuse, and were disappointed that the Roosevelts did not wish to see them. The President felt particularly hurt; as his mother said, love of approval was his "besetting fault."[3]

Once the letter-reading formalities were over, Edith took Captain Butt to the rail to see if they could see any of her children sailing in the welcoming armada. Presently, they spotted Archie and Quentin, and then Ted and his slight, fair fiancée of two months, Eleanor Alexander, dwarfed by the great liner.

The couple had been engaged just before Edith left for Egypt. At that time she had written her future daughter-in-law: "One of the hardest things I ever did was to sail away and leave you and Ted in these happy days which can never come again. Even happier ones lie in the future I am sure, but never the same."[4] Now as she saw her family again, she looked to Archie Butt as if she might jump overboard. "Think," she exclaimed; "for the first time in nearly two years I have them all within reach!" Returning to the cabin, she called out, "Come here, Theodore, and see your children. They are of far greater importance than politics or anything else."[5]

To her, certainly, but were they really to him? Many of the former President's welcomers, including his admiring fifth cousin, Franklin, must have wondered what his political thoughts were as he saw the spires of New York, his lifelong constituency, looming up ahead.

Cornelius Vanderbilt, who headed a Committee of One Hundred which had organized the review of the fleet as well as a street parade for the former President, welcomed the Roosevelts officially when they transferred to the launch *Androscoggin*. Edith and Theodore were led immediately to the bridge to watch the formation of the battle cruisers. Every siren in the harbor shrieked in salute as they

"Every siren . . . shrieked in salute."
Theodore and Edith in New York harbor, June 1910.
Franklin and Eleanor Roosevelt stand by the funnel.

appeared, and the warships (gray, not white as they had been previously) began to steam proudly up the Hudson toward Twenty-fifth Street. As the returning hero prepared to land at the pier, a deafening shout rang out, loud enough, wrote Butt, "to waken the stones."[6] The bulk of the volume came from some five hundred newly uniformed Rough Riders, who had come to escort their Colonel in procession.

"I am more glad than I can say," Theodore said in reply to Mayor Gaynor's welcoming speech, "to be back in my own country. And I am ready and eager to be able to do my part," he said significantly, "so far as I am able in helping solve problems which must be solved if we of this greatest democratic republic are to see its destinies rise to the highest level of our hopes and opportunities."[7]

Seated in the carriage of honor with the Mayor and Vanderbilt, Roosevelt led a long line of vehicles and marchers up Broadway and Fifth Avenue, past thousands who had gathered to accord him "one continuous heartfelt ovation."[8] Bands on the sidewalks played enthusiastically. Theodore, waving and grinning as if he were having the time of his life, actually felt "a little uncomfortable" with the "slightly hysterical" reception, for he knew that "there always comes a revulsion after hysteria."

Edith, meanwhile, had gone ahead by automobile with the family and a few friends to watch the parade from Mrs. Alexander's townhouse at 433 Fifth Avenue. Here gifts from well-wishers, including an ornamental pitcher from the Tafts, awaited her, and a favorite Georgian lunch of creamed chicken and rice had been prepared for Theodore.

Butt had reminded himself earlier to address his former employer as "Colonel." He had heard that Edith (who infinitely preferred the simple "Mr. Roosevelt"), became quite angry at the use of "Mr. President," to which she felt he was no longer entitled. But the Captain, stationing himself at Theodore's side, found himself saying, "Let the President pass," and "The President desires," long before the day was out.

Being in close proximity throughout the welcoming ceremonies, Butt had ample opportunity to reassess Theodore Roosevelt. Though in manner, appearance and expression he seemed the same, Archie sensed that he had undergone something of a sea change. During his

triumphant tour of Europe he had clearly "become a world citizen
. . . capable of greater good or greater evil . . .".[9]

Though Lodge, the Cabinet officers, Nick and William Loeb (now
head of the New York Custom House) probed for an inkling of what
Theodore thought or intended to do, politically, in the face of Taft's
disappointing progressive record, he gave no hint. For two months he
would keep his own counsel. (When Taft heard this he said bitterly,
"I don't care if he keeps silent forever").[10]

Since there was, as yet, no pension for former Presidents, Theodore
now had to find work. Several possibilities were open to him. He
could run for the Senate, or the Mayoralty of New York City; he
could become the president of a university, or simply write his
memoirs for a fat advance. None of these appealed to him, and he
settled on becoming an editor of the *Outlook,* a weekly magazine
which most closely reflected his own opinions. For an annual salary
of twelve thousand dollars, he would be required to write just one
article a month.

As a "consolation prize" to Edith and Ethel for his year's absence
Theodore asked Ted to purchase them an automobile. But he became
so attached to it himself that he virtually abandoned the Long Island
Rail Road for trips to the magazine office in New York. By the time
winter set in the car was already nearly worn out.

Mail by the ton continued to arrive at Sagamore Hill. Reporters
were shown thousands of letters, hundreds of books and magazines
piled high on tables, sofas, chairs, and even on the floor. It would
take an army of clerks at least six months to answer it all. There were
requests to criticize speeches, to demonstrate patent window devices
and to restore the unemployed to lost positions, as well as countless
demands for autographs and money.[11] Theodore Roosevelt was
expected to solve all the problems of the citizenry, from launching
careers to saving murderers from execution. As Butt had divined, he
now aroused such expectations and possessed such power as could be
used for good or evil.

On June 20, only two days after the Roosevelts' return to the
United States, Ted and Eleanor were married by Episcopal rites at
the Fifth Avenue Presbyterian Church. Edith wore a dress in "a

pretty soft shade" of lilac, which she knew Eleanor would like. The atmosphere in the crowded nave was swelteringly hot. Five hundred gallery seats were reserved for the Rough Riders, and at the reception afterward the old stalwarts were seen making off with most of "the little boxes of wedding cake."[12]

The couple headed west immediately after their nuptial breakfast. Ted was to begin work in a month's time in the San Francisco office of the Hartford Carpet Company, up whose corporate ladder he was now climbing rapidly.

On June 22, Theodore went in to New York to see Scribners about his book *African Game Trails*. No one appeared to notice him as he entered the store, but when he came out much later dense crowds had formed, which tried to prevent him from passing. "They wanted to carry me on their shoulders," he told Corinne later; "and I realized at once that this . . . represented a certain hysterical quality which boded ill for my future . . ."[13]

During his first twelve days at home Theodore conferred with a great number of influential political figures. They included his old White House guest Booker T. Washington, the Washington *Star* columnist Mark Sullivan, Robert Collier, publisher of *Collier's Weekly*, a delegate from the Chicago Hamilton Club, former colleagues James R. Garfield and Gifford Pinchot, Wisconsin progressive leader Robert La Follette, New York State progressive Henry L. Stimson, and New York State Governor Charles Evans Hughes.[14]

After seeing Hughes, Theodore broke his political silence and made a public commitment to support the Governor's fight for a reform bill to ensure direct primaries for nomination to state offices. The next day, June 30, accompanied by Lodge, he met with President Taft himself at his summer home in Beverly, Massachusetts. Taft, trying not to show resentment, offered drinks, and Theodore, who seemed to be under some stress, accepted, saying he "needed rather than wanted a Scotch and soda." The three men chatted about Theodore's European trip, discussed New York State politics (the ostensible reason for the call), and announced to the press that the meeting had been friendly. Theodore, however, arrived home looking "very tired and hot." These first steps back into politics inevitably led to others. On July 1, the Primary Bill was defeated.[15] Sixteen days later, Theodore suffered another setback, when the chairmanship of the New York State Republican Convention, for which he had announced himself a contender, went to Vice-President James Schoolcraft Sherman. Since President Taft had been equivocal publicly about which candidate he supported, but in private he hoped for Roosevelt's defeat, the rift between the two old friends grew even wider.

"Taft is utterly helpless as a leader," Theodore complained to Ted. "He has just enough strength to keep with him . . . the good conservative unimaginative people who never appreciate the need of going forward, and who fail to realize that unless there is some progressive leadership, the great mass of the progressives will follow every variety of demagogue and wild-eyed visionary."[16]

Such outspoken comments to public figures and to the press filled the newspapers. Columns about Theodore outstripped columns about the President by two to one. "Politics," Edith wrote Kermit, "are seething abominably."[17]

"I do so wish I had a grandchild," she added in another letter. The yearning was compounded at the end of August, when Archie (who had been expelled from Groton for writing a letter ridiculing the headmaster) came home before leaving for a school in Arizona. "It is a dreadful wrench for me," sighed his mother. "I look back regretfully to the days when the old hen could brood you all under her wings." It was a sad summer for both parents, marking as it did, said Theodore, "the definite end of the old Oyster Bay life" now that most of the children and their cousins were grown and scattered.[18]

On August 23 the former President began a nineteen-day speaking tour of sixteen states stretching from New York to Kansas. He traveled in a private railroad car provided by the *Outlook*, and at Osawatomie, Kansas, gave what many considered the most radical speech of his entire career, entitled "New Nationalism." It was a text that made Bryanist Democrats and progressive Republicans alike rejoice, while the Old Guard and other opponents of socialism trembled. Beginning with a quote from Lincoln, to soften the impact of what followed, he said: "'Labor is prior to and independent of, capital . . . Labor is the superior of capital, and deserves much the higher consideration.'" Then, continuing with his own words: "The essence of any struggle for liberty has always been, and must always be to take from some one man or class of men the right to enjoy power, or wealth, or position, or immunity, which has not been earned by service to his or their fellows." This was to become the cry of the growing progressive movement: to put "national need before sectional or personal advantage."[19]

Edith spent the last week of August with Corinne at Henderson House, the Robinsons' ancestral home in Herkimer County, New York, which Douglas had recently inherited.[20] The silvery stone mansion, built in 1832 on land granted by George II, was a replica of Gleiston Castle in Scotland, and at seventeen hundred feet above sea level offered magnificent views of the fertile Mohawk Valley. Inside it was full of improbable relics: a large, hand-piped organ, a Dresden chandelier, a collection of Bohemian ruby glass, Canton china bowls, Sir Walter Scott's wine glass, a presidential waffle iron, handwoven Douglas tartan rugs, and a huge conch shell which the senior parlor maid would blow loudly to bid departing guests a safe journey and early return.

The long-established rituals of Henderson were a relaxing change for Edith, reminding her of the ordered world into which she had been born. She was summoned every morning to breakfast by small gongs chiming "Up with the Bonnets of Bonnie Dundee." At eight-thirty she sat down to a meal of gargantuan proportions: a lavish spread of Scottish oatmeal and finnan haddie, English kedgeree and deviled kidneys, Southern hominy grits and chicken hash, lashings of thick cream over fresh fruit, and copious quantities of coffee.

Corinne had recently returned from a round-the-world voyage, which Douglas had fondly hoped would ease the pain of Stewart's death, just over a year before. It did not. Corinne was never to be her old natural self again, but she acted the part of "delightful hostess" valiantly. Her face in repose, however, was mostly sorrowful. Caught unawares, she was, to Archie Butt, "the saddest woman I ever looked upon." It was "just as if someone had picked her up and broken her."[21]

Edith returned to Sagamore Hill on September 1, and Theodore rejoined her there on the eleventh. Just over a week later he crossed Long Island Sound to lunch with President Taft at Henry White's house in New Haven. The purpose was for the two leaders of the divergent wings of the Republican Party to make a show of solidarity before the November elections. The time of the meeting was physically and emotionally inauspicious for Taft. His weight had soared to 330 pounds, his heart was weak and he suffered from gout, while his emerging rival was in robust health. Furthermore, Theodore's activity on behalf of progressives, and his obvious disapproval of Administration policies, had "seared" the President "to the very soul." [22]

The two men talked alone this time, and the atmosphere when they parted appeared strained. Nevertheless, presidential pique did not prevent Theodore from being elected temporary chairman of the State Convention in Saratoga, and he continued to campaign all over the country for progressive Republican candidates. In St. Louis, Missouri, he even dared to go up in an airplane during a personal appearance requested by Governor Herbert Spencer Hadley. But his efforts on behalf of social reform were to no avail. In New York State the Republican machine made little effort to get out the voters for Roosevelt's gubernatorial choice, Henry L. Stimson, and the party lost heavily in the election. The Democrats won every state office, carried both Houses of the Legislature, and elected twenty-three of thirty-seven Congressmen. In the country at large, the Democratic sweep was tremendous, and included even Taft's home state of Ohio. The collapse of the Republicans, in the opinion of party regulars, was due to Roosevelt's failure to give Taft an unreserved endorsement, and, in the opinion of insurgents, to the fact that he neglected to attack the President outright. However, in nine western states progressive Republicans won. This, according to a progressive historian, "boded ill for the . . . Taft administration [and] effectually silenced for a time the lion of Oyster Bay." [23]

That fall, with Theodore almost constantly away on his political travels, Edith occupied herself uneasily. As a true Republican she did not like the way things were going, and keeping busy was one way of steering her mind off politics. She saw Quentin off to begin his second year at Groton, arranged books, planted bulbs, put up double windows and laid huge tiger and leopard skins sent her from China, in the North Room. "Winter is coming on," she wrote Kermit, who had just turned twenty-one. "I am glad to think I have Father safely caged at Sagamore." [24]

"Safely caged" or not, Theodore vowed to "continue the fight exactly on the lines along which I have been fighting." But "in strict confidence," he told his old crony William Allen White, editor of the *Emporia Gazette,* "I don't feel at all comfortable about the result in 1912."[25]

On November 19 he went to Washington to give a lecture on Africa to the National Geographic Society. Knowing that the Chief Executive was in Panama, and that Mrs. Taft was in New York City, he revisited the White House for the first time since quitting it in 1909. He toured the servants' quarters, remembering everyone by name, and munched on the cook's corn bread, before heading for the Executive Wing. There he found that Taft had built himself a new office, oval in shape and directly over the old tennis court. Theodore could not resist trying out the presidential chair, saying "how natural it seemed to be there." Chief Usher Ike Hoover was moved to tears. "It is the only happy day we have had in nearly two years," he said afterward, "and not one of us would exchange it for a hundred-dollar bill."[26]

Twenty-Eight

You can put it out of your mind, Theodore, you will never be President of the United States again.

—Edith Kermit Roosevelt[1]

On January 2, 1911, Lloyd Griscom lunched with the Roosevelts and found both of them sadly lacking in their old buoyancy. News of their depressed state found its way to Taft, who attributed it to the location of Sagamore Hill—"a dreary spot in winter," which no doubt had "a bad effect on both of them." But the President added: "What [Roosevelt] is undergoing now may be the thing most needed to get him back to a normal frame of mind . . . If only he could fight! That is what he delights in, and that is what is denied to him now."[2]

It was clear to others that the "books and pictures and bronzes, and big wood fires, and horses to ride," which Theodore claimed made him "thoroughly happy," were not enough to satisfy a man of such abnormal energy.[3] As it happened, that January was the first period of rest from travel and speechmaking he had had since returning from Europe, but the inactivity did not suit him. However, he still held off from a direct challenge to Taft for leadership of the

371

Republican Party, and refused to attend a meeting of insurgents wishing to form a National Progressive Republican League to promote Robert La Follette or some other candidate to run against Taft for the nomination in 1912. Some people complained that the former President was sulking, or merely playing coy. But the truth was that men such as Gifford Pinchot had become so identified with extremists that Roosevelt could work with them only "to a very limited extent."[4]

By March, Theodore's general frustration began to show in the time-honored way. He wrote to ask the President if, in the event that the brewing Mexican revolution turned into an international war, he might raise and command a cavalry division.[5] Taft agreed, while doubting it would ever be necessary.

In the continued absence of demanding political work, Theodore decided to embark on another speaking tour to tout the "New Nationalism," or progressive philosophy. During the summer and fall of 1910 he had covered the entire country with the exception of the South, the Southwest and the Pacific Coast; this lack he now proceeded to rectify, starting for Washington, D.C., on March 8 for a thirty-four-day swing. It was agreed that Edith would join him at Albuquerque, New Mexico, after visiting Bob Ferguson in nearby Silver City. (Bob had contracted tuberculosis, and was now compelled to live in a high, dry climate.)

On Thursday, the sixteenth, they arrived in Williams, Arizona, where sixteen-year-old Archie, looking "well but thin," joined them from school.[6] Friday morning he and his father rode down the Grand Canyon, while Edith rested on its banks, watching the changing colors in the vast depths. In the afternoon they all left for Phoenix, and motored from there to Roosevelt Dam, which the dedicatee had been invited to open.

Edith was astonished at the hold her husband still had on people. At every tiny station crowds turned out to see him, "holding out their children so that he might touch them." Very early one morning she awoke in the special car to hear a man on the platform say "in pleading tones 'Oh, Colonel, *do* wake up.'" It was all "so touching and amusing," she told Cecil Spring-Rice, "and I wish I could tell you of all the men who begged to follow him to fight Japan or Mexico or anyone!"[7]

On Sunday, March 19, the Roosevelts motored to Archie's school in Mesa, and the following day had lunch with a crowd of Rough Riders at Phoenix. Afterward they continued on to San Francisco to spend ten days with Ted and Eleanor. The latter was now two months pregnant. When Edith contemplated the expected baby she felt "a very deep and new emotion for the child of my child." Here Quentin met up with the rest of the family. He was nearly fourteen now, "an affectionate, soft hearted, overgrown puppy kind of boy, absorbed in his wireless and in anything mechanical." This included typesetting and learning to play the piano. He was doing very well at Groton, repeatedly standing first in his class.[8]

From San Francisco Theodore went north to Washington, Idaho, Montana and Wisconsin, while Edith and Ethel took a four-day trip to Yosemite. They started for New York on April 9. "The American eagle flaps its wings when I think of all I have seen since leaving home," Edith wrote Springy. "Country and countrymen I am proud of them both. . . . This is a great, big overgrown, hobbledehoy of a nation, and may it be long before its angles wear off."[9]

On August 6, 1911, Edith turned fifty. Eleven days later Eleanor gave birth to a girl, Grace. The new grandmother immediately planted a little grove of pine trees at Sagamore Hill where the baby could play when she came to visit.[10] It was otherwise a quiet summer. Kermit went to visit the Fergusons; Ethel vacationed in Maine; Archie spent most of the day in his room cramming for Harvard preliminaries. When he emerged it was to be coached in French by his mother, and in history and civics by his father. Quentin spent much of his time tinkering with gadgets. And so the long hot days dragged on into fall.

On September 30 Edith was riding at a gallop with Theodore and Archie when, for no apparent reason, her horse Pine Knot suddenly swerved and shied. She was thrown onto the macadam road in front of Cove School, and knocked senseless. Try as Theodore might to revive her, she showed no signs of coming to. Frantically, he hailed a passing delivery van, and transported her home. She remained completely comatose for an agonizing thirty-six hours, before regaining a glimmer of consciousness, and for nine days afterward was lucid only at intervals.[11] When she finally revived she had no recollection of the fall, and found that she had no sense of taste or smell. Her head ached excruciatingly for days, and Theodore summoned a nerve specialist and two nurses to watch her around the clock. It was many weeks before she felt strong enough to venture outside. In time she regained her sense of taste, but not that of smell. Never again would she be able to luxuriate in the perfume of honeysuckle and roses, the aroma of bread baking, and the salty tang of the ocean.

Edith Wharton wrote twice to inquire after her, and sent a copy of her latest book, *Ethan Frome*. But the grim subject matter, (particularly at the story's climax, when Mattie Silver, in a suicidal pact with her lover, crashes into an elm, crippling herself for life) was hardly guaranteed to cheer Edith in her present condition.[12]

On December 2 Edith and Theodore celebrated their silver wedding anniversary. Christmas that year was "old style," with Alice, Nick, Kermit, Archie, Quentin, and Laura Roosevelt and her children joining them. But age and the absence of small children cast a certain pall over the occasion. As Theodore remarked, the festival "loses some of its fine edge when the youngest child is a boy a half inch taller than his father!"[13]

By early 1912 Theodore had, to all intents and purposes, begun to run for President. Progressive Republicans, forecasting the impossibility of nominating La Follette over Taft, were turning increasingly to Roosevelt to champion their cause of reform. Theodore, seeing a party split develop, sent messages to old friends warning them of a coming, potentially disastrous conflict. Through Alice he advised Archie Butt "to get out of his present job" and not wait for the convention or the election. Alice added her own advice: "Get from under the edifice before the crash." The implication was that Taft might be defeated by her father for the nomination. The aide ignored this advice, feeling that he could not honorably abandon the President. He thus risked Theodore's displeasure, for as he himself had once written, "Roosevelt likes to have his way with horses, as with men."[14] However, Butt was not one to flinch from unpleasantness, and on January 28 he drove up the newly-paved driveway to Sagamore Hill.

He found the French Ambassador, Jules Jusserand, with Theodore and Edith, as he had so often been in the days of the Roosevelt White House. Next day Butt wrote his sister:

> They were just the same dear people. The woodwork part of the house has been painted drab instead of red,

but otherwise there was no change from the last time I
was there. The fireplaces were filled with huge logs
which the Colonel cuts down for exercise; the dogs were
following one all over the house, and Mrs. Roosevelt was
moving in and out like some delicate shuttle, keeping
everything in harmony and laughing to herself as she
passed—a little trick she has that always keeps her clear-
cut before my eyes. She has entirely recovered and looks
just as young and as lovely as she did the day she left the
White House. He greeted me at the door with the same
cheery handshake . . . Mrs. Roosevelt asking a hundred
questions and I tripping up myself in my haste to tell her
of all her friends, from Mrs. Townsend down to Alice,
the black scullery maid at the White House.

The Colonel heard us laughing once, and he rushed in
and made us repeat what had just been said. He never
could stand being left out of a good laugh . . .

One incident during the luncheon will amuse you. It
seems that the telephone had been out of order, and
word had been sent to the office to have it repaired. Just
before luncheon was over the colored man, one of those
who preferred to work for the Roosevelts in private life
than to remain at the White House, said:

"Colonel, the telephone man has been here, sir, and
he says you cut down all the trees this morning which
had the wires on them, and he said too, sir, that you
didn't even pull the wires out after the trees fell."

The Colonel looked guilty as Mrs. Roosevelt began to
laugh, but he stopped her quickly by saying:

"Now, Edie, don't you say a word. It was your own
fault. You always mark the trees I am to cut down, and
you did not do it. No, Edie, you did not do your duty as
forester of this establishment, and you ought to be
punished, but I will say nothing more about it and not
hold you up to scorn before your children if you will let
the subject drop once for all."

"It seems to me," said the ambassador, "that no one
has said a word but yourself."

"Ah! But you don't know my wife. She has a language
all her own. That telephone will never ring now that my

wife will not begin to chuckle to herself, and if the cursed thing ever gets out of order, which it most frequently does, she will tell the servants to see if the wires are still up or if the trees are down. No, my dear Mr. Ambassador, people think I have a good-natured wife, but she has a humor which is more tyrannical than half the tempestuous women of Shakespeare."

He continued to talk for about two hours in this jocular vein, until it was time for Archie to leave. Edith sent her love to President Taft, and thanked him again for the sofa. But Theodore made no mention of his successor.[15]

As it happened, the President's health was worsening. Butt wrote that his skin was like wax, he had heavy bags under his eyes, and was habitually drowsy. Henry Adams, himself the victim of a recent stroke, met Taft one night that winter in Lafayette Square, and found him "more tumble to pieces than ever," with a sad deterioration in the quality of his mind. In contrast—perhaps in anticipation of a Convention fight—Theodore had a good rosy color, and even after days of strenuous work professed to feel "fine as silk."[16]

At the beginning of February, Edith took Laura Roosevelt's town house on East Thirty-first Street for a few weeks. She said she wanted to see a few plays and operas and friends, but in effect she was upset with Theodore's growing involvement in politics, and wished to disassociate herself from the Republican intriguers thronging Sagamore Hill. On February 2, 1912, Robert La Follette, frail from an attack of ptomaine poisoning, made a meandering, sometimes incoherent speech to a group of publishers in Philadelphia, which gave his disillusioned progressive supporters a final excuse to turn their attentions to Roosevelt. On February 10, Theodore received a letter, signed by seven progressive Governors, asking him to accept the nomination for Republican candidate. The pressure on him to run mounted daily, in the belief that the Democrats would assuredly beat Taft. "Politics are hateful," Edith wrote Kermit next day. "Father thinks he must enter the fight definitely since La Follette's collapse . . . and there is no possible result which could give me aught but keen regret."[17]

At a speech before the Constitutional Convention in Columbus,

Ohio, on February 21, Roosevelt further alienated conservative party friends like Lodge and Root by advocating one of the most controversial progressive tenets, namely the right of the people to vote in referendum for or against all court decisions affecting the constitutionality of state laws. Then, compounding their antagonisms, he casually remarked to a reporter, "My hat is in the ring."

On Saturday, February 24, he wrote the seven progressive Governors: "I will accept the nomination for President if it is tendered to me." [18]

About this time, Henry Adams began to perceive Roosevelt as a prophetic poseur, drunk with cloudy visions. "Even so clear-headed a man as Root thinks that Theodore has not the Presidency in his mind, but that he aims at a leadership far in the future, as a sort of Moses and Messiah for a vast progressive tide of a rising humanity," he wrote Elizabeth Cameron. "Edith is so much disturbed by the 'mess' that she has taken Ethel off to Panama." [19]

The former First Lady had indeed left for South America on February 24, although she remained diplomatically silent on why she was going. She had not been at sea two days before the newspapers officially announced Theodore's candidacy. "I see nothing for him but the asylum," commented Adams, while Taft said that Roosevelt would be "the most bitterly discredited statesman in American politics" if he defeated an incumbent President for the Republican nomination. [20]

Edith revisited the Culebra Cut, Balboa and the Island of Tobago, which she had first seen in happier times. She and Ethel were guests of the Government of Costa Rica before returning to New York on March 19. She was amused to note that Theodore's hair, which had been quite straight and flat for a year, was now "curling vigorously,—due to psychical electricity doubtless!" [21]

He did not pause long in his frenzied pursuit of the nomination to welcome them home. The following evening he made a major policy speech at Carnegie Hall reaffirming his position on the recall of judicial decisions. It had nothing to do with ordinary civil or criminal suits, he said, nor did he favor the recall of judges. He merely proposed that in landmark cases involving police power "the question of the validity of the law . . . be submitted for final determination to a vote of the people." [22]

Four days after this speech the Roosevelts met Cabot and Nannie

Lodge in New York City. Theodore had realized for a time now that on some domestic issues he and his old friend were heading in different directions, but he was philosophical about the split, and protested a continuing warm personal affection. "Apparently the meeting was as though nothing had happened," Adams reported to Mrs. Cameron. "Edith has come back from Panama quite well again, and the Napoleon of our small society is in excellent form, but much bigger . . ."[23]

The strain of being loyal to two masters proved too much for Archie Butt. He was by now "completely tuckered out," and his doctor recommended a rest. Accordingly the Captain sailed for Rome on March 2, 1912. After a month in Italy and England he felt much better—so much so that in mid-April he sailed for home from Southampton. The name of his chosen vessel was S.S. *Titanic.*[24]

If Theodore's stand was difficult for Henry Cabot Lodge, it was impossible for Nick Longworth. He and his Cincinnati family were old friends of William Howard Taft, and being married to the daughter of Taft's challenger for the GOP nomination was embarrassing in the extreme. He was also by nature a stalwart Republican. In spite of his father-in-law's admonition, "Of course you must be for Taft," Nick's dilemma was real; even Alice, who would support no one but her father, felt sorry for her husband. Edith was irritated with both of the Longworths. "Sister arrived talking like molasses blobbing out of a bottle and rocking as if she were a boarder in a summer hotel," she told Ethel that spring. "I wish to goodness that Nick would come out flat footed and work for Taft, or do something! It is hard on everyone."[25] Occasionally, mother and stepdaughter communicated by long-distance telephone, neither seeing how Theodore could win the nomination.

It became harder still for the Longworths in late April, when Theodore defeated Taft in the Nebraska, Pennsylvania and Illinois primaries. The President fought back with an anti-Roosevelt speech in Boston. It was one of the most painful duties of his life, he confessed afterward, and wept. In spite of his efforts, however, Taft lost New Jersey and Ohio—his own state—when thirty-seven out of forty delegates elected to support Roosevelt.

It was an unkind April. Following fast on the drowning of Archie Butt, and Henry Adams's half-crippling stroke, came the passing of Edith's close friend Aunt Lizzie. These bereavements and worries, coupled with concern over Theodore and the imminent convention, made Edith increasingly irritable. "I fear I seemed cross and stern to my little girl today," she apologized to Ethel, "but she must forgive me. I have much to bear."[26]

Theodore arrived in Chicago on Saturday, June 15, three days before the Republican National Convention, with several volumes of Roman history under his arm, and 1,157,397 primary votes behind him—compared to Taft's 761,716. Translated into delegates, this majority, theoretically, assured Roosevelt the nomination; but not all the delegates now flocking to the city were to be permitted access to the Convention floor. About five hundred, in fact, were locked in competition for half that number of seats, and the White House–controlled Convention Committee had already shown an alarming tendency to rule in favor of delegates committed to Taft. The result was that on Sunday, the sixteenth, less than forty-eight hours before the opening of the Convention, Roosevelt found himself seventy delegates short of the nomination. All his aggressive instincts boiled up in a furious desire to destroy the President whom he himself had created only four years before. That day, Theodore sat down with Edith, who had accompanied him to Chicago, and went over the draft of the most fighting speech he had ever made in his life.

She suggested that some of the more bellicose paragraphs be modified or omitted. Purged of rancor, the final speech proved to be both noble and inspiring when he delivered it the following night, Monday, June 17, to a massive rally of progressives in the Chicago Auditorium.

> Friends, here in Chicago at this time you have a great task before you. I wish you to realize deep in your hearts that you are not merely facing a crisis in the history of a party. You are facing a crisis in the history of a nation ... We fight in honorable fashion for the good of mankind; fearless of the future; unheeding of our individual fates; with unflinching hearts and undimmed eyes; we stand at Armageddon, and we battle for the Lord.[27]

Next day at the Coliseum Elihu Root was elected temporary chairman of the Convention. Notwithstanding the great lawyer's services as Secretary of War and Secretary of State in both Roosevelt

"I have lived, most reluctantly, through one party split."
Edith in Chicago, 1912.

Administrations, he was now pledged to President Taft, and his
election boded ill for the progressives. Root set the tone for the
proceedings with a ruling that permitted the seating of a majority of
Taft delegates. From that moment on, the swing of the Convention
away from Roosevelt was irreversible.

Depressed and worried at the prospect of having to split his
progressives away from the GOP, Theodore held a meeting of
advisers at his hotel. Somebody suggested that the popular Governor
Herbert S. Hadley of Missouri, who combined progressive principles

with party loyalty (he had had a ten-minute ovation on first entering the Convention Hall), might make a good compromise candidate, uniting both Roosevelt and Taft supporters. Theodore, reluctant to abandon the fight, called his wife into the room and miserably asked, "I wonder if it would be better for Hadley to head the party?" Her answer was decisive: "Theodore, remember that often one wants to do the hardest and the noblest thing, but sometimes it does not follow that it is the right thing."[28]

So, on Saturday, June 22, 1912, William Howard Taft was renominated for President by the Republican Party, while 344 of Theodore's 451 delegates stalked grimly off the floor. That evening, at a "rump" convention held in Orchestra Hall, Theodore Roosevelt provisionally accepted nomination as a candidate of the newly formed Progressive Party. He said that if someone else was formally selected at a full Progressive Convention, to be held in Chicago in August, he would gladly support him. But there was little doubt in anybody's mind that come November he would run against Taft in the national election.

In Baltimore, on July 2, Woodrow Wilson, the austere fifty-five-year-old former Princeton professor and Governor of New Jersey, was nominated for President by the Democratic Party.

Shortly afterward, E. A. Van Valkenberg, publisher of the Philadelphia *North American*, arrived at Sagamore Hill to get Roosevelt's reaction, and, if possible, details of his campaign plans.

> "Telegrams and letters have been pouring in by the hundreds," said Theodore, "but I couldn't make up my mind until yesterday. Then I had the family all in and I talked it over with them and decided I've got to run. Here's the situation as I see it. Wilson has been nominated. If I should happen to want the regular Republican nomination in 1916 all I'd have to do now would be to keep still. Wilson will beat Taft hands down. I've got to run because while there's no chance of my success the cause of liberal government would be advanced fifty years. I've figured up the cost pretty well. I know it's going to be a bitter campaign—a vindictive one from the other side—there's going to be lots of lying

about me . . . a lot of my lifelong friendships will be
broken up." He mentioned especially Root and Lodge.
"But I've got to do it because if I don't everything I've
tried to work for politically will be lost." He paused a
moment. "Wait a minute," he went on, "till I get
Edith." He brought her in and he and she stood there
hand in hand like a couple of children. "Edith," he said,
"tell Van what we decided yesterday." She said practically what he had detailed . . . in a regretful tone that
spoke sincerely of personal and family sacrifices.[29]

To her the whole year so far with its breakup of old loyalties, and
petty political wrangling, had been distasteful, so much so that she
had made no daily diary entries—the first such lapse since entering
the White House in 1901. But for a few precious weeks that summer
she was able to enjoy life again, with her family all around her and
politics temporarily in abeyance. Even Ted, Eleanor and Baby
Gracie were able to join the throng at Sagamore Hill. Ted had quit
his job with the carpet company in San Francisco, and, impatient to
make more money, had joined an investment banking firm on Wall
Street. He intended to rent a house in town for the winter, but in the
meantime was anxious to introduce his wife to the delights of country
life at Oyster Bay. For Eleanor, it was no easy adjustment. Nothing
in her upbringing as an only child had prepared her for the
Rooseveltian frenzy of activity.

> Something was going on every minute of the day. The
> house was always full of people . . . At first I thought
> everyone would be tired when the day was over and
> would go to bed early, but I soon found out nothing of
> the kind could be expected. The Roosevelt family
> enjoyed life too much to waste time sleeping. Every
> night they stayed downstairs until nearly midnight;
> then, talking at the top of their voices, they trooped up
> the wide uncarpeted stairs and went to their rooms. For
> a brief moment all was still, but just as I was going off to
> sleep for the second time they remembered things they
> had forgotten to tell one another and ran shouting
> through the halls . . . By six the younger ones were up,

and by seven I was the only one who was not joyously beginning the day.

When Eleanor joined the family for a picnic, she anticipated dainty sandwiches and chicken salad, elegantly packed and eaten under a shady tree. Instead she was forced to trek through woods where mosquitoes seemed "as big as bats," then climb into a seatless boat and row for two hours in scorching sun before arriving at a beach "precisely like the one we had started from," except that it was ringed with poison ivy.

Here Theodore built a roaring fire to roast clams, and presented the first one to Eleanor. It was large and rubbery and "gritty with sand." After vainly chewing it for some minutes, she "slipped it under a log." Since wedgelike ham sandwiches and a demijohn of water were the only other fare, Eleanor went hungry. "As we packed up to go home a head wind started to blow. It had taken us two hours to get there; it took four to get back. Faces and necks were sunburned, hands were blistered. My father-in-law had a difficult time reaching shore, as the boat in which he was rowing Mrs. Roosevelt was leaking badly."

Everybody except Eleanor agreed afterward that it had been "one of the best picnics we ever had."[30]

On July 27, the Roosevelts' brief period of full family harmony came to an end with the departure of the twenty-two-year-old youth who many suspected was Edith's favorite son. Her diary entry for the day—the first that year—reads simply: "Kermit sailed for Brazil via England to begin work on R.R." After graduating from Harvard with his original class of 1908 (completing four years' work in the equivalent of two and a half) he had accepted a management position with the Brazil Railroad Company. Like Ted, he hoped to make money in business, but unlike Ted he had no real taste for corporate life. At heart Kermit was an adventurer and a dreamer, with nascent literary ambitions; time would show whether he had self-discipline enough to reconcile these warring extremes.

Alice was at Sagamore Hill to see him off, and to make known her plan to go to the Progressive Convention the following week. Neither her father nor her husband thought this wise, and they took her out onto the piazza to discuss it. While sympathizing with Alice's divided loyalties, both men decided it would be unfair to Nick if she did go. Alice, rocking violently in her chair, felt very sorry for herself and cried, but "promised to abide by their decision."[31]

Edith went to Chicago with Theodore again on Sunday, August 4, and the Progressive Party Convention opened the following day. "It was far more serious as well as more enthusiastic than the last," she told Kermit. "The red bandanas flapped and waved, . . . the two great songs were the 'Battle Hymn of the Republic' and 'Onward Christian Soldiers.' The delegates were younger than those in June. Albert J. Beveridge made a splendid chairman and a sounding board had been arranged over the platform so the speeches could really be heard."[32]

Needless to say the speaker listened to with the most breathless interest was Theodore Roosevelt, who stood up before the Convention on August 6. For fifty-two minutes the assembled delegates cheered him with adoration that reminded impartial observers of mass religious rapture. When he at last attempted to stop the demonstration, the entire hall burst into song:

> *Thou wilt not cower in the dust,*
> *Roosevelt, O Roosevelt!*
> *Thy gleaming sword shall never rust,*
> *Roosevelt, O Roosevelt!*

Buoyed by this reception, Theodore went on to give an updated version of his great speech on the eve of the Republican Convention, ending with the same resounding line, "We stand at Armageddon and we battle for the Lord."

"If they treated Theodore as they deal with certain composite substances in chemistry," Owen Wister wrote afterward, "and melted him down . . . [to] his ultimate, central, indestructible stuff, it's not a statesman they'd find, or a hunter, or a historian, or a naturalist—they'd find a preacher militant."[33]

On Wednesday, August 7, Theodore was nominated for a third term in the presidency, with Governor Hiram Johnson of California as his running mate. The campaign now began in earnest. "I am in what is in all probability a losing fight," Theodore wrote Cecil Spring-Rice, "and although I have all the press and nine-tenths of what regards itself as cultivated opinion against me, I really do not think I was ever in my life better contented. I never could feel happy when I possessed the uneasy subconsciousness that I was not doing all I ought to help out those who were not given fair play." [34]

As the summer passed, and more and more disenchanted Democrats as well as Republicans grouped behind the Progressive banner, Edith began to feel that Theodore might, after all, stand a chance. One morning after her husband had demolished a huge plate of liver and bacon and was sitting in his rocking chair drinking yet another cup of coffee, she began to read a few headlines from the *Times* which showed that the Wilson campaign officials had doubts about winning, particularly in New York State. "Don't you think that's good news, Theodore?" she asked. He grinned and said, "By George, you know, we've really got a chance." [35]

"Theodore left yesterday in fine spirits," Edith wrote Corinne on August 22 after he set out to open his campaign in Pennsylvania, "but I can't say that he is looking forward to the month of September with joy. If you come across any book which he would care to read on the trip do send it to him, and if you wish it returned he is most conscientious. He likes a new book on history or science or a novel which is not a problem novel, but one in which he can consistently act the hero's part, or a good novel of trash . . ." [36]

September saw Theodore Roosevelt cross the country in a mammoth speaking odyssey via the Midwest to Washington and Oregon, looping through California, the Southwest and the Plains States, and ending up in the Deep South. On October 2 he was back in Oyster Bay, but only briefly; five days later he set off again on a tour of the Great Lakes states.

By Monday October 14 he had arrived in Milwaukee, while Edith moved to New York City to stay with Aunt Laura. That evening the two women went to the theater. They were seated on the aisle, with Edith on the inside. There was a spare seat next to her for Laura's son, Oliver, who was working at the city's Progressive Party headquarters and had not yet arrived. He did not do so until after the curtain rose. As he sat down, Edith reached out and touched his knee in greeting, only to find that he was "shaking violently." She realized at once that something had happened to Theodore.

In silent inquiry she gripped Oliver's hand. Steadying his voice, he told her that telegrams had come from Milwaukee saying that her husband had been shot at, but not hit. Edith gasped and asked Oliver to go back to headquarters and make sure the news was not worse. He did so and soon reappeared to admit that Cousin Theodore had in fact "been scratched but had kept on with his speech."

Edith continued to sit numbly in her seat. For years, since Theodore first ran for Governor in 1898, she had dreaded such a catastrophe as this. Now that it had happened the shock was paralyzing. Laura wanted her to leave the theater, but Edith insisted on staying, saying vaguely "that he couldn't be hurt if he went on with his speech."[37]

Reporters waiting outside for her to emerge after the performance were foiled when she slipped out of a side entrance and took a car to Progressive headquarters in the Hotel Manhattan. By now details of the assassination attempt were coming in. Apparently Theodore had been leaving the brightly lit Gilpatrick Hotel in Milwaukee, and was standing in his car waving his hat to the crowd when a shabby little man approached. His name was John Schrank; he was a disgruntled and deranged former New York saloonkeeper from Theodore's Police Commissioner days, and he sought revenge. Leaning over the edge of the car, he fired a gun point-blank at his victim's chest. Theodore recoiled as if hit with a sledgehammer; by some miracle the bullet had hit his steel spectacle case and the typescript of his speech, thickly folded in his breast pocket. This did not prevent it from penetrating the flesh, but the deflection had saved his life. He had the presence of mind to call out, "Don't hurt him. I want to look at him," as enraged bystanders grappled with the attacker. Roosevelt stared penetratingly at the cowering Schrank, and then turned silently away.[38]

Since no blood issued from his mouth, Theodore assumed that the bullet had not perforated his lungs. Consequently he decided to go ahead and make his planned address. He arrived at the hall still wearing his gore-stained shirt, took the perforated speech from his breast pocket, and spoke for an hour and a half.[39]

Edith stayed at headquarters until word came just after midnight that Theodore's wound had been dressed at the Emergency Hospital in Milwaukee. He was now sleeping quietly in a rail car on his way to Chicago's Mercy Hospital, where doctors would consider whether to remove the bullet.

In spite of a personal telegram from Theodore telling her that the wound was "trivial" and not "a particle more serious than one of the injuries" the boys used to have, she decided to go to Chicago the next day. First she went back to Laura's to snatch a few hours sleep. By now she had recovered her famous poise, and seemed "absolutely calm and self-possessed."

On the morning of Tuesday, October 15, Edith returned to headquarters and heard that Theodore was safely in bed in Chicago. The bullet had entered half way up his right side, broken a rib, and continued about four inches to the left, where it finally lodged, a mere quarter of an inch from his heart. Absolute rest had been ordered to mitigate the possible effects of blood poisoning.[40]

If Edith had time to scan the daily newspapers, even those which had bitterly opposed her husband in his campaign, she must have been touched by the sympathetic tone in all of them. "Mr. Roosevelt," the *Times* commented, "showed the indomitable courage that is engraved in his being. It was rash . . . but it was characteristic, and the judgment of the country will be that it was magnificent." The *Sun* headline read: "No Thought of Self . . . Smiles Through It All." A *Herald* cartoon of the Colonel flourishing his bullet-riddled speech was captioned: "We are against his politics, but we like his grit."

That afternoon at four o'clock, Edith, accompanied by Ted, Ethel, and Dr. Alexander Lambert, climbed aboard the Chicago-bound Twentieth Century Limited. Would Mrs. Roosevelt be strong enough to make the trip, an *Evening Mail* reporter inquired of the doctor? "A woman is always able to do anything she wants to do at any time," he replied.

Next morning, Wednesday, the party arrived in Chicago at about eight-thirty and alighted at a suburban station to avoid crowds. Alice was waiting for them. They went directly to Mercy Hospital on Prairie Avenue. "Theodore looks splendidly," Edith wrote at once to Bamie, "but of course we must not stop being anxious until seventy-four hours have elapsed." By that time any danger of infection from the bullet (the doctors had decided not to remove it) would have passed. As a precaution, the patient had been given "anti lock jaw serum."

On Thursday morning Edith saw Theodore's wound for the first time. "It is about the size of a dime," she told Emily, "and no signs of suppuration." The surrounding muscles were black and blue.[41]

For five nights she slept in an airy and tastefully furnished room right next to Theodore's. Her days were occupied in reading cables from all over America and the world, including two gentlemanly messages from Taft and Wilson announcing that they were halting their campaigning until more was known about Roosevelt's condition. Edith vigilantly kept visitors and newsmen away from the sick room. The only exceptions were Governor Hiram Johnson, the Progressive Vice-Presidential candidate, and the women's-rights advocate and social worker Jane Addams, a favorite of Theodore's. "All the bosses that had gone before [Mrs. Roosevelt]—Quay, Platt, Hanna and Hill—were amateurs to her," wrote correspondent Charles Willis Thompson.

> That sedate and determined woman, from the moment of her arrival in Chicago, took charge of affairs and reduced the Colonel to pitiable subjection. Up to her advent he was throwing bombshells into his doctors . . . and directing his own medical campaign . . . The moment she arrived a hush fell upon T.R. . . . he became as meek as Moses. Now and then the Colonel would send out secretly for somebody he knew and wanted to talk to, but every time the vigilant Mrs. Roosevelt would swoop down on the emissary . . . No such tyrannical sway has ever been seen in the history of American politics.

Theodore pleaded and grouched in vain. "This thing about ours being a campaign against boss rule is a fake," he said after Edith's first day in the hospital. "I never was so boss-ruled in my life as I am at this moment." But Thompson saw him grin fondly at her and remarked, "It is evident that the Great Unbossed likes being bossed for once." Theodore, in fact, was enjoying himself hugely. He looked on his time in the hospital as "a positive spree." As for being shot, it was "a trade risk which every prominent man should accept as a matter of course."[42]

On Monday morning, October 21, Edith bundled Theodore into a wheelchair, transported him to a rail car and tucked him into a bunk. The broken rib had already begun to mend; he no longer suffered discomfort from it, and spent most of the journey to New York reading magazines, "in a most contented frame of mind." [43] Five days after reaching Sagamore Hill he celebrated his fifty-fourth birthday, and three days after that Edith heard him make one of the greatest speeches of his career, at an enormous Progressive Party rally in Madison Square Garden. One hundred thousand people crowded the arena and streets outside, and the roar that greeted Roosevelt's appearance on the platform lasted for forty-one solid minutes. When silence at last descended, the candidate, who looked in robust health, began to speak, his voice reaching all corners of the vast auditorium:

> . . . Our people work hard and faithfully. They do not wish to shirk their work. They must feel pride in the work for the work's sake. But there must be bread for the work. There must be a time for play when the men and women are young. When they grow old there must be certainty of rest under conditions free from the haunting terror of utter poverty . . . We here in America hold in our hands the hope of the world, the fate of the coming years, and shame and disgrace will be ours if in our eyes the light of high resolve is dimmed, if we trail in the dust the golden hopes of men. [44]

On November 5 Woodrow Wilson won the presidential election by more than two million popular and 347 Electoral College votes over Theodore Roosevelt. Taft finished a poor third. The final figures were: Wilson 6,301,254; Roosevelt 4,127,788; Taft 3,485,831. Simple analysis showed that if the Republican National Convention had nominated Theodore and not precipitated a fatal split in party voting strength, he would now once again be President-elect of the United States.

"The result is only what we expected all along," Edith wrote Kermit in Brazil next day, "but for about ten days after Father's wound a great change in popular feeling caused many of our leaders to feel that a Progressive landslide was possible. I don't think they ever went so far as to actually believe this . . . Father is as brave as he can be, but you know him well enough to realize that he will paint the situation in his letter to you in the blackest colors . . ." [45]

Quentin, of all her sons the most like Theodore, felt the defeat just as acutely. "Things up here are gloomy, gloomy, gloomy," he wrote from Groton. "I am reading Racine . . . Don't you think it was pretty good of the rector to come out for the progressives? He said to me after the election, 'Well, Quentin, I guess we'll all have to wait for 1916 . . . My but I'm glad [the] election is over. I had a rotten time up here."

A minor casualty of the voting, but major as far as the Roosevelts were concerned, was Nick Longworth's loss of his Congressional seat. Alice looked "horribly ill and worn," Edith wrote, "and has had a dreadful time with Nick. He can't seem to face his defeat."[46]

As for Theodore, he was not optimistic about his own political future. Whether he knew it or not, his life had already begun to take on the shape of a classical drama. It had reached its heroic climax in the White House years, and by breaking from the Republican Party he had committed his act of hubris. The assassination attempt and subsequent election defeat were the direct consequences of that fatal insolence. Only the tragic last act remained to be played out.

Shortly after the election news arrived at Sagamore Hill that Cecil Spring-Rice had, at last, won the post of his desires: he had been appointed British Ambassador to Washington. "Now I feel horribly at not being President," Theodore wrote in a sad letter of congratulation. "Under the circumstances it will not do for you to see very much of us, I fear!"[47]

Edith never made her views on the election of 1912 public. Once she had made up her mind to support Theodore, she did so with all the eagerness she could muster. But her heart was not in the fight, as she privately revealed many years later. "I trust the Republican party will cling to its name and reform from within," she wrote Ted. "I have lived, most reluctantly, through one party split and no good comes of it. That tremendous enthusiasm—Oscar Straus singing 'Onward Christian Soldiers' with all his heart and soul, which amused him immensely after all was over,—all wasted."[48]

Twenty-Nine

*I feel a trifle down for I have not been able to help Father, and
Kermit does not need me now.*

— Edith Kermit Roosevelt[1]

The eighteen months immediately following the defeat of the
Progressive Party saw little lessening of activity in the Roosevelts'
lives. It was a time of happiness and unhappiness, health and
sickness, success and failure, much like any other. It was also a time
of transition. Edith would never again see her husband scale the
heights of political or military achievement; nor would she enjoy the
luxury of having all her children near at hand. As a family they had
passed their peak. Henceforth, though there were minor inclines to
surmount, the road led inevitably downhill.

Now that Theodore was, if temporarily, out of public life, he
turned, as he had so often in the past, to writing. During the winter of
1912 and early 1913 he prepared a lecture for the American
Historical Society entitled "History as Literature," collaborated with
the naturalist Edmund Heller on a two-volume work called *Life
Histories of African Game Animals,* and began a series of articles for the

Outlook, which were ultimately published as his *Autobiography*. In this last he omitted any mention of Alice Hathaway Lee and of his first marriage, but described life at Sagamore Hill with Edith and the children in his best prose style.

> The house stands right on the top of the hill, separated by fields and belts of woodland from all other houses, and looks out over the bay and the Sound. We see the sun go down beyond long reaches of land and water . . . We love all the seasons; the snows and bare woods of winter; the rush of growing things and the blossom-spray of spring; the yellow grain in the ripening fruits and tasseled corn, and the deep leafy shades that are heralded by "the green dance of summer"; and the

"She found herself once again simply the mistress of Sagamore Hill."
Sagamore Hill, Oyster Bay, Long Island.

sharp fall winds that tear the brilliant banners with
which the trees greet the dying year.[2]

To keep his fighting spirit in trim, he engaged in a libel suit against
George A. Newett, the editor of *Iron Ore,* a Michigan weekly
newspaper. In the fall of 1912, Newett had printed a column in which
he accused Roosevelt of lying, cursing and drunkenness. Theodore
would admit to occasionally telling less than the whole truth for
political reasons, and was capable of a profanity or two when roused,
but intemperance—never. He detested cocktails and beer, had no
liking for whiskey, and took brandy only when sick. A rare glass of
celebratory champagne or Madeira, a sip of sherry with soup, a little
watered wine with dinner, and port with cheese—all these he
enjoyed. The closest he came to gin was in a mint julep after a hot
game of tennis; that was all. If his exuberant enthusiasm and ruddy
complexion gave an impression of insobriety, that could not be
helped. But he was tired of the old charge of being a toper, and this
time intended to rebuke it publicly.

And so, in the last week of May 1913 Robert Bacon, Gifford
Pinchot, James R. Garfield, George B. Cortelyou, William Loeb,
Admiral George Dewey, General Leonard Wood, Jacob Riis, Dr.
Alex Lambert, Dr. Presley Rixey, Lawrence Abbot, Lyman Abbot,
Emlen Roosevelt and Phillp Roosevelt all made their way to Marquette, Michigan, to testify on behalf of Theodore Roosevelt. Newett
failed to produce a single defense witness, and the jury found for the
plaintiff. Theodore was not vengeful. He asked merely that a token
six cents for damages be levied against his accuser, and telegraphed
his wife the good news. It felt good, he said, to have dealt "with these
slanders, so that never again will they be repeated."[3]

Abstemious as Theodore might be, Edith was not reassured that
his eldest son was of similar bent. During the winter Ted had begun
to spend increasing amounts of time in various hard-drinking New
York clubs. Edith rather wished that he had not left California. "I
think he goes too much to the Brook Club," she wrote Kermit, "and I
don't think Eleanor realizes and can act accordingly." In her opinion,
"the lowest point" had come at Christmas, when Ted lunched at the
Ritz with business acquaintances instead of coming to Sagamore Hill.
If he was content to be "a tin pin in a pin cushion," she wrote bitterly

to Kermit, that was his affair. "I realize that each child must lead his or her own life after leaving home and those who don't care to be the pearl in the satin box have at least the right of choice."[4]

The unaccustomed vehemence of this attack on her son was followed shortly afterward by a strangely possessive reaction when Ethel, now twenty-one, announced that she intended to make a trip to Brazil. Edith told her that while she "would not be selfish and *forbid* her going," she herself was "not strong" at the moment, and Ethel was the only person she could turn to for help "in the really heavy work of keeping accounts etc. straight." Beside, she went on weakly, Theodore was still inclined to entertain large numbers of his friends at Sagamore Hill, "and I might not have the strength to see that all went smoothly for them."[5] Ethel disappointedly agreed to stay, perhaps sensing why her mother, at fifty-one, was beginning to feel emotionally fragile. The family doctor, indeed, had already prescribed a course of thyroid tablets.

But Ethel had her own way that spring of 1913 in choosing a husband. She had fallen in love with Richard Derby, a tall, dark-haired Manhattan doctor whom she had met at Roosevelt Hospital. "Dick," at thirty-one, was ten years her senior, but he came from a fine old Massachusetts family. More to the point, he had, on top of his salary as a practicing surgeon, a private income of between twelve and fourteen thousand dollars a year. Edith at first found Dick taciturn and ill-at-ease, but later attributed to him many of Kermit's introspective characteristics. (The latter, as it happened, had long ago picked the doctor as a suitable husband for his sister.) Theodore, who always employed superlatives to describe any member or prospective member of his family, told Bamie that Dick was "the best young fellow I know," and happily agreed to their marriage in April.[6]

Alice arrived at Sagamore Hill a week before the wedding. She produced a "dark blue satin and dingy yellow" dress from her suitcase, and said she intended to wear it at the ceremony. Edith considered it inappropriate, and sent her back to New York to buy something "light and becoming."[7] But the original gown more nearly reflected Alice's mood. The political split of 1912 was having continued repercussions. The loss of Nick's Congressional seat had inevitably been followed by a move to Cincinnati to live with Mrs. Longworth Senior. It had been a painful adjustment for Alice, who sorely missed her Washington friends. Edith was understanding, but felt little sympathy. She sensed that Alice was not, and had never really been, a true Progressive. Like Nick, the girl was basically a conservative Republican. "Our life and convictions have no real interest for her. The bonds were a deep and true family affection and political sympathy; and now the first is what keeps up, a mere semblance of reality in the last."

Nick, still sulking about the loss of his seat, clearly laid the blame on his father-in-law's defection. He sent no message of congratulation to Ethel, and made floods in Ohio an excuse for not attending the wedding. "Unfortunately we did not care," Edith wrote, 'but poor dear Sister was deeply hurt."[8]

Ethel and Dick were married at Christ Church, Oyster Bay, at twelve noon on Friday, April 4. Edith had had the church freshly painted for the occasion, decorated it with spring flowers, and arranged for the five hundred guests to be entertained at Sagamore Hill afterward. The air was warm and summerlike, and a huge crowd waited outside the church while a band played "Pride of America." "Ethel never looked prettier," Edith wrote Emily, who to everyone's relief ("She is unintentionally so very requiring") had elected not to come over.[9] The bride wore Aunt Kermit's Victorian stockings and Grandma Carow's white India shawl as her "something old." Her "something new" was Dick's wedding present of an emerald pendant matching her engagement ring.

At the reception guests were seated at tables on the piazza, in the dining room, and the North Room. Many old friends were there, including Henry Cabot Lodge, Owen Wister, and Winthrop Chanler, whose daughter Hester was one of the bridesmaids. "The atmosphere of youth and love was everywhere," Edith sighed to Emily.

Into Ethel's trunk she slipped a length of white silver brocade which had long ago been a gift to herself from Sturgis Bigelow. Worth was to make a gown and matching coat from it when the honeymoon couple reached Paris. "Will you ever forgive me?" Edith wrote the donor. "I should have given it to no one else in the world."

Exhausted, she stayed in bed next day until lunchtime, and spent the afternoon wandering through the woods. The only companion she could find was Emlen's daughter, Margaret Roosevelt. "I had thought Sister might care to be with me," she wrote Ethel, "but she preferred to go to Dorothy Straight's and Margaret was very dear and understands so much . . ."

Life was quiet now at Sagamore Hill. "Mother and I have dear evenings together," Theodore wrote Ethel. "But I wish I played cards and was more of a companion to her."[10]

Cecil Spring-Rice, wearing a beard to conceal erysipelas scars, arrived in the United States at the end of the month to take up his duties as British Ambassador. A note from Edith and Theodore awaited him, inviting him and his family to Sagamore Hill. But Ambassador Jusserand cautioned that for the time being it was politically expedient to avoid meeting with President Wilson's former opponent. The Roosevelts understood. "If ever you think it safe," Theodore wrote, "do come out and visit us . . . and if you don't think this advisable, let us know when you are passing through New York and we will come in and lunch or dine unobtrusively with you." Edith wrote later: "If you make the trip from New York by motor, it could be done without the knowledge of the reporters."

Springy, the diplomat and friend, was frustrated. "I propose to have a real long talk as soon as I can get the chance. It is sufficiently tantalizing. Damn it all . . . Oh, T.R., how I wish I could see you. I nearly wept in Rock Creek Park . . . I could *hear* you . . ." Five months were to pass before the Spring-Rices felt free to spend a weekend at Sagamore Hill.[11]

An urgent message from Emily, to say that she had to undergo an operation in Switzerland for removal of her appendix, took Edith to Europe on June 10. Ethel and Dick met her on the nineteenth in Lausanne and escorted her to a room in the Hotel Mirabeau overlooking the lake. Emily's surgery was successful, and after three weeks' convalescence she and her sister traveled south to Porto Maurizio, arriving there on July 13.

Disturbing letters from Oyster Bay prevented Edith from enjoying her Mediterranean sojourn. "Just when everything should be managed to shield Father," she complained to Kermit, "Ted has brought his family including mother-in-law [to Sagamore Hill], Sister hers, including Nick and Cross Anna her maid, and settled upon him like vampires; filling the house with the people they want to know, using Father as a bait!"[12]

The truth was that Theodore was having a thoroughly good time while his stern keeper was away. "Ted and Eleanor and Alice had a feeling as if in the absence of mother they could impose all their least desirable friends on pagan old father," he in turn wrote Kermit. "Accordingly they planned various delightfully wicked feasts of friends whom they thought mother would not like to have, . . . as a matter of fact nothing ever happened except two very small and stodgily virtuous dinners!"[13]

What probably irked Edith more than not being at home to protect Theodore from *personae non gratae* was that in his letters to her he was preserving "a sphinx-like silence" about his plans to sail for South America in the fall, to head an expedition into the Brazilian wilderness. It was his "last chance to be a boy," he explained to friends who protested that he was too old and the jungle too dangerous. It was also an opportunity to make money. He expected to clear twenty thousand dollars from articles and lectures and books about the trip, and believed this sufficiently justified any risk. But Edith understood the real reason. "Father needs more scope," she pointed out to Ethel, "and since he can't be President must go away from home to have it; and I feel so like the homesick schoolboy. 'Life is short. Let us spend it together.'"[14]

Edith, Richard and Ethel (who was now expecting a baby) sailed home together in mid-August, and arrived in New York on the twentieth. Theodore was not there to welcome them: he had gone out to the Southwest on a five-week trip with his two younger sons. Edith had encouraged this venture in the hope that it would reduce her husband's expanding waistline and bring him into a "close association" with Quentin, an increasingly "complex sort of person." The three returned on August 26. Edith found Theodore no thinner, but Quentin decidedly "more mature."[15]

She had every reason to feel proud of her youngest son. He was doing splendidly at Groton, and still ranked at or near the top of his class. He was the editor and typesetter of the school magazine, and a talented automobile and motorcycle mechanic. His taste in reading was catholic, ranging from detective stories to Greek poetry. Like his father he always had a book in his pocket, and could read anywhere, no matter how much noise was going on around him. He also had a developing political instinct, and a concern for people that matched his father's. The family noticed that Edith's "mental jump was always from Theodore to Quentin, as if the two were one."[16]

Alice came to Oyster Bay in September, the week of Ted's twenty-sixth birthday, and was "very spiteful" with everybody. "It is very hard for her having Nick out of politics," remarked Edith, "but not fair to come to stay at Sagamore and visit it on the family." [17]

Since Theodore seemed determined to go through with his boyish plan to explore the Paraguay River (and justified it, not very convincingly, by explaining that he could combine it with a political lecture tour of Brazil and neighboring countries), Edith agreed to accompany him on the first stage of the trip. Margaret Roosevelt offered to go with her, and they sailed on the *Vandyck* on October 4, 1913. To everyone's surprise Theodore enjoyed the sea voyage, laughing at the deck sports as Edith had not seen him laugh in years. "I think he feels like Christian in *Pilgrim's Progress* when the bundle fell from his back," she wrote Bamie, "—in this case it was not made of sins but of the Progressive Party." [18]

After a brief visit to Barbados, they landed on October 18 at Bahia, Brazil, where Kermit, bleached blond by the sun, was waiting to be picked up. He had recently quit his job with the Brazil Railroad and joined the Anglo-Brazilian Iron Company as a bridge construction supervisor at two thousand dollars a year. Fortunately his new employers were in favor of his taking six months off for exploration of the interior, believing that the experience would "increase his value." [19]

From Bahia the Roosevelts continued south to Rio de Janeiro. Edith found the famous port "as beautiful as a dream, the houses in the folds of the hills covered with thick forests, the great bay with its waves washing the whitest sands." Here they stayed "under Government care" at the palace. But it was not a relaxing visit, for Edith was immediately swept up into the whirlwind of social and official activities that Theodore always generated wherever he went. The next month, during which the Roosevelts moved on through south Brazil, Uruguay, Argentina, and then on across the Andes to Santiago, Chile, saw no slackening of pace. They visited bacteriological institutes, wineries, sugar plantations and bull farms; attended a Russian ballet, celebrated Theodore's fifty-fifth birthday, fought their way through hordes of worshipful schoolchildren, and dined with numerous Presidents. As if all this were not enough, two romantic dramas distracted them en route. In Buenos Aires Margaret Roosevelt began to receive bunches of white roses, sent her every day by a young man named Henry Hunt, who had fallen in love with her on the ship. Here, too, on November 13, Kermit received a cable from a certain Belle Willard, daughter of the American Ambassador to Spain, agreeing to marry him.[20]

Belle was a close friend of Ethel's, and had been courted by Kermit in 1912, before he left for South America. Edith remembered her as blond, "very small and slight," and a beautiful rider. She had dubbed her "the Fair One with Golden Locks," after the heroine of a fairy tale. Belle and the equally blond Kermit had made an attractive couple, and Theodore for one was not surprised to hear of the match. But Edith could not avoid feelings of shock and gloom. "I feel a trifle down," she wrote Ethel, obviously with some foreboding that there were depths in Kermit which the gaily sociable Belle would not satisfy. Earlier in the trip, in a letter to Bamie, she had significantly described her second son as "the one with the white head and the black heart."[21]

Edith and Margaret said goodbye to Theodore and Kermit on November 26, and took ship for Panama. They spent three days on the Isthmus, seeing Gatun and Colon and dining with Goethals, before continuing homeward on December 11. The next day Edith noted casually in her diary: "Margaret miserable with headache. Evidently too much sun." By the time they landed in New York on the eighteenth, Margaret, who had proved an ideal traveling companion, was seriously ill—not with sunstroke, but with typhoid fever. Sixteen days later the young woman was dead. Edith, feeling "more distressed than I can say," attended her funeral on January 5, 1914. A poignant mourner was "poor Henry Hunt."[22]

Another loss shook her on January 14, when a telegram came from Boston announcing the death of Grandma Lee.[23] One consolation, given the present insecurity of the Longworth ménage, was the old lady's establishment of a trust fund awarding Alice an extra ten thousand dollars annually.

Back in Brazil Theodore had abandoned his original plan to probe the Paraguay River, in favor of an even more ambitious expedition, to be sponsored by the Brazilian government, and led by a full-blooded Indian explorer, Colonel Rondon. This was to travel an unknown, thousand-mile waterway—the River of Doubt, which flowed north

from the Brazilian Plateau toward the Amazon itself. On Christmas
Eve, 1913, Theodore wrote to his wife:

> DARLING EDIE,
>
> Kermit is now in first rate shape, and as tough as
> hickory, and I never felt in better health—in spite of
> being covered with prickly heat—so if you do not hear
> from me to the contrary you can safely assume that this
> condition of things is permanent. Of course we have not
> really begun the expedition proper as yet, and there will
> be many extremely disagreeable experiences; but we are
> being hardened under exceptionally pleasant conditions,
> and so far have had no hardship whatever. Kermit,
> Harper, Miller and I, with some of the Brazilians, who
> are capital fellows and great chums of Kermit, are
> returning from a delightful week at a huge ranch in the
> marshes of the Taquery river. There were very few
> mosquitoes . . . the ranch was absolutely bare, no glass
> in the windows even, but clean. The weather was hot,
> but clear; the food was good; and we were in the saddle
> eight or ten hours a day. We each killed a jaguar, his
> being an exceptionally large one and mine a good
> average one; together with other game. The bird life,
> especially as regards the big waders and the macaws,
> was marvellous; and the flat marsh country dotted with
> stretches of palm-covered dry land, was in our eyes most
> attractive. Kermit is his own mother's son! He is to me a
> delightful companion; he always has books with him;
> and he is a tireless worker. He is not only an excep-
> tionally good and hard hunter, but as soon as he comes
> in he starts at his photographs or else at the skins,
> working as hard as the two naturalists. Indeed of our
> whole expedition everyone works hard except good little
> Father Zahn. I have just sent Scribners the third article;
> it seemed to me interesting, but it may not seem so to
> anyone else.[24] Sunsets and lovely marshes, and queer
> birds, are fascinating to those who see them, but may be
> anything rather than fascinating when written about for
> the benefit of those who do not see them.

We are very much pleased with Col. Rondon. He is very hardy, and fitted for this kind of business by twenty-five years experience, and is evidently agreably surprised by our conduct; and he is most anxious to do all in his power for us. Everything possible is done for my comfort, in the little ways that mean so much to a man of my age on a rough trip.

I shall send you a Xmas cable from Corumbá, this evening; we are now in a hot little sidewheel steamer jammed with men, dogs, bags and belongings, partially cured and rather bad-smelling skins, and the like. *I* enjoy it; but my dainty sweetheart most certainly would not. I am drenched with sweat most of the waking hours, and the nights are too hot for really comfortable sleeping as a rule; but there are exceptions. In ten days we shall be at the last post office, San Luis de Cáceres; and then we shall go into the real wilderness.

Kiss Ethel and Eleanor for me; I think of them very, very often, and of you all the time, and it is a real comfort to think of Ted, so hard-working and trust-worthy and efficient. Archie and Quentin are also always in my thoughts, as good Dick—we are so fortunate in him! I am sure we shall love Belle greatly.

YOUR OWN LOVER[25]

On February 27, 1914, Theodore, Kermit, Rondon, and nineteen others including sixteen paddlers in seven dugout canoes, began to descend the uncharted river. After nearly two months of battling an endless succession of jungle rapids and cataracts, their food supplies were sadly diminished, and they were all abjectly weak. Voracious insects bored through their clothes and poisoned their blood with fever and dysentery. One man went mad, killed a companion, and fled into the jungle. Another drowned when a boat capsized. Theodore suffered an injury to his left leg (which had never completely recovered from the Pittsfield accident of 1902) while trying to dislodge two canoes marooned on rocks. After this his health rapidly deteriorated, and, fearing to become a burden, he vainly begged Kermit to continue without him.

At last, toward the end of April, the party arrived at the settlement

of San João, carrying their leader on a litter. Here they took a steamer
first to Manaus and then on to Belém. Theodore lost fifty-seven
pounds, formed another dangerous abscess on his leg, and developed
a virulent fever in his blood. There had been a time, indeed, when he
seemed on the point of death. Yet he had somehow succeeded in
putting on the map a river as long as the Rhine. The Brazilian
government officially named it Rio Roosevelt, in honor of its explorer.
But locally (perhaps because of the difficulty in pronouncing the
Dutch name) it soon became known as Rio Teodoro.[26]

Edith, a hemisphere away from her husband, spent the first
months of 1914 in New York City hotels, so that she could be near
Ethel, whose confinement was drawing near. On March 7, after a
very difficult forty-eight-hour labor, Ethel gave birth to an eight-
pound dark-eyed boy. He was named Richard after his father. A
week later Edith went to Groton for Quentin's confirmation, and on
the twenty-fifth moved back to "lovely and peaceful" Sagamore
Hill.[27]

In April she began to read Theodore's series of articles in *Scribner's,*
entitled *A Hunter-Naturalist in the Brazilian Wilderness.* Thoughts of the
dangers the expedition faced were with her constantly. Only the
beauty of the singing in Gluck's opera *Orfeo* succeeded in distracting
her. "I felt that South America did not exist," she wrote Bamie, "and
I was 'only a little bit of string' after all, and nothing mattered
much."[28]

Kermit sailed directly from Brazil to Lisbon, and then traveled on
to Madrid, where Belle was living with her parents in the American
Embassy. The couple planned to be married in June. Theodore took
ship for New York, arriving on May 19. Edith, Ted and Archie put
out in a tugboat hired by Cousin Emlen, and met him at quarantine.
It was a subdued homecoming: there were no crowds, no welcoming
committees, no parade, as there had been in 1910. The family went
directly to Sagamore Hill, where Ethel, Dick, and the new grandson
were waiting.

Theodore looked well; his emaciation actually became him. Only
the day before he had suffered a recurrence of chills and fever, but
seemed to have shrugged it off. Edith thought that her husband
seemed "younger for every pound he has lost—a year a pound, I

should say."[29] A few days later she wrote Kermit: "I am doing my best to keep his wonderful figure." If by this she implied that he was now going to settle down under her motherly wing, she was mistaken. A mere forty-eight hours after arriving home, Theodore wrote one of his perennial "Personal and Private" letters to General Francis Vinton Greene, saying that "in case of a serious war" with Mexico he would like to raise a division of cavalry, "such as I had in the Spanish War."[30]

On May 26 Theodore went to Washington to give a lecture to the National Geographic Society about Brazil. Ambassador Spring-Rice was there, and cabled Edith: "I don't think I ever saw or heard him in better form!" The former President sailed for Europe and Kermit's wedding on May 30, accompanied by Alice and Cousin Philip Roosevelt, who was to be best man. "I feel sadly that I shall not be with you on the 11th," Edith apologized to her son, "but it just was not possible." To Ruth Lee she vaguely explained, "Things went so badly here last summer when I was away."[31]

The reason for her not going is obscure. She was not feeling strong physically, after her arduous tour of South America. Kermit's surprise engagement, followed by the death of Margaret, and Theodore's long worrying absence, had also left her in a frail emotional state. Analysis of the evidence available, from thyroid pills to frequent depressions, indicates that Edith Roosevelt, in her fifty-third year, was undergoing menopause.

A fragment of a letter from Theodore describing Kermit's wedding has survived:

> DARLING EDIE
>
> . . . Kermit . . . is very well indeed, and very good-looking; and he and Belle are the dearest engaged *[sic]* couple imaginable. I never saw two people more in love with one another; and she is a dear. I am very fond of her; and how proud I am of Kermit! I like the Ambassador, and Mrs. Willard is so pretty, and with such nice manners—Richmond style, and very pleasant, altho of course tired and rather overcome . . .
>
> On Tuesday we went out in motors a couple of hours to the country palace of the King and Queen and took lunch with them, and it was charming; I like the Queen,

and genuinely admire and respect the King; he is also
very amusing, and had been just as much entertained as
I was by the "wake" of King Edward . . . We went to
the Escorial on the way back.

Wednesday was the Civil Marriage; simple, and
rather impressive. Belle and Kermit were so dear!—I
believe she will be his sweetheart almost, but not
entirely, as you are mine. One of the two witnesses was a
very good fellow, the Duke of Alva; it is curious to think
of the whirligig of time, and the terror of madness with
which my Dutch (and doubtless your Huguenot) ancestors three centuries and a half ago regarded his great
and cruel forbear . . . Well, I believe that Kermit and
Belle have as good chance of happiness as any two lovers
can have.

Your lover!T.R.[32]

Just four days later, on June 28, 1914, came news of the
assassination in Sarajevo of the Archduke Francis Ferdinand, heir to
the thrones of Austria and Hungary. The act had no more significance for Edith than for any other American woman at first, and she
did not mention it in her diary or any surviving letters. Yet by August
4, Germany had declared war on Russia, France and Belgium, and in
retaliation England declared war on Kaiser Wilhelm. Before peace
was restored, the world as Edith Kermit Roosevelt knew it would be
irrevocably changed.

Thirty

"They have all gone away from the house on the hill."
—Edith Kermit Roosevelt
quoting Edwin Arlington Robinson[1]

Exploration, big-game hunting, foreign travel, authorship, a happy domestic life—none of these compensated Theodore Roosevelt for loss of power. He would not rest until he was again able to implement his views, organize and control. Edith had seen this after the return from Africa in 1910, when politicians flocked to Sagamore Hill looking for a presidential candidate. Now in the early summer of 1914 she saw it again: the only difference was that this time the politicians were merely seeking a New York State gubernatorial candidate.

For a few weeks Theodore toyed with the idea of running on the Progressive ticket. But to Edith's relief a laryngologist pointed out that his larynx had been so weakened by jungle fever it could not withstand the strain of hundreds of open-air speeches. Confirming this diagnosis on June 27, Dr. Lambert ordered him to rest for four months. Theodore agreed not to run for Governor, but the "rest" lasted precisely two days. On June 29, Theodore resigned his five-year association with the *Outlook*, so as to "take a more or less active part in trying to secure . . . the triumph of those principles embodied in the progressive platform of 1912."[2] Once again he took to the speaking trail, campaigning for Progressive Party candidates in fifteen states, though he realized it was for a hopeless cause.

In November the party suffered a resounding defeat both in New York State and in the nation. Theodore saw in it the party's final death rattle. "They are way ahead of the country as a whole in morality, and the country will need too long a time to catch up with them," he said sadly. "It will be, from the selfish standpoint, a great relief to me personally when and if they do disband. But it is rather pathetic for the remnant who stood fast."[3]

The following month he signed a three-year contract with *Metropolitan Magazine* for an annual salary of $25,000. On its termination in 1917 he hoped to retire, for by then Quentin would be almost twenty-one, and all the other children established in their own careers.

No vacation in the sun relieved the gray winter of 1914–15, with its gloomy news from Europe, so Edith went frequently to town for uplifting operas and concerts. She saw *Il Trovatore, Parsifal, Siegfried, Manon Lescaut,* and heard the great Russian pianist Josef Hofmann. No amount of spiritual satisfaction, however, could compensate for the physical ravages of menopause. On April 14, she entered the Roosevelt Hospital for "a necessary operation."[4]

During her three weeks there Theodore was the successful defendant in a libel suit brought against him by New York State Republican boss William Barnes, whom in 1914 he had publicly accused of corruption. The case cost Theodore $42,000 in legal fees and other expenses. It was worth it, for the battle, any battle, had a salutary effect on his general well-being. "I have never seen Theodore look better," Edith wrote Emily. "He bubbles over with good spirits and I do my best to pant and puff after him."[5] Even a broken rib (the result of his horse plunging off before his foot was firmly in the stirrup) failed to dampen his verve. It was stimulated afresh by the prospect of yet another "bully fight"—as it turned out, the greatest and most tragic of his career.

In the early months of the war in Europe, Theodore had given patriotic lip service to President Wilson's policy of American neutrality, despite strong private sympathy for the Allies. But effective British propaganda about German atrocities (and French

propaganda which Edith read in translation in the London *Mail*),
plus the loss of a thousand American lives when a U-boat sank the
S.S. *Lusitania* on May 7, 1915, and a growing feeling that the people of
the United States sympathized with the Allies, led Theodore to voice
publicly his fears of the danger of an upset in the European balance of
power.

In July he wrote a former Rough Rider saying that in the event of
being drawn into "this European war" he would like to raise a
cavalry division, which, he assured Arthur Lee, could be trained and
shipped over in ninety days.[6]

Through the pages of *Metropolitan Magazine* he began weekly
warnings to his countrymen of the world-wide threat to democracy
when people were not prepared to fight for it. This series of articles
was published in book form in February 1916 under the title *Fear God
and Take Your Own Part*. The phrase, suggested by Edith, was taken
from George Borrow's popular book *Romany Rye*.

Other influential men took up the battle cry, and began to practice
what Roosevelt preached. Early in 1915 General Leonard Wood
established a military training camp for volunteer citizens at Plattsburg, New York. Ted, Archie and Quentin immediately enrolled, and
their father promised to come upstate and address the cadets. During
this first summer at the camp, Ted became a Company First
Lieutenant, Archie a Battalion Second Lieutenant, and Quentin, still
only seventeen, received a certificate stating that with more age and
experience he, too, would make an excellent officer.

Sagamore Hill once more became a mecca for all kinds of war-
favoring political and military advisers and consultants. "He likes the
house full of Tom, Dick and Harry," Edith complained to Kermit,
"and I can't quite keep up with the pace . . ."[7]

Quentin entered Harvard on September 25. Three days later came
unexpected news of the death of Nannie Lodge from heart disease.
The shock left Edith limp. She left next morning for the funeral in
Boston, and found Cabot inconsolable. Nannie had been not only his
closest companion, but his surest critic. "If I have been of any use in
the world," he mourned, "to her I owe it."[8]

The presidential election of 1916, looming against the lurid
backdrop of possible involvement in the war in Europe, began to
throw its shadow fully a year in advance. Political power groups all

over the country sprang up, restlessly intriguing for and against the pacifist President. By now Theodore had conceived a dislike of Wilson bordering on hatred. He could not understand how a man of such supposedly high moral principles could be content with merely registering diplomatic protests against German totalitarianism. After the President's stately note deploring the sinking of the *Lusitania,* Theodore sarcastically asked Alice, "Did you notice what its serial number was? I fear I have lost track myself; but I am inclined to think it is No. 11,765, Series B."[9]

To escape the "boiling political cauldron" with which they found themselves "wholly out of sympathy," Edith and Theodore took a six-week vacation in the Caribbean that winter. They left in mid-February 1916, and were royally entertained on most of the islands between St. Thomas and Trinidad. In Guadeloupe, after dinner with the Governor, "all the population" turned out at midnight to escort them to their boat, the women in bandanas and flounced frocks dancing to a band, and the men shouting, *"Vive Roosevelt!"*[10]

Kermit (now back in South America, and working for the City National Bank) became a father for the first time while they were away. It was a boy, baptized Kermit, but promptly nicknamed "Kim."

By the spring of 1916, Theodore Roosevelt's concern that America lacked sufficient trained men and equipment to counter German belligerency finally communicated itself to large numbers of like-minded countrymen. The result was that Military Preparedness Parades were organized in various cities, including New York. Thousands of individuals and hundreds of groups were invited to take part in a day-long march up Fifth Avenue on May 13. Ted encouraged his wife to raise a battalion of twelve hundred women, who assembled at dusk behind an enormous banner with "INDEPENDENT PATRIOTIC WOMEN OF AMERICA" emblazoned in gold letters. Edith, acting completely contrary to character, took her place in the procession wearing the required white dress and carrying a lantern.[11]

On the same day a four-page advertisement appeared in *The Saturday Evening Post* entitled "Why Roosevelt Would be Our Best Guarantee of Peace." This was one of many public attempts that spring to encourage Theodore to run for President in the November elections. But while there was growing public sentiment for the policies Roosevelt had propounded for the past fifteen months, Theodore knew "it would be utter folly" to nominate him "unless the country was in heroic mood." He therefore declined any Progressive overtures, and encouraged his followers to support the Republican nominees, Charles Evans Hughes and Charles W. Fairbanks, believing that the defeat of Wilson was the paramount need. For all that, he did not have much time for Hughes, whom he called "the Bearded Lady." He told a reporter, "If Judge Hughes is elected I shall be out of it . . . I shall ask nothing from him and will recommend nobody. He will not ask my advice. So I will just be an elderly, literary gentleman of quiet tastes and an interesting group of grandchildren."[12]

Archie and Quentin returned to Plattsburg in the summer of 1916—the former with more enthusiasm than the latter—and numerous grandchildren filled the places they had once held at Sagamore Hill. Theodore amused young Richard Derby by performing the "Dance of Old Man Kangaroo," tried in vain to break baby Ted's habit of putting salt into "Grandpa's soup" (his large mug of morning coffee), and kept picking up little Gracie to cuddle whenever her nurse turned her back.

This peaceful idyll did not last long. In the fall Theodore was off again campaigning for Hughes in a grand sweep of the country. From Phoenix, Arizona, he wrote his "Darling true-love" that his voice was holding out, and that the trip had been "successful enough," but he doubted whether he had been able to "change any votes." Two weeks later his fears were confirmed. Woodrow Wilson defeated Hughes by twenty-three electoral and 594,188 popular votes. It was "a sad blow" for Edith. "Every morning I wake with the feeling of something wrong, and then realize that another four years must pass with this vile and hypocritical charlatan at the head of our Nation." The fact that Corinne's son Theodore Douglas Robinson was elected New York State Senator was a small consolation.[13] Since leaving the White House, Theodore Roosevelt had campaigned in, and lost, no fewer than four consecutive elections.

In early January 1917, Edith and Theodore packed six cases of presidential papers and shipped them to the Library of Congress,

"You have made the real happiness of my life."
Edith and Theodore in 1916.

with the proviso that scholars must seek special permission to see them until after Theodore's death. The consignment was followed by his hasty note: "The Lord only knows where the key is. Break the cases open, and start to work on them!"[14]

At the end of the month, President Wilson severed diplomatic relations with the Kaiser after being served notice by the German Ambassador that all neutral shipping carrying contraband munitions to the Allies would be destroyed. This action brought an inevitable reminder to the Secretary of War that Theodore Roosevelt wished "to raise a Division of Infantry, with a divisional brigade of cavalry in the event of war."[15] A few days later Edith and Theodore canceled an arranged winter vacation in Jamaica, and scrapped plans for a six- to eight-month field trip to Polynesia they had intended to begin later in the year under the auspices of the American Museum of Natural History.

Fatal U-boat attacks that spring upon three American ships carrying contraband cargo finally galvanized President Wilson to call for action "to make the world safe for democracy." Congress responded on April 6, 1917, by passing a War Bill. Four days after this Theodore Roosevelt called at the White House and formally requested presidential permission to take a division to Europe. The hour-long meeting was surprisingly cordial. Wilson even admitted afterward that he had been charmed by Theodore's personality. "He is a great big boy," he said. "There is a sweetness about him that is very compelling."[16]

All the same, the answer was no. White House opinion was that the former President's military experience was too brief, and too dated. A subsequent request from Clemenceau to have Roosevelt come to France to heighten the morale of the fighting men still failed to sway Wilson. The President concurred with the opinion of General John Pershing, Commander of the American Expeditionary Force, that Roosevelt was not sufficiently trained, nor in sound enough health, to withstand the rigors of modern trench warfare. But no argument would ever convince Theodore Roosevelt that Woodrow Wilson had refused him for other than political reasons.

Despairingly, he now diverted all his energy to the enlistment of his four sons. He asked General Pershing to accept Ted and Archie as privates, if they could not win commissions as officers, rather than let them languish at Plattsburg for a third summer. Quentin, with his mechanical and romantic bent, dreamed of entering the war as an airman. His father managed to engineer a place for him at the Mineola airdrome on Long Island. This was not easy, since Quentin had bad eyes and a chronically wrenched back, acquired in Arizona when a pack horse rolled over on him.[17] Theodore also urged Arthur Lee to use his influence in obtaining for Kermit (who was largely untrained) a position in the manpower-hungry British Army. "It is of course, asking a favor," he explained to Cecil Spring-Rice, "but the favor is that the boy shall have the chance to serve, and if necessary be killed in serving."[18]

On April 14, 1917, Archie married Grace Lockwood, a spirited dark-haired girl, at Emmanuel Church, Boston. Quentin was best man. "Choir and all beautifully planned," Edith noted tersely in her diary. There was very little of the usual gaiety attending family weddings, though everyone tried to look cheerful.[19] A certain urgency and worry over the future hung in the air. Edith could not know, but might have sensed, that this was the last time she would ever see all her family together.

By summer the process of attrition was already under way. In mid-July Ted and Archie signed up as officers under Pershing, and Kermit secured a staff position with the British Force in Meso-potamia. Quentin, who quickly proved himself to be a born aviator, prepared to follow on July 23. A week before leaving, he arrived for dinner at Sagamore Hill, bringing with him Flora Payne Whitney, the slender, dark-haired twenty-year-old daughter of Harry and Gertrude Vanderbilt Whitney. The couple were secretly engaged, and Quentin hoped that "Foufie" would be able to join him in Europe later, so they could marry there. Edith and Theodore, although kept in the dark about this, must surely have felt the seriousness of their son's relationship and weighed the pros and cons. The Whitneys had amassed an immense fortune from oil, tobacco and real estate. They belonged to "the out-door sport wing of the smart set" which Theodore considered "kindly" but "self-ab-sorbed."[20] Edith, who disliked the polo-playing, horse-racing type that Harry Payne Whitney personified, was relieved to find that Flora was also out of sympathy with that flashy world, and preferred the more modest one that the Roosevelts inhabited.

On Quentin's last night at home, Edith went upstairs as usual to tuck him in. To her he was always "the baby," and together they still enjoyed reading fairy tales. The following morning she and Theodore went in to New York City to see him off. Flora, who had sprinkled Quentin's uniform with salt water for luck, arrived at the Fourteenth Street dock separately on the Whitney yacht.

Quentin's sailing was delayed, so to cut short the agony of parting, Edith and Theodore said goodbye to him (she hiding in his cabin a paper bundle containing a homemade loaf, a small knife and some chocolate). Then they left the young couple to enjoy the remaining time alone.[21]

A few days later, from Newfoundland, came Quentin's account of his last few hours in America:

> Monday after I left you, Fouf and I had lunch and then hoofled down to the boat. Of course it didn't go at two not till nearly three, so she and I sat on a bale of hides and waited until it was almost time for the boat to go. Then I packed her off for I don't think she could have stood watching the boat pull out. She was wonderfully brave, and kept herself in. I don't know how she did, for I don't mind confessing I felt pretty down myself, when I saw the Statue of Liberty and the New York sky-line dropping below the horizon. Still, I'll be back sometime within a year, I've a hunch, and anyway, I'm gone now, and there's no use objecting.[22]

And so silence and loneliness descended on the mansion overlooking Oyster Bay. "'They have all gone away from the house on the hill,'" Edith wrote sadly, "but it is all quite right and best."[23]

Thirty-One

Only those are fit to live who do not fear to die; and none are fit to die who have shrunk from the joy of life. Both life and death are parts of the same Great Adventure.

—Theodore Roosevelt[1]

Following a custom for families with sons at the front, the Roosevelts hoisted a service flag at Sagamore Hill with four stars on it.

Awareness of the war and all it might mean was spreading, and Americans other than armament manufacturers soon found ways of profiteering. One advertisement that appeared in a local newspaper about this time greatly amused Edith:

MEN ATTENTION!
You are going to the front. Have you made arrangements to have your home defended during your absence? I make a specialty of defending homes during the duration of the war. I guarantee to keep the Hun from your threshold or will make no charges. My terms are as follows:

To defending one home and one wife $25 per month

To defending one home and one dearly beloved wife
                                          $40 per month
To defending one home and one dearly beloved wife
      and one child of either sex $50 per month
An additional charge of $10 per month for each child.
Reduced charges to Rooseveltian families.
Telephone Westbury 139

J. C. Cooley
Maple Avenue
Westbury, L.I.[2]

In the fall of 1917 Theodore traveled the country exhorting young men to volunteer and fight the German menace. Now that his three-year contract with *Metropolitan Magazine* was coming to an end, he began to spread his views in the columns of the *Kansas City Star* for an annual salary of $25,000. In addition he still contributed a short monthly editorial to the *Metropolitan* for an extra stipend of $5,000. These sums, combined with his and Edith's private incomes, made him a rather wealthy man, but he explained that the money would be useful for launching Archie and Quentin in their chosen careers after they came home.[3]

Edith, in an attempt to keep her mind off war, began to learn typing. Theodore laughed until he cried at one of her early efforts— "the spelling, the repetition of letters, the use of capitals, the telescoping of words, and a genial aspect of exhilaration make it a document of priceless worth."[4]

The typing was soon abandoned. Nothing seemed to divert her mind or raise her spirits after the boys sailed; she identified too strongly with the wives who were left behind. It was worse for Belle than for herself, she told Kermit in a moment of deep pessimism, "for my life is over, and I am tired of my old body anyway, and I shall be glad to get rid of it."[5]

Flora came frequently to Sagamore Hill to be with her prospective parents-in-law—so often, indeed, that they soon found out about her secret engagement to Quentin. "I have just returned from spending the afternoon at your place," she wrote her fiancé, "—and how I loved it and hated to leave to come home to a wild house party and an unsympathetic family."[6]

In spite of Edith's good intentions to keep her husband's waistline to post-Brazil proportions, he was, by the fall of 1917, fatter than ever before. Since the early days of their marriage Theodore had been a compulsive overeater. Upon leaving Harvard his weight had been a mere 125 pounds; by the time he entered the White House it had soared to the 200-pound mark—far too heavy for a man only five feet eight inches tall. Now his once-firm muscles had turned increasingly to fat. At Sagamore Hill he was always among the first to appear when the elephant-tusk gong sounded for meals. His breakfasts set the tone of the day, consisting of huge dishes of fruit, fried liver, bacon and eggs, hominy grits with salt and butter, Southern style, and quantities of white bread. He was wont to put so much cream on his peaches and strawberries that it ran through the holes encircling the plate, and he would look up furtively to see if Edith had noticed. Ted once saw him eat a dozen fried eggs, followed by two glasses of milk and four oranges. For stimulation he relied chiefly on coffee, preferring a Huntington and Dorn grind specially ordered from New York. He served himself with great formality, pouring the brew into a huge cup, lacing it liberally with cream and sugar, and taking evident pleasure in each lusty gulp.

Until about 1914 Edith had no objection to these gargantuan eating habits: her typically Victorian theory was that a man who worked as hard with his brains as Theodore did needed plenty of nourishment. But now she could see that the extra poundage was affecting his health. So, with wifely encouragement, Theodore decided to enroll for a two-week diet-and-exercise course at a camp in Stamford, Connecticut, run by Jack Cooper, a former prize fighter. The boxer found Theodore thirty-five pounds overweight (more like eighty-five pounds by modern standards) and suffering from high blood pressure. His heart and lungs seemed sound. Accordingly Cooper devised a regimen in which the Colonel would hike three miles before breakfast, have a massage, and then perform several hours of exercises under the supervision of professional instructors. These men were trained athletes, "touching the underworld on one side, and gilded youth and frayed gilded age on the other." Cooper marveled at Theodore's appetite: "a dragoon would envy it," he said. Since his client was not prepared to eat less, Cooper registered only a three- or four-inch waist reduction at the end of the course. On

October 22, Theodore arrived home very tired, and not looking particularly improved, Edith thought. "I fear it was too much of a strain on his nerves," she remarked. "I had hoped that since he felt that he could do it, it would be the right thing."[7]

Dick Derby sailed for Europe on November 12 to join the American Medical Corps. To console Ethel, and to show public approval of Flora's new place in the family, Edith and Theodore took both young women to Canada on a speaking tour at the end of the month. From Hamilton Flora wrote a letter to Quentin saying she was terrified all the time Mr. Roosevelt was making a speech. She begged her fiancé, "Please do not go into politics." Evidently the girl, like Edith, tended to think of Quentin as the reincarnation of his father.[8]

Quentin's reply, if any, appears not to have survived. Letters from him to anyone that fall were a rare commodity. Edith retaliated by not writing to him. Theodore, as "a hardened and wary old father," advised his errant son that if he wanted to keep Flora he had better write interesting love letters "at least three times a week."[9]

As it happened, Quentin had a valid excuse: pneumonia. Luckily he was being nursed in Paris by none other than his sister-in-law, Eleanor, a member of the Y.M.C.A. service canteen.

December was bitterly cold that year at Sagamore Hill, and the "bird cage" of a house was hard to heat. But logs kept the Christmas hearth warm for those few members of the family who could still sit around it. Ethel was there with Richard and her irresistible six-month old baby, Edith, who "smiles and laughs and crows and waves her little arms and legs and is most alluring," Theodore told Dick.[10]

The Longworths also made an appearance. Nick had at last been reelected to Congress and was "doing exceedingly well," the Colonel wrote Kermit. "As for Sister, she has more political sense than almost anyone I know, and I thoroly enjoy talking matters over with her."[11] Alice kept her ear to the ground in Washington, and passed all inside information on to her father.

It was a rare moment of real communication between father and daughter. Years later Alice would fondly remember him that Christmas, hunched over his book-piled desk and reviewing Osborn's *The Origin and Evolution of Life* as a fire in the North Room blazed.

Christmas did not seem like Christmas with so many of the family away, but they managed to drum up a certain amount of jollity over roast home-reared pig. "We don't buy pork," Theodore explained to Ted, "as [Herbert] Hoover [Chairman of the American Relief Commission] doesn't approve, but we feel at liberty to eat what we raise."[12]

Edith spent a gloomy four days in Washington toward the end of January 1918. Most of her friends there had died or moved away. Those who remained were so old that "she felt as if she were revisiting a scene from which all she knew had vanished."[13] She stayed with Alice, and together they visited Franklin Delano Roosevelt, now Assistant Secretary of the Navy, lunched with Henry Adams (almost eighty and looking shrunken), and heard Senator George E. Chamberlain, one of the few Democrat preparedness leaders, make an address in Congress. On the way back she motored to Catonsville, Maryland, for three days with her White House secretary Belle Hagner, who had married a Baltimore businessman.

Less than a week after she returned home Theodore underwent an operation in Roosevelt Hospital for yet another serious abscess, this time in his buttock, and had treatment for two more in his ears. The surgery was successful, but within twenty-four hours a painful infection developed in his left inner ear, which was to leave him permanently deaf on that side. For three days he lay in a critical condition. Edith left his side only to go to church.

Recovery was slow, and three weeks passed before he could be moved to Sagamore Hill.

It continued to be a sad winter—the saddest they had ever spent together, although a worse was yet to come. On February 14, the thirty-fourth anniversary of Alice Lee's death, Cecil Spring-Rice died. He had recently lost his ambassadorship in Washington to Lord Reading, who was purportedly better versed in European war conditions. The suddenness of this removal, unaccompanied by any announcement of promotion, had stunned the sensitive Springy. He had been in good health when he left the capital, and Henry Cabot Lodge, for one, was convinced that he had died of a broken heart. "We dearly loved Cecil," Theodore wrote Florence Spring-Rice. "He was our close friend for over thirty years . . . only a man of rare unselfishness, a man completely lacking in the vulgar ambition to keep in the public eye, could . . . have rendered the literally invaluable service that his country—and my country too,— needed." [14]

Edith had scarcely absorbed the shock of Spring-Rice's death when word came on March 27 of a stroke that had killed Henry Adams. In recent years the old historian had been unable to read or write, and was more than ready to quit a world with which he had long been out of sympathy. And so yet another of Edith's links with that long-ago Washington "when we were all young" snapped. Only one remained now—Henry Cabot Lodge.

Two pieces of good news, at least, relieved the misery of the winter. Belle Roosevelt gave birth to her second son, Joseph Willard, in January, and on February 18 Grace too had a son, Archibald, Jr. Edith and Theodore now had eight grandchildren, and sought increasing solace in their company as the loneliness of old age advanced upon them.

On Wednesday, March 13, the United Press telephoned Sagamore Hill that little Archie's father and namesake (newly promoted to captain) had been awarded the Croix de Guerre "under dramatic circumstances." Later news revealed that while leading a platoon toward the German lines he had been hit by flying shrapnel. His kneecap was shattered, and one arm broken so badly that its main nerve was severed. [15]

To honor his courage, Edith ordered a bottle of Grandfather Isaac Carow's old Madeira—the finest in New York State outside of the Vanderbilts', according to one professional opinion—to be brought up from the cellar. In company with Theodore, Ethel, and a visiting friend, she drank a toast to her gallant son. Then, Theodore wrote, "her eyes shining, her cheeks flushed as pretty as a picture, and as spirited as any heroine of romance, Edith dashed her glass on the floor, shivering it in pieces, saying, 'That glass shall never be drunk out of again.'" [16]

Proud as she was of the bravery of her sons in battle, Edith was equally solicitous of their emotional life. In March she even suggested to Quentin that before he left his French training camp for the front he should invite Flora to come over and marry him. On April 7 he replied: "Dearest Mother . . . I followed your advice . . . wrote Fouf telling her to come over if she possibly could . . . I know her family will kick, but I really don't think they've got any right to. Heaven knows we'll never know our minds any better than we do now."[17] Flora immediately began to prepare by taking shorthand and typing lessons, and applied for a passport to go to France, where she hoped to do useful work after marrying. Edith wanted to go with her to represent the Roosevelts at the ceremony, but the authorities refused both women permission.

At the end of May, Theodore was dining alone at the Blackstone Hotel in Chicago during a speaking tour of the Midwest, when a very large man with a walrus mustache entered the room. A sudden silence among the other diners caused Theodore to look up, directly into the eyes of William Howard Taft. Without hesitating, Roosevelt threw down his napkin, jumped to his feet, and put out his hand. Taft shook it firmly, and the two men slapped each other on the back. As the former Presidents sat down together, people in the restaurant cheered. They talked intently, and found themselves in agreement on how America should conduct herself in the war. Both remarked how poor a President Woodrow Wilson had turned out to be. By the end of this chance meeting, they were completely reconciled, and Theodore came away "happy as the proverbial lark."[18]

As the war lingered on, Edith came to resent her husband's absences more and more, and decided to try to make him "feel a responsibility about me for that will perhaps cut his flights by tying him to my apron strings." But after a lifetime of allowing him a very long tether, this was easier said than done. The only way to see more of Theodore was to travel with him. Consequently, in early June 1918, she accompanied him on a week-long tour of Illinois, Missouri, and Indiana. When they reached home on the sixteenth there was a telegram from Quentin, announcing that he had been ordered to active duty from Issoudon, where he had been impatiently serving as a flying instructor. "Moving out at last with Ham [Hamilton Coolidge] very glad love to all." It was followed shortly after by a letter to say that he had been transferred to Orly Airfield, near the front. His departure from Issoudon was tearful. As he passed the hangars where all the mechanics were lined up to say goodbye, a sergeant yelled out, "Let us know if you're captured and we'll come after you." A lump came to Quentin's throat. "It's nice to know," he wrote, "that your men have liked you."[19]

"He was sure a prince."
Quentin Roosevelt, top left.
His hand rests on the man who succeeded him as Flora Whitney's fiancé.

One motive behind Quentin's anxiety to see fire was the desire to emulate his three brothers, who had all distinguished themselves in battle, and who were not above taunting him over his involuntary sojourn in camp. Kermit, who had won the British Military Cross for bravery in Mesopotamia, was on his way to France to serve as Captain of Artillery in the American Army. Ted, a Lieutenant Colonel, had been gassed in the lungs and the eyes to the point of blindness at Cantigny. He nevertheless continued to lead his battalion through heavy bombardment, and refused to be evacuated. For this, and for organizing another successful raid, he was awarded the Silver Star and the Croix de Guerre.[20]

Early in July 1918 Theodore Roosevelt requested that his still unspent Nobel Prize money of forty thousand dollars (the proposed industrial peace foundation had never materialized) be returned to him for redistribution to groups and individuals aiding the war effort. Congress complied, and the securities, which now amounted to $45,482.83, were divided into twenty-eight unequal parts. A sum of $6,900 went to the Red Cross, $5,000 to Eleanor and the Y.M.C.A., and $4,000 to the Jewish Welfare Board. Smaller sums of $500 each were given to families of wounded soldiers in countries around the globe, as well as in various American states. One thousand dollars went to Emily "for work in connection with the Italian Red Cross."[21] Emily had thought at the start of the war of returning to America and taking a cottage near Sagamore Hill. But she changed her mind and began to work in Porto Maurizio, nursing wounded soldiers and victims of epidemical influenza.

Quentin had his first "dogfight" on July 5. "You get so excited," he told his mother, "that you forget everything except getting the other fellow, and trying to dodge the tracers, when they start streaking past you."[22] A few days later he downed his first Boche.

On Tuesday, July 16, news flashed round the world that Tsar Nicholas II, the Tsarina and their children had been murdered by the Bolsheviks, bringing to an end the Romanov dynasty in Russia. But a more cryptic and more personal message found its way to Sagamore Hill late that same afternoon.

Theodore was dictating to his secretary, Miss Josephine Stricker, when Phil Thompson, the Oyster Bay correspondent of Associated Press, appeared. He asked to show the Colonel a copy of a puzzling telegram from the front to the New York *Sun*. It read: "WATCH SAGAMORE HILL FOR—" That was all. The rest of the message was censored. Afraid that Edith might be within earshot, Theodore closed the door. "Something has happened to one of the boys."

It could not be Ted or Archie, since both were still recovering from their wounds; nor could it be Kermit, who had been delayed in reaching the front by a bout of malaria. That left Quentin. Lacking any definite information, there was little to do but wait for news bulletins. In the meantime, Theodore asked Thompson to say nothing to Mrs. Roosevelt.

The Colonel dressed for dinner as usual. Until bedtime he talked and read with Edith, as though everything were normal. Yet her maternal instinct seems to have suspected something, for there is a rare blank in her diary for the date.

Before breakfast next morning, July 17, Phil Thompson returned, bringing the first unofficial dispatch that Quentin had been shot down over enemy lines. Theodore took him out on the piazza, and paced up and down silently, struggling to calm himself. "But Mrs. Roosevelt!" he said finally. "How am I going to break it to her?" Presently he went in to see Edith. Thompson, who had asked for a statement of reaction, waited behind on the piazza. Thirty minutes passed. Then the Colonel reappeared, with the promised statement in his hand. It consisted of just one sentence: "Quentin's mother and I are very glad that he got to the front and had a chance to render some service to his country, and show the stuff that was in him before his fate befell him."[23]

With that he went into the library and began to dictate his day's mail, "his voice choking with emotion . . . and the tears streaming down his face." He did not stop until his desk was entirely cleared.[24]

At some point later in the day Edith sought out Phil Thompson on the piazza. Her eyes were red, but she appeared composed. "We must do everything we can to help him," she said. "The burden must not rest entirely on his shoulders." For her part, she could best survive by going about her daily business just as Theodore did. There was no point giving in to grief over the fact that Quentin had plummeted out of the sky to his death. She had always said, "You cannot bring up boys as eagles and expect them to turn out sparrows."[25] The following morning, July 18, she accompanied her husband to New York on the first stage of his journey to the Republican State Convention in Saratoga. Theodore had promised to give the keynote address, and no bereavement could deflect him from his commitment.

When he arrived in Saratoga later that day, and stepped onto the platform to make his speech, an old friend in the audience said that he had never seen a face that depicted such human agony.[26] Theodore began to read a prepared text, but halfway through he set the typescript aside, and spoke extemporaneously while the audience sat hushed.

> The finest, the bravest, the best of our young men have sprung eagerly forward to face death for the sake of a high ideal. . . . When these gallant boys, on the golden crest of life, gladly face death . . . shall not we who stay behind, who have not been found worthy of the great adventure . . . try to shape our lives so as to make this country a better place to live in . . . for the women who sent these men to battle and for the children who are to come after them?[27]

After he finished speaking newsmen and politicians gathered round and asked if he would run for Governor that fall. No, he told them, "my heart is wrapped up in my boys at the front." Privately to Corinne he admitted: "I have only one fight left in me, and I think I should reserve my strength in case I am needed in 1920."[28] Even *in extremis* the White House still beckoned him.

On July 20, a cable from President Wilson confirmed that Quentin had been killed by two shots through the head. German aviators buried him with full military honors because he had fought bravely, and "because he was the son of Colonel Roosevelt, whom they esteemed as one of the greatest Americans." The broken propeller and wheels from his plane were placed near a simple cross marking his grave in the village of Chaméry, a few miles west of Rheims. Here his body would remain. "Where the tree falls," said Theodore, "there let it lie."[29]

"Death is not a black unmentionable thing," Hamilton Coolidge, Quentin's closest friend, wrote to Edith. "I feel that dead people should be talked of just as though they were alive. . . . To me Quentin is just away somewhere. I know we shall see each other again and have a grand old 'hooshe' talking over everything . . . his personality or spirit are just as real and vivid as they ever were."[30] Before the war's end Ham himself was killed by a direct hit from an antiaircraft gun.

Countless other letters of condolence and praise found their way to Sagamore Hill, not all of them directly addressed to Edith and Theodore. Quentin's childhood antics as leader of the White House Gang were still fresh in the memory of millions of Americans, and almost overnight he became one of the war's most famous heroes. Inevitably the simplest words were the most poignant. "I wonder if his dad is anything like him," one Corporal wrote. "If he is I would vote for him . . . He was sure a prince." An Italian barber who had served with Quentin mourned: "He was afraid of nothing . . . the goodest kid I ever saw."[31]

On the same day that President Wilson confirmed Quentin's death, a cable came from Eleanor in Paris to say that Ted had been badly wounded in the leg. After this second blow Theodore wrote Kermit:

> Mother has been as wonderful as she always is in a great crisis. She has the heroic soul . . . she went for a couple of hours row with me out on the still, glassy water towards the sound; there was a little haze, and it all soothed her poor bruised and aching spirit; then we took a swim; and as we swam she spoke of the velvet touch of the water and turning to me smiled and said, "there is left the wind on the heath, brother!"[32]

Try as she might to be brave, Edith could not help seeing Quentin in every room at Sagamore Hill, and Ethel suggested she come to her summer place at Dark Harbor, Maine. Theodore decided to go, too, and they left on July 25. A completely broken Flora joined them in time for Edith's fifty-seventh birthday. Theodore's heart went out to the girl. "She is young, and time will mercifully heal her sorrow," he wrote, "but she has had her golden dream and it has proved only a dream. If only she could have married Quentin!" But the fact remained she had not; all she had to comfort her were memories of courtship and a handful of letters full of the uncertain optimism of youth going into battle: ". . . if I am not killed, there will be a time when I shall draw into New York again, and you will be there on the pier, just as you were when I left, and there will be no parting for us for a long time to come."[33]

Edith tried to keep occupied by reading and knitting and watching little Richard play with trains. She avoided going out on the water.

"A motor boat trip with the rush of the wind precludes all but thoughts." Time passed, but Theodore knew that it brought his wife little relief. "Mother," he wrote Kermit, "will carry the wound green to her grave." As for himself, he told Edith Wharton he could not write about his youngest son, "for I should break down."[34]

The Roosevelts returned to Sagamore Hill on August 10, and found Alice waiting for them, brightening the gloom of the otherwise empty house. It was "everything to have her here," Edith said. She needed all the emotional support she could get, for an agonizing task awaited her: reading Quentin's last batch of letters describing his final crowded hour.[35]

One afternoon a young man in khaki came to say goodbye to her. It was Archie's great friend and cousin Nicholas Roosevelt, about to leave for France. Half a century later he would recall in awe Edith's extraordinary strength as she faced him.

> She personified order, duty, and discipline. I have known no one more completely in command of herself. If she felt fear, she put it behind her. If she ever flinched she never showed it. Only [this] once did I see her upset, and then only for a moment . . . When she saw me in uniform her eyes filled with tears and she turned away. Then she put her hand on my arm and said: "I'm all right, Nick; I'm all right." And she was.[36]

Archie, invalided out of the Expeditionary Force, came back to the United States on September 5, 1918. Edith and Theodore drove to New York to meet him at the Langdon Hotel, and took him to the hospital where he had to report every day for treatment. He looked in better shape than either parent had dared to expect, but another operation on his leg was necessary to remove a piece of lodged shrapnel, and his left arm was still paralyzed. He was fated to suffer from stiffness and pain for the rest of his life.

That fall the Allied forces drove the Germans eastward across the Somme, the Aisne and the Meuse, whence they had come four years before. Ted returned to the First Division as Lieutenant Colonel in the waning days of the action, and Kermit joined him as Captain. Both men were at the front for the last three weeks' fighting of the war.[37]

Sagamore Hill was exceptionally beautiful during these autumn months, with its trees a blaze of color against the still, pale waters of the bay. At a picnic on Eel Creek beach Edith felt her soul at last begin to mend. "The sky was most lovely," she wrote Kermit, "with banks of dark clouds and glimpses of blue, and a thunder shower came, with a rainbow . . . As we walked across the little bridge we saw a fish hawk soar and then make his great plunge to get his supper . . ."[38]

They continued to walk and to row together through late October, when Owen Wister came to stay. "I remember watching the small boat moving outward with them into the placid bay, shining in warm sunlight," the novelist wrote.

> I followed it for a little while, and an over-mastering sadness rose suddenly in me. I turned and took the path away from the water.
>
> At table sometimes, and often in the great room, Roosevelt would fall from animation into silence. Once he came out of his silence and said:
>
> "When I went to South America, I had one Captain's job left in me; Now I am good only for a Major's."
>
> And upon another occasion, without reference to what we had been saying: "It doesn't matter what the rest is going to be. I have had fun the whole time."
>
> . . . While we were talking another time about our own politics after the war, Mrs. Roosevelt said: "If we should ever go back to the White House—which heaven forbid! . . ."
>
> They stood at their hall door as I drove off, stood watching, after their words bidding me to come again soon, she quiet beside him, he waving his hand; Quentin's father and mother, carrying on.[39]

Thirty-Two

The old lion is dead.

—Archibald Bulloch Roosevelt[1]

Two days after Owen Wister's departure from Sagamore Hill, Theodore Roosevelt turned sixty. He welcomed the anniversary, saying that "it somehow gave him the right to be titularly as old as he felt." He also hoped that Kermit, at the same age, would be "as much in love with Belle as I am with your mother, and will feel that you owe her as much as I owe your mother."[2]

As the crisp autumn days turned to wintry damp, Theodore began to suffer crippling attacks of rheumatism. Physical discomfort, aggravated by grief, ate away at his spirit. "Quentin's death shook him greatly," Edith told Kermit. "I can see how constantly he thinks of him and not the merry happy silly recollections which I have but sad thoughts of what Quentin would have counted for in the future."[3]

A perceptive acquaintance who saw the Colonel in those dark days noted for the first time that the "old exuberance" had gone "and the boy in him had died."[4]

On October 28 Theodore struggled in to New York City to make a speech to a packed Carnegie Hall audience in answer to Wilson's latest "gyrations," as Edith called them. The President's talk of peace with Germany without unconditional surrender was anathema to Roosevelt. After speaking for ninety minutes, Theodore paused to comment on the length of time, only to have the audience shout, "Go on." Edith, marveling at her husband's capacity to ignore his aching body, felt that the crowd was glad to have a leader to articulate their own thoughts.[5]

By early November, one of Theodore's feet was so swollen that he could not wear a shoe. Three doctors were summoned to Sagamore Hill, and all ordered him to bed. He disobeyed them on November 5 by hobbling out to vote in the Congressional elections, and afterward felt "wretchedly." But his gesture, matching that of millions of other Republican voters, was worthwhile. The G.O.P. won majorities in both House and Senate. "Wilson rebuked. Hurrah!" Edith wrote in her diary.

Winds of change were also blowing in Germany, where the death of Quentin Roosevelt was said to have affected the morale of the Kaiser's army. Ordinary soldiers complained that it was unjust that the son of a famous American statesman had been killed fighting for his country, while their own Emperor's six sons sat safely at home. On November 9, 1918, Wilhelm II abdicated and sought refuge in Holland.[6] The Armistice was signed on November 11. That same day Theodore returned to Roosevelt Hospital suffering from inflammatory rheumatism—a legacy of his Brazilian fevers and abscesses.

Almost uninterruptedly for the next forty-four nights Edith stayed in a corner room at the hospital separated from her husband only by a shared bathroom. During the daytime she had lunch with friends, or went to matinees and exhibitions, so that in the evening she would have something stimulating to tell Theodore. Otherwise she spent her time reading Shakespeare at his bedside. "Every line is familiar," she told Kermit as she finished *Macbeth,* "and yet ever new."[7]

On December 15 the rheumatism attacked Theodore's left arm so cruelly that his wrist had to be bound and put in a splint. Edith wished she could bear his pain. "It would be a sort of occupation for me," she said, "while there are many things which he wants to do and cannot."[8] Nevertheless the Colonel managed to dictate lengthy letters on a myriad of subjects to such old acquaintances as Rudyard Kipling, Arthur Lee, and Henry Cabot Lodge.

William Allen White called at the hospital one day to see

Theodore, only to be told he was "under the influence of a narcotic" and could not see anyone. The Kansas editor left a message with the bombshell news that General Leonard Wood was thinking of running for President in 1920, and that if Roosevelt had any thought of seeking the nomination himself he should let the party know at once. Roosevelt, indeed, had very definite thoughts, so much so that he sent not one but three messages to White's club—one via Dr. Lambert, one via a hospital official, and the third via Edith—summoning him back to the hospital. "It was so good of you to come again," Edith said sweetly on White's return.[9]

Inside the sick room Theodore told White, "Well, probably I shall have to get in this thing in June." He showed him a manuscript he had already written laying out his proposed campaign platform. This featured an eight-hour working day for the ordinary man, social insurance, and an old-age-pension scheme—a program uncannily similar to that Cousin Franklin would finally introduce some fourteen years later.

Another visitor was Senator Lodge, who came and stayed for two days expressing great suspicion of Wilson's idea of a League of Nations. But, surprisingly, Theodore approved of such an organization, so long as America remained militarily prepared to defend herself.

The waning days of the year brought Theodore no relief from his incessant pain and weakness. Roosevelt Hospital doctors were forced to tell him that there was very little more they could do, and that he must be prepared to spend much of the rest of his life in a wheelchair. The Colonel reacted, as always, pugnaciously. "All right!" he snapped, "I can work and live that way, too."[10]

Later, to a friend of his wife he said, "Do not sympathize with me. Have you ever known any man who has gotten as much out of life as I have? I have seen more than any other man. I have made the very *most* out of my life."

Corinne found her brother in philosophical mood, too. "No matter what comes," he told her, "I have kept the promise that I made to myself when I was twenty-one . . . that I would work *up to the hilt* until I was sixty, and I have done it."[11]

Plenty of fight still remained, especially when Woodrow Wilson's name was mentioned. Taking Margaret Chanler by the hand, Theodore said: "I seem pretty low now, but I shall get better. I cannot go without having done something to that old gray skunk in the White House." In the same vein he ruminated to a doctor, "If this left wrist were a little better I would like to be left alone in this room with our great and good President for about fifteen minutes, and then I would cheerfully be hung."[12]

On December 25, 1918, Dr. John H. Richards, the hospital's rheumatic specialist, allowed Theodore to go home. The patient was still weak from fever and anemia, and was suffering from vertigo—the result of inflammation in the inner ear. But Christmas at home could do him little harm, and perhaps some good. Because the inflammation in the ear affected his balance, the doctor took his arm as they left the elevator. "Don't do that," Theodore said, "I am not sick, and it will give the wrong impression." As the door opened he braced himself and walked steadily past curious onlookers toward the waiting car. Only Edith was allowed to walk beside him.[13]

Alice, Ethel, Archie and Grace were at Sagamore Hill to welcome him, and the Christmas table was laid. Theodore enjoyed watching little Edie Derby running around "exactly as if she was a small mechanical toy," but he soon tired, and was forced to spend the remainder of the afternoon resting.[14]

Each day that followed, he had breakfast in bed, came downstairs for lunch, and afterward lay on the library sofa, reading and dictating letters. "I hope to see you all home as soon as possible," he wrote Ted, who was still on active duty in Europe. "I do not believe in our undertaking a general and indefinite policing of European squabbles."[15]

On December 29 and 30, Edith took Theodore for an hour's drive. Though stiff in the joints, he seemed otherwise better. But next day he was "not as well," and rainy weather on New Year's Day 1919 brought back severe pain in his leg and hand. He began to spend most of his time upstairs, lying on the sofa in the old nursery, which faced south and was the warmest room in the house. On Friday, January 3, Dr. Richards came out and recommended a trained nurse to help Edith.

Josh Hartwell, a young doctor who treated the Whitney family, "stiffened her up," and gave a second opinion. He said that Theodore would eventually recover—but not as soon as Dr. Richards seemed to think.[16]

"The boy in him had died."
Theodore Roosevelt in 1918: the last photograph.

Sunday, the fifth, was still sunny and not too cold. Theodore enjoyed a visit from Flora and dictated a letter to Kermit. He worked for a total of eleven hours, correcting the proof of a *Metropolitan Magazine* article, and finishing an editorial for the *Kansas City Star*.[17] In the latter he said that the League of Nations was desirable, but only if based on an agreement between present allies. Other nations should be admitted as their conduct warranted.

Several friends stopped by, but Theodore was not able to see them. Alfred Noyes, the well-known English poet, called. Edith went downstairs and served him tea, at the same time delivering a message from her husband: "Tell him I'm a pacifist, but I do believe in common sense."[18]

As it grew dusk, Theodore fell to reading and gazing out of his window. He "watched the dancing of waves, and spoke of the happiness of being home, and made little plans" for Edith. As she rose from her game of solitaire, he suddenly looked up from his book and said, "I wonder if you will ever know how I love Sagamore Hill." All in all, it had been, Edith concluded, a "happy and wonderful day."[19]

At about ten o'clock, Theodore was still lying on the nursery sofa, and asked Edith to help him sit up. He felt as if his heart or breathing were about to stop. "I know it is not going to happen," he said, not wanting to alarm her, "but it is such a strange feeling."[20] She gave him sal volatile, and called the nurse, who said his pulse was good. Nevertheless, Edith sent for a local doctor, who confirmed that pulse and heart were excellent. Theodore's hand was also less painful, but the nurse gave a hypo of morphine so that he would not be awakened during the night.

James Amos, his old White House valet, arrived at Sagamore Hill to assist with the night watch. At about twelve o'clock he helped Theodore to bed, and then put out the light and settled down in front of the fire. At 12:30 A.M. Edith went in to take a look at her husband. At two she reappeared. The patient "was lying on his side sleeping so comfortably" that she refrained from going "too near for fear of waking him." At four o'clock she was dozing in her own room when the nurse woke her. The Colonel had stopped breathing. Edith rushed to her husband's bedside. "Theodore, darling!" she called, leaning over him. But there was no reply. He seemed "just asleep, only he could not hear."[21]

It was January 6, the Feast of the Epiphany. Theodore Roosevelt had died from an embolism, "probably in the coronary artery." At his bedside table lay a last scribbled note reminding himself to see Will Hays, the Republican National Committee Chairman, to go to Washington for ten days to see the Senate and the House and prevent a split on domestic policies.

"We can only know," Edith wrote Ted, "that death had no sting for dear Father. I think he had made up his mind that he would have to suffer for some time to come and with his high courage had adjusted himself to bear it."

Going through the motions, she telephoned Corinne at 6 A.M., and in a "gentle and self-controlled voice, though vibrating with grief," told her sister-in-law the news.[22]

When Josephine Stricker arrived to deal with the Monday-morning mail, she was overwhelmed by the deluge of telegrams that were already arriving. Opening the middle side drawer of Theodore's desk to make room for some of them, she found "Cocky-locky—a little stone rooster—fast asleep in his seashell," which the Colonel had tucked away for one of his grandchildren.[23]

At midday, a friend from New York stopped by. He sensed that behind "the crying smile" with which Edith greeted him, "her heart was torn out of her roots." Late in the afternoon Corinne arrived, and she and Edith, two old friends of fifty-four years, "walked far and fast along the shore and woodlands" that Theodore had loved. Twilight had fallen by the time they returned, and airplanes were flying low around the house. "They must be planes from the camp where Quentin trained," said Edith, her voice breaking. "They have been sent as a guard of honor for his father."[24]

"The old lion is dead," Archie cabled his brothers in Germany. Ted replied:

> DICK SAILING HOME IMMEDIATELY. KERMIT AND I
> WILL STAY HERE FOR WE SUGGEST MOTHER MIGHT
> WISH TO COME OVER HERE WITH SISTER IMME-
> DIATELY TO SEE ABOUT QUENTIN'S GRAVE AND COM-
> MEMORATIVE TABLET. WE WOULD MEET THEM. WE
> ARE ALL TOGETHER.[25]

A letter from Kermit followed:

> DEAREST DARLING MOTHER,
>
> There's nothing in the world to say. I had been in to dine at Coblenz, and Ted was waiting when I got back, and we sat up the rest of the night and talked. We finally agreed about cabling you to come and arrange about Quentin's grave; and that Dick should go right home.
>
> Through my mind over and over there runs:
>
> *He scarce had need to doff his pride*
> *Or slough the dross of earth,*
> *E'en as he trod that day to God,*
> *So walked he from his birth*
> *In simpleness, and gentleness and honor, and clean mirth.*
>
> Father somehow seems very near, and as if he would never be far. I don't feel sorry for him; he wouldn't want it, that would be the last thing. There never was anyone like him, and there won't be. You're the only person I feel sorry for; for now you must walk in sad loneliness, for who has lost father, has lost all; but it isn't for long; man's life is but a span, as has been said throughout the centuries; for you it's probably even a shorter run than for me, but for none of us is it very long; and then we shall all be joined together on the other side of the last great adventure; and Quentin too will be waiting over there, with his same smile. It seems fearful for the country to be left without Father; but a sort of faith from I don't know where comes to me, that the "inscrutable design" would not take father away rashly or without premeditation. It is foolish to think of oneself, but you will know how the bottom has dropped out for me; at first it was complete, but then comes the realization that father could never really die, and that even though I can't bother him about every little decision, when a really vital one comes he will be there as unfailing as

ever. Oh my very dearest mother, a letter, or words, or
any other way of expression, is inexpressively futile; but
you know the depth of my sorrow for you; you know it,
and I can't tell it.

KERMIT[26]

Hundreds of other letters came. "The shock of the news is dazing,"
the historian W. R. Thayer wrote Edith. "Yet I see clearly even now
that America is going to appreciate him more and more, and to
understand him better, and I have no doubt that he will stand in
history as our greatest after Lincoln. Let me urge you to take some
consolation in realizing that *you* were indispensable to his full
development. He would have been less, but for you. We old friends
always knew this and we were silently grateful to you."[27]

Corinne heard from Edith Wharton, who was in France working
for the Allies. "When I write of your brother my heart chokes in my
throat and I can't go on. No one will ever know what his example and
his influence were to me."[28]

In the House of Representatives on February 2, a pale and tired
Henry Cabot Lodge made a ninety-minute speech—a miniature
biography of his dearest friend. When the Senator said, "One thing
that endeared Roosevelt to the popular heart was that he had no
secrets in his life—he kept nothing from the people because he had
nothing to hide," there was a spontaneous outbreak of applause. And
when he ended by quoting Bunyan's *Pilgrim's Progress*—"'So he
passed over, and all the trumpets sounded for him on the other
side,'" his voice broke, and he was unable to go on.[29]

Woodrow Wilson received the news of Theodore Roosevelt's death
in a European railway carriage. Reporters watched closely as he read
the telegram. A mixture of emotions crossed his face—surprise, pity,
then triumph.[30]

Theodore's funeral took place on Wednesday morning, January 8,
1919. His oak coffin stood draped with Rough Rider flags in the
North Room, and before the cortege moved off Quentin's favorite
prayer was read: "O Lord, protect us all the day long of this
troublous life, until the shadows lengthen and the evening comes, and
the busy world is hushed, the fever of life over, and our work done.

Then Lord in Thy mercy grant us a safe lodging and peace at the last, through Jesus Christ, our Lord."[31]

Edith, following widow's custom, stayed in the house with Christine Roosevelt and read the funeral service through, while some five hundred villagers and dignitaries attended the simple ceremony in Christ Church, Oyster Bay. There was no music and no eulogy. Only a few garlands and green stars left over from Christmas decorated the chancel.

Political friends and enemies from Theodore's thirty-seven-year career made their way to Youngs' Cemetery afterward. Among them was William Howard Taft. He stood at the snowy graveside, on the wooded hill overlooking the bay, and remained longer than anyone else, his head bowed, his face wracked with emotion, weeping profusely.

At the train station the mourners gathered on their way back to town. They talked, said one, "not in subdued tones, but freely," as Roosevelt himself had always done. They had never left this station before without feeling invigorated and inspired at having seen the Colonel. "Men told this story and that of his amazing vitality, his courage, his humor, his stupendous versatility, his astounding memory, his enticing way with children, his lovableness, his constant humaneness." It would be foolish, said someone, to think that he could ever *really* die.[32]

Edith Kermit Roosevelt by John Singer Sargent, 1921.

Early Widowhood
1919–1927

Thirty-Three

I languish out, not live the day,
Using no other exercise
But what I practise with mine eyes:
By which wet glasses I find out
How lazily time creeps about
To one that mourns . . .

—Henry King[1]

With the death of Theodore came the end of Edith's physical attachment to life. Her remaining twenty-nine years were to be lived out on a more spiritual plane. This did not mean that practical public or family matters were neglected: on the contrary, she entered into these with the same zest as before, taking on more rather than fewer responsibilities as the years went by.

Two days after her husband's funeral, Edith closed Sagamore Hill for the rest of the winter, and motored to Oldgate, Bamie's house in Farmington, Connecticut. She had to get away from her own home and its all-pervading associations with Theodore. Certainly Oldgate could not be more different from Sagamore. A white stone and yellow clapboard structure, it lay in a valley, at the end of an avenue of great Colonial elms. It was, as its name implied, a historic building, with some seventeenth-century rooms and a Wren water gate supposedly brought over by an English soldier during the Revolutionary War. But no sooner had the triple-paneled, brass-knockered door swung open than Edith was confronted by the sight of Bamie, almost completely crippled with arthritis, in a wheelchair—a painful reminder of what had been in store for Theodore had he lived. The likelihood of such a fate was constantly on his mind toward the end, and she rejoiced that he had escaped it.[2]

After six days in Farmington, comforting and being comforted by her sister-in-law, Edith went on to New York City, where, in spite of bureaucratic difficulties, she arranged a passport for herself and her maid to sail on February 5, 1919, for Europe.

Memories of Theodore pursued her as the S.S. *Lorraine* plowed east across the cold Atlantic. The sound of gulls reminded her of mornings when she awoke at Sagamore Hill and heard an unfamiliar note in the "early, early songs"; how she used to "just touch" her husband quietly, "and he was awake and told me." Reading alone in her cabin, she would remember quiet evenings in the library, and Theodore's endearing habit of coming up and saying, "A little bit of chocolate—broken in two." Over and over she turned in her mind the times she had spent with him, and rejoiced "that neither custom nor necessity parted us for longer than his life required: such happy rides and rows . . ."[3]

Ted, Kermit and Belle met Edith at Le Havre, and together they traveled to Paris, where Emily was waiting. Bob Bacon was also there to greet Edith, just as he had been nine years before during Theodore's triumphant tour of Europe. Bacon's opinion was that "the whole French nation would do anything" for Mrs. Roosevelt, because "they worshipped her husband."[4]

A severe headache over the weekend kept Edith from motoring to Quentin's grave at Chaméry until Tuesday, February 18. The sky was overcast, but rain held off as she made the ten-minute walk from the village to the hillside grave. In her arms she carried great bunches of white lilac, lilies of the field, violets and anemones, and Emily marveled at her tearless self-control as she knelt and recited the Lord's Prayer.

Since her son's body was to remain in France, Edith arranged with representatives of the ninety residents of Chaméry for a fountain to be erected to his memory at her expense. She wanted the monument to be both beautiful and useful and asked especially "that the bases of the pillars at each side be made broad enough for seats."[5]

Narcissus, violets and pink daisies were already in bloom on the Ligurian hills when Edith arrived at Villa Magna Quies the last week in February. She intended to spend the rest of the winter and early spring with Emily. Quickly she established a routine that would enable her "not to think." She stayed in bed until noon, read mailed copies of the *Daily News,* took postprandial walks up to the Cloisters, studied Italian, and played rummy with her sister, who had temporarily given up nursing to look after her. She ate well and slept soundly, lulled by "the sound of the waves and the wind in the palms and pines."[6]

But asleep or awake she could not lose the sense of loneliness at the core. Even though Theodore seemed "so very near," she began to long for Sagamore and the very associations she had run away from. She read prodigiously: the works of Anatole France, Edmund Gosse's *Father and Son,* and her favorite metaphysical poets. Again and again she meditated Henry King's *Exequy,* "To his Matchlesse never to be forgotten Friend," and quoted it in letters home. One passage in particular moved her: for the rest of her life tears would come into her eyes when she recited it to her grandchildren.[7]

> *Sleep on my Love in thy cold bed*
> *Never to be disquieted!*
> *My last good night! Thou wilt not wake*
> *Till I thy fate shall overtake*
> *.Till age, or grief, or sickness must*
> *Marry my body to that dust*
> *It so much loves; and fill the room*
> *My heart keeps empty in the Tomb.*
> *Stay for me there; I will not faile*
> *To meet theee in that hollow Vale.*
> *And think not much of my delay;*
> *I am already on the way,*
> *And follow thee with all the speed*
> *Desire can make, or sorrows breed.*
> *Each minute is a short degree,*
> *And ev'ry houre a step towards thee . . .*

In spite of a conscious effort by both sisters to curb their natural antipathy toward each other, life did not run smoothly. Edith, who strongly believed "families must hold together," tried to be appreciative of her sister's attentiveness, but their incompatibility was of too long standing, and the distance between them over the decades had become more than geographical. Though Emily was four years younger, her soft wavy hair was already gray, and her shoulders had

"The distance between them . . . had become more than geographical."
Emily Carow in nurse's uniform, Porto Maurizio, c. 1919.

broadened unbecomingly. She was worn down by solitude, nervous fatigue, and rheumatism, disliked being touched, and had a tendency to babble excitedly in "rather involved" English. When "really launched" she made her sister's head spin. Emily's neighbors offered little light relief: Edith wrote Belle that the Mediterranean climate "must be beyond reproach," for they "range in age from eighty to ninety."[8]

As March passed, Edith began to feel more rested, but deep down suspected that she would never again be whole. "I am dead, but no one but you dearest Corinne must know that," she wrote on the twenty-first, "and I am fighting hard to pull myself together and do for the family not only my part but also Theodore's."

A favorite phrase of her father-in-law's kept running through her head: "Live for the living." Her thoughts turned to the future of Sagamore Hill. The only justification for keeping it on was if it could remain a center for the family—*all* of "Father's children," she stressed to Ethel. ". . . I have felt no difference between the rest of you and Sister."[9]

Homesickness finally overcame Edith, and she sailed on the *Verdi* from Genoa on April 29. Every one of her children was at the dock to greet her when she arrived in New York on May 15.

The first summer at Sagamore Hill without Theodore was too painful for Edith to record. Her diary is blank for two months after her return, and is entered only fitfully for the rest of the year. Events worthy of notice in normal times were the birth of Theodora, Grace and Archie's second child, and the death of Mame on July 19. The passing of the old nurse dredged up yet more happy and painful memories.

On October 27, 1919, the sixty-first anniversary of Theodore's birth, Congress granted his widow a franking privilege. From now on Edith's envelopes need bear no postage stamp: her initials alone would suffice. This privilege pleased her, not because it saved her money, but because she looked on it as a tribute to Theodore Roosevelt. She was also the beneficiary of a five-thousand-dollar annual pension to presidential widows, just established by Andrew Carnegie. Edith disliked the idea of being a recipient of charity, but was reluctant to refuse in case Carnegie withdrew the funding, to the distress of other former First Ladies who might be in need of it. When the first payment came she "crossly" sent it to Mr. Cruikshank to invest.[10]

That fall Ted, following in his father's footsteps, finally took a plunge into politics. On November 4 he was elected to the New York State Assembly by the largest majority ever given to a candidate in Nassau County. The same day his fourth child was born—a son, whom he and Eleanor promptly named Quentin. There had been an agreement in the family that the next male grandchild to appear would be entitled to the honored name, and Belle Roosevelt, who was herself about to give birth, was slightly peeved, especially as Eleanor's baby was two months premature. Four days later, Belle produced her own third child—a girl, baptized Clochette.

In December came a trip to South America for Edith—the first of many winter vacations that she would take during her widowhood and would continue to take until she became too infirm to travel. This time she went with Kermit, who was going to be two months in Argentina, Chile and Brazil as the representative of the American Ship and Commerce Corporation. In Rio they stayed at the International Hotel, a rather pretentiously named little villa with a terrace, halfway up the mountainside behind the city. While Kermit held business meetings, his mother explored downtown Rio on street cars, lunched in local restaurants, browsed peacefully in the English Library, and luxuriated in the semitropical sunshine.

Having thus "laid in a good supply of heat," she was fortified for the remainder of winter, and returned to New York on January 17, 1920. February and March were arduous months. The snow was so relentless that no one was able to visit Sagamore Hill; Edith was as totally isolated in her high, drift-clogged home as a marooned mountaineer. She was forced to take the sleigh whenever the weather cleared enough for her to go down to the village.

After the thaw she gratefully renewed her acquaintance with her grandchildren. There was Kim, "the most engaging little Reynolds baby," Willard, "too fat and heavy and bad tempered," and Clochette, "lovely and always smiling." Ethel's little Richard was "handsome," and Edie "very affectionate and clever and full of fire," while Ted's three boys earned the highest praise of all: they were "very like mine." She wrote them many charming letters, full of fantasy and lively detail. "The cuckoo telephoned to me. He misses you *dreadfully* . . . I went to bathe and found a hornet's nest in the bath house. One hornet came and buzzed at me, but I stood just as still as still and he did not sting."[11]

That winter Flora Payne Whitney surprised all the Roosevelts by announcing her engagement to Rod Tower of Philadelphia. "None of us are very happy about it," Ethel wrote Emily, "though he is a nice boy. Poor child, I think she has just done it in desperation, she was so unhappy. He adores her, but otherwise is a perfectly commonplace youth, doing very well in a banking house downtown . . . But in a way I understand . . . Even with myself I sometimes just cannot believe that all this has come to us and that never again will we be happy, and young as we were. And that always there will be the pain beneath the laughter."[12]

Emily came to America for two months in the summer of 1920, and after she left again in early September Edith plunged into national politics, writing a ringing exhortation for *The Woman-Republican:*

> FROM THEODORE ROOSEVELT'S WIDOW
> Mrs. Theodore Roosevelt, Senior, has issued the following statement:
>
> The country's vital need is the election of the Republican candidates, Warren G. Harding and Calvin Coolidge. Only will the full measure of Americanism in the next administration be attained if the people shall declare for the party which holds true nationalism as its high ideal . . .

Then, in a realization that women were emerging as a political force, she went on:

> The time appeals most strongly to the manhood and the womanhood of America. To woman more than ever before because to her has come the perfected opportunity to make her influence weighty in behalf of the nation . . .
> Steadiness and staunchness of American purpose are

obligatory if we would first bring back our country to its stable place and then by strong endeavor do all that can be done for peace and general welfare in all lands.

EDITH KERMIT ROOSEVELT
Sagamore Hill, Sept. 13, 1920[13]

"Americanism," "nationalism," "duty," "staunchness"—it was Theodore all over again. In November, when women exercised their right to vote for the first time, there was a Republican landslide, and Ted was reelected to the State Assembly.

Then in December, after Ethel was safely delivered of her third child, a daughter, Sarah Alden, Edith prepared for a decade and more of new experiences which would vastly increase her awareness of the world outside Sagamore Hill.

Thirty-Four

"I have salt water around my heart," as the Breton saying goes.
—Edith Kermit Roosevelt[1]

In a travel book entitled *Cleared for Strange Ports,* which Edith published with Kermit, Belle, and Richard Derby in 1927, she wrote:

> Women who marry pass their best and happiest years in giving life and fostering it, meeting and facing the problems of the next generation and helping the universe to move, and those born with the wanderfoot are sometimes irked by the weight of the always beloved shackles. Then the birds fly, the nest is empty, and at the feet of the knitters in the sun lies the wide world.[2]

The "wide world" indeed opened out before her during the decade and a half after Theodore's death, a period in which she had many exotic adventures in all four quarters of the globe. Her first two trips as a widow—to Europe in 1919 and to South America the following winter—were anguished flights from the reality of grief and loneliness

449

rather than recreative travel. Not until January 25, 1921, when she boarded a little ship of the Trinidad Line, did she truly begin to benefit from her new experiences.

After brief stops in Grenada and Port of Spain, she joined a party in British Guiana which included William Beebe, the great zoologist and an old friend of Theodore's, for a voyage up the Demerara River to Kaieteur Falls. Edith had long wanted to see this wonder of nature. Squeezing herself and a few hastily packed belongings into a primitive boat with six traveling companions, ten paddlers, and a "captain," she glided off into the wilderness of South America. For five days the crowded craft sailed past high, densely wooded banks, broken only occasionally by narrow paths leading to mysterious destinations. At night Edith and the other voyagers slept in spartan shacks perched on poles near the water's edge. Through the floor boards came the snores of the paddlers, slung below in hammocks.

On the fifth day they reached the foot of the mountain, whose approach slope was locally known as "Fat Man's Misery." Edith had to clutch at exposed tree roots as she made the precipitous ascent to a broad sandstone plateau. Here was a vast expanse of wavering grass and flowering shrubs, through which flowed the Upper Essequibo River. The placid waters crossed this savannah and wound round a small rocky island thick with golden-leaved shrubs, before plunging through curtains of spray into a wooded gorge eight hundred feet below. With her ornithologist's eye, developed by Theodore, Edith spotted two colorful macaws flying over the falls, and later found swallows incredibly nesting under the very lip of the cataract, in the space between water and rock.

Such sights had a healing effect upon her. She had felt "nervous and wretched" when she started out; here she sensed "the peace that is within the starry sky, the rest that lies upon the lonely hills."[3]

The next few months of 1921 passed pleasantly enough for Edith, if not for family and friends. People came and went, but most of them found Sagamore Hill sadly lacking in vitality without Theodore. "It always seems like a hollow shell," Corinne told her daughter after one visit, "but . . . I think Aunt Edith needed me."[4]

In March, much to Edith's pride, President Harding appointed thirty-four-year-old Ted Assistant Secretary of the Navy, as Theodore had been before him.

Later that spring one of her children came to live permanently at Oyster Bay for the first time. Dick Derby joined the staff of the Long Island Insane Asylum in May, and he and Ethel searched out a home only four miles from Sagamore Hill. It was "Old Adam House," a shingled, buff-colored Victorian structure surrounded by pines on Lexington Avenue. Ethel settled down contentedly (she would spend the rest of her life in this house, dying there over half a century later).[5]

On Saturday, July 9, Edith motored to Southampton for the wedding of Bamie's twenty-two-year-old son, Lieutenant Sheffield Cowles, to a bright, attractive, artistic girl named Margaret Krech. She wholeheartedly approved of "Bobbie," as everyone called the bride. This approval did not extend to all the guests, particularly Franklin Delano Roosevelt, last fall's unsuccessful Democratic Vice-Presidential candidate. The "featherduster" boy of the past was now nearly forty, a lusty womanizer and noisy celebrant at parties. His behavior on this occasion was so "uproarious" as to shock the Oyster Bay Roosevelts.[6] But Sheffield, who had worked as an aide to Franklin during his Assistant Secretaryship of the Navy, knew that many naïve frustrations lay behind the jovial façade. Once, on a ship returning from the Versailles Peace Conference, Franklin had confessed to him that the greatest disappointment of his life was not being admitted to Harvard's Porcellian Club.[7]

Exactly one month later a far greater tragedy struck Franklin. He contracted polio at Campobello Island, Maine. The agonizing convulsions that followed brought about a change in his character. He read widely, studied intensely, and conceived an overwhelming ambition to return to politics at the higher levels.

That August Edith Kermit Roosevelt turned sixty.

Arthur and Ruth Lee were among the visitors to Sagamore in the fall of 1921. Arthur was now Britain's First Lord of the Admiralty, and was on his way to Washington for an international naval conference on the limitation of armaments. The Lees had just made a grand gesture in donating their beautiful Buckinghamshire mansion, Chequers, to the nation, to be used as a country residence for the Prime Minister. They hoped Edith would visit them wherever and whenever they settled. "It was a great pleasure to see the Lees," Edith wrote, "but brought many memories."[8] She recalled standing next to the young Captain Lee and watching Theodore galloping across the pine flats of Tampa; she thought of Theodore walking under the great beech trees at Chequers and demolishing Lord Kitchener over dinner afterward . . . Always memories of Theodore, Theodore, Theodore.

Yet she welcomed the Lees' company, because, as she pointed out to Arthur, it was her season of painful anniversaries. "All the autumn is hard to bear. Beginning October 27th, Theodore's birthday, Quentin's [November 10], the date of our engagement [November 17], the date of our marriage [December 2], and then January 6 . . ."[9]

On the last-named day in 1922, three years after Theodore's death, Edith led a memorial visit of his friends to the grave. This "Pilgrimage" was so cathartic that it became an annual event, in which she would participate (but not always march) for the next two decades. Every year, after placing a wreath in Youngs' Cemetery, the pilgrims would assemble in the North Room at Sagamore Hill to read and discuss various Rooseveltian texts. "Usually," one remembered, "Mrs. Roosevelt would bring out some letter or some memorandum or tell some story that was usually off the record and quite secret, but illustrated the kind of man that TR was." After light refreshments the group would sit around and wax nostalgic. "I wanted it, and love having it, and it is pain too," Edith told Ted, after one Pilgrimage, and after another she jotted cryptically, "So right again."[10]

On January 17, 1922, Edith accompanied Archie on a business trip to Europe. First they visited Paris, where she wandered up and down the quays chatting to booksellers, and revisited Sainte Chapelle to see the restored glass which had been removed for safety during the war. They made a side trip to Berlin before taking an airplane to London. This, Edith's first flight, was, she noted drily, "a great pleasure in itself, but slightly *accidenté.*" Stormy weather battered the little plane until they had to return to Paris "to change a machine." Darkness descended on their second hop over the English Channel, and they were forced to land on the coast at Folkestone and take "a motor" for the remaining seventy miles to London.[11]

Unfazed, Edith left alone next day on a voyage to South Africa. The Cape enchanted her, with its "exquisite pink amaryllis," its white stretches of beach, its "jade-green ocean varied with splashes of wine-color from the seaweed-covered rocks," its "great wide plain, with always the chance of a glimpse of the big baboons," its spacious vineyards and its Dutch-style white plaster houses. "Nothing can give an idea of the porcelain beauty of the atmosphere," she told Bamie. "I am fitter to face the world than I have been for a long time."[12]

In October 1920 Edith had accepted a kind offer by the Arthur Lees to have a gift copy of the first portrait of Theodore by Philip Laszlo shipped to Sagamore Hill, just as soon as she could feel that the pleasure of having it would be greater than the pain. She had always thought the Rough Rider portrait by Enke, taken with them from the White House, "very inadequate," and the numerous photographs in her collection were in no way a substitute for a work by such a distinguished artist as the Hungarian.

The Laszlo arrived sometime in 1922, and Edith hung it "over the little platform" in the North Room to balance the *Seats of the Mighty*. The copy was "in every way equal to the original," she told the Lees. "The likeness is so vivid, so alive, that I am forced to turn off the burners when I am alone in the room." Often, after she had been working at her desk all evening, she ran in "to say goodnight to it."[13]

In September, after summer at Sagamore Hill with Emily, she went to Warm Springs, Virginia, to take the waters. Here, on October 2, heartbreaking news reached her. Eight-year-old Richard Derby, Jr., who had been suffering from asthma and tubercular glands when she left home, had died of septic poisoning.

The death of her adored grandchild hit Edith hard. She had been especially fond of the delicate boy, who reminded her of Theodore in his own early asthmatic years. Once again she sought the healing rays of the sun, and in January 1923 sailed for Pará in Brazil. The city, edged with mango trees, sprawled lazily at the mouth of the Amazon. On an excursion into the surrounding country she was directed to a jungle hideaway "all dropping with moisture behind its locked gates." She gave a few pennies to a small boy who produced a key and led her "across perilous bridges and through dark paths to a muddy port." Here the boy whistled "and a hideous head reared itself from the depths in answer to his call, and submitted to his caresses." The weird creature was a manatee, a species which Edith

"The likeness is so vivid, so alive . . .
I am forced to turn off the burners."
Arthur Lee's memorial gift to Edith:
Theodore Roosevelt by Philip de Laszlo.

had seen once before in the public gardens at Georgetown, but not "in such intimacy." [14]

She was back in New York by March 20, and in April workmen began a month-long repair and redecoration of Sagamore Hill, largely financed with Theodore's life insurance. In the middle of all the resultant chaos a telegram arrived from Bamie to say that Will Cowles was critically ill after a stroke. Edith left next morning for Farmington. Being at Oldgate always depressed her—she and Bamie got on no better now in age than in youth—and since Will's condition appeared static, she took the first opportunity of escaping and beginning a motor tour of rural Connecticut. On April 25, almost by instinct, she came upon a small town in the Quinebaug Valley, named Brooklyn. Here her Tyler ancestors had settled in the early eighteenth century. Strange inherited emotions stirred in Edith as she explored the cemetery and found the grave of her centenarian great-great-grandfather, Daniel Tyler II, who had had three wives, twenty-one children, fifty grandchildren, and 120 great-grandchildren. Engraved on his tomb was a rhyme:

> *Although a hundred years I've seen,*
> *My life was short,*
> *'Twas all a dream.*

Returning to the village center, she admired two fine old Tyler houses on Main Street. Then she drove on to Norwich to see her own birthplace on Washington Street, whence, sixty-four years before, Gertrude Tyler had set forth in white silk and point lace to marry Charles Carow.

Two days after getting back to Sagamore Hill, Bamie telephoned to say Will was unconscious, and Edith hurried north again. Three days later, on May 1, her brother-in-law died. Bamie, crippled but still a courageously striking figure, received the mourners in the library after a military funeral. Corinne was there to help Edith comfort the bereaved woman. The three old friends were all widows now (Douglas Robinson had died in 1918). Edith could not help but reflect how much more cruelly life had treated the Roosevelt sisters than herself. Bamie, at sixty-seven, was almost paralyzed by the rheumatoid arthritis that had been strengthening its grip on her joints for over a decade. This, plus the infantile deformity of her spine, confined her to a wheelchair, and Hopkinson, her faithful butler, had to lift her in and out of it like a baby. She was, besides, increasingly deaf, so much so that visitors were obliged to speak into an "acousticon" box in order to communicate with her. Yet somehow Bamie had still continued to entertain, dressing each day in one of her innumerable white high-necked tea gowns, and managing to attract crowds of guests to tea at Oldgate. Regulars understood that at various times they were expected to leave the room briefly, while Hopkinson came in to adjust the position of her legs. The process was so agonizing for her she could be heard whimpering, "Oh, Hopkinson! Hopkinson! Oh, Hopkinson!"[15]

Corinne, at sixty-one, was smitten with a Job-like variety of ailments. Her own childhood inheritance was asthma, combined with the Rooseveltian tendency to skin eruptions, from carbuncles to eczema. She had also (like Theodore before her) lost the sight of one eye, and now had failing vision in the other. Enduring grief over her dead son Stewart was now complicated by worry over his brother Monroe, an alcoholic whose personality and life seemed to be a carbon copy of the doomed Elliott Roosevelt.[16] But Corinne managed to hide her sadness and discomfort to an unusual degree, laughing, talking and wheezing her way through countless poetry readings and parties, at which no one was a better raconteur. Since women had won the vote she had been expending her immense energies in the work of a New York State Republican Committee woman, and addressing rallies all over the country. The climax of this late career had come in 1920, when she achieved the distinction of being the first woman ever to address a Republican political convention.[17]

Saying goodbye as soon as she decently could, Edith left Farmington, painfully aware of the ravages of time.

The visits to Brooklyn and Norwich stirred Edith's interest in her own ancestry, and she felt a strong desire to reestablish her own roots, now that the trunk that had so long supported her was fallen. As a result, she began to sift through old family papers, which she found so absorbing that she decided to publish some of them. With Kermit's help she selected an assortment of diaries, travel journals, nautical logs, letters and book lists. Chronologically arranged, these told part of the story of both Tylers and Carows, from the time of their arrival in the New World in the seventeenth century through the marriage of her own parents in 1859 and the death of Daniel Tyler IV in 1882. The resultant book, published by Scribners in 1928 under the title *American Backlogs,* was profusely illustrated with family portraits, and pictures of Tyler architecture and Carow ships. It was favorably reviewed by *The New York Times,* and, to Edith's surprise, her valetudinarian mother emerged as a heroine, in the august opinion of the critic:

> It was a happy thought which moved Mrs. Theodore Roosevelt to compile, with the assistance of her son Kermit, the schoolgirl letters of her mother, Gertrude Tyler Carow. . . . They are letters full of individuality, ingenuousness, observation and charm, and they paint a delightful portrait of an eighteen-year-old American girl whose education is being 'finished' in the Paris of the beginning of the Second Empire . . . she is vividly and lovably alive.[18]

In spite of this praise, the book did not sell well—perhaps understandably, given its limited appeal. The only royalty Edith appears to have received was one hundred dollars, most of which she felt came from her own pocketbook when she purchased copies for friends. Emily wrote and asked, pointedly, if the book was to be published before Christmas. "I shall not answer," Edith told Ethel. "If she cares for the book she can buy it for five dollars."[19] Evidently she had already begun to feel the ruthless rapacity of authors who contend that a book worth reading is a book worth buying.

With plans under way to publish a memorial edition of Theodore's works, as well as selections from his correspondence with Henry Cabot Lodge, Edith began to worry about the invasion of privacy that would result if Theodore's letters to her should ever be exposed to public scrutiny. No sooner had she finished editing and approving the Lodge letters, than she began to go through her personal collection and ruthlessly destroy them. "Painful though it is," she wrote her sister, "I do not dare do otherwise. I have been able to keep a few for the children." She had just been reading the letters of Elizabeth and Robert Browning, and "the exposure of their intimate thoughts" was "horribly distasteful" to her. "I could not bear the idea that this should happen to me," she told her good friend Eleanor Robson Belmont.[20]

The fall of 1923 saw the completion of the reconstruction of Theodore's birthplace with funds raised by the Woman's Roosevelt Memorial Association and its masculine counterpart, the Roosevelt Memorial Association. Edith visited the house on Twentieth Street where she had spent so much of her childhood and found the restoration and the exhibition rooms (built on the site where the Robert Roosevelt home once stood) "excellent." The carefully matched wallpapers, carpets and hangings, though of a period no longer fashionable, were "quite perfect."[21]

On Christmas Eve that year, Edith and Kermit set off on a two-month trip round the world, which took them from California to Hawaii, on to Japan and China, and then to Russia via the Trans-Siberian Express.

Arriving in Yokohama on January 14, 1924, a few months after the great Japanese earthquake, Edith found the fires of devastation still smoldering. She was relieved that their rooms in Tokyo had been reserved at the new quake-proof Imperial Hotel. This revolutionary floating-cantilever structure, designed by Frank Lloyd Wright, had been completed only two years earlier. As the only large, safe building in the capital, it now served as a refuge for all foreign embassy staffs whenever Tokyo experienced the slightest tremor—for seismic repercussions of the earthquake were still occurring.[22]

Kermit went to Osaka on business on their first day ashore, and Edith was left alone. About five o'clock on the morning of January 15, she awoke to the sound of workmen chatting in the garden below her window. Suddenly there "came a shiver which threw down houses" all around the hotel, yet the only initial effect the catastrophe outside had on the Imperial was to put out the lights. Deciding it was more dignified to be crushed in bed than to run through the labyrinthine corridors in her nightgown, Edith stayed where she was, praying that if a ceiling fell her end would be rapid. As the first rays of dawn came through the window, her government-supplied interpreter tapped on her door and entered. He was immaculately dressed, as though nothing had happened, in a "perfectly adjusted kimono," and presented Edith with a candle and a flask of water for washing. She was assured that the hotel was safe and unharmed, but the earth continued to move uneasily all through the rest of her stay in Japan.

Later in the morning Kermit arrived, having ridden part of the way from Osaka on a bicycle because the railroad was disrupted. Mother and son then set off for the Meiji shrine: they were curious to see "a manifest of the inner soul of Japan." At the entrance a Shinto priest greeted them, in his symbolic robe of purity. After visiting the shrine, he escorted them on a stroll through the peaceful surrounding park.

The Noh drama impressed Edith more than anything else in Japan. "I had long read and studied it," she wrote later, "and to find myself in a Japanese temple with the most eminent of the two companies of actors employing every resource of an art refined to the highest point from traditionary years, was a dream realized to an incredible height."

Sumida Gawa, one of the greatest dramas, had particular significance for her. It told the story of a mother's long search for her stolen son. While crossing a river she hears that an anniversary ceremony for a lost child is about to take place at a nearby grave site, and realizes that her search is over. As the woman walked slowly to the center of the sparse stage to a few twigs representing the grave, Edith felt "the love and sorrow of all the mothers of all the ages."

She was reluctant to leave Japan, where the feeling for her husband as the peacemaker of Portsmouth was "most touching." China, in contrast, was a keen disappointment; the new Republic, with its fierce squabbling between Nationalists and Communists, held no charms for a religious, patrician American. At the Summer Palace in Peking she thought nostalgically of the old Empress, who had sent her such beautiful gifts during the White House years. "The great spaces of the Temple of Heaven," she mused, "still mark the searching for spiritual light which no longer exists in China."

As for Communist Siberia, it was "a leap from a worn out civilization to none at all." People at home had warned her that those snowbound wastes were too hazardous for a woman traveler, but the six-thousand-mile train ride from Harbin to Moscow turned up a few pleasant surprises, such as the meals provided en route by a chef who had formerly served a Grand Duke. One of his breakfasts consisted of a perfectly cooked plump Siberian partridge; and his idea of a light hors d'oeuvre before dinner was *sakouska*—a lavish spread of fish, caviar and cold pheasant—accompanied by the finest wines. There was also the ever changing landscape: forests of birch and pine glistening with icy tracery in the thin sunlight; rugged lake country crisscrossed by sleighs laden with fish caught through thick ice; barren stretches of snow on the steppes as far as the eye could see. At the stations, red-cheeked women in high felt boots and colorful smocks offered turkeys for sale, and young boys skated across the frozen snows on steel bars fastened to slabs of wood.

Other aspects of the journey were less pleasing to her sensibilities. The smell of unwashed bodies and stale tobacco in third class (through which she and Kermit had to walk en route to the dining car) was unbearable; the washroom often froze solid and had to be thawed by a porter brandishing a hot poker; one of the passengers died of smallpox. Edith comforted herself with the stoical philosophy: "When I was at home I was better off, but travellers must be content."

Moscow, first seen under a cold moon, on February 17, 1924, had a "strange barbaric beauty." Rather than risk the doubtful facilities of government-run hotels, the Roosevelts stayed in an old aristocrat's mansion. Family portraits hung on the walls in memory of past glory, and the bed linen, though ornamented with crests, was heavily darned. In Red Square, Edith was conscious of "an ever-present fear" as people hastened about their business.

Leningrad (which Edith, in her diary, insisted on still calling Petrograd) was a gentler place. She spent a morning at the great Kirov Ballet school, a recipient of relief from Herbert Hoover during the war and consequently hospitable to any American visitor. Edith watched classes, ate with the students, and noted that Fanny Essler's slippers in the museum were no larger than a child's.

In the Winter Palace the Tsar's apartments were intact "even to the pencils on his writing desk and the chessmen ready to play." Only one imperial picture appeared to be missing; by an odd coincidence, the original was later offered for sale to one of Edith's traveling party in New York. Part of the palace had been cleared for government propaganda—a grisly photographic exhibit of the Terror, showing mangled and executed corpses. Edith had a moment to recall Spring-Rice's letters to her in the early days of the century, when he had forecast exactly this. Russia was "no place to linger," she concluded.[23]

Edith spent a good part of the summer of 1924 working on the manuscript of *American Backlogs.* Part of the research took her to Red Bank, New Jersey, to look up Barbary Brae, Grandfather Tyler's old house, where she had spent much of her childhood. She arrived none too soon, for the house was about to be greatly altered, and "the pretty planting of the grounds" had already been swept away.[24] Three cottages at Oceanic, which the Carows had also used, were still intact.

Mental absorption in her genealogical project seemed to have a salutary effect, for she "picked up a lost habit of sleeping at night,"[25] and had a series of happy picnics at Eel Creek with her grand-children.

Now that Quentin's memorial at Chaméry had been erected, she set about creating one at Groton. It consisted of an alcove to hold his books as well as a few by and about his father, and two chairs and a table for the boys to sit at while reading them. On the walls hung a picture of Quentin and his grave, its headstone carved with lines she had chosen from Shelley's *Adonais:*

> *He has outsoared the shadow of our night;*
> *Envy and calumny and hate and pain,*
> *And that unrest which men miscall delight,*
> *Can touch him not and torture not again.*

The pain of Quentin's death would never lessen. Years later she would write in her diary on July 14: "Still so hard."[26]

Incidents involving several of the Roosevelts caused Edith some concern in the fall of 1924. Ted quit his post as Assistant Secretary of the Navy (after serving for three and a half years) in order to run for Governor of New York State against the incumbent Democrat, Al Smith. The odds in favor of the latter were formidable. Earlier in the year the name of Theodore Roosevelt, Jr., had been unjustly smeared in the "Teapot Dome" scandal. The Assistant Secretary, it was revealed, had once held stocks in the Sinclair Oil Company, to which the Navy Department, acting at the request of Secretary of the Interior Albert B. Fall, subsequently leased some naval oil fields at Teapot Dome in Wyoming. Sly references were also made to the fact that Archibald Roosevelt worked for Sinclair. To the huge relief of the family, Ted's wife, who handled her husband's finances, was able to prove that in 1921, long before the leasing, she had sold the stocks in question. As for Archie, he not only promptly resigned from Sinclair Oil, but was a key witness for the prosecution at the subsequent Congressional hearings. He even attempted, without success, to persuade a former colleague at Sinclair to bring further damaging evidence to light, specifically involving Secretary Fall. In any case, extra proof of corruption was not needed. Fall was convicted of accepting bribes and sent to prison.[27]

Despite Ted's obvious innocence in the affair, the specter of Teapot Dome inevitably raised its ugly head during the gubernatorial campaign. Governor Smith and Mayor Jimmy Walker of New York told their supporters to "lay off the oil," for it might boomerang into a sympathy vote. But Franklin Roosevelt's wife, Ted's cousin Eleanor—now an ardent Democrat—ignored the warning, and toured the state making anti-Ted speeches in a specially-constructed truck shaped like a huge teapot. Edith did not deign to counter the innuendo of her niece. In November Ted lost the gubernatorial race by 108,589 votes out of one million cast.[28]

Five days after the election that staunchest of Republicans and oldest of family friends, Henry Cabot Lodge, died of a cerebral hemorrhage. He was seventy-four years old, and had been continuously in Congress for thirty-eight years. Edith made no mention of his passing in her diary. Only her family really mattered to her now. Besides, she had never quite forgiven Cabot for not supporting Theodore in 1912.

A shock of a different kind presented itself only three days after Cabot's death. Alice arrived at Sagamore Hill and casually announced that, in her forty-first year, she was almost six months pregnant. *"Bouleversé,"* wrote Edith in her diary, without distinguishing who was emotionally upset, herself or her stepdaughter. It is not known if she subsequently became privy to the rumors then sweeping Washington that Nick Longworth (recently elected Speaker of the House) was not the father. But in a letter to Bamie on November 22, regarding a projected trip to Cuba, she wrote: "Alice's news was rather a blow, and I daresay a few days at sea are good for me."[29]

Alice gave birth in Chicago to a girl on February 14, 1925. The date, St. Valentine's Day, was a painfully memorable one to both mother and grandmother, being the anniversary of the death of Alice Lee Roosevelt.

Edith arrived at the hospital just a few hours before, but did not see Alice until the next day. "A pretty little baby and a real Roosevelt," was her verdict. The mother, she wrote in some surprise, "looks younger than she has done for years." She bravely hoped that her stepdaughter would call the baby Alice, but the Longworths chose the name Paulina, after a favorite apostle.[30]

Edith felt so relieved "that Alice's troubles are over" that she decided to treat herself to a vacation in Italy. She sailed on March 27, and after a few days in Nice with a friend, went on to Sicily and Malta with Emily.

The summer of 1925 was a quiet one as far as family companionship was concerned. Archie's and Eleanor's children were in Vermont, and Ted and Kermit were off on a six-month hunting expedition in Central Asia, sponsored by the Chicago Field Museum of Natural History. Their aim was to capture large mammals, in particular the great wild sheep *Ovis polis,* rarely seen since the days of Marco Polo.

When Ted returned to America he had no job and no political prospect, so he wrote two books. The first was an account of life at Sagamore Hill entitled *All in the Family;* the second was a collection of stories about World War I called *Rank and File,* one of which Ernest Hemingway later selected for his anthology *Men at War: Best War Stories of All Time.*[31]

Edith observed rather than celebrated her sixty-fourth birthday on August 6, 1925. By now the seasons and the years were beginning to accelerate and run together into the dread monotony of old age. There were long periods at Sagamore Hill when no visitors came; and at other times the arrivals of annual house guests seemed shockingly close together. Noisy intrusions by her grandchildren (now numbering fifteen) were welcome to begin with, but left her exhausted before long. "I like to see their little faces," she was fond of saying, "but I prefer to see their backs."

Since she was by nature reclusive and sedentary, she had to fight all the harder to be socially and culturally active—but fight she did, with courage that Theodore himself would have admired. She forced herself to go to Oyster Bay parties and receptions, and weekly gossip sessions at the Needlework Guild. Instead of listening to concerts over the radio, she made frequent excursions into the city to hear the opera and the Philharmonic.

Yet try as she might she could not avoid a creeping feeling of sameness. "I have been swinging in and out of New York like a pendulum," she wrote one day.[32] Evidently her life needed a major stimulation, a project into which she could throw all her declining energies. It would be a while yet before she found it; for the time being she continued to seek diversion in travel.

In January and February of 1926, for example, she was in Yucatán to explore the Maya ruins. She climbed the pyramids at Chichén Itzá, wandered through their deserted rooms, and gazed across the forests where other ancient cities lay buried. A year later she was ferrying along Argentina's Paraná River, and then crossing marshland thick with water fowl and "frogs that cried *Breck-e-kex kex* as I had supposed they did only in the pages of Aristophanes."[33] Her destination was the legendary Iguaçu Falls in Brazil.

Reaching there on February 4, 1927, she stood next morning on the brink of a stupendous chasm which awed her as nothing else but the Grand Canyon of Arizona. "The same majesty and power. Silence, a lump in the throat, and my heart beating: 'How amiable is Thy dwelling place, Thou Lord of Hosts.'"[34]

Edith speaking for Hoover at Madison Square Garden in 1932.

Old Age
1927–1948

Thirty-Five

Being happy is a state of unconscious mind.
—Edith Kermit Roosevelt[1]

Edith was sixty-six years old in August 1927, and had already begun to suffer from what she loosely called "heart attacks." These could be described more accurately as flutters or murmurs, but they were, nevertheless, the beginning of a serious heart disturbance which was to restrict her more and more as the years went by.

Realizing that her days of foreign travel were numbered, Edith began to look for a place closer to home where she could escape the familial and social pressures of Long Island whenever she felt the need. Accordingly she returned to Brooklyn, Connecticut, to look at the old Tyler homes with a view to possible purchase. As luck would have it one was for sale that summer. For many years it had been a hostelry known as the Putnam Inn, after her great-grandfather Tyler's first wife's father, the Revolutionary War General, Israel Putnam. Such intricate genealogical connections were child's play to the author of *American Backlogs;* and in answer to the powerful longings that had stirred in her when she had first visited the town of her forebears, she bought the property.[2]

The inn, or Mortlake Manor, as she promptly renamed it (its original title) was an immense, three-story white clapboard structure built for Daniel Tyler III in the late eighteenth century, on two and a half acres of ground on the old Worcester Turnpike. A sixty-foot-wide lawn with shady trees separated the front stoop from the highway, while its north-facing side door looked onto an equestrian statue of General Putnam. A macabre feature of the exterior was a line of black waves painted on the baseboard by Daniel III, in memory of a son who had died at sea.

Edith's first impression on entering the hallway was of decorative wooden ceilings, and massive white board paneling with Corinthian pilasters on either side embellished with Greek motifs. The sitting room and library opened out to her left; the dining room was situated at the back of the house. Exploring these and Mortlake's other barnlike, sparsely furnished chambers, Edith noted that though there was no central heating system there were many elegant wood-burning fireplaces. Since the house would be used chiefly as a summer refuge, she saw no need to improve on the old system of heating the place.

One of the most attractive features of the house was its huge twenty-four-pane sash windows full of trembling sunlit leaves. Edith was delighted to find portraits of three Daniel Tylers in the hall, and one of General Putnam in the parlor, not to mention a secret panel in the staircase, a corner cupboard in the upstairs bedroom she chose for herself, and an old cabinet and knife box built into the woodwork. She signed the deeds to Mortlake on August 25, 1927, and immediately felt at peace there. "I find that I am content to lie awake resting, and do not need to play solitaire or knit or read when I can't sleep," she wrote Ethel.[3]

Stimulated by the cavernous spaces of the old house, she began to "snoop" for pieces of furniture at local auctions, in the happy knowledge that no matter how long she lived, she would never completely fill it. From Mr. Blake, the local carpenter, she ordered several hand-carved tip-top tables, from five to fifteen dollars apiece. She was so pleased with this work that many subsequent commissions flowed from her, including the construction of an arbor over the south door for a climbing rose.[4]

Edith's purchase of Mortlake Manor was something of a puzzlement to her family—particularly the more businesslike ones, who saw its maintenance as an unnecessary drain on her finances. Nobody, except Ethel, who had a profound sense of family history, could imagine why an old lady should want to spend her high summer days in an empty house in a hot valley, when she could spend them on a hill above the cool shores of Long Island.

But Edith felt no need to explain. Every July 4, or thereabouts, and at various other times in spring and fall, she would pack her black and white dresses, and motor north from Oyster Bay onto the mainland with her "three musketeers"—Clara the mulatto maid, Bridget the cook, and Lee (later Dyer) the chauffeur.

After settling in, Edith would slip into a simple routine which changed little over the years. In the mornings she read or knitted with a pair of smooth applewood needles Mr. Blake had made for her. In the afternoon she went for long walks in the fields opposite, or visited with the village gossip, Miss Gracie Bowen, who could usually be found rocking on her porch across the street. Sometimes she sewed with the local Needlework Guild, and on Fridays went antique hunting. On Sunday she went either to the stone Episcopal church, or to the clapboard Meeting House built by her great-grandfather.[5] Every evening she sat down to a formal meal consisting of soup, a roast, and, in summer, fresh raspberries bought by the quart from an old lady on an adjoining property. It was, in effect, a solid bourgeois existence, contrasting sharply, and perhaps deliberately, with the sophisticated, frenetic pace of her political years with Theodore. Even though Mortlake was in easy reach of Farmington, she saw Bamie infrequently. Her sister-in-law's condition depressed her, and she missed seeing Will's kindly face. Her reluctance to visit was not lost on Bamie. "Edith Roosevelt has in a snarkish mood 'silently vanished away,'" she wrote Corinne, "while I with my old habits continue to make lace in the bow. I really suppose that she is very happy in [the] isolation of her new ancestral home . . ."[6]

Edith was well able to afford to indulge her "folly" in Connecticut, since she was now a wealthy woman. Her income amounted to over $21,000 a year in 1928. It included a new $5,000 widow's pension, over and above her annual $5,000 from the Carnegie Trust. When Congress first voted the appropriation, she reacted much as she had done to the millionaire's generosity. "I thought of refusing to accept it," she told Edwin Emerson, a former Rough Rider, "because I didn't need it, but then I came to the conclusion that would be an

"I really suppose that she is very happy
in the isolation of her new ancestral home."
Mortlake Manor, Brooklyn, Connecticut.

ungracious thing to do, since it would cause embarrassment to the
other Presidential widows now receiving such pensions. Then I
bethought myself how much good I could do with scattered parts of
that money to the poor . . . So I decided to accept the pension money
with due gratitude, but to give it away piecemeal . . ." Later,
Emerson "learned from certain luckless former members of TR's
regiment, who happened to have been in dire need, that they, as well
as other poor comrades of our regiment, had indeed received from
Mrs. Roosevelt, 'the Mother of the Regiment,' needed sums of
money . . ."[7]

Her concern for presidential widows was genuine. She well knew
the history of such unfortunates as Dolley Madison, who had been
compelled to sell her husband's notes of the Constitutional Con-

vention to Congress for $30,000; or Mrs. Lincoln, so desperate for a stipend that she had to live abroad; or Mrs. Ulysses S. Grant, who depended on the sale of her husband's memoirs to survive. In contrast, Edith Kermit Roosevelt was very comfortably off, and took pleasure in being magnanimous.

Total strangers were often the recipients of her largesse, from substantial sums of money to minor acts of generosity and concern.[8] Another, more subtle form of Edith's beneficence was her patronage of the arts. Between 1926 and 1936 the struggling poet Elbert Newton came to Sagamore Hill intermittently in the early summer months to give poetry readings to a "class" she assembled. Members included Mrs. Emlen Roosevelt, Mrs. Philip Roosevelt, Eleanor Robson Belmont, Mrs. Henry Frick, Miss Alice Weekes, Grace Roosevelt and Ethel Derby. The works heard and discussed ranged from Emily Dickinson and Yeats to Edith Sitwell and Archibald MacLeish. The "fee" for admission was supposed to be ten dollars per person, but the cash total somehow always exceeded the numbers attending. The poet was commensurately grateful. "In no other group," he marveled, "do I feel such a spirit of love of poetry for poetry's sake . . . And I never saw so much money. Where does it come from?" Newton, showing the artist's traditional indifference to material appetites, spent much of the money on books written by his contemporaries. "I am hoping for that day when you will allow me to try new poets on you," he wrote Edith, "so much regard do I feel for your sensitiveness to poetry." He willingly dropped poems for audience use if Edith disliked them, but there were few artistic clashes, since their tastes were similar. He admired John Donne, as she did, as "the most intriguing mind of them all." Edith became fond of her personal bard. The letters from "funny little Newton" were among the few that she could never bring herself to destroy.[9]

To Edith's quiet distress, Emily visited Mortlake for the first time in the fall of 1927. "The whiskered brigand," as the grandchildren now called her, was growing increasingly deaf, had a pinched white face, and was emotionally fragile. She was "always near to tears," said Edith, "but I could do nothing." The obvious sisterly solution would have been to invite Emily to share Mortlake, and even her life at Sagamore Hill, but she could not bring herself to do it, and was therefore "fretted" by feelings of guilt.

Emily spoke of little else than nursing the wounded during the war.

This had been the high excitement of her life. "She will talk of it incessantly and tear me to pieces," Edith complained to Ethel. The sisters were more incompatible than ever, as the isolation of Brooklyn emphasized. Edith could only pray for the Lord to deliver her from hardness of heart, for she felt like "a worm and a whited sepulchre." [10]

After Emily sailed at the end of November, Edith felt a lightening of spirits, but no real joy. Falling into a philosophical mood, she began to ponder the meaning of the word *happy*—"which I had been for so long that I thought no more of it than the air I breathed," she told Ethel. "Suddenly a few days ago I realized I had only felt that way twice since Father died." Both times, she acknowledged, had been in dreams. "While I can have pleasure and enjoyment, interest and amusement . . . being happy is a state of unconscious mind." [11]

Throughout the twenties, books about Theodore continued to trickle from the press, including *The Rough Rider,* a novel by Hermann Hagedorn, the indefatigable director of the Roosevelt Memorial Association, and a copious author of books and pamphlets about his hero. Something about Hagedorn's avid appetite for snippets of family information irritated Edith, and this latest book, with its starry-eyed mixture of fact and fiction, struck her as distasteful. "You know how I dislike cheap novels," she wrote Ethel, "and more than I can express that one should be written in which Father figures!" This "finished" Hagedorn and his ilk for her. "Well meaning, not *de notre monde;* they don't understand.'" [12]

She reacted even more violently to Henry Pringle's *Theodore Roosevelt: A Biography*, published in 1931. It was a witty, well-written, but iconoclastic book, portraying Roosevelt as a war-mongering imperialist and sometime clown. (The bulk of the illustrations were cartoons.) Pringle's work went on to win the Pulitzer Prize, but it infuriated Edith. "On each page is a sneer or a slap at Father," she complained again to her daughter. "I can not read it; Mr. Loeb says it is packed with false statements. I should like to burn it and mail the ashes to its author. Nothing has made me as angry for a long time. I wish the estate had put a prohibitive price on use of the papers . . ."

Nevertheless, Edith continued to help other authors with works about or connected with her husband. Stephen Gwynn's book on Cecil Spring-Rice, she said with satisfaction, "could scarcely have been written without the letters which I gave." She also helped

Looker on his *The White House Gang* "as much as I could." Edith found it "terribly painful" to read most things about Theodore, except Lewis Einstein's *Roosevelt: His Mind in Action*, which she could not put down. "How anyone whose personal contact was so slight can have reasoned so correctly I am at a loss to understand," she wrote Arthur Lee.[13]

Edith visited Panama, Guatemala, and San Salvador in the winter of 1927–28, and in the spring sailed for England with Ethel to stay with the Lees. On the night of their arrival, June 22, Ruth Lee wrote in her diary:

> Edith seemed a little more frail and more easily tired than she used to be, but, in truth, she was generally tired in the old days, because she always had to do more than she had strength for . . . I think it is partly her limited strength, as well as her natural reserve, that make her shrink from involving herself with new or unnecessary people or things. She knows so well what she likes and what she wants that she saves up for them.[14]

A week later, the former First Lady, looking "very distinguished" in a simple black dress, awarded Roosevelt prizes to the scholars of Cheltenham College. Arthur Lee, an Old Boy and now President of the college, had endowed the prizes annually for the best essay "on Theodore's gospel of public service." Afterward, Edith surprised the audience with "a most touching speech," wrote Ruth. "The effect was very emotional, and when Arthur followed in a moving little speech about Theodore, Ethel and I held hands harder than ever, and had some difficulty in refraining from crying."[15]

"When the smoke is cleared away there will be a great many Humpty Dumpties," Kermit Roosevelt wrote Ted in a mixed metaphor his mother would not have tolerated, after the financial crash of October 1929. Edith suffered less than most Americans in the subsequent depression—indeed less than most Roosevelts: Archie's stocks, for example, were seriously eroded, and Aunt Laura "lost everything." Thanks to Edith's excellent inherited investments, and sound management of her portfolio over the years by Cruikshank and Sons, her income dropped only slightly during the year that followed, by some $1,400. In 1931 it incredibly rose to a new height of $25,264.73, and would not drop again substantially until President Franklin Delano Roosevelt began to implement his New Deal policies.[16]

At least one of her sons was able to ride out the storm on a Federal salary. Shortly before the crash, President Hoover appointed Ted Governor of Puerto Rico, and he took up his post that fall. Having learned Spanish in advance of arrival, he showed immediate concern for the nutrition and health problems of the island, and set about correcting some of them. When a run on the banks was threatened as a result of the depression, he put up $100,000 in personal funds to avert it—a quarter of what he was worth.

This did not prevent Eleanor from lavishly redecorating the Governor's sixteenth-century palace, La Forteleza, a Spanish fortress overlooking San Juan harbor, with tapestry wall-hangings, Tibetan paintings, and masses of banquet silver brought down from Long Island. Ted arranged to have a liqueur box made from elephants' feet, although he feared the cost might take a good part of his $10,000 salary. "I am trying," he told Kermit, "to be a combination of democracy and swank."[17]

In January 1930, Edith arrived in Puerto Rico for a two-week stay. She rested in the luxurious palace gardens, lush with tropical plants, took a daily swim in the ocean, and had such a delightful time on a trip to Haiti with her daughter-in-law, "flying around the citadel in pursuit of planes," that she returned to San Juan in September for almost a month. Ted was surprised at his mother's energy and capacity for enjoyment, and amused to find that he was out of her favor. "She likes you and me moderately," he told Kermit, "and Archie a great deal. She likes Belle and Eleanor moderately also, and Gracie a great deal." The reason for this, according to Ted, was that "Archie sees the best people and that you and I just have friends."[18] Archie was also a more solicitous son, living close to Sagamore Hill (he had moved into a Colonial house in Cold Spring Harbor in 1921) and acting as a willing escort to musical and theatrical events. He was usually in attendance to put his mother on a steamer and meet her when she got off.

No matter how in or out of favor Ted was, Edith returned to Puerto Rico yet again in December. The timing of her Christmas disappearance from New York brought an acid comment from Bamie to Corinne: "I suppose she is gleefully getting out of the way of having to get or give presents."[19]

While on the island Edith read the recently published letters of Henry Adams "with great interest and thought sadly of how much he would have suffered had he seen them in print." Some of the letters made poignant reading: "Theodore Roosevelt was at Lodge's," Adams had written on May 19, 1889. "You know the poor wretch has consented to be Civil Service Commissioner and is to be with us in Washington next winter with his sympathetic little wife . . ."[20]

Edith arrived back in New York on January 6, 1931, the twelfth anniversary of Theodore's death. But the isolation of Sagamore Hill at that time of year proved too much to bear. Besides, she felt a few worrying flutters in her chest, and on March 11, therefore, sailed on the *Topeka* for Jamaica. "Peace perfect peace," she wrote in her diary on board ship. "No more thumps from the heart."[21] She returned to Oyster Bay on April 2. A week later came the startling news of the death of Nick Longworth, at the age of sixty-one. He had recently been replaced after serving six years as Speaker of the House, and while visiting friends in Aiken, South Carolina, developed fatal pneumonia. Alice had arrived to find Nick already in a coma, and sat with him during his last hours. Kermit and Archie immediately flew south to be with their sister, while Edith made her way to Cincinnati for the funeral next day. Throughout the obsequies Alice maintained "splendid poise." She appreciated the support of "Mother especially," who, she told her Aunt Corinne, "was her own very best self."[22]

In his brief will, drawn up shortly after the birth of Paulina, Nick left his wife almost $780,000. This included Rookwood, and the house on Massachusetts Avenue in which they had lived for the past five years. Alice decided to keep on the Longworth family home in Ohio until Paulina had completed her education there: after this she would sell it.[23]

Edith felt tired and depressed for weeks after Nick's death. Then on August 25, 1931, another piece of distressing news summoned Edith north to Farmington. Bamie, now seventy-six years old, was lying comatose at Oldgate. She showed no sign of recognition as Edith entered her room, and she died the same evening without regaining consciousness. Perhaps, for Edith, it was just as well. The two women had never been close, and it had been left to Theodore to keep the relationship between them sweet. After his death, given the difference in their tastes and temperaments, it had inevitably soured.

In October 1931, Hermann Hagedorn dined with Edith to discuss the Theodore Roosevelt Memorial Association's purchase of Analostan Island in the Potomac River opposite Rock Creek for the sum of $364,000. The Association's idea was to convert it to a public park and then present it to the nation in memory of Theodore. Edith approved, but she had decided views on what should be done with the ninety acres of land. "No pompous architectural efforts" should mar the natural landscaping. John Burroughs supported Edith in her views. "Give the grass time to grow on his grave before we pile up the marble," he said when hearing of a plan to raise ten million dollars for a memorial to Theodore.[24]

The spring of 1932 was a menacing one to Edith and others of her prosperous class. Charles Lindburgh's son was kidnapped and found dead; New York real-estate business fell stagnant, and the economy was so generally weak that Edith Wharton had to accept $750 for the kind of story that she had previously sold for $3,000. In June the Democrats nominated Governor Franklin Delano Roosevelt of New York as their presidential candidate. This proved to be a bitter pill for the Oyster Bay Roosevelts, particularly those who remembered Cousin Eleanor's mudslinging campaign against Ted in his gubernatorial race.

To Edith's dismay, over three hundred messages arrived at Sagamore Hill congratulating her on Franklin's nomination, in the mistaken belief she was his mother, or grandmother, or even his wife. She could not help feeling that the Democrats were "making deliberate propaganda of the name Roosevelt."[25] In an attempt to correct the record, she bought envelopes printed with a picture of Hoover (who was running for reelection on the Republican ticket) and used these along with her own franking signature.

But the letters continued to come. In a last-ditch effort to make it perfectly clear whose side she was on, Edith entertained three hundred of the Edith Kermit Roosevelt Republican Club to lunch at Sagamore Hill on August 10 to celebrate President Hoover's birthday. Her welcoming speech made the front page of *The New York Times* next day, sharing space with another dramatic headline: "Hitler is Expected to be Chancellor in Cabinet Shake-up."

The day after the Club reception, Edith made a further gesture in support of Hoover. With Ethel and Dick Derby she went to Long Island's Roosevelt Field [named in memory of Quentin] to await the arrival of a plane which would transport her to Washington and the President's Notification Ceremony. Reporters, photographers, and movie newsreel cameramen surrounded her as she stepped from her car. She declined to be interviewed, but promised "to say something for the movies" before takeoff. A giant Curtiss Condor landed, and she began to walk toward it. Someone pushed a microphone at her for the promised speech, which consisted of six smiling words. "I'm on my way to Washington." Then she broke away, ran across the grass, and, with the help of a stewardess, hopped aboard the plane.[26]

In Washington she was again pestered by newsmen for a statement. "I haven't talked to the press, not in seventy-one years, and it's too late to begin now," she said.

After a buffet luncheon served under a gaily striped marquee on the south lawn of the White House, Edith received with the Hoovers in the Blue Room at 1 P.M. It was twenty-three years since she had last set foot in the Mansion, and she found the experience painful. The present occupant, the son of an Iowan blacksmith, had made a fortune as a mining engineer and was now a millionaire. As President he could afford to turn his salary back to the Treasury, and spend lavishly refurnishing the Executive Mansion. Edith hardly recognized the once-familiar rooms. "The house itself is swept and garnished and no ghost of the past remains to haunt me," she wrote Kermit after the "hateful" visit was over.[27]

She had had the best of intentions in going to Washington, but her appearance there boomeranged. Letters of abuse—generally anonymous—now began to pour in condemning her for coming out against a relative. "They all seem to know what father would do under the present conditions," she told Ted, "and vilify me for doing otherwise. 'Coming out of my retirement' . . . I did not know that I had retired. I had thought that Aunt Emily was the only person who would reprove and exhort me, but I find she has many companions. The scrap basket fortunately is capacious."[28]

"At the feet of the knitters in the sun lies the wide world."
Edith Kermit Roosevelt, 1932.

Undeterred, Edith made another public appearance for Hoover. This time it was in a much larger arena, and in a more prominent role. On October 31, eight days before the presidential election, she spoke to the largest political audience ever assembled in Madison Square Garden, on behalf of the Republican ticket.

The speech brought requests from radio networks to broadcast an address on Mr. Hoover's achievements during his first term in office. But she professed to be too busy with prior commitments—as Chairman of the Long Island Needlework Guild. "If only I had known last May the kind of campaign it was to be," she told Ted, "I should have done differently." [29] Instead of campaigning she found herself with a crowded timetable of lectures to Guild members on such lofty themes as: "Great is tribulation for scouring off sin."

On November 8, 1932, Edith voted early. By the time the polls closed Franklin Delano Roosevelt had been elected President of the United States by a popular majority of seven million. This event, which ultimately changed the structure of American society, was full of omens for the Oyster Bay Roosevelts. For Edith in particular, it was the beginning of the end of the hierarchical world in which she had spent all her life. She could not know it yet, but the country was on the threshold of a new era: that of the working man.

Earlier that year, Ted, who had performed successfully in Puerto Rico, had been appointed Governor-General of the Philippines by President Hoover. When Cousin Franklin came to power and reporters asked Ted what was the exact relationship of the two like-named men, he quipped that he was the President-elect's "fifth cousin, about to be removed." [30]

Actually he was secure—at least until Franklin was inaugurated in March 1933. Seizing this last opportunity to visit Manila as her son's guest, Edith arrived there on January 2. Malacañan Palace, the Governor's house, did not compare with La Fortaleza "in charm and atmosphere," but it was "far, far more comfortable." The Filipinos, with their Oriental veneration of age, treated her like visiting royalty, and commented on her "charm, dignity, and grace." [31]

Ted held a large evening reception for his mother, arranging for an armchair where she could sit with a bouquet and merely smile at people as they went by. She scorned this plan, however, and stood up shaking hands with everyone for nearly two hours.

During Edith's stay in Manila, the newspapers published reports that Kermit and Belle were cruising on Vincent Astor's yacht with Franklin. Ted was embarrassed, for it appeared that his brother might be wooing the new President so that Ted could remain as Governor. In an attempt to clarify the matter, Ted invited newsmen to lunch to meet his mother, and one reporter was bold enough to ask him why Kermit was boating with the President-elect. There was a pregnant silence as everyone strained to hear the reply. But before Ted could speak Edith's gentle voice came from across the table: "Because his mother was not there!"[32]

Thirty-Six

If I could not have both I should choose my children's respect rather than their love.

—Edith Kermit Roosevelt[1]

Edith sailed from Manila on February 1, 1933, and on the seventeenth day at sea received a cable telling of Corinne's death from pneumonia at the age of seventy-one. She had been in ill health for years, but the suddenness of her passing was a blow. "I should have taken the field first," Edith wrote in her diary. "V. lonely."

All through their girlhood and the early years of marriage, Corinne and she had been the closest of friends. It was not until Theodore went to Washington that they had begun to see less of each other. In recent years, indeed, the friendship had dwindled to almost nothing. Edith had little left but bundles of letters to remember her by. These, unfortunately, did not reflect Corinne's full personality. They were sentimental and colorless, and consisted largely of favorable descriptions of her children, not all deserved. But face to face, as Fanny Parsons remarked, Corinne "had the power of entering into the emotional and spiritual mood of another and of imparting a certain radiance to the experience." Alice Longworth felt the same: "One wanted to tell her everything, sure of her perfect comprehension and response whether it was a serious problem or an indulgence in family malice." For herself, Edith wrote simply and sadly: "So many memories we shared. So much we saved to tell each other when we met."[2]

Franklin Roosevelt's crushing defeat of Herbert Hoover in November 1932 seems to have aroused Edith's sympathy for that unhappy Republican, and she wrote him a warm letter, as one former occupant of the White House to another:

> MY DEAR MR. PRESIDENT
> This is to remind you of your house on Long Island. At Oyster Bay in point of fact—called Sagamore Hill, and I am the housekeeper. If you wish to bring some friends to a place where you can talk quietly, or you have papers to write undisturbed, I hope you will telephone. The number is not listed so I put it below.
> Believe me
>
> Sincerely yours
> EDITH ROOSEVELT[3]

Hoover responded to her invitation on March 12, 1933, a mere eight days after quitting the presidency. Clearly bruised by the catastrophic events of his Administration, he preferred to remember his brilliant record as Chairman of the American Relief Commission in World War I, and "talked most interestingly of his European experiences."

Edith was too old, and too entrenched in her class and habits, to welcome all aspects of the New Deal, and she haughtily let it be known that the liberalism of the Bull Moose movement "in no way resembles the policies of the present Administration in Washington." Privately, however, she wrote Arthur Lee: "As to public affairs, I am hopeful, for I believe Franklin is a shrewd statesman." Alice, on the other hand, was scathing in her denunciation of the new President. "He has the cripple's psychology . . . he puts his disability out of his mind and makes the most of what is left to him. He treats the American people in the same way, distracting them with anything which he thinks will keep them happy for the moment, but without any deep thought behind it."[4]

But no matter how disapproving Alice might be of Franklin's politics, Edith was sympathetic to the domestic problems of the new First Lady, who was, after all, her niece. In response to a letter from Eleanor full of feminine gossip about the Executive Mansion, Edith tactfully replied: "Your letter was an answer to prayer, full of things which I wanted to know. Much such conditions met me in the White House, and I am quite sure that I did not deal with them as efficiently as you have done."[5]

Edith's standard of living was not proof against the continuing effects of the depression. Although her Carow investments, handled by Cruikshank and Sons, remained fairly secure, Theodore's estate, managed by Roosevelt and Sons, soon showed alarming signs of erosion. She therefore took steps to shore it up, investing in Canadian bonds, and reviewing her insurance policies. It turned out that she had been paying employers' liability for "hotel servants" on Mortlake, though it had not been a hotel since she bought it, and for some years before that employed no servants. There were other "worrying entanglements" in the estate which had actually forced her into debt. Mr. Cruikshank was summoned to help straighten things out. They scrutinized her expenditures closely, and several long-paid philanthropies were abandoned.

Her sons and daughters were less fortunate. Even Alice, amply provided for by the Lees and by Nick, professed to be feeling the pinch, and was obliged to publish a best-selling memoir, *Crowded Hours*. In a gloomy moment Edith envisaged the whole family living on the Sagamore Hill property in "individual shacks built by hardy grandchildren."[6]

The last-named, visiting Sagamore summer after summer, scrutinized their formidable grandmother with the intense curiosity of the very young for the very old. They were intrigued by the neatness and discipline of her appearance and habits. She would lie every morning on a chaise longue in her bedroom wearing a white or lilac shawl, a linen nightgown, and a lace nightcap on her *ondulé* gray hair, polishing her nails with a tortoiseshell buff until the ends of her fingers were "glassy." Then she would begin to read or play solitaire. As the children stopped by on their way down to breakfast, she would present her parchmentlike cheek to be kissed, giving off a faint fragrance of Pear's soap and eau de cologne. One grandchild calculated that her chin had "a thousand wrinkles."[7] Later in the morning she would descend to her drawing room to deal with correspondence, firmly closing the door behind her. Occasionally a privileged child would be allowed in to play on the white polar-bear rug. Half a century later Archie's daughter Nancy remembered sneaking sideways glances at her from floor level, and marveling at "the old-fashioned grace of her slender white hands, still beautiful in spite of the enlarged knuckles and heightened blue veins, flying swiftly over intricate embroidery or carefully penning a note in her angular Spenserian script."

Sometimes a grandchild would be asked to recite or sing a song. "Billy Boy" always reminded her of Quentin, and the tears would trickle down her face in "a steady flow."[8]

Granddaughters on the whole were drawn to Edith more than grandsons. Most of the latter found her unsympathetic. They resented the fact that she always allocated them the hardest beds in the house. "Which one have you got?" they would ask one another. "The Rock of Ages or Pharaoh's Heart?" Any boy who left his room untidy with apple cores or dried fruit pips would find them on his dessert plate at the next meal. When Archie Junior nearly cut his hand off playing with his grandfather's sword, she told him "not to fuss and to go in to lunch." (This caused no surprise among the adults in the family, who remembered one occasion when Theodore had cut his head climbing the windmill and, seeking his wife's sympathy, was dismissed with: "Please, Theodore, go and drip in the bathroom.")[9]

In the afternoon, Grandmother would emerge wearing a straw hat and carrying a large basket, and would proceed to clip flowers. If it was not too hot she would take the dogs for a walk. Even if the animals got into a fight, she never lost her self-possession. Nancy recalled being ordered once to "grab one tail while I hold the other to separate them."

Edith's walks almost invariably led her toward the seashore. Beaches, buoys, boats, fountains, cataracts—anything associated with water appealed to her. She still loved to swim, as she had done with Theodore, and could often be seen in Oyster Bay in a ballooning black bathing suit, surrounded by numerous grandchildren playing "impudent minnows to her indifferent whale."[10]

In the evening, Edith would sit in white dress and pointed shoes, on the piazza, knitting and reminiscing about her girlhood: how as a teenager she used to wish on the first star, and how vain she had been, matching the color of a dress to the fur of her red setter dog.[11]

On Sundays, Edith would don "a heavy old fashioned widow's veil tossed back over her head" and implacably lead children and grandchildren to church. "She would glare at family whispers," said Nancy, or produce candy for the coughers "from a dainty chaste silver box. . . . She followed the service with attention . . . passing out to the children and more sluggish members of her family the correct passage and page."[12]

As Edith moved on into her seventies, she began to have more frequent attacks of heart thumping. Dr. Alexander Johnston, a stately young physician recommended to her by Dick Derby, diagnosed this as paroxysmal tachycardia, a functional disturbance during which the normal heart rate of, say, seventy or eighty beats a minute changes to exactly double. The malfunction (not necessarily brought on by overexertion) would begin abruptly, often last several hours, and cause her pain and sometimes prostration until the beat returned, just as abruptly, to normal. There was no drug at that time to alleviate the condition, and Edith spent many uncomfortable days and sleepless nights which she graphically described as "white."[13]

In spite of declining health, she kept up a punishing schedule of letter-writing (dozens of them to the unemployed who sought her aid); of reading to invalid neighbors, entertaining, and making public appearances, some of them not without their lighter moments. She wryly told Ted about one Roosevelt House tea where she was mobbed by "old old friends dating back to my girlhood who put their arms about me as we met. Total strangers with their tales of having shaken hands with Father, and several guests whose minds must have wandered a bit. One whose mother was intimate with my family at Chestnut Hill, one whose mother had been present at my marriage in that house . . ."[14]

At a luncheon of her old Comstock School classmates, Edith was amused to be toasted as "the embodiment of the highest ideals of American Womanhood." This was one accolade to which she would never lay claim, since she had a grand contempt for the kind of housewifely duties most women boasted about. "Thank goodness the Lord never asked that sort of thing of me," she said tartly to a young relative complaining of domestic drudgery. The latter's private feeling was that "it would have required more nerve than even the Almighty possessed" to have submitted Edith "to such indignities."[15]

From time to time she was plagued by the threatened publication of childhood letters of her own and Theodore's. She despised "the flourishing of nursery annals before the world," and hoped that Kermit could buy them for her, or "exact payment for the Estate which may act as deterrent."[16]

Theodore Roosevelt, Jr., duly replaced as Governor-General of the Philippines, arrived home from Manila in September 1933. He had won the respect and gratitude of the islanders by keeping their banks open during FDR's "holiday" closing earlier in the year. Though he was returning with no prospect of a political post, he was not unemployed for long. He accepted the job first as director and then as chairman of the board of the American Express Company. Edith occasionally met some of Ted's business acquaintances, but she found them dull. "A pleasant time was had by none," she wrote after one unsuccessful luncheon.

Her relationship with her eldest son was in fact deteriorating. "I wonder what I can have done to offend Ted," she asked Kermit. "As far as he is concerned it had been better if I had been dead . . . I have been no possible use, merely an ignored liability."[17] Apparently it did not occur to her that at forty-six her eldest son and heir, securely established in business with four children and as yet no permanent home, might be casting longing glances at Sagamore Hill, and wondering when his seventy-two-year-old mother was going to tire of running such an enormous household.

"Such a year of despair," Edith wrote enigmatically in her diary on March 4, 1934. As usual she sought comfort in a warm climate, and took ship for Greece two days later with Ethel. She felt too weary to disembark at all points along the Ionian coast "unless for a great reason such as Olympia." Here she was rewarded with a vision of paradise, as ravishing as it was unexpected. Walking among the pine woods, the wildflowers and the broken columns she came upon a river crossed by a tiny footbridge. As she stepped out upon it the sound of music echoed across the water. "A little lad was piping on the bank of the river."

For two days she could not shake the beauty of the scene from her mind. "There's a wonderful sentence in Sidney's *Arcadia,* I think," she wrote Ted. *'Piping in the Golden Age, as if the world would ever be young.'* That's not quite it. Perhaps you remember . . ."[18]

In the fall of 1934, Archibald Roosevelt hit upon a way of supplementing his diminished income, and at the same time educating his daughters (Archie Junior was already at Groton). He opened a small private school for ten- to sixteen-year-olds in the garage adjoining his house on Turkey Lane in Cold Spring Harbor. Grace was the official headmistress, but certified teachers were brought in to do the actual instruction. The curriculum featured French, German, and Latin, with heavy emphasis on English and American literature. Sometimes in the evenings Archie would come in and regale the weary students with long recitations of his father's favorite poems, such as *The Saga of King Olaf* and the more recondite lyrics of Kipling.[19]

The school thrived, and after Edith had been to see it she wrote in her diary: "A problem solved." It was always a relief to see her children making money, especially in these financially troubled times. Remembering Theodore's expensive gambles with politics, she confessed to being "unambitiously satisfied when the comforting thought of Kermit and Archie established in business careers crosses my mind."[20] Ted she was not quite as easy about, for she knew that at heart his great ambition in life had been to achieve the same heights as his father.

In January 1935, Edith traveled to South America. Stopping as usual in the Canal Zone, she was pleased to find that it was still a part of the world where her husband was revered. "'Dear old Teddy,'" the man in the street says . . . he has become a conglomerate of Santa Claus and a tribal deity."[21] She continued on to Guatemala, soaking up sunshine and sea air. On her way back at the end of January she received word of the birth of her first great-grandchild, William McMillan, Jr., to Ted's daughter Grace.

This was Edith's last visit to Latin America, and as she sat in the majestic isolation of Mortlake in the waning summers of her life she would be glad to have so many odd corners of that part of the world "to flash before the inward eye." For the immediate future, at least, travel of any kind had to be sacrificed, because for the first time in

"It was always a relief to see her children making money."
Archibald Bulloch Roosevelt and his family, 1935.

years her annual income had dropped below twenty-thousand
dollars. That fall she was much frustrated by this calamity, for she
had to refuse an invitation to join Kermit on a trip to Belfast,
Northern Ireland. (Her son was now Vice-President of International
Mercantile Marine, and had to make the crossing to plan for direct
weekly passenger and cargo services to the United States, just as his

great-grandfather Carow might have done a hundred years before.)
But Edith's financial adviser said bluntly she could not afford to go.
"I would have found myself a good maid who could trot sightseeing
with me, and have been no bother at all," she moaned. "O cruel
George [Cruikshank] thou wert unkind!"[22]

Instead, she found herself on September 16, 1935, the 148th
anniversary of the adoption of the Constitution, making a speech to
the National Conference of Republican Women, which was broadcast
nationwide. By some miracle a recording of the speech has survived.
Though crackly and occasionally indistinct with age, the old discs
vividly reproduce the unique quality of Edith's voice, and even
something of her regal "presence." The timbre of her high, clear
tones, and many of her enunciations, uncannily resemble those of the
British royal family, although the sentiments expressed—in a plea for
loyalty to the ideals of George Washington—are defiantly American.
"To them in this crisis we dedicate our lives . . . never to fall back in
our purpose to leave to our children, and to our children's children,
the freedom of life and thought which has been ours. For if we fall, we
fall like Lucifer, never to hope again."

The applause that followed was resounding. Evidently Edith was
in full command of her audience. For all her reticence, she was a born
public speaker, able to manipulate emotions without being moved
herself. "Shall I make them laugh or shall I make them cry?" she
would ask humorously before making an address.[23]

In early November Edith went to New York to see the new
operetta *Porgy and Bess*. "Exciting music," was the verdict, "but not
to compare artistically with play."[24] During the same week she was
somewhat preoccupied making a list of possessions she wanted to
leave as gifts in her will to each of her children. Her heart was
"thumping" increasingly now, and she had trouble sleeping. Then on
the night of November 12, 1935, the accident that all old people
dread befell her. She rose from her bed in the dark to open a window,
stumbled, and fell heavily on her right hip. She could hardly crawl
back into bed, and the following morning was taken to North County
Community Hospital, where a severe fracture was diagnosed, and she
was sentenced to a prolonged stay under medical care. The hip bone,
brittle with age, stubbornly refused to knit, and she remained in the
hospital for the next five months. This long inactivity depressed her

so much that she even discontinued her daily diary jottings, not to resume them until January 1937. Ted, visiting her, found her "much weaker than I had hoped . . . All she wished to hear . . . dealt with old times, she did not want to know of the present."[25]

Edith fought against a natural inclination to be morbid and crotchety. Over and over she repeated to herself the French phrase: *"On sourit. La gaieté c'est une politesse."*[26]

Thirty-Seven

Dark morning a tired old child facing a robbed life. Praying for its end.

—Edith Kermit Roosevelt[1]

In April 1936, hospital doctors put Edith into a heavy brace, and, with the aid of a "walker" and a nurse, she managed to traverse the whole length of her corridor and back. "There is a glow of light ahead," she wrote Kermit after he had visited her. "I am thinking of Sagamore! Dearest love. I hated to have you see me at my worst."[2]

She herself had not been seeing her favorite son at *his* best. Radiation treatment for persistent warts on his hand had turned his left thumb cancerous, and it had had to be amputated at the first joint. For years, moreover, he had shown signs of succumbing to "the curse of the Roosevelts"—alcohol. Now he was drinking heavily, and had begun to take drugs to dull the pain in his thumb, the discomfort of recurrent malarial fever (contracted in South America) and the spiritual ache in his heart. This last was caused by a variety of factors: frustration in his career (the business world did not really suit him), fundamental dislike of the frantic social life enjoyed by Belle

491

and the circle in which he moved, and the need he still felt for his father's guidance and advice, as if he had never quite grown up. "You will know how the bottom has dropped out for me," he had told Edith after Theodore's death. People had often noticed similarities of manner, taste and temperament between Kermit and his father. Theodore himself had said, "Kermit and I are so much alike."[3] In recent years the son had even begun to resemble his father physically. The slight blond appearance that Kermit had kept through his teens had by now given way to a darker, thicker persona, and the once-sensitive face was jowly. One day Edith unexpectedly sighted him coming toward the house, walking with a cane, his head bent. He "looked so like Father," she told Ethel, "that my heart gave a jump."[4]

Kermit had always been happiest when searching for rare books, writing some of his own *(War in the Garden of Eden, The Happy Hunting Ground, Trailing the Giant Panda)*, studying languages, and exploring the nether reaches of the world. But there was less and less time for these pursuits as the responsibilities of work and family grew. His four children were very different personalities, and although they found their father fun to be with, did not feel that he invited closeness.[5]

Woodrow Wilson's aide Colonel House once told Fanny Parsons that of all Theodore Roosevelt's children Kermit was "the most brilliant," who if he "showed" could be President of the United States.[6] But Kermit did not "show." Far from attempting to scale the summit of society and politics, he preferred to seek refuge in drink, and solace in the company of simple, sympathetic women outside his own class for the most part (one of them was a masseuse)—much as his Uncle Elliott had done. He had too much of the sensibility and introspection of his mother, and too little of the driving ambition of his father and elder brother, to have sought high office. One member of the Knickerbocker Club said he loved to watch Kermit come in "because all the old gentlemen immediately put down their papers and sat on the edge of their chairs" waiting for a story, or an account of some adventure.[7]

His physical stamina, even in his forties, was legendary. The natives in the Tian Shan mountains of China insisted on one day's rest for every day spent exploring with him because he set such an impossible pace. He was also, like his father, a skillful taxidermist, allegedly able "to skin a mouse while riding on a pad elephant."[8]

"You will know how the bottom has dropped out for me."
Kermit Roosevelt in the 1930s.

Kermit spoke several languages (including Portuguese, Swahili, Hindustani and Urdu) with great enthusiasm and fluency, though little regard for grammar. One winter he read Cervantes in the original as he traveled to and from his office by subway.[9]

There was never any doubt, after Quentin's death, that Kermit was the son Edith found most *sympathique*. Even when he came in flushed from drinking she would say, "I know he's a naughty boy, but I just love him." He was indeed infinitely lovable, and worth saving from the abyss that gaped ever wider before him. But whether he himself wanted to be saved, she could never determine.[10]

Edith spent the early winter of 1937 in a cottage in St. Andrew's, Florida, a fishing village on the Gulf of Mexico near Panama City. The house, rented on the slim evidence of a photograph, was grandiloquently called Magnolia Manor. But it proved to be something less than baronial. For one thing it was in a poor neighborhood, and for another the kitchen cabinet was "a cockroach apartment." Edith could do little about the former, but depended on her Irish cook, Bridget Turbidy, to get rid of the infestation. Her only other companions were her two maids, Mary Sweeney and Clara Lee— who had been the wife of her old White House coachman Charlie. She had hoped to have Belle, who "has always been a daughter to me," with her, but she was ill and Kermit had taken her to Switzerland instead.[11]

The quiet days were spent walking stiffly and slowly along the beach, listening to mockingbirds singing in the *magnolia grandiflora* in front of the house, and watching the glorious sunsets over the bay. After two weeks Edith began to feel herself again "for the first time in fifteen months."[12] Villagers brought fresh fish, quail and vegetables, and Edith gave a tea party for the editorial staff of the local high school newspaper, *The Tornado Whirl*. One polite, low-voiced girl asked Edith for the story of her life. Such questions always struck the former First Lady as intrusive. "Is there *anything* that can't be asked about?" she said in mock surprise.[13]

Archie and Grace came for a couple of days in late March, and the latter expounded on the awfulness of Magnolia Manor in a letter to Belle:

> The house is dark with large trees all about, dripping moss which keeps every bit of sunlight from penetrating. The house is gloomy beyond words and furnished more terribly and in the same style as Yellowbanks. It is surrounded with poor white shacks and when our m-in-l

> [*sic*] gives a pea hen shriek, as she does very frequently.
> now for Clara, or pounds on the floor with her cane, all
> the near neighbors come to the door to see what is going
> on. . . . The maids all loathe it and wept on our
> shoulders about it . . .[14]

Archie added acidly that his mother's house was in a suburb
"something like the road between the Queensboro Bridge and
Jamaica."[15]

By early April Edith herself had had enough of St. Andrew's.
"Florida is in no way my mind," she told Belle. "Heaven helping me
I shall never see it again but it exactly served my turn this
winter . . ."

When she got back to New York in late April she bought a Buick
automobile, and in June motored to Mortlake, where she stayed until
August 4. In the meantime, Kermit's continuing battle with alcohol
caused an understandable estrangement with his mother. She was
"bitterly anxious" about him through the fall of 1937, and welcomed
any overture toward her which seemed a gesture of a return to
normality. "Dearest Kermit I am always thinking about you," she
wrote on October 24, "and should you ever want to see me I will
appear."[16]

Nineteen thirty-eight began on a somber note. "Dark morning
tired old child facing a robbed life. Praying for its end," Edith wrote
in her diary. The Christmas and New Year celebrations at Sagamore
Hill had exhausted her slender resources of energy. "I could have
cried with fatigue," she confessed to fourteen-year-old Nancy. It was
a relief to have the Pilgrimage over on January 6 so that she could sail
for a vacation in Madeira. Yet even the sea voyage, so beloved in the
past, had become a trial because of her continuing lameness and
fragility. "The extreme difficulty of moving when there is the least bit
of motion makes it a languorous joy," she told Ethel.[17]

Madeira failed to improve her mood: the island was windy and
boring, and she considered her bill at the Ritz appallingly expensive.
"Robbers all," she fumed as she sailed away to Lisbon. She was more
contented in that exquisite city, and made sightseeing visits to the
Mausoleum of Portuguese Kings, the fortress tower of Belém, from
whence Vasco da Gama had made his epochal sea voyage to the East,

and the palace of Sintra, which Byron once described as the most beautiful place in the world. Edith also had a delightful picnic in the pine woods beyond Estoril, and read, as she always did when away from home, Shakespeare—usually the historical plays, or *Hamlet* or *Macbeth,* but never *Lear* nowadays, with its "too tragic" treatment of old age.[18]

She arrived back in New York on March 17, still tired and lame and frequently incapacitated by heart trouble. Her doctor recommended brandy, an effective cardiac stimulant. Edith skeptically tried it, found it did not go to her head, and was so pleased by its effects that she began to understand Kermit's weakness for it. She even went so far as to tell him so.[19]

In 1937, Ted and his wife decided that after twenty-seven years of living in rented houses, they did not want to wait any longer for Sagamore Hill. There had been an understanding in the family that when Edith died her eldest son would inherit the house. As early as 1920, when Elihu Root had asked the widow to turn her home over to the Roosevelt Memorial Association to be preserved in honor of Theodore, she had refused, saying it must be kept for Ted.[20] But Edith's amazing resiliency after her accident persuaded Eleanor that it was time to build a home with more up-to-date facilities. Ted agreed, and acquired the old orchard adjacent to Sagamore Hill from his mother. Bill McMillan, his architect son-in-law, was brought in to design a $90,000 Georgian-style mansion and ground was broken that year. By April 1938 "Old Orchard House" was complete, and Eleanor furnished and decorated it with colorful scrolls from Tibet, porcelain, embroideries and carpets from China, stone heads from Cambodia, a carved amber wood fourposter bed from the Philippines, and other treasures collected on her travels round the world. Edith liked the house, but was not pleased to receive a bill from Eleanor amounting to $140 for new trees to separate the two properties, nor when she learned she was expected to "rebuild the dock" on her own shore, but not for her own convenience.[21]

During the next few years, her relationship with Eleanor became more and more strained. There were times when Edith felt that her daughter-in-law wanted "to say goodbye as soon as I came into the room." "I understand her less than any of my three in-laws," she complained to Ethel, "and really it should be the other way round."

She suspected that Eleanor was the kind of person who was happy only when she had a definite job to do, and would become increasingly restless now that Old Orchard House was finished. Her son's wife, she concluded, "did not have 'a heart at leisure with itself/ To soothe and sympathize.'"[22]

On the afternoon of Edith's seventy-seventh birthday, Kermit came to see her at Sagamore Hill. No word survives as to his physical and mental condition during the visit, except Edith's despairing diary entry afterward: *"La tristesse au fond de tout."*[23]

Emily was in the United States that summer, but Edith saw little of her. She traveled about the Eastern seaboard visiting relatives and friends, and appeared at Sagamore Hill only for brief periods. The message that she was not really welcome there appeared finally to have sunk in. Her incompatibility with her sister now bordered on outright estrangement, a situation which Edith would soon have cause to regret.

The weather that fall was violent and ominous. A September hurricane wrought havoc in the Northeastern states (Sagamore Hill itself somehow escaped), cutting off electricity in Oyster Bay, blowing in windows, tearing down trees. The three big elms in front of Mortlake were uprooted, and a little provost house was lifted from its foundations and dumped in Edith's garden.[24] With her Shakespearean awareness of pathetic fallacy, she could hardly have avoided a sense of foreboding.

As fall turned to winter, her isolation increased, and she welcomed letters from her grandchildren. Nancy Roosevelt, who was now fifteen and at school in Maryland, was one of her favorites, a slender, sensitive, voluble girl with "a loving and unselfish heart." Nancy really loved her grandmother, who in turn confided her innermost feelings in a way that she was too proud to do to other people. "I was rather down," she wrote in November 1938, "for winter is on the way and the North Room is cold, and I felt alone and a thousand years old." By the end of that month the hill was covered in a thick blanket of snow, and she confessed her perennial longings to board a ship and sail away to a warm country. As the old woman worked at her desk, a kitten lay "purring furiously" in her lap. Suddenly it jumped on the table and started playing with her pen. There was otherwise, she told Nancy sadly, "not much news."[25]

The tropical sunshine of Haiti in February 1939 was just beginning to ease Edith's stiff bones and muscles when she received a cable telling her that Emily was seriously ill with pneumonia. A subsequent message said that her sister was out of danger and convalescent, but on March 10, after Edith had returned to Oyster Bay, Emily took a turn for the worse. On March 13 a message came: "No hope." Edith at once made plans to sail, but a final cable forestalled her. Emily had died on March 19. She was seventy-three years old, and had lived in Italy for over fifty years.[26]

The granddaughter of her closest friend, Madame Rappis, was with her at the end, and wrote describing the dying woman's last hours:

> One day she told me: "God bless my sister, nephews and nieces." Poor Emily, she needed love! Quite lately she asked me to call her Aunt Emily . . . Tomorrow morning we'll accompany her to the cemetery; like she wished, she'll rest near her dear friends, my Granny and Father.[27]

The subtle reproof in this letter would not be lost on Edith. Another letter, from the president of the Italian Red Cross, reassured her that at least some people had cared for her sister at the end, and been moved by her death. Fellow nurses had dressed her for burial in a white uniform "as a last token of love and homage."

Ted was the chief beneficiary of Emily's will. He inherited Villa Magna Quies and its olive grove, valued at $5,000, along with government bonds valued at $800, and half of her Carow silver. The other half went to Ethel, who also received jewelry and all articles of gold.

Several Italians, claiming to have served Emily in some capacity, wrote to her sister claiming they had been promised money or goods as remuneration for their various services. Edith resisted their overtures. Only the dead woman's personal maid and cook were permitted gifts of furniture and clothing.[28]

Edith would feel guilt over Emily's lonely death for the rest of her life. "This is Aunt Emily's birthday," she wrote on one anniversary, "and I am wondering if I could have made her life happier and fuller.

The Bible says somewhere 'Love is the fulfillment of the law,' and I suppose I should have loved her more deeply; but that little impish quality that she had put me off. And that is no excuse at all!"[29]

Edith's unusual sensitivity to nature sharpened as she entered extreme old age. She noted the changing seasons, and was profoundly affected by them. Snow depressed her with its white bleakness, and she welcomed the renewal of life brought by spring. She watched intently for the first signs of the vernal season—a daffodil in Smith's Field, or a dandelion in the meadow; the first asparagus in the vegetable garden, and the first bloodroot in the woods. "No! No! Not even one bud," she wrote crossly in her diary on April 11, 1939.

It was a late and trying spring. The North Room was shorn of its treasures for an exhibition at Roosevelt House. Since most of the exhibits were mementos of Theodore, Edith hated to lose them, even temporarily. Then Sagamore Hill itself was reassessed for local taxes at $1,200 an acre on seventy-nine acres, and her one acre of shoreline revalued at $29,000. To crown it all, Kermit came back from an unsuccessful alcoholic cure. "He seems to have broken down nervously into pieces," Archie told Arthur Lee. In her diary his mother wrote: *"Miserere nobis."*[30]

The summer sojourn at Mortlake restored Edith's strength for the first time in months, but the news of September 1 set her back again. Germany attacked Poland, and on the third Britain and France declared war on the aggressor. But Poland was completely conquered in four weeks. "Can only pray it may not be a great war," Edith wrote.[31]

At least one person in her family rather hoped it might be. The spreading European conflict presented a challenge to Kermit Roosevelt that was lacking in his everyday life, and in early September he sailed for England to offer his military services to Winston Churchill.

Thirty-Eight

I strove with none; for none was worth my strife;
Nature I loved, and, next to Nature, Art;
I warmed both hands before the fire of life;
It sinks, and I am ready to depart.
                                    —Walter Savage Landor[1]

Although Winston Churchill was not yet Prime Minister of Great Britain in the autumn of 1939, he had just been named First Lord of the Admiralty, and was able on the strength of Kermit Roosevelt's distinguished name to secure him a commission in the British Army. On October 24 Edith heard over the radio that her son had been made a major in his old regiment from Mesopotamian days, the Middlesex.[2]

Early in 1940 it became clear to British Intelligence that Hitler intended to invade Scandinavia. A special reconnaissance mission was therefore sent to Norway, and Kermit was part of it. When the Germans attacked in April, he fought in the Battle of Narvik, performing amazing feats under fire to rescue equipment and men, "in many instances carrying the wounded on his back."[3] But in less than two months the Germans drove the British out, and Kermit was transferred to Egypt. Here in September he fell ill with malarial fever and dysentery. Edith read about this collapse in the newspaper and wrote worriedly in her diary: "Kermit always on my mind."[4]

Continued physical weakness, combined with what was officially described as a "heart condition," resulted in his being invalided out of the Army at the end of the year. Kermit appealed to Churchill (now Prime Minister) early in 1941 to reinstate him, but was tactfully refused:

> MY DEAR MAJOR ROOSEVELT:
> I have made enquiries about the possibility of your remaining on the active list, but I am afraid that after reading the medical reports I cannot feel that you are at present fit for active service. . . .

Still unable to accept that physically he was a ruined man, Kermit asked Churchill for a position on a minesweeper. The Prime Minister replied on March 25:

> . . . While I have nothing but admiration for your anxiety to serve in any capacity . . . I am sorry that the medical reports on your case make it impossible for me to recommend you for anything of this kind . . . I hate to disappoint you because I know how truly your heart is with us.[5]

Kermit disconsolately returned to the United States in late June 1941. If he had drunk heavily before, he now began to drink as if he were bent on self-destruction.

By the summer of 1941, Ted, too, had applied for active duty—in *his* old regiment, the 26th Infantry, First Division, then in training at Fort Devens, Massachusetts. He was now fifty-four years old, and before the year was out would be promoted to Brigadier General and Deputy Divisional Commander. His youngest son, twenty-one-year-old Quentin, also enlisted, and was assigned to the Field Artillery in the same division.

Edith, meanwhile, to whom the whole year was a nightmare repeat of 1914, grew physically and mentally frailer, to the point where she could not always manage to balance her own checkbook and answer her own mail. Ethel and Archie and the dependable Mr. Cruikshank helped straighten out her finances, while her granddaughters Edith Derby Williams and Sarah Derby Gannett could be relied on to help with letters. Edith had always prided herself on her ability to handle finances. ("Mamma says I must tell you that I am very practical and know a great deal about money," she had written Theodore fifty-five years before during their engagement.) Now she felt "ashamed" at the diminution of her powers.

One thing at least happened to cheer her during the summer. At Mortlake, on August 6, 1941, she opened *The New York Times* to find herself the subject of an editorial.

> Mrs. Edith Kermit Carow Roosevelt is 80 today. The general regard, or should we say affection, that the public has had for her so many years will deprive of any air of intrusion a congratulation on this anniversary. To the elder among us the mention of her name calls back the years when the White House rang with the shouts and laughter of children. Never had it been, nor is it likely to be again, so noisy and so happy. And it was through her good offices that the White House was restored according to the plans of its architect. A well-stored mind, a gracious presence and nature, kindness as well as dignity are hers. She has had an easy gayety at the proper time; in the hour of sorrow a tranquil courage. She has, too, a sense of humor, sometimes exercised pleasantly at the expense of the extraordinary man or compound of several kinds of men that was the elder Theodore Roosevelt. He is nobly commemorated by statue, by building, by many memorials and visits to his birthplace and his home. Let us not wait too long to say it: This is a great as well as a beloved woman.

Sagamore was lovelier than ever in the fall of 1941. Roses were still blooming, raspberries ripening, and the sun so warm through September that Edith spent much of the day out of doors. But on October 4 the sharp sound of a telephone bell shattered her tranquillity. The caller was a doctor in New Jersey, who told her that

Kermit had been found in a local dive so prostrated with alcohol as to need emergency treatment. Numb with shock, she called Archie, who had long been concerned about his brother, and he promised to go at once and pick Kermit up.[6]

"Anxious and in great suspense," Edith wrote in her diary. "Worked at a confused check book, for steadiness." Next morning, Sunday, she went to church alone. The weather was very hot when she arrived home, and she stayed indoors the rest of the day. That evening Archie returned "greatly exhausted." Over dinner he told her what he had been doing during the last twenty-four hours. Finding Kermit incapable, he had hired an ambulance, taken him to an alcoholic-treatment center, the Hartford Retreat, in Connecticut, and had him committed. Whether the treatment would be effective or not no one could say. "I have but little hope," Edith wrote afterward.

During the night she was awakened by heart pain, and had to summon her doctor for morphine. Under its influence she drowsed for most of the following day on a sofa.

The events of the next five weeks are best deduced from Edith's terse diary entries.

October 8	. . . Heart very heavy for one problem.
October 9	Always one thought on my mind.
October 10	Sent K. birthday message.
October 16	A letter from Kermit gave me great happiness. Suffers, but no resentment. v. loving.
October 20	Archie in p.m. with sad papers etc.
October 22	. . . At peace again—but without hope.
October 25	Letter from Kermit asking me to come up.
October 31	Troubled by Kermit's letter—answered it as I could.
November 1	All Saints' Day . . . prayed for K. . . . Archie in p.m. troubled about my inevitable trip to see K.
November 6	Saw Kermit in a.m. Cannot write.
November 7	Saw K. in morning. Started for home arrived early afternoon. Cannot write. God grant me wisdom.
November 9	Too tired when I went to bed for prayers.
November 13	Very tired and sad. Cannot put Hartford away.

What had happened was that Kermit, after his initial recovery from his binge, had demanded to be released. When Edith and Archie would not agree to this, he sued his brother for unjust incarceration. But Archie won the case, and Kermit remained for the time being in the Hartford retreat.[7]

The Nazi advance across Europe over ground long familiar to Edith was yet another source of distress to her during the winter of 1941–42. She felt as though she "were watching the desperate illness of one whom I loved."[8]

Soon after the attack on Pearl Harbor on December 7, 1941, and President Franklin Roosevelt's subsequent declaration of war on Japan, Archie began to talk of going to fight in the Pacific. Edith tried to discourage him: she was not in favor of upholding "English rule in Australia."[9] But she knew the futility of trying to keep back any son of Theodore's when war beckoned. "Heart heavy with sorrow," she wrote on January 2, 1942.

But a joyful telegram from Kermit, who had finally been released from Hartford, lifted her spirits only three days later. Next morning, January 6, was the twenty-third anniversary of Theodore's death. In deference to her frailty, the Roosevelt Pilgrimage was not observed for the first time. Edith did not mind. "Wrote checks and am quite myself again. So happy to be alone with my memories."

On February 10 another telephone call from a doctor's office in New Jersey rudely jerked Edith back to the present. But this time the voice on the line was Kermit's. He announced that he was about to enter Overlook Hospital in Summit, for what *The New York Times* later described as a "general checkup,"[10] and asked if he could bring a Dr. Stevens and a Dr. Lee to see his mother at Sagamore Hill. Edith agreed, and the two physicians duly arrived on February 14 in time for lunch. Kermit, however, did not appear until three. Nothing is known of the subject discussed during this mysterious meeting except what can be inferred from Edith's enigmatic diary entry for the day: "A hard blow."

The situation in Southeast Asia was calamitous in the first nine months of 1942. Japan had swept through the Pacific islands, taking Thailand, Singapore and Hong Kong, and was now preparing to attack the Philippines. "The last news has been so bad," Edith wrote Ted in mid-February, "that I cannot write of it and it is all I can do to hold myself together. Today I walked down the back road and turned toward the tennis court and stopped and looked at this dear house where we have had such happiness. It is better to live in the past for old ladies like me." [11]

During this winter of worldwide discontent, her wispy gray hair, which she was always unsuccessfully trying to anchor in "a strict Grecian knot" became "a fluff of white," and her weight fell to below one hundred pounds. [12] Kermit was always in her consciousness, although she by now decided that there was absolutely no hope for him. He remained at Overlook through April but the treatment there seems to have been unsuccessful, and Archie was obliged to recommit him to the Hartford Retreat at the end of the month. On May 1 Edith wrote in her diary: *"Qui tollit peccatur mundi miserere nobis."* Then she took from her bookshelf a copy of *Cleared for Strange Ports,* the book they had written together, and began to reread his vivid account of their journey across Siberia. Determinedly she tried to think only good thoughts of him.

Sometime in early summer Archibald Roosevelt received a telephone call from the President of the United States. "What are we going to do about Kermit?" Then, in the manner of a man who preferred to answer his own questions, Cousin Franklin went on to suggest that he commission Kermit as a major in the American Army, and have him sent somewhere well out of harm's way. Archie approved the suggestion, but was unprepared for just what theater of operations FDR had in mind. When Kermit's orders arrived, it was found that he had been posted to Alaska. [13]

Kermit telephoned to say goodbye to his mother at Mortlake on July 14, 1942. By one of those curious coincidences of fate which cast a shadow over so many of the Roosevelt family's anniversaries, it was twenty-four years to the day since Quentin had been killed. Something in Kermit's conversation or tone of voice made Edith uneasy. She was not optimistic about his future, she told Ethel. [14]

The Japanese had occupied the islands of Attu and Kiska in the western Aleutians, and it was feared that they might use these as a steppingstone to attack the American mainland. Consequently a defense force had to be stationed there as the country's northwestern bastion. As far as Kermit was concerned, local duty would not be too onerous, consisting mainly of reconnaissance flights across the Aleutians. He had hunted the Kodiak bear there in 1937, and was familiar with the terrain.

Edith's pessimism about him was dispelled somewhat on September 4, when *The New York Times* called to say that in a counteroffensive against Japan Kermit had done well. But after this initial success winter settled down over the Aleutians, leaving Kermit and his fellow officers little to do. They grew so bored that they began to bribe the Air Force to fly in cases of liquor.[15]

By January 1943, Kermit had already suffered several internal hemorrhages, and he was flown on a stretcher to Barnes General Hospital in Vancouver Barracks, Washington State. Here it was found that he had a severe case of secondary anemia. Belle went out to see him, and was told by the Medical Board that there was no possibility of her husband returning to active service. In spite of this he soon talked his way out of the hospital on sick leave, and in late March headed east.[16]

It was a cold day when fifty-three-year-old Major Roosevelt climbed Sagamore Hill to see his mother again for one brief hour on April 4, 1943. Edith noted that his eyes were clear and his skin good. But he was puffy about the jowls, and had lost the taut abdominal muscles that he had once had in common with his father. She also detected a personality change. Gone were the last vestiges of his old gaiety and charm; he was no longer "my Fiddler of Dooney."[17]

> *For the good are always the merry,*
> *Save by an evil chance,*
> *And the merry love the fiddle,*
> *And the merry love to dance . . .*

Yeats's fiddler had been in paradise, but Kermit was demonstrably in hell.

After he left, Edith walked about the house admiring the rare, unusual gifts that had been his trademark over the years. A pretty red wood tray on her dressing table, a pink rabbit in the drawing room, a bag hanging from the library screen. "In each room," she wrote him afterward, "I can think of you."[18]

She would never see her son again. He returned to Alaska,

"bewitched" the doctors into allowing him back on active duty, but inevitably ended up hospitalized—this time in Anchorage. On May 31, his colleagues wiped out the Japanese garrison on Attu, and the threat to mainland America was finally removed. With this went Kermit's last hope of useful service to his country. Four days later, unable to bear the life of inaction to which he was condemned, helpless to tame the demons which plagued him, Kermit Roosevelt put a .45 revolver under his chin and shot himself through the head.[19]

The following afternoon, June 5, Edith was talking to her grandson Quentin, who was at home recovering from wounds suffered in Tunisia, when Grace Roosevelt came into the room. It had been decided in the family to break the news of Kermit's death gently and not quite truthfully: Edith heard only that her son had died of heart failure.[20] After everyone had gone, she wrote Kermit's epitaph in her diary.

June 4th, 1943
Ft. Richardson, Alaska.
K.R.

O God, my God, where'er Thou art,
Keep my beloved in Thy Heart
Fold in thy Heart that head so bright
Heal him with Thy most gentle light
And since Thou mad'st forgetfulness
Forget what'er Thou find'st amiss
And since Thou mad'st remembering
Remember every lovely thing,
And then my God look down and see,
And pityingly remember me.

At Communion next day, Edith could think of only one phrase to comfort herself. It was: "Triumphant over pain."

Kermit was buried in the military cemetery at Fort Richardson on June 8. His mother tried to be brave, but the last glimmer of light had gone from her life, and she felt lonely and restless. But, she told Ethel, "mercifully all my instinctive memories of Kermit are happy. Those desperate days at Hartford have left my mind and no longer haunt me."[21]

On December 26, the doctor examined Edith and told her he wanted her to stay upstairs "for some time." She rebelled. "No! No! No!" she wrote in her diary. Feeling no more substantial than "a rag and a bone," she defiantly entertained her newlywed grandson Willard and his bride to lunch on New Year's Day 1944.[22]

In February, word came from Europe that Brigadier General Theodore Roosevelt, Jr., had been awarded France's highest military prize, the Legion of Honor. For the first time in months Edith felt a return of vitality. She had lunch with Alice (who came north more frequently now that Paulina was at Vassar) and they had a long chat about politics in general and congressional rejection of the President's tax bill in particular. Edith enjoyed her adder-tongued stepdaughter, especially when she did her famous imitation of the toothy First Lady and destroyed the reputation of Washington stuffed shirts.

In March, Ted, moving with the help of a cane on account of an arthritic hip, went to England to begin amphibious training with the Fourth Division for the coming invasion of Normandy. In April he was best man at Quentin's wedding, which took place at a small English country church. The bride was Frances Webb, a Kansas City girl who was working with the American Red Cross Clubmobile.

Two months later, on the eve of D Day, Ted wrote Eleanor from his transport:

> We are starting on the great venture of the war . . .
> We are attacking by daylight the most heavily fortified
> coast in history, a shore held by excellent troops . . . I
> go in with the assault wave and hit the beach at H Hour.
> I'm doing it because it's the way I can contribute most.
> It steadies the young men to know I am with them, to
> see me plodding along with my cane.
>
> Quentin goes in, I believe, at H plus 60. That's bad
> enough. Frankly, it may be worse than when I go in.
>
> We've had a grand life and I hope there'll be more.
> Should it chance that there's not, at least we can say
> that in our years together we've packed enough for ten

"We are starting on the great venture of the war."
Brigadier General Theodore Roosevelt, Junior, 1944.

ordinary lives. We've known joy and sorrow, triumph and disaster, all that goes to fill the pattern of human existence. Our children are grown and our grand-children are here. We have been very happy. I pray we may be together again.

This will be the last for the present. The ship is dark, the men are going to their assembly stations. Before

going on deck they sit in darkened corridors to adjust
their eyes. Soon the boats will be lowered. Then we'll be
off.[23]

At dawn next morning, Ted's boat was first ashore on Utah Beach.
By some miscalculation his troops were landed three quarters of a
mile too far south. Not much more than a hundred yards away the
enemy was entrenched, bristling with heavy and light artillery. Ted
rushed his men over a nearby wall to a safer inland position, and
then, under heavy fire, returned to direct wave after wave of other
troops in the same direction. For this act of supreme courage (cited
by General Omar Bradley as the bravest he had ever seen) Ted was
recommended by three superior officers for the Congressional Medal
of Honor—the same decoration his father had been denied after the
battle of San Juan Hill.[24]

Slowly, and at terrible cost to life, the Germans were pushed back.
Throughout June and on into July the exhausted Ted continued to
direct operations from his mobile headquarters—a made-over truck
captured from the enemy. Inside the vehicle one of the General's
aides erected a bed and desk and installed electric light. Here, in spite
of a doctor's warning that he was taxing his already overstrained
heart, Ted went on with preparations for the next attack. As he
worked, reverberations from German gunfire shook his insubstantial
shelter.

On the night of July 11, 1944, Quentin stopped by to see his father.
He found him suffering from battle fatigue, but in good spirits, and
left at about ten o'clock. Shortly afterward, Ted died of sudden heart
failure. He was buried with full military honors in the cemetery of
Sainte-Mère-Eglise, with Generals Patton and Bradley among the
pallbearers. At fifty-six, Theodore Roosevelt, Jr., had been the oldest
man in the first invasion wave on D Day. His service in two world
wars had brought him all the combat medals awarded by the United
States Army Ground Forces.

Edith was at Mortlake when the news came. She had not even
known that Ted had a weak heart. At church later she wept silently
throughout the service.[25]

A mysterious fire at Sagamore Hill in early July destroyed the
garage and a servant's cottage adjoining it. Fortunately, no one was

hurt, and Edith had the Buick with her in Brooklyn, otherwise the estimated damage of thirty thousand dollars would have been much greater. Plans for reconstructing the burned-out buildings were a distraction for her, and she began to lose the terrible sense of oppression that descended after Ted's death. But as the month wore on further, emotional paralysis set in. "Ted's death did something to me from which I shall not recover," she told Ethel, and for the first time she "dreaded to go home."

Back in Oyster Bay on August 7, she withdrew more and more into her memories so that they seemed more real than reality. When Quentin brought his wife to see her, she confused him by saying, "You were the first of my babies to die." And when Eleanor asked her what she thought of plans for a movie about Theodore, she wrote that she was "too removed from life to judge."[26]

Archibald Roosevelt, now in his fifty-first year, had been serving for nearly two years as a battalion commander with the 162nd Infantry in New Guinea. He had been awarded the Silver Star for gallantry, and promoted to Lieutenant Colonel. By a cruel twist of fate he had also been wounded by a grenade in the same knee that shrapnel shattered in the First World War. In January 1945 he suffered a recurrence of malarial fever contracted in the South Pacific, and after two months of prostration was sent to the West Coast on sick leave.[27]

The following month, General MacArthur returned, as he had promised, to the Philippines. By now the end of the war, both in Europe and the Pacific, was in sight. But the nation's Commander in Chief did not live to see it. On April 12, in Warm Springs, Georgia, Franklin Delano Roosevelt collapsed suddenly and died of a massive cerebral hemorrhage.

It was a beautiful spring day in Oyster Bay when Edith heard the news. She was stunned. During the years of war she had changed her mind about "Cousin Franklin" to the extent of saying that though he was "on the wrong side of the fence" he was, nevertheless, "a nice man," who, to her satisfaction, had turned out to be as conservative as Alexander Hamilton, and as democratic as Lincoln. "Could he but have lived until Peace," she mused in her diary, and telegraphed her niece in the White House, "Love and sympathy." Eleanor replied: "Many thanks for your kind wire. It was a shock, but I am glad he died working without pain or long illness."[28]

"He had been awarded the Silver Star for gallantry."
Lieutenant Colonel Archibald Roosevelt in World War II.

Edith approved of Truman's "intelligence and tact" in the transition period, and admired the radio speech he made five days after taking over the reins of government.[29]

In May the European war wound to its conclusion. On the third, Hitler was reported dead, and on the fifth came news of Germany's surrender. At Oyster Bay church victory service Edith felt very faint, and continued to feel weak for the next two months. Her trip to Mortlake was delayed until July 18, and while there she began to tear up some of her more recent letters, to protect them from "Little Bright Eyes." She longed now "for restful death," and hoped she might be spared "physical disgrace."[30]

On August 6, 1945, her eighty-fourth birthday, United States airplanes dropped the first atomic bomb on Hiroshima, killing 6,175 people. Three days later 36,000 more died when a second bomb exploded in Nagasaki. Neither event was recorded by Edith, who "lost track of time" between July 27 and August 12, and "entered everything wrongly." It was as if the cosmic detonations, unseen, unheard, but somehow felt, had thrown her old world off its axis. Her only later comment on the end of the war with Japan was succinct: "Hirohito has slowly come down."[31]

In September 1945, Edith employed Jessica Kraft, a cheerful part-time secretary from Oyster Bay, to help her with checks and correspondence. Mrs. Kraft usually went to Sagamore Hill in the afternoon, and if it was fine had tea with Edith on her bedroom balcony. On cooler days they often sat in the North Room, and watched birds in the bird bath under the great elm. She found her employer "meticulous over her expenses and accounts," and scrupulously faithful in answering any mail with questions about Theodore. Since she could no longer do close needlework, Mrs. Kraft would sometimes bring a box of rags from the Needlework Guild, and the old lady would occupy her hands by winding them into balls. One day when the two women were walking in the garden, the younger one remarked, "Mrs. Roosevelt, you've had such a sad life." Edith instantly replied, "I have no regrets; it's been a full one."[32]

One of her last visitors from the outside world was the talented photojournalist Stefan Lorant, author of *I Was Hitler's Prisoner*. He was an attractive, witty, cultivated man of about forty-five, who found her in turn "charming and warm." Afterward, he remembered with admiration her "sparkling blue eyes" and the "steel rod in her spine." She was a woman "who knew what she wanted."

Lorant was preparing an illustrated biography of Theodore, and wanted her to identify a historic picture he hoped to use. It was of two small boys in a window looking down on Lincoln's funeral

"La gaité c'est une politesse."
Edith Kermit Roosevelt in her last years.

procession in the year 1865. To his amazement Edith recognized it straight away. She pointed out the two boys as Theodore and Elliott Roosevelt, and told him the story of how the elder "horrible" one had pushed her into a back room because the somber parade had made her cry. She recalled with meticulous detail the dark hangings, the mournful tunes and herself as "Spotless Edie" with golden curls.

As they sat before the library fire, the journalist found himself increasingly enchanted. Getting up to leave at the conclusion of the interview, he said, "Mrs. Roosevelt, if I were ten years older, I would propose to you." Edith, smiling, came right back at him. "And, Mr. Lorant, if I were ten years younger, I would accept."[33]

The past was constantly brought back to Edith in the final years of her life. One spring, Tranquillity, the white-pillared house where her early romance with young Teedie had blossomed and withered, was pulled down to make way for a modern structure. An old friend from Albany days stopped by and evoked memories of Edith as First Lady of New York State, dancing cotillions with Governor Roosevelt's aides, and tucking favors under the pillows of her children. An even older friend, Fanny Parsons, announced that she was planning to write a volume of memoirs entitled *Perchance Some Day*. "I can't possibly guess the subject," Edith teased Ethel, aware of Fanny's youthful crush on Theodore.[34]

Her diary began to peter out in October 1945. It came to an end altogether on December 11 with: "Lovely sunny day, but I am not to be braced!" She was no longer well enough by 1946 to compose a really coherent letter, and her last surviving written communication with Ethel asks for someone to "answer stacks of mail for an incompetent mother at any price."[35]

Edith made her last will and testament in September 1946, leaving the bulk of her estate ($414,517.90) to be divided equally among Archie, Ethel, Eleanor and Belle. To Alice, who had income from other sources, she bequeathed $1,000 and the John Singer Sargent painting of the White House. Mary Sweeney, her personal maid, was left $1,500; Bridget Turbidy, her cook, $1,000, and Clara Lee, her housekeeper, $1,000.[36] All others who had served her were allotted fifty dollars for each year or fraction of a year of service.

Various grandchildren had already received substantial amounts to avoid inheritance tax. In a poignant paragraph Edith added: "It is my hope and my wish that some or all of my children and grandchildren may wish to occupy from time to time my house at Brooklyn, Connecticut." She directed it to be held in trust "for use without payment of rent and without liability for damage."[37]

With the signing of her will Edith, in effect, severed her formal attachment to life. The four seasons of 1947 found her largely bedridden, as did the spring and summer of 1948, the last she was to see. As the leaves began to fall in September and the days shortened, the final weakness stole upon her. She had long been prepared for death. Sixteen years before, at a meeting of the Oyster Bay Needlework Guild, she announced that she had chosen her own epitaph. "Nothing would please me more," she had said, "than when I die they put this inscription on my tombstone: 'Everything she did was for the happiness of others.'" Thirty-seven years before, after she had been thrown from her horse in front of Cove School, she realized she might well have been killed, and asked for a plot to be set aside in Youngs' Cemetery for Theodore and herself. She could not bear the thought of being buried in Greenwood or some other commercial graveyard. Accordingly she left instructions for her funeral, taking responsibility for dying as she had for living. "Simplest coffin possible. If the church has no pall, cover with one of my crepe shawls. Nothing on coffin but bunch of pink and blue flowers from my children. Processional Hymn No 85 'The Son of God.' *Not* slow tempo. Recessional Hymn No. 226 'Love Divine.' The anthem from Beethoven's Ninth Symphony. Service as in Prayer Book. Do not take off my wedding ring and please no embalming."[37]

Death, when it came, was swift. During the last week of the month she began to suffer from shortness of breath, and had to sleep propped up. The pain in her limbs, caused by years of arteriosclerosis, increased, and on September 29 she fell into a coma. Her maids stayed with her throughout the night, and summoned Dr. Johnston when the end seemed near. At 6:30 A.M. on September 30, 1948, Edith Kermit Roosevelt died. She was eighty-seven years old. It was her second passing from this world. The first had been on January 6, 1919.

Acknowledgments

In the summer of 1975 I happened to be seated next to Mr. P. James Roosevelt at a dinner party in his Oyster Bay home. During the course of conversation he told me that Mrs. Ethel Roosevelt Derby, the eighty-four-year-old daughter of President and Mrs. Theodore Roosevelt, had recently deposited in the Theodore Roosevelt Collection at Harvard some of the very few surviving letters from her father to her mother. At this something clicked in my head, signaling that I had found my next writing project. Four years later, with the help and constant encouragement of my host, and of Dr. John Allen Gable, Executive Director of the Theodore Roosevelt Association, I finished this biography of Edith Kermit Roosevelt.

My quest for the much admired but greatly elusive personality of Theodore Roosevelt's second wife led in many directions. As an intensely private person, Edith Roosevelt was an inveterate letter-burner. Fortunately recipients of *her* letters were not. The Theodore Roosevelt Collection at Harvard contains thousands of letters from her to her mother, sister, and sisters-in-law; and the papers of her sons Theodore, Jr., and Kermit and her stepdaughter Alice in the Library of Congress are a prodigiously rewarding source of family correspondence for the White House years and beyond. I must thank Miss Joanna Sturm, Alice Roosevelt Longworth's granddaughter, for allowing me access to her grandmother's sealed papers. Months of combing through Theodore Roosevelt's correspondence with his sister Anna Roosevelt Cowles ("Bamie"), as well as large quantities of uncatalogued material at the Theodore Roosevelt Birthplace, proved most rewarding. Equally productive were the numerous journeys I made to the basement of Sagamore Hill, Mrs. Roosevelt's home for sixty-one years, where Jessica Kraft, her part-time secretary and a former Curator, and Gary Roth, the present Curator, kindly allowed me a free run of miscellaneous Tyler and Carow papers, National Park Service interviews, news clippings, scrapbooks, photograph albums and some of Edith's personal belongings, including her size-six white leather gloves, Parisian clock stockings, and ivory fans. Mr. Roth's help was invaluable in the selection of illustrations.

Written inquiries to various near and distant relatives were also fruitful. Mr. John Alsop, a grandson of Theodore Roosevelt's sister Corinne, hospitably allowed me to spend two weekends at his Connecticut home looking through his family's personal collection of letters and photographs, the bulk of which is now transferred to Harvard.

Archibald Bulloch Roosevelt, Edith's eighty-five-year-old son, responded to my *New York Times Book Review* request for information, saying he thought his mother "deserved" a biography. He subsequently entertained me in his Florida home on two separate occasions, talked tirelessly of family matters, recited humorous anecdotes, and showed me letters, scrapbooks, and photograph albums. My debt to him and his daughter Nancy Roosevelt Jackson is very great.

Mrs. Jackson also responded to the *Times* advertisement, sending me her own beautifully written memoir of her grandmother, "A Sense of Style." She, too, showed me letters. We have met on countless occasions, and she has related some of the family stories to be found in the book.

Nancy Jackson's sisters, Theodora Rauchfuss and Edith Roosevelt, have also provided keen and telling observations, and added lively detail to this portrait of their grandmother. The other eight surviving Roosevelt grandchildren responded with generosity. Mr. Archibald Roosevelt, Jr., and his wife talked with me at length, showed me family papers, and have been unfailingly helpful. Mr. Roosevelt also sent me a copy of his *American Heritage* article, "The Ghost of

Sagamore Hill," describing childhood days with Edith. Kermit and Willard Roosevelt gave me many insights into her character and family relationships, and their sister Clochette Roosevelt Palfrey supplied me with letters and numerous anecdotes. So did Ethel Roosevelt Derby's daughters Edith Williams and Sarah Alden Gannett. The children of Theodore Roosevelt, Jr., namely Theodore Roosevelt III, Cornelius Roosevelt and Grace Roosevelt McMillan, were all most cooperative. The last-mentioned permitted me to look through all twenty-five large volumes of her mother's meticulously kept albums.

The help I received from Mrs. Edna Kunkel of Brooklyn, Connecticut, has been invaluable. We met by chance while I stood staring at the site opposite her house once occupied by Mortlake Manor. Mrs. Kunkel turned out to be a knowledgeable student of Tyler history, and had a collection of photographs showing the interior of the Manor just before it was demolished. She most kindly arranged interviews with several Brooklyn residents who had known Edith Kermit Roosevelt in old age, and provided me with nuggets of information which added richness to my last chapters. Mrs. Richard Hatch very graciously consented to be interviewed, along with Florence and Dorothy Blake, and provided space and refreshments in her own house for the occasion.

My gratitude to Dr. John Gable is immense. He has conscientiously supplied me with new material when it came to his attention, suggested potential sources, allowed me access to the Theodore Roosevelt Birthplace collection, read the completed manuscript, and written copiously detailed notes for additions and changes.

I must also thank Wallace Finley Dailey, the extraordinarily efficient Curator of the Theodore Roosevelt Collection at Harvard; Clement Conger, Curator of the White House, and Betty C. Monkman, Registrar, for answering questions, checking my chapters on the White House alterations of 1902, and supplying this book's cover illustration and other visual material.

Perhaps my greatest debt is to the late Mrs. Ethel Roosevelt Derby, who talked to me at length several times before her death in December 1977 at the age of eighty-six. She showed me family portraits, albums, books and china, and promised to look for "further documents." After she died her daughters Edith Williams and Sarah

Alden Gannett fulfilled that promise, summoning me to Oyster Bay in the great ice storm of 1978 to go through trunks and boxes of material they had discovered in their mother's attic. When it became clear that I would need several weeks to absorb the mass of papers, they insisted that I take everything home—an act of phenomenal trust and benevolence. My gratitude to them can hardly be expressed, for the Ethel Roosevelt Derby Collection encompasses Edith Kermit Roosevelt's personal diaries dating from 1901 to 1945, as well as hundreds of important letters from eminent friends and acquaintances. It contains a batch of movingly intimate letters from Edith to Theodore Roosevelt at the time of the Spanish-American War, and some earlier love letters, revealing a passion in the former First Lady which I had long suspected, but had hitherto been unable to verify. The discovery of this cache came when I was halfway through the manuscript, and led to much rewriting. If I have caught anything of the complexity and depth of Edith Roosevelt's character, it is in large part because of the thoughtfulness of Mrs. Williams and Mrs. Gannett.

Thanks are also due to my agent, Ann Elmo, and Peggy Brooks, who together arranged the contract for this book. To my editor, Joseph Kanon, who patiently waited for the manuscript, and prepared it for publication with all his renowned finesse, I am forever indebted.

Others who contributed in large or small ways to the book are so numerous that I can only list them alphabetically, and acknowledge their contributions in appropriate places in the Notes:
John Winthrop Aldrich; Elswyth Thane Beebe; Robert Bennett, Superintendent of the Executive Mansion in Albany; Patricia Bradford, Archivist at Churchill College, Cambridge; Allan Churchill; Mr. and Mrs. William Sheffield Cowles; Gypsy da Silva; Herbert Dowd; Mary Hagedorn Du Vall; Leon Edel; Dr. William R. Emerson; Dr. Ivan V. Jacobson; Cynthia Jay; Dr. Alexander Johnston; David Kahn; William Loeb; Stefan Lorant; Agnes Nagel; Helen Newman; Dr. Mary Pitlick; Doris and Stanley Rich; Elizabeth Roosevelt; Frances Roosevelt; Jean Roosevelt; Philippa Roosevelt; Michael Small; Michael Teague; William Royall Tyler; Laura Chanler White; David Wigdor of the Library of Congress; Robert Wood, Archivist, Herbert Hoover Presidential Library, and Mitchell York.

Bibliography

Sources of primary materials are divided into public and private collections, and listed in their order of importance to this book. Bracketed codes will be used in the Chapter Notes below. Secondary materials are listed alphabetically, and will be short-listed in the Notes, along with full citations of minor sources.

Primary Sources: Public Collections

(TRC) Theodore Roosevelt Collection, Widener and Houghton Libraries, Harvard, Cambridge, Mass. An enormous archive, including not only TR's personal papers, but also those of his sisters Anna ("Bamie") and Corinne. Among the last-mentioned papers are several thousand letters to and from Edith Kermit Roosevelt. Correspondence with her mother and sister alone runs to about 1,000 items.

(KR) Kermit Roosevelt Papers, Library of Congress, Washington, D.C. Includes the copious, lifelong correspondence between Edith Roosevelt and her favorite son.

(TR Jr.) Theodore Roosevelt, Jr., Papers, Library of Congress, Washington, D.C. Includes an equally copious but rather less intimate correspondence with Edith Roosevelt.

(TRB) Theodore Roosevelt Birthplace National Historic Site, New York City. The remains of the Woman's Roosevelt Association Library are rich in random materials collected by the scholar Hermann Hagedorn, including transcribed interviews, family reminiscences and photographs, as well as TR's complete, unexpurgated correspondence with his sister Anna ("Bamie").

(SH)   Sagamore Hill National Historic Site, Oyster Bay. Archives contain
                a wealth of Edith Roosevelt documents and memorabilia, including
                her personal scrapbooks, photograph albums, and a box of Quentin
                Roosevelt correspondence.

(LEE)   Arthur Lee (Viscount Lee of Fareham) Papers, Courtauld Institute,
                London. Includes half a century of correspondence with the
                Roosevelts, as well as Lord Lee's privately-printed autobiography
                (see book list below).

(CSR)   Cecil Spring-Rice Papers, Churchill College, Cambridge, England.
                Includes many letters of Edith and Theodore Roosevelt not to be
                found in Gwynn (see book list below).

(MHS)   Massachusetts Historical Society, Boston, Mass. Contains the
                Henry Cabot Lodge Papers and Henry Adams Papers. The latter
                collection includes scores of letters to and from Adams, John Hay,
                Cecil Spring-Rice, and Elizabeth Cameron.

(FDRL)   Franklin Delano Roosevelt Library, Hyde Park, N.Y. Contains
                most of the few surviving papers of Elliott and Anna Roosevelt, as
                well as those of Edith Roosevelt's niece Eleanor.

(TRP)   Theodore Roosevelt Papers, Library of Congress, Washington, D.C.
                A gigantic collection, mainly of official correspondence, including
                Edith Roosevelt's own papers as First Lady.

(NA)   National Archives, Washington, D.C. Contains Edith Roosevelt's
                impressive *White House Record of Social Functions, 1901–1909,* a 13-
                volume illustrated history of presidential entertainment at its most
                splendid.

(WH)   The White House Curator's Office, Washington, D.C. Comprehen-
                sive architectural and furnishing records, plus picture and photo-
                graph files.

Primary Sources: Private Collections

(ERD)   Ethel Roosevelt Derby Papers. An archive of transcendent impor-
                tance to this book, featuring Edith Roosevelt's complete diaries,
                1901–1945, and hundreds of personal letters.

(ALS)   Alsop Family Papers. The bulk of this collection, consulted pri-
                vately, has now been transferred to TRC. The citation (ALS)
                therefore applies only to the documents still held by the donor, Mr.
                John Alsop.

(NRJ)   Nancy Roosevelt Jackson Papers. Letters from Edith Roosevelt to
                her grandchild.

(ABR)   Archibald Bulloch Roosevelt Papers. A small collection of letters to
                and from immediate family members. Since ABR's death in Oct.
                1979, the bulk of this has been transferred to TRC.

(EER)   Elizabeth Roosevelt Papers. Numerous letters from Edith Roosevelt
                to Elizabeth Emlen Roosevelt ("Aunt Lizzie").

(EW)   Edith Derby Williams Papers.

(CRP)   Clochette Roosevelt Palfrey Papers.

(ARL)   Alice Roosevelt Longworth Papers, Library of Congress. Mrs. Longworth's White House diaries, and some letters from Edith Roosevelt and others, are currently to be seen only with permission.

Interviews

The author has interviewed the following children, grandchildren, other relatives, friends, and associates of Edith Kermit Roosevelt, listed alphabetically:

Mr. and Mrs. John Alsop; the Misses Florence and Dorothy Blake; Mr. and Mrs. William S. Cowles, Jr.; Mrs. Ethel Roosevelt Derby; Mrs. Sarah Derby Gannett; Mrs. Richard Hatch; Mrs. Nancy Roosevelt Jackson; Mrs. Cynthia Jay; Mrs. Theodora Rauchfuss; Mrs. Jessica Kraft: Mrs. Edna Kunkel; Mrs. Alice Roosevelt Longworth; Mr. Stefan Lorant; Mrs. Grace MacMillan; Mrs. Clochette Roosevelt Palfrey; Mr. Archibald Bulloch Roosevelt, Sr.; Mr. and Mrs. Archibald Roosevelt, Jr.; Mr. Cornelius Roosevelt; Miss Edith Roosevelt; Mrs. Frances Roosevelt; Mrs. Jean Roosevelt; Mr. Kermit Roosevelt; Mr. P. James Roosevelt; Mr. Theodore Roosevelt III; Mr. Willard Roosevelt; Miss Joanna Sturm; Mrs. Edith Derby Williams; Miss Mary Young.

Secondary Sources

Adams, Henry, *The Education of Henry Adams*. Modern Library, 1931.

————*Letters*, ed. Worthington Chauncey Ford, 1892–1918. Houghton Mifflin, 1938.

Barrus, Clara, *The Life and Letters of John Burroughs*, 2 vols. Houghton Mifflin, 1925.

Butt, Archibald W., *Letters*, ed. Lawrence F. Abbot. Doubleday, 1924.

————*Taft and Roosevelt*, 2 vols. Doubleday, 1930.

Cassini, Marguerite, *Never A Dull Moment*. Harper & Bros., 1956.

Chanler, Margaret T., *Roman Spring*. Little, Brown, 1934.

Chanler, Winthrop, *Letters*, ed. Margaret T. Chanler, New York, 1951.

Colman, Edna, *White House Gossip*. Doubleday, 1927.

Daggett, Mabel P., "Mrs. Roosevelt, The Woman in the Background," *The Delineator*, March 1909.

Gable, John A., *The Bull Moose Years: Theodore Roosevelt and the Progressive Party*. New York: Kennikat Press, 1978.

Garraty, John A., *Henry Cabot Lodge*. Knopf, 1953.

Green, Constance M., *Washington: Capital City, 1879–1950*, Vol. 2. Princeton University Press, 1962.

Gwynn, Stephen, ed., *The Letters and Friendships of Sir Cecil Spring-Rice*, 2 vols. Houghton Mifflin, 1929.

Hagedorn, Hermann, *The Roosevelt Family of Sagamore Hill*. Macmillan, 1954.

Harbaugh, William H., *Power and Responsibility: The Life and Times of Theodore Roosevelt*. Farrar, Straus and Cudahy, 1961.

Hoover, Irwin H., *Forty-two Years in the White House*. Houghton Mifflin, 1934.

Lash, Joseph P., *Eleanor and Franklin*. Norton, 1971.

Leary, John J., *Talks With TR*. Houghton Mifflin, 1920.

Lee, Arthur (Viscount Lee of Fareham), *A Good Innings,* 3 vols. Privately printed, 1940.

————,*A Good Innings,* selected and ed. Alan Clark. London: John Murray, 1974.

Lodge, Henry Cabot, *Selections from the Correspondence of Theodore Roosevelt and Henry Cabot Lodge, 1884–1918,* 2 vols. Scribners, 1925.

Longworth, Alice R., *Crowded Hours.* Scribners, 1933.

Looker, Earle, *The White House Gang.* N.Y.: Fleming H. Revell, 1929.

Lorant, Stefan, *The Life and Times of Theodore Roosevelt.* Doubleday, 1959.

Parsons, Frances ("Fanny") R., *Perchance Some Day.* Privately printed, 1951.

Pringle, Henry F., *Theodore Roosevelt: A Biography.* Harcourt Brace, 1931.

Putnam, Carleton, *Theodore Roosevelt: The Formative Years, 1858–1886.* Scribners, 1958.

Quereau Genealogy. Privately printed, 1928.

Randolph, Mary, *Presidents and First Ladies.* Appleton-Century, 1936.

Rixey, Lilian, *Bamie: Theodore Roosevelt's Remarkable Sister.* David McKay, 1963.

Robinson, Corinne R., *My Brother Theodore Roosevelt.* Scribners, 1921.

Roosevelt, Edith K., *American Backlogs: The Story of Gertrude Tyler and Her Family, 1660–1860.* Scribners, 1928.

————, *et al., Cleared for Strange Ports.* Scribners, 1924.

Roosevelt, Kermit, ed., *Quentin Roosevelt: A Sketch with Letters.* Scribners, 1921.

Roosevelt, Nicholas, *TR: The Man as I Knew Him.* Dodd, Mead, 1967.

Roosevelt, Theodore, *Autobiography.* Macmillan, 1913.

————, *Cowboys and Kings: Three Great Letters,* ed. Elting E. Morison. Harvard University Press, 1954.

————, *Diaries of Boyhood and Youth.* Scribners, 1928.

————, *Letters,* 8 vols., ed. Elting E. Morison and John Blum. Harvard University Press, 1951–54.

Roosevelt, Theodore, Jr., *All in the Family.* Putnam, 1929.

Roosevelt, Mrs. Theodore, Jr., *Day Before Yesterday.* Doubleday, 1959.

Samuels, Ernest, *Henry Adams,* 3 vols. Harvard, 1958–64.

Sewall, William W., *Bill Sewall's Story of TR.* Harper & Bros., 1919.

Singleton, Esther, *The Story of the White House,* Vol. 2. McClure, 1907.

Slayden, Ellen M., *Washington Wife: Journal, 1891–1919.* Harper & Row, 1962.

Strong, George T., *Diaries, 1835–1874,* 4 vols, ed. Allan Nevins. New York, 1952.

Sullivan, Mark, *Our Times: America Finding Herself.* Scribners, 1927.

Tyler, Gen. Daniel, *Memoirs,* ed. Donald G. Mitchell. Privately printed, 1883.

Wagenknecht, Edward, *The Seven Worlds of Theodore Roosevelt.* Longmans, Green, 1958.

White, William A., *Autobiography.* Macmillan, 1946.

Willets, Gilson, *Inside History of the White House.* New York: Christian Herald, 1908.

Wister, Owen, *Roosevelt: The Story of a Friendship, 1880–1919.* Macmillan, 1930.

Wood, Frederick S., ed., *Roosevelt as We Knew Him: Personal Recollections of 150 Friends.* John C. Winston, 1927.

Notes

Since certain names appear frequently in these notes, the following abbreviations will be used:

INTRODUCTION

1. *Wealth and Wealthy Citizens of New York City,* pamphlet in New-York Historical Society (1845), gives Cornelius Van Schaak Roosevelt's estimated wealth as $500,000. At his death in 1871 he was worth some $7 million. William Sheffield Cowles, Jr., and Corinne Robinson Alsop to Hermann Hagedorn, Dec. 1954 (TRB).

2. Based on *New York Times,* April 26, 1865; Stefan Lorant to author, June 1976; Lorant's article, "The Boy in the Window," *American Heritage,* VI.4 (June 1955).

3. Abraham Lincoln Second Inaugural Address, March 4, 1865.

4. EKR to TR Jr., May 21, 1944 (SH).

5. Butt, *Letters,* 62.

6. EKR to ARC, March n.d. (TRB). Until EKR went to Albany with TR as governor, she steadfastly refused to allow any picture of herself and the children to be published. "A

lady's name," according to her philosophy, "should appear in print only three times: at her birth, marriage, and death." TR told newsmen in 1898, "If I were to give you her picture for publication, Mrs. Roosevelt would consider it sufficient cause for divorce."

7. EKR to TR, June 8, 1885 (ERD).
8. Carpenter, Frank G., *Carp's Washington* (McGraw-Hill, 1960), 3.
9. EKR to TR Jr., Aug. 7, 1929 (TRB).

10. Theodora Rauchfuss to author, Feb. 1979.
11. Daggett, "Mrs. Roosevelt."
12. Roosevelt, N., *TR*, 28.
13. Washington *Evening Star*, Aug. 11, 1932.
14. Butt, *Letters*, 127.
15. Ibid., 235.
16. Jan. 13, 1906.
17. Butt, *Taft*, I, 181.
18. Butt, *Letters*, 75.

CHILDHOOD: 1861–1872
Chapter One

1. Unidentified newspaper clipping (TRB).
2. EKR, *Backlogs*, 199.
3. Ibid., 200.
4. From an advertisement for Kermit & Carow (SH).
5. James West Roosevelt to Mrs. Eliza Kermit, Jan. 8, 1872 (SH).
6. *The St. Nicholas Society of the City of New York: 100 Year Record 1835–1935*, pamphlet, 22–23 (NYC Municipal Archives).
7. EKR, *Backlogs*, 233.
8. Charles Carow to Gertrude Tyler, July 24, 1858 (TRC).
9. (SH).
10. May 31, 1859 (SH).
11. EKR, *Backlogs*, 234; Gale clipping (see n. 1 above).

12. Tyler, *Memoirs, passim.*
13. EKR, *Backlogs*, 234.
14. Gale clipping (see n. 1 above).
15. Ibid. Gertrude could look forward to a prosperous way of life with Charles. Of his father's estate of $258,277, he had received one seventh, i.e., $36,670, plus a seventh of the remaining silver, furniture, pictures, jewelry, wines, and real estate. He also inherited shares in the Hudson River Railroad, Ohio Canal, U.S. bonds, Bank of Commerce, New York Gas and Light Company, and other excellent stocks. (Isaac Carow will, NYC Surrogate Court.)
16. The house still stands, an imposing but dilapidated mansion, broken up into thirteen apartments.

Chapter Two

1. Verse from *The Children's Hour.*
2. ARL to Hermann Hagedorn, Nov. 9, 1954 (TRB).
3. The reason given by EKR to her own children was that Charles Carow's ill health was caused by his fall. In the Roosevelt family generally his decline was attributed to drink.
4. TR Jr., *Family*, 24.
5. TR qu. by Maurice Egan, in a letter to EKR, Nov. 30, 1907 (ERD).
6. Edith Williams to author, April 1976.

7. (TRB mss.)
8. EKR in speech to the Woman's Roosevelt Memorial Association, March 15, 1933, *Roosevelt House Bulletin*, Spring 1933.
9. Amy Belle (Cheney) Clinton to Hermann Hagedorn (TRB).
10. Putnam, *Formative Years*, 51.
11. Pronounced "Bammie"—short for *bambina*.
12. ARC to William S. Cowles, Jr., Aug. 19, 1929 (TRB).
13. This was before the tales were edited and published by Joel Chandler Harris.
14. (TRB mss.).
15. TR. *Autobiography*, 17.
16. EKR to WRMA (see n. 8 above).
17. TR Jr., *Family*, 58.
18. EKR to KR, April 28, 1912 (KR mss.).
19. Chanler, *Spring*, 203.
20. EKR to WRMA (see n. 8 above). Bamie's ailment disclosed in a letter from her to Dr. Russell Hibbs of NY Orthopedic Hospital, n.d. 1928, qu. in news clipping (TRC).
21. EKR to Edith Williams, May 6, 1946 (EW).
22. The crashes of 1869 and 1873 diminished his resources further.
23. EKR to KR, n.d. 1938 (KR).
24. TR, *Letters*, 1. 3.
25. ARC to William S. Cowles, Jr., Oct. 28, 1924 (TRB).
26. TR, *Autobiography*, 7–8.
27. Now on display at TRB.
28. Parsons, *Perchance*, 25.
29. Robinson, *TR*, 1.
30. CRR diary, Oct. 6, 1876 (TRC).
31. ". . . a very curious dark color. She was like that chair she was so brown." Mrs. Richard Aldrich to Mary Hagedorn, March 30, 1955 (TRB).
32. Parsons, *Perchance*, 27.
33. EKR to ARC, Friday 14th n.d. [1895?] (TRC).
34. TR, *Letters*, 1.3.
35. Robinson, *TR*, 40. "Supple jacks" are shrub stems suitable for walking sticks.
36. Parsons, *Perchance*, 29. Elliott himself, however, was always conscious of his intellectual and moral inferiority to TR. "What will become of me when I are a man?" he once wrote his father. "Are they not a very large number of partners in the store . . . I think Tedie would be the boy to put in the store [Roosevelt & Son] if you wanted to be shure of it because he is much quicker and a more shure kind of boy though I will try my best." (FDRL).
37. TR, *Boyhood*, 13.
38. Mittie to Anna Bulloch Gracie, June 1869 (TRC); EKR to TR Jr., March 12 [1929?] (TRB).
39. TR, *Boyhood*, 99, 100, 103.
40. TR to EKR, from Rome, c. 1869–70 (TRC).
41. N.d. (ERD).
42. EKR to TR, Nov. 24 [1869?] (ERD). Teedie was not only troubled by asthma in Europe; he also suffered from chronic boils and *cholera morbus* (a kind of nervous diarrhea).
43. TR, *Letters*, 1.4–5.
44. EKR to CRR, Nov. 19, 1869 (TRC).
45. EKR to CRR, Feb. 1, 1870 (TRC).
46. Corinne Robinson Alsop, unpublished memoir (ALS).
47. Parsons, *Perchance*, 36–37.
48. Mrs. Ellen Fanshawe to EKR, Jan. 28, 1932 (ERD).

Chapter Three

1. Qu. in Tyler, *Memoirs,* 119–20.
2. Edith Wharton and EKR were descended from Joshua Quereau. He was EKR's great, great, great grandfather and Mrs. Wharton's great, great grandfather. Wharton, Edith, *A Backward Glance* (Appleton-Century, 1934), 55.
3. The Stewart house, designed by John Kellum, later became the Manhattan Club. Soon the houses of the rich were moving up Fifth Avenue at the rate of two blocks a year. *New York Times* "Urban Annals," July 9, 1978.
4. Strong, *Diary,* 4.271.
5. Dickens, Charles, *American Notes* (Chapman & Hall), 52.
6. The Roosevelt livery was claret and green. Mittie to TR Sr., Oct. 15, 1873 (TRC).
7. Strong, *Diary,* 3.422.
8. EKR to Charles Carow, Aug. 9, 1871 (TRC).
9. Charles Carow to EKR, Aug. n.d., 1871 (TRC).
10. EKR to Charles Carow, Aug. 21, 1871 (TRC).
11. Gertrude Carow to Charles Carow, Aug. 12 and 21, 1871 (TRC).
12. EKR to Charles Carow, Aug. 21, 1871 (TRC).
13. Gunther, B. B., *Memories of School Days Nearly Half a Century Ago,* pamphlet dated Nov. 23, 1926 (SH).
14. EKR, School Composition Notebook, 1871–74 (ERD).

15. Parsons, *Perchance,* 20.
16. See n. 14 above.
17. EKR to KR, Nov. 14, 1907 (KR). She told TR Jr., however, that as a schoolgirl she could easily "recite the Kings of Jerusalem with their dates." Nov. 11, 1931 (SH).
18. EKR to Nancy Roosevelt Jackson, Nov. 1 and 15, 1938 (NRJ); EKR to KR, June 14, 1904 (KR).
19. EKR to KR, June 8, 1907 (KR).
20. EKR Reading Notebook (ERD).
21. EKR to KR, April 10, 1938 (KR).
22. EKR to KR, n.d., and Feb. 24, 1938 (KR); EKR to TR Jr., March 6, 1942 (TR Jr.).
23. EKR to KR, April 21, 1907 (KR).
24. Ibid., Jan. 6, 1918 (KR).
25. Fanny Parsons in an address to the Woman's Roosevelt Memorial Association, Oct. 27, 1948, *Roosevelt House Bulletin,* Fall 1948 (TRB). In 1875 Louise Comstock graded EKR "A" for ability in composition, "9" for neatness, and "10" each for "Effort, Good Thoughts, and Regularity" (ERD).
26. Graphologist Andrew Glaze, analyzing EKR's handwriting on March 4, 1979, sees "Considerable character, intelligence, and self-assertiveness. She is confident, adventurous, logical, well-organized, and practical (most of her energy is dispensed on the latter). She is unathletic, and has a tendency to depression when her energy flags.

YOUTH: 1872–1886
Chapter Four

1. CRR diary, Nov. 12, 1876 (TRC).
2. Robinson, *TR,* 55.
3. (TRC.)

4. Robinson, *TR,* 67–68.
5. Louise Vierick, "Roosevelt's German Days," *Success Magazine,* Oct.

1905. Mittie's reaction was a mixture of scorn, amusement and disbelief.

6. TR, qu. in Hermann Hagedorn, *The Boys' Life of Theodore Roosevelt* (Harper & Bros., 1922), 39.

7. Copybook of the Dresden Literary American Club, qu. in Putnam, *Formative Years*, 100.

8. Bamie's actual debut took place in Philadelphia in Jan. 1874, because 6 West Fifty-seventh Street was not finished.

9. P.O.R.E. Notebook (TRC).

10. Ibid.

11. N.d. (TRC).

12. EKR composition, "Port Washington," Nov. 12, 1873 (ERD). Presidents Grant and Hayes were habitués of Long Branch in the 1870s.

13. EKR, "Port Washington" (see n. 12).

14. Wilson, Harold F., *The Jersey Shore: A Social and Economic History* (New York, 1953); *Ocean Grove Guidebook*, 1874.

15. EKR to CRR, fragment of letter, n.d. (TRC).

16. TR, "Notes on Natural History," July 23–30 (TRB).

17. Parsons, *Perchance*, 26.

18. Robinson *TR*, 90.

19. Ibid.; TR to ARC, Aug. 6, 1876 (TRB); TR to EKR, Aug. 6, c. 1875 (ERD).

20. Parsons, *Perchance*, 29. In July 1875, TR, not yet 17, had passed the rigorous Harvard entrance examinations, doing well in all eight subjects. See Putnam, *Formative Years*, 127.

21. CRR diary, Nov. 12, 1876; ibid., Nov. 1, 1876 (TRC).

Chapter Five

1. From "The Four-Leaved Clover," by EKR, aged 16, P.O.R.E. Notebook (TRC).

2. TR had no idea yet what career he would pursue. It would not be the family glass business, because that had been given up on account of the 1876 financial panic. TR, *Letters*, 1.14.

3. TR, *Letters*, 1.16, 18.

4. Parsons, *Perchance*, 35.

5. Fanny Parsons to Woman's Roosevelt Memorial Association, Oct. 27, 1948, *Roosevelt House Bulletin*, Fall 1948 (TRB); EKR to TR Jr., Aug. 19, 1930 (TRB).

6. TR to ER, Jan. 7, 1877, and Anna Bulloch Gracie to ER, Jan. 5, 1877 (FDRL); CRR diary, Jan. 10, 1877, (TRC).

7. TR to CRR, Jan. 14, 1877, qu. in Putnam, *Formative Years*, 168–69;

TR, *Letters*, 1. 29, 23.

8. P.O.R.E. Notebook, Jan. 27, 1877 (TRC).

9. See Lewis, R.W.B., *Edith Wharton* (Harper & Row, 1975), 66.

10. TR to ARC, May 6, 1877 (TRB); CRR diary, Oct. 27, 1877 (TRC); TR diary, May 27, 1877 (TRP); TR, *Letters*, 1.28.

11. (ERD.)

12. CRR diary, Oct. 27, 1877 (TRC).

13. ARC to William S. Cowles, Jr., n.d. (TRB); Anna Bulloch Gracie diary (TRC).

14. TR diary, Jan. 1, 1878 (TRP).

15. CRR to EKR, n.d. 1878 (TRC).

16. TR diary, Dec. 11, 1877 (TRP).

17. TR diary, May 16, July 9, 1878 (TRP).

18. (TRC.)

19. TR diary (TRP).

20. TR to ARC, Sept. 20, 1886 (TRB); TR diary (TRP).
21. Putnam, *Formative Years*, 170; Corinne Robinson Alsop, unpublished memoir (ALS); CRR to EKR, Aug. 30, 1878 (TRC).
22. CRR to EKR, Aug. 30, 1878 (TRC).
23. TR did well in his examinations, achieving an 87 percent average, and ranking 13th in a class of 166. He led in zoology and political economy.
24. TR, *Letters*, 1.36.
25. TR diary, Nov. 28, 1878, and Jan. 25, 1880 (TRP).
26. TR diary (TRP); TR, *Letters*, 1.38.
27. TR, *Letters*, 1.40.
28. Book now in possession of Edith's granddaughter, Sarah Alden Gannett.
29. TR to ARC, Sept. 29, 1879 (TRB).
30. TR diary, Oct. 10, 1879 (TRP).
31. TR had ridden his horse lame earlier in the year, on fierce rides to and from Chestnut Hill. He was once found wandering in the woods at night, too restless to sleep and apparently suicidal.
32. TR diary, Nov. 16, 1879 (TRP).
33. Ibid., April 1879 (TRP).
34. Ibid., Dec. 24, 1879 (TRP).
35. Ibid., Jan 25, 1880 (TRP).
36. Ibid., Jan 31, 1880 (TRP); Daggett, "Mrs. Roosevelt."
37. Corinne Robinson Alsop notebook (TRC). "I know that Aunt Edith gave the impression . . . that she had not loved Uncle Ted [at first], and said that she had danced at his wedding, but my mother always spoke of the shock to Aunt Edith when she received a letter to say that he was engaged to Alice Lee."
38. (ERD.)
39. Hagedorn, Hermann, *The Boys' Life of Theodore Roosevelt* (Harper and Bros., 1922), 63; TR to Mittie, Aug. 1, 1880 (TRC).
40. Parsons, *Perchance*, 43.
41. Ibid.
42. Ibid.; ERD to C. Putnam, Putnam, *Formative Years*, 210.

Chapter Six

1. Nancy Roosevelt Jackson, granddaughter of EKR, to author, Feb. 1976.
2. Parsons, *Perchance*, 44.
3. Hagedorn, *Family*, 11.
4. CRR to ER, Dec. 6, 1880 (FDRL).
5. McAllister, Ward, *Society as I Have Found It* (Cassell, 1890), 157.
6. TR diary, Dec, 20, 1880 (TRP).
7. ARC to Jack [Lee?], Dec. 10, 1880 (TRC).
8. Ibid.
9. Holt, G., *TR*, typed extract (TRB).
10. See n. 1.
11. Mittie to Mrs. Hilbourn West, March 9, 1881 (TRC).
12. EKR to CRR, Feb. 15, 1881 (TRC).
13. Corinne Robinson Alsop, unpublished memoir (ALS). Mrs. Theodore Douglas Robinson, daughter-in-law of CRR, told Hermann Hagedorn that it was because CRR loved TR too much.
14. TR diary, Dec. 31, 1880 (TRP). ER left on Nov. 7, before TR returned from Oyster Bay. Mittie to ER, Dec. 7 (FDRL).
15. TR diary, April 1 and July 6, 1881 (TRP). Garfield died Sept. 19. TR, *Letters* 1.55. His constituency was known as the "Silk Stocking" or "Diamond Back" District.
16. Mittie to ER, Dec. 10, 1881 (FDRL).

17. EKR to CRR, May 1, 1882 (TRC).
18. Sarah Edwards Henshaw to Gertrude Carow, qu. in Tyler, *Memoirs*, 132–33, 105.
19. N.d. (SH). Also EKR, *Backlogs*, 40.
20. Will filed at New Yok City Surrogate Court.
21. TR diary, Jan 3, 1883 (TRP). His income in 1883, from salary, shares, and royalties on *The Naval War of 1812* was a comfortable $13,920.
22. Anna Bulloch Gracie diary, Jan 5, 1883 (TRC).
23. ERD, "Ingersoll Interview," 1962 (SH); EKR to Dr. Frank Chapman, May 29, 1933 (ERD).
24. *New York Times*, March 18, 1883.
25. EKR to KR, June 23, 1918 (KR); EKR to ERD, Feb. 13, 1937 (ERD).
26. Crandall, Charles H., *The Season* (New York, 1883), 295.
27. TR to Mittie, July 9, 1883 (TRC). ER's daughter, Eleanor, would marry her Hyde Park relative in 1905.
28. ER to CRR, Jan. 1, 1882; Anna

29. Rebecca Hall to ER, July 25, 1883 (FDRL).
29. TR also bought a few hundred head of cattle in North Dakota, the first of several ranching investments.
30. Mittie to Mrs. Hilbourn West, Sept. 30, 1883 (TRC).
31. On a letter to TR, c. 1901, from an alleged former maid of Mittie's, referring to the latter's "grey" hair, EKR wrote that she in fact died with "not a single white hair" (TRP). After the death of TR Sr., Mittie had become increasingly eccentric and would disappear into a closet with a maid to tie up mysterious parcels. Corinne Robinson Alsop, unpublished memoir (ALS).
32. TR, *In Memory of My Darling Wife* (TRC).
33. Arthur Cutler, TR's old tutor, qu. in Sewall, *TR*, 11.
34. He did however discuss it with ranchers. Daggett, "Mrs. Roosevelt," says that TR took EKR's letter of condolence with him to North Dakota.

Chapter Seven

1. TR, *Letters*, 1.66.
2. Each inherited $62,500 from Mittie's estate.
3. ARC to William S. Cowles, Jr., n.d. (TRB). Bamie also disbanded TR's house on West Forty-fifth Street.
4. TR to ARC, June 17, 1884 (TRB).
5. TR paid off a $3,000 mortgage on Sewall's Maine property. He and Dow were to receive a salary, plus a percentage of the Dakota profits. They were not to be held responsible for any losses.
6. TR to ARC, June 17, 1884 (TRB).
7. Sewall, *TR*, 47.
8. William Merrifield to Hermann

Hagedorn, June 1919, in the Bad Lands. Notes taken by stenographer (TRC). "We talked over domestic affairs a great deal and likewise personal affairs. He told me that I was the only man he ever talked to about his first wife. He told me about her death . . . I had just lost mine and there was a sort of common bond between us. The loss of his first wife shot him to pieces. He was tremendously fond of her."
9. Pittsburgh *Dispatch*, April 15, 1885.
10. St. Paul *Pioneer Press*, June 23, 1885.
11. Merrifield to Hagedorn, June 1919 (see n. 8). ". . . She used to visit

some people there in New York and he'd avoid meeting her; and they kept that up for years. Then he met her in the hall one time. He met her there by accident." Also see Putnam, *Formative Years*, 556–57.

12. Fanny Parsons told Hagedorn in October 1948, "Edith and I both went to Theodore Roosevelt's wedding. There was no indication then that Edith was heartbroken about the marriage. When they fell in love not two years after Alice Lee's death, they were both amazed and rather shocked to think that it could happen so soon." (TRB).

13. Roosevelt, N., *TR*, 23.

14. Fanny married Will Dana in 1884. After his death she married James Russell Parsons in 1896.

15. The timing of the name change is probably significant. Sagamore Mohannis was the Indian chief who signed away his tribe's rights to the land two and a half centuries before.

16. Lodge, *Correspondence*, I,35.

17. The ring and watch were left to EKR's daughter ERD. The pearls went to her granddaughter Sarah Alden Gannett.

18. CRR to ARC, March 29, 1886 (TRC).

19. TR, *Letters*, 1.96.

20. (ERD.)

21. TR, *Letters*, 1.101, 107.

22. Hagedorn, Hermann, *Roosevelt in the Badlands* (Houghton Mifflin, 1921), 409, 411. Similarly when TR asked Sewall one day that fall if he should go into politics or law, Sewall advised politics, because men like TR were needed. "If you go into politics and live," Sewall added, "your chance to be President is good." TR laughed and said, "That looks a long ways ahead to me." Sewall, *TR*, 93–94.

23. EKR to TR [c. Aug.], 1886 (ERD).

24. TR to CRR, Aug. 7, 1886, qu. in Robinson, *TR*, 138.

25. "Society Topics of the Week," *New York Times*, Aug. 29, Sept. 5, 1886.

26. (TRB.)

27. Wagenknecht, *Seven Worlds*, 87–88; TR, *Letters*, 1.108.

28. TR qu. in CRR to ARC, Oct. 12, 1886 (TRC). CRR told ARL that she and ARC were against the union, because they knew EKR would come between them and their brother. ARL to Hermann Hagedorn, Nov. 9, 1954 (TRB); CRR to ARC, Oct. 12, 1886 (TRC).

29. (ERD.)

30. Rixey, *Bamie*, 62. When Fanny Parsons received her own note from TR, she was thunderstruck. She had seen the couple many times during the previous winter, but "had not the slightest suspicion of this denouement." Parsons, *Perchance*, 65.

31. Roosevelt, N., *TR*, 23.

MARRIAGE AND MOTHERHOOD:
1886–1901
Chapter Eight

1. Verse from poem "Two in the Campagna."

2. TR to ARC, Aug. 11, 20, 1886 (TRB).

3. Qu. in Lorant, *TR*, 458; TR's senior year dissertation, June 1880 (TRC).

4. See n. 8 below.

5. Gwynn, *CSR*, 1.50.

6. Ibid.; TR, *Letters*, 1.116.

7. ARC to William S. Cowles Jr., n.d. (TRB).

8. A copy of the marriage certificate now hangs in the Roosevelt room at Brown's Hotel. The original is still at St. George's.

9. Nov. 20, 1886.

10. TR to ARC, Dec. 4 and 13, 1886 (TRB); EKR to TR recalling their honeymoon, Jan. 16, 1901 (ERD). Few places on the Roosevelts' itinerary coincided with TR's honeymoon trip with Alice Lee.

11. Taken from a bill dated Dec. 22 and 23 (SH).

12. TR, *Letters*, 1.117.

13. Ibid.

14. Ibid., 1.119; TR to ARC, Jan. 10, 1887 (TRB).

15. TR, *Letters*, 1.119.

16. Ibid., 121.

17. Ibid., 122.

18. Ibid., 123.

19. Ibid., 126; TR to ARC, March 12, 1887 (TRB).

20. Jan. 15, 1901 (ERD).

Chapter Nine

1. TR to ARC, May 10, 1891 (TRB).

2. Gwynn, *CSR*, 1.61.

3. HCL to EKR, Oct. 23, 1895 (MHS); TR to ARC, Feb. 12, 1893 (TRB).

4. Memoranda to HCL, qu. Lodge, *Correspondence*, I, 25; Lodge, diary, March 20, 1885 (MHS); HCL to CSR, Aug. 12, 1898 (CSR); TR to HCL, April 15, 1896 (MHS).

5. TR, *Letters*, 1.126–27.

6. TR to ARC, May 16, 1887 (TRB).

7. EKR to KR, Jan. n.d., 1908 (KR).

8. Lodge, *Correspondence*, I,55.

9. Ibid., 56. Despite some shared favorites in literature, EKR said many years later, "Theodore never could be sure of my liking a book he chose. We had quite different tastes; perhaps that is one reason why I love him so much . . ." EKR to Arthur Lee, Jan. 24, 1928 (LEE).

10. TR, *Letters*, 1.129.

11. TR to ARC, Sept. 11, 1887 (TRB).

12. TR, *Letters*, 1.132; TR to ARC, Sept. 18, 1887 (TRB).

13. EKR to TR Jr., Aug. 4 [1932?] (TRB).

14. EKR to ERD, July 25, 1945 (ERD).

15. TR, *Letters*, 1.133; TR to ARC, Sept. 29, 1887 (TRB).

16. TR, *Letters*, 1.136.

17. EKR to TR Jr., n.d. (TRB).

18. TR to TR Jr., n.d. (TRB).

19. CRR to ARC, Aug. 1, 1888 (TRC).

20. ABR to author, Feb. 1976.

21. TR to ARC, July 1, 1888 (TRB).

22. Lodge, *Correspondence*, 1.68–69.

23. July 11, 1888 (MHS); TR to ARC, July 15, 1888 (TRB).

24. CRR to ARC, Aug. 1, 1888 (TRC).

25. Ibid., Aug. 13.

26. TR, *Letters*, 1.147.

Chapter Ten

1. Adams, *Education*, 353.

2. TR, *Letters*, 1.167.

3. Ibid., 173.

4. Ibid., 174; TR to ARC, July 24, 1889 (TRB).

5. (ERD.)

6. TR to EKR, Sept. 7, 1889 (TRC). The words "no pregnancy" are the author's conjecture; they have been heavily crossed out in the original.

7. TR to ARC, Oct. 13, 1889 (TRB).
8. EKR to EC, n.d. (TRC).
9. TR, *Letters*, 1.208.
10. Mrs. Reginald de Koven, qu. in Green, *Washington*, 2.199.
11. Washington *Post*, Jan. 2, 1891.
12. Ibid.; TR, *Letters*, 1.230.
13. Feb. 13, 1890 (TRB).
14. TR to ARC, Jan. 28, 1890 (TRB); TR, *Letters*, 1.215.
15. Chanler, *Spring*, 195, 203.
16. Adams, *Letters*, 398.
17. Wister, *TR*, 148; Adams, *Education*, 317.
18. Adams had an income of between $25,000 and $50,000 a year. "All the chairs were of a nursery altitude," said one visitor. It was from Adams's house that the decorator Elsie de Wolfe conceived the idea of extremely low chairs, "nothing more than a cushion on the floor." Samuels, 3.339. See also de Wolfe's *After*

All (New York, 1935), 107.
19. Cater, Harold D., *Henry Adams and His Friends* (Houghton Mifflin, 1947), lxx: "Adams liked Mrs. Roosevelt especially."
20. Adams, *Letters*, 445.
21. Adams, *Education*, 322, 355; Winthrop Chanler to CSR in Gwynn, *CSR*, 2.187.
22. Chanler, *Spring*, 192–93.
23. TR, *Letters*, 1.215.
24. CRR diary (TRC); Hermann Hagedorn, Badlands Notes (TRC); William Sewall to Hagedorn, 1919 (TRC).
25. TR, *Autobiography*, 116.
26. Robinson, *TR*, 40.
27. EKR to EC, Sept. 5, 1890 (TRC). This letter encloses a sketch of the ranch house. CRR diary; EKR to EC, Sept. 22, 1890 (TRC).
28. CRR diary (TRC).
29. TR, *Letters*, 1.233.

Chapter Eleven

1. EKR to EC, Aug. 10, 1894 (TRC).
2. TR to ARC, Dec. 26, 1890 (TRB).
3. Elizabeth Cameron to Henry Adams, Jan. 10, 1891 (MHS).
4. Tripple, tripple, little toes,
   In the beans the chicken goes.
   The calves are in the clover,
   The foals are in the oats,
   The ducks are in the puddle,
   I wish baby was taller. [Translated by Edmund Morris.]
5. TR to ARC, April 4, 1890 (TRB).
6. Ibid., May 2, 1890. Anna wrote to ER in a letter (n.d., FDRL): "I shall never feel you are really your dear old self until you can give up all medicines and wines of every kind. I believe the latter has led to your great difficulty in giving up morphine and laudanum. . . . Do dear

throw your horrid cocktails away . . . I wonder if this last is asking too much."
7. Elizabeth Cameron to Henry Adams, Jan. 10, 1891 (MHS); TR, *Letters*, 1.236.
8. ARC to William S. Cowles, Jr., n.d. (TRB).
9. July 12, 1891 (TRB).
10. The Carows met ARC in Paris and were appalled at how careworn she looked. TR to ARC, June 7, 1891 (TRB).
11. CSR to Elizabeth Cameron, June 26, 1891 (MHS).
12. Ibid., Aug. 14, 1891.
13. EKR to TR Jr., Feb. 13 [1935?] (TRB).
14. EKR to Gertrude Carow, Nov. 21 [1891?] (TRC).

15. N.d. (SH).
16. EKR to ARC, May 18, 1894; EKR to Gertrude Carow, Nov. 4, 1893 (TRC).
17. TR, *Letters*, 8.1430.
18. EKR to EC, Aug. 25, 1892 (SH). "He would rather stay with me in a dim room than go to walk with anyone else" EKR in *The Baby's Journal* (TR Jr.).
19. TR, *Letters*, 8.1429; EKR to EC, July 19, 1892 (SH).
20. EKR to ARC, n.d. (TRC); n.d. [1890] (ERD).
21. Isabella Hagner James in New York *Tribune*, Oct. 30, 1932.
22. EKR to Gertrude Carow, April 22, 1892; Gertrude Carow to EKR, June 4, 1892 (TRC).
23. EKR to EC, July 26, 1892 (TRC).
24. EKR to ARC, n.d. (TRC).
25. Ibid., Dec. 14, 1893 (TRC); ABR to author, Feb. 1976.
26. TR to ARC, Dec. 17, 1893 (TRB), Jan. 6, 1894 (TRC).
27. EKR to EC, Aug. 27, 1899 (TRC).
28. Aug. 10, 1894 (TRC).
29. EKR to Gertrude Carow, n.d. (TRC).
30. TR to ARC, Aug. 22, 1891 (TRB).
31. Ibid., Aug. 24.
32. Ibid., Jan. 21, 1892 (TRB). From Paris he wrote: "He signed the deed for two thirds of all his property (including the $60,000 trust); and agreed to the probation. I then instantly changed my whole manner and treated him with the utmost love and tenderness. I told him we would do all we legitimately could to help him to get through his two years (or thereabouts) of probation." (TRB.)
33. TR to ARC, July 12, 1891 (TRB).
34. ER to Mrs. Hall, July 1892 (FDRL).
35. EKR to EC, Jan. 9, 1893 (TRC).
36. TR to ARC, Feb. 4, 1893 (TRB).
37. Fragment, n.d. (TRC).
38. EKR to ARC, fragment, n.d. (TRC).
39. EKR to Gertrude Carow, Aug. 10, 1894 (TRC); TR to ARC, July 29, 1894 (TRB).
40. CRR to ARC, Aug. 15, 1894 (TRC).
41. Aug. 18, 1894 (TRB).
42. N.d., 1894 (TRC).

Chapter Twelve

1. Aged three to TR qu. in Hagedorn, *Family*, 22.
2. EKR to EC, March 7, 1893 (SH).
3. Ibid., May 16, 1893 (TRC).
4. Ibid.
5. TR, *Letters*, 1.334.
6. Roosevelt, N., *TR*, 23.
7. Sept. 13, 1893 (ERD).
8. An older half brother of FDR.
9. EKR to ARC, Feb. 3, 1894 (TRC).
10. N.d. (TRC).
11. The name "Sister" was now frequently used instead of Alice. Later generations of nieces and nephews still illogically address ARL as Aunt Sister.
12. April 9, 1894 (TRB).
13. EKR to ARC, May 13, n.d. (TRC).
14. TR in *The Baby's Journal* (TR Jr.).
15. EKR to Aunt Lizzie, Nov. 27, 1908 (EER). Also based on ERD's and P. James Roosevelt's memories of the old lady, given to author, April 1976.
16. Hagedorn, *Family*, 36.
17. TR Jr., *Family*, 171.
18. EKR to ARC, Sept. 28, 1894 (TRC).

19. TR, *Letters,* 1.407; 8.1433.
20. EKR to EC, Jan. 3, 1895 (SH); TR, *Letters,* 1.420, 439.
21. EKR to Gertrude Carow, Jan. 25, 1895 (SH). The milk gave out in December; EKR put it down to worry over KR and ARL. TR to ARC, Jan. 20, 1895 (TRB).
22. Ibid., Feb. 3, 1895 (TRB); EKR to Gertrude Carow, March 6, 1895 (SH).
23. TR to ARC, March 9, 1895 (TRB). Henry Adams, who crossed from Europe with Kipling in 1892, re-marked on the author's "undeniable vulgarity," but respected his art and became friendly. The year of the Roosevelts' meeting with Kipling is mistakenly dated in TR, *Letters.*
24. EKR to EC, April 10, 1895 (SH).
25. TR, *Letters,* 1.446; Mary Moore (Gertrude Carow's sister), writing from Turin to EKR, April 24, 1895 (ERD).
26. Gertrude Carow to EKR, Oct. 2, 1892 (TRC).
27. TR, *Letters,* 1.456.

Chapter Thirteen

1. Notes (TRB).
2. TR, *Letters,* 1.469.
3. Robinson, *TR,* 157.
4. "Theodore Roosevelt and the Problem Before Him," *Leslie's Weekly,* Oct. 10, 1895.
5. Bob Ferguson, qu. in Rixey, *Bamie,* 92.
6. Ibid., 93.
7. EKR to ARC, Jan. 6, 1894 (TRC).
8. TR to ARC, July 19, 1895 (TRB).
9. ARC to William S. Cowles, Jr., Oct. 27, 1925 (TRB). Mrs. Theodore Douglas Robinson, CRR's daughter-in-law, told Mary Hagedorn on Nov. 17, 1954, "I don't think she was in love with him [Lieut. Cowles], really." (TRB).
10. ARC to William S. Cowles, Jr., n.d. (TRB).
11. CRR to EKR and TR, Nov. 24, 1895 (ERD).
12. ARC to William S. Cowles, Jr., n.d. (TRB).
13. EKR to ARC, Oct. 13, 1895 (TRC).
14. William Sturgis Bigelow, qu. in Rixey, *Bamie,* 89; TR to ARC, Nov. 18, 1895 (TRB).
15. EKR to ARC, Jan. 20, 1896 (TRC).
16. March 4, 1896 (TRC); TR to ARC, April 12, 1896 (TRB); EKR to ARC, April 8, 1896 (TRC).
17. Notes (TRB).
18. TR to ARC, May 24, 1896 (TRB).
19. EKR to ARC, n.d. (TRB); EKR to ARC, Feb. 17 [1896?] (TRC); EKR to CSR, Dec. 2, 1896 (CSR).
20. Ibid.
21. The Republicans spent over $7 million on the campaign; Bryan spent only $300,000. Nannie Cabot Lodge to CSR, qu. in Gwynn, *CSR,* 2.197–98; EKR to CRR, Dec. 26, 1896 (TRC).
22. Leary, *TR,* qu. in TR, 27.
23. EKR to ARC, Dec. 28, 1896 (TRB).
24. TR, *Letters,* 1.619.

Chapter Fourteen

1. Butt, *Letters,* 146.
2. EKR to EC, May 10, 1897 (TRC).
3. William Sturgis Bigelow to HCL, April 13, 1897 (MHS).

4. Rixey, *Bamie*, 106.
5. Corinne Robinson Alsop, unpublished memoir (ALS).
6. TR, *Letters*, 1.642, 655.
7. Ibid., 676–77.
8. Ibid., 521, 677.
9. Ibid., 718, 745.
10. TR to ARC, n.d. (TRB); EKR to EC, Feb. 15, 1898 (TRC).
11. Feb. 24, 1898 (MHS).
12. TR, *Letters*, 1.786. Such an inflammatory sickness can be a symptom of puerperal (childbed) fever, of tuberculosis, or of typhoid. In the last case, small ulcers in the intestinal tract burst and release infection into the peritoneum. In the 1890s medical procedure was to drain the pus from the muscle by leaving the wound open. It would close of its own accord when the abscess had been drained. The infection would nowadays be treated either with antibiotics or by drainage, or, in extreme cases, if there was danger of the infection recurring or spreading, by hysterectomy. It appears that Edith was suffering from either puerperal fever or typhoid: since she lived to a ripe old age she was clearly not tubercular. Dr. Ivan V. Jacobson to author, Jan. 1977. Chanler, *Letters*, 65; Elizabeth Cameron to Henry Adams, March 21, 1898 (MHS); TR, *Letters*, 1.789.
13. TR, *Letters*, I.790.
14. Ibid., 798.
15. Ibid., 2.804; EKR to TR Jr., July 25, 1939 (TRB).
16. EKR to EC, Feb. 15, 1898 (TRC).
17. TR, *Letters*, 1.795. Spanish responsibility for the sinking of the *Maine* has never been proved.
18. (TRB.)
19. April 4, 1898 (TR Jr.).
20. Thomas, Lately, *A Pride of Lions* (New York, 1959), 249.
21. TR, *Letters*, 2.817, 808.
22. Butt, *Letters*, 146.
23. TR, *Letters*, 2.824.
24. Ibid., 831; KR to EC, n.d. (SH).

Chapter Fifteen

1. EKR to TR, July 1, 1898 (ERD).
2. Ibid., May 28, 1898 (ERD).
3. Ibid., May 20 (ERD).
4. EKR to EC, June 5, 1898 (TRC).
5. Ibid.
6. Ibid., June 3, 1898 (ERD).
7. Lee, ed. Clark, *Innings,* 61.
8. Ibid., 68.
9. Chanler, *Letters*, 81–82.
10. TR to EKR, June 15, 1898 (TRB). This and the following letters, parts of which were copied by ARL and sent to CRR, are mistakenly attributed as letters to the latter by Morison (TR, *Letters*, 2.843). EKR refused CRR permission to print extracts from the texts in New Jersey newspapers, explaining to TR, "I cannot wish that they should be made so public." July 18, 1898 (ERD).
11. TR to EKR, June 25, 27, 1898 (TRB). Also see TR, *Letters*, 2.844 and n. 10 above.
12. TR to EKR, June 25, 27, 1898 (TRB); TR, *Letters*, 2.845.
13. EKR to TR, June 27, 1898 (ERD). EKR inked out this sentence before giving it to ERD as a souvenir. But the ink has faded and the words show through.
14. Hagedorn, Hermann, *Leonard Wood: A Biography* (Harper, 1931), 1.152, 157.

15. TR, *Letters*, 8.907.
16. EKR to EC, Aug. 13, 1899 (TRC).
17. TR, *Letters*, 2.863.
18. July n.d. (TRB).
19. EKR to TR, July 5 and 14, 1898 (ERD).
20. Ibid., July 18; EKR to EC, July 1 and 3, 1898 (TRC).
21. TR, *Letters*, 2.855; EKR to EC, Aug. 8, 1898 (TRC).
22. Qu. Stallman, R. W., *Stephen Crane* (George Braziller, 1968), 384.
23. EKR to ERD, July 16, 1944 (ERD).
24. Riis, Jacob, "Mrs. Roosevelt and Her Children," *Ladies' Home Journal*, Aug. 1902.
25. EKR to EC, Aug. 15, 1898 (TRC).
26. Eva Trenholm Green to EKR, Jan. 22, 1925 (ERD).
27. Ibid.
28. EKR to EC, Aug. 22, 1898 (TRC).
29. Ibid.
30. Hagedorn, *Family*, 52.
31. EKR to EC, Sept. 23, 1898 (TRC).
32. Hagedorn, *Family*, 61; Wood, *Roosevelt*, 64–65; EKR to EC, qu. in Hagedorn, *Family*, 64.
33. EKR to EC, Sept. 11, 1898 (TRC).
34. TR, *Letters*, 2.876.

Chapter Sixteen

1. EKR to CSR, March 25, 1899 (CSR).
2. New York *Herald*, Oct. 4, 1898. Frank S. Black, the incumbent Governor, was rejected as a candidate for a second term, because he had allowed excessive, and probably corrupt, spending on Erie Canal repairs, thus losing voter support.
3. EKR to EC, Oct. 7, 1898 (TRC).
4. TR, *Autobiography*, 127.
5. Riis, Jacob, "In the Roosevelt Home," New York *Sun*, Jan. 1, 1899.
6. EKR to EC, Oct. 19, 1898 (TRC).
7. Amy Cheney to Hermann Hagedorn, n.d. (TRB).
8. Rixey, *Bamie*, 128. "Bamie believes no one has noticed," EKR had written at the end of May, "and I confess that I should myself only think our Caesar had fed upon some fattening meat, but I am stupid about such things." EKR to TR, May 28, 1898 (TR Jr.).
9. EKR to EC, Oct. 19, 1898 (TRC).
10. Joe Murray to EKR, Nov. 8, 1898 (ERD); TR, *Letters*, 2.888.
11. Isaac Hunt, TR's old Assembly colleague, to Hermann Hagedorn, Sept. 20, 1923 (TRB).
12. EKR to EC, n.d. Dec. 1898 (TRC). Description of Executive Mansion also based on a personal tour by author in August 1978, and on Isabelle K. Savelle's guide, *The Executive Mansion* (New York, 1960).
13. Adams, *Letters*, 208.
14. Parsons, *Perchance*, 123.
15. ARC to FDR, n.d. (FDRL); New York *Sun*, Jan. 3, 1899.
16. New York *World*, Jan. 3, 1899.
17. EKR to EC, Jan. 3, 1899 (TRC).
18. This was a practice that would continue in the White House.
19. EKR to EC, Jan. 3, 1899 (TRC).
20. Parsons, *Perchance*, 124. He also wrote Mrs. Selmes, two weeks later: "Whatever comes, I have been Colonel and been Governor!" TR, *Letters*, 2.916.
21. Ibid., 944.
22. March 27, 1899 (TRC).
23. Dec. 3, 1898 (TRC).
24. Feb. 19, 1899 (TRC).

25. Feb. 15, 1899 (TRC).
26. Donovan said that TR's stance and pugilistic behavior were those of a typical fighter. Colman, *Gossip*, 287–88.
27. Parsons, *Perchance*, 125–26. Fanny had just published a successful book entitled *How to Know the Ferns*.
28. EKR to her granddaughter Edith Williams, May 6, 1946 (EW); EKR to EC, April 30, 1899 (TRC).
29. Roosevelt, N., *TR*, 13; Corinne Robinson Alsop, unpublished memoir (ALS). Hermann Hagedorn repeats the story, quoting CRR, in *Roosevelt House Bulletin*, Fall 1948 (TRB).
30. Ibid.
31. William S. Cowles, Jr. to author, Dec. 16, 1976.
32. Mrs. Theodore Douglas Robinson to Mary Hagedorn, Nov. 17, 1954 (TRB); ABR to author, Feb. 1976; Parsons, *Perchance*, 125; Gwynn, *CSR*, 1.294.
33. ERD to author, Oct. 1977. Hagedorn has a slightly different version of the story in *Family*, 105.
34. TR, *Letters*, 2.1424.
35. Qu. in Harbaugh, *Power*, 319.
36. Mary Youngs to Hermann Hagedorn, Jan. 11, 1949 (TRB).
37. EKR to ARC, n.d. (TRC).
38. Longworth, *Hours*, 26–30; EKR to EC, Aug. 13, 1899 (TRC).
39. EKR to EC, April 30, 1899 (TRC).
40. TR, *Letters*, 2.1022–1023.
41. EKR to EC, July 8, 1899 (TRC).
42. *Cromwell* was serialized between Jan. and June of 1900 in *Scribner's Magazine*. TR received $5,000 plus 15 percent royalty for the book. A friend, probably Elihu Root, described it as "a fine imaginative study of Cromwell's qualifications for the governorship of New York." See TR, *Letters*, 2.1043.
43. EKR to EC, Sept. 30, 1899 (TRC).
44. Churchill, who dined at the end of December with the Roosevelts in Albany, incensed his hosts by slumping in his chair, puffing on a cigar, and refusing to get up when women came into the room. ARL in *Saturday Evening Post*, Dec. 4, 1965.
45. TR, *Letters*, 2.1079.
46. EKR to TR Jr., Aug. 12, 1931 (SH); EKR to Aunt Lizzie, Dec. 27, 1905 (EER). TR was frequently away hunting on his wife's birthday. EKR's watch was in blue enamel with an anchor of diamonds in the center. She wore it around her neck or pinned to a dress "always" and left it to Nancy Roosevelt Jackson. The watch was recently stolen.
47. EKR to CSR, Dec. 15, 1899 (CSR).
48. Longworth, *Hours*, 34; TR, *Letters*, 2.1108.
49. Lodge, *Correspondence*, 1.424; TR, *Letters*, 2.1160.
50. Ibid., 1153, 1161.
51. Beale, Howard K., *Theodore Roosevelt and the Rise of America to World Power* (Johns Hopkins Press, 1956), 64; EKR to CSR, March 16, 1900 (CSR).
52. EKR to ERD, March 12, 1900 (ERD).
53. TR, *Letters*, 2.1272.
54. Parsons, *Perchance*, 132.
55. Wood, *Roosevelt*, 72–75.
56. TR, *Letters*, 2.1337.
57. June 22, 1900.
58. TR, *Letters*, 2.1337.
59. June 22, 1900.
60. TR, *Letters*,, 2.1337; Leech, Margaret, *In the Days of McKinley* (Harper, 1959), 542.
61. New York *World*, June 22, 1900.

Chapter Seventeen

1. Qu. in EKR speech to the Woman's Roosevelt Memorial Association, October 20, 1933, *Roosevelt House Bulletin*, Fall 1933 (TRB).
2. Cassini, *Moment*, 140. Both President and Mrs. McKinley had been ill.
3. Mr. Dooley in *Harper's Weekly*, Oct. 13, 1900; EKR to EC, n.d. (TRC); TR, *Letters*, 2.1451.
4. EKR to EC, Dec. 7, 1900 (TRC).
5. Charles Moore to EKR, Dec. 14, 1934 (ERD).
6. EKR to EC, March, 1901 (SH); Hagedorn, *Family*, 107; EKR to ARC, Feb. n.d. 1901 (TRB).
7. EKR diary, March 4, 1901 (ERD); TR, *Works*, XIV, 342–45.
8. Hagedorn, *Family*, 107; EKR to EC, n.d. (SH).
9. Longworth, *Hours*, 36.
10. EKR to EC, n.d. (SH).
11. TR, *Letters*, 3.60, 58.
12. Parsons, *Perchance*, 136–37.
13. EKR remembered the artist, and in 1902 invited her to paint a splendid portrait of herself as First Lady. The painting is now in the possession of Edith Williams.
14. TR, *Letters*, 3.427; ERD to author, April 1976. Sienkiewicz wrote blood-curdling romances set in medieval Poland.
15. Longworth, *Hours*, 39.
16. EKR to EC, Sept. 9, 1901 (SH). The anarchists, who desired to create a stateless society in the U.S. by means of breaking down all organized government and laws, had been flourishing as an increasing threat to national security since the mid-1880s.
17. EKR to EC, Sept. 9, 1901 (SH).
18. See n. 1 above.
19. Ibid.
20. Robinson, *TR*, 204–5.
21. (TRB.) The cause of death was gangrene, due to a bullet buried so deeply that doctors could not remove it.
22. EKR diary, Sept. 15, 1901 (ERD).
23. Winthrop Chanler to EKR, Sept. 16, 1901 (ERD); Gwynn, *CSR*, 1.346; Mrs. Lee to EKR, Sept. 15, 1901 (ERD).

FIRST LADY: 1901–1909
Chapter Eighteen

1. EKR to CSR, Jan. 27, 1901 (CSR).
2. New York *World*, Sept. 17, 1901.
3. EKR diary, Sept. 16, 1901 (ERD); EKR to EC, Sept. 18, 1901 (TRC).
4. EKR to Woman's Roosevelt Memorial Association, Oct. 20, 1933, *Roosevelt House Bulletin*, Fall 1933.
5. *Washington Post, New York Times,* Sept. 18, 1901.
6. *New York Times,* Sept. 18, 1901; EKR to EC, Sept. 18, 1901 (TRC).
7. Ibid. Ida McKinley returned to Canton, and was thereafter cared for by her younger sister. She visited her husband's grave almost daily, until her death in 1907.
8. EKR to EC, Sept. 18, 1901 (TRC).
9. EKR to TR, Sept. 21, 1901 (ERD).
10. TR to William Allen White, qu. White, *Autobiography*, 341. Under Jefferson the Executive Mansion was known as "the President's House." In 1834 the nickname "White House" appeared in print

for the first time.

11. First established as a family library by Mrs. Fillmore (1850–53).

12. EKR to EC, Sept. 29, 1901 (SH).

13. Ibid. At the end of 1904 Mame moved in (after a protracted visit with Emily in Italy) as Ethel's personal maid. The White House was by then enlarged.

14. EKR to EC, Sept. 29, 1901 (SH).

15. TR, *Letters*, 3.178. Presidential equipage was not provided by the government; incumbents were expected to supply their own.

16. Maud Rochon to Hermann Hagedorn, interview, n.d. (TRB).

17. Baker, Abby G., "Social Duties of Mrs. Roosevelt," *Pearson's Magazine*, Dec., 1903; Randolph, *Presidents*, 184–85.

18. Parsons, *Perchance*, 139, (Oct. 1, 1901); TR, *Letters*, 3.161.

19. *Town Topics*, Sept. 19, 1901.

20. Adams, *Letters*, 367; John Hay to Henry Adams, qu. Samuels, *Adams*, 3.251; TR, *Letters*, 3.181.

21. Washington, Booker T., *My Larger Education* (Doubleday, 1911), 168–69.

22. Dunne, Finley Peter, *Mr. Dooley's Opinions* (New York, 1906), 207–8. The controversy as to whether the educator was at lunch or dinner is settled by EKR's diary entry on Oct. 16: "Mr. Booker Washington at dinner."

23. CRR to Charles Munns, Nov. 29, 1901; ARC to CRR, Nov. 13, 1901 (TRC).

24. EKR to Woman's Roosevelt Memorial Association, Oct. 20, 1933, *Roosevelt House Bulletin*, Fall 1933.

25. CRR to Mrs. Henry Parrish, Jan. 4, 1902 (TRC).

26. Longworth, *Hours*, 47. Edith did, however, splurge on 2,000 roses and

50 azalea trees to perfume and decorate the East Room. Washington *Post*, Jan. 4, 1902.

27. See n. 25 above.

28. Misspelled "Selores" in the Ford edition of Adams's letters.

29. Henry Adams to Elizabeth Cameron, qu. Samuels, *Adams*, 2.364.

30. Qu. Sullivan, *Our Times*, 2.441.

31. Gwynn, *CSR*, 1.347.

32. (CSR.)

33. Parsons, *Perchance*, 140.

34. German–U.S. relations had soured during the Spanish-American War.

35. TR, *Letters*, 3.220; Longworth, *Hours*, 48.

36. March 6, 1902; Cassini, *Moment*, 169.

37. EC to ERD, n.d. (ERD).

38. Baker, Abby G., "Social Duties of Mrs. Roosevelt," *Pearson's Magazine*, Dec. 1903.

39. *Harper's*, Jan. 6, 1906. "Rag-time is said to be what he really appreciates. Chopin particularly sets him on edge, but he dutifully attends the musicales and tries to be good. Sometimes he gets to shifting uneasily in his seat, his gaze wanders, and before he knows it he is bowing and smiling and showing his teeth to acquaintances across the room. Then suddenly he encounters his wife's reproving glance, and lapses quickly into a polite, if bored, attention." Daggett, "Mrs. Roosevelt."

40. Washington *Star*, March 4, 1901.

41. Beaux, Cecilia, *Background with Figures* (New York, 1930), 230–31.

42. Musicale programs (TRC); Cassini, *Moment*, 174.

43. Beaux, *Background*, 227–28; EKR to EC, n.d. (TRC).

44. EKR to EC, April 24, n.d. (TRC); *Message of the President of the U.S. transmitting the Report of the Architects*,

Washington, 1903 (U.S. 57th Congress, 2nd Session, Senate Document 197); TR to McKim, May 10, 1902 (TRP).

45. Qu. Hagedorn, *Family*, 156.
46. Whole account based on ibid., 168–70, and Colman, *Gossip*, 281–83.

Chapter Nineteen

1. Qu. in Slayden, *Wife*, 46.
2. Ibid.
3. (TRP.)
4. Sept. 18, 1902 (TRP).
5. Ibid.
6. Lorant, *TR*, 382.
7. EKR to TR, Sept. 28, 1902 (KR).
8. Qu. Roosevelt, K., *The Happy Hunting Grounds* (Scribners, 1920), 21; Butt, *Letters*, 101.
9. EKR to KR, Oct. 1, 1902 (KR); EKR to EC, Dec. 7, 1902 (TRC). Belle Hagner wrote in an article in the Boston *Transcript*, May 24, 1933: "It is credited to her [EKR] that largely through her influence Congress passed the bill which laid the foundation of a national gallery now housed in the National Museum in Washington." The Watts painting, which brought a protest from the Woman's Christian Temperance Union, is now in the Smithsonian Institution. EKR's desk is being used, at time of writing, by Amy Carter.
10. Formerly called the Cabinet Room; now the Treaty Room.
11. Inscription on the desk.
12. This bedroom is now the President's private upstairs dining room, created by Mrs. John F. Kennedy.
13. Originally designated the Temporary Office Building, the structure remains more or less in its original form. The Oval Office was added by President Taft. The West Terrace, which previously served as garden workshops, was redesigned for servants' quarters and laundry rooms. This freed the ground floor of the house proper for extra visitors' facilities.
14. Hale, William B., *A Week in the White House* (New York, 1908), 10.
15. The Oval Office now stands on the site of the court.
16. W. B. Hale, qu. Willets, *White House*, 192.
17. Wagenknecht, *Seven Worlds*, 152; Crook, Col. W. H., "The Home Life of Roosevelt," *Saturday Evening Post*, March 11, 1911; Butt, *Taft*, 250. TR received 1,500 letters a day during his second term.
18. Crook, "Home Life." Isabella Hagner James in New York *Herald Tribune*, Oct. 30, 1932.
19. EKR to EC, Oct. 19 and Nov. 14, 1902 (TRC).
20. Qu. Colman, *Gossip*, 299–302. The portrait, by Encke, now hangs at Sagamore Hill. It was a gift from Maria Longworth Storer, and shows TR in military uniform. See TR, *Letters*, 3.391.
21. At TR's request these were changed to buffalo heads in 1908, three months before he left the White House. This fireplace is now in the Harry S. Truman Library at Independence, Mo.; a copy of it was reinstalled during the Kennedy Administration.
22. Adams, *Letters*, 2.387.
23. Since President Wilson's tenure, White House china has always been American made. In TR's time, na-

tive potteries were not yet able to do such fine work as European. Mrs. Taft decided not to purchase a new set for her husband's Administration, being "entirely satisfied with the quiet taste displayed by Mrs. Roosevelt." Taft, Helen, *Recollections of Full Years* (Dodd, Mead, 1914), 351–52.

24. The Collection continued to grow, and by 1921 a separate China Room had to be created to house it. A few of the pieces can now be seen in the Smithsonian Institution in Washington, D.C.

25. Adams, *Letters*, 382; EKR, qu. Butt, *Letters*, 189. She "sent it to Veerhorf to be restored," because the canvas was in poor condition. The fireplace referred to is one of three that date back to the 1814 reconstruction. The others are in the Green Room and a second-floor bedroom.

26. In 1965 this space, where the Roosevelts had entertained special friends, was renamed the Jacqueline Kennedy Garden. As designed by Edith, there was a great preponderance of yellow flowers, this being the color that she loved. (Mrs. McKinley had disliked yellow to such an extent that there was none to be seen in and around the White House in 1901; but since she liked blue, "the grounds were literally covered with blue flowers.") Butt, *Letters*, 28.

27. First found in plans drawn by Latrobe in 1807.

28. Now exhibited in the Smithsonian Institution, Washington, D.C.

29. Brown, Glenn, "The New White House," *Harper's Weekly*, July 14, 1906; EKR to Aunt Lizzie, Jan. 26, 1903 (EER); TR to Maria Longworth Storer, TR, *Letters*, 3.392; TR to Cass Gilbert, President of the American Institute of Architects, ibid., 6.1431.

30. Mr. Dooley in *Collier's Magazine*, Feb. 28, 1903.

Chapter Twenty

1. Qu. by Mark Sullivan in Washington *Evening Star*, Aug. 11, 1932.
2. TR, *Letters*, 3.392.
3. The dinner of 1901 was canceled because of mourning for McKinley.
4. Slayden, *Wife*, 46.
5. Ibid., 47.
6. See also Longworth, *Hours*, 162. "The pleasantest part of a reception was the supper afterward . . ."
7. Wister, *TR*, 107–14. EKR's first diplomatic reception in the redesigned White House was not an unqualified triumph as far as the staff was concerned, since 2,000 people could never be comfortably accommodated in a space sufficient for only 1,000. A double column of visitors passing on the grand stairway merged at the bottom, and created a massive jam. "In addition," wrote the official White House archivist, "for some reason not fully understood, guests were too tightly packed in the State Dining Room." *White House Functions*, I. (1902–3).

8. Ibid.
9. Ibid.
10. Butt, *Letters*, 246.
11. Butt, *Taft*, 375.
12. EKR diary, Feb. 13, 14, 15, 19, 1903. (ERD).
13. (TRC).
14. Butt, *Letters*, 329; TR, *Letters*, 3.428; Adams, *Letters*, 398.
15. EKR diary, April 4, 1904 (ERD);

Carpenter, Frank G., *Carp's Wash-ington* (McGraw-Hill, 1960), 265. The *Mayflower* was usually used only by the Admiral of the Fleet and the Secretary of the Navy.

16. EKR to EC, April 12, 1903 (TRC); TR, *Letters*, 3.401; Hoover, *Forty Years*, 28. Far from exaggerating White House stories for entertain-ment purposes, as had been custom-ary in the past, the press, according to Hoover, often toned down Roose-velt tales, on the grounds that read-ers would not believe the truth.

17. Brown, Glenn, *Memories* (New York, 1931), 125. See also Washington *Herald,* Jan. 2, 1903.

18. Qu. Stanley Olmsted in Washington *Herald,* July 27, 1931; TR, *Letters*, 3.406.

19. EKR to TR, May 3, 1903 (ERD).

20. EKR to Aunt Lizzie, April 11, 1903 (EER).

21. TR, *Letters*, 3.484; TR, *Autobiography*, 356.

22. Barrus, *Burroughs*, 2.109; TR, *Letters*, 3.630.

23. Ibid., 3.485–86.

Chapter Twenty-one

1. Qu. in Foraker, Julia, *I Would Live It Again* (Harper, 1932), 192.

2. TR, *Letters*, 3.604.

3. Lee, *Innings*, 1.320.

4. Smalley, George W., *Anglo-American Memories* (Putnam, 1912), 343.

5. ARL diary, Jan. 27, 1903 (ARL). Other entries that month are full of despair. "I don't think I ever make an impression on anybody." Earlier she wrote: "I pray for a fortune. I care for nothing except to amuse myself in a charmingly expensive way."

6. Wister, qu. in Hagedorn, *Family*, 186.

7. TR, *Letters*, 3.408.

8. Ibid., 5.149.

9. ARL diary, May 3, 1904 (ARL); Cassini, *Moment*, 200. TR often teas-ingly addressed Marguerite as "Anna Karenina."

10. Adams, *Letters*, 418. John Hay had warned Adams on Oct. 19, 1902: "When he was one of us we could sit on him—but who, except you, can sit on a Kaiser? Come home and do it or we are undone." (MHS).

11. Gwynn, *CSR*, 1.376.

12. Ibid., 411.

13. Samuels, *Adams*, 3.461.

14. Sullivan, Mark, Washington *Star,* Aug. 11, 1932.

15. TR, *Letters*,, 4.751–53.

16. Ibid. The Roosevelts had three yachts at their disposal. The *Sylph* (152 tons displacement); the *Dolphin* (1,465 tons displacement); the *Mayflower* (2,690 tons displacement). *The Presidential Yacht:* Historical Data White House Curator's office.

17. Qu. Hagedorn, *Family*, 189.

18. EKR to EC, Oct. 29, 1904 (SH); Daggett, "Mrs. Roosevelt"; Wister, *TR*, 108.

19. Beer, Thomas, *Hanna, Crane, and the Mauve Decade* (Knopf, 1941), 605–6.

20. Ibid.

21. Adams, *Education*, 417.

22. Adams, *Letters*, 428.

23. Qu. Hagedorn, *Family*, 209.

24. TR, *Letters*, 4.807.

25. Butt, *Taft*, 167.

26. July 30, 1904 (TRB).

27. EKR to EC, Oct.1, Nov. 6, 1904 (SH).

28. Butt, *Letters*, 220, qu. CRR. Also see Robinson, *TR*, 218.

29. TR to ARC, Oct. 18, 1904 (TRB).
30. Harbaugh, *Power*, 232.
31. Hagedorn, *Family*, 272; Robinson,

TR, 244, gives TR's own views on the third-term question.
32. TR, *Letters*, 4.1025.

Chapter Twenty-two

1. EKR to CSR, Sept. 10, 1905 (CSR).
2. EKR to EC, March 5, 1905 (SH); TR, *Letters*, 4.1131.
3. EKR to EC, March 5, 1905 (SH).
4. Ibid.
5. New York *World*, March 5, 1905.
6. Longworth, *Hours*, 67.
7. Colman, *Gossip*, 295.
8. Her maid removed the mark; the gown, somewhat faded, is now displayed in the Smithsonian Institution.
9. Robinson, *TR*, 226; EKR to EC, March 5, 1905 (SH).
10. Lee, *Innings*, 1.327.
11. Jan. 29, 1905 (SH).
12. Gwynn, *CSR*, 1.394, 446.
13. TR, *Letters*, 4.760; Gwynn, *CSR*, 1. 453.
14. Ibid., 456, 458.
15. Ibid., 470.
16. Ibid., 498.
17. HCL diary, Jan. 15, 1905 (MHS).
18. Qu. Edel, Leon, *Henry James* (Rupert Hart-Davis, 1972), 5.275–76.
19. EKR to EC, Jan. 15, 1905 (SH); TR to HCL, Feb. 15, 1887 (MHS).
20. Qu. Edel, *Henry James*, 5.276.
21. EKR diary, May 1, 1905 (ERD); EKR qu. in Hermann Hagedorn, *Roosevelt House Bulletin*, Fall 1948. On the Mount Vernon excursion the Tafts, the Jusserands, and Charles McKim accompanied them. They explored Washington's house, and had tea in the *Sylph*'s cabin on the way back.
22. EKR diary, Jan. 21, 1905 (ERD).
23. EKR to Eleanor Roosevelt, Dec. 28, 1904 (FDRL).

24. Corinne Robinson Alsop, unpublished memoir (ALS); Eleanor Roosevelt, qu. in Lash, Joseph, *Eleanor: The Years Alone* (Norton, 1972), 303.
25. Lash, *Eleanor*, 141; *Current Biography*, June 1943. ARL was a bridesmaid at FDR's wedding.
26. EKR to EC, Feb. 7, 1905 (SH).
27. EKR to Aunt Lizzie, May 12, 1905 (EER).
28. TR, *Letters*, 4.1209–10.
29. Burroughs, John, *Under the Maples* (Houghton Mifflin, 1921), 101.
30. EKR to ABR, May 9, 1908 (ABR).
31. Burroughs, *Maples*, 106.
32. EKR to KR, May 22, 1907 (KR); Burroughs, *Maples*, 106.
33. The picture was a gift from the Lees after TR left the Presidency.
34. Hagedorn, *Family*, 233.
35. EKR to EC, July 2, 1905 (TRC).
36. TR, *Letters*, 4.1258–59.
37. Ibid., 6.1489–90. Adams was inconsolable, and wrote that Hay "had solved nearly every old problem of American statesmanship" during his eight years in office. Henry Adams to Mrs. Hay, qu. in Samuels, *Adams*, 3.828.
38. TR, *Letters*, 4.1259.
39. Longworth, *Hours*, 71.
40. Howard, Eleanor V., "This Week's Wedding at the White House," *Harper's Weekly*, Feb. 17, 1906.
41. Longworth, *Hours*, 88.
42. TR to EC, Sept. 23, 1905 (ERD); EKR to ARC, n.d. (TRB); TR Jr., *Family*, 58–59. EKR wrote to Kermit on Oct. 11, 1905, rather enig-

matically: "I think that you have made great strides in manliness and strength of character in this past year, and all in the direction of overcoming your besetting sin. My prayer for you is . . . 'that you may be *true* and just in all your dealings.' . . . it comes to us all—at least all the *real* people,—when we put aside childish things, to realize the beauty of absolute truth." (KR).

43. Sept. 23, 1905 (ERD).
44. Ibid.
45. Hagedorn, *Family*, 222.
46. New York *Sun*, Aug. 6, 1905; Gwynn, *CSR*, 1.483.
47. Hagedorn, *Family*, 230.
48. New York *World*, Aug. 31, 1905.

Chapter Twenty-three

1. A professor of law and politics, and a friend of TR speaking of Edith and Theodore in a memo dated Dec. 31, 1948 (TRB).
2. EKR to Aunt Lizzie, Oct. 22, 1905 (EER).
3. EKR to KR, Oct. 21, 1905 (KR); EKR to EC, Oct. 22, 1905 (SH).
4. Oct. 22, 1905. (EER).
5. TR, *Letters*, 5.60.
6. EKR diary, Oct. 27, 1905 (ERD).
7. EKR to KR, Oct. 30, 1905 (KR).
8. Longworth, *Hours*, 108.
9. "I love you with everything that is in me Nick, Nick my Nick." ARL diary, July 22, 1905 (ARL); EKR to Aunt Lizzie, Nov. 27, 1905 (EER).
10. *Town Topics*, Feb. 1, 1906; Charley McCauley, qu. in Butt, *Letters*, 329; EKR to KR, Feb. 4, 1906 (KR).
11. EKR's dress described in a letter from a Mrs. Lambert to "Dora" (TRB).
12. Feb. 18, 1906.
13. Ibid.
14. Interview with ARL by Sally Quinn, Washington *Post*, Feb. 12, 1974.
15. *New York Times*, Feb. 18, 1906.
16. Hoover, Irwin H. (Ike), "Four Stormy Years," *Saturday Evening Post*, March 17, 1934.
17. Willets, *White House*, 287; Longworth, *Hours*, 114.
18. Ibid., 128.
19. TR, *Letters*, 5.81, 164–65; EKR to KR, March 4, 1906 (KR).
20. Lee, *Innings*, 1.340; Leary, *TR*, 20–21; TR, *Letters*, 7.748. Moore was a naval aide to the President.
21. TR, *Letters*, 5.346.
22. March 15, 1906 (wrongly dated 1904 in TRC).
23. Wells, H. G., *Experiment in Autobiography* (Macmillan, 1934), 648–49.
24. The waterway saved 8,000 nautical miles for U.S. vessels by eliminating the Cape Horn route.
25. See articles in *Harper's Weekly*, Nov. 24 and Dec. 8, 1906, for descriptions of the trip. Also *Collier's*, Dec. 8, 1906.
26. EKR to Aunt Lizzie, Nov. 11, 1906 (EER).
27. EKR to KR, Nov. 18, 1906 (KR).
28. TR, *Letters*, 5.507; *Colliers*, Dec. 8, 1906.
29. TR, *Letters*, 5.498.
30. Ibid., 502; Philadelphia *Daily Ledger*, Dec. 3, 1906.
31. Isabella Hagner James, New York *Herald Tribune*, Oct. 30, 1932.

Chapter Twenty-four

1. Qu. in Wagenknecht, *Seven Worlds*, 165.
2. TR, *Letters*, 5.261.
3. Looker, *Gang*, 165; EKR to Aunt Lizzie, Oct. 11, 1905 (EER); Looker, *Gang*, 208–13.
4. TR, *Letters*, 5.788.
5. Looker, *Gang*, 16, 137–39.
6. Ibid., 152.
7. Seeley, Bromley, "Presidential Roughhouse," clipping, n.d. (TRB).
8. Looker, *Gang*, 26–27.
9. Ibid., 164.
10. Ibid., 21.
11. TR, *Letters*, 4.773.
12. TR to ARL, qu. in Hagedorn, *Family*, 254–55; Looker, *Gang*, 13–14.
13. *Munsey's Magazine*, July 1907; TR, *Letters*, 7.345.
14. Ibid., 4.1317.

15. Ibid., 8.1444; EKR to KR, Dec. 6, 1909 (KR).
16. TR, *Letters*, 5.811.
17. Ibid., 524, 520–21.
18. Adams, *Letters*, 475.
19. TR, *Letters*, 5.696.
20. Ibid., 5.800.
21. Ibid., 4.1193.
22. EKR to EC, Oct. 12, 1907 (TRC). In December ABR was circumcised in the hope of alleviating his head pains.
23. EKR to Aunt Lizzie, Oct. 15, 1907 (EER).
24. (TRC.)
25. EKR to Aunt Lizzie, Oct. 15, 1907 (EER).
26. EKR to KR, Oct. 27, Dec. 3, 1907 (KR).
27. TR, *Letters*, 6.922.
28. Butt, *Letters*, 127.
29. TR, *Letters*, 6.891.

Chapter Twenty-five

1. Butt, *Letters*, 380.
2. TR, *Letters*, 6.995. TR hung the Laszlo of EKR in his study at Sagamore Hill so that he could see it when he looked up from his desk. In 1953 it was moved to EKR's sitting room so that the public could see it. Laszlo painted many prominent figures, including Edward VII, George V, Wilhelm II, President Harding, President Wilson, Mussolini, and Pope Leo XIII. He died in England in 1937.
3. White, *Autobiography*, 339.
4. EKR to KR, April 26, 1908 (KR).
5. Ibid., May 9.
6. TR was offered $100,000 by *Collier's* but was content to accept $50,000 from *Scribner's*, which he thought a more dignified magazine. See TR, *Letters*, 6.1105.
7. Butt, *Letters*, 380.
8. Ibid., 9. Butt wrote with eventual publication in mind. After his death the *Letters*, and a second volume, *Taft and Roosevelt*, were published. Note that the first two letters in Abbot's edition of the former are mistakenly dated April 8 and 11. They should be May 8 and 11.
9. Butt, *Letters*, 15.
10. Ibid., 118.
11. Ibid., 160.
12. TR, *Letters*, 6.1330. Ted was put on probation again for cutting lectures in March 1908.

13. EKR to KR, Sept. 26, 1908 (KR); TR, *Letters*, 5.422.
14. QR to EKR, Sept. 24, 25, 1908 (SH).
15. EKR diary, Sept. 26, 1908 (ERD); QR to ABR, Oct. 29, 1908 (ABR).
16. EKR to ABR, Nov. 2, 1908 (ABR).
17. Andrews, Marietta M., *My Studio Window: Sketches of the Pageant of Washington Life* (New York, 1928), 196–97.
18. Riis, Jacob, *Town and Country Magazine*, March 2, 1901; also in "Mrs. Roosevelt and Her Children," *Ladies' Home Journal*, Aug. 2, 1902.
19. The day was Nov. 26, 1901 (TRP); Butt, *Letters*, 324.
20. Randolph, *Presidents*, 198.
21. Butt, *Letters*, 103, 148.
22. Ibid., 221.
23. Ibid., 156, 42.
24. Sept. 29, 1908 (CSR).
25. TR, *Letters*, 6.1241–42.
26. Butt, *Letters*, 153.
27. Ibid., 206, 207, 234.
28. Ibid., 255; "The President's Christmas Turkey," *Christian Herald*, Dec. 9, 1903.
29. TR, *Letters*, 6.1472.
30. Butt, *Letters*, 327, 328.
31. Ibid., 239.
32. Ibid., 302.
33. (ERD.)
34. Butt, *Letters*, 237, 329, 349, 350. Butt burned the painting as ordered, although he was sorely tempted to salvage the beautifully painted hands.
35. Corinne Robinson Alsop, unpublished memoir (ALS).
36. Butt, *Letters*, 354.
37. Feb. 26, 1909 (KR).
38. Butt, *Letters*, 367.
39. Ibid., 377.
40. Ibid., 378. The Abbot edition has marcaronis, an obvious misspelling.
41. Ibid., 380.
42. Adams, *Letters*, 514, 515; Henry Adams to EKR, March 11, 1909 (ERD).
43. TR, *Letters*, 6.1476.
44. EKR to Aunt Lizzie, Feb. 13, 1909 (EER).
45. TR, *Letters*, 6.1084; Butt, *Letters*, 382.
46. March 6, 1909 (ERD).

MISTRESS OF SAGAMORE HILL:
1909–1919
Chapter Twenty-six

1. EKR speaking of TR to Archie Butt, qu. in Butt, *Letters*, 323.
2. Butt, *Taft*, 29.
3. Ibid., 122.
4. TR, *Letters*, 7.6.
5. EKR to KR, March 31, 1909 (KR).
6. Ibid., April 14, 7, 1909 (KR).
7. Butt, *Taft*, 122.
8. June 16, 1909 (KR).
9. Butt, *Taft*, 168.
10. EKR to KR, July 21, 1909 (KR).
11. EKR to TR, Aug. 2, 1909 (KR).
12. Aug. 8, 1909 (EER).
13. EKR diary, Nov. 5, 1909 (ERD); EKR to CSR, DEC. 17, 1909 (CSR).
14. (TRC.) The letter reached New York on Dec. 24.
15. Nov. 28, 1909 (KR).
16. Adams, *Letters*, 531.
17. TR, *Letters*, 7.44.
18. Ibid.; EKR diary, March 14, 1910 (ERD). TR's African expedition was the first systematic and comprehensive investigation and collection of the flora and fauna of the area. It

cost $75,000. Of this, $30,000 came from Andrew Carnegie; $20,000 from TR. See TR, *Letters*, 7.13. KR's photographs of the wild elephant herd were considered by his father to be the best ever taken. Ibid., 35.

19. EKR to CRR, March 18, 1910 (TRC); TR, *Boyhood*, 304; EKR diary, March 30, 1910 (ERD).
20. TR, *Kings*, 35.
21. Ibid., 37–41.
22. EKR diary, April 4, 1910 (ERD); TR, *Kings*, 47.
23. TR, *Letters*, 7.73.
24. EKR to KR, Jan. 7, 1910 (KR); EKR to CRR, April 18, 1910 (TRC).
25. EKR diary, April 29, 1910 (ERD).
26. TR, *Letters*, 7.81.
27. TR, *Kings*, 41, 43, 44.
28. Stefan Lorant to author, Feb. 1976; Lorant, *TR*, 513.
29. Pringle, *TR*, 518. The pictures are in the North Room at Sagamore Hill.
30. Grandfather Lee died March 21,

1910. Half of the $500,000 that he left went to his widow for life; the rest was divided into six parts. Alice received her mother's share, $41,600. Since her marriage she had received no allowance from her father, so this was a welcome increase in income. See ARC to CRR, May 19, 1910 (TRC).
31. Butt, *Taft*, 348.
32. Ibid., 332.
33. TR, *Kings*, 115. "I hate when people touch me," EKR told a granddaughter many years later, "except family. Then I like a nice long hug." Theodora Rauchfuss to author, Feb. 1979.
34. TR, *Kings*, 105.
35. Lee, ed. Clark, *Innings*, 109; TR, *Kings*, 105.
36. Gwynn, *CSR*, 2.151.
37. TR, *Letters*, 7.88.
38. Edward Grey, qu. in Roosevelt, N., *TR*, 60.

Chapter Twenty-seven

1. Butt, *Taft*, 562.
2. June 16, 1910 (ERD).
3. Butt, *Taft*, 472.
4. March 4, 1910 (TRB). It pleased EKR later when Ted said that Eleanor and his mother were the two people whose judgment on a point of right and wrong he "regarded as conclusive." TR, *Letters*, 7.121.
5. Butt, *Taft*, 399. Also on the welcoming boat were Mr. and Mrs. Franklin D. Roosevelt.
6. Ibid., 400.
7. *New York Times*, June 19, 1910.
8. Butt, *Taft*, 401; TR, *Letters*, 7.196. EKR elected not to ride in the parade. From Europe she had written to officials that she would watch

the water parade from a boat, but "I will not ride in a procession." To TR Jr. she added, "Penelope will seek a room in a hotel and bow gracefully to Ulysses from a balcony while he receives the plaudits of the people." May 14, 1910 (TRB).
9. Butt, *Taft*, 385, 396.
10. Ibid., 416.
11. *New York Times*, June 26, 1910.
12. EKR to TR Jr., May 1, 1910 (TRB); Mrs. TR Jr., *Yesterday*, 50.
13. Robinson, *TR*, 262.
14. Hughes was appointed to the Supreme Court by Taft in April 1910, when he decided he could not afford to run again for Governor.
15. Butt, *Taft*, 419; EKR diary, July 1,

1910. TR knew that coming out in support of Hughes committed him to further political action. See TR, *Letters*, 7.169. A combination of Democrats and Republicans defeated the Primary Bill. Significantly, both Taft and TR were losers on this issue.

16. TR, *Letters*, 7.120–21.
17. Butt, *Taft*, 495; EKR to KR, n.d., 1910 (KR).
18. Ibid., July 17, Aug. 22, 1910 (KR); TR, *Letters*, 7.121.
19. TR, *Works*, XVII, 8.
20. From his father, Douglas Robinson II, a distant relative of President James Monroe.
21. EKR to KR, Aug. 29, 1910 (KR); Butt, *Taft*, 397.
22. Ibid., 516.
23. Ibid., 519; TR, *Letters*, 7.156. Nationally, the Democrats held twenty-six governorships, plus a 228–162

majority in the House. The Republicans lost ten Senate seats. A postscript to fears for TR on his airplane flight: the pilot, Arch Hoxsey, crashed fatally a year later.

24. Oct. 30, 1910 (KR). KR received $500 from TR on his birthday, half of what TR Jr. had received on his 21st, because he had "had all the travels." In congratulating her younger son, EKR wrote: "Many happy returns, and my wish that you may in years to come grow more and more like your Father in character." At TR's suggestion TR. Jr. continued to receive an allowance from home until 1911; his father reckoned he could afford it, since he expected to earn at least $40,000 from his book *African Game Trails*. TR, *Letters*, 7.161.
25. TR, *Letters*, 7.161.
26. Butt, *Taft*, 562.

Chapter Twenty-eight

1. Qu. in Morison, Elting E., *Henry L. Stimson* (New York, 1960), 179.
2. Butt, *Taft*, 579–80.
3. TR, *Letters*, 7.181.
4. Ibid., 199.
5. Ibid., 243.
6. EKR diary, March 16, 1911.
7. April 5, 1911 (CSR).
8. EKR to CSR, April 11, 1911 (CSR); TR, *Letters*, 7.316; QR's school reports (SH).
9. April 5, 1911 (CSR).
10. TR, *Letters*, 7.344.
11. EKR diary, Sept. 30, 1911 (ERD).
12. Among EKR's first visitors were Mrs. Selmes and Lady Gregory, patron of Irish artists and writers, who was in New York for a performance of Synge's *Playboy of the Western World*.

13. TR, *Letters*, 7.468.
14. Butt, *Taft*, 776.
15. Ibid., 828–34. EKR's "recovery" mentioned by Butt was not from her accident, but from a subsequent attack of erysipelas. Jusserand's impression of EKR was "gentle, refined, distinguished, with, as I noticed . . . a will of her own, never forcefully exerted, but which, however, was felt." Jusserand, Jules, *What Me Befell* (Houghton Mifflin, 1934), 221.
16. Butt, *Taft*, 839; Adams, *Letters*, 577; TR, *Letters*, 8.1457.
17. Feb. 11, 1912 (KR).
18. TR, *Letters*, 7.508, 511.
19. Adams, *Letters*, 586. "At first it was pretty hard," EKR wrote to Arthur Lee that April, "and at the worst of

it I was forced to be away . . . in all my life I was never more unhappy." (LEE).

20. Adams, *Letters,* 587; Butt, *Taft,* 843.
21. EKR to Arthur Lee, April 19, 1912 (LEE).
22. TR, *Works,* XVII, 151–71.
23. Adams, *Letters,* 2.589.
24. Butt, *Taft,* 847, 848. At midnight on Sunday, April 14, the "unsinkable" liner brushed against an iceberg off the Grand Banks of Newfoundland. Its double hull of steel caved in, flooding the "watertight" compartments, and in two and a half hours she sank, taking 1,500 passengers with her. Captain Butt was among them. "Don't forget that all my papers are in the storage warehouse," he had written his sister-in-law before leaving, "and if the old ship goes down you will find my affairs in shipshape condition."
25. N.d., 1912 (ERD).
26. May 27, 1912 (ERD).
27. Gable, *Bull Moose Years,* 16–17.
28. Mrs. TR Jr. to Hermann Hagedorn, n.d. (TRB).
29. E. A. Van Valkenberg to David Hinshaw, a manager of the Progressive Party, who in turn told J. F. French, 1922 (TRB).
30. Mrs. TR Jr., *Yesterday,* 60–62.
31. Longworth, *Hours,* 211–12.
32. Aug. 8, 1912 (KR).
33. Gable, *Bull Moose Years,* 108–9; Wister, *TR,* 232.
34. Aug. 10, 1912 (CSR). Only two of the seven governors who had urged TR to run now joined the Progressive Party—Hiram Johnson of California and Chase Osborn of Michigan. The bulk of the Progressive rank and file were successful middle-class people—lawyers, doc-

tors, professors, suffragettes, and farmers. All resented the commercialism of the new rich.
35. Roosevelt, N., *TR,* 100, qu. from his own diary.
36. Aug. 22, 1912 (TRB).
37. Roosevelt, N., *TR,* 67.
38. Schrank was later declared insane and put into an asylum.
39. Leary, *TR,* 30.
40. TR, *Letters,* 8.1449; Roosevelt, N., *TR,* 67; EKR to EC, Oct. 17, 1912 (TRC). Later a second telegram arrived telling EKR that TR was going to Chicago "to find out what I could do on the rest of the trip," and urging her "not to come out" because "I am not nearly as bad hurt as I have been again and again with a fall from my horse." Oct. 15, 1912 (KR).
41. EKR to ARC, Oct. 16, 1912 (TRB); EKR to EC, Oct. 17, 1912 (TRC); Roosevelt, N., *TR,* 68.
42. TR, *Letters,* 7.629; Thompson, W. S. *Presidents I've Known* (Bobbs-Merrill, 1929), 150–55.
43. EKR to KR, Oct. 21, 1912 (KR).
44. Gable, *Bull Moose Years,* 128–29.
45. Nov. 6, 1912 (KR).
46. QR to EKR, Nov. 16, 1912 (SH). (The Rector of Groton was Endicott Peabody.) EKR to KR, Dec. 1, 1912 (KR). Nick's defeat was made more bitter by Alice's appearance (after her father was shot) at a Progressive rally in Cincinnati. She thus seemed to be endorsing her husband's Bull Moose opponent. ARL herself always attributed the loss of Nick's seat to this apparent endorsement. ARL to John Gable and retold to author.
47. Gwynn, *CSR,* 2.173, 174.
48. N.d. (TRB).

Chapter Twenty-nine

1. EKR to ERD, Nov. 14, 1913 (ERD).
2. TR, *Autobiography*, 328.
3. *Roosevelt v. Newett: A Transcript of the Testimony taken and Depositions read at Marquette, Michigan* (privately printed, 1914, by W. Emlen Roosevelt), 357–58.
4. EKR to KR, Nov. 17, Dec. 29, 1912 (KR).
5. Ibid., March 2, 1913 (KR).
6. TR to ARC, April 4, 1913 (TRB). Edith Williams says that her parents probably met even earlier at the White House.
7. Longworth, *Hours,* 228.
8. EKR to KR, May 24, 1913 (KR).
9. Ibid., March 9.
10. EKR to EC, April 6, 1913 (TRC); EKR to Bigelow, April 6, 1913 (ERD); EKR to ERD, April 6, 1913 (ERD); TR, *Letters,* 8.1450.
11. Gwynn, *CSR,* 2.187; EKR to CSR, May 30, 1913 (CSR); Gwynn, *CSR,* 2.190–91.
12. July 6, 1913 (KR).
13. TR, *Letters,* 7.733.
14. EKR to KR, July 15, 1913 (KR); qu. Wagenknecht, *Seven Worlds,* 11. EKR to ERD, n.d., 1913 (ERD).
15. EKR to KR, Aug. 3, 31, 1913 (KR).
16. Nancy Roosevelt Jackson to author, Feb. 1976.
17. EKR to KR, Sept. 14, 1913 (KR).
18. Oct. 15, 1913 (TRC).
19. TR to ARC, Nov. 11, 1913 (TRB).
20. EKR to a Miss Eustis, Oct. 25, 1913

(ERD); EKR to ARC, n.d. (TRC).
21. EKR to Ruth Lee, Dec. 14, 1913 (LEE); EKR to ARC, Oct. 15, 1913 (TRC).
22. EKR diary, Jan. 5, 1914 (ERD). "Margaret drank only bottled water and ate no salad; can't imagine how she got the typhoid." EKR to EC, Dec. 21, 1913 (TRC).
23. EKR diary, Jan. 14, 1914 (ERD).
24. These articles became a book entitled *Through the Brazilian Wilderness.*
25. Dec. 24, 1913 (KR).
26. TR, *Letters,* 7.766. The party collected 1,000 birds and some 250 mammals, including an anteater as big as a bear, and a rare white-lipped peccary.
27. EKR diary, March 25, 1914 (ERD).
28. April 3, 1914 (TRC).
29. EKR to Ruth Lee, April 27, 1914 (LEE); EKR to KR, May 24, 1914 (KR).
30. TR, *Letters,* 7.763.
31. EKR to Ruth Lee, May 27, 1914 (LEE); EKR to KR, May 24, 1914 (KR); EKR to Ruth Lee, May 27, 1914 (LEE). She also told Ruth that Philip Roosevelt was "of all that generation of cousins . . . the most sympathetic and companionable to Theodore." Ibid.
32. June 11, 1914 (KR).
33. Strictly speaking, he was TR IV— TR's father having been the first of that name.

Chapter Thirty

1. EKR to ERD, July 23, 1917 (ERD), quoting from Edwin Arlington Robinson's "House on the Hill."
2. TR, *Letters,* 7.768.
3. Ibid., 8.831–32. Nick Longworth,

however, was reelected, and Alice reopened their Washington home at 1735 M Street.
4. Probably a hysterectomy; the records no longer exist at the Roosevelt

hospital. EKR to KR, April 3, 1915 (KR); EKR diary, *passim* (ERD).

5. June 21, 1915 (TRC).
6. TR, *Letters*, 8.970.
7. June 19, 1915 (KR).
8. Privately printed memorial, qu. in Garraty, 102.
9. Thompson, C. W., *Presidents I've Known* (Bobbs-Merrill, 1929), 169, 170.
10. EKR to KR, Feb. 20, 1916 (KR).
11. Mrs. TR Jr., *Yesterday*, 68–70.
12. TR, *Letters*, 8.1023; Leary, *TR*, 76. Root, HCL and Leonard Wood had all contemplated the Republican presidential nomination.
13. TR to EKR, Oct. 21, 1916 (ABR); EKR to Ruth Lee, Nov. 29, 1916 (LEE). Theodore Douglas Robinson served until 1918 and was reelected in 1920. In 1924 he followed his uncle into the post of Assistant Secretary of the Navy.

14. TR, *Letters*, 8.1133. Little cataloguing was done, however, until the Roosevelt Memorial Association contributed funds in 1922.
15. TR, *Letters*, 8.1149.
16. Pringle, *TR*, wrongly dates this meeting April 9. "It is quite useless," Edith wrote afterward, "to dwell on how this forced inactivity hurts [Theodore]. He said at an address at one of the Long Island camps that the war was an exclusive club where he had been blackballed." EKR to Ruth Lee, Sept. 26, 1917 (LEE).
17. TR, *Letters*, 8.1193, 1199, 1202.
18. Gwynn, *CSR*, 2.396–97.
19. Longworth, *Hours*, 254.
20. TR, *Letters*, 8.1276.
21. QR to Flora Payne Whitney, n.d. (SH).
22. QR to EKR, n.d. (SH).
23. See n. 1.

Chapter Thirty-one

1. TR, *Works*, XIX, 243–47.
2. (ERD.)
3. TR, *Letters*, 8.1230. "I am very satisfied," EKR wrote regarding TR's *Kansas City Star* contract, "for he gets immediate publicity instead of being hushed to silence until the beginning of the month." EKR to Ruth Lee, Sept. 26, 1917 (LEE).
4. TR, *Letters*, 8.1231.
5. Sept. 15, 1917 (KR).
6. Flora Payne Whitney to QR, Sept. 30, 1917 (ERD).
7. TR, *Letters*, 8.1246; Jack Cooper to J. F. French (TRB); EKR to ERD, Oct. 22, 1917 (ERD).
8. Nov. 27, 1917 (ERD). ERD had already been to France in 1915 with Dick, to serve with the American Ambulance Corps for a few months.

9. TR, *Letters*, 8.1266–67.
10. EKR to ARC, Jan. 29, 1918 (TRC); TR, *Letters*, 8.1262.
11. Dec. 25, 1917 (KR).
12. Dec. 25, 1917 (TRB).
13. TR, *Letters*, 8.1277.
14. Gwynn, *CSR*, 2.431, 436.
15. At Archie's urging, TR and EKR supplied his regiment with 200 pairs of shoes. See ABR, "Lest We Forget," in *Everybody's Magazine*, May and June 1919, criticizing the Administration for failure to train and equip American soldiers adequately.
16. TR, *Letters*, 8.1301.
17. April 7, 1918 (SH). At first QR was supply officer at Issoudun Army Camp near Bourges, "the most forsaken little hole," he told EKR. Hearing frequently from Flora made

it "a lot easier" to bear. He was glad his mother liked his fiancée, now that she "had got past the fact that she was one of the Whitneys and powdered her nose." N.d. 1917 (SH).

18. Leary, *TR*, 203.
19. EKR to KR, June 16, 1918 (KR); Roosevelt, K., *QR*, 148, 149.
20. Mrs. TR Jr., *Yesterday*, 99.
21. TR, *Letters*, 8.1364.
22. Roosevelt, K., *QR*, 60.
23. Hagedorn, *Family*, 412.
24. Stricker, Josephine, "Roosevelt At Close Range," *Delineator*, Sept. 1919.
25. Hagedorn, *Family*, 412; grandchildren to author on various occasions.
26. Isaac Hunt, qu. in Hagedorn, *Family*, 423.
27. Ibid.
28. TR, *Letters*, 8.1355; Robinson, *TR*, 346.
29. Roosevelt, K., *QR*, 176; TR qu. a clergyman he once knew, *Letters*, 8.1381. QR's body was in fact moved after World War II to Normandy to be next to Ted's. The stone from the first grave is now on the lawn at Sagamore Hill by the flagpole.
30. Roosevelt, K., *QR*, 169.
31. Ibid., 235, 236.
32. July 21, 1918 (KR). EKR was refer-

ring to a favorite passage from George Borrow's *Lavengro:*

There's night and day, brother, both sweet things;
Sun, moon, and stars, brother, all sweet things;
There's likewise a wind on the heath. Life is very sweet, brother; who would wish to die?

TR Jr. had been shot through the leg above and behind his knee. Dick Derby made sure the wound was cleaned properly, otherwise TR Jr., might have been paralyzed. Mrs. TR Jr., *Yesterday*, 102.

33. TR to TR Jr., July 21, 1918 (TRB); QR to Flora Payne Whitney, July 29, 1917 (SH).
34. EKR to CRR, Aug. 8, 1918 (TRC); TR to KR, Aug. 10, 1918 (KR); TR, *Letters*, 8.1363.
35. EKR to CRR, Aug. 14, 1918 (TRC).
36. Roosevelt, N., *TR*, 20.
37. On Jan. 28, 1918, TR Jr.'s Brigadier General recommended he be promoted to lieutenant colonel, saying he "considered him an officer of unusual ability." Two other senior officers also recommended him, but HQ turned them all down. Mrs. TR Jr., *Yesterday*, 82–83.
38. Oct. 6, 1918 (KR).
39. Wister, *TR*, 371–72.

Chapter Thirty-two

1. ABR cable to his brothers, Jan. 6, 1919 (KR).
2. Oct. 27, 1918 (KR).
3. Oct. 29, 1918 (KR).
4. Hagedorn Notes (TRC), qu. in Pringle, *TR*, 601.
5. EKR to KR, Oct. 29, 1918 (KR).
6. Roosevelt, K., *QR*, 196–97.
7. Dec. 15, 1918 (KR).
8. Ibid.

9. White, *Autobiography*, 549.
10. John T. Faris memo (TRB).
11. C. E. Young to EKR, Jan. 6, 1919 (ERD); Robinson, *TR*, 362.
12. Chanler, *Spring*, 202; Hermann Hagedorn, quoting Dr. Richards, in *Saturday Evening Post*, Dec. 9, 1922.
13. Hagedorn, qu. Dr. J. H. Richards (see n. 12).
14. TR to ARC, Dec. 28, 1918 (TRB).

15. Dec. 29, 1918 (TRB).
16. EKR diary, Dec. 31, 1918 (ERD); EKR to ERD, Jan 4, 1919 (ERD).
17. EKR to KR, Jan 12, 1919 (KR).
18. Noyes, Alfred, *Two Worlds for Memory* (Lippincott, 1953), 112.
19. EKR to TR Jr., Jan 12, 1919 (TR Jr.); Colby, Major Everett, address in Trinity Cathedral, Newark, N.J., Feb. 9, 1919 (TRB); EKR diary, Jan. 5, 1919 (ERD).
20. EKR to KR, Jan. 12, 1919 (KR). In her diary, EKR wrote simply, "At four a.m. T. stopped breathing. Had had sweet, sound sleep." (ERD).
21. EKR to KR, Jan. 12, 1919 (KR); Amos, James, *TR: Hero to His Valet* (New York, 1927), 157.
22. Hermann Hagedorn, qu. Dr. Richards, *Saturday Evening Post,* Dec. 9, 1922; EKR to TR Jr., Jan. 12, 1919 (TR Jr.); Robinson, *TR,* 365.
23. Stricker, Josephine, "Roosevelt at Close Range," *Delineator,* Sept. 1919.
24. George Syran to "Mr. and Mrs. Osbourn," Jan. 11, 1919 (ARL). Robinson, *TR,* 365.
25. (TR Jr.)
26. (KR.)
27. Jan. 7, 1919 (ERD). TR currently rates fourth after Washington, Lincoln, and FDR, according to an American Historical Society poll, 1977. Many other friends recalled TR's virtues, among them Arthur Lee: "I loved him more than I ever loved any man . . . and I was more proud of his friendship than of anything else . . . That gift of sympathy—almost feminine in its delicate intuition—has never failed to move and fill me with wonder. . . . Two of the greatest tragedies of these latter years will have been that he was not President at the outbreak of the war, and that the world should be bereft of his counsel at this dangerous dawn of Peace." Charles G. Washburn, TR's old college friend, wrote: "The mere mention of his name quickens the circulation of my blood and brings tears to my eyes. I miss him so. I believe there never was a more *overpowering* personality than his. I think *enthralling* expresses it better. There is no need of speaking of it to those who knew him, and no use doing so to those who did not." Lee to EKR, Jan. 1919 (LEE); Washburn to EKR, March 18, 1927 (ERD).
28. N.d. (TRC). Edith Wharton wrote a poem, "The Lamb," in memory of TR; so, too, did Kipling, calling his eulogy "Greatheart."
29. Mary Cadwalader Jones to EKR, Feb. 13, 1919 (TRC).
30. Pringle, *TR,* 602.
31. For a discussion of "Quentin's Prayer," see *The Oxford American Prayer Book Commentary,* 595.
32. "And the Mourners Go About the Streets," by "The Happy Eremite," memo, n.d. (TRB).

EARLY WIDOWHOOD: 1919–1927
Chapter Thirty-three

1. Extract from "To his Matchlesse never to be forgotten Friend."
2. EKR to ERD, April 13, 1919 (ERD).
3. EKR to TR Jr., May 15, 1929 (TRB); EKR to ARC, Dec. 16, 1923 (TRC); EKR to TR Jr., July 31, 1929 (TRB).
4. Bacon, Robert, *Life and Letters,* ed. James Brown Scott (Doubleday, 1923), Feb. 7, 1919.
5. EC to ERD, Feb. 18, 1919 (ERD);

EKR to KR, March 1, 1919 (KR).

6. EKR to CRR, March 21, 1919 (TRB). When EC went back to nursing, at the end of 1919, she took a position at the Children's Tubercular Hospital in Genoa. A ward there was named after QR. EKR to KR, Feb. 13, 1920 (KR).
7. EKR to ERD, March 30, 1919 (ERD); Nancy Roosevelt Jackson to author, Aug. 1936.
8. EKR to KR, April 20, 1919 (KR); EKR to ERD, March 4, 1919 (ERD); EKR to Belle Willard Roosevelt, April 20, 1919 (KR).
9. EKR to CRR, March 21, 1919 (TRB); EKR to ERD, April 2, 1919 (ERD).
10. Edwin Emerson in a letter to *The New York Times*, Oct. 4, 1948; EKR to KR, Feb. 13, 1920 (KR).
11. EKR to EC, March 14, 20, 1920 (ERD); EKR to Richard Derby, Jr., Aug. 13, 1921 (ERD).
12. ERD to EC, Feb. 27, 1920 (ERD). The marriage took place on April 19, 1920. The couple divorced in 1925, and Flora married "Cully" Miller, an architect, in 1927. She is still alive.
13. In 1920, Congress added the Women's Suffrage Amendment to the Constitution.

Chapter Thirty-four

1. EKR, *Strange Ports*, 37.
2. Ibid., 5.
3. Ibid., 8–11; EKR to KR, Feb. 9, 1921 (KR).
4. April 24, 1921 (TRC).
5. Dick Derby died in 1963, ERD in 1977.
6. Lash, *Eleanor and Franklin*, 265.
7. William S. Cowles, Jr., to author.
8. EKR to EC, Nov. 6, 1921 (TRC). "All she cares for now," Ruth Lee wrote in her diary later, "are the people who cared for Theodore, and she lives altogether in her memories." Lee, *Innings*, 2.916.
9. Jan. 14, 1930 (LEE).
10. Memo (TRB); EKR to TR Jr., Jan. 9, 1929 (TRB); EKR diary, Jan. 6, 1932. The headstone for Theodore's grave was designed by the sculptor Beatrix Ferrand, a daughter of EKR's close friend Mary Cadwalader Jones. "All her ideas were carried out," said Beatrix of EKR later, "so the design is hers, rather than anyone else's." Ferrand to ERD, n.d. (ERD).
11. EKR to EC, Jan. 31, 1922 (TRC); EKR diary, Jan. 31, 1922 (ERD).
12. EKR, *Strange Ports*, 13; EKR to ARC, March 12, 1922 (TRC).
13. EKR to Arthur Lee, March 31, 1921, Aug. 30, 1922, July 14, 1923 (LEE).
14. EKR, *Strange Ports*, 14, 15.
15. Roosevelt, N., *TR*, 31.
16. In July 1919 the always charming Monroe was released from Bloomingdale's alcohol treatment center and went to work on the Robinson family property in Virginia, just as his uncle Elliott had done in similar circumstances nearly thirty years before. "Quite hopeless," EKR told EC, Aug. 2, 1919 (ERD). She was wrong, for Monroe, under the influence of a Roman Catholic friend, eventually gave up alcohol, and was sober for at least five years before his death in December 1947.
17. Chanler, *Spring*, 254. CRR was a published poet who would have distinguished literary grandsons: the writers Joseph and Stewart Alsop.

18. *New York Times,* Dec. 30, 1928.
19. "An idea," EKR added. "I shall tell her the price and ask if she wants it for Christmas." Oct. 28, 1928 (ERD). Earlier in the year she had elaborated on her poor relationship with EC in a letter to ERD. "Don't believe a word she tells you about me. She knew neither my life nor my thoughts when I was young, and disliked my friends. Four years is a gap unless there are congenial tastes . . ." Jan. 6, 1928 (ERD).
20. EKR to EC, Nov. 6, 1924 (TRC); Belmont, Eleanor Robson, *The Fabric of Memory* (New York, 1957), 108.
21. EKR to ARC, Nov. 29, 1923 (TRC).
22. In spite of worldwide protests, the hotel was torn down in the late 1960s.
23. EKR, *Strange Ports,* 18–20, 87–114, 95, 22, 110, 22.
24. EKR to EC, Aug. 21, 1924 (TRC).
25. EKR to ARC, July 16, 1924 (TRC).
26. 1931 (ERD).
27. For a complete account of Teapot Dome see Werner, M. R., and John Starr, *Teapot Dome* (Viking, 1959). Also Mrs. TR Jr., *Yesterday,* 147–64.
28. For accounts of the campaign see *Yesterday,* 162–66, and Lash, *Eleanor and Franklin,* 291.
29. (TRC.)
30. EKR to EC, Feb. 18, 1925 (TRC); EKR to ARC, Feb. 17, 1925 (TRC).
31. Still at a loose end in late 1928, TR Jr. went to Burma with Kermit to hunt the giant panda. Pressing shipping business curtailed the expedition for Kermit, but not before he and TR Jr., caught a panda as well as 2,000 small mammals for the Chicago natural-history museum.
32. Various Roosevelt grandchildren to author; EKR to KR, March 27, 1927 (KR).
33. EKR, *Strange Ports,* 28–46.
34. Ibid., 31–32.

OLD AGE: 1927–1948
Chapter Thirty-five

1. EKR to ERD, Dec. 1, 1927 (ERD).
2. Probably for as little as $1,500, according to the Town Clerk of Brooklyn. She signed the deed on August 25, 1927. Originally she had attempted to buy the smaller and older house of Daniel II nearby, but its owners were not prepared to sell. The new house was called Mortlake, "after the English place where they [Tylers] came from." Ingersoll Interview, 1962 (SH).
3. Aug. 22, 1927.
4. Mr. Blake's daughters to author, May 1977.
5. Both churches still stand.
6. Sept. 1, 1927 (TRC).
7. Edwin Emerson in a letter to *The New York Times,* Oct. 4, 1948.
8. Helen Linn, Margaret Snowden Knapp, and Edward Plummer have given author other instances of EKR's generosity and graciousness.
9. Newton to EKR, June 27 and 24, 1928; May 26, 1933; EKR to ERD, Jan. 20, 1928 (ERD).
10. EKR to ERD, Nov. 6, 12, 27, 30, 1927 (ERD).
11. Ibid., Dec. 1, 1927.
12. Ibid., Dec. 23, 1927.
13. Ibid., Nov. 8, 1931 (ERD); EKR to TR Jr., Dec. 18 [1930?] (TRB); EKR to CRR, Dec. 14, 1932 (TRC); TR Jr. to the Lees, Dec. 28, 1930 (LEE).
14. Lee, *Innings,* 3.1241–42.
15. Arthur Lee to EKR, Jan. n.d. 1919 (LEE); qu. Lee, *Innings,* 3.1241–42.

16. KR to TR Jr., Oct. 30, 1929 (TR Jr.); EKR accounts of finances from her personal diaries (ERD).
17. Nov. 25, 1929 (KR). ARL in *Plain Talk*, June 1930, said she obtained for TR Jr., "for whom success has been so dilatory," his post in Puerto Rico by speaking in Kansas City for President Hoover.
18. TR Jr., to KR, Jan. 29, Sept. 26, 1930 (KR).
19. Dec. 9, 1930 (TRC). This letter was written on the same day that EKR had visited ARC, and found her confined to her room. "Desperately sad," she wrote in her diary.
20. EKR to ERD, Dec. 23, 1930 (ERD); Adams, *Letters*, 398.
21. March 14, 1931 (ERD).
22. EKR diary, April 11, 1931 (ERD); ARL to CRR, April 16, 1931 (TRC).

23. Brough, James, *Princess Alice* (Little, Brown, 1975), 286–87.
24. Barrus, *Burroughs*, 2.371–72. Burroughs said the "Road of the Loving Heart" dedicated to Robert Louis Stevenson in Samoa was an ideal kind of monument.
25. EKR to TR Jr., April 13, Aug. 10, 1932 (TRB).
26. *New York Times*, Aug. 11, 1932.
27. Ibid.; EKR to KR, Aug. 14, 1932 (KR).
28. Sept. 1, 1932 (TRB). EKR was often very depressed at this time. A diary entry for Oct. 3, 1932, reads: "Archies left. House very empty. No use. Better out of the world."
29. Oct. 18, 1932 (TRB).
30. Mrs. TR Jr., *Yesterday*, 304.
31. EKR to ERD, Jan. 4, 1933 (ERD).
32. Mrs. TR Jr., *Yesterday*, 301–2.

Chapter Thirty-six

1. EKR to ERD, Sept. 22, 1927 (ERD).
2. EKR to TR Jr., n.d. (TRB); Parsons, *Perchance*, 29; Longworth, *Hours*, 31; EKR to Dr. Frank Chapman, March 19, 1933 (ERD).
3. N.d. (Herbert Hoover Presidential Library, West Branch, Iowa).
4. EKR to James R. Garfield, repudiating a statement by Senator Vic Donahey of Ohio that FDR represented the same ideals as TR; EKR to Arthur Lee, Sept. 29, 1933, and ARL to Lee, Aug. 1935 (LEE).
5. Nov. 17, 1933 (ERD).
6. EKR to KR, Oct. 4, 1935 (KR). In 1931, EKR's total income was $25,264.73; in 1932, $24,048.34; in 1933, $21,781.57; in 1934, $20,255.19; in 1935, $19,327.56. When the government introduced

an inheritance tax she began to give substantial sums to her grandchildren.
7. Keogh, Theodora, *The Tattooed Heart* (Farrar, Strauss and Young, 1953), 220.
8. Nancy Roosevelt Jackson in an unpublished memoir of EKR, "A Sense of Style."
9. Theodora Rauchfuss to author, Feb. 4, 1979; granddaughter Edith Roosevelt to author, Feb. 1976; Archibald Roosevelt, Jr., to author, April 1977; Corinne Robinson Alsop unpublished memoir (ALS). Joseph Alsop found EKR *"very intimidating."* Granddaughter Grace McMillan to author, July 1979.
10. Nancy Roosevelt Jackson, "A Sense of Style."

11. Keogh, *Tattooed Heart,* 22–29.
12. Nancy Roosevelt Jackson, "A Sense of Style."
13. Dr. Alexander Johnston to author, April 1, 1977.
14. EKR to TR Jr., Dec. 11, 1929 (TR Jr.).
15. Nancy Roosevelt Jackson, "A Sense of Style." To Archie Jr. EKR once said of servants: "If they had our brains they'd have our place." ABR Jr. to author Oct. 1979.
16. EKR to KR, Sept. 18, [1933?] (KR).
17. EKR diary, June 1, 1935 (ERD); EKR to KR, July 19, 1936 (KR). Later TR Jr. joined Doubleday, the publishers, where he became a vice-president.

18. March 29, 1934 (TRB).
19. Mrs. Robert Jay, formerly Cynthia White, a granddaughter of Stanford White and pupil in Turkey Lane School, to author, Dec. 16, 1978.
20. EKR to Arthur Lee, July 6, 1931 (LEE).
21. EKR to KR, Jan. 13, 1935 (KR).
22. EKR to KR, qu. Wordsworth's "Daffodils," July 14, 1935, and on Sept. 8, 1935 (KR).
23. Edith Williams to author, April 1976. The tape of EKR's address is at TRB.
24. EKR diary, Nov. 7, 1935 (ERD).
25. TR Jr. to Ruth and Arthur Lee, March 29, 1936 (LEE).
26. EKR diary, Jan. 1, 1937 (ERD).

Chapter Thirty-seven

1. EKR diary, Jan. 1, 1938 (ERD).
2. EKR to KR, March n.d., 1936 (KR).
3. TR, *Letters,* 8.1453–54. Another reason for Kermit's malaise was that he had lost the investment money of several Oyster Bay friends and relatives, notably in a Manhattan coffee-shop venture. Before going out of business the coffee shop had acquired a reputation for being a homosexual hangout. ABR Jr. to author, April 1977.
4. Nov. 19, 1927 (ERD).
5. Kermit ("Kim") and Willard Roosevelt, and Clochette Roosevelt Palfrey to author at various interviews.
6. Fanny Parsons to Hermann Hagedorn, 1948 (TRB).
7. Unidentified memoir in Belle Roosevelt's papers (KR).
8. TR Jr., *Family,* 61.
9. Willard Roosevelt to author, April 27, 1978; see also n. 7.

10. Nancy Roosevelt Jackson to author, Feb. 1976.
11. EKR to ERD, Jan. 20, 1937 (ERD); EKR to KR, March 1, 1937 (KR).
12. EKR diary, Feb. 18, 1937 (ERD).
13. EKR to Mrs. William Loeb, Easter 1937 (TRB).
14. March 26, 1937 (CRP).
15. March 29, 1937 (CRP).
16. EKR to Belle Willard Roosevelt, April 5, 1937 (CRP); EKR diary, Oct. 22, 1937 (ERD); EKR to KR, Oct. 24, 1937 (KR). "Mother is in gorgeous shape," TR Jr. wrote Arthur Lee about this time, "willing and able to hit from any angle at anybody, including all of her devoted family." Sept. 20, 1937 (LEE).
17. EKR diary, Jan. 1, 1938 (ERD); EKR to Nancy Roosevelt Jackson, Jan. 18, 1938 (NRJ); EKR to ERD, Jan. 25, 1938 (ERD).
18. EKR diary, Feb. 4, 1938 (ERD);

EKR to KR, Feb. 24, 1938 (KR).

19. April 10, 1938 (KR).
20. Mrs. TR Jr., *Yesterday,* 390.
21. EKR diary, June 6, 1944 (ERD). The land was not purchased until 1945. Old Orchard is open to the public as part of Sagamore Hill National Historic Site, but the bulk of the furnishings are no longer there.
22. EKR to Edith Williams, Jan. 10, 1946 (EW); EKR to ERD, July 24, 1942 (ERD).
23. EKR diary, Aug. 6, 1938 (ERD).
24. EKR to Nancy Roosevelt Jackson, Nov. 1, 1938 (NRJ).
25. EKR to Dr. Frank Chapman, Oct. 20, 1944 (ERD); EKR to Nancy Roosevelt Jackson, Nov. 1 and 29, 1938 (NRJ).
26. EKR diary, March 13, 1939 (ERD). EC had been worried about money since the depression and asked her

sister for advice about her investments. EKR told her to keep what she could in Italy.
27. Maud Rappis to EKR, March 20, 1939 (ERD).
28. It seems that EC's affection for TR Jr. was unrequited. In a letter to KR, July 28, 1930 (KR), he had written, regarding an impending visit by EC, that he hoped she would dive into the Atlantic en route. "It would be hard on the barracuda, that's all. Supposing she bit one!" He gave Villa Magna Quies to his Italian maid on her retirement. Cornelius Roosevelt to author, May 14, 1979.
29. EKR to KR, April 18, 1943 (KR).
30. ABR to Arthur Lee, Sept. 18, 1938 (LEE); EKR diary, June 28, 1939 (ERD).
31. EKR diary, Sept. 1, 1939 (ERD).

Chapter Thirty-eight

1. *Epigrams,* canto "Death."
2. EKR diary, Oct. 24, 1939 (ERD).
3. Belle Willard Roosevelt papers (KR). A friend in the Horse Guards wrote to Kermit: "It was a great asset to me to have a chap like you there, who did not mind how many bullets cracked around his head, or how many hours a day he had to work." Porcellian Club Obituary (KR).
4. EKR diary, Sept. 28, 1940 (ERD).
5. March 2 and 25, 1941 (KR).
6. ABR to author, Feb. 1979.
7. Ibid.
8. EKR diary, June 7, 1940 (ERD).
9. Ibid., Jan. 27, 1942.
10. *New York Times,* Feb. 12, 1942.
11. Feb. 16, 1942 (TRB).
12. Nancy Roosevelt Jackson to author, May 21, 1977; EKR to Dr. F. Chap-

man, March 13, 1944 (ERD).
13. ABR to author, Feb. 1979.
14. July 24, 1942 (ERD).
15. EKR diary, Sept. 4, 1942 (ERD); Peter Lacey, member of 328 Regular Combat Team, to author, Nov. 1978.
16. Belle Willard Roosevelt to Mr. Joy, Feb. 1, 1946. (KR).
17. EKR diary, April 4, 1943 (ERD).
18. EKR to KR, April 5, 1943 (KR).
19. ABR and various other members of the Roosevelt family to author. The night before his death Kermit went to Nellie's Diner on E Street in Anchorage. "He always sat at the counter so he could talk with me," Nellie recalled. "He had wine here [that night]; I think wine was the only alcoholic beverage he could take." After "making the rounds"

with a friend, Muktuk Marston, KR arrived back late at the post. Marston announced his intention "to get some sleep," whereupon KR said wistfully, "I wish *I* could sleep." He then went down the corridor into his cubicle, never to emerge alive. Lyman L. Woodman, "A Roosevelt in Alaska," *Alaska Living*, June 2, 1968. While Mr. Woodman failed to mention KR's suicide in his article, he confirmed it in a telephone conversation with Dr. John Gable, Executive Director of the Theodore Roosevelt Association, in 1979.

20. A later letter from Belle said that KR "was found with his head on his pillow, gone." EKR diary, July 27, 1943. Kermit's youngest child, Dirck, also committed suicide, at the age of 28.

21. EKR diary, June 5, 1943; EKR to ERD, Oct. 14, 1943 (ERD).

22. EKR now had 16 grandchildren and 15 great-grandchildren.

23. Mrs. TR Jr., *afl7Yesterday*, 453–54.

24. TR Jr. received the Medal of Honor posthumously, thus becoming the most decorated soldier of World War II.

25. Reverend J. R. Jones to Associated Press, July 14, 1944.

26. EKR to ERD, July 30, 1944; EKR diary, July 31, 1944 (ERD); Mrs. Frances Roosevelt to author, May 21, 1979; EKR diary, Aug. 19, 1944. Quentin, like the first Quentin, was fated to die in a plane crash.

27. New York *Herald Tribune,* Aug. 5, 1945. From New Guinea ABR wrote his mother, complaining he had no books to read. With serene indifference to his jungle habitat, she sent him a check for $10, and suggested he choose some titles "at the nearest store." Australia was a thousand miles away. ABR to author Feb. 1979.

28. EKR to Jessica Kraft; EKR diary, April 14, 1945; Eleanor Roosevelt to EKR, n.d. (ERD).

29. EKR diary, April 14, 1945 (ERD).

30. EKR to ERD, July 25, 1945; EKR diary, Sept. 19, 1945 (ERD).

31. EKR diary, Aug. 12 and 28, 1945 (ERD).

32. Jessica Kraft to author, April 8, 1976.

33. Stefan Lorant to author, Feb. 2, June 7, 1976.

34. EKR to ERD, May 31, 1946. Tranquillity was pulled down in the same month.

35. N.d. (ERD).

36. EKR will, Nassau County Surrogate's Court, Long Island. Clara predeceased EKR in Sept. 1947. Nobody wanted the old Tyler home which had meant so much to EKR. After her death it was sold, turned into tenements, and, in April 1965, pulled down.

37. EKR, *Backlogs,* 84; Mary Frances Youngs to Hermann Hagedorn, Jan. 11, 1949 (TRB); EKR's handwritten funeral instructions (ERD). The epitaph, a variation of an inscription EKR had seen on the tomb of a Tyler governess, was not used on her own gravestone.

Illustration Credits

Index